THE
RESTITUTION LAW REVIEW
1998

The Editors and Publishers gratefully acknowledge
the generous support of

CLIFFORD CHANCE

in the production of
The Restitution Law Review

RESTITUTION LAW REVIEW

CONTENTS

Articles
An Essay on the Action for Money Had and Received *Sir William Evans*	1
The Law of Restitution and the Proceeds of Crime: a Survey of English Law *Graham Virgo*	34
Third Party Cheques – Security or Snare? *Professor Andrew Tettenborn*	63
Cross-Border Tracing *George Panagopoulos*	73
Improvements and Enrichment: A Comparative Analysis *Dirk A Verse*	85

Comment
Restitution and the Conflict of Laws in the House of Lords (*Kleinwort Benson v Glasgow City Council*) *Andrew Dickinson*	104
Clarifying Restitution for Wrongs (*Attorney-General v Blake*) *Graham Virgo*	118
Indefeasible Title as a Bar to a Claim for Restitution (*Pyramid Building Society v Scorpion Hotels Pty Ltd*) *Robert Chambers*	126
Restitutionary Compensatory Damages for Breach of Fiduciary Duty? (*Swindle v Harrison*) *Steven B Elliott*	135
Subrogation, Unjust Enrichment and Remedial Flexibility (*Banque Financière de la Cité v Parc (Battersea)*) *Charles Mitchell*	144
Equitable Title and Common Law Conversion: The Limits of the Fusionist Ideal (*MCC Proceeds v Lehman Brothers International (Europe)*) *Kit Barker*	150
Failure of Consideration and Reliance in Contract (*Stocznia Gdanska SA v Latvian Shipping*) *Peter Jaffey*	157
Transfers into an Overdrawn Account in Breach of Trust — The Bank's Liability for Receipt (*Citadel General Assurance Co v Lloyds Bank Canada*) *Craig Rotherham*	162
A Trace of *Chase Manhattan* in the Netherlands? (*Ontvanger v Hamm*) *Professor HLE Verhagen and NED Faber*	165

Regional Digest
Asia Pacific *T M Yeo*	169
Australia *Peter Butler*	176
Canada *Lionel Smith and Kenneth Fitz*	198
England and Wales *William Swadling*	209
European Union *Alison Jones*	228
Israel *Professor Daniel Friedmann*	247
New Zealand *Professor Peter Watts*	253
Scotland *William Stewart*	258
South Africa *Professor Daniel Visser*	263
U S A *Professor Andrew Kull*	267

Review Article
Chambers, *Resulting Trusts* (*Rt Hon Lord Millett*)	283

Book Reviews

Smith *The Law of Tracing* (*Rt Hon Sir Robert Walker*)	286
Burrows and McKendrick *Cases and Materials on the Law of Restitution* (*Eoin O'Dell*)	287
McMeel *Casebook on Restitution* (*Eoin O'Dell*)	287
Rose (ed) *Failure of Contracts: Contractual, Restitutionary and Proprietary Consequences* (*Professor Andrew Tettenborn*)	290
Swadling (ed) *The Limits of Restitutionary Claims* (*Professor Robin Evans-Jones*)	291
Ashe and Rider (eds) *International Tracing of Assets* (*George Panagopoulos*)	293
Howard (ed) *Butterworths Money Laundering Law* (*George Panagopoulos*)	294
Cato *Restitution in Australia and New Zealand* (*Ross Grantham*)	295
Jackson *The History of Quasi-Contract in English Law* (FDR)	295

THE RESTITUTION LAW REVIEW

General Editor

F.D. ROSE, M.A., B.C.L., Ph.D., M.A., Barrister
*Professor of Commercial and Common Law,
University of Buckingham*

Consultant Editor

P.B.H. BIRKS, Q.C., D.C.L., LL.D., F.B.A.
*Regius Professor of Civil Law,
University of Oxford;
Fellow of All Souls College, Oxford*

Regional Editors

P.A. BUTLER, *University of Queensland*
Professor D. FRIEDMANN, *University of Tel-Aviv*
E. O'DELL, *Trinity College Dublin*
A. JONES, *King's College London*
Professor A. KULL, *Emory University*
Dr L.D. SMITH, *St Hugh's College, Oxford*
W.J. STEWART, *Macmillans*
W.J. SWADLING, *Brasenose College, Oxford*
Professor D.P. VISSER, *University of Cape Town*
Professor P. WATTS, *University of Auckland*
T.M. YEO, *University of Singapore*

Assistant Editor
A.W.J. STEVENS, *University of Birmingham*

The *Restitution Law Review* reflects the increasing recognition and rapid development worldwide of the law of unjust enrichment and restitution. It is designed to provide a comprehensive expert information service by regional reporters from major jurisdictions in the common law and civil law worlds. They will produce annual surveys of developments within their jurisdictions, accompanied by summaries of cases, legislation, law reform proposals, articles, books and other information. The RLR will include original source material together with critical comments and articles analysing and discussing matters of practical and theoretical interest.

All correspondence should be sent to:
>Professor F.D. Rose,
>School of Law,
>University of Buckingham,
>Buckingham MK18 1EG,
>United Kingdom.

Views expressed are not necessarily those of the Editors and Publishers of the *Restitution Law Review*.

Annual Subscription. One issue of the *Restitution Law Review* is published annually in September. The subscription for each annual volume is Standard Rate: UK and Europe £45.00; Rest of the World (except North America) £48.00. Reduced Rate For Individual Academics: UK and Europe £25.00; Rest of the World (except North America) £28.00. Student rate available on application. Prices include postage at surface rate. Subscribers can receive their copies of the *Review* by airmail, the cost of which will be charged at the appropriate rate. Orders to

>**Mansfield Press, P.O. Box 639, Oxford OX3 7HD, UK**

North American subscriptions. Subscriptions for the USA and Canada are dealt with by our exclusive distributor for North America. All enquiries should be directed to:
>Wm W Gaunt & Sons Inc, Gaunt Building, 3011 Gulf Drive, Holmes Beach,
>Florida 34217-2199, USA.

Citation. This issue should be cited as: [1998] RLR.
Citations within the *Review* are to pages except to entries in the *Regional Digest*, where § numbers are used.

© **1998 Mansfield Press, P.O. Box 639, Oxford OX3 7HD** except where otherwise indicated. The copyright in official publications is acknowledged.

All rights reserved. No part of this publication may be stored in any form of retrieval system or reproduced or transmitted in any form or by any means without prior authorisation.

>Typeset by Hope Services (Abingdon) Ltd
>Published by The Mansfield Press
>Printed in Great Britain by Biddles Ltd., Guildford and King's Lynn

Notes for Contributors

1. Contributions are invited and received on the understanding that they are not being considered for publication elsewhere.

2. All communications are at the risk of the author, who should retain copies.

3. The latest issue of the *Restitution Law Review* or the *Company, Financial and Insolvency Law Review* should be consulted for style. Contributions should be submitted in English in the house style. The editors reserve the right of final decision on matters of style, grammar, punctuation, citation etc.

4. Contributions should be in the forms both of (a) a 3.5 inch disk in Word Perfect 5.1 format and (b) typed (text and footnotes) single side, double spaced, A4 paper with one inch margins.

5. The asterisked footnote to the author's name should contain only higher degrees and honours, a brief description of the author's current position, relevant general information about the contribution (*eg* that it was a public lecture) and acknowledgement of assistance.

6. Articles should be preceded by an abstract of approximately 100 words digesting the central theme(s).

7. Citations must always be given (book reviews included, for which, however, they should be kept to a minimum). Citations in the RLR Regional Digest and book reviews will be in the text. All other citations should appear in the footnotes. The first reference to an authority, or to a generally unfamiliar series of reports or serial, should give its full title (including *eg* "*& Co Ltd*"); thereafter, a suitably abbreviated form should be used. Citations should generally remain specific (*eg* "[1994] RLR 73, 875" not "*supra* n 3, at p 75"), except that "*ibid*" should be used when the immediately preceding citation is repeated.

8. Where frequent reference to one or more citations (particularly, lengthy ones) is necessary, it may be convenient for the first footnote to specify an abbreviation or list of abbreviations to be used subsequently.

9. Cross-references should not use "above", "*ante*", "*loc cit*", "*op cit*", "below" or "*post*" but "*supra*" and "*infra*." They should be kept to a minimum. Where used, they should if possible identify the place not by page number (which may alter more than once during printing) but by the relevant part of the article or nearest footnote number, *eg*: "*infra* Part A(2)(c)" or "*supra* text to n 9."

10. Where reference is made to part of a cited source, first and last page numbers should be given, eg *Launchbury v Morgans* [1971] 2 QB 245, 253–257 (not "235 ff" or "235 et seq").

11. Where possible, case citations should be given of the official series of Law Reports (*eg* "AC", "Ch" or "QB" or, failing that, "WLR"). For older cases, there should be citation of both the nominate reports and (on the first citation only) the English Reports (*eg* "*Moses v MacFerlan* (1760) 2 Burr 1005; 97 ER 676"). Where an unofficial series of reports is commonly used internationally, that citation should generally be included (*eg* "*Deglman v Guaranty Trust of Canada* [1954] SCR 725; [1954] 3 DLR 785"). In US citations the date should appear first. The "*v*" is italicised.

12. Articles should commonly be cited thus (with abbreviated forms for repeated citations where necessary): WR Cornish, "Colour of Office: Restitutionary Redress against Public Authority" [1987] *J Malaysian & Comparative Law* 41 (full name for less familiar sources; otherwise abbreviated) [thereafter, *eg*: Cornish [1987] JMCL 41, 50]. Books and papers therein should commonly be cited thus: J Bird, "Choice of Law": ch 2 of FD Rose (ed), *Restitution and the Conflict of Laws* (Mansfield Press, Oxford, 1995) (hereafter "*Rose*") [or hereafter "Bird" if reference is to chapter only], 72. Authors initials should be given on first citation.

13. Punctuation in citations should generally be avoided.

14. In books and articles, authors should endeavour to use up to three levels of (sub-)headings only. A. First Level; **1. Second level**; *(a) Third level*.

15. All references, citations and quotations should be verified before submission. The accuracy of the contribution and of the proof is the author's responsibility.

AN ESSAY ON THE ACTION FOR MONEY HAD AND RECEIVED

Sir William Evans

Editors' Note

We reprint here the *Essay on the Action for Money Had and Received*, written by Sir William David Evans and published in 1802.

The author

William David Evans (1767–1821) was a barrister and a prolific legal writer. The briefest acquaintance with his work shows that he was deeply committed to legal scholarship, able to draw not only on a close study of the common law but also on wide learning in civilian writings. His first work (1795) was an enlarged edition of Salkeld's reports. He next wrote the *Essays* (1802), which are further discussed immediately below; and then *A General View of the Decisions of Lord Mansfield* (1803). This was followed by a translation of Pothier's *Treatise on Obligations* (1806), with extensive comparative notes and essays. He went on to write number of other works on a variety of subjects, including a popular annotated collection of statutes. He was a stipendiary magistrate in Manchester from 1813–1818, and Vice-Chancellor of the County Palatine of Lancaster from 1815–1818. In 1819 he was knighted and appointed Recorder of Bombay. He arrived there in 1820 but died soon after. (Source: *Dictionary of National Biography.*)

The book

The full title of the book is *Essays: On the Action for Money Had and Received, on the Law of Insurances, and on the Law of Bills of Exchange and Promissory Notes*. It was published in Liverpool in 1802, in octavo. The book is dedicated to Sir Edward Law, then the Attorney-General, later to be Lord Ellenborough. According to the preface (at iii), the essays were originally printed with the intention of separate publication; this explains why each essay is separately paginated, and has its own table of contents. There is also a "Preliminary Essay," which is a sort of reflection on the nature of law and legal systems.

The text of the essay is reprinted by kind permission of the British Library from its copy of the book (shelfmark 515.c.21).

The Essay

The *Essay On the Action for Money Had and Received* is the first in the book. The structure of the essay appears clearly to have been derived from a passage in *Moses* v *Macferlan* (1760) 2 Burr 1005, 1012; 97 ER 676, 681. Lord Mansfield, in the context of some general observations on the action for money had and received, said, ". . . it lies for money paid by mistake; or upon a consideration which happens to fail; or for money got through imposition, (express, or implied;) or extortion; or oppression; or an undue advantage taken of the plaintiff's situation, contrary to laws made for the protection of persons under those circumstances." The first four chapter titles reflect these words.

1

No attempt has been made to produce a full commentary on the text, but some points are worth noting briefly. Evans appears to be the first writer in the common law tradition to accept that unjust enrichment can be a source of obligations (at **[8]**). There is a lengthy discussion of the recoverability of payments made under void contracts (at **[48]**–**[80]**); this includes an analysis of some of the annuities cases (at **[70]**–**[80]**), whose importance to the modern law of unjust enrichment was emphasised by the recent decision of the Court of Appeal in *Guinness Mahon* v *Royal Borough of Kensington and Chelsea* §102. Evans, like others in the legal profession, was clearly troubled with the actual result in *Moses* v *Macferlan* (1760) 2 Burr 1005; 97 ER 676, in the light of the principle of *res judicata,* and he addressed this in detail (at **[92]**–**[102]**).

Perhaps the most topical subject considered in the *Essay* is mistake of law (at **[11]**–**[22]**). Evans, who was opposed to Pothier's view that a mistake of law could not ground recovery, gives an invaluable account of the law immediately preceding *Bilbie* v *Lumley* (1802) 2 East 469; 102 ER 448, which decision came too late for the *Essay*. Evans returned to the topic, disappointed and unpersuaded by the holding in *Bilbie,* in one of the appendices to his 1806 translation of Pothier.

The text

The work of preparing the text has been done by Professor Peter Birks, Professor Francis Rose and myself. Evans included a list of errata, and these have been incorporated but identified so that the reader can discern how the text appears as corrected and in the original. We have made a small number of amendments in cases where there appears to have been an obvious error, but again the original text is shown. In order that the text appear as readable as possible, it is printed as corrected by the author and editor, alterations being indicated in the footnotes.

All the footnotes are numbered consecutively. The majority of footnotes are the editors'. Some indicate corrections, marked to show whether they come from the editors or from Evans' errata. Others give citations, either in a fuller version than those provided by the author or where none was supplied by the author. The original text included a few footnotes by the author, marked by an asterisk or, where a second footnote appeared on a page, by a dagger; these footnotes are now numbered in series with the editors' footnotes but are marked [*Author's footnote:*].

It should be noted that Evans was not consistent in his Latin orthography; for example, he sometimes wrote *"bona fidê",* sometimes *"bonâ fide",* and sometimes *"bona fide".* In this we have made no amendments. Moreover, when quoting from other authors, Evans did not always reproduce the quoted text verbatim; we have not drawn attention to this in individual cases.

Lionel Smith
St. Hugh's College, Oxford

THE ACTION FOR MONEY HAD AND RECEIVED

[1] AN ESSAY ON THE ACTION FOR MONEY HAD AND RECEIVED.

[2] CONTENTS.

INTRODUCTION	3
CHAP. I. — *Of Money paid by Mistake*	11
SECTION I. — *Mistakes of Law*	ibid.
II. — *Mistakes of Fact*	22
CHAP. II. — *Of Money paid on a consideration which has failed*	25
SECTION I. — *Of Failure by Misconduct of the Defendant*	ib.
II. — *Of Failure by change of Intention in the Plaintiff*	28
III. — *Of a Failure from Accidental Circumstances*	29
CHAP. III[.][1] — *Of Money paid through imposition or extortion*	35
IV. — *Of Money paid on Illegal Contracts*	37
SECTION I. — *Of Contracts attended with Criminality, Turpitude, or Oppression*	ibid.
II. — *Of Contracts which are Void, but not Criminal*	48
PART I. — *Void Insurances*	51
II. — *Of Wagers*	63
III. [—][2] *Of Annuities*	70
CHAP. V. — *Of Cases in which the Action is not maintainable*	81
SECTION I. — *Miscellaneous Cases*	ibid.
II. — *Of Compromises*	86
CHAP. VI. — *Of the Effect of Judicial Proceedings*	91
VII. — *By what Persons the Action may be maintained*	103
VIII. — *Against what Persons the Action may be maintained*	106
IX. — *Of the Damages*	119

[3] INTRODUCTION.

IF one person receives a sum of money for the purpose of paying it over to another, his obligation to make such payment is too plain to require any comment. The general obligation to refund money, which has been paid under a mistake, or obtained by fraud or extortion, or given for a purpose to which it has not been applied, is equally evident. According to the Roman law, actions of different denominations were adapted to the several cases, in which such payment was unduly made. The English law has adopted a general supposition, that the money which ought to be refunded was received for the use of the party by whom it was paid, and that the person receiving it [4] made a promise to pay it on request. And the action used for this purpose is called AN ACTION FOR MONEY HAD AND RECEIVED. This action has also an extensive latitude as a mode of trying adverse rights; for if a person sells my property under a claim of title or otherwise, I may in point of form consider him as my agent, and charge him with having received the money for my use and made a promise to pay. I have no intention at present of examining the different cases in which this is the proper form of action, where it is agreed that a right of action in some shape certainly exists. I shall only observe, that the extension of it has of late years been considerably favoured, and a party may now obtain redress upon this general allegation, in many cases where it was formerly deemed necessary to make a particular and circumstantial statement of his

---

[1] Editor's insertion.
[2] Editor's insertion.

demand, whereby the danger of failing from an error in the statement was considerably increased: and that in the cases where a person has his election to bring his action as for a wrong, or waving the injury, to consider the conversion of [5] his property as an agency, and an obligation to account, he must act consistently throughout, and not treat the same act as licit for one purpose, and tortious for another. If I charge a man with converting my corn or timber to his own use, and sue him for damages, it will be no justification that I owe him a sum of money; but if I proceed against him in an action for money had and received, in order to recover the produce, he may set off his debt, and I cannot oppose the argument that his being my creditor does not warrant his taking and disposing of my property. Where death or bankruptcy has taken place, the choice between these two remedies is often very important.

The present essay will be chiefly confined to the action for money had and received, as enforcing an obligation to refund money which ought not to be retained. The Roman system of jurisprudence ranked this as a *Quasi* contract, being an intermediate order between contracts properly so called, which were founded upon actual consent, and wil-[6]ful wrongs. And without particularising their technical distinctions, I shall, in referring to that law, in general consider the term *Solutio indebiti*, as comprising the general distinctions arising from a liability to refund.

This obligation was enforced according to the general principles of natural equity, the foundation of it being a retention by one man of the property which he had unduly received from another, or received for a purpose, the failure of which rendered it improper that he should retain it. The mere legal liability to the original payment was the question in consideration, but the injustice of permitting the money or other property, under all the circumstances, to be retained. The introduction of the action for money had and received into the English courts, is not novel, and several cases had occurred previous to the appointment of Lord Mansfield, in which it had been properly applied, so that it was familiar in point of practice. But it was reserved to that eminent judge, to trace the nature and principles of the action, with a most [7] instructive perspicuity, and to direct the general application of it in its proper channel.

In some instances the particular decisions may be reasonably questioned, but the utility resulting from his general discussions must be universally allowed. In the case of Moses *v*. Macferlan, 2 *Bur*. 1005,[3] which gave him the first opportunity of expressing his opinions upon this ground of action; he very compendiously stated the nature and principles of it, coinciding in effect with the institutes of the civil law. The following extract, from his opinion, will furnish a proper introduction to a more minute examination of the subject. — "This kind of equitable action to recover money, which ought not in justice to be kept, is very beneficial, and therefore much encouraged. It lies only for money, which *ex aequo et bono*, the defendant ought to refund, it does not lie for money paid by the plaintiff, which is claimed of him as payable in point of honour and honesty, although it could not have been recovered from him by any course of law; as in payment of a debt [8] barred by the statute of limitations, or contracted during his infancy, or to the extent of principal and legal interest upon an usurious contract, or for money fairly lost at play: because, in all these cases the defendant may retain it with a safe conscience, though by positive law he was barred from recovering. But it lies for money paid by mistake; or upon a consideration which happens to fail; or for money got by imposition, (express or implied) or extortion or oppression; or an undue advantage taken of the plaintiff's situation, contrary to laws made for the protection of persons under these circumstances. In one word, the gist of this kind of action is, that the defendant, upon the circumstances of the case, is obliged by the ties of natural justice and equity, to refund the money."[4]

The maxim of the civil law, that it is naturally just that one man shall not be enriched to the detriment of another, *Hoc naturâ aequum est, neminem cum alterius detrimento fieri locupletiorem,* is particularly applied to the claim which we are at present examining.

[3] *Moses v Macferlan* (1760) 2 Burr 1005; 97 ER 676.
[4] (1760) 2 Burr 1005, 1012.

[9] The Commentary of Vinnius upon the title in the institutes, *De solutione indebiti*, contains a very instructive view of the subject. His general exposition of it, which agrees in substance with the preceding observations of Lord Mansfield, is as follows:[5] "In order to induce an obligation in favour of the person paying, and a right to reclaim what has been paid, two things are required. That what is paid should not be due; that it should be paid through error. In respect of the first; there is no repetition of what is really due: and nobody can suppose that there is a right of repetition if what was paid was due both in point of law and of natural justice. But supposing it only due according to one of these: if it is only by strictness of law, without any obligation in point of equity, and could be repelled by a perpetual exception, the right of repetition is allowed; as such a sum cannot be said to be due except in name. But what is due according to natural justice is considered as being really due; and, although the payment of it could not be enforced, yet if it is actually paid, though by a person who supposes himself to be **[10]** liable in point of law, it cannot be reclaimed. If a debtor has a perpetual exception, but which is founded upon some reason that does not remove his natural obligation, and not being apprized of it, pays the debt, he has no claim to repetition. Such is the exception of a judgment in his favour, as the sentence of the judge cannot destroy the obligation founded on the consent of the party, and therefore it was decided, that a person really indebted, but liberated by a judgement in his favour, could not insist upon a repetition. Also, if a person under the power of his father, borrowed money, from the payment of which he was protected by the *Senatus consultum Macedonianum*, and after he became his own master (*pater* [*familias*][6]) paid the money he was bound, as there was a natural obligation subsisting.["][7]

[11]
CHAP. I.
Of Money paid by mistake.

WITH respect to money paid under a mistake, Vinnius observes,[8] that "error is twofold, of fact, that is, when there is an ignorance of the fact, [out][9] of which the law arises, or of law when the fact is known; but there is an ignorance of the legal consequence."

SECTION I.
Mistakes of Law.

"Hence it becomes a question how the maxim is to be understood, which is laid down simply and generally, that whatever has been paid by mistake **[12]** may be reclaimed, whether it applies to error of fact only, or extends to error in point of law? The opinion of the old interpreters is, that if no natural obligation intervenes, even what is paid under a mistake in law, may be recovered back, in which opinion I concur. I am principally influenced by this reason, that the right to recover back what has been unduly paid, is founded upon equity and moral rectitude, of which it is an universal consequence, that it can only be repelled by an exception founded upon the same principles. But what pretence of equity can a person have, or what colour has he for excepting to the injustice of being required to refund what has been paid to him, though under an ignorance of the law, but what was nowise due to him upon the principles of natural justice; as if a person was induced by fraud or force to enter into an engagement, I cannot be brought to think that what has been paid in the execution of such engagement can be retained, and that any man can

---
[5] Arnoldus Vinnius, *In quatuor libros institutionum imperialium commentarius academicus ac forensis* (1642) on J.Inst 3.28.6, p 699 col.2—p 700 col 1. This work is cited henceforth as Vinnius, *Commentary* (n 5). Page references are to the 4th ed (Amsterdam, 1665). In modern notation J.Inst. 3.28 is 3.27, the division of 3.6 having been abandoned.
[6] Author's substitution of "familias" for "familius".
[7] Editor's addition of closing quotation marks.
[8] Vinnius, *Commentary* (n 5) p 700, col 2.
[9] Author's substitution of "out" for "and".

avail himself of his own iniquity, under the single pretence that the person who made the payment mistook the law, [13] and was ignorant that an engagement so obtained, was of no legal efficacy: and lest this should seem to be an assertion without authority, the text of the law is evidently applicable, wherein Julianus following Nerva and Atilinius, elegantly answers, that money paid by one who though it was due from him, but might have protected himself by an exception of fraud, might be recovered back. And this is paid under an error of law. And there are other similar instances. I am also influenced in this opinion by the consideration that in the whole title of the pandects *de condictione indebiti* though it is diffuse, the right of reclaiming is never limited to payments made under an error in fact, or excluded from those which are made under an error in law, but is constantly referred to payment through error generally, whether the payment was nowise due, or whether it was barred by reason of a perpetual exception[10], [14] from which it may be understood that the nature of the error is no bar to the recovery, but the knowledge of the person who pays, and that alone is an impediment. And this is also proved by the reason which is given for precluding a person from recovering what he has paid, knowing it not to be due; that he is considered as having made a donation, which cannot be affirmed of a person who conceives himself to be under an obligation, and necessarily bound to pay. Lastly, I am influenced, and that in a principal degree by what is stated in the 8th law of the title, *De juris et facti ignorantia*, that an error of law shall not prejudice any person, so far as to induce the damage of losing his property, which seems clearly to denote that what is paid under a mistake in point of law, may be reclaimed; because, if that be denied, it must admitted, that an error in point of law, does extend to prejudice a person by inducing the loss of his [15] property contrary to the opinion of Papinian, in the law which has been been cited. For the answer of those who dissent from this argument is a mere cavil; they insist that the person claiming a right to be repaid, does not contend in respect to the losing of property, but in respect to property which is already lost; *(non de re amittenda sed de amissâ)*, for if a person who pays his money under a mistake of the law, so far loses it, that he has no remedy for recovering it back, then an error of law does induce the damage of losing his property. Neither does the question refer to the time of instituting a suit for the recovery, but that in which the payment is made. And Papinian denies that a person, in consequence of an error of law, can lose his property, that is, by being precluded from recovering it. And what the same Papinian lays down in the preceding law, that ignorance of the law is of no avail to those who wish to acquire, but does not prejudice those who only seek their own, *(juris ignorantia non prodest adquirere volentibus suum vero petentibus non nocet)* is to be understood as an universal proposition. Neither is the 29 law [16] D.Mandati[11], any obstacle to this course of reasoning: for there a case is proposed of two persons, contesting which shall avoid a loss that been incurred: the debtor who could have availed himself of a perpetual exception, and the surety, who not being ignorant of the fact, paid the money: and it is decided, that the surety has no right of action. But there is not a word in that law about the obligation to refund: and where it is said in the ninth law, *de juris et facti ignorantiâ*, that an ignorance of the law shall be prejudicial it is to be understood that it shall give no advantage; that it shall not entitle a man to any gain, neither shall it subject him to any loss[12]. But still it is to be remembered that the pay-

---

[10] [*Author's footnote*:] Payment is considered to be unduly made, not only if it is nowise due, but if it could not be recovered in consequence of any perpetual exception. Wherefore, such also [14] may be reclaimed unless it is made with the knowledge that the party is protected by the exception *De condic. indeb.* 26. S. 3 [*ed*: D.12.6.26.3]. Whoever has a perpetual exception, may reclaim what he has paid by mistake, l. 40 [*ed*: D.12.6.40]. If a payment is made through error upon any of those considerations, which have no legal effect, it may be reclaimed, l. 54 [*ed*: D.12.6.54].

[11] [*Author's footnote*:] Non male tractabitur, si cum ignoraret fidejussor [*editors' substitution for* "fidejessor"] inutiliter se obligatum solverit an mandati actionem habeat? Et si[ ]quidem [= *editors insertion of space*] factum ignoravit recipi ignorantia ejus potest, si vero jus, aliud dici debet [*ed*: D.17.1.29.1].

[12] [*Author's footnote*:] The passage in the digest relates to heirs, paying a legacy without availing themselves of the Falcidian law, by which a testator was restrained from giving away above a certain portion of his property in legacies.

ment made under an ignorance of the law can only be reclaimed if it **[17]** was unaccompanied by any natural obligation. But if the person making the payment was naturally under such an obligation as may afford the party receiving a just cause for retaining it, a distinction is to be made between an ignorance of law and of fact; and a right to recover shall be denied in the first case, but allowed in the last. If I pay a legacy according to the will of a testator, though it has not the requisite formalities: if I am not apprized of the fact of its wanting those solemnities, I may reclaim it; but not if knowing the facts, I was ignorant of the legal consequences. But this is not founded upon the single reason that a man shall be bound by his ignorance of the law, but because there is a natural obligation founded upon the will of the testator. And to this principle may be referred the passages in the code, wherein a right to recover is denied upon a mistake in law, or confined to a mistake in fact[13]: for in truth, you **[18]** cannot merely in consequence of my having made a mistake respecting a matter of law, have any just cause of retaining what nowise belonged to you. And here we should attend to the rule, that it is better to favour a person reclaiming his own, than the adventitious gain of another[14].["][15]

Pothier adopts the opposite conclusion, and states without reserve, that a person cannot be allowed to alledge an ignorance of law, which is not to be presumed, and is inexcusable, because he ought to take advice, and inform himself of the law respecting the business in which he is concerned. He refers to the law 10 *de jur. et fact. ignor.* above cited, as deciding the question, and to the case in which the heir was not allowed to **[19]** reclaim the Falcidian portion that he had omitted to deduct in payment of a legacy, as illustrating the difference between an error of law and an error of fact.[15a]

It is singular that a question, open to so much discussion, has passed with very little attention in the cases affected by it in the English courts. The opinion of Vinnius appears to be best founded, as it arises from the application of the rules of natural justice, upon which this right of action rather depends, than upon any positive rules or artificial reasoning. I conceive it may now be positively stated, that this opinion is adopted in the English law. In the case of Archer *v.* the Bank of England, Doug. 638,[16] the payee of a bill had restrained its negotiability by an endorsement, that the drawees must place it to a particular account. Afterwards it was negotiated with a forged endorsement of the name of the person to whose credit it was to be placed; and the drawer, for whose honour it had been paid to the bank, was allowed to recover the amount. This case was fully open to the question **[20]** under discussion. The person who paid the bill, and who must be considered as the drawer (the act having been adopted by him) could not be deemed ignorant of the fact, for he had only to read the endorsement; but the argument, though there was a difference of opinion, did not embrace this general question, and turned wholly upon the effect of the endorsement. The principle was more evidently adopted in the case of Bize *v.* Dixon, 1 T.R. 285.[17] An insurance broker was indebted to a bankrupt in a considerable sum of money, but had counter-demands for losses, due to persons, on whose behalf he had effected insurances on commissions *del credere*. These he had a right to set off, but under the mistaken idea that he

---

[13] [*Author's footnote:*] C. l. 6. de jur. et fact. ignor [*ed*: C.1.1.18.6]. Si non transactionis causâ, sed indebitam errore facti, olei materiam vos Archantico stipulanti [dare] [= *editors' insertion*] spopondisse Rector provinciæ animadverterit: reddito quod debetis, residui liberationem condicentes **[18]** audiet id. l. 10 [*ed*: C.1.1.18.10]. Cum quis jus ignorans indebitam pecuniam solverit cessat repetitio; per ignorantiam enim facti tantum repetitionem indebiti soluti [competere] [= *editor's correction of* "competre"] tibi notum est. De condic. indeb. l. 6 [*ed*: C.4.5.6]. Si per ignorantiam facti non debitam quantitatem pro alio solvisti, et hoc adito rectore provinciæ fuerit probatum hanc et cujus nomine soluta est restitui eo agente providebit.

[14] [*Author's footnote:*] Melius est favere repetitioni quam adventitio lucro.

[15] Vinnius, *Commentary* (n 5), p 701, col 2, where Vinnius derives the statement in the preceding note from D.50.17.41. Editors' closing quotation marks.

[15a] RJ Pothier, *Traité du quasi-contrat appelé promutuum et de l'action condictio indebiti* para 162 (we have used the edition in *Oeuvres de Pothier*, vol 5, ed M Bugnet (1861)). This book is hereafter cited as Pothier, *Quasi-Contrat* (n 15a).

[16] *Archer v The Bank of England* (1781) 2 Doug 637; 99 ER 404.

[17] *Bize v Dickason* (1786) 1 TR 285; 99 ER 1097.

had no such right, he paid the whole debt from himself to the assignees: he afterwards gave them notice of the mistake, cautioning them not to make a dividend. Lord Mansfield said, "that the general rule had always been, that if a man has actually paid what the law would not have compelled him to pay, but what in equity and conscience he ought, he cannot recover it back again in an action for **[21]** money had and received. But where money is paid under a mistake, which there was no ground to claim in conscience, the party may recover it back again by this kind of action."[18] Still there was no *express* reference made to a mistake in point of law. But in a late case before Lord Kenyon, the point was more explicitly mentioned. The drawer of a bill of exchange paid the amount to the holder, knowing that he had given time to the acceptor, who had become bankrupt. His lordship said, "it is not only necessary that the plaintiff should know all the facts, but he should know the legal consequences of them. It seems to me that the plaintiff did not know the legal consequences of them, and he paid the money under an idea that he might be compelled to pay it. Where a man, knowing all the facts explicitly, and being under no misapprehension with regard to any of them, nor of the law acting upon them, chooses to pay a sum of money, *volenti non fit injuria,* he shall not recover it back again. — Chitty on Bills, 102.[19] The case came before the court of King's Bench, who confirmed Lord Kenyon's opinion, **[22]** but it is not reported. Lord Chief Justice De Grey said, in the case of Farmer *v.* Arundel, 2 Bl. Rep. 825,[20] that when money is paid by one man to another on a mistake, either of fact or law, the action would lie; but this was an *obiter dictum,* the decision of the particular cause being in favour of the defendant.

I shall have occasion in a subsequent part of this essay, to allude to some other cases in which an ignorance of the law became in some degree, the object of consideration; but they turned upon a different principle from that which has been hitherto the topic of enquiry.

SECTION II.
Of Mistakes in Fact.

It will be unnecessary to attempt a particular enumeration of the several cases, in which there may be a right of reclaiming money paid under a mistake of fact: whether upon a supposition that **[23]** something has occurred to induce a liability of payment, which in point of fact, has not occurred; as if an [insurer][21] has paid for the loss of a vessel not heard of for an unusual length of time, but afterwards found to be safe; or from an ignorance of some fact which has actually taken place; as if the endorser of a bill paid the amount to the holder, not having the notice to which was entitled, of its having been refused acceptance. It is in general immaterial whether the person receiving was under equal ignorance or not, provided he had no right to the payment which has been erroneously made; the obligation to refund is, in either case, equally strong. But a mere error in the motive for transferring a sum of money, does not necessarily induce a right to reclaim it, if there is no error with respect to the nature of the act, and this is the rule in regard to contracts in general. Therefore if I gratuitously give a person a sum of money under the notion that he has rendered me some valuable service, and afterwards discover that the notion was ill founded: this affords me no right to reclaim it, because I intended a donation, though **[24]** that intention was induced by an erroneous supposition.

The principle that what a man pays with full knowledge, and without any undue influence, cannot be recovered back, being established: Pothier puts the case of its being uncertain, whether a man paid what was not due from him knowingly or erroneously, and decides, that it ought to be presumed that the payment was made erroneously, and that he should be allowed to reclaim it according to the general principle; that where the circumstances are obscure, the right of repe-

---

[18] (1786) 1 TR 285, 286–287.
[19] J Chitty, *Bills of Exchange,* 1st ed (1799), 102.
[20] *Farmer v Arundel* (1772) 2 W Bl 824; 96 ER 485.
[21] Editor's substitution of "insurer" for "insured".

tition is to be rather favoured than an adventitious gain. *In re obscurâ melius est favere repetitioni quam adventitio lucro.*

[25]
CHAP. II
Of Money paid on a consideration, which has failed.

MONEY paid under a condition which happens to fail, is, in the civil law, the subject of a distinct title, *De condictione*[22] *causâ datâ causâ non secutâ*. This may happen through the misconduct of the defendant, through a change of inclination in the plaintiff, or from accidental circumstances.

SECTION I.
Of Failure by Misconduct of the Defendant.

In the first class may be placed the case of Dutch v. Warren,[23] which is particularly adverted to by Lord Mansfield in Moses v. Macferlan.[24] The defendant agreed to sell the plaintiff five shares [26] in some copper mines, and received the purchase money, but afterwards refused to transfer the shares, telling him that he might take his remedy: and upon an objection that there should have been a special action for the non-performance of the contract; the court said, that "the extending these actions depends upon the notion of fraud. If one man takes another's money for doing a thing, and afterwards refuses to do it, it is a fraud, and it is at the election of the party injured, either to affirm the agreement by bringing an action for the non-performance it, or to disaffirm the agreement ab initio by reason of the fraud, and bring an action for money had and received to his use."[25] It is customary in a declaration, to combine these charges; but the distinction is not merely technical, for there may be an important difference in the amount of damages: and in case of a bankruptcy, a debt may be proved under the commission, for money paid without consideration; but there can be no redress for accidental damages. If a person sells an estate by auction, giving a description which is found not to coincide with the pre-[27]mises put to sale, the purchaser may bring this action for a return of the deposit. This occurred a few years ago, in an action against Mr. Chinstie, who described a country mansion in his particulars, as possessing every beauty and accommodation, but which the buyer, upon going to view his purchase, found to be totally destitute of all the recommendations ascribed to it. In a late case, the defendant agreed to sell the plaintiffs cord wood, and proceeded so far with part of the wood, that, according to the general custom in such cases, it had become the property of the purchaser. The plaintiffs paid a sum of money on account, but upon the defendant neglecting to cord the remainder of the wood; brought an action to recover back the money, as having been paid upon a consideration that had failed; and it was held, that the action was maintainable. Lord Kenyon said it was an entire contract; and as by the defendant's default, the plaintiffs could not perform what they had undertaken to do, they had a right to put an end to the whole contract, and recover back the money [28] that they had paid under it. They were not bound to take a part of the wood only. — 7 T.R. 183.[26]

SECTION II.
Of Failure by change of intention in the Plaintiff.

The failure of consideration by a change of intention on the part of the plaintiff, may induce the right of repetition, provided he was under no obligation to the defendant in respect to its com-

---

[22] Author's insertion of second "c" into original "*conditione*".
[23] *Dutch v Warren* (1721) 2 Burr 1010; 97 ER 680; 1 Str 406; 93 ER 598.
[24] (1760) 2 Burr 1005, 1010.
[25] *Ibid*, 1011.
[26] *Giles v Edwards* (1797) 7 TR 181, 182 [*sic*]; 101 ER 920.

pletion. A common instance of this, is the return of the premium upon a policy of insurance, the risque never having commenced. If I employ an attorney to institute a cause, or a broker to purchase a parcel of goods, and change my intention at the outset of the cause, or before the purchase is made, they must return the money which was advanced, subject to a proper deduction for the trouble and expence already incurred. Ulpian puts the case of a person employing another to take a journey, and decides, that if the employer is, [29] under the circumstances, at liberty to change his intention, he may reclaim what he has advanced for the expences; but if the person employed has been at any expence in preparing for his journey, he is bound only to refund the balance.

Where a person bought a chaise, with liberty to [return][27] it, paying 3s. 6d. per day for the [hire],[28] and returned it accordingly. It was held, that he might bring this action to recover the purchase money, the consideration having wholly failed by his availing himself of the condition. Towers v. Barrett, 1 T.R. 133.[29]

SECTION [III].[30]
Of a Failure from accidental circumstances.

A failure from accidental circumstances may happen several ways. If a person supposing himself to be upon the point of death, makes a donation *causa mortis*, and afterwards recovers, he may reclaim what he has given. If an insurance is made with a warranty, and is void from the war-[30]ranty not being complied with, the premium must be returned. If a sale has been put an end to by the mutual consent of both parties, the deposit money must be refunded. Where money is paid for the purchase of property, to which the seller cannot give a sufficient title, the case may fall under this division, or be imputable to the fault of the defendant, according to the circumstance of his being acquainted with, or ignorant of the defect. In case of the purchase of land, I think it may now be considered as an established point of law, that after a conveyance is made, the purchaser, in case of eviction, has no claim to a repetition, for want of title in the seller, (unless the seller was guilty of fraud, by knowingly concealing the defect.) Mr Fonblanque, who seems to consider the subject as in some degree open to argument[31], contends in favour of what I have above supposed to be the rule of law; observing that the opposite decision would lead to the most serious inconvenience, as every contract, however guarded and bounded in its terms, would be liable to be opened at any dis-[31]tance of time, The particular inference which he draws from an expression in Bree v. Holbeach, Doug. 657,[32] "that the assigner of a mortgage did not covenant for the goodness of the title, but only that he had not incumbered the estate, it being incumbent on the plaintiff to look to the goodness of it," is not fully supported; because the question in that case turned upon the statute of limitations, and the suggestion of fraud. It is not said that if the action had been commenced within six years, it would not have lain in consequence of the nature of the demand. The opinion of the profession, however, seems to regard the point as settled; though it has not been the direct ground of any determination. I have always entertained considerable doubt of the utility which results from adopting this maxim. As to the inconvenience that the contract might be opened at any distance of time, the right of recovery is by the determination in the case of Bree and Holbeach, restricted to the period allowed by the statute of limitations; and viewing the subject in any other respect, the purchaser, who acquires no effective title, parts [32] with a large sum of money to the seller, who by reason of his want of title, in effect parts with nothing, yet is allowed to retain that sum. Thus he derives a clear gain, and the

---

[27] Author's substitution of "return" for "reclaim".
[28] Author's substitution of "hire" for "time".
[29] *Towers v Barrett* (1786) 1 TR 133; 99 ER 1014.
[30] Editors' substitution of "III" for "II".
[31] [*Author's footnote:*] I B. C. 5. S. 8. [*ed*: J Fonblanque, *A Treatise on Equity* (1793), vol 1, ch 5, §8; esp 363–366].
[32] *Bree v Holbech* (1781) 2 Doug 654, 657; 99 ER 415, 417, *per* Lord Mansfield.

purchaser sustains a clear loss of the whole amount. *Unus ex alterius detrimento locupletior fit.* In a late case, a person sold a leasehold interest in some premises, from which the purchaser was evicted for want of title: but no regular conveyance having been made, he was allowed to recover the purchase money, and the ground of the decision was, that the whole passed by parol, Cups v. Read, 6 T.R. 606.[33] This case shews, that the rule is founded upon the principle, that no engagement shall be implied which is not expressed where there is a formal contract; and the rule is reasonable as far as regards the warranty of the title, and the right to consequential damages. But the money was paid upon a consideration which has failed, and therefore it is only on the ground of technical authority, contrary to general principles, that it can be retained. *Caveat emptor*, when applied to a retention of the purchase money, may be translated "The devil take the hindmost."

[33] In a case which arose early in the 18th century, the court of Chancery, decreed one hundred guineas as part of an apprentice fee, to be paid back to the father of the apprentice, his master having died within three weeks after the sealing of the articles, though it was expressly provided by the articles, that if the master should die within the year, only sixty pounds should be returned. — 1 Vern, 460.[34] Lord Kenyon, when Master of the Rolls, observed, that this decision carried the authority of the court as far as could be. — 3 Bro. Ch. 480.[35] And Mr Fonblanque observes, that if it be a rule of equity, as in many cases it is stated to be, that equity will not alter or extend the agreement of the parties, the decree seems irreconcilable with such rule. — B. I. C. 5. S. 8.[36] A suit in equity must, in respect to this subject, be considered as being merely equivalent to an action for money had and received, and there can be no pretence for referring the decree to any other principle than that of money paid upon a consideration which has happened to fail; and the court, in decreeing the apprentice fee to be refunded, seems to have thought the consideration [34] for which it was given, was the entire performance of the articles, whereas it was the fact of contracting the relation, and the entering into the consequent engagements. In that view the consideration was complete and entire, and could not partially fail. I much doubt whether the precedent would now be followed, but think it certainly would not be allowed by analogy to govern any other case.

[35]

CHAP. III.
Of Money paid through imposition or extortion.

AS to money got through imposition, it will not be material to enter into much discussion. The general principle is sufficiently intelligible, and there can be little difficulty in the application of it to particular instances as they arise. The taking a premium for the insurance of a vessel, knowing of her safe arrival; the representation by a person employed to buy a horse that he had paid 50l. when in fact he paid only 40l. and thereby fraudulently obtaining ten, are cases falling within this division of the subject. These cases also generally involve the circumstance, which has been already considered, as sustaining a principal ground of repetition, that the money is paid under a mis-[36]take. It may be proper to add, that persons knowingly and designedly obtaining money of goods by false pretences, and with intent to cheat, are, upon a criminal prosecution, subject to very serious punishment.

Cases of extortion and oppression, are the taking of exorbitant fees, by officers of the customs; the detention of property pledged until more is paid than the principal and legal interest. —

---

[33] *Cripps v Reade* (1796) 1 TR 606; 101 ER 728.
[34] *Newton v Rowse* (1687) 1 Vern 460; 23 ER 586.
[35] This appears to be a reference to *Hale v Webb* (1786) 2 Bro CC 78, 80; 29 ER 44, 45.
[36] See *supra*, n 31, at 364.

Astley v. Reynolds, 2 Str. 915.[37] The detention of a surrender by the steward of a manor, until an improper demand was satisfied: the extortion of a sum of money for restoring money seized by mistake. — Irwing v. Wilson, 4 T.R. 485.[38] In some of these cases it was contended, that the payment was voluntary. But it was truly answered that the rule *volenti non fit injuria,* only holds where the party has the freedom of exercising his will, which he has not when his legal rights are withheld from him. Every thing exacted as a condition for refraining from an unlawful or injurious act, falls within the same general observation.

[37]
CHAP. IV.
Of Money paid on illegal Contracts.

THE illegality of contracts, upon which any sum of money has been paid, is a subject that requires a distinct consideration; and there are two divisions to which it will be convenient to refer; the first comprising contracts infected with criminality, turpitude, or oppression; the other, such as are merely void, so as not to induce any right of action, but not attended with those exceptions.

SECTION I.
Of Contracts attended with criminality, turpitude, or oppression.

Upon the first division I shall insert the following extract from [Domat],[39] which clearly shews **[38]** the grand distinctions of natural justice, as recognized by the civil law, and afterwards state their adoption and application in the law of England.

He observes, that by unlawful facts, we understand here, not only those which are prohibited by some express law, but all those which are contrary to equity, honesty, and good manners, although there be no written law, which makes mention of them: for whatever is contrary to equity, honesty, or good manners, is contrary to the principles both of divine and human laws. It may happen three ways; that by an unlawful fact, one may receive a sum of money, or other thing, from another person; for the fact may be unlawful either only on the part of him who gives, or only on the part of him who receives, or on the part of both the giver and receiver. Thus he who, under pretext of civility, should make a present to one who he knew would be his judge or arbitrator, and who, on his part, was altogether ignorant of the motives of the said present, would give unlawfully what the said **[39]** person might receive without any offence to justice. When any person, by himself or others, exacts a sum of money, or other things, to hinder him from committing some great violence, or makes one deliver up to him the titles to some debt or some right which he owes, the said fact is unlawful only on the part of the person who commits the violence, and not on the part of him who suffers it. When a person receives money of another, either himself, or by a third hand, to commit some crime, some offence, or some injustice, the fact is unlawful both on the part of him who receives, and of him who gives.

If the fact be unlawful only on the part of him who gives, he who has received will not be obliged to give it back, unless it be that the circumstances regulate his duty in another manner. Thus, in the case of him who had received a present, being ignorant of the unjust motive of giving it, as has been explained: if the motive chanced afterwards to come to his knowledge, he would be obliged either to abstain from the function of judge or **[40]** arbitrator, or to give back the present which he had received, or even to do both the one and the other, according as prudence and equity might require, under the circumstances of the quality of the persons, and of that

---

[37] *Astley v Reynolds* (1731) 2 Str 915; 93 ER 939.
[38] *Irving v Wilson* (1791) 4 TR 485; 100 ER 1132.
[39] Editors' sustitution of "Domat" for "Dornat" (J Domat, *Les Lois Civiles dans leur Ordre naturel* (1689–94)).

of the fact. When the fact is unlawful only on the part of him, who has received a thing from an unjust cause, he who has given it may recover it again, although the receiver may have performed what he was bound to do by his engagement; and nothing can excuse the receiver from making the restitution, even although the thing were not demanded of him, nor from the other punishments which the fact may deserve, if it comes before a court of justice. If the fact be unlawful both on the part of him who gives, and of him who receives, the giver shall lose deservedly what he has employed to so ill a purpose, and shall have no action for recovering it[40]."[41]

Where all the criminality is on the part of the person paying the money, it seems evident, that he [41] can have no claim to the restitution of it, whatever may be the obligations of the receiver in respect of other persons, or however he may deem it improper to retain what has been so advanced.

The distinction between the illegality, which affects both parties, and that which only affects the receiver, is of the highest importance. In the first case, both parties transgressing a law made for the welfare of the public, or arising from the rules of public order, neither can have any pretence for calling in aid the assistance of a court of justice. If money is engaged to be paid upon such a contract, the courts will give no assistance in demanding it. If it is actually paid, they will give no assistance in reclaiming it. In the other case, the receiver only is regarded as an offender, and cannot alledge his own offence as a bar to the demands of the party to whom his conduct is deemed injurious.

This was clearly stated in an action tried before Lord Mansfield, where a creditor had refused to [42] sign a bankrupt's certificate without a sum of money being paid to him, in contravention of the statute which prohibits the payment of money for the signing a certificate, and the bankrupt's sister having paid the money, sued for repetition of it; and Lord Mansfield said, it was argued, that as she founded her claim upon an illegal act, she should not have relief in a court of justice: but she did not apply to the defendant to sign the certificate upon an illegal or improper consideration; but as the defendant insisted upon it, she, in compassion to her brother, paid what was required. If the act is in itself immoral, or a violation of the general laws of public policy, there the party paying shall not have this action; for where both parties are equally criminal against such general laws, the rule of law is *potior est conditio defendentis*. But there are other laws which are which are calculated for the protection of the subject against oppression, extortion, deceit, &c. If such laws are violated, and the defendant takes advantage of the plaintiff's situation or condition, there the plaintiff shall recover; and it is astonishing that the reports do [43] not distinguish between the violation of the one sort and the other. If a lender takes more than the principal and legal interest, an action will lie to recover the surplus. The case of money given to a solicitor, to bribe a custom-house officer, is against his own agent, and therefore the person giving it cannot recover. But the present is the case of a transgression of a law made to prevent oppression to the bankrupt himself, or his family; and the plaintiff is in the case of a person oppressed, and from whom money has been extorted, and advantage taken of her concern for her brother. It is absurd to say, that any man transgresses a law, made for his own advantage, willingly. Smith *v.* Bromley, Doug. 697.[42]

In subsequent cases his lordship has followed the same course of reasoning, observing upon the two sorts of prohibitions; that where the prohibition is founded upon general reasons of policy and public expedience, the parties offending are equally [44] guilty, and there the defendant has the better condition. For instance, in bribery, if a man pays a sum of money, by way of a bribe, he can never recover it in an action, because both plaintiff and defendant are equally

---

[40] [*Author's footnote:*] Ubi dantis et repetentis turpitudo versatur non posse repeti dicimus si pecunia detur ut male judicatur ff. de cond. ob. turpem vel injustam causam. 3. [*Ed:* the Latin text, which is D.12.5.3, has been garbled. Worst, *dans* and *repetens* are the same person, the original having *dans* and *accipiens.*]

[41] Author's closing quotation marks. There are no opening quotation marks.

[42] *Smith v Bromley* (1760) 2 Doug 696; 99 ER 441.

criminal: but where contracts or transactions are prohibited by positive statutes, for the sake of protecting one set of men from another set of men; the one from their situation and condition, being liable to be oppressed and imposed upon by the other; there the parties are not in equal fault, and in furtherance of these statutes, the person injured, after the transaction is finished and completed, may bring his action, and defeat the contract. The case of a person paying money to a lottery office keeper for illegal insurances, like those of paying money for signing a certificate, and usury falls within the latter of these descriptions, for the statutes upon that subject, are made to protect the ignorant and deluded multitude, who, in hopes of gaining prizes, not conversant in calculation, [45] are drawn in by the office keepers. Vi. 2 Bl.1073. Cowp. 197. — 790.[43]

In a case before Lord Northington, it appeared, that the defendant had, by means of Admiral Boscowen's mistress, procured the plaintiff to be appointed a lieutenant of marines, and received from him 200l. After the plaintiff was appointed, the other officers refused to roll with him, discovering that he had been a livery servant; and having been in consequence discharged, he filed a bill to be repaid the money; and Lord Northington decreed it to be returned with interest. He laid it down as a rule, that if a man sells his interest to procure a person an office of trust or service under the government, it is a contract of turpitude; it is acting against the constitution, by which the government ought to be served by fit and able persons, recommended by the proper officers of the crown, for their abilities, and with purity. By this means, the most innocent and pure officer of the crown, whose business it is to recommend, may have his honour tainted and scandalized. [46] It has been argued, that the defendant was to have had the appointment himself, and only sold his commission; but his lordship did not give credit to the fact. He said, that if the defendant might sell his interest, the plaintiff had been imposed upon, and that the defendant knew the plaintiff was incapable of it by having worn a livery. Ambler, 432.[44] Of the turpitude of this contract, no doubt can be entertained; the imposition of it is not equally clear. The impropriety of appointing a livery servant an officer of marines, was equally known to both parties, and although the degree of turpitude attached to a person selling his interest, may, so far as affects the public, be greater than that of the person buying it, the case of the latter seems sufficiently unfavourable to preclude him from any assistance in a court of justice.

There was a case in the King's Bench, where a sum of money had been paid in order to procure a place in the customs. The place was not procured, [47] and the party who had paid the money having brought his action to recover it back, it was held, that he should recover, because the contract remained executory.[45] And this was afterwards referred to by Mr. Justice Buller, as shewing a sound disctinction between contracts executed and executory, and as supporting the position, that if an action is brought to rescind a contract, you must do it while it continues executory. Vi. Doug. 471.[46] The decision itself is not reported,[47] and it is not very easy to think it could be sustained upon any principles of general reasoning, for, divesting the case of the technical terms *executed and executory*; a sum of money was given for a purpose not merely void but criminal; each of the parties was affected by the objections founded upon public policy; every thing to be done on the one side was complete; but the other party not having fulfilled his engagement, the person who advanced the money would, in case it had been a lawful agreement, have been entitled to an action either for a return, or for incidental da-[48]mages. But it being an illegal engagement, the law assisted one of the parties implicated in the illegality against the other. The corrupt price not having been productive, was decreed to be restored, though the performance of the agreement certainly could not have been enforced. All the meaning that the

---

[43] *Jaques v Golightly* (1776) 2 W Bl 1073; 96 ER 632; *Clarke v Shee* (1774) 1 Cowp 197; 98 ER 1041; *Browning v Morris* (1778) 2 Cowp 790; 98 ER 1364.
[44] *Morris v M'Cullock* (1763) Amb 432; 27 ER 289.
[45] *Walker v Chapman* (1773) Lofft 342; 98 ER 684.
[46] *Lowry v Bourdieu* (1780) 2 Doug 468, 471; 99 ER 299, 300-301, *per* Buller J.
[47] But see *supra*, n 45.

word *executory* can have in such case is, that the man, who had received money for the illegal purpose, had not carried such illegal purpose into execution; but between such parties acting in opposition to the law, it is not the province of courts of law to interpose. They rest their confidence in each other, and the law leaves the fulfilling or transgressing it to themselves.

SECTION II.
Of Contracts which are void, but not criminal.

The cases where contracts are void, but not attended with any circumstances which are illegal or immoral, are involved in some confusion, and will hardly admit of any settled principle, being **[49]** confidently ascribed to them in respect to the obligation of returning money actually paid. It however seems to me that the true course should be to enquire what natural equity requires to be done, and whether under all the circumstances the money can be fairly and conscientiously retained.

Where the money is paid in contemplation of deriving some advantage upon a future event, and the event still continues uncertain, and every thing is entire, Mr. Justice Buller's distinction may be very fairly applied. I lay a wager upon the event of a prohibited horse race, paying Titius 5l. to receive 10l. Before the race is run, and whilst the event of it is uncertain, I may rescind the contract, and require the five pounds to be repaid: but after I have lost it, and run the chance of his honourably fulfilling his engagement, if I had won, I have no pretence of justice to require the stake to be returned upon the allegation that he would not have been under any legal compulsion to pay: but if I have won the wager, and he should take ad-**[50]**vantage of the legal exception, refusing to pay me the 10l. the question arises, Whether he is compellable to return the [five]?[48] And I think (viewing the subject at present, as not affected by any positive authorities) that he is. He has elected to treat the contract as a nullity, and consequently the payment as made, without consideration. Public policy protects him from paying what he has lost, but natural justice requires him to refund what he has received. Whilst the event was uncertain, I was entitled to insist upon a return, and the case ought not to be altered to my prejudice, when the event has terminated in my favour. Suppose Titius having lost the money, pays the amount of it, he has no claim to a return; it was due in point of honour; and not having availed himself of the assistance of the law to evade the payment, he is not in this action, which is universally allowed to be founded upon the principles of natural justice, (and he has no other mode of address) entitled to sue for a repetition.

I shall now advert to the cases which have **[51]** arisen upon this subject as applicable to void insurances, to illegal wagers, and to annuities void for want of registry.

PART I.
Void Insurances.

In the case of Lowry v. Bourdieu, Doug. 451,[49] the plaintiff made an insurance upon an East India voyage, not having any direct interest in the ship, but being a creditor of the captain by bond, and the bond being stated as the subject of the insurance. It was one question, Whether the chance of losing his debt by his debtor not making a successful voyage, was not an insurable interest, but upon principles not connected with the present discussion? It was rightly held that it was not. After the voyage had been performed, and all risk (supposing the policy valid) was at an end, he brought his action for return of the premium, insisting that as he would not have been entitled to recover in case of a loss, it had been paid without considera-**[52]**tion. Lord Mansfield's opinion fluctuated upon this case, but he finally held, that the money could not be recovered;

---

[48] Author's substitution of "five" for "fine".
[49] *Lowry v Bourdieu* (1780) 2 Doug 468; 99 ER 299.

observing that insurances, without interest, were mere games of hazard, like the cast of a die, and that it was a gaming policy against an act of parliament; and therefore the court would not interfere to assist either party, according to the well known rule, that *in pari delictô, &c.* not that the defendant's right was better than that of the plaintiff, but they must draw their remedy from pure fountains. Mr. Justice Willes differed from the rest of the court. He observed, that it did not appear to him that the parties had an idea that they were entering into an illegal contract. The whole was disclosed, and they thought there was an interest. This was a mistake; but it was a new point of law. Mr. Justice Ashurst was of opinion against the plaintiff, but his only observation was, that the contract was a gaming policy; not adverting to the circumstance, that that very supposition was the whole foundation of the plaintiff's claim. Mr. Justice Buller was clear that the plaintiff ought not to recover. There was no fraud on the part [53] of the underwriter, nor any mistake in matter of fact. If the law was mistaken, the rule applied that *ignorantia juris non excusat.* He then adverted to the distinction already stated, between contracts executed and executory; observing, that if the plaintiff had brought his action before the risk was over, and the voyage finished, he would have had a ground for his demand; but he waited till the risk (such as it was, not indeed founded in law, but resting upon the honour of the defendant) had been completely run. — The propriety of this decision seems to be extremely clear, but it is to be regretted that the precise ground of it was not distinctly ascertained; or rather that the judges who concurred in it, did not precisely agree in the ground of their opinion. Lord Mansfield proceeded upon the ground of the parties being *in pari delictô*; and it may be therefore supposed, that the distinction which I have presumed to suggest between contracts which are criminal, and founded upon an immoral purpose, and those which are merely void, as being deprived of any legal efficacy, is without foundation. But I [54] conceive the distinction to be founded upon those principles of natural justice which are principally to be regarded in discussing the right of repetition. The argument of Mr. Justice Willes appears to be well founded to a certain extent; for whilst the event was uncertain, or if it had terminated in favour of the plaintiff, an innocent mistake of the law by parties not having any corrupt intention, might be fairly urged in support of reclaiming what could not produce in point of legal efficacy, the benefit intended; or what from the refusal to complete the contract, appeared to have been paid without consideration. Mr. Justice Buller's opinion, that the mistake of law could afford no excuse, is in opposition to this argument. — I have, in a former part of this essay, discussed the question, how far money supposed to be due by a mistake in point of law, and not due in respect of natural justice, was the subject of repetition, adopting the argument that the nature of the mistake did not prejudice the substantial right. Applying this to the present subject, I conceive, that if a man pays a sum of money for some consideration supposed to be the [55] object of a legal contract, but which, by reason of some impediment, could not be effective, there being no criminal or fraudulent motive, it does, not furnish any right to the person receiving, to catch at the advantage, and retain the money for which he has given no equivalent. The distinction between executed and executory contracts, seems to be well supported in respect of such contracts as these, which are merely void; and it is here that Mr. Justice Willes appears to have fallen short in his opinion. I say *in such contracts as these*, for if my former observations are correct, the distinction does not hold where a criminal purpose intervenes. The person who paid his money upon the void insurance, might recover it during the voyage, but a candidate who had bribed an elector, could not sue him for a return before the day of election; but when Mr. Justice Buller adverts to the circumstance that the plaintiff waited till the issue, such as it was, resting in the honour of the defendant, had been completely run, we see a principle, which puts the propriety of the decision beyond the reach of reasonable doubt. Turning [56] to the case of Moses and Macferlan;[50] the grand expositor of the principles upon which this right of action is founded; we see that it was money fairly lost at play, and which the

---

[50] *Moses v Macferlan* (1760) 2 Burr 1005.

defendant, upon the circumstances of the case, was not obliged by the rules of natural justice and equity to refund. I have deemed it particularly necessary to attempt this analysis of the case of Lowry and Bourdieu, as the authority of it is frequently relied upon, and has, I conceive, in some cases, been misapplied; more especially in the case of Andree v. Fletcher, 3 T.R. 266.[51] A reassurance was made upon a foreign vessel; this was, upon a special case, adjudged to be void, as falling within the general prohibition against reassurances; the assured then sued for a return of the premium. His counsel was arguing, that the defendant had received the money without risk, and therefore retained [it][52] against conscience. The objection to the plaintiff's recovering, must be that the original transaction was illegal, because it is contrary to a statute; but that statute is merely an act *juris positivi*. In Martin v. Sitwell, 1 Str. 156,[53] where the policy was originally void for **[57]** want of interest, it was held, that the premium was received without any consideration, and was therefore money had and received to the plaintiff's use, which the court held he might recover; and it is immaterial whether the contract be void at common law [or][54] by statute; for in Jaques v. Golightly, 2 Bl. 1073,[55] it was held, that the premium paid for insuring lottery tickets, might be recovered back, though the contract of insurance was void by statute. In Wharton v. De la Rive, Park, 428,[56] where an action was brought on an insurance that America would be declared independent within a certain time; Lord Mansfield being of opinion that the contract was illegal, was going to nonsuit the plaintiff on the opening; but it appearing that the defendant had not paid the premium into court, he permitted the plaintiff to take a verdict for that sum. This course of argument seems to be not only judicious and plausible, but a correct examination of legal principles: BUT WHILST THE PLAINTIFF'S COUNSEL WAS PROCEEDING, the court thinking that this case could not be distinguished from Lowry v. **[58]** Bourdieu, ordered, that the *postea* should be delivered to the defendant. — Certainly, if the mere circumstances of the two cases are considered without reference to any expressions used in determining Lowry and Bourdieu, no cases could be more dissimilar. Lowry paid his money upon a wager; he waited till the wager had been won by Bourdieu, taking the chance of his honour for the payment, in case it had been lost, and then sued to recover his stakes, alledging that Bourdieu, in case of loss, could have availed himself of a legal exception. Andree paid his money upon a wager which he won. Fletcher, who lost it, availed himself of a legal exception, to avoid paying the loss, and then insisted most unconscientiously upon retaining what he had received as a consideration for that contract, by which he had refused to be bound. In the one case no unfairness whatever could be imputed to the defendant. In the other, no reprobation of the iniquity of the defendant's conduct could be too severe. The cases cited in the argument of Andree and Fletcher, are much more nearly analogous to the principal case, and **[59]** two of them[57] are directly in point, (that if a man pays a premium for a contingent engagement, and on account of some legal exception, cannot enforce the engagement, having, according to the terms of it, succeeded, the premium shall be returned,) unless there is some technical distinction between contracts void by the common law, and under a statute, of which I am not aware; (for the distinction between contracts being partially or wholly void, in respect to the acts engaged to be performed, has nothing to do with the present argument.) The case of Jaques v. Golightly, is not equally applicable, for there the defendant was regarded as a person criminally deluding the plaintiff. But it is partially applicable, as that was not the only ground of the decision. The balance upon the account, supposing the transaction to

---

[51] *Andree v Fletcher* (1789) 3 TR 266; 100 ER 567.
[52] Author's insertion.
[53] *Martin v Sitwell* (1690) 1 Show KB 156; 89 ER 509.
[54] Author's insertion.
[55] *Jaques v Golightly* (1776) 2 W Bl 1073; 96 ER 632.
[56] *Wharton v De La Rive* (1782), discussed in JA Park, *A System of the Law of Marine Insurances* (4th ed. ? *cf* n 60), 428; see 3rd ed (1796), 376.
[57] [*Author's footnote*:] Martin v. Sitwell, and Wharton v. De la Rive.

have been legal, was in favour of the plaintiff, and Lord Chief Justice de Grey, is reported to have said, "This is an application for favour, by a man knowingly transgressing. He says, and says right-[60]ly, that the insurance contract was null and void. ["][58]He has therefore a scruple of conscience, not to pay the money won by the plaintiff, because the play was illegal; but he has no scruple to retain the consideration money." On the other ground alluded to of criminality and imposition, the defendant would have been compellable to have refunded the premiums, even if the balance had been in his favour.

The right of the assured to recover the premium in the case of Andree v. Fletcher,[59] considered according to the principles of natural equity, divested of any positive municipal authority, is still more evident from analogy to the case of an insurance void for fraud. The premium is commonly restored; and, as I conceive, ought always to be so, because, otherwise a penalty would fall on the assured, and an undue advantage accrue to the insurer: the underwriter cannot be defrauded out of his subscription; but having taken the exception, he cannot, without consideration, retain the premium. (There is indeed one case in which [61] Lord Mansfield said, that the fraud was so gross, that the premium should not be recovered from the underwriter; but if the premium of an insurance defeated for fraud, is to be generally returned gross fraud, or slight fraud, which differ not in principle, but only in degree, can never make the distinction.)[60] But if a man, who has advanced his money, intending to defraud another, [62] shall be allowed to sue for a return when the fraud is detected and defeated, though he must necessarily be conscious of acting wrong, (a corrupt intention being included in the very supposition,) how much stronger and more clear, must his case be, who has paid his money upon a contract not naturally vicious, but merely rendered inefficacious for some reason of public expediency, and in respect of which, the person receiving the money, has availed himself of an objection, founded upon positive law, and in the private application of it, though perhaps not in the public enactment, contrary to natural justice.

Where one man retains money under circumstances, the mere statement of which shows that he unjustly seeks to acquire an adventitious gain to the prejudice of another, every presumption and inclination should be in favour of the rights of repetition, and nothing should be allowed to defeat the substantial claims of justice, except the most direct and imperious authority, or the necessary tendency to introduce a rule which might [63] more frequently produce detriment, by supporting iniquitous demands, than benefit by enforcing such as are just, and incapable of being accurately distinguished in its application to the one case or the other.

---

[58] Opening quotation marks in original removed by editor.
[59] *Andree v Fletcher* (1789) 3 TR 266; 100 ER 567.
[60] [*Author's footnote:*] I find that it has been decided, in the case of Chapman v. Frazer, Park, Jus. 4 ed. 218 [*Chapman v Fraser* (1763), JA Park, *A System of the Law of Marine Insurances*, 3rd ed (1796), 218], that in all cases of actual fraud, on the part of the insured, the underwriter may retain the premium. This case is not reported at length; but I cannot think it consistent with general principles. It, at the same time, treats the contract as inducing, and not inducing a risk; since, if there was a risk, the loss was payable; if there was not, the premium was paid without consideration, or it introduces a penal consequence of an anomalous character. The more particular discussion of that question would be foreign to my immediate subject; but allowing the decision to be correct, it only subtracts one detached particular from the argument upon the direct question under consideration.—Whilst this sheet is passing through the press, I have received the report containing the case of Vandyck v. Hewit, 1 East, 96 [*ed*: *Vandyck v Hewitt* (1800) 1 East 96; 102 ER 39], in which the assured was not allowed to recover the premium on a policy upon trading with the enemy. In that case, there was an illegal act, and the decision accords with what I have submitted to be the true distinctions on the subject.

The Action for Money Had and Received 19

PART II.
Of Wagers.

A wager was laid on the event of a boxing match, and the money deposited in the hands of a third person. One of the parties having lost the wager, gave notice to the stake holder, not to pay over the money, and sued him for his stake; and the court of King's Bench held, that he was entitled to recover. Lord Kenyon took notice, that the action was not brought against one of the parties laying the wager, but a stake holder; and observed, that if the defendant had paid over the money to the winner, perhaps he would not have been answerable again; but here the money was still in his hands. Cotton *v.* Thurland, 5 T.R. 405.[61]

[64] This case will warrant a slight digression concerning the character of a stake holder and his consequent obligations. It must be allowed, on all hands, that he ought not to be allowed in consequence of the money being placed in his hands, upon a contract which is illegal or void, to appropriate it to his own use, but that he is accountable for it in one shape or another. The true way of viewing the case seems to be by considering the deposit of the stakes as a security from the respective parties, and by subjecting the stake holder to the same obligations, and allowing him the same exceptions as would prevail between the parties themselves. If this principle is correct, the following consequences will ensue. *Provided the wager is unexceptionable*, and might be enforced between the parties according to the event, the stake holder must retain the money until the event is decided, and cannot liberate himself by returning the deposit to either party in the mean time, except by mutual consent. *If the subject of the wager is illegal and void*, either party may demand a return *before the event* has happened, [65] because the other party could not maintain an action upon the principal contract; nor consequently after an event in his favour demand more from the stake holder than his original deposit. *After the event decided*, the losing party may require the stake holder not to pay the wager to the other, and may sue for what he advanced, for the same reason which was applied to the preceding hypothesis. If the stake holder, without notice from the loser to the contrary, pays the whole to the winner, the loser cannot reclaim his stakes from either of the others, for having fairly lost the money, though the law would not, in case nothing had been deposited, have enforced the performance of the engagement against him; yet, when he has voluntarily fulfilled it, there is nothing unconscientious in the retention, which can afford him a right of repetition; therefore the stake holder, who pays it over by his authority, implicitly given at the time of the deposit, and continuing unrevoked at the time of payment, is no further accountable to him. And the receipt of the winner, from the stake holder acting under such au-[66]thority, is equivalent to a receipt from the loser himself; and the payment is equally valid[62]. If the winner demands the money, the stake holder may elect to pay each party his deposit, and the winner can found no claim against him for the money won upon the void contract: but if the loser consents to the payment, no objection can be made by the stake holder; as a man may, without consideration, voluntarily direct the application of his money in the hands of another. And if the stake holder is justified in paying the money won, unless he has notice to the contrary, he is necessarily compellable to pay it when there is an express consent by the only person interested to oppose.

A recent case, which appears to have been rightly decided, may, from the observations with which it was accompanied, and a mistake in those reporters, to whose general accuracy the public are so much obliged, lead to erroneous conclusions. The [67] plaintiff paid 100*l*. upon condition to be repaid 300*l*. if peace was not made before the 11th of September, 1797. Having sued for the breach of the agreement, and upon the common count, for money had and received, it was admitted on the trial, that the wager was illegal, and that the 300*l*. could not be recovered;

---

[61] *Cotton v Thurland* (1793) 5 TR 405; 101 ER 227.
[62] [*Author's footnote:*] Since the above was written, the point has been so determined. Vi. Howson *v.* Hancock, 8 T.R. 575 [*ed: Howson v Hancock* (1800) 8 TR 575; 101 ER 1555].

but by the direction of Lord Kenyon, the plaintiff obtained a verdict for the money which he had paid. According to the report of the case, it was argued as if the action had been brought not by the winner, but by the loser; and Lowry v. Bourdieu,[63] was relied upon as an authority, to shew that the party should make his option to rescind the contract while it was executory; otherwise he first takes the chance of the event happening in his favour; and when that is decided against him, he turns round, and insists upon the illegality of the contract. But the court confirmed the verdict; and said it was more consonant to the principles of sound policy and justice, that wherever money had been paid upon an illegal consideration, [68] it might be recovered back again by the party who had thus improperly paid it, than by denying the remedy to give effect to the illegal contract; and the marginal abstract of the report is in these words: — "If a sum be deposited upon the event of an illegal wager, the loser *may recover back* his deposit after the event of the wager." Lacaussade v. White, 7 T.R. 535.[64] Now it is notorious, both on account of the publicity of the subject, (the event in question not having yet taken place after the lapse of several years) and from the action being originally framed to recover what had been lost, that the action was brought not by the loser, but the winner of the wager. It was diametrically opposite to the case of Lowry v. Bourdieu, in which the plaintiff endeavoured to recover back the premium which he had lost by the terms of the contract, and similar in circumstance, but contrary in determination to Andree and Fletcher.[65] The loser of the wager availed himself of the illegality of the contract to avoid performing his engagement, and in addi-[69]tion to this, he wished most fraudulently to retain what he had received as the consideration for a contract that he had elected to vacate, and which therefore was, in effect, paid without consideration. It is therefore by no means to be inferred from this decision, that if the event had been otherwise, and peace had been concluded, the plaintiff could have recovered the deposit, which it was no wise contrary to honour, or justice in the defendant to retain. The report being substantially wrong, very little stress can be laid upon the supposed expression, that wherever money has been paid upon an illegal consideration, it may be receovered back, as that expression thus indefinitely applied, and still more as applied to the particular case, is in opposition to the authority of preceding cases, and to the general opinion of those who have investigated the subject, by tracing it to its original principles of natural justice.

[70]
PART III.
Of Annuities.

The annuity act having vacated the securities for life annuities, which are not registered according to the directions therein prescribed, many contracts have been frustrated by the mere unskilfulness of those who intended fully to comply with the provisions of the law. An annuity having been set aside for the insufficiency of the memorial, the court of King's Bench decided, that the annuitant might sustain an action to recover back the consideration money, for which it had been granted. Mr. Justice Ashurst said, in delivering the opinion of the court, that as the security was not set aside for any fraud in the transaction, but merely for a mistake or omission in form, it became unconscientious in the party to retain it, and it was therefore recoverable as money had and received to the plaintiff's use. Shove v. Webb, 1 T.R. 732.[66] Mr. Powell, in his treatise on the law of contracts, [71] questions the rectitude of this decision. He founds his argument upon an analogy to the distinctions which have been [made][67] upon the statutes of gaming.

---

[63] *Lowry v Bourdieu* (1780) Doug 467.
[64] *Lacaussade v White* (1798) 7 TR 535; 101 ER 1118.
[65] *Andree v Fletcher* (1789) 3 TR 266.
[66] *Shove v Webb* (1787) 1 TR 732; 99 ER 1348.
[67] Editor's insertion.

The statute 16 Chap. II. enacts that all *contracts* for money exceeding 100l. lost at play, and all *securities* for it shall be void. The 9th of Anne provides that all *securities* for money lent to play with, shall be void. And upon the latter act, which only declares that the *securities* shall be void, it is held, that the contract arising from the loan, shall be obligatory: and as the annuity act only directs that if there is not a registry as prescribed, every *assurance* shall be void without adding that the *contract* for the annuity shall be void. Mr. Powell infers, that notwithstanding all the assurances are vacated, the contract may subsist; and that therefore the supposition of the consideration for which the money was paid, having failed, is founded upon a mistake, as such consideration may remain in the subsistence of the contract, notwithstanding the invalidity of the assurance given for its performance; and he observes, "That a contract should fail of effect, for want of the party **[72]** claiming a benefit, by it being capable to substantiate it by legal evidence, is not unusual, yet in such a case he can have no relief in law or equity."[68] This reasoning seems to me to be chiefly founded upon an analogy which is merely verbal, and extremely fallacious. The loan of money is an *act* in its nature producing an obligation independant of any verbal declaration, and there is nothing inconsistent in the obligation being allowed to subsist, notwithstanding the invalidity of some adventitious engagement, by which the performance of it was intended to be more effectually secured; whereas an obligation solely arising from an express engagement, and necessarily rendered ineffectual by the assurance for its performance being defeated, cannot, in reason or justice, be deemed to subsist for a collateral purpose, when it no longer subsists in respect to its original object. There is also a manifest difference between the accidental circumstance of a failure of evidence, and the express and positive defeasance of the engagement itself. If it could be shewn that notwithstanding the defeasance of the **[73]** assurance, the contract for the payment of the annuity might, in its nature, subsist as an obligation which could be legally enforced, I admit the reasoning in question to be correct; but if they are so identified, that the subversion of the one necessarily induces the extinction of the other, in point of legal efficacy, any argument resulting from the supposed existence of the contract, must lead to consequences inconvenient and unjust. I agree with Mr. Powell, that no distinction is made between an annuity being defeated from the consideration being of a nature which is prohibited, and its being rendered void from a formal defect. This distinction, though mentioned by the learned judge, whose opinion has been cited, did not necessarily form an ingredient in the decision. I think that in neither the one case or the other ought the consideration to be retained.

Mr. Plowden, in his treatise on annuities, strongly controverts the opinion of Mr. Powell, that the contract for the annuity can subsist when the assurance is vacated; but upon another ground, **[74]** he adopts the same conclusion of the annuitant having no right to reclaim the consideration money. He says,[69] "If we reflect that the only motive which can induce a person to yield to the ruinous terms of selling an annuity at the present market price, which varies widely from the real value, is to avoid being thrown into goal for the non-payment of a sum of money larger than he has means to command, and having therefore contracted with his creditor to satisfy him; and the creditor having consented to be satisfied with a species of payment by instalments, which every annuity is." [This I deny; a payment by instalments relates to a precise sum to be absolutely paid in a given number of parts, an annuity is wholly uncertain, it may be much, or it may be nothing].[70] "The legal and equitable question hereupon arises, Can the creditor, by his own neglect, laches, means, or procurement, without the consent or concurrence, and greatly to the prejudice of the debtor, annul at will the annuity, securities and contract, and drive the debtor back to his original desperate situation, of owing a debt which he cannot discharge, and for **[75]** emerging out of which he had legally contracted with his creditor, to pay such an exorbitant consideration annually during his life. This is neither the case of an estate sold under a bad title, nor of money

---

[68] JJ Powell, *Essay upon the Law of Contracts and Agreements* (1790), 229.
[69] F Plowden, *A Treatise upon the Law of Usury and Annuities* (1797), 448–450.
[70] Author's note, in original text.

borrowed under void securities. In the first of these cases the vender must return the purchase money, but he takes back the estate; in the second having borrowed, and actually received a specific sum which the other lent, (and every loan is a contract for payment), he must either repay or effectually secure; and in neither case is he injured, and in both he must do justice. But in case of an annuity, the vender appears actually to contract with the purchaser, that he shall never be liable to be called upon for the principal; particularly at the will of his creditor, who, on his side, shall not profit of his own contempt or neglect of the law." A great part of this reasoning will be answered, by admitting that a man who has neglected to take the measures prescribed by law, for securing his annuity, or to speak more correctly, who has fallen into some mistake in endeavouring to comply with the requisites of the law, [76] shall not be allowed in the first instance, to adduce his own neglect or mistake as a ground of prejudice against the opposite party: he shall not alledge, that in consequence of a blunder in the registry, he will no longer receive his annuity, but reclaim his principal, any more than a person who has made a fraudulent insurance, shall come in the first instance, and shewing, that by his own fraud, the policy was void, insist upon the premium being retained; but when the other party has taken advantage of the invalidity of the contract, has found out some formal technical objection, and refused, in consequence, to adhere to his engagement, can it be contended that he has any right, in point of natural justice, to retain the money that he received for a purpose which he refuses to execute? By the protection of the law he shall not be placed in a situation which he considers less advantageous, than if his engagement had not been made; but shall he be therefore enabled to put himself in a better situation, than if there had been no engagement at all, by the amount of the money which he wishes to retain? He shall not be in-[77]jured; but shall he therefore be allowed to defraud? And as to any suppositious agreement of not reclaiming the principal, it is an essential part of the supposition that the annuity will be duly paid; it is blowing hot and cold to adopt one part of the supposition and reject the other. If the grantee of the annuity does not properly provide for its security, let the granter avail himself of positive law and avoid it: but let him not at the same time retain the purchase money, and withhold the annuity: more especially let not the conduct of the man who requires to be paid either the one or the other, who only *certat de damnô vitando* against the other, *qui certat de lucro captando* be the object of reproach. I have not, in the course of private practice, had much opportunity of making observations upon this subject; but the cases which come before the courts of justice, much more frequently evince a disposition in the seller of the annuity, fraudulently to defeat his deliberate engagements, than in the purchaser to harrass or oppress the seller. When it is supposed that the under value at [78] which these contracts are obtained, is to throw all the favour on one side, I cannot help doubting the truth of the fact. The market value of most commodities, and the real value, are synonymous terms, according to the well known test of Hudibras. If the purchases were necessarily attended with the great advantages supposed, the price would rise by the influx of competitors, until a real level was upon the average attained. In annuities the market value is not the calculated value, merely taking into the account the rates of compound interest and insurance: but the market value being so much below the calculated value, seems to shew that the latter is not the real value, when every circumstance, particularly the disposition so prevalent in the sellers of annuities, to cheat if they can, is taken into consideration.

Subsequent to the decision of Shove and Webb, it was ruled by two of the judges, who concurred in that decision[,][71] Mr. Justice Buller, and Mr. Justice Grose, contrary to the opinion of Mr. Justice Ashhurst, that *a surety* for the payment of the an-[79]nuity, was not upon its being vacated for want of enrolment, liable to refund the consideration money, although he had joined in signing a receipt for it. Stratton *v.* Rustall, 2 T.R. 366.[72] From some of the expressions used by the two learned judges, Mr. Plowden infers, that this case cannot be reconciled with the for-

---

[71] Editors' substitution of comma for full point.
[72] *Straton v. Rastall* (1788) 2 TR 366; 100 ER 197.

mer, but neither of those judges intimates the slightest opinion that their former decision was incorrect. They proceed wholly upon the character of the defendant as being a mere surety for the payment of the annuity, and upon his not having in fact received any of the money which he was required to refund. Holding that he was not concluded by the act of signing the receipt, although that would have been *prima faciê* [evidence][73] against him. This ground of decision is perfectly consistent with the compelling a person to refund a sum of money which he has actually received for an engagement, that he has thought proper to vacate, notwithstanding his power to vacate it arises from the neglect of the other party.

[80] The observations which have been made respecting money paid upon the contracts particularly referred to, can easily be applied to other cases dependant upon the same general principles.

[81] CHAP. V.
Of Cases in which the action is [not] *maintainable.*[74]

I Shall now advert to some cases, in which the action for money had and received, is not maintainable.

SECTION I.
Miscellaneous Cases.

A forged bill was drawn upon Price, in the name of *Sutton*, and Price supposing it to have been really drawn by Sutton, paid the amount to Neale, a fair endorsee. Afterwards, upon the forgery being discovered, he sued for a return. After the [82] plaintiff's counsel had been heard, Lord Mansfield stopped the counsel for the defendant, saying, It was one of those cases which could never be made plainer by argument. It is an action upon the case for money had and received to the plaintiff's use: in which action the plaintiff cannot recover the money, unless it be against conscience in the defendant to retain it, and great liberality is always allowed in this sort of action; but it can never be thought unconscientious in the defendant to retain this money, when he has once received it upon a bill of exchange endorsed to him upon a fair and valuable consideration, which he had *bona fide* paid without the least privity, or suspicion of any forgery. Here was no fraud — no wrong. It was incumbent on the plaintiff to be satisfied that the bill upon him was in the drawers hand before he accepted or paid it; but it was not incumbent upon the defendant to inquire into it. His lordship pointed out some circumstances of neglect on the part of the plaintiff, by which the defendant was encouraged to take the bill, and said, "It is a misfortune which has happened without the defend-[83]ant's fault or neglect. If there was no neglect in the plaintiff, yet there is no reason to throw off the loss from one innocent man to another innocent man: but in this case, if there was any fault or negligence in any one, it certainly was in the plaintiff, and not in the defendant. Price *v.* Neal, 3 Bur. 1354.[75]

A lottery office keeper brought an action for the repetition of what he had paid upon illegal insurances. It was first supposed that he had been the defendant in the cause; and much of the discussion proceeded upon that ground, to shew the right of the person to recover, who had been unwarily induced to pay his money for such insurances, and that that person was not implicated in the criminality of the contract; but when it occurred that the contrary was the case, so that the plaintiff was not only in *pari delicto*, but also stood in the light, and under the description of that

---

[73] Author's insertion.
[74] Author's insertion.
[75] *Price v Neal* (1762) 3 Burr 1354; 97 ER 871.

species of insurer, from whom the statute meant to protect the unwary; the court were of opinion [84] that he could not recover. Browning v. Morris, Cowp. 790.[76]

A person borrowed money upon a respondentia bond, which was void by positive statutes. The executors paid a sum of money in discharge of the bond, and afterwards they brought an action to recover it back, but it was decided against them. Lord Kenyon said, that he thought the executors were bound, both in honour and conscience, to refund the money which had been advanced, though the original contract were contrary to a positive law; for it was not a penalty, but money, which the defendants had actually advanced; and the original contract mas not *malum in se,* but *malum prohibitum*. Though the security on which this money was borrowed was void by the statute, he did not know but that an action for money, had and received, might have been maintained to recover back the money; but the ground on which he went was, that there was no misrepresentation, nor any improper conduct by the defendants, to extort the money from the [85] plaintiffs; but the plaintiffs knowing the whole transaction, and the law also, as they were bound to know[77], voluntarily paid it. There was nothing contrary to conscience in the defendants receiving the money which they had advanced; the plaintiffs, therefore, are not entitled, either in law or in equity, to recover it back again. Munt v. Stokes, 4 T.R. 561.[78] The executors, in the preceding case, appear to have paid rather less than the principal sum advanced; but for what reason, is not stated. I cannot think that the respondentia interest or premium, if paid, could have been reclaimed. It was admitted, that if the money had been paid by the borrower himself, there would have been no right of action.

Many other instances might be adduced, in [86] which there would be no right to reclaim money that could not originally have been recovered by legal process, but which was paid in pursuance of a moral obligation, or for the payment of which there was some real and probable subject. The general principle, recognized in all the authorities upon the subject, can easily be applied to the variations of particular cases.

SECTION II.
Of Money paid by way of Compromise.

Here it will be proper to refer to the payment of money by way of compromise. "From the principle that there is no ground of repetition, when there is a real and probable cause of payment, it follows," (says Pothier,) "that if for the purpose of avoiding a contest which has arisen, or is likely to arise between you and me, respecting what you insist, though without foundation, to be due from me to you; I pay you a part of the demand by way of compromise, when in fact I owe you [87] nothing, I have no right of repetition, because there was a real subject of payment in the preventing a law suit. This rule only applies, if the compromise is unattended with any fraud which renders it void; as if you had used any improper artifices to draw me into it." He adds, "or if the compromise does not take place until after judgment in the last resort, which is conclusive upon the matter in dispute, and of which we are unapprised."[79]

It is held, that a sum of money cannot be reclaimed which a person has paid after a judgment in his favour, whether he was privy to or ignorant of such judgment; and the writer alluded to having put the question, Why a compromise, after a judgment, of which the parties are ignorant, is not equally binding? states, that the reason for the difference is evident. The payment of a sum,

---

[76] *Browning v Morris* (1778) 2 Cowp 790; 98 ER 1364.
[77] [*Author's footnote:*] This observation can only allude to that general knowledge of the law, which every man is presumed to possess; but an inference, deduced from such general knowledge, would be contrary to the principles adopted in an early part of the present Essay; and in respect of which, the direct authority of the noble and learned judge, would outweigh the effect of an incidental remark, not forming the basis of his judicial determination.
[78] *Munt v Stokes* (1792) 4 TR 561; 100 ER 1176.
[79] Pothier *Quasi-Contrat* (n 15a), para 159.

after a judgment which releases me from the demand, induces a presumption that I was under a natural obligation to make it; and though a judgment discharges me from all legal responsibility, it leaves [88] the natural obligation entire; and this natural obligation is sufficient to render the payment valid. But a compromise has no other foundation than the uncertainty of the demand which is in dispute; and the intention of putting an end to the suit to which that uncertainty has given rise. The compromise, in its essence, relates to something which is uncertain and doubtful; whereas, when a judgment has removed that uncertainty, and the suit is finally determined, it follows, that what is done after the judgment, the parties being ignorant of its having taken place, is a nullity, there being no subject upon which a compromise could attach.

There appears to me to be more subtilty than solidity in this reasoning, though I agree that a compromise is essentially different from a payment of money, under the consciousness of its being morally due. A judgment which is not divulged, being so far as the parties are concerned, as much a matter of uncertainty as the issue of a [89] pending suit: and the motives for dividing the matter in contest, for preferring a certain receipt or payment to the mere chance of a total recovery or liberation, as opposed to a total loss, may be equally strong up to the very moment when the event is finally divulged, as in the first outset of the process. I conceive that the contrary reasoning must have originated in some techinical force of the word *transaction*, (which is used in the civil law to denote a compromise) [confining][80] it to the case of an undecided litigation. Pothier adds, that the clause at the end of an account, by which it is said that all claims are mutually discharged, and that neither of the parties shall have any demand upon the other, is not a transaction, (or compromise) and consequently is no bar to reclaiming what has been unduly paid [thereon][81]; and he cites a passage from the digest to the same effect. This is certainly true; neither of the parties supposes himself to pay or receive any thing more or less than is really due; but the account proceeds upon the supposition of the real balance being ascertained. The common provision of "Errors excepted," is per-[90]fectly unnecessary; for though the statement of an account is presumptively correct, it may, by sufficient proof, be shewn to be erroneous, and the parties are not concluded by any admission from asserting their respective rights.

[91]
CHAP. VI.
On the Effect of judicial proceedings.

POTHIER having discussed the effect of a compromise, as was shewn in the preceding chapter, goes on to say, "If I cannot reclaim what I paid without its being due by way of compromise, the reason is much more strong for precluding me, when I have actually been condemned to pay by a legal judgment; for the judgment in this case, forms a civil obligation. *Propter auctoritatem rei judicatae repetitio cessat.* --- D. Mand. 59. *Pecuniae indebitae per errorem non ex causâ judicati solutae esse repetitionem jure condicionis non ambigitur.* --- Cod. de condic. indeb. 1.[82] This, as a general rule, is essentially necessary to support the authority of judicial [92] proceedings, and contests would be infinite, if a case once decided, could, in a collateral way, be again brought into controversy.

The case of Moses v. Macferlan, 2 Bur. 1005,[83] is of great utility, as it expounds with so much accuracy and perspicuity, the general principles which regulate the action for money had and received; but the immediate decision of that cause, if not a deviation from the rule at present under consideration, is a very strong exception to it. The payee of several promissory notes, under 40s. each, endorsed them over, for the purpose of recovering against the drawer. The

---
[80] Author's substitution of "confining" for "confirming".
[81] Author's substitution of "thereon" for "therein".
[82] Pothier, *Quasi-Contrat* (n 15a), para 159. The quoted texts are D.17.1.29.5; C.4.5.1.
[83] *Moses v Macferlan* (1760) 2 Burr 1005.

endorsee agreed, that the payee should not be liable to the payment of the money; but afterwards sued him as endorser, in the court of Conscience, for the amount. The court of Conscience rejected the evidence of this agreement, thinking they had no power to judge of it, and decreed the money to be paid. It being paid accordingly, the payee brought his action in the court of King's Bench, for money had and [93] received, and it was ruled that he was entitled to recover.

Lord Mansfield admitted it to be most clear, that the merits of a judgment could never be overhaled in an original suit, either at law or in equity. He said,[84] "Till the judgment is set aside or reversed, it is conclusive as to the subject matter of it, to all intents and purposes. But the ground of this action is consistent with the judgment of the court of Conscience; it admits the commissioners did right. They decreed, upon the endorsement of the notes by the plaintiff, which endorsement is not now disputed. The ground upon which this action proceeds, was no defence against that sentence: it is enough for us that the commissioners adjudged they had no cognizance of such collateral matter. We cannot correct an error in their proceedings, and ought to suppose what is done by a final jurisdiction, to be right: but we think the commissioners did right in refusing to go into such collateral matter; otherwise, by way of defence, against a promissory note for 30s. they might go [94] into agreements and transactions of great value; and if they decreed payment of the note, their judgment might indirectly conclude the balance of a large account. The ground of this action is not that the judgment was wrong; but that, for a reason which the now plaintiff could not avail himself of against that judgment, the defendant ought not, in justice, to keep the money. And at Guildhall I declared, very particularly, that the merits of a *question*, determined by the commissioners, where they had jurisdiction, never could be brought over again in any shape whatsoever. Money may be recovered by a right and legal judgment, and yet the iniquity of keeping that money, may be manifest, upon grounds which could not be used by way of defence against the judgment. Suppose an endorsee of a promissory note having received payment from the drawer or maker of it, sues and recovers the same money from the endorser, who knew nothing of such payment. Suppose a man recovers upon a policy, for a ship presumed to be lost, which afterwards comes home; or upon the life of a man presumed to be dead, who afterwards [95] appears; or upon a representation of a risk deemed to be fair, which afterwards come out to be grossly fraudulent.

"The admission that an action might unquestionably be brought upon the agreement, is a decisive answer to any objection from the judgment; for it is the same thing as to the force and validity of the judgment, and it is just equally affected by the action, whether the plaintiff brings it upon the equity of his case arising out of the agreement, that the defendant may refund the money he received, or upon the agreement itself, that besides refunding the money, he may pay the costs and expences the plaintiff was put to."

The present Chief Justice of the King's Bench, has lately adverted to this opinion being received with considerable dissatisfaction by the profession;[85] and it certainly is a proposition very difficult to maintain, " *that a sum of money, paid under the direct authority of a court of competent jurisdiction, may be reclaimed as unduly paid.*" That a [96] person should be judicially compellable to pay a sum of money; and as soon as he has paid it, should be allowed to institute another suit to recover it back again. The inferior quality of the court does not seem to induce any substantial difference; and the same rule which could be applied to this small sum of money, recovered in the court of Conscience, must be equally applicable to a recovery of the largest demand in any of the courts of Westminster.

It is said, to be *sufficient that the commissioners adjudged they had no cognizance of such collateral matter*; but if they had such cognizance, and the matter could be proper ground of defence, their erroneous opinion to the contrary, could not convert that ground of defence into a substantive cause of action to defeat their judgment upon the immediate claim before them.

[84] (1760) 2 Burr 1005, 1009–1010.
[85] *Semble Phillips v Hunter* (1795) 2 H Bl 402, 416; 126 ER 618, 625, *per* Eyre CJ.

The opinion *that they did right*, is also very questionable; for if there is any legal defence to the supposed cause of action, that defence must be equally available in one court as another: and though the power of a court of [97] Conscience only extends to debts under 40s.; if any circumstances are material to shew that such debt under 40s. is not due, although these circumstances relate to transactions of the greatest value, they ought to be fully considered. The discussion of them does not import right of deciding matters not within the jurisdiction; it is merely an examination of evidence relating to the demand which is regularly before them, and there can be no pretence for contending that an endorsee of a promissory note can maintain an action against the endorser, for whose use, and {and} on whose account, and as whose agent he has received it, with the express engagement that the endorser should not be molested thereon.

In the several cases supposed by the illustrious judge, there would be iniquity in keeping the money; but I do not think there could be any ground for maintaining an action for money had and received. Indeed any reference to them is only proving *idem per idem*. The supposition, that a man who has recovered money, by a regular [98] judgment, can be compelled in this way to refund on account of a matter of defence afterwards discovered, is contrary to all practical experience; and it would be very difficult to draw the line which should settle what was a final adjudication.

As to the jurisdiction of courts of equity in giving relief against judgments at law, it is a regular known proceeding: though it is not formally an appeal, it is a corrective power attended with the same effects; and being a special jurisdiction, essentially different from that possessed by courts of law, ought not to be drawn into consequences foreign to the objects of its institution.

It may be difficult satisfactorily to distinguish the right of bringing an action on the agreement, and an action for money had and received; but the former attached immediately upon the instituition of the suit; the money paid would be evidence to shew the amount of damages upon violation of the agreement. There may be several instances in which a suit may be brought con-[99]trary to an agreement, and yet the agreement be no defence in the suit; as if there is a covenant not to sue within a given time; if there are two obligers, and there is a covenant not to sue one of them; if there is a covenant not to sue generally, it may be used as a release to defeat the action; but having another power and efficacy, as an agreement, I do not think that a recovery in the action would be a bar to an original suit, directly founded upon the violation of the agreement. Whether the setting up such an agreement may be allowed to shew that money recovered under a regular judgment was unduly paid, and directly subject to repetition, is a very different question. Whether the one mode of proceeding or the other, may be more beneficial to a defendant, is a question not of sufficient magnitude to permit the subversion of a fundamental rule of law depend upon the exposition of it[86].

[100] A recent determination of the King's Bench, goes a great way to destroy the authority of Moses and Macferlan, and certainly is a stronger instance of the right of repetition, being precluded in respect of money paid under a judicial proceeding. Hampton brought an action against Marriott, for goods which had been before paid for, and a receipt given; but Marriott not being able to find the receipt at that time, and having no other proof of the payment, he could not defend the action, but was obliged to submit, and pay the money again. He afterwards found the receipt, and brought an action to be repaid the money so wrongfully obtained, but was not allowed to recover. Moses and Macferlan was cited in his favour, as was a subsequent case, not reported, of Livesey and Rider, where a similar action was held to be maintainable. Lord Kenyon

---

[86] [*Author's footnote:*] At the time of making the above observations, I was not aware of a similar course of argument having been taken by Lord Chief Justice Eyre, in the case of Philips *v* Hunter, 2 H.B. 402 [*ed: Phillips v. Hunter* (1795) 2 H Bl 402; 126 ER 618]. His opinion upon that particular case, [100] was contrary to that of all the other judges of England, but the grounds of decision, upon which the other judges proceeded, were perfectly collateral to the subject of our present enquiry.

said he was afraid of such a precedent: if the action could be maintained he **[101]** knew not what cause of action could ever be at rest. After a recovery by process of law, there must be an end of litigation, otherwise there could be no security for any one. It often happens that new trials are applied for on the ground of evidence supposed to have been discovered after the trial, and they are as often refused, but this goes much further; and Mr. Justice Lawrence said, that if the case cited be law, it goes the length of establishing this, that every species of evidence which was omitted by accident to be brought forward at the trial, may still be of avail in a new action, to over-hale the former judgment, which is too preposterous to be stated. 7 T.R. 269.[87]

In a former case, an endorsee of a promissory note had obtained interlocutory judgment; and a sum of money was therefore paid under a compromise. It afterwards appeared, that the plaintiff had taken the note, knowing that it was given upon an illegal consideration, and an action was brought, reclaiming the money paid. And an objection being made that this action was, in effect, **[102]** to put the same sum in litigation a second time; Lord Kenyon over-ruled it on the ground that the money had been paid under a compromise, and not under the judgment of a court. The case was brought before the court of King's Bench on a question of evidence, but no discussion took place there as to the right of action. Cobden v. Kendrick, 4 T.R. 431.[88]

It has been stated in the preceding chapter, that money, paid under a compromise, is not subject to repetition; but the case last cited, may furnish an exception on the ground of fraud.

[103] CHAP. VII.
By what Persons the [Action][89] may be maintained.

WITH respect to the persons by whom the action may be maintained; if my factor pays a sum of money on my behalf, erroneously supposing it to be due, the right of repetition belongs not to him but to me. If a person paid his own money in my name, and on my behalf, he was allowed by the Roman law, to sue immediately for the repetition, if the money was not due, without having recourse to the circuity of suing me, and leaving me to sue the party who had received it, with which determination I conceive the law of England would coincide; and this right of repetition is still more evident if I disavow the payment; for **[104]** otherwise he would be wholly destitute of redress, not having any claim against me. But it is competent to me to sue in my own name, for money paid on my behalf, though without my authority. Such was the case of Ancher and the Bank of England, Doug. 637.[90] The drawer of a bill was allowed to recover the money which a friend had paid for his honour, and for which the drawer, under the circumstances of the case, was not liable.

In a case where a brewer's clerk had paid his master's money in illegal lottery insurances, the master was allowed to recover it back. Lord Mansfield (being then of an opinion which he afterwards changed, that nothing could be recovered back by the person who had himself paid money upon such insurances) said, he thought that the plaintiff did not sue as standing in the place of his clerk, for the money and notes which the clerk paid to the defendant, were the identical money and notes of the plaintiff. "Where money or notes are paid *bona fide*, and upon a va-**[105]**luable consideration, they never shall be brought back by the true owner; but where they come *mala fide* to a person's hands, they are in the nature of specific property; and if their identity can be traced and ascertained, the party has a right to recover. It is of public benefit and example, that he should; but otherwise, if they cannot be followed and identified, because there it might be inconvenient, and open a door to fraud. Here the plaintiff sues for his identical property, which has

---

[87] *Marriott v Hampton* (1797) 7 TR 269; 101 ER 969.
[88] *Cobden v Kendrick* (1791) 4 TR 431; 100 ER 1102.
[89] Editors' substitution of "Action" for "Actions".
[90] *Archer v The Bank of England* (1781) 2 Doug 637.

come to the hands of the defendants iniquitiously and illegally, in breach of the act of Parliament,["][91] Cowp. 197.[92]

[106] CHAP. VIII.
Against what Persons the Action may be maintained.

AS to the persons against whom the action may be brought, there is some difference between the civil law and the decisions of the English courts, upon the point of a person being individually liable to refund what he may have received as agent for another. According to both systems of jurisprudence, the principal is liable for what has been paid to his agent on his behalf, and by his authority. But in the civil law the agent was not liable if the principal ratified the payment, even if the agent derived an advantage from it; as by being discharged from bringing it into account. *Si* [107] *procuratori falso indebitum solutum sit, ita demum a procuratorê repeti non* [*potest*][93] *si dominus ratum habuerit, sed ipse dominus tenetur. Dig. de condic. causa, &c.* 14.[93a] *His solis pecunia condicitur, quibus quoquomodo soluta est non quibus proficit*[.][94] *de condic. indeb.* 49.[95]

In the case of Jacob v. Allen, 1 Salk. 27,[96] a person received money as attorney, for an administrator, and paid it over to him. The administration being repealed, an action was brought against the attorney, by the executor; and it was objected that the defendant acting only as attorney for him that was in fact administrator, it was the receipt of the administrator, and not of the defendant; but Lord Chief Justice Trevor, before whom the cause was tried, disallowed the objection, for the administration was merely void, and consequently the administrator could give no authority, and then there was nothing to hinder the raising an implied contract. But Lord Chief Justice Holt, in the subsequent case of Pond v. Underwood, 2 Lord Ray-[108]mond 1210,[97] made a contrary decision; for though all acts done by an administrator where there is a will, are void, it was hard to make the defendant liable, having paid the money over to the administrator before he knew of the will.

Where an action was brought against a person to refund a sum of money, which had been paid to him as receiver for Lady Windsor, and for which a receipt was taken as paid for the use of Lady Windsor, Mr. Baron Perrot, before whom the cause was tried, was of opinion, that the action did not lie; that nothing could be more absurd than to make the collector or receiver of another person, liable to an action for every payment that was voluntarily made to him, and to leave him to be defended or deserted by his principal, as such principal should think fit: that if the action lay in this case it, would lie against every attorney, who by his client's direction, should demand and receive money as due to his client, which the supposed debtor might voluntarily pay, and afterwards think fit to dispute. He thought that if the money had [109] been paid over to Lady Windsor, the plaintiff might easily prove it; and if it was not paid over, yet the payment to her receiver was payment to her; and therefore the action might be brought against her. He referred to an action brought against Mr. Kynaston's collector, to recover back a sum paid for tithes, wherein Lord Chief Justice Lee nonsuited the plaintiff upon the principle that the right to an inheritance should not be tried in an action for money had and received against the collector. But whether the money had, or had not been paid over to his principal, that could not be the ground of Lord Chief Justice Lee's opinion, being merely a matter in the knowledge of the principal and receiver, and to make the action maintainable or not, just as the fact should appear on

[91] Editors' closing quotation marks.
[92] *Clarke v Shee* (1774) 1 Cowp 197, 200–201.
[93] Editors' substitution of "potest" for "protest".
[93a] D.12.4.14.
[94] Editors' insertion of full point.
[95] D.12.6.49.
[96] *Jacob v Allen* (1703) 1 Salk 27; 91 ER 26.
[97] *Pond v Underwood* (1705) 2 L Raym 1210; 92 ER 299.

the trial, would make this kind of action a trap for the plaintiff. The case being brought before the court of King's Bench, they were of opinion, that the action ought to have been brought against Lady Windsor, and not against her agent; that the action for money had and received, was a liberal action, founded upon large principles of equity, [110] where the defendant cannot conscientiously hold the money. The defence is any equity that will rebut the action. This money was paid to the known agent of Lady W. He was liable to her for it, whether he had actually paid it over to her or not, he received it for her; and Lord Mansfield expressed a dissent to the case of Jacob v. Allen, and his approbation of Pond v. Underwood. He said he kept clear of all payments to third persons, but where it is to a known agent, in which case the action ought to be brought against the principal, (unless in special cases, as under notice or *male fide*.) 4 Bur. 1984.[98]

In a subsequent case, a sum of money was paid to the defendant as agent for the parties interested under a policy of insurance, who, on the same day, passed it in account to his principals, and gave them credit for it against a larger sum, in which they were indebted to him. On a subsequent day, the underwriter gave the defendant notice that it was a foul loss. The defendant had then accepted no fresh bills, advanced no sum of [111] money, nor given any fresh credit to his principals. On the trial the question was considered to be whether having placed this money to the account of the principals, was equivalent to a payment over? And Lord Mansfield, in reporting the evidence said, that in general the principle of law is clear, that if money be mispaid to an agent expressly for the use of his principal, and the agent has paid it over, he is not liable in an action by the person who mispaid it, because it is just that one man should not be a loser by the mistake of another, and the person who made the mistake, is not without redress, but has his remedy over against the principal. On the other hand, it is just that as the agent ought not to lose, he should not be a gainer by the mistake; and therefore, if after the payment so made to him, and before he has paid the money over to his principal, the person corrects the mistake, the agent cannot afterwards pay it over to his principal, without making himself liable to the real owner for the amount; but the present case turns upon this, that the agent was precisely in the same situation at the time the mis-[112]take was discovered as before; and in conscience the defendant is not entitled to retain the money. After argument by counsel, his lordship in addition, observed, that the defendant had trusted his principals, and given them credit. He trafficked to the country, where they loved, and had had agents there, who knew how to get the money back. The plaintiff is a stranger to them, and never heard of their names. [This cannot be literally true; for then the defendant would have been, to all intents and purposes, so far as related to the plaintiff's claim, not an agent, but a principal.][99–100] Is it conscientious then (he said) that the defendant should keep the money which he has got by their misrepresentation, and should say, though there is no alteration in my account with my principal, this is a hit. I have got the money, and I will keep it? If there had been any new credit given, it would have been proper to have left it to the jury to say, whether any prejudice had happened to the defendant by means of this payment: but here no prejudice at all is proved, and none is to be inferred. Under these circumstances, the [113] defendant has no defence in point of law, and in point of equity and conscience, he ought not to retain the money in question. A new trial was accordingly granted. Buller v. Harrison, Cowp. 565.[101]

The following observations have occurred to the writer of the present essay, as applicable to the preceding case. It is admitted, that no fraud or misconduct was imputable to the defendant; and it is clear, that between two innocent persons, a court of equity, or a court of law, in the equitable action for money had and received, should stand neuter. Supposing the plaintiff had, under the same mistake, paid the money to the holder of a bill of exchange, or by special direction, to

---

[98] *Sadler v Evans (Lady Windsor's Case)* (1766) 4 Burr 1984; 98 ER 34.
[99–100] Author's note in original text.
[101] *Buller v Harrison* (1777) 2 Cowp 565; 98 ER 1243.

any creditor of the insured, or had made the loss the ground of a promise to a third person, or even if such promise or payment had been made to the agent himself in his character of a creditor, in any of these cases the plaintiff would be bound. The case would certainly be the same if the agent had *bonâ fide* paid it to his principal, and had immedi-**[114]**ately received it again. And the present case appears only to differ from that in circumstance and the want of circuity, and not in substance and effect. It is to avoid circuity that a retainer is deemed equivalent to a payment. The argument urged by the defendant's counsel that the agent would be lulled into security, is apparently supported by the principles of reason and justice; for no man who had lawfully received a sum of money on behalf of his debtor, would institute a process, or have recourse to any other measure, for the recovery of his debt, when a decisive answer could be given by setting off the money which he had received. According to the rules of the civil law, which appear to be founded in natural equity, whenever a person who is creditor of another for a given sum, becomes his debtor to the same amount, or in another sum, capable of being brought into compensation, the compensation takes place, and the respective debts are extinguished so far as they concur, by the mere force of the law of compensation. In the English law, a defendant is not bound to avail himself of the statutes of set off, and **[115]** may pay the debt which he owes, and maintain an action for the mutual demand; but as every man would in general consider an indisputable right of set off, as equivalent to an actual payment, this technical distinction does not seem to effect the general principle, as it is founded in substantial justice.

It is observable, that in the civil law there was no distinction founded upon the circumstance of a payment over; the payment was considered as made to the principal, and the agent only regarded as an instrument of transmitting it.

An action was held to be maintainable against an auctioneer for a deposit; the sale being objected to upon sufficient grounds by the purchaser, as the money did not appear to have been paid over by him to his principal; but even if it had, as the objection was made before it either had, or ought to have been paid over, he was held to be a stake holder, a mere depositary of the money, who ought not to have parted with it till such time as **[116]** the sale should be finished and completed; and it should appear in the event to whom it properly belonged. Borough *v.* Skinner, 5 Bur. 2639.[102]

In a very late case the broker, on a policy of insurance, received the money from the underwriters, and refused to pay it over to the assured, alledging that the voyage was illegal; and as he was a stake holder, the plaintiff's right was not greater against him than against the underwriters, and he must stand in the same situation as if he had immediately sued them. Mr. Justice Buller said, "Is the man who has paid over money to another's use, to dispute the legality of the original consideration? Having once waved the illegality, the money can never come into his hands again. Can the defendant, then, in conscience, keep the money so paid? For what purpose should he retain it? To whom is he to pay it over? Who is entitled to it but the plaintiff?" To which Lord Chief Justice Eyre added, "The defendant is not like a stake holder. The question is, Whether a man who has received money to another's use on an **[117]** illegal contract, can be allowed to retain it, and that not even at the desire of those who paid it to him? I think not." Bos. and Pul. 3.[103]

If a person receives in my name, and on my behalf, a sum of money, which the party paying it supposes due from him to me, the payment cannot be deemed to have been made to me, unless I either gave a special authority for receiving it, or ratify and assent to the payment, as being made on my account. If I disavow it, the action cannot be sustained against me, but only against the person to whom the payment was actually made.

Pothier says, that this rule applies even when the person to whom the money is paid, has a general procuration; for such procuration imports an authority to receive what is due, but not to

---

[102] *Borough v Skinner* (1770) 5 Burr 2639; 98 ER 387.
[103] *Tenant v Elliott* (1797) 1 Bos & Pul 3; 126 ER 744.

receive what is not due; therefore, if he receives what is not due, or more than is due, I may disavow the payment, and the action can only be brought against the receiver.[104] I conceive that this **[118]** observation can only be assented to with some qualification, for a receiver of rents, a clerk in a counting house, and other persons of similar characters, might be deemed to receive any sums of money paid to them as such, by virtue of a sufficient authority from their principals.

[119] CHAP. IX.
Of the Damages.

THE same liberality which governs that nature of this action will also regulate the amount of the damages to be recovered. Thus when an action was brought against a person who had received a sum of money for another, it was held, that he might retain a proper compensation for his trouble in receiving it. Lord Mansfield said, "The plaintiff can recover no more than he is in conscience and equity entitled to, which can be no more than what remains after deducting all just allowances, which the defendant has a right to retain out of the very sum demanded. This is not in the nature of a cross demand, or mutual demand, or mutual debt, it is a charge which makes the sum of mo-**[120]**ney, received for the plaintiff's use, so much less.["][105] 4 Bur. 2134.[106]

In the case of Dutch v. Warren,[107] a sum was paid for the transfer of stock, and the stock not being transferred, the plaintiff was only allowed to recover the value of the stock, which was less than the money paid. If, as Lord Mansfield said, in Moses v. Macferlan, the stocks had been considerably higher, the damages could only have been given for the money paid. No redress can be had in this form of action for consequential damages arising from the non performance of an agreement. And it has been very lately determined, that in an action for money had and received, the plaintiff can recover nothing but the net sum received without interest. Walker v. Constable, 1 B.P. 306.[108]

It seems however difficult to reconcile these two decisions, more especially the last, to the principles of general reasoning. Where one party, by his refusal to complete a contract, gives the other a **[121]** right to treat the contract as [a][109] nullity; why should that right, which is allowed in its nature, be restricted in its extent?

And though a recovery of incidental damages for the nonperformance of a contract, would be repugnant to the nature of an action founded upon the disaffirmance of such contract, it is by no means a necessary consequence of that principle, that damages should not be allowed in respect of the interest of the money improperly detained; and this observation, in respect of the action, as it is brought for restitution of money unduly paid, and which is founded upon a legal fiction, will be more forcible where the allegation, which is commonly formal, is literally true: when money is actually received by one man for the use of another, and instead of being paid over, is placed at interest, or employed in business: but if there is a technical rule which governs the action in general, it would be incorrect to dispense with the application of it in particular cases.

[122] Supposing it should appear upon reconsideration that the rule is merely founded upon practice, and not supported by principle, it may be important to attend to the observation of Lord Mansfield, in the case of Robinson and Bland, as reported in 1 Bl. 256,[110] that where an

---

[104] Pothier. *Quasi-Contrat* (n 15a), para 168.
[105] Editors' closing quotation marks.
[106] *Dale v Sollett* (1767) 4 Burr 2133, 2134; 98 ER 112, 113, *per* Lord Mansfield.
[107] *Dutch v Warren* (1721) 2 Burr 1010.
[108] *Walker v Constable* (1798) 1 Bos & Pul 306; 126 ER 919.
[109] Editors insertion.
[110] *Robinson v Bland* (1760) 1 W Bl 234, 256; 96 ER 129, 141.

error has been established, and has taken root, upon which any rule of property depends, it ought to be adhered to by the judges, till the legislature thinks proper to alter it, lest the new determination should have a retrospect, and shake many questions already settled; but the reforming erroneous points of practice, can have no such bad consequences, and therefore they may be altered at pleasure, when found to be absurd or inconvenient.

FINIS

THE LAW OF RESTITUTION AND THE PROCEEDS OF CRIME — A SURVEY OF ENGLISH LAW

Graham Virgo*

The recent recognition by the Court of Appeal in *Attorney-General v Blake*[1] that the Attorney-General can bring a public law claim to prevent a criminal from profiting from the commission of a crime, should renew interest in the potential role of the law of restitution in ensuring that criminals do not profit from their crime.[2] This is a matter which has not previously received the attention it deserves.[3] Indeed, the Law Commission in its recent paper on restitutionary damages, *inter alia*, does not make any reference to the possibility of restitutionary claims for wrongdoing triggered by the commission of a criminal offence.[4] In fact, the law of restitution does have an important role to play in ensuring that criminals do not profit from the commission of their crimes. There is a body of cases from which general principles can be identified, the effect of which should be that restitutionary relief is indeed available where the defendant has committed a crime, in the same way as it may be available where the wrong involves the commission of a tort, breach of contract or equitable wrongdoing.

When an offender has committed a criminal offence restitutionary principles may be relevant in two ways. First, the offender may have received a benefit as a result of the commission of the crime, so the question is whether there is a cause of action which will enable somebody to recover the proceeds of the crime from the criminal. Secondly, a consequence of the offender committing the crime may be that he or she is entitled to obtain a benefit, under a life assurance policy for example. Here the question is whether the offender can be prevented from obtaining this benefit. In both cases the relief which is available will depend upon the application of the same fundamental principle, namely that no wrongdoer should be allowed to profit from the commission of a wrong.[5] Since there is no clearer wrong than the commission of a criminal offence, the application of the "no profit principle" means that, as a general rule, the criminal should not be allowed to retain or to receive the proceeds of the crime. But, if this is accepted, the question which then needs to be considered is who is the most appropriate person to instigate proceedings to ensure that the criminal does not profit from the crime. In particular, should proceedings be instigated by the victim or the State or by both? This raises important questions as to the proper relationship between private law and public law claims.

---

* Fellow of Downing College, Cambridge and Lecturer in Law at the University of Cambridge.
[1] [1998] 1 All ER 833. See "Clarifying Restitution for Wrongs", *infra*, 118.
[2] The question of criminals retaining the proceeds of crime is a continual matter of public interest. See, in particular, the public outrage, in April 1998 concerning the payment to Mary Bell for interviews in connection with her conviction for killing two children in 1968.
[3] It is, however, something which has not completely escaped the attention of authors on the law of restitution. Goff and Jones, in particular, devote a whole chapter to "Benefits Accruing to a Criminal from his Crime": *The Law of Restitution*, 4th ed (London, 1993) (hereafter "*Goff & Jones*"), ch 37. See also Mason and Carter, *Restitution Law in Australia* (Sydney, 1995), ch 19 ("Wrongful Death") and Maddaugh and McCamus, *The Law of Restitution* (Ontario, 1992) ch 22 ("Criminal and Quasi-Criminal Acts").
[4] *Aggravated, Exemplary and Restitutionary Damages*: Law Com. No 247, 1997. The Law Commission explicitly confines its analysis of the law to restitution for civil wrongs: p 28.
[5] This principle was recognised by Lord Hardwicke LC in *Bridgeman v Green* (1755) 2 Ves Sen 627, 628.

I. RESTITUTIONARY CLAIMS BROUGHT BY THE VICTIM

A. *The general principle*

Although it is a fundamental principle of the law of restitution that no criminal can retain a benefit which accrues to him or her as a result of the commission of a crime,[6] it does not follow automatically that the victim of the crime is necessarily entitled to recover the benefit which the defendant had obtained. Whether the victim's restitutionary claim should succeed depends on the resolution of difficult questions of policy and requires consideration in particular of principles of causation and remoteness of benefit. Even if it can be shown that the offender did obtain the benefit as a result of the commission of a crime it is also necessary for the victim to found his or her claim on a cause of action within the law of restitution, whether this be the reversal of the defendant's unjust enrichment, the vindication of property rights or the fact that the commission of a crime involves some form of wrongdoing which is recognised as triggering the award of restitutionary remedies.

B. *Claims founded on the reversal of the defendant's unjust enrichment*

Where the defendant has obtained a benefit from the plaintiff as a result of the commission of a crime the defendant will have been benefited at the plaintiff's expense and so the plaintiff will be able to obtain restitution of the benefit if the claim falls within one of the recognised grounds of restitution. So, for example, if the defendant falsely imprisons the plaintiff and demands the payment of money from him or her as a condition of release, the defendant will have committed the crimes of false imprisonment[7] and blackmail,[8] but the plaintiff will be able to recover the money paid on the ground of duress of the person.[9] Restitution is available in cases such as this because the defendant's threat to continue to restrain the plaintiff, unless the money is paid, is a threat to do something unlawful.

In some circumstances the plaintiff will have transferred a benefit to the defendant pursuant to an illegal transaction. This transfer may itself be criminal and this might prevent the plaintiff from recovering the benefit because of the principle that the parties are *in pari delicto*.[10] But this principle is subject to a number of exceptions, the effect of which is that the plaintiff will be able to recover the benefit transferred to the defendant, despite the fact that the transaction was illegal. For example, the plaintiff may have withdrawn from the transaction[11] or the defendant may have been more responsible for the illegal transaction so that the parties are not in fact *in pari delicto*.[12]

C. *Claims founded on the vindication of property rights*

Sometimes the crime committed by the defendant involves the receipt of property belonging to the plaintiff in circumstances where the defendant does not obtain title to the property. This is invariably the case where the defendant steals the plaintiff's property. In such a case the plaintiff

---

[6] *St John Shipping Corp v Joseph Rank Ltd* [1957] 1 QB 267, 292 (Devlin J). See also *Attorney-General* v. *Guardian Newspapers Ltd (No 2)* [1990] 1 AC 109, 286 (Lord Goff).
[7] This is a common law offence. See Smith and Hogan, *Criminal Law*, 8th ed (1996), 431-442.
[8] Theft Act 1968, s 21.
[9] See, for example, *Duke de Cadaval v Collins* (1836) 4 Ad and El 858.
[10] *Holman v Johnson* (1775) 1 Cowp 341. For general discussion of the defence of illegality in the law of restitution and the exceptions to that defence see GJ Virgo, "The Effect of Illegality on Claims for Restitution in English Law" in WJ Swadling (ed), *The Limits of Restitutionary Claims: A Comparative Analysis* (UKNCCL, 1997) 141.
[11] *Tribe v Tribe* [1996] Ch 107.
[12] See, for example, *Kiriri Cotton Co Ltd v Dewani* [1960] AC 192.

can bring a proprietary claim for restitution founded on the vindication of his or her continuing proprietary rights in the property which was stolen. For such a claim to succeed the defendant must retain the property or its traceable proceeds. Even if the defendant has dissipated the property and is not in possession of its traceable proceeds, the plaintiff will still be able to bring a personal claim to recover the value of the property received, with the cause of action still being founded on the vindication of proprietary rights. This is illustrated by *Lipkin Gorman (a firm) v Karpnale Ltd*,[13] where a partner of the plaintiff firm of solicitors stole money from the firm and gambled it away at the defendant's casino. The plaintiff was able to recover the value of the money from the defendant in an action for money had and received. This was a personal claim, since the defendant no longer retained the money or its proceeds. The preferable explanation of this case is that the plaintiff's claim depended on the fact that, when the defendant received the money, the plaintiff retained a proprietary interest in it.[14] This was because the money was taken from the plaintiff without its consent, so the plaintiff did not intend that title in the money should pass to the thief. It was irrelevant that the defendant in this case was not the criminal, it being sufficient that the defendant had received the proceeds of crime from the criminal.[15]

There are two other routes available to the victim who wishes to bring a restitutionary claim to recover property from a criminal. The first is to establish that the defendant holds the proceeds of crime on constructive trust for the benefit of the victim on the basis that the defendant's conscience will have been adversely affected by the commission of the crime.[16] Secondly, where the defendant has obtained a benefit from the commission of theft or a related offence, the victim of that offence may have a statutory claim to the proceeds of the crime by virtue of the Theft Act 1968, s 28. By this provision, where the defendant has been convicted of any offence with reference to theft, such as theft itself, handling stolen goods, robbery or burglary, the court has discretion to make any of the following orders:

(a) that the person who is in possession or control of the stolen goods, whether this is the criminal or a third party, should return them to the victim;

(b) that the defendant should return goods which have been substituted for the stolen goods or the proceeds of sale of the stolen goods or their substitute to the victim; or

(c) that money which was in the defendant's possession when he or she was arrested should be paid to the victim up to the value of the goods which were stolen.

D. Claims founded on wrongdoing

1. Tort

A number of crimes also constitute torts, so that where the plaintiff is the victim of a crime it will be possible for him or her to found a restitutionary claim on the relevant tort, so long as the tort is of the type for which restitutionary remedies are available. So, for example, the victim of the crime of theft may have a restitutionary remedy founded on the tort of conversion against the thief.[17] Similarly, where the defendant commits a crime involving deception, such as obtaining property by deception, this will also constitute the tort of deceit and so the plaintiff should be able to "waive" the tort and seek a restitutionary remedy.[18]

---

[13] [1991] 2 AC 548.
[14] See further Virgo "Reconstructing the Law of Restitution" (1996) 10 TLI 20.
[15] See *Bridgeman v Green* (1755) 2 Ves Sen 627, 628 (Lord Hardwicke LC).
[16] *Westdeutsche Landesbank Girozentrale v Islington London Borough Council* [1996] AC 669, 716 (Lord Browne-Wilkinson). This is discussed further *infra*, 39.
[17] That restitutionary remedies are available where the tort of conversion has been committed is illustrated by *Lamine v Dorrell* (1710) 2 Ld Raym 1216 and *Chesworth v Farrar* [1967] 1 QB 407.
[18] See *Halifax Building Soc v Thomas* [1996] Ch 217 where the defendant was convicted of conspiring to obtain a mortgage advance by deception. On the facts the plaintiff's claim to retain the proceeds of the crime failed because

2. Breach of fiduciary duty

Where the defendant owes fiduciary duties to the plaintiff and in breaching these duties commits a criminal offence, it will be possible for the plaintiff to bring a restitutionary claim against the defendant based upon the breach of the fiduciary duty rather than the commission of the crime. This is particularly well illustrated by the decision of the House of Lords in *Reading v Attorney-General*[19] where the plaintiff, who was a sergeant in the British Army in Egypt, had received payments in return for him accompanying lorries which were smuggling liquor and was consequently convicted for breaching martial law. The plaintiff always wore military uniform to ensure that the lorries were never stopped by the police. When the military authorities discovered what he had done they confiscated most of the money he had received. He then brought an action to recover this money. His claim failed and, although a number of different arguments were used to justify this decision, it is clear that for a majority of the judges the fact that the plaintiff had breached his fiduciary duty to the Crown was an important consideration.[20]

3. Founding a claim on the crime itself

(a) The crime as a cause of action

Where the victim of the crime is unable to sue the criminal for the commission of a tort or breach of fiduciary duty is it possible to found a restitutionary claim on the crime itself? In principle the answer should be "yes" because the commission of a crime is an even more heinous form of wrongdoing.[21] There are, however, no cases where a plaintiff has brought a restitutionary claim founded on the commission of a crime. The main reason for this is that in many cases the victim of the crime will have a claim for compensation from the defendant. Where the plaintiff's loss is equivalent to the defendant's gain and it is clear that the plaintiff can recover compensation for loss suffered as a result of the crime, whether at common law or by virtue of particular statutory provisions,[22] there is no need to bring a somewhat speculative claim for restitution. Sometimes the defendant's gain might exceed the plaintiff's loss and so a restitutionary claim would be attractive. That such a restitutionary claim might be brought was doubted, however, by Glidewell LJ in *Halifax Building Soc v Thomas*:[23]

> "The proposition that a wrongdoer should not be allowed to profit from his wrongs has an obvious attraction. The further proposition, that the victim or intended victim of the wrongdoing, who has in the event suffered no loss, is entitled to retain or recover the amount of the profit is less obviously persuasive."

it had elected to affirm the mortgage despite the defendant's fraud. But, if the mortgage had not been affirmed and it could have been shown that the defendant had obtained a benefit as a result of the crime, the claim would have succeeded.

---

[19] [1951] AC 507. See also *Attorney-General for Hong Kong v Reid* [1994] 1 AC 324, where the Privy Council held that the proceeds of crime, namely the bribes which had been obtained by the defendant in breach of fiduciary duty, were held on constructive trust for the plaintiff.

[20] See, in particular, [1951] AC 507, 516, *per* Viscount Jowitt LC and Lord Porter, and 517, *per* Lord Normand. Some of the judges also based their decision on the simple fact that the relationship between the parties was one of master and servant, and since the soldier had earned the money by virtue of his position, the Crown, his master, was entitled to retain it, even though it was obtained as a result of a criminal act: *ibid*, 514, *per* Lord Porter.

[21] See *Goff & Jones*, 711, who also argue that anybody who derived a benefit from the commission of the crime should be required to disgorge this benefit to the victim, regardless of whether or not they committed the crime.

[22] Such as the power of a criminal court to order the offender to pay compensation to the victim in respect of personal injury, loss or damage resulting from the offence: Powers of Criminal Courts Act 1973, s 35 (as amended by the Criminal Justice Act 1982, s 67 and the Criminal Justice Act 1988, s 104(1)). Compensation may also be obtained from the Criminal Injuries Compensation Board: Criminal Justice Act 1988, ss 108–117.

[23] [1996] Ch 217, 229.

Two reasons can be suggested for this reluctance to allow the plaintiff to recover the proceeds of the crime.

(i) Identifying a breach of a duty owed to the victim

Although in every case of restitution for wrongs it is necessary to justify why the remedy should be assessed by reference to the defendant's gain rather than the plaintiff's loss, especially where the plaintiff has suffered little or no loss as a result of the wrong, this is particularly difficult to justify where the wrong constitutes the commission of a crime. The award of restitutionary remedies is much easier to justify where the defendant has committed a tort or broken a fiduciary duty simply because it will be clear that the defendant has broken a duty which was owed to the victim. The connection with the victim is more difficult to establish where the defendant has committed a crime because the general attitude of English law is that the defendant has breached a duty which is owed to the State, hence the power of the State to punish the criminal. But, despite this, in those cases where the victim has been harmed by the commission of a crime, either physically or by interfering with the victim's property, it is surely appropriate to conclude that this involves a breach of duty which was owed to the victim, so the victim should be entitled to claim any benefit obtained by the defendant from the crime.

(ii) A matter for Parliament rather than the courts

Another reason for judicial reluctance to recognise that the victim of a crime can recover the proceeds of the crime from the criminal is that the policy of preventing the criminal from profiting from the crime is a matter for Parliament, using the mechanisms of fines and confiscation. It is often asserted that it is not for the courts to interfere with this policy by extending the law to deprive the criminal of the proceeds of crime. This was recognised by Peter Gibson LJ in *Halifax Building Soc v Thomas*:[24]

> "In considering whether to extend the law of constructive trusts in order to prevent a fraudster benefiting from his wrong, it is also appropriate to bear in mind that Parliament has acted in recent years . . . on the footing that without statutory intervention the criminal might keep the benefit of his crime. Moreover, Parliament has given the courts the power in specific circumstances to confiscate the benefit rather than reward the person against whom the crime has been committed."[25]

Whilst it is clear that the State has the prime interest in ensuring that criminals do not profit from their crimes, it does not follow that the judges lack a subsidiary power to deprive criminals of the proceeds of their crimes where the statutory powers of fines and confiscation are inadequate to deprive the criminal of all the proceeds of the crime. The inadequacy of the statutory powers is exemplified by the fact that fines cannot be used to deprive criminals of benefits which they obtained after they had been convicted and sentenced, or benefits which the court might not have been aware had been obtained by the criminal. Also the statutory powers of confiscation are limited to where the crime committed by the defendant was serious and cannot be invoked unless the defendant has been convicted.[26] There is surely a role for the law of restitution as developed by the judiciary to serve an interstitial function to ensure that the criminal does not retain the proceeds of crime.[27]

There is therefore a need for the common law and equity to recognise that the victim of a crime should have a right to obtain the proceeds of the crime from the criminal, although this is

---

[24] *Ibid.* See also *ibid*, 230, *per* Glidewell LJ.
[25] See also *Chief Constable of Leicestershire v M* [1989] 1 WLR 20, 23, *per* Hoffmann J.
[26] As exemplified by *Attorney-General v Blake* [1998] 1 All ER 833.
[27] See Glidewell LJ in *Halifax Building Soc v Thomas* [1996] Ch 217, 230: "The enactment of this legislation does not, of course, lead inevitably to the conclusion that neither common law nor equity provides a means by which [the criminal] could be prevented from enjoying the profit of the crime." Though he did add that "the readiness of Parliament to address the problem by legislation weakens the case for providing a solution by judicial creativity."

subsidiary to the power of the State to obtain such proceeds. This restitutionary right of the victim is justified for two main reasons. First, because of the fundamental policy that no defendant should profit from his or her crime. Where the State has not deprived the criminal of these profits it is entirely appropriate that the victim should be allowed to instigate such an action as "the instrument of a social purpose."[28] A second reason is just as important. In many cases where the plaintiff is the victim of a crime he or she will have suffered harm for which compensation is not available in the normal way. Enabling the plaintiff to obtain the proceeds of the crime will therefore act as some sort of recompense for the harm which has been suffered. So, for example, if a third party paid the defendant £1,000 to assault the plaintiff, it is surely entirely appropriate that the plaintiff should recover £1,000 from the defendant both because the defendant should not be allowed to profit from the crime but also because this operates as some form of compensation for the injury and trauma suffered by the victim. As Birks has said, in such circumstances the recovery of the proceeds of crime which exceeds the plaintiff's loss "is not an undeserved windfall but ... a remedy for an individual wrong."[29]

(b) The nature of the restitutionary relief

If the defendant is held liable to make restitution to the plaintiff as a result of the commission of a crime the remedy which will be awarded will typically be restitutionary damages.[30] In other words, the defendant will be required to account to the plaintiff for the value of the benefits obtained as a result of the commission of the crime. It is, however, possible that the court will conclude that the defendant holds the proceeds of crime on constructive trust for the plaintiff, so it follows that the plaintiff can bring a restitutionary claim to recover the property which is held on constructive trust. The potential importance of the constructive trust in the context of restitutionary claims founded on the commission of a crime arises from the speech of Lord Browne-Wilkinson in *Westdeutsche Landesbank Girozentrale v Islington LBC*.[31] His Lordship recognised that "when property is obtained by fraud equity imposes a constructive trust on the fraudulent recipient: the property is recoverable and traceable in equity."[32] Whether this reflects the state of English law on when a constructive trust will be recognised is a controversial matter;[33] but, if it is correct, it follows that the constructive trust will be particularly important where the defendant has committed any crime, such as theft or deception, which can be considered to involve fraudulent conduct on the part of the defendant. Indeed, Lord Browne-Wilkinson specifically recognised that a thief who stole a bag of coins would hold those coins on constructive trust for the victim.[34] In fact, the commission of any crime can be considered to involve unconscionable conduct with the consequence that the proceeds of the crime could be held on constructive trust for the victim. But it is still too early to be sure exactly when the courts will recognise that property is held on constructive trust.

---

[28] Birks, "The Proceeds of Mortgage Fraud" (1996) 10 TLI 5.
[29] *Ibid.*
[30] A term now recognised by the Court of Appeal: *Attorney-General v Blake* [1998] 1 All ER 833, 845.
[31] [1996] AC 669.
[32] *Ibid*, 716.
[33] Controversial because of the implications of the plaintiff having a proprietary interest in the proceeds of crime rather than merely a personal claim to the proceeds. If, however, as Lord Browne-Wilkinson himself contemplated in *Westdeutsche* [1996] AC 669, 716, the remedial constructive trust is recognised in English law, the unsatisfactory nature of the institutional constructive trust can be tempered because the remedy can be tailored to fit the circumstances of the particular case so that innocent third parties would not be prejudiced. See now *Re Polly Peck International Plc* [1998] *The Times,* May 18 (CA).
[34] [1996] AC 669, 716.

(c) Obstacles to restitutionary claims founded on crimes

If the victim does bring a restitutionary claim to obtain the proceeds of the crime there are three main obstacles which must be surmounted before such a claim can succeed, and these obstacles will dramatically limit the scope of such a claim.

(i) Causation and remoteness

If the defendant is to be required to disgorge the proceeds of the crime to the victim it will be necessary for the victim to establish that, but for the commission of the crime, the benefit would not have been obtained by the defendant. This raises important questions of causation and remoteness of gain. Whilst it can be assumed that the "but for" test of causation should apply here as it does for other restitutionary claims founded on wrongdoing, it is not clear when the benefit will be considered to be too remote from the commission of the crime. In *Halifax Building Soc v Thomas*,[35] where the defendant had obtained a mortgage advance by deception and had used this to purchase a flat which had subsequently increased in value, Peter Gibson LJ said:

> "Further I am not satisfied that in the circumstances of the present case it would be right to treat the unjust enrichment of [the criminal] as having been gained 'at the expense of' [the plaintiff], even allowing for the possibility of an extended meaning for those words to apply to cases of non-subtractive restitution for a wrong . . . I do not overlook the fact that the policy of law is to view with disfavour a wrongdoer benefiting from his wrong, the more so when the wrong amounts to fraud, but it cannot be suggested that there is a universally applicable principle that in every case there will be restitution of benefit from a wrong . . . On the facts of the present case . . . the fraud is not in itself a sufficient factor to allow [the plaintiff] to require [the criminal] to account for it."

This was therefore a case where the plaintiff could not simply rely on the fact that it was the victim of a fraud to obtain the proceeds of the crime. The explanation for this can be found in the earlier case of *Chief Constable of Leicestershire v M*,[36] the facts of which were almost identical to those of *Halifax Building Soc v Thomas*, in that the offender had made profits from the sale of properties he had purchased with the assistance of a mortgage advance which he had obtained by deception. Hoffmann J did not accept that these profits constituted the proceeds of crime because the profit was not itself obtained by deception but rather was made from the money which was obtained by deception. In other words, the profit was too remote from the crime.

The effect of these two decisions is that, if the victim is to recover the proceeds of crime from the criminal, it must be shown that the proceeds were obtained directly from the crime, rather than indirectly, as will occur where the criminal has profited from investing the proceeds of the crime. This strict approach to the question of remoteness of benefit is at least consistent with the approach which is adopted where the plaintiff's restitutionary action is founded on tort or breach of fiduciary duty.[37] If the victim of a crime can only recover those benefits which the defendant obtained directly from the commission of the offence, it follows that the victim should recover all those benefits which were obtained directly from the victim and presumably also those benefits which the criminal was promised as an inducement to commit the crime, such as a bribe to commit an assault, simply because the bribe was only paid to the criminal because he or she had committed the crime.

If, however, the court concludes that, by virtue of the defendant's fraudulent conduct, he or she holds the proceeds of crime on constructive trust for the plaintiff, the question of remoteness of benefit will not arise. This is because all profits obtained as a result of the crime will be subject to the constructive trust, regardless of whether they arose directly or indirectly. This is illustrated

---
[35] [1996] Ch 217, 227.
[36] [1989] 1 WLR 20.
[37] It also accords with the test of remoteness which is adopted for the purposes of the forfeiture rule, examined *infra*, Part III (c).

by the decision of the Privy Council in *Attorney-General for Hong Kong v Reid*,[38] where the court concluded that the defendant held the bribe he had received on constructive trust for the plaintiff. This meant that the plaintiff had an equitable proprietary interest in the bribe and subsequently the property which had been purchased with the bribe. In fact, the recognition of a constructive trust would have avoided the problem of remoteness in *Halifax Building Soc v Thomas*[39] because it could be concluded that the property which the defendant purchased using the mortgage advance was held on constructive trust for the plaintiff building society, since the defendant had obtained the mortgage advance through the commission of a crime involving deception and so had acted fraudulently. If the property was held on constructive trust it would follow that the proceeds of the sale of the house would also be subject to the constructive trust, regardless of the fact that the property had increased in value.

(ii) The operation of the in pari delicto defence

It is an accepted principle of the law of restitution that no court will allow a restitutionary claim to be brought where it is founded on an illegal act.[40] This is known as the *in pari delicto* defence. In principle this means that the victim of the crime will not be able to rely on the commission of a crime to obtain restitution from the criminal. This will not, however, usually be the case, because there is an accepted exception to this defence where the parties are not equally responsible for the illegal act. Usually the victim will not have participated in the commission of the crime, so he or she will not have been tainted by the illegality.[41]

(iii) The relationship with the public law powers of the Attorney-General

It was recognised by the Court of Appeal in *Attorney-General v Blake*[42] that the Attorney-General could bring a public law claim to ensure that criminals were prevented from receiving the proceeds of the crime. Although the Court of Appeal did not specifically consider whether the Attorney-General could bring a claim to deprive the criminal of the proceeds of the crime once they had been received,[43] the court did appear to suggest that such a claim was not available. But, in the light of the fundamental principle of public policy that no criminal should be allowed to profit from their crime, this is a very odd conclusion to reach. In fact, because of that principle of public policy, if the Attorney-General can prevent the criminal from receiving the proceeds of the crime, it should follow that, where the criminal has received the proceeds of the crime, the Attorney-General should be able to bring a restitutionary claim to deprive the criminal of these proceeds. But, if this is correct, would the victim's private law claim not conflict with the Attorney-General's public law claim? Indeed, in *Blake* the Court of Appeal recognised that the Attorney-General was an appropriate person to institute a claim against the criminal, because it was one of the functions of the Attorney-General to enforce the criminal law. It was recognised by the court that, since the Attorney-General would only intervene where it was right to do so, there were adequate safeguards against the abuse of the jurisdiction to prevent the criminal from receiving the proceeds of the crime.

But, whilst it is proper that the Attorney-General is the only person who should be able to intervene to prevent the defendant from obtaining a benefit, it does not follow that the victim of the crime should be prevented from bringing a claim to require the defendant to disgorge those benefits which have been received as a result of committing the crime. Because of the policy that no criminal should profit from the crime and because the victim was harmed by the defendant, it

---

[38] [1994] 1 AC 324.
[39] [1996] Ch 217.
[40] *Holman v Johnson* (1775) 1 Cowp 341, 343 (Lord Mansfield).
[41] See *Kiriri Cotton Co Ltd v Dewani* [1960] AC 192 for discussion of this exception.
[42] [1998] 1 All ER 833.
[43] *Ibid*, 849.

is entirely appropriate that the victim should have a right to sue the criminal for restitutionary relief. This right should only be circumscribed by statute or where the Attorney-General considers that it is not in the public interest for the victim to sue the defendant.

(d) The potential implications of recognising restitutionary claims founded on crimes

The potential application of a claim to recover the proceeds of crime where the cause of action is simply the crime itself can be illustrated by reference to two situations where a benefit has been obtained as a result of the commission of a crime.

(i) Rosenfeldt v Olson

The first example is the decision of the British Columbian Court of Appeal in *Rosenfeldt v Olson*.[44] In this case the accused was suspected of murdering 11 children. In order to secure his agreement to plead guilty to murder and to disclose the location of the bodies, the police agreed to pay $100,000 to be held on trust for the benefit of the accused's wife and their child. The parents of seven of the accused's victims claimed that this money was impressed with a constructive trust for their benefit. Their claim failed on the ground that the accused's wife and child had not been unjustly enriched at the expense of the parents. This was because the money which had been paid had not been subtracted from the victims. But this decision shows the dangers of assuming that the only cause of action within the law of restitution is that founded on unjust enrichment. It is obvious that the recipients of the money had not been unjustly enriched at the expense of the parents, but it could still have been argued that the parents' restitutionary claim should be founded on the accused's crime. It should make no difference that the actual victims were the children and not the parents, since the crucial consideration is that the accused should not be allowed to profit from his crime, and neither should those who obtain a benefit as a direct result of that crime. But, even if a claim which was founded on the crime was recognised, it was clear that the benefit had not been obtained as a direct result of committing the crime, and so, in accordance with general principles of remoteness, it was correct that the restitutionary claim failed.[45] In addition, according to the English notion of the constructive trust, this was not an appropriate case to recognise that the wife should hold the payments on constructive trust for the parents of the victims, simply because the wife and her child could not be considered to have acted fraudulently.

(ii) Recovering the literary proceeds of crime

If a restitutionary claim founded on the commission of a crime is recognised, such a claim would be particularly important where a criminal, usually a killer, obtains money by selling his or her story to a newspaper or television company or publishes a book about the crime.[46] Should the victim, or where relevant his or her personal representatives, be allowed to recover this money? A number of States in the United States and in Australia have enacted laws to prevent convicted criminals from retaining profits by marketing their stories, with the profits usually being made available for the benefit of the victims of the crime and their families.[47] No specific statutory

---

[44] (1986) 25 DLR (4th) 472.

[45] Even though the accused had committed particularly heinous crimes and so perhaps a more liberal test of remoteness of benefit might be adopted, as discussed below, there is no reason why a different test of remoteness should be adopted where the plaintiff seeks to recover the proceeds of crime from a third party, such as the accused's spouse and child.

[46] *Goff & Jones*, 710. See also Freiberg, "Confiscating the Literary Proceeds of Crime" [1992] Crim LR 96. Freiberg gives the example of Pottle and Randle, who obtained £30,000 in respect of the publication of their book *The Blake Escape: How We Freed George Blake and Why*.

[47] See Okuda, "Criminal Antiprofit Laws: Some Thoughts in Favour of Their Constitutionality" (1985) 76 Cal LR 1353 and Freiberg [1992] Crim LR 96, 97.

provision has been made for this problem in this country,[48] but could the common law prevent the criminal from retaining profits by marketing stories in this way? Clearly but for the commission of the crime the defendant would not have had a story to sell and so would not have obtained the money, so the "but for" test of causation is satisfied. But there are two potential objections to the defendant having to make restitution to the victim.

First, the defendant might argue that the money which he or she had received for selling the story was only obtained indirectly from the crime, since the money derived from the story rather than from the commission of the crime itself. The benefit would therefore be too remote from the commission of the crime. One response to this argument is to assert that, as a matter of public policy, a criminal who has obtained any benefit as a result of the commission of heinous crimes, such as murder, should not be allowed to argue that the benefit was too remote from the crime.[49] Alternatively it could be argued that, since the commission of the crime was a vital element of the criminal having a story to sell in the first place,[50] the profits flowed directly from the crime.

Secondly, the defendant might also argue that he or she had assisted in the writing of the story and so may claim that, even if part of the benefit which he or she obtained should be disgorged to the plaintiff, there should be an apportionment to reflect his or her personal contribution. Whilst such an argument would succeed where the plaintiff's claim was founded on the defendant's breach of fiduciary duty,[51] it should be defeated where the plaintiff's claim is founded on a crime committed by the defendant, again for reasons of public policy that a defendant who has committed a serious crime should not be allowed to benefit in any way from its commission.

(e) Restitution from third parties

Whilst the plaintiff might be able to establish a restitutionary claim to recover the proceeds of the crime from the criminal, it will be even more difficult to establish such a claim against anybody else who assisted the criminal in obtaining the proceeds. The plaintiff will have a claim against anybody who was an accessory to the principal offender's crime and obtained a benefit as a result, because an accessory is guilty of a crime in his or her own right. So, for example, if a third party pays A and B £10,000 each to kill the victim and A strikes the fatal blow, encouraged by B, then B is an accessory and by directly participating in the criminal conduct should be liable to disgorge the £10,000 obtained to the personal representatives of the victim. But a person, such as a ghost writer or publisher who assists in the writing and publication of the defendant's story, should not be liable to disgorge the benefits they obtained from the publication of the story.[52] This is because any benefit which the ghost writer or the publisher obtained was surely too remote from the commission of the crime in the first place. The reach of restitution will be too wide if it embraces claims against both the criminal and anybody who assisted the criminal in obtaining an indirect benefit from the crime without themselves being guilty of a crime in their own right.

Where, however, a third party has received the proceeds of the crime from the criminal, it has been recognised that the third party may be liable to make restitution to the victim. As Lord

---

[48] Although such profits may be the subject of a confiscation order being made under the Criminal Justice Act 1988, discussed *infra* Part II.
[49] Note the similar principle that the court will never allow a plaintiff to obtain restitution on the ground of unjust enrichment where he or she has committed a serious crime, simply for reasons of public policy. See *Tappenden v Randall* (1801) 2 Bos & Pul 467, 471(Heath J); *Kearley v Thomson* (1890) 24 QBD 742, 747 (Fry LJ).
[50] Okuda (1985) 76 Cal LR 1353, 1360.
[51] See eg *Boardman v Phipps* [1967] 2 AC 46 and *O'Sullivan v Management Agency and Music Ltd* [1985] QB 428.
[52] Invariably those States in the United States which have statutes prohibiting the criminal from profiting from the commission of the crime do not prohibit the publisher, ghost writer or producer from retaining profits derived from the criminal's story: Okuda (1985) 76 Cal LR 1353.

Commissioner Wilmot said in *Bridgeman v Green*:[53] "Let the hand receiving it be ever so chaste, yet if it comes through a corrupt polluted channel, the obligation of restitution will follow it . . ." This will certainly be the case where the third party receives property from the criminal in which the plaintiff has a continuing proprietary interest.[54] Where the third party receives property from the criminal in which the plaintiff does not have a continuing proprietary interest, but the third party is aware that the property represents the proceeds of crime, the third party may be considered to have acted fraudulently or unconscionably so that he or she will hold the property on constructive trust for the victim. It is even possible to contemplate circumstances where the criminal holds the proceeds on constructive trust for the victim and the third party could be liable for knowingly receiving property in breach of trust or dishonestly assisting the criminal in breaching the trust.[55]

II. RESTITUTIONARY CLAIMS BROUGHT BY THE STATE

There are a number of statutory mechanisms whereby benefits obtained by an offender as a result of committing a crime may be liable to be disgorged to the State. Disgorgement of the proceeds of crime to the State should be considered to fall within the law of restitution, since, by committing a crime, the offender has committed a wrong against the State by breaching his or her duty to abide by the criminal law of the land. Since detailed analysis of these provisions concerning disgorgement to the State is adequately dealt with in specialised works on the subject,[56] it will be sufficient here simply to identify the key provisions relating to confiscation of the proceeds of crime.

A. Confiscation orders

The most important of the statutory mechanisms to recover the proceeds of crime concerns the duty of the court to order that benefits obtained by an offender as a result of the commission of certain crimes should be confiscated by the State.[57] Essentially, where an offender has been convicted of an indictable offence,[58] which is not a drug-trafficking offence, and the prosecutor has given written notice to the court that he or she considers a confiscation order to be appropriate or the courts considers such an order to be appropriate, the court must make an order that the offender should pay such sum to the Crown as the court thinks fit.[59] The sum which is ordered to be confiscated is limited to the lesser of the benefit which the defendant obtained or the amount which appears to the court to be the amount which might be realised at the time the order is made.[60] Although confiscation orders cannot be made in respect of profits obtained from drug-trafficking offences, this is only because a more draconian power to confiscate profits exists in respect of such offences.[61] Where the victim of the crime has instituted or intends to institute civil

---

[53] (1757) Wilm 58, 65.
[54] Subject to the defence of bona fide purchase for value.
[55] See Oakley, *Constructive Trusts* (1997), 3rd ed (London), 222-239.
[56] See in particular *Mitchell, Taylor & Talbot on Confiscation and the Proceeds of Crime*, 2nd ed (Sweet and Maxwell, 1997).
[57] Criminal Justice Act 1988, Part VI (hereafter "CJA 1988") as amended by the Proceeds of Crime Act 1995. Note also the power of forfeiture: Powers of Criminal Courts Act 1973, s 43 (as amended by the Criminal Justice Aact 1988, s 107). The power of forfeiture is not, however, restitutionary, since the court is confined to depriving the offender of property which was used or was intended to be used to commit a crime, and this does not cover benefits which were obtained as a result of committing the crime.
[58] A Magistrates' Court may also make a confiscation order in respect of a limited number of summary offences.
[59] CJA 1988, s 71, as amended by the Proceeds of Crime Act 1995, s 1.
[60] *Ibid*, s 71(6).
[61] Drug Trafficking Act 1994, s 2(3). This is a more draconian power because of the statutory assumption that all of the drug trafficker's assets are the proceeds of crime and so are liable to confiscation.

proceedings against the defendant in respect of loss, injury or damage sustained in connection with the defendant's criminal conduct, the court has a power rather than a duty to make a confiscation order.[62] Where the defendant has been convicted of one offence and the court considers that the defendant has obtained benefits from a course of criminal conduct, the court may order that all of these benefits should be confiscated even though some of the benefits arise from crimes in respect of which the defendant has not been convicted and which have never been formally taken into consideration in criminal proceedings.

This statutory obligation to make confiscation orders applies regardless of the value of the benefit which the defendant obtained. "Benefit" for these purposes include pecuniary advantages as well as property obtained as a result of the commission of the crime.[63] In other words, if the offender has saved money as a result of the crime this negative enrichment constitutes a benefit for the purposes of the Act. The benefit must be obtained "as a result of or in connection with" the commission of the crime.[64]

The power to make a confiscation order is particularly important where the offender has committed so-called "victimless" crimes, such as insider dealing,[65] where there is no victim who can claim compensation or restitution from the offender. The power to make a confiscation order will also be available to confiscate profits made by a criminal in respect of the publication of a book about the crime or the sale of the story to a newspaper or a television company.

B. Ancillary powers

Even before the offender is convicted the High Court has power to make a restraint order,[66] to prevent the offender from dissipating his or her property, or a charging order,[67] to secure a future confiscation order.[68] In *Chief Constable of Leicestershire v M*[69] Hoffmann J recognised that there was a power at common law to order an injunction to restrain an offender from disposing of the proceeds of crime, but this power could only be invoked in respect of those proceeds which arose directly from the commission of the crime, such as money which had been obtained by deception and its traceable substitute. But Hoffmann J emphasised that the intervention of Parliament in the field of confiscation of the proceeds of crime by the State, particularly where the accused had not yet been convicted of an offence, "suggest that the courts should not indulge in parallel creativity by the extension of general common law principles" beyond the existing power.[70] It is for this reason that Hoffmann J refused to grant an interlocutory injunction which was being sought by the Chief Constable to prevent the accused, who was awaiting trial for obtaining mortgage advances by deception, from dissipating profits which he had made by the use of property which he had obtained by dishonest means. This was because such profits were not made directly from the commission of the crime. Today, a charging order could be made in a case such as this,[71] particularly because the test under the Criminal Justice Act 1988 relates to whether the proceeds

---

[62] CJA 1988, s 71(1C) as inserted by the Proceeds of Crime Act 1995, s 1.
[63] CJA 1988, s 71(4), (5).
[64] *Ibid*, s 71(4).
[65] Contrary to the Criminal Justice Act 1993, Part V.
[66] CJA 1988, s 77.
[67] *Ibid*, s 78.
[68] A charging order was made over the houses of Potter and Randle on the ground that the benefit which they obtained from the publication of a book about their part in George Blake's escape from prison was a benefit which arose from the commission of the crime. No confiscation order was made, because proceedings against Potter and Randle were discontinued. See Freiberg [1992] Crim LR 96.
[69] [1989] 1 WLR 20.
[70] *Ibid*, 23. See also *Malone v Metropolitan Police Commissioner* [1980] QB 49.
[71] As was awarded in the similar case of *Halifax Building Soc v Thomas* [1996] ch 217. Such an order was not available in *Chief Constable of Leicestershire v M* because the Criminal Justice Act 1988 was not in force.

resulted from the commission of the crime without any requirement that they were a direct result of the crime. But the effect of Hoffmann J's decision is still relevant, namely that, in respect of those crimes which are not serious enough to be caught by the statutory schemes of confiscation, the common law will intervene at the request of the organs of the State to prevent the dissipation of profits but only where those profits directly arise from the commission of a crime.

III. DENIAL OF BENEFITS ARISING FROM THE COMMISSION OF CRIMES

A. Does the denial of benefits to a criminal form part of the law of restitution?

Where one consequence of an offender committing a crime is that he or she is entitled to receive a benefit, the general principle that no offender should profit from wrongdoing means that the benefit should be denied to him or her. But does the analysis of this application of the no profit principle properly fall within the law of restitution? Burrows has suggested that it does not, simply because the law of restitution is concerned with the transfer of benefits to the plaintiff, whereas the question which is being considered here is whether the conduct of the offender is such as to prevent the benefit from being received by the criminal in the first place.[72] Goff and Jones disagree[73] and they are right to do so. This is because both preventing the defendant from receiving the proceeds of the crime and transferring the proceeds of crime to the victim or to the State are motivated by the same policy consideration, namely that no criminal should be allowed to profit from the crime. The same question of public policy arises regardless of whether it is considered before or after the defendant has obtained the proceeds of the crime.

B. The Attorney-General's public law claim

It is now clear as a result of the decision of the Court of Appeal in *Attorney-General v Blake*[74] that the Attorney-General can bring a public law claim to ensure that no criminal receives the proceeds of crime.[75] Such a claim is justified as a means of enabling the Attorney-General to vindicate the criminal law.[76]

C. The forfeiture principle

1. The ambit of the forfeiture principle

It is a fundamental principle of English law that a criminal is not able to enforce rights or to recover benefits which accrue to him or her as a result of the commission of certain types of criminal offence.[77] This is a rule of public policy. As Fry LJ said in *Cleaver v Mutual Reserve Fund Life Association*:[78]

> "The principle of public policy invoked is in my opinion rightly asserted. It appears to me that no system of jurisprudence can with reason include amongst the rights which it enforces rights directly resulting to the person asserting them from the crime of that person."

---

[72] Burrows, *The Law of Restitution* (London, 1993), 380.
[73] *Goff & Jones*, 703.
[74] [1998] 1 All ER 833.
[75] See Virgo, "Clarifying Restitution for Wrongs" [1998] RLR 118.
[76] *Ibid*, 847.
[77] *Cleaver v Mutual Reserve Fund Life Association* [1892] 1 QB 147, 156 (Fry LJ); *Beresford v Royal Insurance Co* [1938] AC 586, 598 (Lord Atkin).
[78] [1892] 1 QB 147, 156.

Where the defendant is entitled to benefits as a result of an unlawful killing, the rule which precludes him or her from obtaining those benefits is called the forfeiture rule.[79] But the principle which underlies the forfeiture rule is not confined to where the crime which has been committed is an unlawful killing. Fry LJ recognised in *Cleaver* that the general principle may also be invoked where the criminal has committed a crime involving fraud.[80] The forfeiture principle is in fact potentially applicable in respect of all crimes, but the courts have accepted that it is only the commission of certain types of criminal conduct which will trigger its operation.[81] The test which the courts have adopted is whether the offender intentionally committed the crime.[82] This was recognised by Lord Denning MR in *Hardy v Motor Insurers' Bureau*,[83] where he said that "no person can claim reparation or indemnity for the consequences of a criminal offence where his own wicked and deliberate intent is an essential ingredient in it."

Whilst the application of the forfeiture principle prevents the criminal from obtaining all benefits which accrue as a result of the commission of the crime, the vast majority of the cases are concerned with whether the criminal can obtain an indemnity under an insurance policy. Consistent with the forfeiture principle, such an indemnity will be denied where the criminal intentionally committed the crime,[84] but not where it was committed negligently or innocently.[85] So, for example, it has long been recognised that a criminal who deliberately sets fire to his or her own property to obtain insurance money for damage to the property will not be able to recover the money from the insurance company.[86] The application of the forfeiture principle is also illustrated by *Fauntleroy's Case*,[87] where the offender was convicted of forgery and was executed. The plaintiff was the offender's trustee in bankruptcy who sought to obtain payments under a policy of life assurance which became due on the death of the offender. It was held that, by virtue of public policy, the plaintiff was not able to obtain the benefits of the policy, because the execution of the assured was a consequence of the commission of the crime and no benefits which arose from the crime could be recovered by the criminal or any one who claimed through the criminal, such as the trustee in bankruptcy in this case. This general principle preventing the offender from receiving benefits which arise from the intentional commission of a criminal offence could have been relied on in *Reading v Attorney-General*[88] to prevent the army sergeant, who had been convicted for breach of martial law for taking bribes, from recovering these bribes once they had been confiscated, since they represented the proceeds of a crime which had been committed intentionally.

---

[79] *Re K (deceased)* [1986] Ch 180, 185 (Ackner LJ).
[80] [1892] 1 QB 147, 156.
[81] See Lord Wright in *Beresford v Royal Insurance Co Ltd* [1937] 2 KB 197, 220.
[82] The same test has been adopted to determine whether the forfeiture rule is applicable where the criminal has committed the crime of unlawful killing. But now see *Dunbar v Plant* [1997] 3 WLR 1261. See *infra*, 49.
[83] [1964] 2 QB 745, 760.
[84] *Haseldine v Hoskin* [1933] 1 KB 822. See also *Geismar v Sun Alliance and London Insurance Ltd* [1978] QB 383, 395 (Talbot J).
[85] *Tinline v White Cross Insurance Association Ltd* [1921] 3 KB 327; *James v British General Insurance Co Ltd* [1927] 2 KB 311. See also *Euro-Diam Ltd v Bathurst* [1990] QB 1, 40 (Kerr LJ). Cf *Askey v Golden Wine Co Ltd* [1948] 2 All ER 35 where Denning J held that, even though the criminal had committed a crime by conduct which was grossly negligent, he would be prevented from obtaining an indemnity, contribution or damages "in respect of expenses which [he had] incurred by reason of being compelled to make reparation for his own crime.": *ibid*, 38. But this decision is itself justified on the ground of public policy, namely that, if a criminal is punished by the imposition of a fine, he or she should not be allowed to recover money to offset what he or she has paid to the State.
[86] *Beresford v Royal Insurance Co Ltd* [1938] AC 586, 595 (Lord Atkin).
[87] *The Amicable Society for a Perpetual Life Assurance Office v Bolland* (1830) 4 Bligh (NS) 194.
[88] [1951] AC 507.

2. The relationship between the forfeiture principle and the in pari delicto defence

The principle that criminals, or those claiming through criminals, are not able to obtain benefits arising from a crime, is closely related to the principle that a court will not enable a party to obtain restitution of benefits transferred pursuant to an illegal transaction: the *in pari delicto* defence.[89] Indeed, both of these principles are founded on the same general principle of *ex turpi causa non oritur actio*, namely that the courts will not assist criminals and similar wrongdoers.[90] Also both principles are principles of public policy rather than principles of justice.[91] Consequently, the principles may sometimes lead to unfair results.

Nevertheless, the forfeiture principle and the *in pari delicto* defence remain distinct, there being a number of important differences between them. For example, a transaction may be illegal without necessarily involving the commission of a crime; also the issue of restitution only arises once a benefit has been transferred, whereas the principle preventing the criminal from obtaining the proceeds of crime applies before any benefit has been received. Most importantly, it is much easier to defend the forfeiture principle because the criminal is clearly a wrongdoer, whereas the plaintiff who seeks to recover a benefit which has been obtained by the defendant under an illegal transaction may have been an innocent party. The effect of these differences is that, whilst it is necessary to acknowledge the common policy behind the forfeiture principle and the principle denying restitution on the ground of illegality, the two principles should be kept separate because they apply in different circumstances.

3. The rationale of the forfeiture principle

A number of explanations have been given for the existence of the forfeiture principle.[92] One explanation is that it exists to deter potential criminals from committing crimes in order to obtain benefits as a result.[93] This may explain why the application of the forfeiture principle is confined to where the criminal has intentionally committed the crime, since it is only in this situation that the threat of forfeiture of benefits is likely to have any deterrent effect at all. But it is most unlikely that this principle of the civil law would constitute any greater deterrent than that already provided by the criminal law. Another explanation of the principle is that it stems from a desire to punish the criminal for committing the crime, but it is surely inappropriate for the civil law to punish the criminal, this being a function for which only the criminal courts are well suited. If the civil courts seek to punish the criminal in addition to the punishment which is imposed by the criminal courts, there is an obvious danger of excessive punishment.[94] A final explanation for the forfeiture principle is that it is justified on the ground that no criminal should be able to resort to the law to recover benefits to which they have become entitled as a result of their crimes.[95] This is probably the main reason for the existence of the rule, namely a general distaste that the law should be used to assist criminals in any way.[96]

---

[89] *Holman v Johnson* (1775) 1 Cowp 341, 343 (Lord Mansfield).
[90] See *Euro-Diam Ltd v Bathurst* [1990] QB 1, 35 (Kerr LJ).
[91] *Dunbar v Plant* [1997] 3 WLR 1261, 1270 (Mummery LJ).
[92] See Shard, "Unblinkering the Unruly Horse: Public Policy in the Law of Contract" (1972) 30 CLJ 144.
[93] *Beresford v Royal Insurance Co Ltd* [1938] AC 586, 598 (Lord Atkin); *Gray v Barr* [1971] 2 QB 554, 581 (Salmon LJ); *Re H (deceased)* [1990] 1 FLR 441, 446 (Peter Gibson J).
[94] As recognised by Devlin J in *St John Shipping Corp v Joseph Rank Ltd* [1957] 1 QB 267, 292.
[95] *Gray v Barr* [1970] 2 QB 626, 640 (Geoffrey Lane J). See also *Euro-Diam Ltd v Bathurst* [1990] QB 1, 35 (Kerr LJ).
[96] As Wilmot CJ said in *Collins v Blantern* (1767) 2 Wils 347, 350: "no polluted hand shall touch the pure fountains of justice."

C. The forfeiture rule[97]

It is in connection with the commission of unlawful killings where the forfeiture principle has proved to be most important. Here the principle is called the forfeiture rule, as has been recognised by the Forfeiture Act 1982. Section 1 of the Act states that

> "the 'forfeiture rule' means the rule of public policy which in certain circumstances precludes a person who has unlawfully killed another from acquiring a benefit in consequence of the killing."

The forfeiture rule is particularly important in respect of unlawful killings because it is the commission of this type of crime which is most likely to result in benefits accruing to the criminal. Originally any benefits which accrued to an offender as a result of the commission of murder and other felonies were forfeited to the Crown, but this rule was abolished by the Forfeiture Act 1870. Consequently, the effect of the forfeiture rule today is that the benefits which accrue to the criminal as a result of an unlawful killing are forfeited to the person who is entitled to them once the claims of the criminal, or those claiming through the criminal, are discounted. The uncompromising rigidity of this forfeiture rule has often been criticised[98] and its application has now been qualified by the Forfeiture Act 1982.[99]

1. The types of unlawful killing which trigger the forfeiture rule

It is clear that the forfeiture rule applies in respect of benefits which accrue as the result of the defendant committing the crime of murder,[100] in other words where the defendant has caused the death of a person intending either to kill or to cause serious injury to the victim.[101] It is irrelevant that the murderer was not motivated by a desire to profit from the killing, the very fact of committing murder being sufficient to preclude the killer from obtaining any benefits as a result.[102]

Whether the forfeiture rule is applicable to all forms of manslaughter has been a controversial matter. In *Dunbar v Plant*[103] the Court of Appeal accepted by a majority that the forfeiture rule should apply to all cases of manslaughter, since there was no logical basis for distinguishing between different types of unlawful killing. If this is correct, it follows that the forfeiture rule is potentially applicable where the defendant commits voluntary manslaughter and also where the killer commits involuntary manslaughter, whether constructive manslaughter or gross negligent manslaughter. The rule would even apply, as was accepted in *Dunbar v Plant* itself, where the defendant was guilty of aiding and abetting a suicide.

It is not, however, correct to say that there is no logical basis for distinguishing between different types of unlawful killing, for it has been recognised on a number of occasions that a distinction can be drawn by reference to the killer's culpability.[104] Consequently, it has been recognised that the forfeiture rule should only be applicable where the killer committed a crime

---

[97] For general discussion of this rule see Earnshaw and Pace, "Let the Hand Receiving It Be Ever So Chaste" (1972) 37 MLR 481.
[98] See *eg* Chadwick, "A Testator's Bounty to His Slayer" (1914) 30 LQR 211.
[99] But the rule continues to be applied strictly in other jurisdictions which have no equivalent statutory provision. See *eg Troja v Troja* (1994) 33 NSWLR 269 (NSW CA).
[100] See *eg Cleaver v Mutual Reserve Fund Life Association* [1892] 1 QB 147.
[101] The forfeiture rule will not be applicable to a person who committed murder or any other unlawful killing but was found to be insane, simply because such a person is acquitted of the crime by virtue of insanity: Criminal Procedure (Insanity) Act 1964, s 1. See *Re Houghton* [1915] 2 Ch 173; *Re Pitts* [1931] 1 Ch 546.
[102] *Cleaver v Mutual Reserve Fund Life Association* [1892] 1 QB 147.
[103] [1997] 3 WLR 1261. That the forfeiture rule should apply to all cases of manslaughter had been recognised previously. See *eg In the Estate of Hall* [1914] P 1, 7 (Hamilton LJ) and *Re Giles (deceased)* [1972] ch 544.
[104] *Gray v Barr* [1970] 2 QB 626, 640 (Geoffrey Lane J). See also *Gray v Barr* [1971] 2 QB 554, 569 (Lord Denning MR); *R v Chief National Insurance Commissioner, ex p Connor* [1981] 1 QB 758, 766 (Lord Lane CJ); *Re K (deceased)* [1985] Ch 85, 98 (Vinelott J); *Re H (deceased)* [1990] 1 FLR 441 (Peter Gibson J).

intentionally or deliberately and it is irrelevant that the actual killing was unintentional or that the crime did not involve violence or threats of violence.[105] This test covers all cases of murder and voluntary manslaughter, which is simply murder committed in certain extenuating circumstances, namely where the killer was provoked, was suffering from diminished responsibility or was acting in pursuance of a suicide pact.[106] So, for example, if the defendant is convicted of manslaughter by reason of diminished responsibility, then the forfeiture rule will prevent him or her from obtaining any property under the victim's will.[107] Constructive manslaughter would also be caught by the rule, since that crime requires the defendant to have committed an unlawful act intentionally.[108] It would also cover the case where the defendant was guilty of aiding and abetting the victim to commit suicide, since the defendant would have been committing the crime intentionally.[109] The test will not, however, cover the crime of gross negligence manslaughter, since that crime does not require proof of any intentional conduct.[110]

Even though a distinction can be drawn between different types of unlawful killing on the basis of culpability, the majority in *Dunbar v Plant* concluded that the forfeiture rule should apply to all types of unlawful killing. This was because the enactment of the Forfeiture Act in 1982 has meant that the forfeiture rule can be modified where justice demands. Whilst such an argument is attractive, it does have drawbacks. Most importantly, it means that a fundamental division is created between the forfeiture principle and the forfeiture rule. For, whereas the forfeiture principle will continue to apply only where the defendant has intentionally committed a crime, the effect of *Dunbar v Plant* is that the forfeiture rule will apply to all forms of unlawful killing, regardless of the defendant's culpability. If this is correct it follows that the forfeiture rule will apply to crimes such as causing death by dangerous driving,[111] even though this does not require proof of intent to commit the crime and even though the courts have not applied the rule previously to cases of motor manslaughter.[112] A further disadvantage of the wide interpretation of the forfeiture rule is that it means the regime under the Forfeiture Act will be applicable in a greater number of cases and, as will be seen, the application of that regime is a matter of great uncertainty. Consequently, it would be preferable to interpret the application of the forfeiture rule restrictively from the outset.

Regardless of whether the forfeiture rule is interpreted widely or restrictively, it is clear that that rule applies to other forms of liability relating to unlawful killing, all of which require proof of intention. For example, if the defendant is an accessory to murder, whether by procuring, counselling, aiding or abetting somebody else to kill the victim, then the forfeiture rule should prevent him or her from obtaining any benefit as a result. Similarly, where the defendant has attempted to kill or is involved in a conspiracy to kill or has incited an unlawful killing, then the forfeiture rule should in principle be applicable.[113] Some support for this can be found in the decision of *Evans v Evans*,[114] where the former wife of the plaintiff had been convicted of inciting third parties to murder him. The Court of Appeal held that the plaintiff, who had been making periodical payments to his former wife for 35 years, was no longer required to make these

---

[105] See *Dunbar v Plant* [1997] 3 WLR 1261, 1273 (Mummery LJ).
[106] See the Homicide Act 1957, ss 2-4.
[107] *Re Giles* [1972] Ch 544; *Re Royse* [1985] Ch 22. Cf *Re H (deceased)* [1990] 1 FLR 441, where the trial judge wrongly assumed that a defendant who was guilty of voluntary manslaughter by reason of diminished responsibility was not caught by the forfeiture rule because the defendant had not been guilty of deliberate, intentional and unlawful violence.
[108] *R v Church* [1966] 1 QB 59.
[109] *Dunbar v Plant* [1997] 3 WLR 1261, 1273 (Mummery LJ).
[110] *Adomako* [1995] 1 AC 171.
[111] Contrary to the Road Traffic Act 1988, s 1 (as substituted by the Road Traffic Act 1991, s 1).
[112] See eg *Tinline v White Cross Insurance Association Ltd* [1921] 3 KB 327.
[113] Even though the modifying regime under the Forfeiture Act is not applicable to such inchoate liability.
[114] [1989] 1 FLR 351.

payments in the future because of his former wife's criminal conduct to him. But this case did not in fact involve the application of the forfeiture rule, because the wife was not being deprived of any benefits to which she had become entitled as a result of the crime. Rather, the effect of her criminal conduct was to deprive her of benefits which she had been receiving for a number of years. The reason for this was simply that, for reasons of public policy, it would not be just to expect the plaintiff to continue to make payments to his former wife who had sought his murder. The forfeiture rule will only be applicable where it can be shown that, but for the commission of the relevant crime, the defendant would not be entitled to claim the benefit. It is for this reason that the forfeiture rule is unlikely to be triggered by the commission of an inchoate offence, simply because the commission of such crimes is unlikely to result in any benefit accruing to the criminal.

Usually the crime of murder is committed in circumstances where the killer intends to kill or seriously injure a particular victim who is actually killed. But it is also possible for the crime to be committed where the killer intends to kill or seriously injure one person and the actual victim is somebody else who is accidentally killed. In this type of case the killer is convicted of murder by reference to the principle of transferred malice, whereby the intention to kill one person is transferred to secure conviction in respect of the death of the person who is actually killed.[115] If the killer is entitled to obtain benefits as a result of this killing, should he or she be deprived of them by virtue of the forfeiture rule? For example, if the killer shoots at his wife, intending to kill her, but misses and kills his mother, is the killer still entitled to obtain his mother's estate under her will? The preferable view is that the forfeiture rule has no role to play in such circumstances, simply because the killer lacked the intention to kill the person who died and from whom the benefits were obtained.[116] Whilst the doctrine of transferred malice is perfectly acceptable as a means of securing the criminal conviction of the killer, there is no reason why it should be used to deprive the defendant of any benefits to which he or she is entitled effectively as the result of an accident, in the sense that the killer did not actually intend to harm the person who died.[117]

When determining whether the forfeiture rule is applicable the moral culpability of the killer is irrelevant.[118] So, in *Re Giles (deceased)*[119] it was held that the forfeiture rule prevented the killer from benefiting under her husband's will, even though she had killed him in circumstances where she could successfully plead diminished responsibility and was given a sentence which was remedial in nature and not intended to punish her. The type of punishment and the killer's moral culpability were specifically rejected as relevant considerations in determining whether the forfeiture rule should be applicable.

2. Proving the killer's guilt

For the forfeiture rule to apply it must be shown that the killer was guilty of an unlawful killing. As a general rule, if the killer has been convicted of an unlawful killing in criminal proceedings,

---

[115] *R v Latimer* (1886) 17 QBD 359.
[116] Such a conclusion is more difficult to justify if the Court of Appeal's wide interpretation of the forfeiture rule in *Dunbar v Plant* [1997] 3 WLR 1261 is considered to represent the law.
[117] T Youdan, "Acquisition of Property by Killing" (1973) 89 LQR 235, 244. See also PD Maddaugh and JD McCamus, *The Law of Restitution* (Canada Law Bank Inc, 1990), 495. Salmon LJ, however, in *Gray v Barr* [1971] 2 QB 554, 581 did say that the forfeiture rule would remain applicable despite the reliance on the transferred malice doctrine. But this observation was confined to the particular facts of the case, which concerned whether a killer could recover an indemnity from his insurance company in respect of his liability arising from the killing. It does not follow that the forfeiture rule should prevent the killer from obtaining benefits from the victim's estate.
[118] Though it is a relevant consideration when the court determines whether the application of the forfeiture rule should be modified under the Forfeiture Act 1982.
[119] [1972] Ch 544. See also *Re Hall (deceased)* [1914] P 1, 7 (Hamilton LJ); *Re K (deceased)* [1985] Ch 85, 98 (Vinelott J).

then this conviction is admissible evidence in civil proceedings and will be sufficient proof of guilt for the purposes of those proceedings, though it is still possible for the killer to show in the civil proceedings that he or she was not guilty of the unlawful killing.[120] But if the defendant is acquitted in criminal proceedings, all this means is that the guilt of the defendant was not proved beyond all reasonable doubt. It is still possible for the defendant to be deprived of benefits arising from the crime in civil proceedings where the standard of proof is the more easily satisfied test of the balance of probabilities.[121] So, in *Gray v Barr*[122] although the killer had been acquitted of homicide, he was still denied an indemnity from his insurers by virtue of the forfeiture rule. The forfeiture rule will even be applicable if the killer had never been tried for the particular offence.[123]

3. Application of the forfeiture rule

(a) *Entitlement to the benefit must be caused by the killing*

For the forfeiture rule to be applicable to prevent the criminal from obtaining benefits, it must be shown that the unlawful killing directly caused the criminal to become entitled to the benefits.[124] The usual "but for" test of causation is applicable for these purposes. So it must be shown that the consequence of the killing is that the killer became entitled to benefits to which he or she would not otherwise have been entitled or that the killer had become entitled to benefits sooner than he or she would otherwise have done.[125] The forfeiture rule should be applicable where the killer has simply accelerated the acquisition of the benefit because, by killing the victim, the killer has deprived the victim of the opportunity to change his or her mind as to the destination of the benefit and has removed the possibility that he or she would have predeceased the victim.[126] In certain circumstances it will be difficult to show that the killer became entitled to benefits because of the unlawful killing. For example, if the killer unlawfully wounded the victim who, before he or she died, made a will in favour of the killer, it is not possible to say that the killer had become entitled to the benefits as a result of the killing, since the benefits accrued as a result of the victim's acts after the fatal injury had been caused. Similarly, if before he or she dies the victim had the opportunity to alter the devolution of his or her estate to the killer but failed to do so, it could be argued that the killer became entitled to benefits as a result of the victim's omission rather than the killing.[127] But it would only be possible to conclude that the victim's omission had broken the chain of causation where the victim knew that he or she had the opportunity to alter the devolution of property and consciously failed to do so. In the absence of clear evidence to this effect, this will be a very difficult matter to prove.

There will be a point where the killing is too remote a cause of the benefits accruing to the killer and in such circumstances the forfeiture rule will not operate to deprive the killer of such benefits. This is illustrated by a South African case[128] where a father killed his parents, who had bequeathed property to his child and the child died shortly after the grandparents had been

---

[120] Civil Evidence Act 1968, s 11.
[121] *Dunbar v Plant* [1997] 3 WLR 1261. The Court of Appeal has recently affirmed that the standard for proving in civil proceedings that the killer was guilty of murder is the civil standard on the balance of probabilities: *Francisco v Diedrick* [1998] *The Times*, 3 April.
[122] [1971] QB 554.
[123] *Dunbar v Plant* [1997] 3 WLR 1261.
[124] *Cleaver v Mutual Reserve Fund Life Association* [1892] 1 QB 147, 156 (Fry LJ); *St. John Shipping Corp v Joseph Rank Ltd* [1957] 1 QB 267, 292 (Devlin J). Cf *Re H (deceased)* [1990] 1 FLR 441, 442, where Peter Gibson J said that the forfeiture rule prevented the killer from benefiting directly *or indirectly* from the crime.
[125] Youdan (1973) 89 LQR 235.
[126] Maddaugh & McCamus, *supra* n 117, at p 486.
[127] Youdan (1973) 89 LQR 235, 236.
[128] *Ex p Steenkamp* (1952) (1) SA 744 (T).

killed. It was held that the father could inherit the property which the child had been bequeathed by its grandparents. Although it could be argued that, but for the father killing his parents the child would not have received the property and so the father would not have been able to inherit, the killing had ceased to be an operative cause, since the father did not receive the property from his parents directly. Consequently, the forfeiture rule was held to be inapplicable.

(b) The types of benefits to which the forfeiture rule may apply

Where the forfeiture rule is applicable it may prevent the killer from obtaining a number of different benefits. For example, a killer is not entitled to benefit under the will[129] or intestacy[130] of the deceased. Similarly, a killer is not entitled to benefit from a life insurance policy on the victim's life.[131] In *Davitt v Titcumb*[132] it was accepted that the effect of the forfeiture rule was to prevent the killer from benefiting under a mortgage protection policy. The forfeiture rule has even been applied to deprive a killer of social welfare payments, such as a widow's pension, to which he or she would otherwise have been entitled.[133]

(c) Application of the forfeiture rule to cases where the victim is prevented from changing a will

In certain circumstances it may be possible to show that the victim was intending to change his or her will and so deprive the killer of property which had been bequeathed to him or her under the will. In such a situation the forfeiture rule does not strictly apply. This is because the killer was already entitled to the benefits and so did not become entitled to them as a result of the killing. Consequently, the forfeiture rule will not prevent title to the benefits from passing to the killer. But, because of the killer's actions in preventing the victim from changing his or her will, a constructive trust could be imposed so that the killer holds the property on trust for the "person who, in the view of equity, has the best right to it."[134]

(d) Application of the forfeiture rule to cases where there is a joint tenancy

A particular problem arises in respect of the application of the forfeiture rule where there is a joint tenancy. For example, where a husband and wife are joint owners of the matrimonial home and the wife kills her husband, what happens to the respective interests in the property? The effect of a joint tenancy is that each joint tenant is assumed to own the whole of the legal interest over the relevant property, subject to the co-existing and co-extensive rights of the other joint tenants. This means that, if there are two joint tenants and one of them dies, the other is automatically entitled to the property absolutely. But, if one of the joint tenants dies as a result of being unlawfully killed by the other joint tenant, should the forfeiture rule come into operation and so prevent the killer from obtaining the property? This problem does not arise where there is a tenancy in common, since in such a case the property is owned equally by the tenants in common, so that, if one tenant kills the other, the killer will not be deprived of the interest which he or she already possesses, but the forfeiture rule will prevent him or her from obtaining the interest of the deceased to which he or she might otherwise have been entitled.[135] Yet the application

---

[129] *Re Giles (deceased)* [1972] Ch 544.
[130] *Re Sigsworth* [1935] 1 Ch 89.
[131] *Cleaver v Mutual Reserve Fund Life Association* [1892] 1 QB 147; *Re S (deceased)* [1996] 1 WLR 235. In *Gray v Barr* [1971] 2 QB 554 the forfeiture rule prevented the killer from claiming an indemnity from his insurers in respect of his liability for the unlawful death of the victim.
[132] [1990] Ch 110.
[133] *R v Chief National Insurance Commissioner, ex p Connor* [1981] 1 QB 758.
[134] Youdan (1973) 89 LQR 235, 257.
[135] *Davitt v Titcumb* [1990] Ch 110.

of the forfeiture rule is more complicated where there is a joint tenancy, essentially because the effect of killing the other joint tenant is that the killer's rights are enlarged rather than created as a result of the commission of the crime. There are two possible solutions to this problem:

(i) The killer should be allowed to retain his or her beneficial interest in half of the property for life, but on his or her death the interest should revert to the beneficiaries of the victim's estate. This has the advantage that the killer's estate is eventually deprived of the beneficial interest in his or her half of the property and this is justified because, by killing the victim, the killer has deprived the victim of the chance of surviving him or her and so of becoming entitled to the whole of the property.[136] Consequently, it should be assumed that the victim would have survived the killer and so would have taken the property absolutely by virtue of survivorship. But this smacks of double punishment since, in addition to the punishment of the killer for the unlawful killing, the killer's estate will also be deprived of property to which the killer was already entitled before the crime was committed. There is no warrant for extending the operation of the forfeiture rule in this way. To make matters worse, the effect of this punishment of depriving the killer's estate of the property is that the killer's beneficiaries are effectively being punished for the killer's crime, whereas the killer was allowed to enjoy the benefit of half of the property.

(ii) The second, and preferable, solution to the problem is that the killer should be entitled to retain half of the beneficial interest in the property, but the other half of the beneficial interest should pass to the deceased's next of kin.[137] There are two mechanisms by which this solution can be reached. In both cases the usual rule of survivorship will mean that the entire legal interest in the property is vested in the killer. However, as regards the beneficial interest in the property, one solution, which has been adopted in a number of Commonwealth countries,[138] is to treat the killer as holding an undivided half share of the beneficial interest on constructive trust for those other people who are entitled to the victim's estate. The second mechanism, which was preferred by Vinelott J as more appropriate in the light of the 1925 property legislation, is to treat the killing as a severance of the joint tenancy so that the beneficial interest vests in the deceased and the killer as tenants in common.[139] This is much the more simple and elegant solution.[140] Where there are three joint tenants, one of whom kills the other, then again the killer should not be deprived of his or her existing proprietary interest, but the principle of survivorship should still operate in favour of the other joint tenant, who would consequently obtain the victim's interest in the property.[141] The advantage of this solution to the problem of joint tenants who kill is that the forfeiture rule prevents the killer from benefiting from the commission of the crime without depriving the killer, or those claiming through him or her, of an existing proprietary right. Consequently, in the case of a wife who has killed her husband, the forfeiture rule should not be used to deprive her of her own interest in the matrimonial home, since this right did not arise as a result of the killing of her husband. Rather, she should be prevented from acquiring her deceased husband's share of the matrimonial home. Of course, it might be argued that this solution does deprive the killer of an existing right, since all joint tenants have the right to gain the

---

[136] Jones, *Restitution in Public and Private Law* (1991), 69.
[137] *Re K (deceased)* [1985] Ch 85, 100 (Vinelott J). This issue was not discussed by the Court of Appeal [1986] Ch 180.
[138] *Schobelt v Barker* (1967) 60 DLR (2d.) 519; *Rasmanis v Jurewitsch* (1970) 70 SR (NSW) 407; *Re Pechar (deceased)* [1969] NZLR 574.
[139] This solution was approved in *Dunbar v Plant* [1997] 3 WLR 1261, 1266 (Mummery LJ).
[140] As Napier J recognised in *Re Barrowcliff* [1927] SASR 147, 15. Since the risk that one joint tenant will unlawfully kill the other is not contemplated, the killing repudiates the terms of the joint tenancy and so effects a severance.
[141] See Street J in *Rasmanis v Jurewitsch* [1968] 2 NSWLR 166, 168. *Cf* the judgment of Jacobs JA in the appeal from this decision, where he held that the victim's interest should pass to the victim's estate: (1970) 70 SR (NSW) 407, 412. But there is no reason why the forfeiture rule should operate to deprive the surviving joint tenant who is innocent of any crime of his or her rights under the joint tenancy.

entire estate should the other joint tenant predecease him or her. But it is entirely appropriate that the killer should be deprived of this right since, by virtue of the killing of the other joint tenant, any chance that he or she would have naturally predeceased the killer has been removed.

(e) Application of the forfeiture rule where the victim is a life tenant

A similar problem to that of killings by joint tenants arises where property has been settled on one person for life with remainder to another person, and that person unlawfully kills the former.[142] The effect of the death is that the killer is entitled to the estate immediately, but this would mean that the killer would be profiting from the crime and this is contrary to public policy.[143] Yet if the forfeiture rule is invoked to prevent the killer from obtaining the property then he or she would be deprived of a proprietary interest which already existed before the killing. To reconcile these conflicting policies it is necessary to identify the true benefit which the killer obtains by unlawfully killing the life tenant. This benefit is that the killer accelerates the enjoyment of the life interest. The best method for preventing the killer from enjoying this benefit is by determining what the life tenant's life expectancy was and preventing the killer from enjoying the property until it was likely that the victim would have died naturally.[144] Consequently, the killer should hold the property on a constructive trust in favour of the victim's estate until the victim was expected to have died naturally.

The position is more complicated where the killer's interest is contingent on his or her surviving the life tenant. It could be argued that, in such circumstances, the act of killing the victim means that it should be presumed that the killer would not have outlived the life tenant, so the killer should be deprived of his or her whole interest in the property. But this constitutes a forfeiture of an existing proprietary interest, since even a contingent remainder is alienable and valuable.[145] A preferable solution is to have regard to the victim's life expectancy.[146] Until the end of the period of the victim's life expectancy the property should be treated as though the victim had not died and so should be held on constructive trust for the benefit of the victim's estate. If at the end of this period the killer is still alive, the contingency should be treated as fulfilled and the killer should take the property. If the killer dies before the end of this period, the victim's beneficiaries should take the property absolutely.

(f) Claims of third parties

Whether third parties are able to claim benefits which accrue as a result of the commission of an unlawful killing depends on whether the third party is claiming benefits which accrued to the killer as a result of the crime. If the claim is so dependent it will be defeated by the forfeiture rule, because the effect of the rule is that the killer cannot obtain the benefit, and if he or she does not have the benefit then the third party cannot claim it either.[147] Such benefits are tainted by the crime and so are caught by the forfeiture rule. If, however, the third party has an independent claim to the benefit, which is not dependent on whether the killer has been able to obtain the benefit, the third party will not be affected by the forfeiture rule because the claim is untainted by the crime.

The typical example of a case where the third party's claim is tainted by the crime is where personal representatives of the killer are prevented from obtaining benefits to which the killer was

---

[142] This problem has not been discussed in any case, although it was recognised in *Re Calloway* [1956] Ch 559.
[143] *Cleaver v Mutual Reserve Fund Life Association* [1892] 1 QB 147, 157 (Fry LJ).
[144] Youdan (1973) 89 LQR 235, 250.
[145] *Ibid.*
[146] *Ibid*, 251.
[147] *Cleaver v Mutual Reserve Fund Life Association* [1892] 1 QB 147, 155 (Lord Esher MR); *In the Estate of Cunigunda (otherwise Cora) Crippen (deceased)* [1911] P 108, 112.

entitled if the forfeiture rule had not been applicable. If the killer could not have obtained the benefits then neither can the personal representative.[148] This is illustrated by *In the Estate of Cunigunda (otherwise Cora) Crippen (deceased)*,[149] where the estate of the wife who had been killed by her husband should have passed to the husband on an intestacy. It was held that, after the husband had been executed for the murder, his mistress, who was the sole executrix of his estate, was not entitled to a grant of the administration of the wife's estate because the right to do so arose as a result of the murder. Similarly in *Beresford v Royal Insurance Co*[150] the personal representatives of a person who had committed suicide were unable to recover policy monies from an insurance company, with whom the suicide had obtained a life insurance policy, because at the time suicide was a crime[151] and it was contrary to public policy that the personal representatives should recover the fruits of the crime, namely the money which was due as a result of the death of the suicide victim. It was irrelevant that the insurance policy made specific provision for the payment of money even where the assured had committed suicide, because such a provision was contrary to public policy and so was unenforceable.

An example of a case where a third party was able to claim benefits because the claim was untainted by the commission of the crime is the decision of the Court of Appeal in *Cleaver v Mutual Reserve Fund Life Association*,[152] where a wife killed her husband who had a policy of life insurance with the defendants. The executors of the deceased claimed the sum insured from the defendants. Whilst it was admitted that the wife could not receive this money, because of the operation of the forfeiture rule, this rule could not be relied on to prevent the defendants from paying the money to the deceased's executors, whose claim was based on the estate's entitlement to the money under the insurance policy. It was only once the executors had received this money that they would have been prohibited from paying it to the wife by virtue of the forfeiture rule.

Another example of a case where the third party's right is untainted by the crime is where the killer has assigned his or her rights under an insurance policy for value before the commission of the crime; then the assignee could still enforce those rights even though the killer could not.[153] The reason for this was suggested by Diplock LJ in *Hardy v Motor Insurers' Bureau*:[154]

> "[The contract] is capable of giving rise to legally enforceable rights if, apart from the [forfeiture] rule, the rights of the assured are capable of becoming vested in a third party other than one who is regarded in law as the successor of the assured, such as the personal representative... or his trustee in bankruptcy... an assignee for value before the occurrence of the event would not be prevented from enforcing the contract notwithstanding that the event was caused by the anti-social act of the original assured."

In other words, it does not matter that the event which triggered the legally enforceable rights arose from the commission of the crime by the killer, so long as the assignee acquired these rights before the crime was committed. This means that the right which the assignee wishes to enforce was not tainted by the crime. He or she is in the position of a bona fide purchaser for value, and like such a person is able to enforce the rights so long as he or she has given value without notice of the crime. Although an assignee could still satisfy this test if the assignment took place after

---

[148] This principle was also applied in *The Amicable Society for Perpetual Life Assurance Office v Bolland* (1830) 4 Bligh (NS) 194, where a trustee in bankruptcy was treated as a successor of the assured, just like a personal representative.
[149] [1911] P 108.
[150] [1938] AC 586.
[151] Suicide is no longer a crime: Suicide Act 1961, s 1.
[152] [1892] 1 QB 147.
[153] *Beresford v Royal Insurance Co* [1938] AC 586, 600 (Lord Atkin). See also *Davitt v Titcumb* [1990] Ch 110, where a building society, to which an endowment policy had been assigned, was able to enforce the policy after the murder of the person whose life was insured under the policy.
[154] [1964] 2 QB 745, 768.

the crime had been committed, in such a case the operation of the forfeiture rule would mean that the killer had no rights to assign, and so such an assignee would not be able to claim the benefits which, if the forfeiture rule had not applied, would have accrued to the killer.[155]

(g) Allocation of benefits which are caught by the forfeiture rule

If the killer and those claiming through the killer are unable to obtain benefits by virtue of the forfeiture rule, such benefits should be considered to be retained by the victim's estate and so should be transferred to those people who are beneficiaries of that estate, except for the killer. Normally benefits, such as property, will pass to the victim's residuary legatee[156] or to those who are entitled to the property if the victim died intestate.[157] If the killer was the sole residuary legatee then the property should be distributed as though the victim had died intestate.[158] If the property was left to a class of beneficiaries, one of whom was the killer, then the killer's share should be divided equally between the other members of the class.[159] If the killer is the beneficiary under the victim's life insurance policy, then the proceeds of the policy should be held for the victim's estate.[160]

It has sometimes been suggested that, rather than the victim's estate passing to the next person in succession after the criminal, it should pass as *bona vacantia* to the Crown. This question was canvassed and was reluctantly dismissed in *Re Callaway*.[161] But there was no need for any reluctance in reaching this decision. There is no reason why the forfeiture rule should be used to deprive the successor of his or her rights to the estate, since these rights were not created by the commission of the crime, but rather arise, as in that case, from the law of intestacy or by virtue of the terms of the victim's will.[162] In other words, the successor's rights are not tainted by the commission of the crime.

(h) An alternative approach to the allocation of benefits: the constructive trust

A consequence of the principle that no criminal should profit from his or her crime is that title to property which would otherwise accrue to the criminal, or to those claiming through him or her, cannot pass to the criminal. But this response is not free from difficulty. This is because in many cases, whether by virtue of statute or the common law, legal title should indeed pass to the criminal, and there is no provision in the statute or common law to the effect that an exception should be made where the passing of property is triggered by the criminal's own act. For the forfeiture rule to work it must be assumed that, for reasons of public policy, every legal rule contains an implied term to the effect that no criminal who, by the commission of the crime, has triggered the passing of property should be allowed to benefit from the crime.[163] It would be a much more honest response to apply the relevant statutory and judicial laws literally, without artificial interpretation. This would mean that title to property would pass to the criminal. But, because of the

---

[155] *Re Cash (deceased)* [1911] 30 NZLR 577.
[156] As occurred in *Re Peacock* [1957] Ch 310.
[157] *Re Sigsworth* [1935] Ch 89.
[158] *Re Pollock* [1941] 1 Ch 219; *Re Callaway* [1956] Ch 559.
[159] *Re Peacock* [1957] Ch 310.
[160] *Cleaver v Mutual Reserve Fund Life Association* [1892] 1 QB 147.
[161] [1956] Ch 559.
[162] Megarry (1956) 72 LQR 475. See *Davitt v Titcumb* [1990] Ch 110, where the trial judge commended the decision of the Crown not to pursue a claim in *bona vacantia*.
[163] See *eg Re Royse* [1985] Ch 22, where it was assumed that the application of the Inheritance (Provision of Family and Dependants) Act 1975 was subject to the forfeiture rule, even though the Act makes no provision for this rule. Similarly in *Re Sigsworth* [1935] 1 Ch 89 the Administration of Estates Act 1925 was interpreted as though its provisions relating to intestacy were subject to the forfeiture rule.

principle that no criminal should profit from his or her crime, equity should ensure that because of the killer's unconscionable conduct an equitable interest in the property is created in favour of the victim, with the result that the criminal should hold the property on a constructive trust for the victim's estate.[164] This would be consistent with Lord Browne-Wilkinson's interpretation of the constructive trust in *Westdeutsche Landesbank Girozentrale v Islington LBC*.[165] Such an approach would have a number of advantages.

(i) The operation of the forfeiture rule would not conflict with the clear words of statute and judicial precedent but would continue to fulfil the policy that no criminal should profit from his or her crime.

(ii) If it is accepted that legal title to the victim's estate should pass to the killer, then a constructive trust will be imposed in favour of the people who equity regards are entitled to the estate. Usually it will be clear who such people are, because the normal rules of succession will be applied, with the obvious qualification that the killer and those claiming through the killer will not have a beneficial interest. But in certain circumstances the flexibility of equity will enable the beneficial interest to be created in favour of another party. The most obvious example of this will be where there is clear evidence that the victim had intended to change his or her will, or to make a will, so as to leave the estate to a particular person, but was killed before he or she was able to do so.

(iii) If the property which had been acquired by or through the criminal had been received by a third party then the victim of the crime, or the beneficiaries of the victim, would be able to recover the property. But this is subject to an important qualification, namely that the property could not be recovered from a third party who was a bona fide purchaser for value. This is consistent with the general principles relating to the operation of the bona fide purchase defence in the law of restitution. An example of a case where this defence might have been applicable is the New Zealand decision of *Re Cash*,[166] where the husband who murdered his wife had subsequently assigned his interest in her estate to a firm of solicitors to pay for their costs in defending him in his trial. It was held that the firm could not enforce these rights simply because the husband's crime meant that he did not obtain any title to the wife's estate and so had nothing to assign to the solicitors. But it is clear that, if the husband had assigned his rights to the wife's estate before he had committed the crime, then the assignee would be able to enforce the rights.[167] It should make no difference to the position of the assignee that the assignment for value took place after the crime had been committed, subject to the important qualification that the assignee lacked notice that the crime had been committed, for otherwise the assignee would not have been acting bona fide. This would in fact have meant that the bona fide purchase defence would not have been applicable in *Re Cash* because, if the assignee firm of solicitors were defending the killer from whom the rights had been assigned, presumably they must have known that the rights had been obtained as a result of the commission of a crime.[168] But in other cases assignees will obtain rights from the killer for value after the crime had been committed and in circumstances where they are unaware that the assignor had committed a crime to obtain the rights. The claims of such assignees should prevail and this will be achieved by accepting that legal title to the victim's property passes to the killer and any constructive trust will be defeated by the bona fide purchase defence.

---

[164] Youdan (1973) 89 LQR 235, 253.
[165] [1996] AC 669, 716.
[166] [1911] 30 NZLR 577.
[167] See *Beresford v Royal Insurance Co Ltd* [1938] AC 586, 600 (Lord Atkin).
[168] Surprisingly, in the light of the reported facts, the trial judge did characterise the assignment as bona fide and for value: [1911] 30 NZLR 577, 581. But surely, at the very least, the firm of solicitors were put on notice that the husband might not be entitled to the beneficial interest in his wife's estate.

D. The Forfeiture Act 1982[169]

1. Application of the Forfeiture Act

The inflexible common law forfeiture rule has now been modified by the Forfeiture Act 1982. Although this Act does not apply where the defendant has committed murder,[170] in virtually every other case where the forfeiture rule has precluded a person who has unlawfully killed another person from acquiring any interest in property, the application of that rule may be modified by order of the court.[171] Obviously this power to modify the forfeiture rule will only be relevant where that rule is applicable in the first place, so it remains necessary to consider the application of the forfeiture rule at common law. But the Forfeiture Act is not automatically applicable simply because the forfeiture rule applies. The Act will only apply where the killer has committed an unlawful killing either as principal or accessory,[172] but it does not apply to inchoate offences which relate to unlawful killing, such as attempts to kill the victim.[173] The Act only applies where somebody is prevented by the forfeiture rule from acquiring an interest in property. The notion of "interest in property" includes any beneficial interest in property which the offender would have acquired under the will of the deceased or on his or her intestacy,[174] or on the nomination of the deceased under any statute or as a *donatio mortis causa* made by the victim.[175] "Interest in property" also includes property which was held on trust for any person and which the offender would have acquired as a result of the death of the deceased.[176] This would cover the case where one joint tenant kills the other and, subject to the operation of the forfeiture rule, would have obtained the property absolutely by virtue of the principle of survivorship. The definition of "interest in property" means that the Act does not apply to benefits which would have been obtained under an insurance policy had not the forfeiture rule been applicable, save where the proceeds of the policy are held on trust for the killer.[177]

The Forfeiture Act is applicable even though the killer has not been convicted of a criminal offence.[178] However, an important distinction exists depending on whether or not the killer has been convicted of a crime in respect of the unlawful killing. For, if the killer "stands convicted of an offence of which unlawful killing is an element", the power of the court to modify the forfeiture rule will only apply if proceedings under the Act are brought within three months of the conviction.[179] If the killer has not been convicted of a crime then there is no limitation period within which an application must be made. Similarly, if the killer's conviction has been quashed, it seems that there is no longer any limitation period in respect of the making of an application, since he or she no longer "stands convicted" of an offence.

---

[169] For commentary on the Act see Kenny (1983) 46 MLR 66.
[170] Forfeiture Act 1982, s 5.
[171] *Ibid*, s 2(1). The Act applies regardless of when the unlawful killing occurred: s 7(4).
[172] *Ibid*, s 1(2).
[173] The Act is also inapplicable where the killer has committed suicide, because the killer has not killed "another person". But this is consistent with the present law relating to the forfeiture rule itself, since that rule does not apply where the killer has committed suicide, since suicide is no longer a crime: Suicide Act 1961, s 1. The Forfeiture Act will, however, be applicable where the crime of aiding, abetting, counselling or procuring suicide has been committed: *Dunbar v Plant* [1997] 3 WLR 1261.
[174] Or under the Inheritance (Provision for Family and Dependants) Act 1975: Forfeiture Act 1982, s 3(1)(a).
[175] Forfeiture Act 1982, s 2(4)(a). "Property" includes any chose in action: *ibid*, s 2(8).
[176] *Ibid*, s 2(4)(b).
[177] *Dunbar v Plant* [1997] 3 WLR 1261.
[178] See the social security case (1990) 87/24 LS Gaz 47.
[179] Forfeiture Act 1982, s, 2(3).

2. Modification of the forfeiture rule

The court will only modify the forfeiture rule if it is satisfied that, having regard to the conduct of the killer and of the deceased and of any other circumstances of the case which appear to be material, the justice of the case requires the rule to be modified.[180] The forfeiture rule may be disapplied completely[181] or it may be modified in part.[182] In exercising his or her discretion as to whether or not the forfeiture rule should be modified the trial judge must not seek to do justice between the parties to the dispute but rather should rather consider whether the culpability of the defendant justified the strict application of the forfeiture rule.[183] In *Dunbar v Plant*[184] Mummery LJ said that:

> "The court is entitled to take into account a whole range of circumstances relevant to the discretion, quite apart from the conduct of the offender and the deceased: the relationship between them; the degree of moral culpability for what has happened; the nature and gravity of the offence; the intentions of the deceased; the size of the estate and the value of the property in dispute; the financial position of the offender; and the moral claims and wishes of those who would be entitled to take the property on the application of the forfeiture rule."

The application of the Forfeiture Act is well illustrated by the decision of the Court of Appeal in *Re K (deceased)*,[185] where a wife, having killed her husband, was convicted of manslaughter for which she received a sentence of two years' probation. This lenient sentence was justified because of the particular circumstances of the killing. The wife had been battered by her husband for a number of years. On the day of the killing her husband had beaten her again and, intending to frighten him away, she picked up a loaded shotgun, released the safety catch and aimed it at him. The gun accidentally went off and killed him. The wife claimed that she was entitled to an interest under her husband's will and was also entitled to the matrimonial home. The court, having accepted that the forfeiture rule was applicable, held that the wife should be granted complete relief from the forfeiture of all the benefits which had accrued to her on the death of her husband. A number of factors were considered to be relevant to the exercise of the court's discretion.

(a) The most important factor was the degree of moral culpability of the wife in committing the crime; her offence was considered to be at the least serious end of the spectrum of manslaughter offences. This was because she had been provoked to kill her husband and this had been reflected in the sentence of probation which she had received,

(b) The moral culpability of the wife and of her husband was compared. Whilst the wife had been loyal to her husband, it was considered to be relevant that he had abused her for a number of years.

(c) The relative financial position of the wife as compared with the other people who were entitled under the husband's will was taken into account. The court stressed that the husband had made appropriate provision for his wife and was under no moral duty to make provision for anybody else.

(d) The conduct of the other beneficiaries under the husband's will was also considered, particularly since a number of them had confirmed, after the death of the husband, that the terms

---

[180] *Ibid*, s 2(2).
[181] *Ibid*, s 2(1). See eg *Dunbar v Plant* [1997] 3 WLR 1261.
[182] Forfeiture Act 1982, s 2(5). If the effect of the forfeiture rule is to prevent the killer from obtaining social security benefits, such as a widow's pension, the discretion to modify the rule is given to the Social Security Commissioner and not to the court: Forfeiture Act 1982, s 4, as amended by the Social Security Act 1986, s 76.
[183] *Dunbar v Plant* [1997] 3 WLR 1261.
[184] *Ibid*, 1275.
[185] [1986] Ch 180.

of the husband's will should be respected, despite the potential application of the forfeiture rule.[186]

Further, in *Dunbar v Plant*[187] a majority of the Court of Appeal exercised its discretion to disapply the forfeiture rule completely in a case where the defendant had aided and abetted the suicide of her fiancee, where he had killed himself pursuant to a suicide pact. It was held that the forfeiture rule should not be applied to prevent the defendant from obtaining benefits from the deceased's estate for a number of reasons. The most important reason was that the nature of the defendant's crime was such that she had not received any penal sanction for it, consequently her culpability did not justify the application of the forfeiture rule. Also the deceased had intended that the relevant benefits, namely the proceeds of an insurance policy and his interest in their house, should be received by the defendant on his death.[188]

3. A critique of the Forfeiture Act 1982

By virtue of the enactment of the Forfeiture Act 1982 the injustice which arose from the strict adherence to the principle that no criminal could benefit from the commission of a criminal offence has been alleviated to some extent. But that Act is not totally satisfactory. The Act should, for example, be extended to cases of murder, since there are some cases of murder where the killer's true culpability does not warrant the strict application of the forfeiture rule. For example, in certain cases of mercy killing, where one spouse kills another spouse to alleviate his or her suffering, there is no reason why the killer should be prevented from obtaining benefits which would otherwise have accrued to him or her on the death of the victim. In the same way as not all forms of manslaughter involve the same culpability, the same is also true of the crime of murder and this should be reflected in the way the forfeiture rule is applied in such cases. It is also most unfortunate that the Act does not apply to relieve the forfeiture of benefits which would have been received under an insurance policy had not the forfeiture rule been applicable. Most importantly, the Forfeiture Act places the judiciary in a particularly difficult position, since the Act gives no assistance as to how the judges' discretion should be exercised. In fact, in all reported cases concerning the application of the Act the judges have disapplied the forfeiture rule completely.[189]

IV. CONCLUSIONS

Gradually the potential for the law of restitution to ensure that criminals do not profit from the commission of their crimes is being recognised. How this develops in future will depend very much on whether there is any more statutory intervention and also how the constructive trust develops. As the law stands it is clear that the constructive trust could be used to ensure that criminals do not profit from their crimes.

---

[186] See also *Re H (deceased)* [1990] 1 FLR 441, where the trial judge stated that, had the forfeiture rule been applicable to the case, he would have exercised his discretion under the Forfeiture Act to disapply the rule completely. Relevant factors which he would have taken into consideration in exercising his discretion included that the husband who had killed his wife had not been in control of his actions because of the adverse effects of taking antidepressant drugs. Also the couple were happily married, there were no other moral claimants for the wife's assets and, if the husband received those assets, they would assist him in paying for his rehabilitation treatment.
[187] [1997] 3 WLR 1261.
[188] Mummery LJ dissented on the ground that weight should be given to the moral claims and wishes of the deceased's family.
[189] The only case where the forfeiture rule was modified rather than disapplied was the decision of the trial judge in *Dunbar v Plant*, but the Court of Appeal overruled this decision: [1997] 3 WLR 1261. Other cases where the rule was disapplied completely include *Re K* [1986] Ch 180 and *Re S* [1996] 1 WLR 235.

What this survey of the law has sought to show is that, whether the law is being used prospectively to ensure that criminals do not receive the proceeds of the crime or retrospectively to require criminals to disgorge these proceeds, the policy of the law is the same. Consequently, the granting of prospective and retrospective relief to ensure that criminals should not profit from their crime should simply be treated as different sides of the same coin, a coin which can properly be placed under the general heading of restitution for wrongs.

THIRD PARTY CHEQUES — SECURITY OR SNARE?

*Andrew Tettenborn**

Suppose A provides goods or services to B and accepts payment by a building society cheque. Received wisdom has it that A is in virtually the same position as if he had taken cash. Barring the possibility of forgery (possible but unlikely) or failure of the building society that drew the cheque (almost unthinkable), he has a cast-iron guarantee of getting paid.

Or has he? Suppose the building society countermands the cheque. Has A, the payee, any right at all against the society, or is he thrown back on his right of action against B, who may well be of doubtful solvency? More drastically, what if the society asks for its money back after the cheque has been met, for example because B obtained the issue of it by fraud? Has A necessarily got a defence to such a claim, or is he at risk of having to repay what he thought — no doubt justifiably — that he could treat as money in the bank? The answers to these questions as a matter of English law are surprisingly unclear: a matter which is, to say the least, odd in a legal system that prides itself on the clarity of its rules of commercial law. In addition, it stands in stark contrast with the position in (for example) the USA under the Uniform Commercial Code.[1]

Not only is the law somewhat uncertain here: in addition, the point is also rather significant. Countless suppliers accept payment by building society cheque on the basis that this gives them an assurance of payment: and a not inconsiderable number similarly rely on other third party cheques — for example, from employers or the like.[2] More importantly still, exactly the same issue also affects anyone accepting payment by banker's draft. Such drafts are in law treated as promissory notes, and for these purposes are largely subject to the same rules on enforceabiloity and recoverability as bills of exchange.[3]

There are two situations where the problems outlined above are likely to arise. One is where B obtained the instrument from the drawer[4] by fraud. Suppose, for example, that B persuades a building society to give him a cheque in favour of A by forging X's signature in X's pass-book; or that he uses some means or other to deceive a bank into providing a draft made out to A.[5] It is by no means inconceivable that the bank or building society would, having found out the truth, seek to refuse payment of the cheque or even, if it is met, to recover the amount of it from A as money paid by mistake. Another example is where, even in the absence of fraud, the consideration provided by B for the issue of the instrument itself fails; for instance, where B obtains the issue of a banker's draft by the deposit of another instrument that, unknown to him, turned out to be forged or worthless.

This article will deal with two issues: first, the right to enforce the instrument, and secondly the right of recovery by the drawer if the instrument is actually paid.

---

* Bracton Professor of English Law, University of Exeter.
[1] Referred to in more detail below.
[2] A straightforward example is where an employer provides a cheque to cover an employee's removal costs.
[3] See Bills of Exchange Act 1882, s 89(1).
[4] The word "drawer" is used here for convenience to refer to a building society which draws a cheque and also a bank issuing a draft. Strictly speaking the position of the latter is assimilated to that of the acceptor of a bill of exchange and not the drawer, since it is the "maker" of the note in question: see Bills of Exchange Act 1882, s 89(2). But nothing turns on this.
[5] Compare the facts of *Citibank NA v Brown Shipley* [1991] 2 All ER 690, in which a draft was obtained by impersonating a customer of the bank concerned (though the draft was paid, and the action was framed in conversion against the recipient).

1. The right to enforce the instrument: defences available

In all the scenarios described above, A is assumed to be the original payee of the instrument concerned, and not an indorsee. If the instrument was originally drawn in favour of B and B endorsed it to A for value,[6] there is no doubt that A is a holder in due course and able to sue on it without reference to issues such as fraud in obtaining its issue. However, if A is a mere payee, the case is more difficult. Unlike the position in the US, where anyone — payee or otherwise — who takes a bill innocently and for value is comprehensively protected,[7] it is clear as a matter of English law that his status remains only that of holder, and not holder in due course, however innocent he was and whether or not he gave value: see the House of Lords' decision in *RE Jones v Waring & Gillow Ltd*[8] in 1925. The question, therefore, boils down to this: how far can a mere holder, not being a holder in due course, enforce the instrument, and to what extent is he affected by fraud or failure of consideration affecting the drawing of it?

Unfortunately, the actual decision in *Jones's* case itself is not very helpful here, since it was concerned not with enforceability of the instrument but with recovery of money paid under it (though, as will appear below, there may be a connection between the two questions). Nor is there much more help from the Bills of Exchange Act 1882, which is singularly silent on the rights of holders. The only right specifically given to a holder as such is the right to sue on the bill in his own name (s 38(1)), which is obvious but unhelpful. True, in s 38(2) there is a list of matters that do *not* affect the rights of a holder in due course, and which therefore (it could be argued) are intended to affect any other holder: namely, "mere personal defences available to prior parties among themselves", and "defects in title of prior parties". As to the latter, further guidance is given as to the latter by s 29, stating that it includes the case where a person negotiating a bill obtained it, or its acceptance, by fraud, duress or unlawful means, or for an illegal consideration, or where any negotiation of it amounted to a fraud or a breach of faith. But neither of these provisions really helps in determining the rights of a payee. The reference to defects in title of prior parties is clearly aimed at the title of prior *holders*; it is entirely inapposite where there are none of these and the only relevant prior party is the drawer himself. Nor, for the same reason, can much sense be made of the the reference to personal defences applicable between prior parties. This obviously envisages the case where there are at least two such parties, not that where there is only one, that is the drawer himself.

In fact, once the provisions of the 1882 Act are out of the way, it is a matter of going back to first principles and looking at the position of the drawers of the various instruments in the various scenarios involved; that is, fraud, failure of consideration and the conduct of the person seeking to enforce the instrument.

(a) A preliminary point: difficulties over "value"

Before doing this, however, there is one further defence which may catch the plaintiff unawares even where there is no other irregularity, namely lack of consideration — the contention, that is, that the person seeking to enforce the instrument (*ie* A) is not a holder for value at all. This is particularly important in the context of English law's surprisingly narrow definition of what counts as consideration for these purposes. The difficulty arises in two contexts: payment of debts, and consideration provided by parties other than the person suing. Concerning payment of debts, one might have thought this raised little difficulty, given that s 27 of the 1882 Act specif-

---

[6] Which is unlikely. Virtually all building society cheques and many bankers' drafts are crossed "a/c payee", which renders them unendorsable anyway because of the effect of the Cheques Act 1992.
[7] See UCC, §3-302(a)(1), providing that a holder in due course is anyone to whom an instrument is *issued or negotiated*, who takes in good faith, etc. (Italics supplied). Those systems, such as French law, that are based on the Geneva Convention of 1930 equally do not distinguish between payees and indorsees in this respect.
[8] [1926] AC 670.

ically provides that consideration includes any "antecedent debt or liability" in discharge of which the instrument is given. However, this reference has been consistently construed as being more limited than it looks, and in particular as restricted to debts existing *as between parties to the bill*.[9] It follows that where A accepts a building society cheque or banker's draft in payment of a pre-existing debt owed to him by B, he is regarded as a gratuitous holder *vis-a-vis* the financial institution concerned and cannot enforce it, unless he can show some further act on his part, such as a distinct promise to forbear to sue B — something that will not be inferred in the absence of specific evidence.[10]

A similar problem of narrow interpretation occurs in the case of the plaintiff who has not himself provided consideration, but seeks to rely on a *quid pro quo* provided by someone else. Section 27(2) of the 1882 Act says that

> "where value has at any time been given for a bill the holder is deemed to be a holder for value as regards the acceptor and all parties to the bill who became parties prior to such time."

Nevertheless, despite some earlier doubts,[11] it now seems clear from *MK International v Housing Bank*[12] that consideration does not count for these purposes unless it was provided *by someone who was himself a party to the instrument.* Consideration provided by a non-party will not do. This is obviously highly relevant where A is seeking to enforce a building society cheque or banker's draft provided by B, since here he will not be able to rely on anything done by B, such as the deposit of an instrument by B with the building society or bank concerned to cover the cheque.

(b) The defence of fraud

Assuming no problem of lack of consideration arises, how far is it open to the drawer of a building society cheque or the issuer of a banker's draft to refuse payment of it on account of fraud affecting its issue to which the payee was not party? The cases are unfortunately unclear.

The starting point is the actual decision in *Jones v Waring & Gillow,*[13] referred to above, which seems to suggest that it can. The facts, slightly simplified, were these. A plausible fraudster called Bodenham owed Warings £5,000 for furniture supplied, which the latter were wisely retaining in their possession pending payment. Bodenham approached Jones (a firm of Welsh car dealers) with a story that he represented the importers of a new make of American car, that this operation was backed by Warings, and that he was authorised to offer Jones exclusive distribution rights provided they agreed to pay Warings £5,000 as a "good faith deposit" on 500 cars. Needless to say, none of this was true. Jones nevertheless swallowed the bait and obligingly armed Bodenham with a cheque for £5,000 made out in favour of Warings. Warings took the cheque from Bodenham in payment of his personal debt to them, cashed it and released the furniture. When the truth came out, Bodenham went to prison and Jones went to the High Court to demand their money back from Warings, alleging payment by mistake of fact. The House of Lords held that their claim succeeded, on the basis (1) (unanimously) that Jones's mistake was sufficient to ground recovery for money paid by mistake under the principle in *Kelly v Solari*;[14] (2) (again unanimously) that Warings were not holders in due course; and (3) (by a majority) that Warings could not resist the claim on the basis that they had changed their position.

---

[9] See *Oliver v Davis* [1949] 2 KB 727; *Hasan v Willson* [1977] 1 Lloyd's Rep 431; *AEG (UK) Ltd v Lewis* [1993] 2 Bank LR 119. The UCC, once again, avoids this problem, by providing that a debt owed to the holder by anyone, whether or not a party, counts for these purposes: see §3-303(a)(3) and Note 4 thereto.
[10] See *Hasan v Willson* [1977] 1 Lloyd's Rep 431, where the court was asked to infer such forbearance merely from the payment, but declined to do so.
[11] Notably certain dicta of Danckwerts LJ in *Diamond v Graham* [1968] 1 WLR 1061, 1064.
[12] [1991] 1 Bank LR 74.
[13] [1926] AC 670.
[14] (1841) 9 M & W 54.

We will return to this decision later. But for these purposes the odd feature of the case is that hardly any attention seems to have been paid to a fourth point which one might have thought of considerable importance, and is of course vital to the subject of this article. Assuming the order of events had been different, could Warings have sued on the cheque had Jones discovered Bodenham's fraud and countermanded the instrument before payment? Although the matter was not discussed, the assumption nevertheless must have been that they could not. This is because otherwise the decision makes no sense: if you can be sued for a sum of money if you refuse to pay it, it is absurd to allow you to use the law of restitution to claim it back once you have paid it over.[15] And indeed, in 1939 Hallett J in *Ayres v Moore*[16] considered *Jones*'s case and drew this precise conclusion. A person induced to accept a bill of exchange by the fraud of a third party did indeed (he said) have a defence to an action to enforce it, except where the person suing was a holder in due course.

Other authority, however, suggests the opposite. There is a clear decision dating from 1911[17] that third-party duress, which is in many ways equivalent to fraud, cannot be pleaded against any holder, whether or not in due course. And in *Hasan v Willson*[18] in 1977 similar reasoning was applied to fraud. One S dishonestly persuaded Willson to draw a cheque in favour of Hasan by giving Willson another cheque which he knew to be worthless. Willson countermanded his cheque when he found out about S's deception, and Hasan sued him on it. In the event Hasan's action failed on the ground that he was not a holder for value. Nevertheless, Robert Goff J was highly sceptical about Hallett J's view in *Ayres*'s case and expressed the plain view that, had Hasan given value, S's fraud would have been irrelevant. The only fraud that would compromise the title of an innocent holder was, he said, fraud committed by a previous holder: the fact that the drawer of a cheque might have been duped by a third party into writing it was irrelevant to his liability to pay it.[19] And indeed this view seems more consonant with ordinary contract principles. Whatever other transactions may lie behind it, the actual contract on a cheque or bill of exchange is between the drawer (or the acceptor, as the case may be) and the holder for the time being:[20] and, just as one cannot plead third party fraud as a defence to an action on an ordinary contract, there seems no reason to accord any more generous treatment to a defendant whose contract happens to be contained in commercial paper.

It is respectfully submitted, therefore, that on principle a building society or similar drawer of a third party cheque or banker's draft should not be entitled to refuse payment on the ground only that he was induced to do so by the fraud of a non-party, and that in so far as *Ayres v Moore* suggests the contrary it should not be followed. The difficulty, of course, is *Jones v Waring & Gillow*, which — however perversely — does seem to imply the opposite result. This was a decision of the House of Lords, and unless and until disapproved by that House must presumably be acepted as good law.[21] The least unsatisfactory way of dealing with it in this connection would seem to be to distinguish it on the basis that, however ill it may sit with the suggestion just made, it did not directly decide the issue of enforceability. As for its curent status on the related question of recovery of money paid, we deal with that below.

---

[15] *Pace* Lord Sumner [1926] AC 670, 695, who did mention in passing the possibility of an action on the cheque but — incredibly — went on to suggest that this had little or no relevance to the point at issue.

[16] [1940] 1 KB 278.

[17] See *Talbot v von Boris* [1911] 1 KB 854.

[18] [1977] 1 Lloyd's Rep 431.

[19] See *ibid* 444. Note that his Lordship was clearly aware of *Jones*'s case, which he cited without comment elsewhere.

[20] A point made by McKay J in the course of an impeccable analysis in the New Zealand case of *Yan v Post Office Bank* [1994] 1 NZLR 154. The case actually concerned failure of consideration (see below): but the point remains valid for fraud too.

[21] It has moreover been cited frequently without disapproval, including twice in the House of Lords (though not on this actual issue): the cases concerned being *Fibrosa v Fairbairn* [1943] AC 32, and *Lipkin Gorman v Karpnale Ltd* [1991] 2 AC 548.

Before leaving the question of instruments procured by fraud, however, it is worth dealing with two other arguments that might be raised by the victim-drawer where fraud is involved. The first is based on a little-discussed subject in bills of exchange law, namely the need for delivery of the instrument in order to for it to be valid at all. Under the Bills of Exchange Act 1882, s 21, a bill[22] cannot be enforced, even by a payee, in the absence of a proper delivery of it by or on behalf of the drawer. To take a simple example, there is no doubt that a person who unlawfully abstracts a cheque from the drawer's office cannot sue on it, even though it may have been made out to himself.[23] The second argument, which as will appear is closely related to the first, is based on the holder's title to the instrument. Although the Act does not say so in so many words, it seems to be a general rule (and certainly one accepted at common law[24]) that in order to sue on a bill of exchange one has not only to be a holder of it but to have title to it as well: one without the other will not do.[25]

At first sight these seem highly relevant to the case of the third party cheque or draft obtained by fraud, at least in the case where B obtains a cheque in favour of A by impersonating a customer of the building society involved. Take the delivery argument. Although the mere fact that delivery is procured by fraud will presumably not invalidate it, could it not be argued that the error as to B's identity vitiated the drawer's intention to part with possession of the instrument at all, so as to enable him to plead "no delivery" in exactly the same way as if it had been abstracted from his office without his knowledge? And similarly with A's title. In the ordinary course of events a person who without fraud gets a building society cheque no doubt obtains title to it, even if it is made out to a third party: a customer of a building society must surely be able to change his mind about using the cheque he has just procured in order to pay the gas bill without facing an action by gas supplier for conversion. But if the intermediary does obtain title, does it not follow that in our example A's title to the instrument depends on that of B who got it in the first place, and that if B obtained it by impersonation he got no title and hence had none to pass to A?[26]

It is suggested, however, that neither of these pleas has much prospect of success.

Take first the title point. To begin with, even where B masqueraded as X, the courts would undoubtedly strain to hold that the building society's mistake was insufficiently fundamental to prevent title — albeit, of course, a voidable title — from passing to him. The analogous case of *Citibank NA v Brown Shipley*[27] nicely illustrates the point. Fraudsters impersonated a customer of the plaintiff bank, which was thereby induced to issue a draft in favour of the defendants and to hand it over to a confederate of the fraudsters. The defendants received it from the latter and allowed the fraudsters to draw cash against it, with which they vanished. Dismissing an action by the plaintiffs against the defendants for conversion of the draft (in which of course the question of who owned it was directly in issue), Waller J rejected an argument based on *Cundy v Lindsay*[28] that the fraudsters got no title to the instrument and hence the defendants, who claimed through them, got none either. Since the plaintiffs had clearly intended that the defendants should eventually obtain possession, and the middle-man who gave it to them purported

---

[22] Including, for these purposes, a promissory note, thus covering the case of the banker's draft.
[23] Compare the common law decision in *Bromage v Lloyd* (1847) 1 Ex 32 (drawer died while still in possession of instrument: his executrix delivered it without authority to the payee: payee's action failed).
[24] See eg *Bell v Lord Ingestre* (1848) 12 QB 317 (indorsee cannot sue where precondition to passing of title not satisfied)..
[25] To take a straightforward example, suppose B obtains a building society cheque made out in favour of A, but then changes his mind about giving it to A. Were B to steal the instrument from A, it is inconceivable that he would be allowed to sue on it.
[26] This point is touched on in a perceptive article by Profesor Geva, "The Autonomy of the Banker's Obligation on Bank Drafts and Certified Cheques" (1994) 73 Can Bar Rev 21, 40 *et seq.*
[27] [1991] 2 All ER 690.
[28] (1878) 3 App Cas 459.

to act merely as a messenger, it could not be said that the identity of the latter was of fundamental importance to anyone. Moreover, there is another point (not in fact argued in *Citibank*, though it might well have been). It is surely arguable that in any case A's title to the instrument in our example is itself original and not derivative from that of B. The building society (or bank) intended all along that A should obtain title to the instrument as and when he got it, and for that purpose entrusted it to B: when B handed it to A, it is suggested that A would get title by virtue of that intent. Put another way, title to chattels passes when they are delivered to the person intended to have them by, or with the consent of, the owner: and this is exactly what happens when a building society furnishes B with a cheque made out to A in the expectation that B will hand it over in due course.

And, it is submitted, similar principles must apply to the delivery argument. Given the relative unimportance of the identity of the middle-man transporting the cheque or draft from drawer to payee, it is almost inconceivable that the identity of the former would be regarded as vital enough to vitiate the drawer's intention to effectuate delivery to him, even in the case of impersonation. And even if it was, there is a further point available to the payee. Even if there was no sufficient delivery to the *soi-disant* customer, the bank or building society must have authorised that person to deliver the instrument to the eventual payee: that is the very point of the transaction.

(c) A second defence? — failure of consideration

The second conceivable plea which may be available to the issuer of the instrument against the payee is failure of consideration. Suppose that A has sold and delivered goods to B against a banker's draft, thus indubitably constituting himself a holder for value. Imagine further, however, that B obtained the draft from the issuing bank by depositing with it a further draft which turned out to be unenforceable or worthless. If sued on its draft, can the bank refuse to pay A on the basis that the consideration in exchange for which it was issued has totally failed? The difficulty here is that, whereas it is quite clear that failure of consideration is on principle a defence to an action on a bill of exchange, the issue normally arises in the context of consideration moving between two parties to the bill. A straightforward example is where X gives Y a cheque for goods which X then rightfully rejects: Y cannot sue X on the cheque. But this does not answer the question in our example, where the matter is more complex, since there are not one but two considerations to consider. One, which moves from a party to a stranger, is that provided by A to B (*ie* the goods): the other, moving *e converso* from a non-party to the drawer, is that furnished by B to the bank (*ie* the other draft). Now, it seems pretty clear that if the former fails — for example, if B having paid A for goods with the cheque then rightfully rejects them — A's right to sue is lost. But is this equally true of the latter?

The decision in *Hasan v Willson*,[29] already referred to, can be read as suggesting that it is. There, it will be remembered, a con-man named Smith persuaded Willson to draw a cheque for £50,000 in favour of Hasan by giving Willson a worthless draft; Willson stopped the cheque when he found out the true facts, and Hasan sued on it. Apart from fraud, Willson raised the defence that the consideration he had received for the cheque had failed — a defence which Robert Goff J seems to have thought would have been good[30] (though in the event he did not have to decide the matter). But this reasoning is, with respect, questionable, and it is suggested that the better view is that failure of consideration can only be pleaded as a defence to an action on a bill if the relevant consideration moves from a party to it. This is for two reasons.

The first is that, if this was indeed what Robert Goff J intended to say, such a view sits somewhat ill with the standard contractual analysis of a bill of exchange or banker's draft. An action on such an instrument by the holder must needs be based on the contract embodied in it: and this

---
[29] [1977] 1 Lloyd's Rep 431.
[30] See *ibid*, 444.

contract can only be between the drawer (or maker) and the holder for the time being. True, there may be other contracts involved in the transaction in question: in particular, the drawing of the instrument may well have been procured by agreement between the drawer and a stranger under which the latter provided separate consideration to the former. But this latter agreement, it is submitted, is analytically entirely separate from the contract in the instrument itself; and if so, it is hard to see why the failure of the consideration provided under it should have any effect on the rights of the holder. Put another way, where A has a contractual right against B, the state of accounts as between B and some third party X, including any failure of consideration moving from X to B, ought to be irrelevant.

Secondly, there is a powerful argument based on the interpretation that has been put on the Bills of Exchange Act 1882, s 27(2), dealing with what counts as consideration in the context of negotiable instruments. This (it will be remembered), while stating that the relevant consideration for the purpose of rendering a bill enforceable may consist of value given "at any time", has been said to apply only to value furnished by a party to the instrument. If (as seems likely) the consideration whose presence makes the bill enforceable is the same as the consideration whose failure bars the holder's action, it seems to follow that the consideration given by B, not coming from a party to the instrument, should indeed be out of account.

2. The right to recover money paid on the instrument

Having dealt with enforceability of the instrument, we now deal with the situation where the boot is, as it were, on the other foot. If payment is made on a banker's draft or building society cheque, can the bank or building society recover the sum paid if the cheque turns out to have been extracted by fraud or mistake, or as a result of a failure of consideration moving from the person obtaining it? This, of course, is a matter of, if anything, greater moment to the payee: it is one thing to know that there is a risk — however small — of a third party cheque not being met, but quite another to have to take account of the possibility of having to reimburse the amount of it even if it is cleared. One might be forgiven for thinking that the two situations ought to be mirror images one of another, and that recovery ought to depend on whether the instrument was enforceable in the first place. But, as we shall see, matters are not as simple as that.

(a) Instruments obtained by fraud

The difficulty here, of course, arises directly from the decision in *Jones v Waring & Gillow*.[31] That case, it will be remembered, specifically allowed recovery against A where a cheque was obtained by deception on B's part, on the basis of money paid by mistake of fact: the reasoning being that, even though A might be a holder for value, he was not as payee a holder in due course or entitled to the privileged position inherent in that status. Now at first sight this decision, which emanates from the House of Lords, seems to clinch the issue — short of an exercise by the House of its powers under the Practice Direction of 1966.[32] Or does it? When looked at more closely, the matter becomes slightly less clear-cut, for two reasons.

To begin with, one vital point is that all involved in *Jones*'s case in the House of Lords seem to have assumed, rather than decided, that recoverability depended on whether Warings were indeed holders in due course. The point simply went by default: it never seems to have been discussed whether they might have had a defence based on other matters, such as their having been holders for value or taken the cheque in *bona fide* payment of a debt.[33] Leaving aside the question whether Warings were holders in due course, the argument was directed to other matters:

[31] [1926] AC 670.
[32] [1966] 1 WLR 1234.
[33] This is doubly odd, since in the Court of Appeal both Scrutton and Sargant LJJ pointed out that receipt under a valid contract was generally a defence to an action for money paid by mistake: see [1925] 2 KB 612, 637, 644–645.

notably, whether Jones's mistake (which did not, of course, go to their liability to pay Warings) was sufficient as a matter of the general law of restitution to ground recovery, and if it did whether a defence of change of position was available to Warings in respect of the claim against them. This being the case, it is suggested that it may be open to another court to regard *Jones*'s case as having proceeded on a tacit admission by the defendants, rather than deciding the issue directly, and for that reason as open to reconsideration.

If *Jones v Waring & Gillow* can be thus sidestepped, the issue becomes much more open. And, it is respectfully suggested, the idea that recovery is available from anyone other than a holder in due course is open to a number of serious objections. One we have already covered. If, as suggested by more recent authorities, third party fraud is no defence to an action on a negotiable instrument, it is absurd to allow that same fraud to be invoked as a ground for recovery against the holder once the instrument has been paid. But there are at least two others.

First, there is a point on chage of position. What divided the majority from the minority in *Jones*'s case was whether, even if the money was recoverable, Warings could plead that they had changed their position by releasing the goods to Bodenham; the majority holding that they could not. But it now seems clear that this no longer represents the law. At least since *Lipkin Gorman v Karpnale*[34] in 1990, if not earlier,[35] it is now established that change of position is a general defence to any restitutionary action based on mistake. It follows that where A, the payee of the cheque in our example, has changed his position by releasing goods against it he now does have a defence, at least to the extent of the value of the rights he has lost.[36]

Secondly, whatever the definitions of different types of holder under the provisions of the Bills of Exchange Act 1882, there is clear authority that as a matter of restitution law as a whole, including actions for recovery of money paid by mistake, *bona fide* purchase for value is a general defence.[37] It also seems clear that *bona fide* purchase for these purposes is widely defined, and in particular includes the situation where the money concerned has been used to discharge an existing debt owed to the defendant by anyone. The old case of *Aiken v Short*[38] illustrates the point straightforwardly. The plaintiffs bought a property from a seller without title, who had earlier purported to charge it to the defendant to secure a debt of £200. Having paid off the defendant with the authority of the seller, they then discovered the truth and sought to recover the £200 as money paid by mistake. They failed. As Platt B (with whom Pollock B agreed) put it, "The money which the defendant got from her debtor was actually due to her, and there can be no obligation to refund it."[39] And a similar principle was accepted by Robert Goff J in *Barclays Bank v WJ Simms*[40] in 1979. A customer of the plaintiff bank owed the defendants £24,000; he sent them a cheque for that amount but later stopped it. The bank overlooked the stop order and paid the cheque; it then sought to recover what it had disbursed from the defendants as money paid by mistake. The action succeeded, but only because the bank's payment, having been made without the customer's authority, did not go to discharge the debt. Had the debt been discharged, Robert Goff J explicitly stated that the defendant would have had a complete answer to the claim

---

[34] [1991] 2 AC 548.
[35] See in particular the judgment of Robert Goff J (as he then was) in *Barclays Bank v WJ Simms* [1980] QB 677.
[36] A further complication in *Jones v Waring & Gillow* was that, having parted with the goods against the cheque, Warings later in some unspecified way managed to regain possession of them. This raises a nice point as to whether the defence of change of position should be regarded as lost in such circumstances: but that is beyond the purview of this article.
[37] See Burrows, *Law of Restitution* (1993), 472 *et seq.*
[38] (1856) 1 H & N 210. Compare too *Foster v Green* (1862) 7 H & N 881.
[39] (1856) 1 H & N 210, 215. Pollock, Bramwell and Martin BB also held that the action failed for another reason, namely that the plaintiffs' mistake did not go to their own liability to pay. This is now accepted to be unsound (see Burrows. *Law of Restitution*, 95 *et seq.*); but that does not affect the point in the text.
[40] [1980] QB 677.

on the basis of *bona fide* purchase.[41] Admittedly, neither *Aiken v Short* nor *Barclays Bank v Simms* involved actions by the drawer of a cheque against a payee who had received it from a third party: but, it is respectfully suggested, there is no reason why this should make any difference. True, the 1882 Act provides carefully drawn (and narrow) designations of who counts as a "holder for value" and "holder in due course". But these are, it is submitted, concerned with the specific issues arising under the Act: in particular, who has title to an instrument, and who is able to enforce it against whom. Save in the case of the right of a party who pays a bill to recover against others liable on the instrument, the Act has nothing to say about the general law of unjust enrichment, and there is no reason to think that they were intended in any way to narrow the category of those entitled to the defence of *bona fide* purchase.

If this is so, it is submitted that the result is clear. it follows that, whatever his status, a person who in good faith provides any kind of consideration for a third party cheque, or receives it in payment of a debt owed to him, must be entitled to keep what he gets and to be correspondingly immune to any action for recovery of it.

(b) Failure of consideration

So far we have been dealing with mistake as a ground of recovery. It remains to deal with a possible claim based on total failure of consideration. To take a previous example, suppose that A obtains from his bank a draft in favour of B by depositing with the bank a separate draft which turns out to be worthless, for example because it is a forgery. Can A's bank seek recovery from B by arguing that the consideration for which it issued the draft has failed?

The answer, it is submitted, must be No, for two reasons. One has already been hinted at in the discussion of whether the cheque can be enforced by A: the consideration furnished by B was pursuant to the contract between B and his bank, whereas the bank's payment to A was made under a different contract, that between the bank and A. Although there is no authority directly in point, it is suggested that, in a contractual context, failure of consideration means failure of the consideration promised in respect of the contract concerned: the non-materialisation of something promised under a different contract will not do.[42] But even waiving this point, there is a further reason to deny the action here, since there is authority that, where X pursuant to a contract with Y pays Z a sum of money, in the event of Y's failure to provide the promised exchange X's only action for recovery is against him and not Z. This at least seems to be the result of the House of Lords' decision in *The Trident Beauty*.[43] Shipowners assigned their right to charter hire to a bank; the charterers paid an instalment in advance to the bank, but the shipowners failed to make the ship available and then became insolvent. The charterers' action against the bank for return of the hire failed, on the basis that they already had a claim (albeit worthless) against the shipowners. There was no reason, their Lordships said, to duplicate this claim by giving the charterers an additional claim against the bank, even though the latter had actually received the money concerned. In the same way, where a bank in pursuance of a contract with its customer B makes a sum of money available to A, it is submitted that, if the consideration provided by B turns out to be worthless, the bank's exclusive remedy must be against B and it cannot look to A.

Conclusion

The suggestions made in this article can be briefly encapsulated. First, the recipient of a building society cheque or banker's draft who provides consideration (other than by accepting it in

---

[41] See *ibid*, 700.
[42] As indeed two members of the Court of Appeal pointed out in *Jones v Waring & Gillow*: see [1925] 2 KB 612, 629 (Pollock MR), 636 (Scrutton LJ). The point was not dealt with in detail in the House of Lords.
[43] [1994] 1 WLR 161.

discharge of a pre-existing obligation) can enforce the instrument and cannot have pleaded against him either the fraud of the person from whom he obtained it, or failure of any consideration moving from the latter. Secondly, despite the difficult decision in *Jones v Waring & Gillow*, it is suggested that the better view is that the recipient of such an instrument is largely immune to any action for recovery of the amount paid, provided only he received it *bona fide* and for value. Furthermore, this protection extends even to the recipient who took the instrument in payment of a debt, even though owing to the narrow definition of "value" under the Bills of Exchange Act 1882 he could not have enforced the instrument.

CROSS-BORDER TRACING: *CONFLICT OF LAWS ISSUES*

*George Panagopoulos**

The question of cross-border tracing (*ie* tracing in the context of claims involving international elements) is one for which there is no clear guidance. Is tracing to be treated as an adjunct to the related claim and thus governed by the same choice of law rule; or is it to be treated as raising a separate issue, thereby attracting its own choice of law rule? These are questions which require answering, for more and more recent cases combine matters involving the conflict of laws and tracing. These difficulties are amplified by virtue of the fact that the role of restitutionary claims in private international law has not been fully settled. Some of the answers to this larger quest may lie in resolving the issue of tracing. Cross-border tracing can be addressed separately, as a self-contained issue. Moreover, not all claims involving tracing will necessarily be restitutionary. An example of a claim involving tracing which is restitutionary is where a mistaken payor brings a claim in relation to the identifiable proceeds of a mistaken payment.[1] At the other end of the spectrum, a seller might claim proprietary rights in the proceeds of a buyer's sale of goods, where the relevant sales contract provides that the seller retains legal or equitable ownership of the goods.[2] Although tracing is relevant to both claims, it cannot be confidently said that they both raise restitutionary issues. Whilst the former claim is clearly restitutionary, the latter is not; yet both raise a potential tracing issue.

1. THE NATURE OF TRACING

a. What is tracing?

Tracing may be employed whenever a party has an interest in showing that the value received in one form at one moment is held in another form at another moment. That is, although property or money are no longer held in their original form, their value has survived. Characteristically, Millett LJ stated in *Boscawen v Bajwa*:[3]

> "Tracing ... is neither a claim nor a remedy but a process. ... It is the process by which the plaintiff traces what has happened to his property, identifies the persons who have handled or received it, and justifies his claim that the money which they handled or received (and if necessary which they still retain) can properly be regarded as representing his property".[4]

As noted by Professor Birks, tracing is never a hunt for the original asset. It is a process which is distinct and separate from that of claiming.[5]

---

* Barrister and Solicitor of the Supreme Court of Victoria; Baring Scholar and Junior Dean, Hertford College, Oxford. Many thanks to Adrian Briggs and Lionel Smith for their helpful comments.

[1] See *eg Chase Manhattan Bank NA v Israel-British Bank (London) Ltd* [1981] ch 105.

[2] See *eg Aluminiumm Industrie Vaasen BV v Romalpa Aluminium Ltd* [1976] 1 WLR 676 (CA); N Palmer "Reservation of Title" (1992) 5 JCL 175; B Collier, *Romalpa Clauses: Reservation of Title in Sale of Goods Transactions* (Law Book Company, Sydney, 1989); G McCormack, *Reservation of Title*, 2nd ed (Sweet and Maxwell, London, 1995).

[3] [1995] 1 WLR 328 (CA).

[4] *Ibid,* 334. Similar distinctions have been previously drawn between the claim and the means of identification or ascertainment in other cases; see *eg Taylor v Plumer* (1815) 3 M & S 562; *Sinclair v Brougham* [1914] AC 398, 419, *per* Viscount Haldane; *Re Diplock* [1948] ch 465, 536-537; *Chase Manhattan Bank NA v Israel-British Bank (London) Ltd* [1981] Ch 105, 122D.

[5] P Birks, "Overview: Tracing, Claiming and Defences": ch 11 of P Birks (ed), *Laundering and Tracing,* (Clarendon Press, Oxford, 1995), 291–295 (hereafter "Birks"). See also LD Smith, *The Law of Tracing* (Clarendon Press, Oxford, 1997), 11–14 (hereafter "Smith").

The nature of tracing is further illustrated by the distinction drawn between "tracing" and "following".[6] "Following", is the process of identifying property in its original form. On the other hand, "tracing" is the process of identifying any new asset acquired in exchange for the original property. Thus, where a plaintiff's car is stolen, the plaintiff may try to locate, through the various transactions, where the car has ended up. This is following. Where however the plaintiff's car is stolen and then substituted for money, the plaintiff may assert a claim in relation to the money. It is the process of tracing which determines that the money represents the value of the car. Tracing is therefore the law's way of determining when one asset stands in the place of another. However, unlike the process of following, tracing is not an exclusively factual process. It will inevitably involve the application of legal rules, namely the rules of tracing, to the particular facts.

b. Why do we trace?

We often trace so as to claim. The purpose of tracing is to bring a claim in relation to a new asset, which would have been available in relation to an original asset. Upon a successful tracing exercise, the plaintiff may for example establish either a proprietary or personal claim against the defendant.[7] The process of tracing is therefore distinct from the actual claim.[8] The conventional reasons why someone may wish to trace are as follows:

(a) The plaintiff may wish to bring a proprietary claim. Such a claim may be on the basis of unjust enrichment,[9] an equitable wrong,[10] or of a reservation of title clause in a sales contract.[11]

(b) The plaintiff may seek a personal claim. This may be a claim for an order that there be an account on the ground of knowing receipt[12] or for an order for money had and received.[13]

(c) Finally, tracing may be employed outside the field of personal and proprietary claims. For example, it may be employed in the context of the Theft Act 1968.[14] Alternatively, it may be used to show that an asset is exempt from a statutory scheme for the division of matrimonial property,[15] or property of a bankrupt,[16] on the ground that it is the traceable proceeds of an exempt asset.

In addition to the above, tracing may be employed in a restitutionary claim so as to show that the defendant was enriched at the plaintiff's expense and not at someone else's.[17] This will be particularly the case in three-party situations where the defendant was not enriched directly at

---

[6] See Smith 6–10; Birks, 291–292.

[7] Birks, 300–302, 395–307; Smith, 24–33; K Mason QC and J Carter, *Restitution Law in Australia* (Butterworths, Sydney,1996) (hereafter "Mason & Carter"), 95.

[8] Birks, 290–292, 300–302; Smith, 10–14, 130–132.

[9] *Chase Manhattan Bank NA v Israel–British Bank (London) Ltd* [1981] Ch 105.

[10] *AG for Hong Kong v Reid* [1994] AC 324. See also *LAC Minerals Ltd v International Corona Resources Ltd* (1989) 61 DLR (4th) 14 (Can SC); *Kartika Ratna Thahir v PT Pertambangan Minyak dan Gas Bumi Negara (Pertamina)* [1994] 3 SLR 257 (Sing CA) (hereafter *Thahir v Pertamina*).

[11] *Aluminium Industrie Vaasen BV v Romalpa Aluminium Ltd* [1976] 1 WLR 676 (CA).

[12] *Agip (Africa) Ltd v Jackson* [1990] Ch 265; *Eagle Trust Plc v SBC Securities Ltd* [1992] 4 All ER 488, 500, *per* Vinelott J; *El Ajou v Dollar Land Holdings Plc* [1993] 3 All ER 717, 739, *per* Millett J (reversed on different grounds [1994] 2 All ER 685).

[13] *Banque Belge pour l'Etranger v Hambrouck* [1921] 1 KB 321; *Lipkin Gorman v Karpnale Ltd* [1991] 2 AC 548. *Cf Trustee of the Property of FC Jones & Sons v Jones* [1997] Ch 159.

[14] See Theft Act 1968 (c 60), ss 24(2) and 28(1)(b).

[15] See *Gasparetto v Gasparetto* (1988) 15 RFL (3d) 401 (Ont HC); *Mitller v Mitller* (1988) 17 RFL (3d) 113 (Ont HC); *Deyell v Deyell* (1991) 90 Sask R 81 (CA).

[16] See Bankruptcy and Insolvency Act 1985 c B-3 (Canada), s 67(1)(b), Bankruptcy Act 1966 (Cth), ss 116(2), 116 (2D)-(4)

[17] *Lipkin Gorman v Karpnale Ltd* [1991] 2 AC 548, 559H–560A, *per* Lord Templeman, 572E, *per* Lord Goff; See also AS Burrows, *The Law of Restitution* (Butterworths, London, 1993) (hereafter "Burrows"), 28–29; Mason and Carter, 95.

the expense of the plaintiff. In such circumstances, a successful tracing exercise will show that the value of the plaintiff's impoverishment can be traced into the defendant's hands. It may not still be in the defendant's hands so as to constitute surviving enrichment. Yet, whether a personal or proprietary claim is brought, it will be necessary that the defendant was "enriched", and that such enrichment was "at the plaintiff's expense". This causal connection between the plaintiff's impoverishment and the defendant's enrichment can be shown through a process of tracing.

c. Tracing at law and in equity

The tracing rules differ as between law and equity. The existence of such separate rules may have ramifications for the conflict of laws. It may potentially add another problem when an issue of tracing arises in private international law. Although it is not the purpose of this article to examine the law of tracing from a domestic law point of view, it nevertheless will be useful to note the different rules.

The common law recognises the tracing of property into substitute products.[18] In tracing the plaintiff's property into substitutes, no distinction is drawn between a chose in action, such as the debt of a bank to its customer, and any other asset. Tracing may therefore follow a cheque or its proceeds.[19] Tracing is also possible when the property, or its substitute, is money going in and out of bank accounts.[20] However, the main limitation of common law tracing is that money cannot be traced once it has been mixed with other money.[21] The rationale for this is that in such circumstances the money ceases being identifiable. The common law therefore takes a strict approach to tracing, being limited to cases of clean substitutions. Thus, due to these limitations there is little resort to common law tracing.

Equity has been more flexible than the common law in relation to tracing.[22] The significant difference between tracing at common law and equity is that equity allows the plaintiff to trace into, and out of, a mixed fund.[23] In tracing into a mixed fund, equity draws a distinction between mixture of the plaintiff's money with that of a trustee and with that of an innocent volunteer. Where the plaintiff's money is mixed with that of an innocent volunteer, the monies in the fund belong *pro tanto* to the parties' contributions.[24] However, where a mixed fund is held in a current bank account, the anomalous "first in first out" rule applies.[25] Thus, the beneficiary's monies that first go in are presumed to go out first. Where the plaintiff's money is mixed with that of a trustee, equity makes a presumption in favour of the plaintiff beneficiary in respect of any identifiable part of the fund remaining.[26] Equity's flexibility in allowing a plaintiff to trace into a

---

[18] *Taylor v Plumer* (1815) 3 M & S 562; *Banque Belge pour l'Etranger v Hambrouck* [1921] 1 KB 321; *Lipkin Gorman v Karpnale Ltd* [1991] 2 AC 548; *Trustee of the Property of FC Jones & Sons v Jones* [1997] Ch 159.
[19] *Cf* P Millett, "Tracing the Proceeds of Fraud" (1991) 107 LQR 71, 73–74.
[20] *Banque Belge pour l'Etranger v Hambrouck* [1921] 1 KB 321; Scrutton LJ in *Banque Belge* held that money could not be traced into and out of a bank account at common law, on the basis that it is not the plaintiff's money that is drawn out.
[21] *Re Diplock* [1948] Ch 465, 518; *Agip (Africa) Ltd v Jackson* [1990] 1 Ch 265, 285; *Lipkin Gorman v Karpnale Ltd* [1991] 2 AC 548, 573, *per* Lord Goff.
[22] It should be noted, that although there are some strong arguments in favour of not distinguishing between tracing at law and in equity (see Smith, 120-130, 165-174; Birks, 295-300), the division is alive and well according to recent authority. See *eg Trustee of the property of FC Jones & Sons v Jones* [1997] Ch 159.
[23] *Re Hallett's Estate* (1880) 13 Ch D 696; *Brady v Stapleton* (1952) 88 CLR 322; *Agip (Africa) Ltd v Jackson* [1991] Ch 547; affg [1990] Ch 265.
[24] *Sinclair v Brougham* [1914] AC 398.
[25] *Clayton's Case* (1815) 1 Mer 572. In *Barlow Clowes International Ltd v Vaughan* [1992] 4 All ER 22, it was held not to extend to a fund intended to be held as a common investment fund. Smith argues that the rule in *Clayton's Case* is a presumption of intention and has in fact nothing to do with tracing: Smith, 185–194. This was the position adopted by the Supreme Court of Canada in *Re OSC and Greymac Credit Corp* [1988] 2 SCR 172. Furthermore, in *Barlow Clowes International Ltd v Vaughan* [1992] 4 All ER 22, 44, Leggatt LJ also considered that the rule in *Clayton's Case* was irrelevant to tracing.

mixed fund, does not allow tracing into property that has been dissipated and subsequently restored.[27]

It is said that, as a prerequisite to tracing in equity, a fiduciary relationship must be established which calls the equitable jurisdiction into being.[28] According to Goff and Jones, the plaintiff must show that the defendant or a third party, through whose hands the trust money passed through on the way to the defendant, stood in a fiduciary relationship to him.[29] The correctness of the rule requiring the existence of a fiduciary relationship so as to trace in equity has been questioned,[30] whilst it is doubted whether the House of Lords will uphold it.[31] In *Westdeutsche Landesbank Girozentrale v Islington LBC*,[32] Lord Browne-Wilkinson stated that an owner may trace in equity as against a thief.[33] It therefore can be argued that this does away with the need for a fiduciary relationship, as a thief cannot be a fiduciary. At any rate, the rule has been eroded, in that the courts have often little difficulty in finding a fiduciary relationship.[34]

2. INTERNATIONAL TRACING

a. The tracing problem

Claims of the type set out above may contain international elements and thus the process of tracing may collide with the conflict of laws. For example, a plaintiff may wish to bring a personal or proprietary claim in relation to value received or surviving outside the jurisdiction.[35] That is, stolen monies may have been used to acquire property in a foreign jurisdiction. Alternatively, the plaintiff may need to trace through foreign jurisdictions into value received or surviving in the defendant's hands within the jurisdiction.[36] For example, stolen monies may have been channelled through several foreign bank accounts before being returned to the jurisdiction. In such cases, a potentially separate issue of tracing may arise. Although the relevant issue in the plaintiff's claim may have been characterised in a particular way and thereby attracted its own choice of law rule, it could be argued that the question of whether the plaintiff can successfully trace is a separate issue, which could potentially attract its own choice of law rule.

---

[26] *Re Hallet's Estate* (1879) 13 Ch D 696; *Re Oatway* [1903] 2 ch 356.
[27] *James Roscoe(Bolton) v Winder* [1915] 1 Ch 62; *Lofts v Macdonald* (1974) 3 ALR 404; *Re Dover* (1981) 6 ACL R 307; *Bishopsgate Inv Management v Homan* [1995] Ch 211.
[28] *Re Diplock* [1948] Ch 465; *Chase–Manhattan v Israel–British Bank (London) Ltd* [1981] 1 Ch 105; *Agip (Africa) Ltd v Jackson* [1990] 1 Ch 265; *Boscawen v Bajwa* [1996] 1 WLR 328. The Court of Appeal in *Re Diplock* [1948] Ch 465, 532 540, interpreted *Sinclair v Brougham* [1914] AC 398 as standing for the proposition that a fiduciary relationship is a prerequisite to tracing in equity. There is doubt as to whether *Sinclair v Brougham* does in fact stand for this proposition: see Lord Goff of Chieveley and GH Jones, *The Law of Restitution*, 4th ed (Sweet and Maxwell, London, 1993) (hereafter "Goff and Jones"), 84; Parker and Mellows, *The Modern Law of Trusts*, 6th ed by AJ Oakley (Sweet and Maxwell, London, 1994) (hereafter "Parker and Mellows"), 613.
[29] Goff and Jones, 93.
[30] Goff and Jones, 85, 93–94, 101; Birks, 297; Smith, 120–130, 162–174; Parker and Mellows, 613; P Millett, "Tracing the Proceeds of Fraud" (1991) 107 LQR 71, 75. See also Meagher, Gummow and Lehane, *Equity: Doctrines and Remedies*, 3rd ed (Butterworths, Sydney, 1992) (hereafter "Meagher, Gummow and Lehane"), 134.
[31] Goff and Jones, 85.
[32] *Westdeutsche Landesbank Girozentrale v Islington LBC* [1996] AC 669.
[33] *Ibid*, 716.
[34] See eg *Chase-Manhattan v Israel–British Bank (London) Ltd* [1981] 1 Ch 105; *Agip (Africa) Ltd v Jackson* [1990] Ch 265, 290, per Millett J; Parker and Mellows, 614. See also *Aluminiumm Industrie Vaasen BV v Romalpa Aluminium Ltd* [1976] 1 WLR 676, 687–690, per Roskill LJ, 693, per Goff LJ, where the Court of Appeal inferred a fiduciary relationship from the provisions of the relevant sales contract.
[35] See eg *Chase Manhattan Bank NA v Israel–British Bank (London) Ltd* [1981] Ch 105; also *Macmillan Inc v Bishopsgate Investment Trust Plc (No 3)* [1996] 1 WLR 387. See also the facts of *A–G for Hong Kong v Reid* [1994] AC 324.
[36] See *El Ajou v Dollar Land Holdings Plc* [1993] 3 All ER 717 (reversed on different grounds [1994] 2 All ER 685).

In practical terms, an international tracing issue should only arise in two particular types of situations. First, there is the situation where, although the *lex fori* may recognise a successful tracing exercise, it is not recognised under one of the potentially applicable foreign laws. For example, monies may have been mistakenly paid from an English bank account into a German bank account and then transferred into an Austrian bank account. The plaintiff may therefore have to trace through, or into, foreign jurisdictions which do not recognise tracing.

Secondly, there is the situation where a difference exists between the tracing rules of the *lex causae* and of the *lex fori*. That is, although tracing may be recognised by both potentially applicable laws, one may be more flexible or liberal, or allow tracing in circumstances where the other will not. For example, in this case, monies may have mistakenly been paid from an English bank account into an Australian one. A question may arise as to whether a fiduciary relationship is required as a prerequisite to tracing in equity. There is no requirement of a fiduciary relationship to trace in equity under Australian law.[37] Thus, if the plaintiff is unable to demonstrate the existence of a fiduciary relationship, the success of the claim may depend on whether the tracing exercise is governed by Australian or English law. It will therefore be significant to determine which law applies to the tracing exercise if the success of the plaintiff's claim depends on the relevant tracing rules.

b. The approaches

Where a cause of action has an international element added to it, the first step in determining the applicable law to the relevant issue, or issues, is the process of characterisation.[38] We must know the nature of the matter before us for the purposes of private international law so as to determine whether it is procedural or substantive; and, if substantive, what the relevant choice of law rule or rules might be.

There are three main approaches which could be adopted in relation to the characterisation of tracing. First, it could be said that, as tracing is a process and not a right or remedy, it is a procedural mechanism employed by the court to identify the whereabouts of value. That is, tracing in itself does not create any rights; it merely raises certain evidentiary presumptions. Being procedural, it therefore should be governed by the *lex fori*. Other potentially applicable laws have nothing admissible to say on the matter. Secondly, tracing could be seen as an issue in its own right which may attract its own choice of law rule. Finally, it could be said that, although a substantive issue, tracing is an extension of rights with an independent source, and therefore it is an issue which should be governed by the *lex causae*. In other words, the tracing issue is to be governed by the law governing the substantive issue to which the tracing exercise relates.

i. Procedural or substantive issue?

It could be argued that, as tracing is merely a process, which in itself does not create any rights, it should be characterised as procedural and thus governed by the rules of the *lex fori*.[39] However, it is submitted that, where a tracing issue arises, it should be characterised as a substantive issue to be governed by the *lex causae*.[40] First, tracing is not a matter which is directed

---

[37] *Black v Freedman* (1910) 12 CLR 105, 110, *per* O'Connor J; *Australian Postal Corporation v Lutak* (1991) 21 NSWLR 584, 589.
[38] See *Macmillan Inc v Bishopsgate Investment Trust Plc (No 3)* [1996] 1 WLR 387, *esp* 391–392, *per* Staughton LJ.
[39] For the proposition that matters of procedure are governed by the *lex fori* see generally L Collins (ed), *Dicey and Morris on The Conflict of Laws*, 12th ed (Sweet and Maxwell, London, 1993) (hereafter *Dicey and Morris*), Rule 17. See also *Huber v Steiner* (1835) Bing NC 202; *Leroux v Brown* (1852) 12 CB 801; *Mahadervan v Mahadervan* [1964] P 233; *Boys v Chaplin* [1971] AC 356; *McKain v Miller* (1991) 174 CLR 1 (HCA); *Stevens v Head* (1993) 176 CLR 433 (HCA).
[40] See also Smith, 275; J Bird, "Choice of Law": ch 3 of FD Rose (ed), *Restitution and the Conflict of Laws* (Mansfield Press, Oxford, 1995) (hereafter "Bird"), 86. *Cf* R Stevens, "The Choice of Law Rules of Restitutionary

at governing or regulating the mode or conduct of court proceedings. Only those issues which "[form] part of the mechanism of the machinery of litigation, or [are] directed to the regulation of the mode or conduct of court proceedings"[41] should really be characterised as procedural.

Secondly, if the *lex causae* relating to the claim does not recognise tracing, the ability to trace will be pointless, irrespective of whether it is recognised by the *lex fori*. As noted above, the process of tracing and claiming are separate. However, where the law applicable to the relevant claim does not recognise claims contingent on tracing, there is nothing the *lex fori* can add to the matter.

Thirdly, tracing exists both at law and in equity, each one governed by slightly different rules. Thus, the type of tracing rules which are employed will need to be determined by whether the plaintiff is claiming at law or in equity. Furthermore, some of the tracing rules and presumptions in equity depend on whether the defendant is innocent or a wrongdoer.[42] These distinctions in the tracing rules suggest that tracing should be viewed as an issue of substance to be determined by the *lex causae* applicable to the particular claim. Moreover, whether one can trace in equity must surely depend on whether the *lex causae* recognises equitable claims. At least on present authority, a fiduciary relationship is a prerequisite to a successful tracing exercise in equity. It would be ludicrous if the *lex fori* were searching for a fiduciary relationship to allow tracing in equity, when under the *lex causae* no such requirement was necessary. The pre-requisite of a fiduciary relationship makes the tracing process seem more like an issue of substance than procedure. This last argument can be extended by saying that, if tracing were governed by the *lex fori*, a degree of double actionability may arise. Although a plaintiff may be able to trace the value of his property into the defendant's hands pursuant to the *lex causae's* tracing rules, his claim may fail if the tracing process is thwarted by the *lex fori's* stricter requirements.[43] It must be contrary to common sense to defeat a claim which would succeed under the *lex causae* but fails due to a procedural characterisation of tracing. Similarly, where the converse applied, such that the *lex causae's* tracing requirements are stricter, it would also be inappropriate to allow a claim on the basis of the *lex fori's* more liberal tracing rules, when such a claim would not succeed under the *lex causae*

Finally, it is submitted that in *Chase Manhattan v Israel-British Bank*,[44] the plaintiff's ability to trace was governed by the *lex causae*, namely the law of New York.[45] Goulding J relevantly described the issue as "whether the equitable right of a person who pays money by mistake to trace *and* claim such money under the law of New York is conferred by substantive law or is of a merely procedural character".[46] His Lordship found that under New York law the defendant had become a constructive trustee of the monies and that this arose "by a rule of substantive law and is not the mere result of a remedial or procedural rule".[47] Although Goulding J further held that there was no significant difference between the law of New York and England,[48] in relation to the imposition of a constructive trust for mistaken payments, and thus that no conflict arose, the finding that the constructive trust arose as a matter of substantive law was crucial.[49] As the defendant's assets had already been impressed with a trust, as a result of the winding-up proceedings, the plaintiff needed to show that the constructive trust had arisen as a matter of

---

Obligations": ch 5, in FD Rose, *Restitution and the Conflict of Laws* (Mansfield Press, Oxford, 1995) (hereafter "Stevens"), 211–212.
[41] *McKain v Miller* (1991) 174 CLR 1 (HCA), 27, *per* Mason CJ.
[42] See *eg Re Hallet's Estate* (1879) 13 Ch D 696; *Re Oatway* [1903] 2 Ch 356.
[43] See *supra* §2 (a).
[44] [1981] Ch 105.
[45] *Cf* Smith, 275.
[46] *Chase Manhattan Bank N.A. v Israel-British Bank (London) Ltd* [1981] 1 Ch 105, 122D (emphasis added).
[47] *Ibid*, 127B.
[48] *Ibid*, 118E, 120A, 128A–B.
[49] *Cf* Burrows, 497.

substantive law and not under a remedial rule, governed by the *lex fori*. In this way the plaintiff's money would have remained unaffected by the winding-up proceedings. As it was agreed that the substantive law was that of New York, the plaintiff therefore had to show that the constructive trust had arisen by the law of New York, prior to the winding-up proceedings.[50] As already illustrated, the constructive trust which arose, consequent upon both the process of tracing *and* claiming, and thus both were governed by the *lex causae*.

ii. *A separate choice of law rule?*

Assuming that tracing is a not a procedural issue, the next question is whether it attracts its own separate choice of law rule. The view that tracing may attract its own distinct choice of law rule was rejected by Millett J in *El Ajou v Dollar Holdings Plc*.[51] It was recognised by his Lordship that tracing could be characterised either as procedural, and therefore governed by the *lex fori*, or as a substantive issue to be governed by the law governing the restitutionary obligation.[52] It was not necessary to give a final decision on that point in *El Ajou*, as on either footing it was to be governed by English law. What is clear is that tracing is not to be separately characterised and thus governed by its own choice of law rule. As a consequence, a plaintiff may be able to trace through jurisdictions which do not recognise tracing. It was relevantly stated that:[53]

> "[w]here [assets] have passed through many different hands in many different countries, they may be difficult to trace; but . . . neither their temporary repose in a civil law country not their receipt by intermediate recipients outside the jurisdiction should prevent the court from treating assets in the legal ownership of a defendant within the jurisdiction as trust assets".

Therefore, according to Millett J, the ability to trace, at least in equity, does not require that every intermediate recipient be amenable to the court's jurisdiction but only that the defendant is. This is because the plaintiff's ability to trace is "dependent on the power of equity to charge a mixed fund with the repayment of trust monies, not upon any actual exercise of that power".[54] Although the dicta of Millett J are in terms of jurisdiction and tracing in equity, they nevertheless help to illustrate how an international tracing issue should be treated.

It is submitted that the approach of Millett J is correct and that an issue of tracing should not be characterised as a separate issue, attracting its own choice of law rule. First, although tracing is an issue of substance, it is not a source of rights. As discussed, tracing may be relevant to a wide variety of claims. Tracing merely extends, to other assets or defendants, rights with an independent source.[55] As noted by Birks: "Anyone can have a go at tracing. If you have a go, you may or may not succeed in locating the value of one asset in another. If you do succeed, it does not follow that you can make any claim. The background facts are important to claiming, not to tracing."[56] Thus, the most logical approach in relation to international tracing is to apply the choice of law rule relating to the relevant claim contingent on tracing.

Secondly, if a separate choice of law rule were to apply to tracing issues, what would it be? It would be difficult to imagine something other than some form of recognition by the relevant

---

[50] This is also consistent with Lord Browne-Wilkinson's reinterpretation of *Chase-Manhattan* in *Westdeutsche Landesbank Girozentrale v Islington LBC* [1996] A 669, 714, where he concludes that the law of New York and England were in fact different.
[51] [1993] 3 All ER 717 (rvrsd [1994] 2 All ER 685 (CA) on different grounds).
[52] *Ibid*, 736.
[53] *Ibid*, 737.
[54] *Ibid*.
[55] Smith concludes that, although a matter of substance, tracing should not attract a separate choice of law rule. Although "it is a substantive part of proving a right or claim, nonetheless it is not essentially a source of rights": Smith, 276. Although the author agrees with this proposition, it is essentially based on our domestic law understanding of tracing. As will become apparent, there are further compelling arguments for adopting this position from a private international law perspective, as well as certain ancillary issues which also need to be addressed.
[56] Birks, 297.

alternative jurisdictions. This would raise the further problem of whether the plaintiff must show a vested proprietary interest under the law of each intermediate jurisdiction, or whether he would merely need to show that the particular tracing exercise is recognised by the relevant jurisdictions. The dictum of Millett J in *El Ajou* makes perfectly good sense. Where a plaintiff merely needs to trace *through* foreign jurisdictions, the success of his claim should not depend on whether the foreign jurisdictions recognise tracing, or that he has a valid claim under the law of each jurisdiction. Fraudsters could thereby defeat legitimate claims merely by channelling funds through the right jurisdictions.

Thirdly, a choice of law rule which reflects the interests of the foreign intermediary jurisdictions could not be said to be protecting certainty and security of transactions. One of the main policy arguments in favour of the *lex situs* rule is based on its efficacy *vis-à-vis* third parties. So as to ensure certainty in relation to real rights, a third party intending to acquire an interest in property must be protected from the risk that such a thing might be subject to a foreign law.[57] Such an argument can hardly be said to be a legitimate policy consideration in relation to funds, which often only notionally pass through a particular jurisdiction.

Furthermore, where someone traces *into* a foreign jurisdiction, such that the value received, or surviving, is in a foreign jurisdiction, there is again no real reason for separately characterising the tracing issue. If the concern was to protect the interests of the *lex situs*, this would presumably be taken care of by any proprietary issue raised through the plaintiff's claim. For example, where stolen monies are used to purchase a car in a foreign jurisdiction, a plaintiff's claim to the beneficial title of such a car may be seen as raising an issue of title and therefore attract the choice of law rule for the transfer of tangible moveables.[58] Such issues would raise proprietary characterisations and therefore attract the *lex situs* or a choice of law rule reflecting the proprietary nature of the issue. In such an event, it would be the proprietary choice of law rule which should determine if tracing were available.

A separate choice of law rule for tracing issues which took into account the interests of the alternative jurisdictions would, it is submitted, be inconsistent with our understanding of tracing. What is being traced is value and not property or assets. The tracing process does not create any rights or remedies in itself. A claim may however be brought in relation to the traceable proceeds. As recognised by Millett J in *El Ajou*, it must be the tracing rules of either the *lex fori* or the *lex causae* (of the relevant issue arising in the claim) which should apply.

iii. Characterisation of tracing

It is therefore submitted that tracing should neither be characterised as a matter of procedure, to be governed by the *lex fori*, nor as a separate issue attracting its own choice of law rule. Tracing is best viewed as an extension of rights with an independent source. The choice of law rule governing the issue arising out of such rights must govern any tracing issues.[59] Where a restitutionary claim contingent on tracing is brought, the restitutionary choice of law rule ought to govern the ability to trace. For example, where the plaintiff's monies are stolen and paid into the defendant's bank account, with which the defendant has subsequently bought bonds, the plaintiff's claim that the defendant make restitution of the value of the bonds may be seen as raising a restitutionary issue. If so the restitutionary choice of law rule, which governs the defendant's liabil-

---

[57] *Re Anziani* [1930] 1 Ch 407, 420; *Macmillan Inc v Bishopsgate Investment Trust Plc (No 3)* [1996] 1 WLR 387, 424-425, per Aldous LJ; M. Wolff, *Private International Law*, 2nd ed (Clarendon Press, Oxford, 1950), 511-512; PM North and JJ Fawcett (eds) *Cheshire and North's Private International Law*, 12th ed (Butterworths, London, 1992), 798.

[58] See *Dicey and Morris*, Rule 118.

[59] See also Smith, 276; Bird, 86; cf Stevens, 212-213. This is also the position adopted by Sir P Millett, "Jurisdiction and Choice of Law in the Law of Restitution", a paper delivered at the 8th National University of Singapore Conference on International Business Law — *Current Legal Issues in International Commercial Litigation*: [1997] RLR §12.

ity to make restitution, will also determine whether the plaintiff can trace into the bonds. Alternatively, if the issue arising out of a claim contingent on tracing is characterised as a proprietary issue, thereby attracting the *lex situs* or some other rule applicable to the particular property in question, the law applicable under that particular choice of law rule must also determine the tracing issue. The above approach applies *mutatis mutandis* to other types of claims contingent on tracing, where the relevant issue may, for example, be characterised as contractual, a wrong or a matrimonial issue.

iv. Interest in the tracing process

It has been submitted above that when tracing internationally the plaintiff need not show an interest under the law of each intermediary jurisdiction. There are strong arguments against such a requirement. First, the success of a tracing exercise would depend on the particular jurisdictions through which the traceable proceeds went. If a fraudulent party channelled funds through a jurisdiction which did not recognise tracing, it could easily defeat a tracing exercise, and thus the relevant claim. Furthermore, the more jurisdictions involved, the more complex and costly the international claim. This would be a blessing to the fraudsters and the launderers. Secondly, where the tracing process involves funds moving through various bank accounts via electronic transfers, it becomes rather artificial to speak of the plaintiff tracing "through" a jurisdiction.

It should be noted that the above analysis is consistent with the mere power to revest theory of tracing.[60] According to this theory the interest contingent upon tracing is an incomplete interest, that is "a mere power to revest" — or a mere equity. It is not a vested interest. There are certain advantages in adopting the mere power analysis of tracing, and this is particularly so in the context of private international law. Under this theory, the plaintiff need not show a proprietary interest at every intermediate link of the chain. Thus, in *El Ajou*,[61] Millett J, expressly denied that the plaintiff "must have been in a position to obtain an equitable charge against every successive account";[62] whilst he described the defrauded plaintiff's interest in the funds into which he traced as "entirely notional".[63]

In addition to overcoming the need to establish a proprietary interest at every step in the tracing chain, the mere power analysis of tracing is consistent with the fact that tracing does not create any rights or remedies, and therefore helps explain why a tracing issue should not attract its own choice of law rule. Despite the fact that there remain some unresolved questions in relation to the power analysis, such as when and how such power is exercised,[64] it is nevertheless submitted that such an analysis should be adopted, at least as a matter of private international law.

3. ANCILLARY ISSUES

a. Intermediate purchases or acquisitions

Where one traces through a foreign jurisdiction, an ancillary proprietary issue may arise. Property within the tracing chain may have been sold to an intermediary recipient, or to the defendant, and thus a purchase may have occurred. Alternatively, an accession or specification may have occurred through the process.[65] In such a case, it is submitted that a separate issue will

---

[60] Birks, 307-311; *cf* Smith, 358–361. *Re ffrench's Estate* (1887) 21 LR (IR) 283 is cited as an example of the mere power theory; *cf Cave v Cave* (1880) 15 ch D 639.
[61] *El Ajou v Dollar Land Holdings Plc* [1993] 3 All ER 717, 739, *per* Millett J (reversed on different grounds [1994] 2 All ER 685).
[62] *Ibid*, 737 d-e. *Cf El Ajou v Dollar Land Holdings (No 2)* [1995] 2 All ER 213, 221g, *per* Robert Walker J.
[63] *Ibid*, 737j.
[64] See Birks, 311.
[65] In relation to specification or accession in private international law, see *eg Borden (UK) Ltd v Scottish Timber Products Ltd* [1981] Ch 25; *Zahnrad Fabrik Passau GmbH v Terex Ltd* 1986 SLT 84

arise of whether the ancillary proprietary issue has defeated the claim. Such ancillary issues are to be characterised separately, and are to be determined by the applicable choice of law rule for the acquisition, accession or specification of the particular type of property.[66]

An ancillary proprietary issue will often arise by way of defence: namely, the defendant may be a purchaser in good faith in relation to the property or, alternatively, the defendant may allege that a previous person in the tracing chain was a good faith purchaser. For example, the plaintiff's employee fraudulently forwards money to B, who is in France. B then uses this money to purchase a car. B then sells this car to the defendant. The plaintiff claims that the defendant holds the car as trustee for the plaintiff. However, the defendant will argue that he was a bona fide purchaser for value. Irrespective of whether the plaintiff's claim is seen as raising a proprietary or restitutionary issue, the defendant's defence (that he was a bona fide purchaser for value) raises an ancillary proprietary issue, which should attract the relevant choice of law rule for the particular purchase, in this case the law of the place where the tangible was at the time of transfer, namely France. The plaintiff's claim may be defeated if the ancillary proprietary question can be substantiated under the law applicable to it, and thus the claim may possibly fail.[67] An analogy here can be drawn with the situation of contractual defences to tortious liability under private international law.[68] What is significant for our purposes is to note that the tracing process will still be governed by the law governing the plaintiff's claim. The fact that there has been an intermediate purchase should not affect the treatment of the tracing issue, as the considerations relating to the intermediate purchase can be dealt with as an ancillary proprietary issue.

The existence of a separate characterisation of ancillary proprietary issues alleviates the concern of not only the situation where the defendant was a bona fide purchaser, but also where a previous recipient was. As a result of this safeguard, there is no reason why the plaintiff need show an interest at every link of the tracing process, *ie*, a "charge against every successive account".[69] It is also a logical consequence of the plaintiff not needing to establish an interest under the law of each intermediary jurisdiction. The plaintiff must be able to trace without any gaps, but the exercise of the final *in personam* or proprietary remedy must depend on the state of affairs at the end of the chain, not at every link.

b. Tracing in equity and at law

As already discussed, the rules for tracing in equity are different from those at law. The existence of this bimorphic form of tracing may add an additional problem; namely that of equity at private international law. There is a view that equitable rights and remedies are administered by the court in accordance with the *lex fori*.[70] Therefore an additional argument could be raised that, irrespective of how one may characterise common law tracing, insofar as equitable tracing is concerned, this is to be governed by the *lex fori*. As long as there is jurisdiction, the court can require

---

[66] See *Macmillan Inc v Bishopsgate Investment Trust Plc (No 3)* [1996] 1 WLR 387.
[67] A private international law matter may raise several issues each governed by a different choice of law rule: *Macmillan Inc v Bishopsgate Investment Trust Plc (No 3)* [1996] 1 WLR 387, 399, *per* Staughton LJ, 418, *per* Aldous LJ.
[68] *Coupland v Arabian Gulf Oil Co* [1983] 1 WLR 1136. See also L Collins, "Interaction between Contract and Tort" (1967) 16 ICLQ 103; O Kahn-Freund, "Contractual Defences to Delictual Claims" (1968) II Hague Recueil 129–157; P North, "Contractual Defences to Torts" (1977) 26 ICLQ 914; P Carter (1983) 54 BYIL 301; also A Briggs, "From Complexity to Anticlimax: Restitution and Choice of Law" [1996] RLR 88, 90
[69] *El Ajou v Dollar Land Holdings Ltd* [1993] 3 All ER 717, 737, *per* Millett J.
[70] *Re Anchor Line (Henderson Bros) Ltd* [1937] Ch 483, 488; *National Commercial Bank v Wimborne* (28 April 1978) Unreported (NSW SC Eq) 1546/1978; *United States Surgical Corp v Hospital Products International Pty Ltd* [1982] 2 NSWLR 766 (the case was appealed to the NSW Court of Appeal [1983] 2 NSWLR 157 and to the High Court of Australia (1984) 156 CLR 41, both courts confirming the trial court's finding that no conflict of laws issue arose as there was no material difference between the relevant systems of law).

the parties to act in accordance with the court's equitable principles, because equity acts on the conscience of the parties and *in personam*. Thus, English law has been applied as the *lex fori*, to grant specific performance in relation to foreign land, without any inquiry as to whether it was the proper law of the contract.[71] However, this is to be contrasted with cases where the application of equitable rights, in relation to land overseas, has been governed by the law of the contract under which those equitable rights arose.[72]

Although the issue of equity's role at private international law is beyond the scope of this article, it is submitted that equitable rights and obligations should be characterised in relation to the right or obligation which gives rise to the equity.[73] Therefore, when faced with an international claim contingent on equitable tracing, the court should characterise the issue arising out of the claim, and the law applicable to that issue should also determine the ability to trace in equity.

There is no significant argument for applying a different approach to tracing in equity. As discussed above, it is pointless to apply the *lex fori* in relation to the issue of tracing where it is not recognised by the *lex causae*. Furthermore, it is inappropriate to defeat a claim contingent on tracing, which would be successful under the *lex causae*, as a result of the *lex fori's* stricter tracing requirements; or, alternatively, to allow a claim in circumstances where the *lex causae's* tracing rules would not have recognised such a claim.

Secondly, recent authorities indicate a move away from the treating of equitable rights and obligations in private international law differently from their legal counterparts. More recent authorities support the proposition that equitable obligations do attract a choice of law rule reflecting that of the relevant obligation.[74] It is submitted that equitable obligations should generally be viewed as counterparts to legal obligations, having merely a different historical basis, and therefore should be characterised in accordance with their legal counterparts.[75] It would therefore follow that equitable tracing should not be treated any differently from legal tracing.

CONCLUSION

The following submissions are made by way of conclusion:

(1) Although a process, tracing is not a procedural matter to be governed by the *lex fori*.

(2) As a matter of private international law, tracing does not attract a separate choice of law rule.

(3) In a private international law matter, tracing is to be governed by the *lex causae* of the claim contingent on tracing. Where the issue arising out of the claim contingent on tracing is characterised as restitutionary, this will be the law of the restitutionary obligation; where the issue is characterised as proprietary, this will be the choice of law rule in relation to the particular property to which the claim relates.

---

[71] *Re Anchor Line (Henderson Bros) Ltd* [1937] Ch 483.

[72] *Ex p Holthausen; re Schiebler* (1874) LR 9 Ch App 722; *British South Africa Co v De Beers Consolidated Mines Ltd* [1910] 2 Ch 502, 510, *per* Farwell LJ, 520, *per* Kennedy LJ (rvrsd [1912] AC 52 on different grounds); *Re Smith; Lawrence v Kitson* [1916] 2 Ch 206.

[73] RW White, "Equitable Obligations in Private International Law: The Choice of Law" [1986] Syd LR 92, 108; Bird, 78; *Halsbury's Laws of England*, 4th ed (reissue), Vol 8(1), para 890, p 662; Stevens, 188–189.

[74] *Chase Manhattan Bank NA v Israel-British Bank (London) Ltd* [1981] Ch 105; *El Ajou v Dollar Holdings Ltd* [1993] 3 All ER 717, 736 (rvrsd [1994] 2 All ER 685 (CA) on different grounds); *Arab Monetary Fund v Hashim (No 9)* [1994] *The Times*, October 11; *Thahir v Pertamina* [1994] 3 SLR 257; *Arab Monetary Fund v Hashim* [1996] 1 Lloyd's Rep 589

[75] See *Nelson v Larholt* [1947] 1 KB 339, 343, *per* Denning J; *United Scientific Holdings Ltd v Burnley Borough Council* [1978] AC 904, 925-926; *Mahesan v Malaysia Government Officers' Co-operative Housing Society Ltd* [1979] AC 374, 380, *per* Lord Diplock. See also P Birks, "Equity in the Modern Law: An Exercise in Taxonomy" (1996) 26 UWALR 1; E Peel, "Jurisdiction under the Brussels Convention": ch 1 of FD Rose (ed), *Restitution and the Conflict of Laws* (Mansfield Press, Oxford 1995), 37; A Briggs, "The Unrestrained Reach of an Anti-suit Injunction: *a Pause for Thought*" [1997] LMCLQ 90.

(4) Where an intermediate purchase, specification or accession has occurred during the tracing process, a separate ancillary proprietary issue will arise to be determined in accordance with the choice of law rule applicable to the particular purchase, specification or accession. Such an ancillary proprietary issue may, by way of defence, defeat the plaintiff's claim contingent on tracing.

(5) The existence of distinct tracing rules at law and in equity should be inconsequential to tracing issues as a matter of private international law.

IMPROVEMENTS AND ENRICHMENT: A COMPARATIVE ANALYSIS

*Dirk A Verse**

To establish an enrichment, and hence the first requirement of a restitutionary claim, can constitute an arduous task. The root of the difficulty lies in the commitment which, it is argued, English law adopts towards the issue of "subjective devaluation". The aim of this essay is to explore the exact scope of this concept. Yet, for reasons of space, it is impossible to deal with all instances of subjective devaluation. The ensuing analysis will therefore focus on one important group of cases where subjective devaluation is frequently invoked, namely cases of unrequested improvements of another's property.[1]

For the purpose of this analysis, a comparative method will be used. Civil law countries have long been granting restitutionary claims for unrequested improvements, and they have thus been facing exactly the same problems as those now arising in the emerging English law of restitution. As will be seen, the issue of "imposed enrichment", as most civilians would refer to it, has been broadly discussed, especially by German lawyers. It will be shown that their solutions of the

---

* Research Assistant in Private Law, Roman Law and Comparative Legal History, University of Regensburg. I would like to thank Professor Peter Birks for his generous help and encouragement, and George Panagopoulos for commenting upon an earlier draft of this paper.

The publication of this article was assisted by a grant from the TMR Network Research Project in Common Principles of European Private Law, funded by the European Commission (contract ERB FMRX-CT97-0118).

The following are referred to by the abbreviations indicated:

Beatson: J Beatson, *The Use and Abuse of Unjust Enrichment: Essays on the Law of Restitution* (Oxford, 1991);
Beissner: M Beissner, *Die Verwendungen des Mieters und unrechtmäßigen Fremdbesitzers unter Berücksichtigung des Aspekts der aufgedrängten Bereicherung* (Göttingen, 1994);
Birks: P Birks, *An Introduction to the Law of Restitution,* revd ed (Oxford, 1989);
Burrows: A Burrows, *The Law of Restitution* (London, Dublin, Edinburgh, 1993);
Burrows, Essays: A Burrows (ed), *Essays on the Law of Restitution* (Oxford, 1993);
Dawson: JP Dawson, *Unjust Enrichment, A Comparative Analysis* (Boston, 1951);
Finn: PD Finn (ed), *Essays on Restitution* (Sydney, 1990);
Goff & Jones: Lord Goff of Chieveley & G Jones, *The Law of Restitution,* 4th ed (London, 1993);
Klauser: KA Klauser, *Bereicherung wider Willen, Zur bereicherungsrechtlichen Behandlung von Verwendungen* (Freiburg, 1955);
Larenz & Canaris: K Larenz & CW Canaris, *Lehrbuch des Schuldrechts,* vol II/2, 13th ed (Munich, 1994);
Loewenheim: U Loewenheim, *Bereicherungsrecht* (Munich, 1989);
Maddaugh & McCamus: PD Maddaugh & JD McCamus, *The Law of Restitution* (Aurora, 1990);
Markesinis, Lorenz & Dannemann: B Markesinis, W Lorenz & G Dannemann, *The German Law of Contract and Restitution* (Oxford, 1997);
Mason & Carter: K Mason & J Carter, *Restitution Law in Australia* (Sydney, 1995);
McInnes: M McInnes, *Restitution: Developments in Unjust Enrichment* (Sydney, 1996);
Münchener Kommentar: Kommentar zum Bürgerlichen Gesetzbuch, 3rd ed (Munich, 1993–);
Palandt: O Palandt (ed), *Bürgerliches Gesetzbuch, Kommentar,* 56th ed (Munich, 1996);
Palmer & McKendrick: N Palmer & E McKendrick, *Interests in Goods* (London, 1993);
Reimer: J Reimer, *Die aufgedrängte Bereicherung, Paradigma der 'negatorischen' Abschöpfung in Umkehrung zum Schadensersatz* (Berlin, 1990);
Reuter & Martinek: D Reuter & M Martinek, *Ungerechtfertigte Bereicherung* (Tübingen, 1983);
von Rittberg: FW Graf von Rittberg, *Die aufgedrängte Bereicherung* (Munich, 1969);
Staudinger: J von Staudinger (ed), *Kommentar zum Bürgerlichen Gesetzbuch,* 13th ed (Berlin, 1993–).

[1] In contrast, the paper will not be concerned with the issue of enrichment through "pure" services, *ie* services which leave no relevant end-product. On such cases see, *Beatson,* 21–44; P Birks, "In Defence of Free Acceptance", ch 5 of *Burrows, Essays,* 105, at 132–135.

enrichment issue are often quite similar to those advocated in the common law jurisdictions. Nevertheless, there are differences in detail which give reason to rethink the exact boundaries of subjective devaluation.

I. INTRODUCTION

Traditionally, the common law has been reluctant to allow claims in cases of unrequested improvements, even where the improver has not acted "officiously" in the strict sense, such as where he has, for example, acted under a mistake or an emergency. The reason for this is plain: it is the maximisation of freedom of choice — the owner shall not be forced to bear the cost of an improvement which he did not choose to have. A well-known judicial statement expresses the same idea "Suppose I clean your property without your knowledge, have I then a claim on you for payment? How can you help it? One cleans another's shoes; what can the other do but put them on?" That is Pollock CB, in *Taylor v Laird*.[2] Another *locus classicus* is Bowen LJ's statement in *Falcke v Scottish Imperial Insurance Co*: "Liabilities are not to be forced upon people behind their backs any more than you can confer a benefit upon a man against his will".[3]

Dawson once remarked that this rule has lain on the consciences of lawyers for hundreds of years and lies on our consciences still.[4] Yet the rule is not (and has never been) as rigorous as these statements may suggest. Thus, in the case of the mistaken improver, it has for long been established, and is now partly laid down by statute,[5] that the improver can rely upon the value of his improvements as a *defence* to a claim in tort brought by the owner.[6] Whilst more recently, one has finally gone so far as to advocate an independent active claim for the improver. The prime example is the judgment of Lord Denning MR in *Greenwood v Bennett*.[7] In that case the Master of the Rolls found support for an independent claim in the principle against unjust enrichment. Thus he stated:[8]

> "There is a principle at hand to meet the case. It derives from the law of restitution. The [owners] should not be allowed unjustly to enrich themselves at [the improver's] expense ... No matter whether [the owners] recover [the improved *res*] with the aid of the courts, or without it, the innocent [improver] will recover the value of the improvements he has done to it."

Unfortunately however, Lord Denning did not attempt an exact conceptual analysis of the various stages of a restitutionary claim; not without justice, his approach has been said to be "rather cavalier".[9] As a result, many questions remain unanswered. Most notably, Lord Denning did not explain why he considered the owner in *Greenwood* to be enriched. The owner made no request for the improvements — could he not have argued that to him, personally, the improvements were not of any use at all? And how can *Greenwood* be reconciled with the owner's freedom of choice so prominently celebrated in *Taylor v Laird* and *Falcke*? Moreover, to what extent does Lord Denning's reasoning in *Greenwood* (which was concerned with improvements of a chattel) also apply to improvements to land?

---

[2] *Taylor v Laird* [1856] 25 LJ Ex 329, 332.
[3] *Falcke v Scottish Imperial Insurance Co* (1886) 34 Ch D 234, 248.
[4] Dawson, 51.
[5] Torts (Interference with Goods) Act 1977, s 6 (1).
[6] *Cf* the 19th century mining cases *Wood v Morewood* [1841] 3 QB 440; *Livingstone v Rawyards Coal Co* [1880] 5 AC 25, 40, *per* Lord Blackburn. See also *The Peruvian Guano Co Ltd v Dreyfus Brothers & Co* [1892] AC 166, 175-176, *per* Lord Macnaghten, and *Munro v Willmott* [1949] 1 KB 295.
[7] [1973] 1 QB 195. The facts are set out *infra*, III (A).
[8] *Ibid*, 202.
[9] E McKendrick, "Restitution and the Misuse of Chattels — The Need for a Principled Approach", ch 23 of *Palmer & McKendrick*, 599, 602. *Cf* also the harsh criticism by P Matthews, "Freedom, Unrequested Improvements and Lord Denning" (1981) 40 CLJ 340, 351-358.

These are the questions that the present article seeks to tackle from a comparative point of view. In doing so, we will focus only on the enrichment issue, *ie* the first of the four stages of the restitutionary claim.[10] Enrichment alone is certainly not enough to establish a restitutionary claim, but it is the enrichment issue which represents the specific difficulty in cases of unrequested improvements. Once it is established that the improvement constitutes an enrichment, the other stages of the restitutionary claim should not be treated any differently from a claim for restitution in money.[11]

II. TWO DEFINITIONS OF ENRICHMENT

Definitions of enrichment can vary between two extreme positions. One position is that a person is enriched when the benefit conferred enhances the market value of his or her assets; this may be called *objective* enrichment. The other extreme is to define enrichment exclusively in relation to the particular recipient of the benefit; this is referred to as *subjective* enrichment or enrichment susceptible to the argument of "subjective devaluation". It is obvious that these definitions can produce very different results. If I build a skyscraper on your piece of land, its market value will rise dramatically and your objective enrichment may run into millions. However, you might have preferred to use the land as a football pitch for your children; if you can subjectively devalue, your subjective enrichment will be nil.[12]

Some civil law jurisdictions, such as France and Italy, have, in principle, adopted the objective approach.[13] An advantage of this approach is certainly its practicability; for objective market values are in general easy to establish. But it is clear that such an approach also entails considerable hardship for the owner. Not only does he have to bear the cost of an unwanted improvement, he might even be compelled to sell the improved asset if he did not have sufficient disposable funds to pay for large-scale improvements. This result has been much deplored. Already some hundred years ago, an Italian writer observed that under the objective approach "the easiest way to ruin someone is to enrich him".[14] Similar statements can be found in France.[15] However, little was done to smooth the rough edges of the objective approach. The only attempt to mitigate the owner's plight, which (at least initially) gained some support, goes back to Pothier. He suggested that in those cases, in which the owner had not enough disposable funds to meet his obligation towards the improver, the sum due ought to be transformed into many moderate instalments.[16] But even this modest adjustment has largely fallen into oblivion in the 20th century. French and Italian writers now seem to consider it as self-evident that the bona fide improver's interest in restitution should prevail over the owner's freedom of choice;

---

[10] The four stages are (i) enrichment, (ii) at the plaintiff's expense, (iii) a ground for restitution that renders the enrichment unjust, (iv) defences.
[11] If seen in this light, a dictum by Lord Denning in *Greenwood* in relation to mistake as an unjust-factor appears doubtful. The Master of the Rolls requires the mistake of the improver to be innocent: [1973] 1 QB 195, 202B–C; see also *Wood v Morewood* (1841) 3 QB 440, 441, *per* Parke B. But that is inconsistent with the general rule as laid down in *Kelly v Solari* (1841) 9 M & W 54, 59, *per* Parke B, allowing restitution in cases of mistake "however careless the party [conferring the benefit] may have been".
[12] As long as you do not sell the estate and realise its appreciation in value.
[13] *Cf, eg*, G Bonet, "Quasi-contrats, Enrichissement sans cause", in *Juris Classeur, Droit Civil* (Paris, 1988), app art 1370–1381, n 67; P Trimarchi, *L'arricchimento senza causa* (Milano, 1962), 8–17.
[14] G Pacchioni, *Trattato della gestione d'affari altrui secondo il diritto romano e civile* (Lanciano, 1893), 679: "il mezzo più semplice e facile per rovinare una persona è quello di arricchirla".
[15] *Cf* L Audiat, note on Cass Civ 28 Mar 1939, S 1939.I.265, 266: "Il est bien évident [. . .] qu'imposer à quelqu'un qui ne l'a pas demandé le remboursement d'un enrichissement tout à fait hors de proportion avec ses ressources, serait, sous couleur de l'enrichir, le conduire à la ruine."
[16] RJ Pothier, *Traité du droit de domaine de propriété*, in *Oeuvres*, vol VIII (Paris, 1827), n 347 *in fine*. For support of this solution see C Demolombe, *Cours de Code Napoléon*, vol IX (Paris, 1870), n 690; V Marcadé, *Explication théorique et pratique du Code Civil*, vol II, 7th ed (Paris, 1873), art 555, n IV.

though they laconically admit that having to pay for a house built on one's land against one's will means a "réstriction considérable à son droit de propriété".[17]

It is only in respect of enrichment claims by *mala fide* improvers[18] that these jurisdictions give weight to freedom of choice and subjectivity of value. Thus, the French *code civil*, art 555 provides that an owner who dislikes the improvement — or at least dislikes paying for it — can defeat the *mala fide* improver's claim by insisting on the removal of the improvement. The same rule is laid down in the Italian *codice civile*, art 936.

But let us return to the improver in good faith and the objective enrichment approach. It is at least surprising that civil law jurisdictions such as France and Italy have been inclined to take this purely improver-sided point of view. For Roman law favoured a much more refined and owner-orientated approach. Thus, Celsus D 6, 1, 38 reads:[19]

> "In fundo alieno, quem imprudens emeras, aedificasti aut conseruisti, deinde evincitur: bonus iudex varie ex personis causisque constituet. Finge et dominum eadem facturum fuisse: reddat impensam, ut fundum recipiat, usque eo dumtaxat, quo pretiosior factus est, et si plus pretio fundi accessit, solum quod impensum est. Finge pauperem, qui, si reddere id cogatur, laribus sepulchris avitis carendum habeat: sufficit tibi permitti tollere ex his rebus quae possis, dum ita ne deterior sit fundus, quam si initio non foret aedificatum. [. . .] finge eam personam esse domini, quae receptum fundum mox venditura sit: nisi reddit, quantum prima parte reddi oportere diximus, eo deducto tu condemnandus es."

> "You inadvertently bought land belonging to another, built or planted on it, and then were evicted by the owner; the good judge's order will vary according to the persons involved and the facts of the case. Suppose the owner would have done the same as you. In that case, in order to get his land back, he must pay your expenses to the extent that the value of the land has been increased, or if the increase in value is more than the expenses, then only the amount you expended. Suppose the owner is a poor man who, if made to pay such a sum, would have to give up his household gods and ancestral graves. In that case it is enough that you be allowed to take away what you can from the building materials, so long as the land is not thus put in a worse condition than it would be in, if there had been no building. [. . .] Suppose the owner is someone who wants to sell the land as soon as he gets it back; unless he pays what he said should be paid in the first case, then the judgment against you is reduced by that amount".[20]

This is a clear statement in favour of a subjective enrichment test, for it emphasises the importance of the owner's individual situation: if the owner has saved expenses that he would otherwise have incurred himself, he will be liable.[21] The same applies when he intends to sell the improved property and thereby realises its enhanced value. In both cases, the owner either saves or receives money which is, as we would now say, incontrovertibly beneficial. But it is very different when the benefit is not turned into money. Celsus takes the case of a *dominus* who is too poor to pay for the improvement and who would thus be forced to sell the improved asset. In such a situation, in order to save the owner from an unacceptable financial sacrifice, Celsus accepts the argument of subjective devaluation, *ie* he holds the owner not liable to pay despite a

---

[17] J Carbonnier, *Droit civil, Les biens,* 15th ed (Paris, 1992), n 213 (b).

[18] The availability of such claims reflects one of the main discrepancies between the civilian and the common law of restitution. It is due to the fact that the common law always requires a special ground for restitution (mistake, duress etc) that renders the enrichment unjust (an "unjust factor"). Civilian systems, in contrast, grant enrichment claims if only there is no legal ground (contract etc) for the transfer of the benefit.

[19] Recent views treat the substance of the text as classical. See G MacCormack, "Ius tollendi" 85 (1982) *Bulletino d'Istituto di Diritto Romano* 77, 78 n 6; D Liebs, *Die Klagenkonkurrenz im römischen Recht* (Göttingen, 1972), 187, n 326; A Bürge, *Retentio im römischen Sachen- und Obligationenrecht* (Zurich, 1979), 59–60, n 216.

[20] The translation is taken from P Stein, in T Mommsen, P Krueger, A Watson (ed), *The Digest of Justinian,* vol I (Philadelphia, 1985), 207.

[21] But note that Roman law did not provide the improver with an active claim (see Julian D 12, 6, 33, *supra*, n 3); rather his rights were confined to a *ius retentionis*, see *ibid, in fine*: "nullo alio modo quam per retentionem impensas servare posse".

considerable increase in market value. However, the improver is at least given a right of removal, provided of course, that the removal can be effected without causing damage.

Celsus's statement has proved to be particularly influential in Germany. It had already been applied in the German *ius commune*,[22] and even though its rules were not explicitly adopted by the BGB, modern doctrine has relied upon them when carving out the concept of enrichment.[23] Thus, despite some critics who still advocate an objective test,[24] it is now the prevailing opinion among German lawyers that in cases of imposed benefits *(aufgedrängte Bereicherung)* enrichment has to be defined not just as a rise in market value but with regard to the particular recipient.[25,26] That seems to bring German law in line with the law in this country; for the English law of restitution, it is argued, also accepts that subjective criteria have to be taken into account.[27] This common starting-point renders a closer comparison with German law particularly promising; it can serve as a check and an inspiration as to how to solve (or how not to solve) the problem of imposed enrichment in the law of restitution.

Before we undertake this comparison, however, two preliminary remarks need to be made. First, it has to be borne in mind that, in German law, a claim in unjust enrichment is not the only relief which may be granted in cases of mistaken improvements. Thus, the BGB contains particular provisions (994–1003) for improvements made by a possessor who is exposed to the *rei vindicatio*.[28] However, we will not deal with these provisions in any greater detail. They are of some significance for German law, but from the perspective of English law, which does not have similar provisions, they are of relatively little interest. Therefore, we will only focus on the issue as to when improvements constitute an enrichment for the purposes of the unjust enrichment claim.[29] Secondly, it should be noted that the subjective notion of enrichment is not the only device German law has developed in order to protect people from imposed enrichment. For instance, the courts have in some cases held that the erection of a building on another's premises amounts to an interference with the recipient's property rights, on the ground that the existence of the building restricted the freedom to use the land. In such cases, the recipient was held

---

[22] *Cf*, *eg*, Reichsgericht, 43 *Seufferts Archiv* n 262 where the Reichsgericht explicitly refers to D 6, 1, 38.

[23] *Cf*, *eg*, Klauser, 47–57.

[24] See, in particular, KH Gursky in *Staudinger*, BGB 951, n 43–45.

[25] See, *eg*, D Lieb in *Münchener Kommentar*, BGB 812, n 262; P Bassenge in *Palandt*, BGB 951, n 21; *Loewenheim*, 100–102; *von Rittberg*, 115; Klauser, 47-57. The subjective approach was judicially approved in Oberlandesgericht Stuttgart [1916] *Das Recht* n 1109; Oberlandesgericht Stuttgart [1972] *Baurecht* 388; Oberverwaltungsgericht Münster, 25 *Entscheidungen des Oberverwaltungsgerichts Nordrhein-Westfalen* 286, 294. Though not explicitly using the language of subjective enrichment, the Bundesgerichtshof also caters for the individuality of value; see *infra*, III (A)(2). *Cf* also §3.2 of the draft law of unjustified enrichment prepared by Professor König at the behest of the German Minister of Justice: "Whoever [. . .] spends anything on an object belonging to another, can claim restitution for his outlays from that other person, insofar as the latter is enriched as a result of that expenditure, *taking into account his own plans concerning his estate.*" (The translation is taken from R Zimmermann, "Unjust Enrichment: The Modern Civilian Approach", 15 (1995) OJLS 403, 428).

[26] It may well be that, under the Nieuw Burgerlijk Wetboek (enacted in 1992), Dutch law will take a similar path. For, in order to protect the recipient from imposed enrichment, the new code now grants the court discretionary power to deny a claim, where, despite an objective enrichment, restitution would place the recipient at an unfair disadvantage; see Book 3, art 120 (2); Book 3, art 121 (2), in conjunction with Book 6, art 212 (1), and the official explanation of these provisions in CJ van Zeben & JW du Pon, *Parlementaire geschiedenis van het Nieuwe Burgerlijk Wetboek*, vol III (Deventer, 1981), 452.

[27] *Cf Birks*, 109–132; *Goff & Jones*, 18-26; *Burrows*, 9–16.

[28] BGB 994 (1), 996 provide that the *bona fide* possessor is entitled to compensation for necessary expenditure and all improvements which raise the value of the improved asset. The decisive question then of course is how "value" is to be defined. There is much to be said for the view that exactly the same subjective valuation as in unjust enrichment should prevail; *cf* D Medicus in *Münchener Kommentar*, BGB 996, n 2 (with further references on this disputed issue).

[29] Nor will we consider the special statutory rights which English law provides for improvements made by business and agricultural tenants; *cf* Landlord and Tenant Act 1927, ss 1–17, Landlord and Tenant Act 1954, ss 47–50, and Agricultural Holdings Act 1986, ss 64–69.

entitled to defeat the improver's claim by insisting on the removal of the improvement.[30] However, the present essay will not deal with these special cases; rather it concentrates on the subjective interpretation of enrichment.

III. THE ROLE OF SUBJECTIVE BENEFIT IN GERMAN AND ENGLISH LAW

If the subjective approach were taken to its extreme, an improvement would only constitute an enrichment if the defendant actually requested the work to be done; in all other cases he would be able to resort to subjective devaluation. However, it appears that neither German nor English law is willing to accept the argument of subjective devaluation in such a radical way. Rather both systems look for its limitations and try to curb its excesses. In the English law of restitution, academics have deduced from the case-law two main tests to overcome subjective devaluation: (A) incontrovertible benefit and (B) free acceptance. As we will see, German law has restricted subjective devaluation in a similar way.

A. Incontrovertible benefit

The concept of incontrovertible benefit seeks to isolate objective benefits that are so obviously beneficial that no reasonable man would deny an enrichment.[31] The most obvious example is certainly the receipt of money. In cases of benefits in kind (such as improvements) the application of the concept is more problematic. Restitution scholars generally agree that it encompasses two situations which, borrowing Birks' terminology,[32] can be referred to as "anticipation of necessary expenditure" and "realisation in money". The exact boundaries of these categories, however, are still subject to debate.

1. Anticipation of necessary expenditure

This is the less complicated of the two categories. Where A provides a benefit which was necessary to B in the sense that he would have had to seek it himself, or would have sought it if he had not been deprived of the opportunity (as by absence or disability), no reasonable man would deny that B has been enriched by the amount which he himself would have had to lay out. The necessity of B's expenditure may arise from a legal obligation,[33] but it may also be a matter of factual compulsion.[34] While the existence of legal necessity is generally readily ascertainable, caution is required regarding merely factual necessities as they can fluctuate according to a person's tastes and circumstances. Moreover, a defendant will often have more latitude as to how and when he fulfils a factual necessity.[35]

Nevertheless, the courts have taken the view that a factual necessity does not have to be absolute. That is to say, a plaintiff can claim to have anticipated inevitable expenditure even though it cannot be said to be absolutely certain that the defendant would have incurred the

---

[30] See Bundesgerichtshof decisions *Lindenmaier & Möhring* BGB 1004 n 14; (1965) *Neue Juristische Wochenschrift* 816; (1966) *Wertpapier-Mitteilungen* 765-766. See also Oberlandesgericht Celle (1954) *Monatsschrift des Deutschen Rechts* 294, 295.

[31] Although originally the construct of academic lawyers trying to explain the cases, the concept of incontrovertible benefit has now found its way into the language of the courts; see *Proctor & Gamble Philippine Manufacturing Corp v Peter Cremer GmbH & Co (The Manila)* [1988] 3 All ER 843, 855; *Marston Construction Co Ltd v Kigass Ltd* (1989) 46 Build LR 109, 126.

[32] *Cf* Birks, 117–124.

[33] For an example involving improvements under a legal obligation, see *Gebhardt v Saunders* [1892] 2 QB 452 (the plaintiff, a tenant, carried out works to repair the plugged drains of the defendant's house, thereby discharging a legal obligation incumbent on the defendant).

[34] See, *eg*, *Craven-Ellis v Canons Ltd*, discussed *infra*, at n 37.

[35] *Cf* M McInnes, "Incontrovertible Benefit in the Supreme Court of Canada" (1994) 23 Can Bus LJ 122, 135.

expenditure anyhow. Thus, in the famous case of *Craven-Ellis v Canons Ltd*,[36] the Court of Appeal took the view that the services of a managing director were necessary to a commercial company, although, of course, a company is not bound by law, or obliged by nature, to provide for the active management of its affairs. So, by saying that a given expenditure was factually necessary, one excludes "unrealistic and fanciful" possibilities of a defendant doing without it.[37]

This relatively liberal definition of factual necessity may also serve to explain Lord Denning MR's famous judgment in *Greenwood v Bennett*. Bennett was a manager of a garage who had purchased a car which required some repair work before being put up for sale. He delivered the car to Searle, who had agreed to repair it. But, instead of doing so, Searle used the car for his own purposes, he crashed it and then sold it as a near-wreck to Harper. Harper, believing the car to be his, brought it back into good condition and sold it on. Finally, the police took possession of the car and took out an interpleader to establish who was entitled to it. The County Court judge held in favour of Bennett. On appeal, while acknowledging that Bennett had the legal title to the car, Harper claimed that he should receive at least some £226 for labour and materials used in the repair. His claim was successful. As discussed, Lord Denning MR did not attempt an analysis of the enrichment issue.[38] However, it is possible to explain his decision on the ground that Harper saved Bennett a factually inevitable expense.[39] For Bennett was a dealer in cars, and the repair of a car may be said to be a necessary expenditure for the purpose of a profitable re-sale. Indeed, the fact that Bennett had initially given the car to Searle in order to repair it shows that Bennett wanted the car repaired before selling it on. Under these circumstances, the possibility that Bennett would have left the car virtually wrecked can be excluded as unrealistic.

Turning to German law, we can see that it has developed along similar lines. Thus, in a case involving a tenant who had considerably improved the leased building, the *Oberlandesgericht Stuttgart* held: "The improvement of a thing entails an enrichment of the owner if [. . .] the owner would have effected, or would have had to effect, the improvement himself; in these cases the enrichment amounts to what the owner himself would have had to expend for the improvement."[41] In support of its view, the court referred to the *ius commune*, making an allusion to the famous fragment of Celsus[42]. Moreover, outside the general law of unjust enrichment (§§ 812–822), the BGB contains some scattered provisions that explicitly allow compensation for necessary expenditure.[42] The legislator explicitly justified these provisions on the ground that the anticipation of necessary expenses always constitutes an enrichment for the owner.[43]

As to the degree of inevitability, German law, like the common law, does not take too strict a view. It does not have to be completely certain that the owner would have incurred the same cost. It suffices if the expense was factually necessary to save the substance and the usefulness of the improved asset. The courts have even gone so far as to consider a change-over of a firm in order to keep up its profitability a necessary expenditure.[44] Some decisions, however, show greater

---

[36] [1936] 2 KB 403.
[37] *Birks*, 120. This was approved in the Australian case *Monks v Poynice Pty Ltd* 8 (1987) NSWLR 662, 665, *per* Young J. It remains to be seen how the courts will apply this test. Birks himself advocates a liberal approach, *ie* he does not insist on too high a degree of inevitability; *cf ibid*, 120–121.
[38] Nor did the other judges; for both Phillimore and Cairns LJJ based their judgments on other grounds than unjust enrichment.
[39] *Cf Birks*, 124; McKendrick in *Palmer & McKendrick*, 604-605.
[40] Oberlandesgericht Stuttgart (1916) *Das Recht* n 1109.
[41] *Supra*, nn 20–21.
[42] See for necessary expenses made by lessees, borrowers, depositees, and bona and mala fide possessors BGB 547 (1), 601 (1), 693, and 994.
[43] See the protocols of the second BGB commission, in B Mugdan (ed), *Die gesamten Materialien zum Bürgerlichen Gesetzbuch für das Deutsche Reich*, vol III (Berlin, 1899), 681.
[44] Reichsgericht, 117 *Entscheidungen des Reichsgerichts in Zivilsachen* (hereafter RGZ) 112, 115 (conversion of a restaurant to a hotel); 139 RGZ 353, 357–358 (switch from a spirit factory to the fabrication of screws, albeit only if the owner had planned to do the same).

reluctance. Thus, according to the *Bundesgerichtshof*, in a case resembling *Greenwood v Bennett*, repairs to make a car ready for sale cannot be regarded as necessary.[45] In contrast, minor repairs at the occasion of a routine check-up were held inevitable.[46] These cases show that the German courts still struggle to draw an exact and coherent line between necessary and unnecessary expenditure. However, the general principle, namely that in cases of inevitable expenses the owner can have no recourse to subjective devaluation, is beyond question.

2. Realisation in money

The other limb of the incontrovertible benefit test is more controversial. The basic idea, however, is far from difficult: if the recipient of a benefit in kind turns it into money he can no longer resort to subjective devaluation, since money is "the very measure of enrichment".[47]

Greenwood v Bennett, in this respect, is relatively easy to explain. For, as Birks points out,[48] counsel for Harper in the Court of Appeal stated that Bennett had in fact sold the car at its full improved value,[49] *ie* he had realised the value of Harper's input in money. However, what should have been the decision if Bennett easily could have sold the car, but had not yet done it? The answer to that question turns on the extent to which the law respects the value of freedom of choice. Birks suggests a strict view; he insists upon the *actual realisation* of a monetary benefit.[50] Goff and Jones, however, advocate a considerably more liberal approach and merely require that the defendant received a benefit which is *readily realisable* without detriment.[51] Burrows, ultimately, stakes a middle ground by arguing that an incontrovertible benefit is established once the plaintiff proves that he conferred a benefit from which the defendant is "reasonably certain" to realise a financial gain.[52]

There are difficulties with either view. The Birks view means that the restitutionary claim is postponed until the actual realisation of the benefit. This is certainly consistent with the idea of subjective devaluation, but, as Birks himself acknowledges,[53] it obviously meets considerable practical difficulties in the event of a long delay before realisation. For instance, wily defendants may be encouraged simply to wait before realising the benefit. In such cases, the improver would have to set spies on the defendant in order to observe whether or not he finally sells the improved asset. That is hardly practicable, let alone desirable. On the other hand, the problem with the Goff and Jones model is that they do not give a sufficient explanation as to why the defendant ought to be compelled to realise a merely realisable benefit if he does not have the least intention of doing so.[54] Moreover, the definition of what is to be considered as readily realisable does not always seem to be entirely convincing. Goff and Jones draw a distinction between land and chattels, with chattels being more readily realisable than land.[55] The reason given is that, unlike chattels, which are usually fungible and replaceable, land is typically unique; to require its sale will therefore often mean a severe hardship for the owner.[56] However, while this is true in many cases,

---

[45] Bundesgerichtshof, 5 *Entscheidungen des Bundesgerichtshofs in Zivilsachen* (hereafter "BGHZ") 337, 341. *Cf* also Reichsgericht 1930 *Juristische Wochenschrift* 2655, 2656.
[46] Oberlandesgericht Schleswig (1951) *Schleswig-Holsteinische Anzeigen* 32.
[47] *Birks*, 109.
[48] *Birks*, 124.
[49] [1973] 1 QB 195, 198.
[50] *Birks*, 121–124. *Cf* also *Mason & Carter*, # 215 *in fine*.
[51] *Goff & Jones*, 23, 175–176.
[52] *Burrows*, 9-10. See also *Maddaugh & McCamus*, 44.
[53] *Birks*, 124. *Cf* also the criticism by *Burrows*, 10; R Sutton, "What Should be Done for Mistaken Improvers?", ch 8 of *Finn*, 241, 255; and McInnes (1994) 23 Can Bus LJ 122, 136.
[54] They only state that, in their view, "the equities of [the improver's claim] are more appealing"; *Goff & Jones*, 176. But see for a possible explanation *infra*, text to n 77–86.
[55] *Goff & Jones*, 23, 175–176, and, more pointedly, 3rd ed (London, 1986), 147–148.
[56] The same applies to chattels which are unique. Consequently, *Goff & Jones* indicate that such chattels are often not readily realisable; *cf ibid*, 176, n 65.

one can also think of contrary examples. Take the case of an owner who had already evinced an intention to sell the improved land.[57] For him the realisation of the benefit does not cause any hardship at all. He should not therefore be allowed to obstruct the improver's claim by merely postponing the sale and by alleging that improvements to land were not readily realisable.

The Burrows approach, finally, also encounters considerable intricacies. True, it would provide a satisfactory solution in a situation like *Greenwood v Bennett*, irrespective of the fact that, incidentally, Bennett had already sold the car at the time of the Court of Appeal hearing. For it could be said to be "reasonably certain" that Bennett, being a dealer in cars, would sooner or later sell the improved vehicle. But apart from such cases it will nearly always be impossible to forecast the defendant's willingness to realise the benefit. Such a prognosis always entails a considerable degree of uncertainty. Moreover, even if the prognosis were reliable, the practical results would still not always be appealing. Take again the case of an owner who originally wanted to sell the asset, but now gives up his intention to do so, merely because he wants to escape the improver's claim. It is now certain that he will not realise the benefit. But should the law really respect such a change of intention?

There is an additional problem with all three of these views. Thus, at the date of trial, the benefit may be held neither likely to be realised nor readily realisable. But eventually the owner does realise it. Should the improver then be allowed to bring a second action? One is inclined to answer in the negative, for obvious practical reasons. However, a convincing explanation is yet to be given.

Although the differences of view between Birks, Goff and Jones, and Burrows are of considerable practical significance, the English courts have not yet resolved this conflict. True, there is an interesting *dictum* by Bowsher J in *Marston Construction Co Ltd v Kigass Ltd*[58] stating that His Honour was "not convinced" by the argument of Professor Birks; rather he thought that "in appropriate cases, the benefit may consist in a service which gives a realisable and not necessarily realised gain to the defendant . . ." On the facts of the case, however, it was not necessary to engage in such analysis. For a plaintiff need only resort to incontrovertible benefit when he cannot establish that the defendant requested the benefit, and in this case it was found that there had been an implied request. So, as McKendrick has emphasized,[59] Bowsher J's statement was only *obiter* and it cannot be taken to have resolved the position under English law.

Given this unsettled situation, let us now explore the German solutions in order to see whether they can be of any assistance in finding an appropriate test. As was mentioned above,[60] these solutions are not to be found explicitly laid down in the BGB; instead, we will have to rely on the relevant case law (which exclusively deals with improvements to land[61]) and the works of academics. It should be noted from the outset that what will be said is not always uncontroversial.[62] In a paper as brief as this, we can only provide a sketch of what currently is the predominant view in the German law of unjust enrichment.

---

[57] As McInnes (1994) 23 Can Bus LJ 122, 133 points out, such a situation might arise if the improver acted pursuant to an agreement with the owner for the sale of the latter's land which ultimately failed. An example is *Lee-Parker v Izzet (No 2)* [1972] 1 WLR 775 (Ch D) where a purchaser had effected considerable improvements before the contract of sale was held void for uncertainty. Goulding J seemed inclined to allow compensation in such a case; however, it was not necessary for him to decide this point because the vendor had a right to set off the reasonable value of the use of the land, which in this case exceeded the value of the improvements.
[58] (1989) 46 Build LR 109, 125–126.
[59] See McKendrick in *Palmer & McKendrick*, 606.
[60] *Supra,* text to nn 23–24.
[61] There is not a single reported case that deals with the problem of imposed enrichment in the context of improvements to chattels. The reason probably is that, in contrast with improvements to land, the value in dispute is relatively small. Thus, if at all, only lower courts will be concerned with such cases.
[62] Thus, as has been mentioned (*supra,* n 25), some authors still advocate an objective approach, *ie* they define enrichment irrespective of whether the value of the improvement is actually realised or at least readily realisable.

Let us begin with a straightforward case. As in English law, it is well-established that an improvement constitutes an enrichment when the owner has actually realised a financial gain by way of selling the improved asset.[63] The same was held to apply — once again with reference to the *ius commune* and Celsus — if the owner merely intended to sell.[64] In such cases, the enrichment consists of the surplus of the selling-price.[65]

Apart from that, the general rule (at least with regard to land) is that it is not incumbent on the owner to realise the increase in sales value *(Verkaufswert* or *Verkehrswert)*. However, this does not necessarily mean that the improver's claim for compensation will wholly fail, since the owner might still have to compensate for the rise in income-value *(Ertragswert)*.[66] This has become particularly relevant in cases that involve improvements to property which is held (or ready to be held) under tenancy. For such improvements often have the effect of enabling the owner to demand a higher rent from future tenants. The capitalised sum of this additional income, which, in times of inflation, is usually less than the rise in sales value,[67] is then held to be the owner's enrichment. A very clear example of this method of calculation is *Oberlandesgericht Stuttgart* (1972) *Baurecht* 388. In that case, the plaintiff had been asked by an architect to add a cellar to a house owned by the defendant. However, after the work had been completed, it turned out that the architect had acted without the defendant's authority. There being no valid contract, the plaintiff based his claim on unjust enrichment. He was denied recovery of the full increase in sales value which he had effected. But the court then went on to say that the cellar would probably raise the future rent 10 DM per month, *ie* 120 DM per year. This sum was then capitalised for the time-span for which an increase in rental value was to be expected.[68] On the facts, the court held that a period of 30 years would be appropriate. That capitalised amount was still considerably lower than the rise in selling value.

If, however, the improvement does not affect the *Ertragswert*, but could only be realised by way of sale, the improver's claim will fail. Such a case was dealt with by the *Oberverwaltungsgericht Münster*: the defendant, a public authority, had let sale-rooms to the plaintiff who effected large-scale installations and thereby enhanced the sales value of the premises. However, the *Ertragswert* remained unaffected, for local legislation had fixed the rent to a certain amount and thus prevented the defendant from demanding higher rents from future tenants. Accordingly, the court held that, despite an objective increase in sales value, the defendant was "subjektiv nicht bereichert" (not subjectively enriched).[69]

---

[63] See, for instance, Bundesgerichtshof (1987) *Neue Juristische Wochenschrift* 3001-3002: the improved building had subsequently been sold in a public auction. It was held that the defendant owners were enriched "so far as the improvement raised the proceeds of the auction".

[64] Oberlandesgericht Stuttgart (1916) *Das Recht* n 1109: "... wenn die Sache dem Eigentümer feil ist; dann besteht die Bereicherung in dem Mehr des erzielten oder zu erzielenden Kaufpreis." See also *Klauser*, 52-53, and *idem* (1965) *Neue Juristische Wochenschrift* 512, 516.

[65] See *supra*, nn 64–65.

[66] Some decisions rely on the notion of *Ertragswert* merely as a factor to calculate the *Verkehrswert*; eg 10 BGHZ 171, 180; 17 BGHZ 236, 240-241. However, as will be shown by the cases discussed in the text, there is a substantial difference between the two concepts; *cf* Klauser (1965) *Neue Juristische Wochenschrift* 513, 516; D König, "Ungerechtfertigte Bereicherung" in Bundesminister der Justiz (ed), *Gutachten und Vorschläge zur Überarbeitung des Schuldrechts*, vol II (Cologne, 1981), 1515, 1570.

[67] *Cf* Klauser *ibid*, 516; König, *ibid*, 1570.

[68] Instead of awarding a capitalised lump sum it would have been more consistent with the subjective approach if the court had granted an annuity as to the rise in rental value which is realised in each single month; *cf* W Pinger, *Funktion und dogmatische Einordnung des Eigentümer-Besitzer-Verhältnisses* (Munich, 1973), 129; *idem* (1972) *Monatsschrift des Deutschen Rechts* 187, 189. Nevertheless, for obvious practical reasons, most scholars share the court's preference for a lump sum; see Koller (1974) *Der Betrieb* 2385, 2389; *Klauser*, 53; G Feiler, *Aufgedrängte Bereicherung bei den Verwendungen des Mieters und Pächters* (Karlsruhe, 1968), 101, n 13.

[69] Oberverwaltungsgericht Münster, 25 *Entscheidungen des Oberverwaltungsgerichts Nordrhein-Westfalen* 286, 295.

The same applies if the owner would have to incur additional expenditure in order to put the improvement to profitable use. This was the case in 23 BGHZ 61:[70] the plaintiff leased from the defendant a piece of land for the purposes of cultivating agricultural products, and of breeding and keeping of small animals. The terms of the lease specified that the leaseholder was entitled to erect minor constructions on the premises and ought to be compensated for them after the expiry of the lease. Soon after the conclusion of the contract, however, the plaintiff erected a solid building which was not covered by the agreement. Again, there certainly was a rise in sales value, but the *Ertragswert* was doubtful. For the construction was tailored for the plaintiff's special purposes, and thus an additional expenditure of some 8,000 DM would have been necessary in order to convert it to living quarters that were ready to let. The *Bundesgerichtshof* held that under these circumstances the defendant ought not be forced to pay for the improvement. Instead, he was allowed to defeat the enrichment claim, albeit only by granting the improver the right to remove the building. We will return to this right of removal at a later stage.[71] In the present context, it is only important to note that the *Bundesgerichtshof* dismissed the improver's claim for compensation in money.[72]

So far, one could argue, that German law confirms the Burrows approach of incontrovertible benefit. It allows compensation if the owner has actually realised or is at least likely to realise a financial gain, be it by way of sale or (not mentioned by Burrows) by way of lease. But German law goes beyond that. Both courts[73] and academics[74] accept that, as in the Goff and Jones model, the defendant ought not to be protected if the benefit is reasonably realisable. Thus, in the case mentioned above, the *Obverwaltungsgericht Münster* clearly worked on the assumption that the principle of good faith (BGB 242) would debar the argument from subjective devaluation if the defendant could easily realise the benefit.[75] The decision of the *Bundesgerichtshof*, arguably, has to be understood in the very same way.[76] In both decisions, however, this restriction of subjective devaluation did not take effect because, as we have seen, the realisation of the benefit would have required the sale of the premises or the completion of additional improvements; neither, it was held, could reasonably be expected from the defendants.

Apart from these cases, the courts have not yet given any exact criteria as to when a benefit can be considered reasonably realisable. Nor have they attempted to explain why the owner should ever be compelled to realise a merely realisable benefit. The allusion to a principle as broad as good faith (BGB 242) hardly suffices to accomplish this task.

However, these issues have been extensively dealt with by academics. As has been said,[77] they unanimously agree that, in some circumstances, the owner should be compelled to realise the benefit. It is submitted that they have found a very convincing argument for this contention.[78] It draws on the coherence between the law of unjust enrichment and the law of damages. In the law

---

[70] For an English translation of this decision see Markesinis, Lorenz & Dannemann, case 141.
[71] *Cf infra*, III (B) and V.
[72] Unfortunately however, the court did not explicitly apply the subjective definition of enrichment, but drew a rather strained analogy with BGB 1001, s 2, a provision that allows to defeat the improver's claim by giving up the improved asset. The court extended this to the case in which solely the improvement is given up. This analogy is now almost universally rejected (see *eg Reimer*, 166–167; *Reuter & Martinek*, 546), and so today the case appears to be better explained in terms of the subjective approach to enrichment. Note also that in English law it would have been difficult for the plaintiff to find even a ground for restitution since, apparently, his improvement was not based on mistake, nor was it freely accepted by the defendant.
[73] See *infra*, nn 76–77.
[74] Lieb in *Münchener Kommentar*, BGB 812, n 264; *von Rittberg*, 116; *Klauser*, 52–53; *Koller* (1974) *Der Betrieb* 2385, 2458.
[75] Oberverwaltungsgericht Münster 25 *Entscheidungen des Oberverwaltungsgerichts Nordrhein-Westfalen* 286, 294.
[76] It also invokes the principle of good faith, and it stresses the fact that the realisation was difficult in the circumstances; see 23 BGHZ 61, 64–65.
[77] *Supra*, n 75.
[78] On the following, see Koller (1974) *Der Betrieb* 2385, 2458; *Reimer*, 97-98. *Cf* also *Larenz & Canaris*, 291.

of damages, it is well established that the injured party has to take all reasonable steps to mitigate its loss.[79] This can mean a severe restriction of the victim's freedom of choice. If, for instance, a personal injury renders the victim unable to pursue its prior profession it might even be obliged to change its occupation and residence.[80] And, where property has been damaged and the cost of repairs would considerably exceed the value of the property, the victim must mitigate the loss by replacing the property.[81] Now, if such a duty is incumbent on the owner even in view of a grossly negligent tortfeasor, then, *a maiore ad minus*, the owner's freedom of choice must suffer the same restrictions *vis-à-vis* an innocent improver.

There is an alternative way of putting this argument.[82] Enrichment and damage are closely related; the one is the opposite of the other. An enrichment claim is concerned with disgorging a gain, while a claim for (compensatory) damages seeks to make up for a loss. Thus both try, though from different angles, to restore the affected party to its prior position. But they must not go further than that. That is to say that a claim for (compensatory) damages is confined to the loss suffered; to exceed this limit would entail enriching the injured party. *Vice versa*, an enrichment claim may not exceed the factual gain; it must not leave the recipient worse off than he was before the transfer of the benefit. That is, it must not leave the recipient with a loss. If that is correct, the interdependence between enrichment and damage becomes apparent: the plaintiff in unjust enrichment can recover just as much as he can skim off without causing a loss to the defendant. Hence, in the present case, we have to ask whether the defendant would suffer a loss if he had to pay for an unwanted improvement. The answer depends on the rules on mitigation. They tell us that there is no relevant loss if the owner could easily avert his loss by selling and replacing the improved property. Accordingly, there is then no obstacle to acknowledging an enrichment.

Drawing on this correlation between damage and enrichment, the latest monograph on imposed enrichment suggests that the criteria relevant for establishing a duty to mitigate ought to be transferred to the law of unjust enrichment.[83] Among these criteria, the fungibility of the asset is, as in the *Goff & Jones* model, particularly important. Thus, assets which are not unique but easily replaceable ought to be replaced. If the owner refuses to do so, he should bear the cost of such extravagance. However, it should be taken into account whether the property is of some special sentimental value for the owner.[84] A further criterion relates to the amount of the increase in value that could be realised. The higher it is, it is argued, the more reasonable it is to expect the owner to realise it, either by way of sale or — as in cases of non-replaceable assets such as land — by way of lease.[85] Finally, since German law does not only provide a claim for the innocent improver, the degree of fault is considered to be relevant: the higher the degree of fault, the less the owner should be required to restrict his freedom of choice.[86]

As has been mentioned, the courts have not yet explicitly relied on these criteria. However, they may serve to fill out the vague notions of good faith and reasonably realisable benefit which have been used by the courts.

Before we sum up the position in German law a special question remains to be dealt with. How does German law cope with the problem of a realisation after the date of trial? Consider a case like 23 BGHZ 61. At the date of trial, the benefit is held not to be reasonably realisable. But then the owner does incur additional expenditure to convert the building into living quarters and

---

[79] *Cf* BGB 254 (2) s 1, 2nd alt. On the equivalent position in English law, see *infra*, text to n 95.
[80] H Heinrichs in *Palandt*, BGB 254, n 37.
[81] If he (or she) chooses to repair the property none the less, only the cost of a replacement can be recovered; Heinrichs in *Palandt*, BGB 251, n 25 *in fine*.
[82] *Cf Reimer*, 97–98.
[83] *Reimer*, 97–98, 100–118.
[84] *Reimer*, 107–109. *Cf* also (1974) Koller *Der Betrieb* 2385, 2458, and, for a different view, *von Rittberg*, 125.
[85] *Reimer*, 100–106.
[86] *Reimer*, 109–112.

lets them for a highly profitable fee. Is the improver now entitled to that gain? So far, there is no case law in this point. However, those scholars who have discussed the problem at some length agree that German law does not allow a second trial.[87] Again, one tries to draw an analogy with the law of damages. There, it is established as a matter of *res judicata* that the tortfeasor cannot take advantage of the fact that, after the end of the trial, the injured party has taken more steps in mitigation than were originally required.[88] *Mutatis mutandis*, it is said that the plaintiff in unjust enrichment cannot rely on the fact that, after the end of the trial, the defendant has realised a benefit although he was not compelled to do so.[89]

The conclusion up to this point is that German law does not insist on the actual realisation of a financial benefit at the date of trial. Rather it is held sufficient that the owner can reasonably be expected to realise such gain. We can deduce from the case law that the owner of land will in general not be expected to sell his land. Thus, he does not have to compensate for the rise in market value; but he might still be liable so far as the improvement has raised his current income (*eg* the rent he receives from letting the improved asset). Furthermore, we have noted that, in trying to find criteria as to when a benefit is reasonably realisable, scholars have drawn an analogy with the rules on mitigation of damages. And finally, it has been shown that German law arguably does not allow a new trial if an unexpected realisation occurs after the date of the first trial.

Do these comparative observations bear any immediate relevance for the position that should be taken in English law? One should certainly be careful not to rush to conclusions. German law has a different background; it has always been more willing to grant improvers relief, and it is generally less reluctant to award claims for uninvited intervention.[90] Nevertheless, it seems that at least two important points should be kept in mind in respect of the future discussion of English law.

The first concerns the possible ways of realisation in money. Hitherto, one has principally thought of realisation by way of sale. But German law shows us that it can equally occur by way of lease, that is by realising the enhanced income value. The case of the *Oberlandesgericht Stuttgart*,[91] however, also illustrates that this rise in income is often difficult to assess. Moreover, it is delicate to grant a lump sum for the expected proceeds since the owner might not have sufficient disposable funds to pay in advance. On the other hand, an annuity as to the extra income that is realised each month is not very practicable.[92] The concept of realisation by way of lease is thus certainly far from unproblematic. However, it should not be totally dismissed; rather, it deserves careful consideration.[93]

The second point refers to the analogy which is drawn with the law of damages and the rules on mitigation. It is as well established in English law, as it is in German law, that the aggrieved party must take all reasonable steps to mitigate the loss which he has sustained. Take again the case of a damaged car. If the cost of repairs exceeds its value, just as in German law, the owner is obliged to replace it, even though he never voluntarily chose to do so.[94] Hence the argument

---

[87] Lieb in *Münchener Kommentar*, BGB 812, n 264; *Reimer*, 98–99. But *cf* also *Reuter & Martinek*, 574-575.
[88] Zivilprozeßordnung (ZPO) 323 only provides for an exception of *res judicata* when damages are awarded as an annuity.
[89] *Cf Reimer*, 98–99.
[90] Thus German law, as all civilian systems, grants claims based on *negotiorum gestio* (BGB 677–687), a principle that has not — at least not generally — been recognized in this country. A different attitude towards uninvited intervention can also be found in penal law: the failure to intervene in cases of necessity can even entail criminal liability under the German penal code (StGB 323c), whereas there is no such liability in English law.
[91] *Supra*, text to nn 68–69.
[92] Most German lawyers therefore prefer the lump sum model; see *supra*, n 69.
[93] Indeed, English law does not seem to be entirely antipathetic to considering a rise in letting value an enrichment; *cf* the statutory rights of business and agricultural tenants to recover the value of their improvements under the Landlord and Tenant Act 1927, s 1 (1).
[94] *Darbishire v Warran* [1963] 1 WLR 1067. It is different when the car is unique; *infra*, n 96.

that we have found in German law also applies to English law: if the law imposes a duty to confine one's freedom of choice in view of a negligent tortfeasor, it must all the more do so *vis-à-vis* an innocent improver. That is to say that the owner must take all reasonable steps to realise the value of the improvement. If he fails to do so he has only himself to blame.

As a consequence, it is submitted that Goff and Jones are right in holding that the owner should not be allowed to rely on subjective devaluation if he does not realise a benefit which is readily realisable without detriment. It is also submitted that the line drawn by Goff and Jones between replaceable and irreplaceable assets (such as land or unique chattels) is appealing in principle, even more so as the rules on mitigation draw exactly the same line.[95] However, one might add that, in special circumstances, it should be possible to deviate from this line. Thus, as in Germany, an irreplaceable asset should nevertheless be held readily realisable if the owner had already evinced an intention to sell it.[96]

It remains to be seen whether the courts will adopt this test. The *dictum* of Bowsher J in *Marston Construction Co Ltd v Kigass Ltd*[97] at least indicates a certain willingness to do so. As a matter of consistency with the rules on mitigation, it is to be hoped that others will follow his example.

A final remark shall be made with regard to the problem of realisation after the date of trial. Again, one could make use of the parallel with the law of damages. There is little doubt, at least so far as damages are awarded as a lump sum, that English law would not allow a new trial if the aggrieved, after the end of the first trial, takes more steps in mitigation than were originally required of him. The same should apply if the recipient of a benefit, after the end of the trial, realises the benefit, even though he could not reasonably be required to do so.

B. Free acceptance

To establish an incontrovertible benefit, it is argued, is not the only way to show that the recipient of an unrequested benefit in kind is enriched. Rather, it appears that an enrichment can also be established by proving that the benefit was "freely accepted". According to Birks, a free acceptance occurs "where a recipient knows that a benefit is offered non-gratuitously and where he, having the opportunity to reject, elects to accept."[98] In such circumstances, the recipient shall not be able to resort to subjective devaluation; for, it is said, if he did not want to have the work done, he should have said so.

However, the concept of free acceptance has come under attack.[99] Most notably, Burrows has argued that it is not clearly established by authority and is unwarranted in principle.[100] In his view, free acceptance "undermines respect for the individuality of values because it is a rational indication of nothing more than indifference to the objective benefit being rendered."[101] For instance, if the owner stands by watching someone clean his car, his mere acquiescence, according to Burrows, does not suffice to show that he values the service; it is at best a sign of indifference. As a consequence, Burrows insists on a positive act of bargaining for the benefit rather than to be satisfied with mere acquiescence. The same argument is even more emphatically made by

---

[95] Thus it was held in *O'Grady v Westminster Scaffolding Ltd* [1962] 2 Lloyd's Rep 238 that the owner of a *unique* car could recover the full cost of repairs although it considerably exceeded the market value of the car. That is to say that the owner was under no obligation to mitigate the damage by selling the car and buying a replacement.
[96] *Cf* McInnes 23 (1994) Can Bus LJ 122, 132–133.
[97] *Supra*, n 59.
[98] Birks, 264. *Cf* also *Goff & Jones*, 19, who do not insist on actual knowledge, but merely require that the recipient, as a reasonable man, *should have known* that the benefit was conferred non-gratuitously.
[99] The attacks refer both to free acceptance as a factor establishing enrichment and to free acceptance as a ground for restitution ("unjust factor"). This paper is only concerned with the former.
[100] A Burrows, "Free Acceptance and the Law of Restitution" (1988) 104 LQR 576–599, and *Burrows*, 12–14.
[101] *Burrows*, 12.

Garner. Stressing the paramount importance of freedom of choice, he argues that an enrichment exists only if the defendant manifested a positive desire to receive the benefit in question and was willing to pay for it as a "present priority".[102]

Responding to those criticisms, the proponents of the concept have admitted that free acceptance does indeed not necessarily indicate that the owner subjectively values the benefit in question. Rather, it is meant to settle the enrichment issue by interposing an obstacle to the argument of subjective devaluation, with the effect that the freely accepting recipient must acknowledge the objective valuation of the benefit. For, indifferent or not, a freely accepting party would act unconscientiously if he (or she) subsequently appealed to the subjectivity of value.[103]

Again, the English courts have not yet clearly resolved this conflict. It was noted in *Marston Construction Co Ltd v Kigass Ltd*, but on the facts Bowsher J found an actual request and not just a mere acceptance, and therefore it was not necessary for him to decide on this "interesting debate".[104] Apart from that case, there is still no single English decision that explicitly uses the language of free acceptance.[105] Thus at present, although many cases seem explicable as an intuitive application of free acceptance, the issue still has to be regarded as unsettled.

However, even assuming for the moment that free acceptance is sufficient to establish an enrichment, as McKendrick has pointed out, it is far from clear whether it will have much of an impact in the case of the mistaken improver.[106] For the owner will generally not have an opportunity to reject the work before it is done; and after that, it has been argued, the benefit can no longer be freely accepted.[107] This is uncontroversial at least as long as the improvement cannot be restored in any way, as is the case when the improver puts fertiliser on the owner's field or paints his house. Having been performed, the work's acceptance is no longer free, but forced, as is clearly expressed in Pollock CB's famous words: "One cleans another's shoes; what can the other do but put them on?"[108]

In contrast, if the improvement can still be detached from the improved property, it seems possible to argue that a free acceptance may still occur after the work has been done. Indeed, it has been suggested by Sutton, that in such cases, the owner continues to have an opportunity to reject in that he has the power to allow the improver to remove the improvement in case he does not regard it as beneficial.[109] If he choses not to take this opportunity, *ie* if he refuses the removal, then according to Sutton he thereby freely accepts the benefit and can no longer resort to subjective devaluation. We will return to this view when discussing the relevant German cases. However, in relation to English law, it has been said that there is no authority to support Sutton's argument,[110] convincing as it may be as a matter of principle. On the contrary, *Leigh v Dickeson*[111] stands for the proposition that the opportunity to reject cannot last beyond the moment that the benefit is conferred. In that case, the improver's claim was dismissed on the

---

[102] M Garner, "The Role of Subjective Benefit in the Law of Unjust Enrichment" (1990) 10 OJLS 42, esp 43–44, 48-52. Free acceptance as a factor establishing enrichment is further criticised by *Beatson*, 21–44. But his criticism merely seeks to exclude free acceptance of "pure" services, *ie* services which leave no relevant end-product; it does not apply to improvements.

[103] Birks, in *Burrows, Essays*, 105, at 128–129; and *cf Goff & Jones*, 19.

[104] (1989) 46 Build LR 109, 124–125.

[105] Other common law jurisdictions, however, have expressly applied the concept; see, *eg*, the New Zealand case *Van den Berg v Giles* [1979] 2 NZLR 111, and the Australian cases *Brenner v First Artists' Management Pty Ltd* [1993] 2 VR 221, 257–259, and *Angelopoulos & Ditara Pty Ltd v Sabatino & Spiniello* (1995) 65 SASR 1 (S Aus Full Ct); noted M Bryan [1996] LMCLQ 377; M McInnes, "Free Acceptance in the Australian Law of Restitution" (1996) 24 Aust Bus LJ 238).

[106] *Palmer & McKendrick*, 603–604.

[107] *Cf* McKendrick in *Palmer & McKendrick*, 604; *Birks*, 280–281.

[108] *Taylor v Laird* (1856) 25 LJEx 329, 332.

[109] Sutton in *Finn*, 252–253.

[110] McKendrick, in *Palmer & McKendrick*, 604.

[111] (1884) 15 QBD 60.

ground that the defendant co-owner, who had no knowledge of the repairs and improvements until the work was done, did not have "an option to decline or adopt",[112] *ie* no opportunity to reject. In so holding, the court did not consider as relevant whether or not the improvements were still removeable.

If one accepts that free acceptance cannot occur after the affixation of the improvement, it is obvious that the doctrine will rarely provide relief to improvers. What remains are cases where the owner knows that the improver will confer the benefit under a mistake or misprediction, but abstains from setting him right. As is well known, equity has indeed granted relief in such cases under the "doctrine of acquiescence".[113] Another case in equity which is suggested to be caught by the principle of free acceptance is *Hussey v Palmer*.[114] A mother-in-law spent money on an extension of her son-in-law's house in the expectation of being able to live there indefinitively. After she had been living in the house for fifteen months, the arrangement broke down. The Court of Appeal held that she was entitled to recover her input. Indeed, this result may be explicable in terms of free acceptance.[115] But it certainly marks a borderline case. For, although he knew that she effected the improvements non-gratuitously, and although he accepted the work on that basis, he did not expect to pay for it. Instead, all he was supposed to do was to let her live in the house. There was thus no positive indication that he valued the improvement in money.[116] But it may be possible to argue that, in the circumstances, it was unconscionable for him to rely on subjective devaluation. For they had both taken the risk of a breakdown of the arrangement, he just as much as her, and there was thus no reason why the material consequences of such breakdown should be suffered only by her.[117]

But let us now turn to German law. There, at least with regard to improvements,[118] cases of free acceptance have been less discussed than in English law. Nevertheless, the position of German law seems to be quite clear: where common lawyers would recognize a free acceptance, German law will also debar subjective devaluation.

Let us start with the case where the owner knows of the improvement *before* the work is done, but refrains from rejecting it. The case law on this issue is relatively scant. All one can find is a line of cases which resemble the *Hussey v Palmer* situation. Thus, in 44 BGHZ 321, the plaintiff had leased a piece of land from his aunt and had paid the legal costs for a will in which the aunt bequeathed this land to the plaintiff. In anticipation of the inheritance, he erected a building on the premises. But the aunt eventually changed her mind and appointed another heir. When this turned out after her death, the plaintiff successfully sued the estate in unjust enrichment. For the aunt, the *Bundesgerichtshof* held, knew perfectly well that the work was done under the presupposition that the plaintiff would become her heir. If she did not want to accept the work in these circumstances, the court continued, she should have said so.[119] Subsequent decisions of the *Bundesgerichtshof* have affirmed this view on similar facts;[120] and it has also found support in

---

[112] *Ibid*, 64–65.
[113] *Cf* the cases descending from *Ramsden v Dyson* (1866) LR 1 HL 83, and *Willmott v Barber* (1880) 15 ChD 96. It has, however, been doubted whether the doctrine of acquiescence is really to be explained as awarding a restitutionary claim. For, at least in some circumstances, it extends to the fulfilment of expectations and thus exceeds restitution. *Cf Birks*, 277–279, 290–293.
[114] [1972] 1 WLR 1286.
[115] *Cf Birks*, 285–286.
[116] Garner, therefore, denies an enrichment and treats the case as being "anomalous": (1990) 10 OJLS 42, 50.
[117] *Birks*, 285–286. On the other hand, the result in *Hussey v Palmer* of course means that the consequences are only suffered by the son-in-law which seems equally problematic. German law, however, has adopted the same solution; see the subsequent paragraphs.
[118] But see for a much debated case of pure services BGH (1971) *Neue Juristische Wochenschrift* 609, and *Markesinis, Lorenz & Dannemann*, 721.
[119] 44 BGHZ 321, at 323.
[120] BGH (1970) *Neue Juristische Wochenschrift* 136; 108 BGHZ 256, 265–266.

academic writings.[121] If the owner abstains from rejecting the work before it is done, it is argued, it would be a *venire contra factum proprium* (and hence contrary to good faith) if he subsequently relied on subjective devaluation.[122] This, it may be noted, seems to be perfectly in line with the way free acceptance is nowadays understood in this country: it does not necessarily mean that the recipient indeed values the benefit in question; rather its role merely lies in precluding the subjective devaluation of objective benefits. In other words, the issue is not one of logic, but rather one of fairness.[123]

Even more interesting, from an English viewpoint, may be the way German law handles cases of acceptance *after* the work has been done. We have seen that, if the improvement cannot be restored in any way, a free acceptance can no longer occur. Yet we have also seen that doubts have been raised in English law whether this should equally apply where the removal of the improvement is still feasible without injury. 23 BGHZ 61[124] indeed affirms these doubts. In that case, it will be recalled, the *Bundesgerichtshof* held that the owner was entitled to subjective devaluation. But this was explicitly made subject to the condition that he must grant consent to the removal of the building that the improver had erected. If he had refused to do so, subjective devaluation would have been barred. That is to say that the *Bundesgerichtshof* took exactly the same view as the one that Sutton has suggested for English law. The owner must choose either of two ways. He can either grant consent to the removal of the improvement; in such a case, he is entitled to subjective devaluation. Alternatively, he can keep the improvement, in which case he has to pay for it.[125]

The logic of this approach indeed appears to be compelling. For, if the owner does not value the benefit in question, there is no reason why he should not give it up. *Vice versa,* if he refuses to give it up this shows that he does value the benefit. It is to be repeated, however, that this only applies where the improvement is removeable without causing an irreparable damage to the improved asset.

In conclusion, whereas the common law would acknowledge a free acceptance, German law equally debars the argument from subjective devaluation. This can be taken as affirming the principal justification of free acceptance as a factor establishing enrichment. Moreover, German law even supports the wider view that, in cases of removable improvements, a free acceptance may still occur after the improvement has been affixed to the principal asset. There is not yet any English authority to share this view. But, as a matter of principle, there seems to be no reason why the owner should be allowed to refuse the removal and at the same time allege that the improvements are of no value to him.

IV. ENRICHMENT AND IMPOVERISHMENT

If the plaintiff has overcome the defendant's argument of subjective devaluation by relying on incontrovertible benefit or (possibly) free acceptance, the question arises as to the exact measure of the enrichment. In particular, it has to be defined whether or not the amount of expenditure incurred constitutes a ceiling for the enrichment claim. Suppose a case where improvements at a cost of 100, lead to a rise in market value of 150, and this enhancement is then realised by way of sale. What is the appropriate measure for the enrichment claim in such a case, 100 or 150?

---

[121] *Cf*, in particular, *Beissner*, 86–87. The criticisms that 44 BGHZ 321 has provoked are on an unrelated point; *cf Beissner*, 82–84; *Markesinis, Lorenz & Dannemann*, 752.
[122] *Beissner*, 86–87.
[123] *Cf* M McInnes, "The Structure and Challenges of Unjust Enrichment", ch 2 of *McInnes*, 17, 25.
[124] *Supra,* n 70.
[125] For support of this view see Bassenge in *Palandt*, BGB 951, n 20, and, in particular, HH Jakobs, "Die Begrenzung des Verwendungsersatzes" (1967) 167 *Archiv für die civilistische Praxis* 350, 376–378.

English courts have not yet openly addressed this issue. True, at first sight, *Greenwood v Bennett* appears to decide the issue in favour of a general "expenditure ceiling". For Harper had improved the value by more than £300,[126] but was allowed to recover only the £226 he had expended. However, a closer look shows that Harper himself had confined his claim to that amount, and a further claim to skim off Bennett's gain was never ventilated in the proceedings. Accordingly, *Greenwood* cannot be taken to contain any authoritative statement on the present issue and thus, again, the matter has to be regarded as unsettled.

One could of course argue that, irrespective of whether the enrichment is 100 or 150, the second requirement of the restitutionary claim, namely that the benefit must have been "at the expense of" the plaintiff, necessarily restricted the claim to the expenditure incurred, *ie* to 100.[127] However, it appears that this is not how the phrase "at the expense of" has been interpreted by the courts in recent times. The role of that phrase, as it seems to be understood today, is merely to identify the plaintiff. That is, to make sure that the enrichment must have come from the plaintiff and not from a third party. It does not mean that only the plaintiff's loss can be recovered.[128]

If that is correct, there should be no principal obstacle to granting the improver a claim which exceeds the expenses he has incurred. Indeed, this is exactly what has been held in Germany by the *Bundesgerichtshof*.[129] Unjust enrichment, it is argued, is *Bereicherungsrecht,* not *Entreicherungsrecht* (enrichment law, not impoverishment law).[130]

However, one should not rush to the conclusion that in our example the enrichment is necessarily 150 as, unfortunately, the *Bundesgerichtshof* seems to suggest. Take the case where the owner could have obtained the same lucrative improvement at a price of 100. If he were held liable to pay for the full rise in value (150) this would mean to neglect the fact that, at the same time as he is enriched, he has also been deprived of the possibility of effecting the same profitable improvement for only 100. The enrichment in such a case should therefore be 100, not 150. Generally speaking, it seems that the enrichment cannot exceed the amount of expenses which the owner would have incurred if he had effected the improvement himself. However, this ceiling refers to the hypothetical expenditure of the defendant, and it should be emphasised that this is not tantamount to saying that the enrichment claim is confined to the plaintiff's loss. Suppose, for instance, the plaintiff has merely expended 100 whereas the defendant would have had to pay 150 to effect the same improvement. In such a case, the enrichment claim can amount to 150, irrespective of the fact that the plaintiff has merely lost 100.

V. CONSEQUENCES OF SUBJECTIVE DEVALUATION

Let us finally turn to the inverse case, *ie* where the improver has *not* overcome the defendant's argument of subjective devaluation. In such a case, no restitutionary claim will lie to compensate for the improvements in money. But as we have seen, German law makes this subject to the con-

---

[126] Harper obtained the car when it was worth only £75, and the improvements effected by him enabled Bennett to sell the car for £400.

[127] *Cf* McInnes in *McInnes*, 17, 32-33, n 98.

[128] See *Kleinwort Benson Ltd v Birmingham City Council* [1997] QB 380, 392-394, *per* Evans LJ; and the Australian case *Commissioner of State Revenue (Vict) v Royal Insurance Australia Ltd* (1994) 182 CLR 51, 73-74, *per* Mason CJ.

[129] 17 BGHZ 236, 239; BGH (1966) *Der Betrieb* 262. These decisions have been criticised by a number of academics; *cf eg* Lieb in *Münchener Kommentar*, BGB 812, n 265; Klauser (1965) *Neue Juristische Wochenschrift* 513, 516–517; but also see *Larenz & Canaris*, 189–190. However, the criticisms do not refer to the court's unjust enrichment analysis, but advocate the "expenditure ceiling" solely as a matter of consistency with other areas of German law (namely the special claims of the owner/possessor model, BGB 994–1003, and *negotiorum gestio*, BGB 683, 670, where the expenditure ceiling is explicitly laid down in the code). *Cf* also the Celsus fragment, *supra*, nn 20-21 (in favour of an expenditure ceiling).

[130] *Cf, eg, Larenz & Canaris,* 128.

dition that the defendant must at least grant consent to the removal of the affixed goods. True, this right of removal is confined to those cases where the detachment is feasible without causing irreparable damage to the improved asset. Moreover, even if the removal is possible without injury, it will often be unattractive from an economic point of view; for the cost of the detachment (which has to be borne by the improver[131]) will frequently exceed the value of the removed goods. The practical value of the right of removal, then, is limited. Nevertheless, at least in some cases, it will ease the plight of improvers who are met with subjective devaluation in German law.

We have seen that Sutton has suggested an identical solution for English law. In his view, the defendant can only avoid free acceptance if he allows the removal of the improvement. However, Sutton linked this with the assumption that "some limited form of property right" remains with the improver.[132] It would go beyond the scope of this paper to evaluate this assumption. Nevertheless, it should be noted that the German right of removal is of a different nature. It does not have any proprietary basis, for it is clear that in 23 BGHZ 61 the defendant had become the absolute owner of the building.[133] The German right of removal is thus better perceived as a personal right arising from unjust enrichment. It is, in a way, a form of restitution in kind where, due to the defendant's subjective devaluation, restitution in money is not available.

VI. CONCLUSION

A careful analysis of the enrichment issue is the key to a proper understanding of the improver's restitutionary rights. In resolving this issue, the law must balance the improver's right to a remedy against the potential unfairness of requiring an owner to bear the cost of an unwanted improvement. It appears that the emerging English law of restitution does not give absolute priority to either of these interests. Rather it seeks to steer a middle course: it protects the owner's freedom of choice, but at the same time it is not willing to prejudice the improver according to mere eccentricities of the owner. The result is a principally subjective approach to enrichment, but one that curbs the excesses of pure subjectivity.

We have seen that a similar approach can be found in the German law of unjust enrichment. There, the predominant view also accepts the argument of subjective devaluation, but in some circumstances precludes the recipient from relying on that argument. This appears to be the case, if (i) the improver has saved the owner a necessary expense, (ii) the rise in sales (or letting) value of the improved asset has been realised or is reasonably realisable, or (iii) the owner refuses to allow the removal of the goods which the improver has affixed to the principal asset. It is to be noted that these exceptions from subjective devaluation have also found some support in English law. While the first seems to be generally accepted, the second has been put forward by Goff and Jones, and the third by Sutton. It may therefore not be beyond the realm of possibility that the English law of restitution will eventually develop along similar lines as its German counterpart.

Be that as it may, the subjective approach to enrichment undoubtedly raises very difficult issues. But that should not lead to the conclusion that it is misconceived as a whole and that an objective approach ought to be preferred. Rather, such difficulties seem to be, as one German court put it,[134] in the "very nature of things" when one seeks to reconcile the colliding interests. Indeed, it would even appear naive to believe that there was a straightforward solution of a case which has lain on our consciences for so long.

---

[131] *Cf* BGB 258 (1). Accordingly, 23 BGHZ 61 merely requires the defendant to grant consent to the removal; he does not have to effect the removal himself.
[132] Sutton in *Finn*, 253 and 266-282.
[133] See BGB 946, 94 (the German equivalent of "*quicquid plantatur solo, solo cedit*") and 23 BGHZ 61, 62.
[134] Oberlandesgericht Stuttgart (1916) *Das Recht* n 1109.

COMMENT

Restitution and the Conflict of Laws in the House of Lords

(Kleinwort Benson v Glasgow City Council)

Andrew Dickinson*

The decision of the House of Lords in *Kleinwort Benson v Glasgow City Council*[1] brought an end to a jurisdictional dispute lasting six years. The decision by a majority (3-2)[2] that the English courts did not have jurisdiction to entertain the claim by Kleinwort Benson (the "Bank") to recover sums paid by it to Glasgow City Council (the "Council") means that the Bank must now pursue its claim in the courts of Scotland. Issues of importance to students of the law of restitution and of the conflict of laws will now fall to be considered (if necessary) by those courts.[3] There is much, however, to reflect upon in the speeches of the majority (which differ in important respects) and in the dissenting speech of Lord Nicholls. In particular, the case seems likely to provoke rather than end discussion (and litigation) about the extent to which the provisions of the Brussels and Lugano Conventions[4] confer jurisdiction upon the courts of Contracting States in respect of proceedings relating to ineffective and abandoned contracts, claims for restitution of benefits conferred in connection with such "contracts" and, indeed, restitution claims generally.

Factual background and course of the proceedings

In September 1982, the Bank entered into seven interest rate swap transactions with the Council. Between March 1983 and September 1987 the Bank made payments to the Council totalling some £807,230. The Council made payments to the Bank totalling £69,152. All five transactions had run their course[5] when, in July 1988, doubts were expressed by the Audit Commission upon the validity of swap transactions entered into by English local authorities. In 1991 the House of Lords held that such transactions were, indeed, beyond the powers conferred upon local authorities by legislation and were therefore void.[6] That conclusion was later echoed by the Court of Session in relation to Scottish local authorities.[7]

On 6 September 1991 the Bank issued proceedings in the English High Court claiming restitution of £807,230 (together with interest). The writ was served upon the Council in Scotland without leave of the court,[8] the Bank asserting that the English courts had jurisdiction under the provisions of the modified version of the Brussels Convention which applies to determine juris-

---
* St Edmund Hall, Oxford.
[1] [1997] 3 WLR 923; noted A Briggs (1997) 68 BYIL 331; E Peel [1998] LMCLQ 22; RH Stevens in P Birks (ed), *Lessons from the Swaps Litigation* (Mansfield Press, Oxford, forthcoming). Unless otherwise stated, page references to in this comment are to [1997] 3 WLR.
[2] Lords Goff, Clyde and Hutton. Lord Nicholls delivered a dissenting speech with which Lord Mustill concurred.
[3] See *infra*, text to nn 116–117.
[4] Brussels Convention on Jurisdiction and the Enforcement of Judgments in Civil and Commercial Matters 1968: see Civil Jurisdiction and Judgments Act 1982, s 2 and Sched 1 (as amended); Lugano Convention: see Civil Jurisdiction and Judgments Act 1982, s 3A and Sched 3C.
[5] The effect of the completion of a supposed swap transaction upon the availability of a restitutionary remedy has recently been considered by the Court of Appeal: see *Guinness Mahon v Royal Borough of Kensington and Chelsea* [1998] 2 All ER 272.
[6] *Hazell v Hammersmith & Fulham LBC* [1992] AC 1.
[7] *Morgan Guaranty Trust Co v Lothian Regional Council* [1995] SLT 299, 301–303 (Ct Sn).
[8] In accordance with Rules of the Supreme Court 1965, Ord 11, r 1(2).

diction between the courts of the constituent parts of the UK.[9] That assertion was challenged by the Council which contended that the claim could be pursued only before the courts of Scotland, the place of the Council's domicile for the purposes of the Modified Convention.[10]

This contention was upheld by Hirst J.[11] The Bank appealed. In May 1993, at the instigation of the Bank, the Court of Appeal referred to the European Court of Justice (ECJ), for a preliminary ruling, questions relating to the interpretation of art 5.1 ("matters relating to a contract . . .") and art 5.3 ("matters relating to tort, delict or quasi-delict . . .") of the Modified Convention.[12] Almost two years later in March 1995, however, the ECJ declared that it had no jurisdiction to consider the interpretation of the provisions of the Modified Convention, noting that its ruling would have no binding effect upon the English courts, which are required only to have regard to decisions of the Court of Justice in this context.[13] The parties renewed their arguments before a differently constituted Court of Appeal, which, by a majority, allowed the Bank's appeal and reinstated the proceedings.[14] The Council sought and obtained leave to appeal to the House of Lords.

The Modified Convention and the Brussels Convention

The jurisdictional dispute in *Kleinwort Benson v Glasgow* required the House of Lords to interpret arts 5.1 and 5.3 of the Modified Convention. It was not (directly) concerned with the corresponding and, for present purposes, identically worded provisions of the Brussels Convention. Nevertheless all four speeches rely heavily upon the jurisprudence of the ECJ in relation to the Brussels Convention and it would be surprising if the reasoning of the majority were not followed in similar cases involving that Convention or, for that matter, the Lugano Convention.[15] It is more difficult, however, to determine what the status of the decision of the House of Lords would be if the ECJ were to reach a different conclusion upon the scope of either art 5.1 or art 5.3 of the Brussels Convention. It is conceivable that the effect of such decision would be to require the lower courts to interpret the Brussels Convention (in accordance with the ECJ decision) and the Modified Convention in contradictory ways. That would be unfortunate.[16]

---

[9] Civil Jurisdiction and Judgments Act 1982, s 16 and Sched 4 (the "Modified Convention"). The Bank initially relied upon a number of provisions of the Modified Convention (arts 5.1, 5.3, 5.8 and 6.1). However, only two provisions (arts 5.1 and 5.3) were in issue before the House of Lords.
[10] Modified Convention, art 2.
[11] [1993] QB 429; noted A Briggs [1992] LMCLQ 283. The Council's summons was heard at the same time as a summons in proceedings between Barclays Bank and the Council raising the same point. It appears that these proceedings were later settled.
[12] [1994] QB 404.
[13] [1995] I ECR 615; [1996] QB 57; noted E Peel [1996] LMCLQ 8.
[14] [1996] QB 687 (Roch and Millett LJJ; Leggatt LJ dissenting); noted J Riley [1996] LMCLQ 182; R Stevens (1996) 112 LQR 391; A Dickinson [1996] LMCLQ 556, 558-563.
[15] At least in respect of claims for restitution arising from void contracts. Lord Hutton (at p 950A) expressed the view that it was desirable that phrases in the Modified Convention taken from the Brussels Convention should be given the same meaning in both contexts. Lord Clyde (at p 942A–B) stated that it was desirable to interpret such phrases in the Modified Convention so as to find solutions "consonant with the principles applicable to the [Brussels] Convention itself". The use, however, of the word "desirable" and both judges' reference to the different rules of interpretation applicable to the Modified Convention suggest, perhaps, that the contrary result is not impossible. Indeed, Lord Goff (at p 934G) would appear to have expressly contemplated differences between the interpretation of the Modified Convention and of the Brussels Convention.
[16] It is tentatively suggested that one possible solution to this dilemma might be to submit that at least one member of the majority was attempting to identify the conclusions which would have been reached by the ECJ had it decided an identical case and that, accordingly, the views of such member(s) should be considered as being conditional upon no later contradictory decision being issued by that court. The speech of Lord Hutton would appear to be most susceptible to this type of analysis.

Interpretation of the Conventions

In interpreting provisions of the Modified Convention, United Kingdom courts are required to have regard to relevant principles laid down by and relevant decisions of the ECJ relating to the provisions of the Brussels Convention dealing with jurisdiction.[17] In the present context, the following matters should be noted:

1. Each provision of the Brussels Convention must be construed "teleologically", *ie* with regard to the objectives and general scheme of the Convention.[18]

2. The first stated objective of the Brussels Convention was to implement art 220 of the EC Treaty by simplifying the procedures for the reciprocal enforcement of judgments. The second stated objective was to strengthen the legal protection of persons established within a Convention state. It was sought to achieve these objectives by introducing rules governing not only the formalities for the enforcement of judgments but also the jurisdiction of courts in the Convention states.[19]

3. To promote uniformity of construction of the Brussels Convention, certain key terms have been accorded an independent interpretation by the ECJ.[20]

4. The basic jurisdictional rule of the Brussels Convention is that a person domiciled in a Convention state must be sued in the courts of that state (art 2). The primacy of this rule is regarded as being essential for the achievement of the second stated objective of the Convention (by ensuring that the EC domiciled defendant is more easily able to defend himself). Accordingly provisions of the Convention which derogate from art 2[21] must be interpreted so as, whilst achieving their purpose, not unduly to derogate from the protection accorded to a defendant by the basic rule.[22] In particular, such rules must be interpreted (a) in such a way as to enable a well informed defendant reasonably to predict the courts in which he may be sued,[23] and (b) in such a way as to avoid a general preference in favour of the courts of the plaintiff's domicile.[24]

5. Article 5 of the Convention contains a number of provisions of so-called "special jurisdiction". The purpose of these provisions is to enable proceedings to be brought before a court having a particularly close connection with a dispute "with a view to ensuring the efficacious conduct of proceedings".[25] In a case falling within the scope of any of the sub-paragraphs of art 5, the plaintiff may elect to commence proceedings in the designated court rather than in the courts of the state of the defendant's domicile. The provisions of art 5, therefore, constitute a derogation from the general principle set out in art 2 and must be construed restrictively.

The correctness of the above principles (and their applicability to interpretation of the Modified Convention) does not appear to have been disputed by any member of the House in *Kleinwort Benson v Glasgow*.[26] The differing conclusions of the majority and the minority resulted from different perceptions as to the extent to which the objectives and general scheme of

---

[17] Civil Jurisdiction and Judgments Act 1982, s 16(3)(a).
[18] This is a technique with which English lawyers are becoming increasingly familiar in view of the ingress of European techniques. Rigid adherence to a literal approach to the construction of statutes and contractual terms is no longer possible. See further *Inland Revenue Commissioners v McGuckian* [1997] 1 WLR 991; *Investors Compensation Scheme v West Bromwich Building Soc* [1998] 1 WLR 896 (*per* Lord Hoffman).
[19] Brussels Convention, Preamble
[20] See *Martin Peters Bauunternehmung GmbH v Zuid Nederlandse Aannemers Vereniging* [1983] ECR 987 ("*Martin Peters*"), 1007–1008 (Opinion of Mancini AG, para 4).
[21] In particular, those focusing upon the subject matter of the claim (*ie* arts 5 and 16).
[22] See *eg Kalfelis v Bankhaus Schröder, Münchmeyer, Hengst and Co* [1988] ECR 5565 ("*Kalfelis*"), 5585 (para 19).
[23] See *Jakob Handte v TCMS* [1992] I ECR 3967, 3995, paras 18–19.
[24] *Dumez France and Tracoba v Hessische Landesbank* [1990] I ECR 49; *Marinari v Lloyd's Bank* [1996] QB 217.
[25] See *eg Martin Peters* [1983] ECR 987, 1002 (para 11).
[26] See Lord Goff (at pp 927G–930H); Lord Nicholls (at p 936D–H); Lord Clyde (at p 942B–943E); Lord Hutton (at p 951C–H).

the Convention permit the interpretation of art 5.1 of the Modified Convention to encompass restitutionary claims arising from (admittedly) ineffective contracts.

Article 5.1

By the Modified Convention, art 5.1, a person domiciled in a part of the United Kingdom may, in another part of the United Kingdom, be sued "in matters relating to a contract, in the courts for the place of performance of the obligation in question; . . .".[27] A court *applying* this provision must, therefore, follow a three stage process: first, it must ask itself whether the dispute (or part of the dispute) involves *matters relating to a contract*; secondly, it must identify the *obligation in question*; finally, it must identify the *place of performance* of that obligation. In doing so, the court would, of course, be required to have regard to the case law of the ECJ relating to the italicised phrases.[28]

It is inappropriate and unacceptable, however, to adopt so mechanical an approach in *construing* art 5. The purpose of the provisions of special jurisdiction and their place within the scheme of each of the Conventions) require that each possible interpretation of the key phrases be judged by the jurisdictional result which it produces or is capable of producing (*ie* in the case of art 5.1, the court identified at the third stage referred to above). If that result is one which in a significant number of cases would give jurisdiction to the courts of a place having no connection with the underlying dispute or would otherwise conflict with the objectives and general scheme of the Conventions,[29] the interpretation in question must be rejected.[30] Thus the interpretation of the phrase *matters relating to a contract* cannot be considered independently of the remainder of art 5.1[31] — a factual connection between a particular dispute and a contract (or other consensual relationship) will not suffice to bring that dispute within the scope of art 5.1.

Lords Goff, Clyde and Hutton

Similarities between the speeches of the majority are more apparent than real. It is proposed, therefore, to deal with each speech separately.

Lord Goff focused upon the meaning of the phrase *obligation in question*. Referring to a number of decisions of the ECJ considering the independent interpretation to be given to this phrase, he concluded that it referred exclusively to the contractual (or other consensual)

---

[27] Modified Convention, art 5.1 (first sentence). The second sentence of the Modified Convention, art 5.1 deals with matters relating to individual contracts of employment. The Brussels Convention, art 5.1 is identically worded save that it refers to "a Contracting State" instead of "a part of the United Kingdom".
[28] For detailed discussion, see Briggs, *Civil Jurisdiction and Judgments*, 2nd ed (1997) (hereafter "*Briggs*"), paras 2.124–2.141.
[29] For instance, by giving undue preference to the courts of the plaintiff's domicile. See further [1996] LMCLQ 556, 562.
[30] It should be emphasised, however, that the absence of any connection between a particular claim and the courts of the place of performance will not prevent those courts from asserting jurisdiction if the claim is of a type to which art 5.1 does apply (*Custom Made Commercial v Stawa Metallbau GmbH* [1994] I ECR 2913, 2956–2957 (paras 16–21); *cf* A Briggs [1996] LMCLQ 27). Considerations of *forum conveniens* fall to be taken into account in identifying the scope of the provisions of art 5 rather than in applying those provisions to individual cases.
[31] *Agnew v Lanförsäkringbølangens AB* [1997] 4 All ER 937, 942B–D. The issue is complicated by the manner in which the *place of performance* of the relevant obligation falls to be identified. In *Tessili v Dunlop* [1976] ECR 1473, the ECJ stated that the court seised of the claim should identify the place of performance by applying its own private international law rules governing the relationship in question.

obligation forming the basis of the plaintiff's claim.[32] It followed that a claim for recovery of money paid under a supposed contract which in law never existed could not fall within art 5.1 because, *ex hypothesi*, there was no contractual obligation, let alone one which formed the basis of the Bank's claim.[33] Lord Goff supported this conclusion with the following arguments:

(a) The existence of jurisdiction under art 5 does not displace the jurisdiction of the courts of the state of the defendant's domicile (in this case, Scotland) under art 2. Accordingly, where a plaintiff is in doubt as to the application of art 5 to some or all of his claim, he may bring the entire claim before those courts.[34]

(b) There is no necessary close connecting factor between the dispute and the courts of the place of performance of any given obligation in a case where the contract is a nullity and the plaintiff's claim is a restitutionary claim to recover money paid under that "contract".[35] In relation to restitutionary claims generally, this argument is, in Lord Goff's submission, supported by the absence of any provision for claims based on unjust enrichment in art 5.[36]

(c) The wording of art 5.1 was influenced by German law.[37] In its submissions to the ECJ in the present case, Germany had argued that art 5.1 did not apply to a claim such as that brought by the Bank.[38]

Lord Goff's consideration of the scope of art 5.1, however, went beyond that necessary to resolve the jurisdictional dispute between the Bank and the Council. Two aspects of that discussion are of note. First, Lord Goff's view that the *obligation in question* was the contractual obligation forming the basis of the plaintiff's claim led (and, indeed, required) him to conclude that art 5.1 almost certainly does not encompass claims by a plaintiff for a declaration that no contract existed.[39] This conclusion did not, in His Lordship's view, conflict with the decision of the ECJ in *Effer SpA v Kantner*,[40] in which it was held that a court must investigate a defendant's denial that a contract existed as a condition of its jurisdiction.[41] It does, however, conflict with existing Court of Appeal authority[42] and with the views of the remainder of the House of Lords (considered further below). Secondly, Lord Goff thought that, very exceptionally, a restitutionary claim might fall within art 5.1.[43] He contemplated that one such exceptional situation (at

---

[32] See pp 928D-930D; 932E-H. Lord Goff relied, in particular, upon the decisions in *De Bloos SPRL v Bouyer* [1976] ECR 1497 ("*De Bloos*"), 1508 (para 11) and *Shenevai v Kreischer* [1987] ECR 239 ("*Shenevai*"), 256 (para 18). However, it should be noted that both these decisions concerned claims in respect of the breach of a specific contractual obligation by act (*De Bloos*) or omission (*Shenevai*).

[33] At pp 931A–B; 932H–933A

[34] At pp 930G–H; 935C. See *Kalfelis* [1988] ECR 5565, 5586 (para 20).

[35] At pp 931B–D; 933A–B. By reason of his basic premise (see *supra*, text to n 32), Lord Goff focused upon *contractual* obligations only. The correctness of the argument in relation to such obligations is considered further below. It might be argued, however, that the *obligation in question* in a restitutionary claim arising from a void contract is the obligation to make restitution (this being the approach adopted by Roch LJ in the Court of Appeal: [1996] QB 678, 694–696). It is submitted that this argument has quite properly been rejected. Applying the decision in *Tessili* (see *supra*, n 31), the *place of performance* of this obligation would be identified in the majority of contracting states as the place of the domicile of the plaintiff (as creditor). This, as noted above, is in direct conflict with the priority given by the Conventions to the courts of the defendant's domicile (see further Peel, ch 1 in Rose (ed), *Restitution and the Conflict of Laws* (1995) ("*Rose*"), 11–20; [1996] LMCLQ 556, 558).

[36] At p 931D. Article 5.4 of each of the Conventions accords jurisdiction in respect of a civil claim for damages or restitution based on an act giving rise to criminal proceedings to the court seised of those proceedings (if competent to hear such claim).

[37] See Jenard Report (OJ C59, 5 March 1979), p 23

[38] Conversely, Lord Nicholls (at p 940F) noted and drew support from the fact that the opposite conclusion had been reached by France, Spain, the United Kingdom and the European Commission in their submissions.

[39] Nevertheless, he left the matter open: see p 934A–B.

[40] [1982] ECR 825.

[41] See further *Tesam Distribution Ltd v Schuh Mode Team GmbH* [1990] ILPr 149, esp 165 (*per* Stocker LJ).

[42] *Boss Group Ltd v Boss France SA* [1997] 1 WLR 351; noted E Peel (1996) 112 LQR 541.

[43] At p 931C.

least in relation to the Brussels and Lugano Convention) might be a restitutionary claim by a plaintiff on the ground of failure of consideration following the termination of a contract for the defendant's breach.[44] This, it is submitted, is not inconsistent with Lord Goff's narrow construction of art 5.1 — this type of claim may reasonably described as a legal consequence of the defendant's failure to perform as promised. In the great majority of cases, the non-performance of the *obligation in question* (*ie* the obligation in respect of which the defendant is in breach) will amount to a partial failure of consideration. In simple cases,[45] it will amount to a total failure of consideration. Again, however, German law may have been influential.[46]

Lord Clyde began from the premise that the approach to construction of art 5 should be "narrow rather than generous".[47] He added that the rules of jurisdiction "should not be construed so as to favour the wishes of the plaintiff" and echoed Lord Goff by noting that a plaintiff may always sue in the courts of the defendant's domicile if there is any doubt as to the availability of art 5.1.[48] Perhaps unfortunately, however, Lord Clyde took the view that the solution could be derived from the text of the Convention and, in particular, from the language of art 5. He noted the following matters:[49] (a) That art 5 makes no direct reference to restitution (save in art 5, dealing with certain civil claims arising in the course of criminal proceedings). (b) That the wording of art 5.1 may be contrasted with art 10(1) of the Rome Convention on the Law Applicable to Contractual Obligations, which provision deals expressly with cases of nullity. (c) That, in the phrase *matters relating to a contract* the use of the present participle "relating", rather than the past participle "related",[50] and the use of the definite article suggested that there must be an identifiable agreement subsisting at the time of the claim. (d) That the phrase *place of performance of the obligation in question* suggested that there was a particular obligation to be performed which was the subject matter of a dispute between the parties. This obligation, in His Lordship's view,[51] must be a contractual obligation and the dispute must concern the performance of the obligation.

Lord Clyde's reasoning is open to criticism in terms both of his literal approach to the construction of art 5.1 (which approach is more suited to the interpretation of domestic legislation[52]) and the soundness of the matters relied upon. As to paragraph (a), the absence of a general provision in art 5 in respect of restitutionary claims might suggest that the authors of the Convention were of the view that there was no close connecting factor consistently linking restitutionary claims with identifiable jurisdictions (or that they regarded such claims as already falling within art 5 — see the discussion in relation to art 5.3 below). It cannot, however, be taken as providing support for the view that specific restitutionary claims are incapable of falling within art 5.1. As to paragraph (b), there is no obvious link between the interpretation of the Rome Convention on choice of law in contract and of the Conventions on jurisdiction. As to paragraph (c), this

---

[44] At p 934C–G.
[45] *Eg* an action to recover a pre-payment for goods sold and not delivered.
[46] Claims for the return of benefits conferred under a contract terminated for breach are characterised under German law as contractual claims. They do not fall within the scope of the sections of the German Civil Code dealing with unjust enrichment claim (see Markisenis, *German Law of Obligations* (1997), Vol I, 44–45; R Zimmerman [1997] RLR 13). See Lord Goff, at pp 934F, 935H–936A.
[47] At p 942G.
[48] At pp. 942H–943A.
[49] At pp. 943F–944D.
[50] See *Strathcaird Farms Ltd v GA Chattaway & Co* [1993] SLT 36, 40 (Sh Ct).
[51] At pp 944B, 944H–945A (drawing support from the decisions of the ECJ in *De Bloos* [1976] ECR 1497 and *Custom Made Commercial* [1994] I ECR 2913).
[52] It is, of course, true that the dispute in *Kleinwort Benson v Glasgow* concerned the construction of a provision contained in an English statute (Civil Jurisdiction and Judgments Act 1982, Sched 4). Nevertheless, given that a literal approach to construction is inappropriate in construing the Brussels and Lugano Conventions (Scheds 1 and 3A to the same Act), it would be surprising, and unfortunate, if the same approach were not adopted in relation to the Modified Convention. See further *supra*, text to n 15.

reasoning indicates the dangers of relying solely upon the wording of a particular language version of the Conventions. The French language version of the Brussels and Lugano Conventions refers to "*en matière contractuelle*", incorporating neither of the features relied upon by Lord Clyde. Finally, as to paragraph (d), it is submitted that, whilst his conclusion may be correct, Lord Clyde failed to focus sufficiently upon why the *obligation in question* must be a contractual obligation or why the dispute must concern the "performance" of that obligation. The answers to these questions require consideration of the compatibility of these (and rival) interpretations with the principles underlying the Conventions.[53] Lord Clyde's literal approach to construction precluded him from embarking upon this type of analysis.

Like Lord Goff, Lord Clyde expressed views as to the application of art 5.1 to classes of dispute other than that between the Council and the Bank. It is clear that he regarded the provision as having a wider scope than his colleague and as extending, *inter alia*, to claims by a plaintiff for a declaration that no contract existed[54] and "any claims arising consequentially on the determination of any issue about performance".[55] Whilst it is not clear what Lord Clyde would consider to be an "issue about performance"[56] or how widely he would interpret the requirement that the claim "arise consequentially" from such issue,[57] it seems probable (although it is not certain) that he considered restitutionary claims arising from the termination of a contract for breach or frustration to be within the scope of art 5.1, the obligation in question being the contractual obligation whose performance was in issue.

Lord Hutton's approach is more closely aligned to that of Lord Goff than that of Lord Clyde. In his view, the ECJ judgments considering the interpretation to be given to Article 5 provided the following guidance:[58] (a) A claim for unjust enrichment is to be regarded for the purposes of the Conventions (as well as under English law) as separate and distinct from a claim in contract.[59] (b) The special jurisdiction given by art 5.1 constitutes a derogation from the general rule contained in art 2 and, accordingly, should be construed narrowly.[60] (c) Jurisdiction under art 5.1 only arises when the claim is to enforce an obligation arising under a contract or a relationship such as a contract for membership of an association.[61] The Bank's claim was not for the enforcement of a contract. (d) The reason for a court having jurisdiction under art 5 is the existence of a "particularly close connecting factor" between the dispute giving rise to the claim and the designated court.[62] In Lord Hutton's view there was no such connection between the dispute before him and the English courts because the Bank's action was brought "not to enforce a con-

---

[53] See *supra*, text to nn 29–31.
[54] At p 945D–F: "Once there is a dispute as to the existence of a contract the performance of which the one party is seeking to enforce or for the non-performance of which he is seeking a remedy, then it should not matter whether procedurally it is the defendant or the plaintiff who raises the issue of the existence of the contract". Lord Clyde would presumably regard the obligation in question in both cases as the particular obligation which one party is seeking to enforce. *Cf Boss Group Ltd v Boss France SA* [1997] 1 WLR 351, 357 C–G (a wider view).
[55] At pp 945F–946C.
[56] For example, how would he regard (a) a construction summons, or (b) a case in which the defendant admitted a breach but denied that any loss had thereby been caused to the plaintiff?
[57] Lord Clyde chose as examples of claims arising consequentially on the determination of an issue about performance (a) a claim for damages, and (b) an award of a *quantum meruit*. It is noted that the latter remedy is sometimes restitutionary in nature and sometimes not.
[58] At p 958C–H.
[59] At pp 950F–H (relying upon *Kalfelis* [1988] ECR 5565, 5581 (para 3). It should be noted, however, that the ECJ in *Kalfelis* was considering whether a court having jurisdiction over a tort claim under art 5.3 should have accessory jurisdiction in relation to connected contractual and restitutionary claims (see further *infra*, text to n 86). The interpretation of art 5.1 was not in issue.
[60] At pp 950H–951H (relying on *Kalfelis* [1988] ECR 5565, 5585–5586 (paras 19–20) and *Somafer SA v Saar-Ferngas AG* [1978] ECR 2188 ("*Somafer*"), 2191 (para 7)).
[61] At pp 951H–953E (relying on *De Bloos* [1976] ECR 1497, 1508-1509 (paras. 8–15), *Handte*, at pp. 3994-3995 (paras. 14-16) and *Custom Made Commercial* [1994] I ECR 2913, 2957 (paras 21–24)).
[62] At pp 953E–954B.

tract to be performed in England, but to recover monies which are repayable to the plaintiff because the contract never existed and because the plaintiff cannot seek to enforce it".[63]

It followed, in Lord Hutton's opinion, that English courts had no jurisdiction in respect of the Bank's claim. It is less clear whether and to what extent his Lordship regarded art 5.1 as being applicable to claims other than claims to enforce a particular contractual obligation. It appears that, like Lord Clyde, he considered that a claim for a declaration that no contract exists does fall within this provision.[64]

Lords Nicholls and Mustill

Lord Nicholls (with whom Lord Mustill agreed) considered that the Bank's restitutionary claim fell squarely within art 5.1 and that the English courts had jurisdiction. Some have preferred the views of the minority to those of the majority.[65] It is argued, however, that Lords Nicholls and Mustill failed to take sufficient account of the nature of the provisions of art 5 and their place within the scheme of the Conventions. The result reached by the majority is, it is submitted, to be preferred.

It is proposed to begin the analysis of Lord Nicholls' speech by emphasising two propositions which the minority did not adopt. First, they did not identify the *obligation in question* as the restitutionary obligation which the Bank was seeking to enforce.[66] Secondly, and more importantly, they appear to have clearly accepted that there is no necessary (or indeed obvious) connection between a claim for restitutionary relief arising from an ineffective contract and the courts for the place of performance of a (supposed) contractual obligation.[67] It is, of course, true that the restitutionary claim is likely to be founded upon the absence of the supposed contract, the claimant's mistaken belief as to the existence of the supposed contract or the matters negativing the existence of the supposed contract.[68] It does not follow, however, that there is any connection between this claim and the place of performance of any supposed contractual obligation (except, perhaps, the supposed obligation whose performance gave rise to the enrichment[69]). Indeed, in many cases involving ineffective contracts, the basis upon which the *place of performance* is often identified (*ie* the consent of the parties) will itself be undermined by the matters negativing the existence of the contract.

The purpose of the provisions of art 5 of the Convention is to confer jurisdiction upon a court having a particularly close connection with the dispute with a view to ensuring the efficacious conduct of proceedings. Lord Nicholls accepted this[70] but submitted that pragmatic

---

[63] At pp 953H–954A. As a result of Lord Hutton's earlier conclusion that the *obligation in question* must be a contractual obligation, he did not consider whether the allegation of a restitutionary obligation to be performed in England provided a sufficiently close connection between the dispute and the English courts (see *supra*, n 35).

[64] At p 957B–C.

[65] Briggs (1997) 68 BYIL 331, 339; Peel [1998] LMCLQ 22; *cf* Collier [1997] All ER Rev 64, 70–71.

[66] *Cf* Roch LJ in the Court of Appeal, *supra*, n 35.

[67] At pp 940A–B.

[68] In certain civil law systems (notably Germany), the nullity of the contract provides, of itself, the basis for the restitutionary claim see Zweigert & Kötz, *An Introduction to Comparative Law*, 2nd ed (1984), 578–583. A similar view was adopted by Hobhouse J and the Court of Appeal in *Westdeutsche Landesbank Girozentrale v Islington LBC* [1994] 4 All ER 972; [1994] 1 WLR 938 (CA); *cf* [1996] AC 669, 683C–H (*per* Lord Goff); see also *Guinness Mahon v Kensington and Chelsea* [1998] (CA). Both mistake (of law) and failure of consideration have also been relied upon as grounds for restitution in the swaps litigation. It is also possible that local authority claimants might rely upon the *ultra vires* nature of their payments as justifying recovery on public policy grounds: see *Auckland Harbour Board v R* [1924] AC 318; *Commonwealth of Australia v Burns* [1971] VR 825.

[69] This connection appears to have been recognised by both Millett LJ in the Court of Appeal [1996] QB 678, 699D and by Lord Nicholls (at p 938E–G). However, neither Millett LJ not Lord Nicholls identified this obligation as being the *obligation in question*.

[70] At p 936E.

considerations[71] and the need for certainty in the allocation of jurisdiction required the court to construe art 5.1 as extending to include the restitutionary claim of the Bank. His reasoning (by reference to hypothetical facts) may be summarised as follows.

(a) Suppose that D (domiciled in a Convention state) agrees to carry out work (in another Convention state) for P. P makes an advance payment to D. Subsequently, D refuses to carry out the work and argues that he lacked the capacity to make the agreement. P sues D for damages for non-performance. It is clear that the courts of the place where the work was to be done have jurisdiction notwithstanding the dispute as to the validity of the contract. The court is required to decide the dispute as to the existence of the contract.[72]

(b) Now suppose that P, anxious to dispose of the dispute once and for all, adds an alternative claim for restitution in the event that D's capacity argument is successful. It would be unthinkable, in Lord Nicholls' view, that this claim should lie outside art 5.1:

"It would be surprising and unfortunate if, having decided that the contract is null and void, the same court cannot proceed to decide on the restitutionary consequences following directly from this . . .".[73]

(c) Next assume that P first takes the view that D's capacity argument is likely to be successful. He first brings a restitutionary claim on the footing that the contract is ineffective. Subsequently, doubting the correctness of his original conclusion, he adds a claim for damages for non-performance. Again, in Lord Nicholls' view, it would be surprising if this reversal of the order of presentation of the alternative claims affected the application of art 5.1.[74]

(d) Should the matter be any different if P makes no claim for damages for non-performance, either because he accepts that D's capacity argument will be upheld or because the invalidity of the contract has been established in earlier proceedings (as in *Kleinwort Benson v Glasgow*)? Lord Nicholls thought not. He stated:

"If a claim for restitutionary relief in respect of payments made in purported performance of a contract is a matter relating to a contract within the meaning of art 5.1, this must be so irrespective of whether there is also an alternative claim based on the existence of the contract."[75]

He expressed the view that the *obligation in question* in such case was the obligation whose existence is (or was) disputed.[76]

Whilst the correctness of the reasoning in paragraph (a) above cannot be doubted,[77] the solution proposed in paragraph (b) requires further explanation and justification. The claim by P would be a restitutionary claim arising from the ineffectiveness of the contract. As noted above, there is no necessary (or obvious) connection between this type of claim (viewed in isolation) and the courts of the place of performance of a supposed contractual obligation. Lord Nicholls accepted this. At first sight, therefore, there would appear to be no good reason why the special jurisdiction of art 5.1 should extend to such a claim.[78] Lord Nicholls, however, considered this conclusion to be impractical and to offend against the spirit of the Convention. He commented:

"The Convention is concerned to promoted the efficacious conduct of proceedings and to avoid multiplicity of closely related proceedings in different contracting states . . ."[79]

[71] At pp 937H–938A: "I say at once that the feature which ultimately has weighed heavily with me is the unattractive practical difficulties which would result from the narrow interpretation urged by the appellant local authority."
[72] At p 938A–B.
[73] At p 938C–D.
[74] At p 938G–H.
[75] At p 939A.
[76] At p 939G.
[77] It represents a straightforward application of *De Bloos* [1976] ECR 1497 and *Effer v Kantner* [1982] ECR 825.
[78] See *supra*, text to nn 29–31: the mere existence of a factual connection between a dispute and a contract (or other consensual relationship) will not suffice to bring that dispute within the scope of art 5.1.
[79] At p 938D.

"What matters is that, however labelled, the [restitutionary] relief is no more than part of the effective determination of a dispute relating to a contract. It is one facet of a single dispute"[80]

"At root the narrow view [urged by the Council] seeks to draw a line between cases where relief is sought for non-performance of a contractual term and all other cases. This would mean than, when the existence of the contract is disputed, a claim for damages for breach of contract is within the article but not a claim for relief consequential upon a successful defence that the contract is void or ought to be set aside. This, in turn, means that the narrow interpretation ascribes to the court an incomplete role in what is a common enough situation. This is unattractive."[81]

Earlier in his speech, Lord Nicholls had referred to the desirability of the whole of a dispute being resolved by one court.[82] He cited the following passage from the judgment of the ECJ in *Martin Peters*:[83]

"It should be noted that multiplication of the bases of jurisdiction in one and the same type of case is not likely to encourage legal certainty and effective protection throughout the territory of the Community. The provisions of the Convention should therefore be interpreted in such a way that the court seised is not required to declare that it has jurisdiction to adjudicate upon certain applications but has no jurisdiction to hear certain other applications, even though they are closely related."

It would appear, therefore, that Lord Nicholls' primary justification[84] for construing art 5.1 as encompassing a restitutionary claim arising in these circumstances was that such a claim would be closely connected with the primary issue (as to whether there was a contractual obligation to perform), which issue would undoubtedly fall within the scope of that article and that what was effectively a single dispute would otherwise be fragmented. He appears to have concluded that the restitutionary claim should be "channelled" with the primary issue and that a court having jurisdiction in respect of that issue should also have jurisdiction in respect of the restitutionary claim. Assuming (for one moment) that this approach is consistent with the principles governing the interpretation of the Convention and with the case law of the ECJ,[85] it would seem to follow that, if the primary issue is no longer disputed, the basis for the restitutionary claim falling within art 5.1 is removed — there is no longer any issue in respect of which the court has jurisdiction under art 5.1 into which the restitutionary claim may be "channelled" nor is there any risk of fragmentation of a dispute. In such circumstances, it is submitted that, in view of the absence of any necessary or obvious connection between the restitutionary claim and the place of performance of any supposed contractual obligation, there is no good reason why the court of the place where the work was to have been performed should have jurisdiction in respect of the restitutionary claim alone — the assertion of jurisdiction would represent an unwarranted extension of art 5.1. If this is correct, then it follows that Lord Nicholls' conclusions, set out in paragraphs (c) and (d) above, cannot be supported. In paragraph (d), there is no primary claim with which the restitutionary claim may be channelled. In the circumstances envisaged in paragraph (c), a "channelling" approach would enable P to bring both claims together in the courts of the place where the work was to be done but only if he could satisfy the court that there was a genuine dispute regarding a contractual obligation which fell within art 5.1 in its own right.

---

[80] At p 938E.
[81] At p 939C–D. See also *supra*, text to n 73.
[82] At p 937D–E.
[83] *Martin Peters* [1983] ECR 987, 1003 (para 17).
[84] In the author's view, it is the only possible justification for such an interpretation. There is some suggestion in Lord Nicholls' speech that he considered it sufficient that restitutionary claims arising from ineffective contracts could be naturally described as *matters relating to a contract* and that he regarded it as being artificial to distinguish between different types of claim capable of being so described (see esp at p 939E–F). This reasoning, it is submitted, is misguided — the phrase *matters relating to a contract* is, essentially, an artificial concept whose meaning is only capable of being determined by reference to the remainder of art 5.1 and the jurisdictional consequences of particular rival interpretations: see *supra*, text to nn 29–31.
[85] As to which, see *infra*, nn 86–91.

Nor is a "channelling" approach such as that apparently adopted by the minority necessarily consistent with the scheme and objectives of the Convention. Similar reasoning was advanced by Darmon AG in *Kalfelis*[86] and in *Shearson Lehman Hutton v TVB*[87] but in neither case was it adopted by the ECJ.[88] In *Kalfelis*, the court rejected this approach in relation to art 5.3, holding that the court having jurisdiction by virtue of that provision in respect of a tort claim did not have jurisdiction in respect of related contractual and unjust enrichment claims.[89] Furthermore, Lord Nicholls' reference to the need to avoid a multiplicity of closely related proceedings is unhelpful in construing art 5.1. The principal objection to this occurrence from the point of view of the operation of the Conventions is that it increases the risk of conflicting judgments, the avoidance of which is essential to ensure the effective reciprocal enforcement of judgments within the Convention states.[90] The Conventions contain rules specifically designed to minimise the possibility of such a conflict.[91] Article 5 is not one of those provisions. It seeks to ensure the efficacious conduct of proceedings by conferring jurisdiction upon the courts of a place having a close connection with the dispute. Whilst it is undoubtedly true that disadvantages (in terms of the conduct of proceedings) may arise from different aspects of a dispute being considered by different courts, the avoidance of such disadvantages is not one of the objectives of art 5.[92] In any event, it should again be emphasised that the plaintiff may bring his entire claim before the courts of the defendant's domicile.

Two further matters should be noted. First, Lord Nicholls did not consider, by way of example, a case in which the plaintiff seeks a declaration that no contract existed. It seems clear, however, that he considered such a case to fall within the scope of art 5.1.[93] This accords with the (*obiter*) views of Lords Clyde and Hutton.[94] Secondly, as noted above, he identified the *obligation in question* in relation to claims to set aside contracts and claims for consequential relief as "the obligation whose existence is in dispute". It is not clear whether his Lordship intended to refer to the obligation whose non-performance gave rise to the original dispute between the parties (in his example, D's obligation to carry out work) or to the characteristic obligation under the contract whose existence was disputed.[95] If the latter, then it is possible that the court having

---

[86] *Kalfelis* [1988] ECR 5565, 5577 (Opinion of Darmon AG, paras 25–30).
[87] *Shearson Lehman Hutton v TVB Treuhandgesellschaft* [1993] I ECR 139, 178–179 (Opinion of Darmon AG, paras 99–111).
[88] In *Shearson Lehman Hutton*, the relevant question did not arise for decision.
[89] *Kalfelis* [1988] ECR 5565, 5585–5586 (paras 19–20). Darmon AG had argued for the same conclusion on the basis that the tortious and unjust enrichment claims should be "channelled" with the contractual claim and that special jurisdiction under art 5 should be accorded only to the courts having jurisdiction under art 5.1.
[90] See *eg Gubisch v Palumbo* [1987] ECR 4861.
[91] Arts 6, 21–22.
[92] The passage from *Martin Peters* [1983] ECR 987 cited by Lord Nicholls (see *supra*, n 83) must be read in context. It was part of the response of the ECJ to the question whether, in construing the phrase *matters relating to a contract* a distinction should be drawn according to whether the obligation in question arose (a) simply from the (consensual) act of becoming a member of an association or (b) from that act in conjunction with a decision made by an organ of the association, it presumably being contemplated that the latter category could be viewed as non-consensual The question was answered in the negative both by the court and by the Advocate General, the latter reasoning [1983] ECR 987, 1011 that such obligations "are founded on the agreement by which a bond of association is created". The close relationship between these two categories of claim is, it is submitted, an entirely different matter from the relationship between a dispute as to performance of a contract and a restitutionary claim arising from the ineffectiveness of that contract. Moreover, it is noted that the language of the first sentence of the passage was relied upon in *Somafer* (at para 7) as justifying a restrictive interpretation of art 5.1.
[93] At p 939E: "Claims to set aside contracts are also of everyday occurrence. Such disputes would fall naturally within the words used in art 5 when defining its ambit: 'matters relating to a contract'. . .". At p 940E: "Disputes relating to the existence of a contract are to be regarded as within the Convention concept of contractual matters . . ."
[94] See *supra*, text to nn 54 and 64.
[95] In Lord Nicholls example, this would also be D's obligation to carry out work.

jurisdiction under art 5.1 would vary depending upon whether the plaintiff pursued a claim for damages for breach of contract as well as a restitutionary claim consequential on nullity. Nor is it clear how Lord Nicholls would identify the *obligation in question* in a case in which there had never been any dispute between the parties as to the existence of a contract.[96]

Article 5.1 and article 13

None of the speeches in *Kleinwort Benson v Glasgow* refers to the relationship between art 5.1 and the consumer contract provisions of the Conventions (Section 4: arts 13–15). By art 13, these provisions apply to determine jurisdiction in "proceedings concerning a contract" concluded by a "consumer" if the contract falls within one of a number of categories. As a general rule, proceedings to which Section 4 extends may be brought by the consumer in the courts of his own domicile as well as those of the domicile of the other party to the contract. The other party to the contract is required to bring such proceedings in the courts of the consumer's domicile.[97]

This omission, especially from the speech of Lord Nicholls, is notable. The purpose of the provisions of Section 4 is to protect the consumer and to avoid any discouragement to his bringing an action which would result from compelling him to sue in the courts of the other (stronger) party's domicile.[98] The achievement of this purpose may obviously be threatened if the phrase *proceedings concerning a contract* were to be construed as excluding a restitutionary claim by the consumer arising from the ineffectiveness of the contract, even if that claim stands alone[100]. However, assuming that a broad interpretation of art 13 is justified by reference to its purpose, it does not follow that art 5.1 (by virtue of the phrase *matters relating to a contract*) should be accorded the same interpretation.[100] Leaving to one side the fact that different words are used in the two provisions, it must be recognised that art 5 and Section 4 of the Conventions have different objectives and achieve those objectives in different ways. Neither the phrase *matters relating to a contract* nor the phrase *proceedings concerning a contract* can be construed independently of the remainder of the part of the Convention in which it is contained or without regard to the objective of that part and its place within the scheme of the Convention. Unlike the provisions of art 5, the purpose of art 14 in permitting the consumer to sue in the courts of his own domicile is not to assist the efficacious conduct of proceedings by enabling them to be brought before a court having a close connection with the dispute. Its purpose is to protect the consumer. Furthermore, the finding that the parties' attempt to contract has failed for whatever reason cannot undermine the basis upon which the courts of the consumer's domicile have been selected. If anything, the need for consumer protection in such case is greater. Again the contrast with the position in relation to art 5.1 is clear.[101] A broad interpretation of the phrase *proceedings concerning a contract* in art 13 may be justified; it is submitted that a broad interpretation of the phrase *matters relating to a contract* in art 5.1 is not.

---

[96] An example of a case in which there may never have been a dispute between the parties upon the issue of nullity was given by Lord Nicholls (at p 940B–D). This example closely resembled the facts of *Kleinwort Benson v Glasgow* itself.
[97] Art 14. See *Briggs*, paras 2.74–2.80.
[98] See *Shearson Lehman Hutton* [1993] I ECR 139, 187 (para 18).
[99] This issue was raised in *Shearson Lehman Hutton* but was not considered by the ECJ. The Advocate General, relying upon a "channelling" approach, concluded that art 13 encompassed a claim based on breach of contractual obligations, breach of pre-contractual obligations and unjust enrichment arising out of one and the same agency contract (at p 179 (Opinion of Darmon AG, para 110)).
[100] *Cf Shearson Lehman Hutton* [1993] I ECR 139, 176 (Opinion of Darmon AG, para 87).
[101] See *supra*, text to n 31.

Article 5.3

By the Modified Convention, art 5.3, a person domiciled in a part of the United Kingdom may, in another part of the United Kingdom, be sued "in matters relating to tort, delict or quasi-delict, in the courts for the place where the harmful event occurred or in the case of a threatened wrong is likely to occur".[102] A court applying this provision must, therefore, consider whether the dispute (or part of the dispute) involves *matters relating to tort, delict or quasi-delict* and, if so, it must identify the *place where the harmful event occurred*. Both italicised phrases have been given independent interpretations by the ECJ.[103]

The Bank argued (in the alternative to its contention under art 5.1) that its restitutionary claim was a *matter relating to tort, delict or quasi-delict*. It relied upon a statement by the ECJ in *Kalfelis* that this phrase must be regarded as "covering all actions which seek to establish the liability of a defendant and which are not related to a 'contract' within the meaning of art 5.1".[104]

If art 5.3 had been interpreted in the manner suggested by the Bank, most restitutionary claims (other than those to which art 5.1 applies) would fall within its scope.[105] The Bank's argument was, however, summarily rejected by the House of Lords as being founded upon a misinterpretation of the passage quoted above in that the word "liability" should be interpreted as meaning a liability in tort, delict or quasi-delict and not a liability to make restitution.[106] This reasoning may be somewhat circular given that the words "tort, delict or quasi-delict" must be given an independent interpretation.[107] It is submitted, however, that a restriction of the scope of art 5.3 to claims founded on a breach of a (tortious or similar) duty by the defendant is capable of being justified not only by the difficulty in identifying a "harmful event" in relation to many (subtractive) unjust enrichment claims but also by the absence of any necessary or obvious connection between such claims and the courts of the place where a particular event (which may be described as a "harmful event" occurred). The diversity and complexity of restitutionary claims preclude either the place of enrichment or the place of impoverishment from being a satisfactory solution in this regard.[108] The inadequacy of the former is compounded by the fact that it is often casual; the inadequacy of the latter by the undue preference which it would give to the courts of the plaintiff's domicile.[109]

Jurisdiction under the Conventions in relation to restitutionary claims

Although the decision in *Kleinwort Benson v Glasgow* has clarified matters somewhat (at least in the short term), the operation of the Conventions in relation to restitutionary claims will continue to raise difficult issues to be decided on a case by case basis. The uncertainty in this area is likely to continue until the application of the Brussels Convention to restitutionary claims has been considered by the ECJ or the Convention is revised to deal expressly with such claims, either

---

[102] Modified Convention, art 5.3. The Brussels Convention, art 5.1 refers to "a Contracting State" rather than to "a part of the United Kingdom" and does not provide expressly for the case of a threatened wrong.
[103] *Kalfelis* [1988] ECR 5565, 5585 (para 18); *Bier v Mines de Potasse d'Alsace* [1976] ECR 1735, 1747 (para 19).
[104] *Kalfelis*, [1988] ECR 5565, 5585 (para 18).
[105] As to the identification of the "harmful event" in relation to restitutionary claims, see Peel, ch 1 of *Rose*, 23–27.
[106] See, in particular, Lord Hutton (at p 958E). Lord Goff (at p 935F) noted that "a claim based on unjust enrichment does not, apart from exceptional circumstances, presuppose either a harmful event or a threatened wrong". It would seem likely that he had in mind as the "exceptional" case either (a) claims to reverse an enrichment secured by wrongdoing, or (b) claims to reverse an enrichment obtained by duress or, perhaps, undue influence. The former category, being founded upon a tort (or other breach of duty), would appear to fall within even the narrow construction of art 5.3 favoured by the House of Lords.
[107] It is also contrary to the view taken by the Advocate General in *Shearson Lehman Hutton* [1993] I ECR 139, 178 (para 102).
[108] *Cf* Peel, ch 1 of *Rose*, 26–27.
[109] See further [1996] LMCLQ 556, 562–563.

by fresh provision or by clarification of the scope of the existing provisions. The current position, however, may be summarised briefly as follows:

1. No single provision of the Conventions (other than art 2) provides an obvious basis for jurisdiction in relation to all restitutionary claims. In particular, neither art 5.1 nor art 5.3 performs this function. It has never been seriously suggested that all such claims should fall within art 5.1 on the ground that the obligation to make restitution is (fictitiously) based upon an implied contract. The decision in *Kleinwort Benson v Glasgow* precludes a wide construction of art 5.3, which treats most restitutionary claims as *matters relating to tort, delict or quasi-delict*.[110]

2. Each of arts 5.1 and 5.3 provides a basis for jurisdiction in relation to certain restitutionary claims, for example:

(a) Article 5.3 ought, in principle, to apply to a claim to reverse an enrichment obtained by the commission of a non-contractual wrong (whether tortious or otherwise). It is suggested that this provision may also be applied to other types of restitutionary claim which, whilst not founded upon a breach of duty, are closely linked to particular conduct by the defendant,[111] the "harmful event" being the conduct complained of.[112]

(b) In the light of comments of Lord Goff and Lord Clyde in *Kleinwort Benson v Glasgow*, it is thought that art 5.1 would be held to be applicable to a claim on the ground of failure of consideration following the termination of a contract for the defendant's breach.[113] In addition, the tone of the majority speeches (and, in particular, of Lords Clyde and Hutton) suggests that art 5.1 may apply to other types of restitutionary claim which are connected with the performance of particular contractual obligation (such as a claim on the ground of failure of consideration following the frustration of a contract, a claim to reverse an enrichment obtained by a breach of contract[114] or, more tentatively, a claim to recover a contractual overpayment).

3. Neither art 5.1 nor art 5.3 provides a basis for jurisdiction in relation to a restitutionary claim arising from an ineffective contract (this being the view of the majority in *Kleinwort Benson v Glasgow*[115]).

Restitution and the conflict of laws again?

After six years, the Bank must now pursue its claim in the courts of Scotland. Lord Goff recorded that the apparent reason why the jurisdictional issue had been so keenly contested was that the Bank was seeking to take advantage of a favourable limitation regime under English law and, in particular, that relating to claims for relief from the consequences of a mistake[116]. It should be noted, however, that the Prescription and Limitation (Scotland) Act 1973 s 23A provides that, where the substantive law of a country other than Scotland falls to be applied by a Scottish court

---

[110] See *supra*, text to nn 93–100.
[111] *Eg* cases concerned with duress or the misappropriation of property.
[112] It is submitted that it is unhelpful to analyse such claims in terms of "damage" or "the event giving rise to damage" occurred and that, accordingly, the autonomous interpretation given to the phrase *place where the harmful event occurred* in *Bier* is inappropriate in this context (*Cf Briggs*, para 2.159).
[113] See *supra*, text to nn 44 and 55. On the same basis, art 5.1 should also apply to a restitutionary claim grounded upon failure of consideration in the event of a breach of contract even if the contract has not been terminated (although the circumstances in which such a claim is available are rare: see *Miles v Wakefield Metropolitan District Council* [1987] AC 539).
[114] As to which, see *Attorney-General v George Blake* [1998] 1 All ER 833.
[115] Which view, it is submitted, is correct both logically (the ineffectiveness of the contract undermines not only the existence of any contractual obligation but also, in many cases, the basis upon which the *place of performance* of a contractual obligation is often identified) and teleologically (such claims lack the necessary close connection with the place of performance of any (supposed) contractual obligation).
[116] At pp 925F–926B, referring to the Limitation Act 1980, s 32(1)(c), for which there is no precisely equivalent provision in Scotland. As Lord Goff noted, in order to rely upon this provision, the Bank must show an entitlement as a matter of English law to recover monies paid under a mistake of law, an issue which subsequently arose for consideration by the House of Lords in *Kleinwort Benson v Birmingham (No 2)* §103.

as the law governing an obligation, the Scottish court shall apply the rules of limitation of that country to the exclusion of corresponding rules of Scots law. This provision raises a further conflict of laws issue, *ie* the need to identify the law governing the claim. Should the courts of Scotland decide that the Bank's claim is governed by English law, then the English limitation regime would apply. It might be thought that the courts of Scotland would be more likely to apply Scots law to such a claim than the courts of England. However, the reasoning of the Court of Session (Outer House) in a similar case (albeit decided in unsatisfactory circumstances) suggests that English law may be favoured, at least in a case where the parties have sought to enter a contract expressly governed by English law.[117] The Council's conflict of laws battle may be only half won.

Clarifying Restitution for Wrongs

(Attorney-General v Blake)

Graham Virgo*

Whilst the fundamental policy underlying the law of restitution for wrongs is clear, namely that wrongdoers should not be allowed to profit from the commission of the wrong, there is great uncertainty as to when particular types of wrongdoing should trigger the award of restitutionary remedies. The Court of Appeal in *Attorney-General v Blake*[1] has done a great deal to clarify the law in this difficult area.

George Blake had been a member of the Secret Intelligence Service but he was also an agent of the Soviet Union. He was consequently convicted of unlawfully communicating information to the Soviets but he escaped to Moscow, where he wrote his autobiography. In this book he disclosed information about the secret service. This breached an agreement not to disclose information gained as a result of his employment by the Crown and it also constituted a breach of the Official Secrets Acts. The book was published in the United Kingdom by Jonathan Cape Ltd without the permission of the Crown. The Attorney-General sued, on behalf of the Crown, to recover all the sums which had been received or were receivable by the publisher. This action failed initially since the trial judge concluded that the defendant had not breached any fiduciary duty which was owed to the Crown in disclosing information which he had agreed not to disclose, simply because that information had ceased to be confidential.[2] Although this point was affirmed by the Court of Appeal, the Attorney-General was given leave to reformulate his claim and this new claim succeeded. The court examined three possible routes which were potentially available to the Attorney-General to prevent Blake from profiting from his wrongdoing.

1. The private law claim: breach of fiduciary duty

The Court of Appeal affirmed that there is more than one category of fiduciary relationship and that different categories of relationship possess different characteristics and attract different kinds of fiduciary obligation. The relationship between Blake and the Crown fell within two categories of fiduciary relationship.

---

[117] *Baring Brothers v Cunninghame DC* [1997] RLR §190 (Ct Sn (OH)); noted J Bird [1997] LMCLQ 182; R Stevens (1997) 113 LQR 249 and in Birks (ed), *Lessons from the Swaps Litigation*; A Dickinson [1997] RLR 66.
* Fellow of Downing College, Cambridge and Lecturer in Law at the University of Cambridge.
[1] [1998] 1 All ER 833.
[2] [1997] Ch 84 (Sir Richard Scott V-C). The Attorney-General had not relied on the defendant's breach of contract or any public law claim.

The first category was the relationship of trust and confidence which arose in this case because Blake was employed to act in the best interests of the Crown and so he owed a duty of loyalty to the Crown. This obligation of loyalty has a number of attributes, including that the fiduciary must not act for his own benefit without the consent of the employer. But this duty only lasts as long as the relationship of trust and confidence continues and such a relationship ends once the employee ceases to be employed by the employer. Consequently, once Blake ceased to be employed by the Crown he no longer owed a duty of loyalty to the Crown as a fiduciary. The only way that a duty of loyalty would subsist despite the termination of employment is where the employee has entered into a contractual undertaking not to damage the employer's interests once the employee has left his or her employment. But if this agreement is breached liability would be founded on breach of contract rather than breach of fiduciary duty.[3] Just because a fiduciary breaches a duty it does not follow that this involves a breach of fiduciary duty, since fiduciaries may owe other types of duty.

The second category of fiduciary relationship which was potentially applicable was that of confidentiality, which will arise whenever information is imparted to one person in confidence. Although such a relationship of confidentiality may arise when one person is employed by another, the relationship does not depend on employment. Consequently, this fiduciary relationship will continue even where the employee is no longer employed by the employer. It had already been recognised by the House of Lords that members of the Secret Intelligence Service, such as Blake, owe a life-long duty of confidence to the Crown, but that such a fiduciary duty only lasted as long as the information remained confidential.[4] Since the information which Blake had published in his book had ceased to be confidential, it followed that he had not breached this fiduciary duty either.

This analysis of the nature of fiduciary relationships is consistent with a number of recent cases which have emphasised that the crucial considerations for identifying a breach of fiduciary duty are whether the particular relationship between the parties can be characterised as falling within one of the recognised categories of fiduciary relationship and whether the particular relationship imposes particular fiduciary obligations which may have been breached.[5] *Blake* shows that the relationship between the parties may fall within more than one category of fiduciary relationship, but the different categories of relationship may last for varying periods and the duties owed by the fiduciary will differ depending on the category of relationship which is being considered.

2. The public law claim: preventing the defendant from receiving the proceeds of crime

In submitting his manuscript for publication Blake had committed the offence of disclosing official information without lawful authority, contrary to the Official Secrets Act 1989, s 1. The royalties which had been paid to Blake and which remained payable by the publisher were therefore the proceeds of crime. The prosecutor can require the court to order that the proceeds of certain crimes, including offences under the Official Secret Acts, should be confiscated by the Crown,[6] but this statutory regime is only available where the defendant has been convicted of the relevant offence.[7] Since Blake had not been convicted of a crime in respect of the submission of

---

[3] [1998] 1 All ER 833, 843.
[4] *A-G v Guardian Newspapers Ltd (No 3)* [1990] 1 AC 109.
[5] See, in particular, *Bristol and West Building Society v Mothew* [1998] Ch 1. For more general analysis of the nature of fiduciary obligations see Sir P Millett, "Equity's Place in the Law of Commerce" (1998) 114 LQR 214, 218–223.
[6] By the Criminal Justice Act 1988, Part VI, as amended by the Proceeds of Crime Act 1995.
[7] A relevant offence is an indictable offence, other than offences which involve drug trafficking, or a limited number of summary offences.

his manuscript to the publisher, the statutory regime was inapplicable. But the Attorney-General, at the invitation of the Court of Appeal, argued that an equivalent power existed at common law. This raised two separate issues: the nature of the Attorney General's claim and the function of the remedy which could be awarded.

(a) The nature of the Attorney-General's claim

The Attorney-General is the guardian of the public interest and has a particular duty to vindicate the criminal law. Consequently, the House of Lords recognised in *Gouriet v Union of Post Office Workers*[8] that the Attorney-General can apply to the civil courts to obtain an injunction to uphold the criminal law. It was assumed in that case that this injunction would be used to restrain the commission or repeated commission of crimes in certain exceptional cases. This jurisdiction to grant an injunction was, however, extended by the Court of Appeal in *Blake* to the case where a crime had already been committed and operated to ensure that the defendant did not benefit from the consequences of that crime. The exercise of such a power was justified on the ground that the criminal courts in this case were powerless to prevent the defendant from benefiting from the crime, because he had not been convicted of an offence relating to the disclosure of information in his autobiography. If the civil courts were also unable to intervene it would follow that Blake could flout the criminal law with impunity and bring it into disrepute by being able to obtain and retain the proceeds of his crime.

The ability of the Attorney-General to obtain an injunction in such circumstances raises two important questions. First, the injunction is granted to vindicate the criminal law and so presumably it is necessary to show that the defendant has committed a crime. Even though no criminal trial had been held, the Court of Appeal concluded that Blake had committed a serious offence under the Official Secrets Act 1989 and presumably it applied the civil standard of proof to determine this. It might be doubted whether it is appropriate for the *civil* courts to determine that the defendant had committed a crime by reference to the civil standard of proof, but this is defensible because the remedy which is awarded does not seek to punish the defendant. Although the Court of Appeal described the injunction which is awarded as a penalty,[9] this is misleading, because the function of the injunction is simply to prevent the defendant from profiting from the crime by ensuring that he or she remains in the same position financially as he or she occupied before the crime was committed.

The second question arising from the ability of the Attorney-General to apply for an injunction to prevent a criminal from profiting from the crime concerns the capacity in which the Attorney-General can bring such a claim. The Court of Appeal recognised that the Attorney-General could bring a public law claim in his own capacity as guardian of the public interest and not as a representative of the Crown. But could the Attorney-General bring a private law claim on behalf of the Crown, to enable the Crown to recover the proceeds of the crime from the defendant? In addition, does the recognition of the Attorney-General's public law claim mean that the victim of the crime is necessarily excluded from bringing a private law claim to recover the proceeds of the crime?

Sir Richard Scott V-C had suggested that the Attorney-General could not have brought a private law claim founded on the breach of the Official Secrets Act, but this was because he considered that the contravention of the Official Secrets Act did not constitute a breach of duty under the civil law.[10] This may be right, but it does not follow that the commission of a crime under that Act cannot trigger the award of private law restitutionary relief. Whilst such a restitutionary remedy would appear to have been unenforceable in this case, because Blake was in Moscow

---

[8] [1978] AC 435.
[9] [1998] 1 All ER 833, 849.
[10] [1997] Ch 84, 95. The Court of Appeal endorsed this conclusion: [1998] 1 All ER 833, 849.

and there was no chance that he would return to this country, the question of whether restitutionary damages should be available in principle where the defendant has committed a crime is a matter of vital importance. The Court of Appeal, however, considered that the Attorney-General could not have obtained restitutionary damages for the commission of a crime in this case, since the court concluded that it only had jurisdiction to grant a remedy which had prospective effect by preventing the defendant from obtaining the proceeds of the crime.[11] But why cannot the court have jurisdiction to award restitutionary remedies which have retrospective effect and so prevent the criminal from retaining the proceeds of the crime? Whilst it is perfectly acceptable to conclude that, where the statutory regime for confiscating the proceeds of crime applies, it is inappropriate for there to be a parallel development of the common law regime,[12] it does not follow that the common law has no role to play where the statutory regime is inapplicable.[13] Otherwise the effect of *Blake* is that the common law can prevent a criminal from receiving the proceeds of crime, but it cannot require the criminal to disgorge the proceeds once they have been received. This is illogical and contradicts the clear policy, specifically recognised by the Court of Appeal,[14] that criminals should not be allowed to profit from their crimes.

If criminals can be required to disgorge the proceeds of their crimes by means of a private law claim perhaps the most appropriate person to bring such a claim is the Attorney-General, since he is the guardian of the criminal law and so is in an appropriate position to determine when an application should be made to the court. Certainly, if the Attorney-General has commenced proceedings, it will not be appropriate for the victim of the crime to make a claim as well. But what of the case where the Attorney-General has not commenced proceedings and the statutory regime is inapplicable? Surely, in such a case, it is entirely appropriate for the victim of the crime to commence proceedings for disgorgement of the proceeds of crime, since being the victim surely gives sufficient *locus standi*. If it is felt that such an action might constitute an abuse of the jurisdiction of the court, one solution is to recognise that the Attorney-General might take over the victim's restitutionary claim and discontinue it, in the same way that the Director of Public Prosecutions can take over and discontinue a private prosecution.[15]

(b) Determination of the remedy

The Court of Appeal recognised that it had jurisdiction to grant an injunction which should be fashioned to ensure that Blake did not receive any benefit which arose directly from the commission of the crime. The injunction which was granted stated that the defendant was restrained from receiving or authorising anybody to receive on his behalf any benefit which resulted from or in connection with the publication of his book. Two observations can be made about this remedy.

First, the Court of Appeal refused to determine what was to happen to the proceeds of the crime. It suggested that, if the unpaid royalties which Jonathan Cape had received but was unable to pay to Blake could be used for a purpose which was not contrary to the public interest, then the court could authorise that use on the application of the Attorney-General. In other words, since Blake's book can still be sold, the publisher can continue to receive Blake's royalties, but it must retain this money until the Attorney-General decides what should happen to it.

Secondly, the court recognised that the injunction would only relate to those benefits which derived directly from the commission of the crime. Although this is consistent with the rules of remoteness which probably apply to other types of restitutionary claim founded on the commis-

---

[11] [1998] 1 All ER 833, 849.
[12] *Chief Constable of Leicestershire v M* [1989] 1 WLR 1015, 1018 (Hoffmann J) and *Halifax Building Society v Thomas* [1996] Ch 217, 229 (Peter Gibson LJ).
[13] This is examined further in "Restitution of the Proceeds of Crime: A Survey of English Law" [1998] RLR 34.
[14] [1998] 1 All ER 833, 849.
[15] Prosecution of Offences Act 1985, s 6(2).

sion of a wrong, it is not consistent with the statutory regime on the confiscation of the proceeds of crime.[16] Is it really appropriate to exclude benefits indirectly obtained from the crime from the operation of the injunction? What if, for example, Jonathan Cape had invested the royalties for Blake in shares and had received dividend payments? Could Blake claim these dividends? According to the Court of Appeal he could, because the dividends were not directly obtained from the commission of the crime. It was the concern that a criminal would retain the indirect proceeds of a crime that probably motivated the Privy Council in *Attorney-General for Hong Kong v Reid*[17] to conclude that the defendant held the bribe he had received on constructive trust for the plaintiff. Whilst the imposition of a constructive trust in such a case is controversial, the desire of the court to strip the criminal of all benefits obtained from the commission of the crime is intuitively correct. One method of obtaining this result, which avoids the problems of the proprietary constructive trust, is simply to prevent the criminal from obtaining any benefits from the crime, whether these benefits arose directly or indirectly. Another solution is to recognise the remedial constructive trust, but this avenue is presently closed.[17a]

3. An alternative private law claim: restitutionary damages for breach of contract

The Court of Appeal also recognised that Blake had breached his contract in submitting his manuscript for publication without first obtaining clearance from the Crown.[18] The Crown had not, however, sought an injunction to prevent publication of the book in breach of contract and it could not establish any loss as a result of the breach. As an alternative, the Crown may have claimed restitutionary damages for breach of contract, but it had not done so, presumably because the state of the authorities suggested that such a claim was unlikely to succeed.[19] Even though the Court of Appeal encouraged the Attorney-General to pursue such a claim, he refused to do so. Undaunted by this inconvenience, the court went on to examine what the result would have been if this restitutionary claim founded on breach of contract had been pursued, and concluded that such a claim would have succeeded. What the court says about restitutionary remedies for breach of contract is *obiter dicta* of the most extreme kind; but, despite this, it is of crucial importance in recognising the potential availability of restitutionary relief for breach of contract. This is the only pronouncement there will be on this matter in this case, because the Crown succeeded on the public law claim and Blake had not taken any part in the proceedings so an appeal to the House of Lords is inconceivable.

(a) The principles underlying the award of restitutionary damages for breach of contract

Analysis of the observations of the court on the availability of restitutionary damages for breach of contract enables the following principles to be identified.

(1) The court affirmed that the basic principle which underlies the award of remedies for breach of contract is that such remedies are intended to compensate the plaintiff for loss suffered. But the court went on to recognise that, in exceptional circumstances, it is appropriate to award remedies which are assessed by reference to the benefit obtained by the defendant as a direct result of the breach of contract. The main justification for the award of such a remedy is that,

---

[16] The Criminal Justice Act 1988, s 71(4) requires confiscation of the value of property which was obtained as a result of or in connection with the commission of the crime without requiring the property to be obtained as a direct result of the crime. See *supra*, 46.

[17] [1994] 1 AC 324.

[17a] *Re Polly Peck International Plc* [1998] *The Times*, May 18 (CA).

[18] The undertaking not to publish information which he had gained from his employment did not constitute unlawful restraint of trade because the agreement was consistent with the policy of the Official Secrets Act 1989, s 1(1): [1998] 1 All ER 833, 843.

[19] See, in particular, *Surrey County Council v Bredero Homes Ltd* [1993] 1 WLR 1361 (CA).

without it, the plaintiff would be deprived of any effective remedy for the breach where a value cannot be attached to the plaintiff's legitimate interest in having the contract performed. The court has therefore recognised the relevance of the performance interest, where the plaintiff's desire to have the contract performed may outweigh the loss which he or she would actually suffer if the contract was not performed.[20] In such circumstances it is appropriate to assess the plaintiff's remedy by reference to the benefit obtained by the defendant as a result of breaching the contract rather than the loss suffered by the plaintiff.

(2) At no point in its analysis of the restitutionary remedy for breach of contract does the court make reference to the unjust enrichment principle. This is to be commended. Restitution in such circumstances does not depend on the reversal of the defendant's unjust enrichment, but is triggered simply by the defendant's breach of contract.

(3) The court had no hesitation in calling the restitutionary remedy which is awarded for breach of contract "restitutionary damages". This accords with the recommendation of the Law Commission that the judiciary should use this term to describe the remedy.[21] Rapid implementation of Law Commission proposals is unusual, but in this case the judiciary adopted the recommendation the day after it was made.[22]

(4) The court emphasised that restitutionary damages for breach of contract would only be available in the most exceptional circumstances and identified two principles which should be relied on to identify these circumstances. The first principle is that the award of compensatory damages should be inadequate in the light of what the plaintiff wanted the contract to achieve. In such circumstances the plaintiff has a particular interest in the performance of the contract. Although the determination of whether compensatory damages are adequate is a matter of some uncertainty, the recognition of this principle is important since it will ensure that the award of restitutionary damages does not undermine the fundamental principle that the usual remedy for breach of contract should be damages which seek to compensate the plaintiff for loss suffered. The second principle is that the benefit obtained by the defendant must have been obtained directly from the breach of contract. Benefits which are too remote from the breach need not be disgorged since they are not considered to be tainted by the defendant's wrongdoing in breaching the contract.

(5) The court acknowledged that the recognition of these two principles means that restitutionary damages should not be awarded in two circumstances where such a remedy has sometimes been advocated. The first situation is where the defendant cynically and deliberately breached the contract. The rejection of restitutionary damages being awarded simply because of the defendant's motive in breaching the contract is surely correct because the defendant's motive is traditionally irrelevant to the assessment of damages for breach of contract.[23] But it can also be defended because it does not follow from the fact that the defendant's breach was deliberate that any benefits obtained necessarily derived from the breach of contract or that compensatory damages are inadequate. The second situation where there is no obvious reason to depart from the compensation principle is where the defendant breached the contract with the plaintiff to enable him or her to enter into a more profitable contract with someone else.[24] This is also consistent with the remoteness principle, since, where the effect of the breach is to place the defendant in a position where he or she is able to obtain a benefit from a third party, that benefit cannot be considered to be obtained as a direct result of the breach of contract. Rather, the breach simply provided the defendant with the opportunity to obtain the benefit from the other party.

---

[20] See D Friedmann, "The Performance Interest in Contract Damages" (1995) 111 LQR 628 and B Coote, "Contract Damages, *Ruxley* and the Performance Interest" (1997) 56 CLJ 537.
[21] Law Commission, *Aggravated, Exemplary and Restitutionary Damages*: Law Com No 247 (1997), pp 51–52.
[22] The Law Commission report was published on 15th December 1997 and the decision of the Court of Appeal was handed down on 16th December.
[23] *Surrey County Council v Bredero Homes Ltd* [1993] 1 WLR 1361, 1370 (Steyn LJ).
[24] As illustrated by the decision of the Supreme Court of Israel in *Adras Building Material Ltd v Harlow and Jones GmbH* (1988) *Israel* [1995] RLR 235.

(6) By applying the two principles that compensatory damages must be inadequate and that the benefit must have arisen directly from the breach of contract, the court was able to recognise two specific circumstances where justice required the award of restitutionary damages for the breach.

(i) Failure to provide what the defendant contracted to provide

Where the defendant agreed to provide a particular service for the plaintiff and charged for this service, but the defendant actually provided a less extensive service, it is appropriate that the defendant is required to disgorge to the plaintiff the amount saved by breaching the contract. So, for example, in the American case of *City of New Orleans v Fireman's Charitable Association*,[25] where the defendant failed to provide as complete a fire-fighting service as it had promised and for which the plaintiff had paid, it would have been appropriate to require the defendant to disgorge what it had saved as a result of this skimped performance. Similarly, in *Ruxley Electronics and Construction Ltd v Forsyth*,[26] where the defendant had built a swimming pool which was not as deep as that which it had promised to build, if it could be shown that the defendant had saved money as a result of this breach of contract this could have been the measure of the plaintiff's damages. This would at least have avoided the artificiality of the court having to value the plaintiff's loss of amenity in having a perfectly useable pool, which was worth what the plaintiff had paid for it, but which was shallower than the plaintiff had wanted. It is because of the artificiality in identifying loss that compensatory damages are an inadequate remedy. Also the award of restitutionary damages is justified because the defendant's benefit, namely what he or she has saved by skimping on the contractual performance, derives directly from the breach of contract.

(ii) Doing what the defendant contracted not to do

Where the defendant obtained a benefit as a result of doing that which he or she had specifically agreed not to do, then it is appropriate for the defendant to disgorge this benefit to the plaintiff, primarily because the benefit was obtained as a direct result of the breach of contract. This actually occurred in *Blake* itself, since the defendant had disclosed information in his book which he had agreed that he would not disclose and obtained benefits, in the form of royalties, as a direct result of this breach of contract. The award of restitutionary damages can also be justified since the plaintiff had suffered no loss and so compensatory damages would not adequately protect the plaintiff's interest in the performance of the contract.

(c) Remaining questions

The approach of the Court of Appeal to the award of restitutionary damages for breach of contract is measured and entirely defensible. It does, however, leave some questions unanswered. The most important of these questions relates to the effect of the court's analysis on previous cases where restitutionary remedies were available where the defendant breached a contract. The award of restitutionary remedies in most of these cases occurred by side-stepping the orthodox bar on the award of restitutionary remedies for breach of contract, and they could still be decided in the same way after *Blake*. So, for example, the plaintiff will still be available to obtain restitutionary remedies where the defendant has breached a contract by founding the claim on the reversal of the defendant's unjust enrichment, the commission of a tort or breach of fiduciary duty. There is, however, one category of case where the plaintiff was previously able to obtain restitutionary remedies by specifically relying on the breach of contract, namely where the defendant has interfered with the plaintiff's proprietary rights as a result of the breach. This appears

---

[25] (1891) 9 So 486.
[26] [1996] AC 344.

to be the best explanation of cases such as *Wrotham Park Estate Co Ltd v Parkside Homes Ltd*,[27] where the defendant breached a restrictive covenant not to develop land without the plaintiff's consent and the plaintiff was awarded damages which can be characterised as restitutionary. The Court of Appeal in *Blake*, however, suggested that the award of restitutionary damages in such cases could not be justified on the ground that the defendant had interfered with the plaintiff's proprietary right arising from the restrictive covenant because "the measure of damages cannot depend on whether the proceedings are between the original parties to the contract or their successors in title".[28] This appears to assume that the restrictive covenant in *Wrotham Park* only bound the original parties, whereas in fact the covenant in that case did bind successors in title because it was registered as a land charge.[29] But this no longer matters. For surely the benefit obtained by the defendant in *Wrotham Park* was obtained as a direct result of the breach of covenant, since, in building houses without the plaintiff's permission, the defendant did what it had promised not to do, and compensatory damages would have been inadequate in such a case because the plaintiff had not suffered any loss.

This analysis can also be used to explain the award of damages in *Jaggard v Sawyer*,[30] where the defendant was held liable to pay damages to the plaintiff for breaching a covenant to use land as a private garden. When the defendant used the land to build a driveway he was doing that which he had promised not to do and the benefit he obtained, namely what he had saved in not having to pay the plaintiff to obtain her permission for the change of use, was obtained as a direct result of the breach of covenant. Although these damages were considered to compensate the plaintiff for loss suffered,[31] and so a restitutionary analysis following *Blake* would appear to be excluded because compensatory damages are an adequate remedy, the better view is that if *Jaggard v Sawyer* were decided now the damages which would be awarded would be restitutionary. This is because the identification of the plaintiff's loss in that case was highly artificial and, as the court recognised in *Blake*, it is simpler and more open to assess the plaintiff's remedy in such circumstances by reference to the defendant's gain rather than the plaintiff's loss.[32] Also the benefit which the defendant obtained clearly derived directly from the breach of contract. More controversially, a further implication of the observations of the court in *Blake* is that the failure to award restitutionary damages in *Surrey County Council v Bredero Homes Ltd*[33] was incorrect. For in that case the defendant had built houses in breach of a covenant to develop the land only in accordance with the planning consent. Since the defendant had done what it had promised not to do, it should have been liable to disgorge to the plaintiffs what it had saved by breaching the covenant.

Even though the observations of the Court of Appeal on the award of restitutionary damages for breach of contract are *obiter*, the recognition of the two key principles which should determine when restitutionary damages are available for breach of contract constitutes an important contribution to the development of a rational law of restitution for wrongs. Whilst the two principles may lack precision, they will enable the courts to determine when restitutionary damages are available with a fair degree of certainty. For example, where the defendant has breached a contract which is specifically enforceable restitutionary damages are potentially appropriate, because compensatory damages are an inadequate remedy, but it will still be necessary to establish that the benefit obtained by the defendant derived directly from the breach of contract. The two principles recognised in *Blake* will only be applicable in exceptional cases, but it is in these

---

[27] [1974] 1 WLR 798.
[28] [1998] 1 All ER 833, 845.
[29] The observation of the court also fails to take into account the rule in *Tulk v Moxhay* (1848) 2 Ph 774.
[30] [1995] 1 WLR 269.
[31] *Ibid*, 281 (Sir Thomas Bingham MR) and 291 (Millett LJ).
[32] [1998] 1 All ER 833, 846.
[33] [1993] 1 WLR 1361.

cases where it is entirely appropriate that remedies are assessed by reference to the defendant's benefit rather than the plaintiff's loss.

Indefeasible Title as a Bar to a Claim for Restitution

(Pyramid Building Soc v Scorpion Hotels)

Robert Chambers*

To what extent will an indefeasible title acquired by registration of an interest in land bar a claim for restitution of unjust enrichment? Although not expressed in those terms, this was the issue before the Victoria Court of Appeal in *Pyramid Building Soc v Scorpion Hotels Pty Ltd*.[1] Unfortunately, it was not addressed directly. The court proceeded on the assumption that the registered interest would be indefeasible unless an exception could be found. Finding none, it concluded without considering the claim to restitution of that interest. This is in marked contrast with many other cases involving registered land, where the courts started by examining the claim for restitution and concluded without considering the effects of registration. These different ways of approaching claims for restitution of interests in registered land have produced glaring inconsistencies among the cases and have left the question at the beginning of this paragraph unanswered.

1. The facts

Five secret agents were made redundant and used money from their separation packages to purchase a guest house through their newly formed company, Scorpion Hotels. One of them, Lewis, caused the guest house to be mortgaged to the Pyramid Building Society. Of the $310,000 advanced on that mortgage, $218,000 was used to discharge an existing mortgage of the property and the remainder appears to have been used by Lewis for his own purposes. The other members of Scorpion were not aware of the mortgage to Pyramid, which was executed by Lewis and his wife. She was not a director of Scorpion at the time and not authorised to execute the mortgage on Scorpion's behalf.

Pyramid attempted to enforce the mortgage, which was registered under a Torrens system of land registration. The trial judge held that the loan and mortgage were void and unenforceable and that Scorpion was liable to Pyramid for $218,000 as money had and received. The Victoria Court of Appeal allowed Pyramid's appeal and held that the mortgage was valid and enforceable and entitled Pyramid to possession of the land, judgment for $1.2M owing on the loan (including compound interest at 24.5% per annum), and costs on a solicitor-client basis.

Hayne JA gave the judgment for the Court of Appeal, basing his decision on the assumptions:[2] (a) "that the mortgage was not properly executed by Scorpion", (b) "that the company never gave authority to anyone to execute the mortgage on its behalf", and (c) "that had Pyramid made further enquiries (enquiries which it should have made) it would have discovered that the mortgage had not been properly executed." Thus, the judgment was given on the assumption that Pyramid had constructive notice of the facts which, apart from the operation of the Torrens system, would have entitled Scorpion to restitution of the mortgaged land.

---

* Senior Lecturer, University of Melbourne Law School.
[1] [1998] 1 VR 188 (CA); rvsg (1996) 136 ALR 166, [1997] RLR §28.
[2] At pp 190, 194.

2. Indefeasibility

The main difference between the trial judge and the Court of Appeal was over the application of the Transfer of Land Act 1958, which establishes a Torrens land registration system in Victoria. Section 42(1) states that:

> "[T]he registered proprietor of land shall, except in case of fraud, hold such land subject to such encumbrances as are recorded on the relevant folio of the Register but absolutely free from all other encumbrances whatsoever".

This is part of the principle of "indefeasibility" which protects the holder of a registered interest in land (the "registered proprietor" in Torrens parlance) from adverse claims. The Court of Appeal reasoned that Pyramid's mortgage would be indefeasible unless it had been guilty of fraud and that constructive notice of Lewis' fraud was not itself fraud within the meaning of the statute. This follows the advice given by the Privy Council, in *Assets Co Ltd v Mere Roihi Pty Ltd*,[3] that "by fraud in these Acts is meant actual fraud, *ie*: dishonesty of some sort, not what is called constructive or equitable fraud".

The Torrens system has two major effects on the common law of real property. First, legal property interests in Torrens land are created by registration. A defective or even forged instrument will, upon registration, produce a good legal title. Secondly, the legal owner is accorded a much stronger defence of *bona fide* purchase than at common law, taking title free of many unregistered equitable interests regardless of any notice or knowledge of the existence of such interests. These two changes to the common law produce the effect which is usually described by judges and commentators as "indefeasibility".[4]

A registered title is subject to any registered interests which appear on that title. It is also subject to a number of unregistered interests, sometimes called "exceptions" to the principle of indefeasibility. Most of the exceptions are expressed in the statute, such as the exception for fraud found in section 42(1), quoted above, and exceptions for a variety of other listed interests, such as easements, charges for unpaid taxes, and the rights of adverse possessors and tenants in possession.

More important for present purposes are the implied exceptions established through judicial interpretation of Torrens statutes. In many Torrens jurisdictions, a person who receives a registered interest in land as a donee is not entitled to the protection of indefeasibility.[5] This "volunteer exception" is the product of a sensible judicial reading of the provision that the registered proprietor of an interest in land shall not "be affected by notice actual or constructive of any trust or unregistered interest" in that land.[6] In *King v Smail*,[7] Adam J noted that the statute protected the registered proprietor, not from the unregistered interest, but from the effect of notice of that interest. Since a volunteer takes subject to prior equitable interests regardless of notice, the statute does not advance his or her position.

3. The "in personam exception"

One of the most important aspects of the Torrens system is commonly referred to in Australia as the "in personam exception" to indefeasibility. Torrens statutes prohibit the registration of most,

---

[3] [1905] AC 176, 210, *per* Lord Lindley.
[4] *Frazer v Walker* [1967] 1 AC 569 (PC).
[5] *Re Passburg Petroleums Ltd* (1984) 8 DLR (4th) 363, 368 (Alta CA); *Rasmussen v Rasmussen* [1995] 1 VR 613, 631-634; see R Carter, "Does Indefeasibility Protect the Title of a Volunteer? A Comment on *Matkowski v Matkowski* and *Sim v Sim*" (1985) 49 Saskatchewan LR 329.
[6] Transfer of Land Act 1958 (Vic), s 43.
[7] [1958] VR 273.

if not all, equitable interests in land. Courts quickly recognised that this did not prevent equitable interests from arising and existing as unregistered interests.[8] Equitable interests continued to be created in much the same way as they were before Torrens. For example, a specifically enforceable contract for the sale of land produces a constructive trust for the purchaser,[9] a loan combined with a deposit of the certificate of title can produce an equitable mortgage,[10] a purchase in the name of a volunteer can produce a resulting trust,[11] and a detrimentally relied upon common intention or reasonable expectation regarding the ownership of a family home can produce a constructive trust.[12]

Torrens statutes change the way in which legal interests in land are created (which is, for most interests, by registration) but have little effect on the creation of equitable interests. The statutory protection from the usual effects of notice of equitable interests makes it unlikely that those interests can survive the registration of a competing interest acquired for value without fraud, but nothing prevents the creation of equitable interests arising on or after registration. In other words, the principle of indefeasibility provides the registered proprietor with powerful protection from pre-existing equitable interests, but should not inhibit the creation of new equitable interests.

The label "in personam exception" is misleading in two ways. First, "in personam" does not mean that rights *in rem* are excluded. It means that the creation of the new right involved the current registered proprietor in some way.[13] If the right is not a right to an interest in the land, it is in no way an exception to the indefeasibility of the registered title. If it is a right to an interest in land, it is best understood as a right *in rem* (even if classified as a "mere equity" for the purpose of determining priorities).[14] In any event, as discussed above, it is clear that unregistered rights *in rem*, such as express or constructive trusts, can be created by a registered proprietor. Secondly, calling it an "exception" to indefeasibility is unhelpful. Indefeasibility describes the effect of a system which cures defects in the vendor's title and protects the purchaser from pre-existing unregistered interests in the property. It does not prevent the creation of new unregistered interests by the purchaser. To call such an interest an exception to indefeasibility is like calling a declaration of trust an exception to the defence of *bona fide* purchaser. While not untrue, it deflects attention from the important issues surrounding the valid creation of such a trust.[15]

4. Restitution in a Torrens system

The application of common law principles to a Torrens system requires some adjustment. The registration of title in the name of the defendant, without the consent of the plaintiff, creates a valid legal title, even though a purported conveyance on that basis would be void at common law. This means that many situations, which could be dealt with at common law through the passive preservation of the plaintiff's pre-existing property interest, will have to be handled in a Torrens system as restitution of unjust enrichment. In both cases, a plaintiff might say, "I want my property back." However, there is a big difference between the recovery of what the plaintiff still owns and the recovery of what he or she used to own. In the former case, the plaintiff seeks to enforce a continuing property right and remedy a wrongful interference with that right. In the latter case, the plaintiff must reverse a transfer of property to the defendant. The right to recover

---

[8] *Barry v Heider* (1914) 19 CLR 197.
[9] *Bunny Industries Ltd v FSW Enterprises Pty Ltd* [1982] Qd R 712.
[10] *J&H Just (Holdings) Pty Ltd v Bank of NSW* (1971) 125 CLR 546.
[11] *Brown v Brown* (1993) 31 NSWLR 582 (CA).
[12] *Sorochan v Sorochan* (1986) 29 DLR (4th) 1 (SCC).
[13] *Bahr v Nicholay* (1988) 164 CLR 604, 613.
[14] See *Breskvar v Wall* (1971) 126 CLR 376, 387-388; P Birks, "Property and Unjust Enrichment: Categorical Truths" [1997] NZL Rev 623, 637-638.
[15] See eg *Bahr v Nicholay* (1988) 164 CLR 604.

that property arises on (or after) the transfer because the defendant has received an enrichment at the expense of the plaintiff which the law considers unjust and reversible.

Where a potentially unjust enrichment consists of a registered interest in Torrens land, a difficult task is to identify the circumstances in which the plaintiff's lack of intention to benefit the defendant will give rise to a right to restitution of that interest, notwithstanding registration in the defendant's name. The fraud exception will be able to cope with many cases, since a forged or fraudulently induced registration will often be made by, or with the knowledge of, the defendant. The dishonesty of the defendant allows for the reversal of the transaction and restitution of legal title to the plaintiff. However, there will be many cases which do not fall within the fraud exception, such as the one under discussion, where the interest was acquired by someone who was not a party to the fraud which led to registration. There will also be cases where the reason for restitution does not involve dishonesty, such as cases of mistake, undue influence or unconscionability.

The volunteer exception will permit relief in many of these situations. So long as the recipient did not give value for his or her interest in land, then (in many jurisdictions) registration of that interest under the Torrens system will not advance his or her position over that of a comparable donee at common law. However, if the defendant has given value (or the land is situated in a jurisdiction, such as New South Wales[16] or Queensland,[17] which allows volunteers the full protection of indefeasibility), then, in the absence of fraud on the part of the defendant, a claim for restitution of an interest in land can only succeed as an "in personam exception" to indefeasibility.

There are at least three potential sources of confusion in cases where Torrens land is transferred from a plaintiff to a defendant in circumstances which give the plaintiff a right to restitution of that land: (i) a new restitutionary unregistered interest in the land can be mistaken for a pre-existing unregistered interest, (ii) a two-party situation can be mistaken for a three-party situation, and (iii) reasons for restitution based on a vitiation of the plaintiff's intention to benefit the defendant (such as mistake or undue influence) can be overlooked or misapplied in the erroneous belief that the "in personam exception" requires some conduct by the defendant. These three pitfalls must be avoided if the "in personam exception" is to be applied properly.

First, the plaintiff's interest in recoverable land can look like a pre-existing interest, which ought to be subject to the principle of indefeasibility. However, the plaintiff does not seek to recover the land through the enforcement of a pre-existing property interest. Prior to the impugned transfer, the plaintiff did not have an equitable interest in the land, but a registered legal title, which carried with it all the rights of beneficial ownership.[18] The registration of title in the defendant's name both destroyed the plaintiff's legal title and created a legal title for the defendant. The plaintiff's right to recover the land is restitutionary, arising for the first time on or after the transfer of legal title and in response to the unjust enrichment of the defendant.[19] It is, therefore, not subject to indefeasibility but falls in the category labelled as the "in personam exception".

The second potential source of confusion is that two-party cases, where the plaintiff seeks to recover property which has passed directly from the plaintiff to the defendant, can look like cases involving three (or more) parties, where the plaintiff seeks to recover property from a defendant who received it, not directly from the plaintiff, but from someone who acquired the property from the plaintiff and then transferred it on in a separate transaction. This happens when the

---

[16] *Bogdanovic v Koteff* (1988) 12 NSWLR 472 (CA).
[17] Land Title Act 1994 (Qd), s 180.
[18] *DKLR Holding Co (No 2) Pty Ltd v Commissioner of Stamp Duties* (1982) 49 CLR 431; *Westdeutsche Landesbank Girozentrale v Islington LBC* [1996] AC 669, 706; see R Chambers, *Resulting Trusts* (OUP, 1997), 51-55.
[19] P Birks, *An Introduction to the Law of Restitution*, rev ed (OUP, 1989), 70-72; P Birks, "Property and Unjust Enrichment: Categorical Truths" [1997] NZL Rev 623, 643-644.

registration of title in the defendant's name is accomplished by the fraud or forgery of a third party. *Pyramid v Scorpion* is just such a case: Pyramid acquired the registered mortgage of Scorpion's land through the fraud of Lewis and his wife. However, it is important to note that registration caused the property interest to pass directly from Scorpion to Pyramid and not through the hands of a third party.

In true three-party cases, where the defendant has acquired legal title from a third person who held it subject to the plaintiff's equitable interest, an important issue normally is whether the defendant had notice of the plaintiff's interest. The Torrens system obviates this inquiry by protecting the defendant from the effect of such notice. However, in two-party cases the defendant will know that the property used to belong to the plaintiff and the question whether the defendant had notice of the plaintiff's interest is simply not relevant. The important question is whether the defendant had notice of the facts which entitle the plaintiff to restitution.

This is precisely the same problem that led to difficulties understanding *Barclays Bank Plc v O'Brien*.[20] In that case, a husband unduly influenced his wife to mortgage her interest in their family home to the bank as a guarantee of his indebtedness. The bank was not a party to the undue influence and the outcome of the case depended on whether the bank had notice of that influence. This was a two-party case, in which the wife sought to recover a property interest which had passed directly from herself to the bank as a result of the intervention of a third party. Therefore, it was a question of whether the bank had notice, not of her prior interest in the property, but of her husband's undue influence.

Unfortunately, a potential source of confusion is found in *Barclays Bank v O'Brien* itself, where Lord Browne-Wilkinson stated:[21]

> "The doctrine of notice lies at the heart of equity. Given that there are two innocent parties, each enjoying rights, the earlier right prevails against the later right if the acquirer of the later right knows of the earlier right (actual notice) or would have discovered it had he taken proper steps (constructive notice)."

The attempt to characterise the wife's right to restitution as the earlier and therefore prevailing right is doomed to failure since it could not have arisen before the bank acquired its interest under the mortgage of guarantee. As Mr Mee pointed out, "there is only one transaction, that which is being attacked on the grounds of undue influence or misrepresentation. When the lender is considering whether to enter into the contract of guarantee, the surety's equity to set aside that transaction has not yet come into being."[22]

There is an important distinction between notice of a pre-existing equitable interest and notice of the vitiation of the other party's intention to enter the transaction. This distinction is crucial for the application of the principle of indefeasibility. The protection from the effect of notice provided by a Torrens system applies to notice of pre-existing unregistered interests and cannot be used to prevent the creation of new equitable interests. In other words, the effect of notice of a pre-existing unregistered interest, arising in three-party cases, is determined by the principle of indefeasibility, while the effect of notice of the unjust factor in two-party cases falls within the "in personam exception".

This leads to the third potential source of confusion mentioned above. Courts and commentators tend to view the "in personam exception" as embracing only those claims based on some conduct of the current registered proprietor.[23] This was the approach taken by the court in

---

[20] [1994] 1 AC 180.
[21] *Ibid*, 195.
[22] J Mee, "Undue Influence, Misrepresentation and the Doctrine of Notice" (1995) 54 CLJ 536, 541–542.
[23] See *eg Secureland Mortgage Investments Nominees Ltd v Harman & Co Solicitor Nominee Co Ltd* [1991] 2 NZLR 399, 410–411; M Hughson et al, "Reflections on the Mirror of Title: Resolving the Conflict between Purchasers and Prior Interest Holders" (1997) 21 Melbourne ULR 460, 489–493.

Pyramid v Scorpion. After deciding that Pyramid had not been fraudulent, it went on to consider briefly whether Scorpion could establish any "in personam remedies" to set the mortgage aside.[24] Unfortunately, the only claim advanced by Scorpion's counsel was for negligence. The court rightly concluded that Pyramid did not owe Scorpion any duty of care and that there was nothing in Pyramid's conduct which could "give rise to a personal equity in Scorpion sufficient to set the mortgage aside".[25] In this the court followed the judgment of the New South Wales Court of Appeal in *Grgic v ANZ Banking Group Ltd*:[26]

> "[T]he expressions 'personal equity' and 'right in personam' encompass only known legal causes of action or equitable causes of action, albeit that the relevant conduct which may be relied upon to establish 'a personal equity' or 'right in personam' extends to include conduct not only of the registered proprietor but also of those for whose conduct he is responsible".

It is true that the creation of most equitable rights depends upon some conduct of the holder of the legal title. However, this narrow view of the "in personam exception" ignores those rights which can arise through no action or fault of the legal-title holder and even without his or her knowledge, such as the creation of an express trust by a transfer of property to a trustee in trust[27] or the creation of a resulting trust by purchase of property in the name of another without the intention to benefit the recipient.[28]

It is in the nature of rights generated by unjust enrichment that they are more likely to be created without the defendant's participation than are rights generated by other events. Rights based on contract or consent normally involve the consensual undertaking of the obligations corresponding to those rights. Liability for wrongdoing, even where that liability is strict (*eg* trespass or breach of trust), depends upon some breach of duty by the defendant. In contrast, an obligation to make restitution of an unjust enrichment can arise without any wrongdoing or involvement by the defendant beyond mere receipt of the enrichment. Courts dealing with rights to restitution of Torrens land need to recognise that those rights fall within the "in personam exception".

5. A problem in need of a solution

This potential for confusion has already worked significant mischief in the form of inconsistency. Like cases are not being treated alike. On one hand is *Pyramid v Scorpion*, where the plaintiff's claim to restitution was denied even though the defendant had constructive notice of the facts giving rise to that claim. On the other hand are cases similar to *Barclays Bank v O'Brien*, where constructive notice of another's undue influence was regarded as a sufficient basis for restitution of registered interests in land under the Torrens system.[29] Even where the claim of undue influence was unsuccessful, this was because the influence had not been proved[30] or the registered proprietor did not have notice of that influence.[31] There was no hint in these cases that the registered interest should be indefeasible in the absence of fraud by, or on behalf of, the registered proprietor.

There is no compelling reason why these cases should not be treated alike. The essential facts are the same in each: the defendant acquired a registered interest in land at the expense of the plaintiff as a result of the intervention of a third party, the plaintiff did not (fully) intend to

---

[24] At p 195.
[25] At p 196.
[26] (1994) 33 NSWLR 202, 222-223, *per* Powell JA.
[27] *Smith v Wheeler* (1671) 1 Lev 279, 83 ER 406; *Mallott v Wilson* [1903] 2 Ch 494.
[28] *Re Vinogradoff* [1935] WN 68; *Re Muller* [1953] NZLR 879.
[29] See *eg Burke v State Bank of New South Wales* (1995) 37 NSWLR 53, 74-79.
[30] *Yerkey v Jones* (1939) 63 CLR 649.
[31] *National Australia Bank Ltd v Garcia* (1996) 39 NSWLR 577, 599 (CA).

benefit the defendant in the circumstances, and the defendant had constructive notice of the plaintiff's lack of intention to confer the benefit. If the unduly influenced plaintiff can obtain restitution in these circumstances on the basis of his or her vitiated intention to benefit the defendant, then so should the victim of forgery or fraud who had no intention to benefit the defendant whatsoever. There does not appear to be any conscious judicial decision to treat these essentially similar cases differently. It appears merely that the presentation of the cases, as problems of either indefeasibility or restitution, has meant that the courts have not been asking the same questions in reaching their solutions. How then should this inconsistency be resolved?

6. Possible solutions

One could choose to follow the path taken in *Pyramid v Scorpion* and hold that a plaintiff cannot obtain restitution unless the defendant has been fraudulent or at least actively involved in the creation of that right to restitution. However, this would prove a difficult road. As discussed above, it has already been decided that equitable interests in Torrens land arise in much the same way as they do under the general law. The "in personam exception" includes all the normal causes of action at common law and equity which might produce a right to land. The exclusion of rights generated by unjust enrichment would require a highly artificial and unsatisfactory barrier. It would also mean uprooting several well established principles. The guarantee cases represent just one area that would be affected. The resulting trust is another. In New South Wales, where a volunteer can rely upon the principle of indefeasibility, it has been decided that the purchase of a registered interest in land in the name of a volunteer will give rise to a resulting trust if the purchaser did not intend to benefit that volunteer.[32] This cannot be explained on the basis of the volunteer's fraud or conduct and could not be continued if the courts in that state adopted the reasoning in *Pyramid v Scorpion*.

The exclusion of claims based on unjust enrichment from the "in personam exception" would place intolerable pressure on the fraud exception, with at least two adverse consequences. First, the temptation to characterise as fraudulent that conduct which falls short of dishonesty would expand the meaning of fraud in Torrens systems. This would dilute the protection afforded by registration in all cases and not just those involving the "in personam exception". Secondly, it would distort the law of unjust enrichment as plaintiffs would need to characterise as dishonest their defendants' involvement in the duress, undue influence, mistake, etc, which formed the basis of their claims to restitution of registered interests in land.

One can see these forces at work as long ago as 1916 in *Taitapu Gold Estates Ltd v Prouse*,[33] where, by a mutual mistake, the plaintiffs transferred more land than intended to the defendants. Under their contract, the plaintiffs were supposed to retain the minerals under the land being sold. However, the minerals were not excepted from the transfer which was registered, thereby giving the defendants legal title to them. The New Zealand Supreme Court decided that the defendants held the minerals on constructive trust for the plaintiffs, even though "they became registered as proprietors without fraud".[34] This trust can be explained as a response to the unjust enrichment of the defendants in the absence of any wrongdoing or dishonesty by the defendants. However, the court felt a need to characterise the defendants' conduct as wrongful, possibly as a justification for interfering with their registered title. Hosking J stated, "In refusing to perform this obligation [to make restitution] and claiming to retain the minerals they are in the wrong, and so the Court has complete jurisdiction."[35]

---

[32] *Brown v Brown* (1993) 31 NSWLR 582 (CA).
[33] [1916] NZLR 825.
[34] *Ibid*, 832, per Hosking J.
[35] *Ibid*, 834.

This will not do. If one can innocently acquire a registered interest in land for value and in good faith and later become a wrongdoer for failing to make restitution of that interest when the facts giving rise to that claim are discovered, then no claim for restitution of such interests should fail unless barred by the passage of time or other supervening events. What seems to have been intended as a means of reducing the incidence of restitution of registered interests in land would have the opposite effect.[36]

Another adverse effect of following *Pyramid v Scorpion* would be the creation of an unnecessary gulf between cases involving interests in Torrens land and cases involving other rights, such as rights to land outside the Torrens system, other forms of property, and personal claims. There should be a compelling reason why, for example, a wife who was unduly influenced personally to guarantee her husband's indebtedness might obtain restitution if the creditor had notice of the undue influence, but not if she also provided a registered mortgage of the family home in support of her guarantee. This path should not be taken unless it can be shown that the integrity of the Torrens system would otherwise be undermined.

Does the other route, taken (perhaps unwittingly) in guarantee cases, provide a better means of regulating claims to restitution of registered interests in land? This strategy limits restitution to cases where the defendant had notice of the unjust enrichment. It recognises that a defendant, who has acquired the enrichment for value and in good faith, has an interest in the security of the transaction which prevails over the plaintiff's interest in obtaining restitution.[37] This is consistent with the approach taken by common law and equity. For example, money paid under a spontaneous mistake (of fact) unjustly enriches the recipient and gives rise to a claim for restitution, subject to defences.[38] This is not true where it is paid under a valid contract.[39] In both cases, the plaintiff was equally mistaken. However, the plaintiff's restitution interest will not prevail in the contractual setting unless there is some additional factor which reduces or eliminates the defendant's otherwise prevailing interest in the security of the transaction. This can occur when the defendant induced,[40] shared,[41] or at least had notice of the plaintiff's mistake.[42] A similar strategy seems to be employed in cases where the plaintiff is suffering from mental incapacity[43] or had a secret qualification of his or her intention to benefit the recipient.[44]

Will this work in a Torrens system? One might assume that a defendant, who has not dealt directly with the plaintiff, but has obtained his or her interest from a forger, would not have a strong claim to the security of his or her receipt. This is the conclusion of the common law and equity, where the normal rule is that persons cannot transfer what they do not have, regardless of how much value is given in good faith in return.[45] However, courts have steered the Torrens system in a somewhat different direction. As mentioned above, registration produces a good title, even if based on a forgery; and, where registration is obtained for value and in good faith, the plaintiff cannot claim restitution.[46]

The protection of the Torrens system embraces more than just transactional security. The courts have decided that the integrity of the system requires that registered interests acquired for

---

[36] See P Birks, "Trusts Raised to Reverse Unjust Enrichment: The *Westdeutsche* case" [1996] RLR 3, 21–22.
[37] *Bainbrigge v Browne* (1881) 18 Ch D 188, 196; *Bank of New South Wales v Rogers* (1941) 65 CLR 42; K Barker, "After Change of Position: Good Faith Exchange in the Modern Law of Restitution", ch 7 of P Birks (ed), *Laundering and Tracing* (OUP, 1995), 191.
[38] *Barclays Bank Ltd v WJ Simms Son & Cooke (Southern) Ltd* [1980] QB 677.
[39] *Bell v Lever Brothers Ltd* [1932] AC 161.
[40] *Newbigging v Adam* (1886) 34 Ch D 582.
[41] *Cooper v Phibbs* (1867) LR 2 HL 149, 170.
[42] *Garrard v Frankel* (1862) 30 Beav 445, 54 ER 961; *Taylor v Johnson* (1983) 151 CLR 422.
[43] *Hart v O'Connor* [1985] AC 1000 (PC).
[44] *Burgess v Rawnsley* [1975] Ch 429 (CA).
[45] See *Northern Counties of England Fire Insurance Co v Whipp* (1884) 26 Ch D 482.
[46] It is said that the registered proprietor is entitled to "immediate indefeasibility": BH Ziff, *Principles of Property Law*, 2nd ed (Toronto, 1996), 415–416.

value and in good faith be secure even in the absence of an underlying transaction. However, as the cases establishing the "in personam exception" show, this does not mean that registered proprietors must be protected from all unregistered claims. The principles governing claims for restitution of unjust enrichment, modified to accommodate the Torrens system, can provide the needed balance between the plaintiff's restitution interest and the defendant's security interest. A defendant who acquires a registered interest in Torrens land from a plaintiff, with notice of the facts giving rise to the plaintiff's claim for restitution of that interest (*ie* notice that the interest is an unjust enrichment at the plaintiff's expense), should not be protected from that claim by the principle of indefeasibility.

This was the approach taken by the New South Wales Court of Appeal recently in *Tutt v Doyle*.[47] Due to a mistake in a plan of subdivision of the plaintiffs' land, they transferred more land than intended to the defendants. The court ordered a new survey and retransfer of the area in dispute, even though the defendants had become registered proprietors of that land. The plaintiffs' claim was handled under the "in personam exception". They had a right to recover the land because the defendants "knew or had reason to know of the mistake prior to completion".[48] In other words, constructive notice of the facts giving rise to the plaintiffs' right to restitution was sufficient to elevate that right above the defendants' interest in the security of their registered title. If this is true in cases of non-induced mistakes, it must also apply in cases where the transfer is caused by the forgery or fraud of a third party.

A primary objective of the Torrens system is the avoidance of the expense, difficulty, and delay of investigating and proving the validity of a vendor's title. The inclusion of claims for restitution of unjust enrichment in the category of "in personam exceptions" does not conflict with this objective. There is a great deal of difference between an investigation into the quality of the vendor's title, which the Torrens system is designed to obviate, and an investigation into the validity of the transaction through which title will be obtained. If the defendant knew or ought to have known that the plaintiff was operating under mistake, duress, undue influence, or in ignorance of the transaction itself, the plaintiff's interest in obtaining restitution of the unjust enrichment can prevail over the defendant's interest in the security of his or her receipt, without undermining the objectives of the Torrens system.

Courts need to recognise that claims for restitution of unjust enrichment are neither exotic nor exceptional and that they need not be dealt with as "exceptions" to indefeasibility. Like a declaration of trust or a contract of sale, unjust enrichment is one of many events which can generate rights to land. Registration of an interest in land cures defects in the vendor's title, but does not immunise the registered proprietor from unregistered rights to that land arising on or after registration. As Ms Langford noted, "the often exclusive reliance on fraud as a grounds for claiming the subsistence of an unregistered interest sometimes overlooks the legitimate principles by which a registered proprietor can be required to honour their legal and equitable obligations".[49]

---

[47] (1997) 42 NSWLR 10.
[48] *Ibid* 15, *per* Handley JA.
[49] R Langford, "The *In Personam* Exception to Indefeasibility of Title" in J Dodds Streeton & R Langford, *Aspects of Real Property and Insolvency Law* (Adelaide L Rev Research Paper No 6, 1994) 91, 120.

Restitutionary Compensatory Damages for Breach of Fiduciary Duty?

(Swindle v Harrison)

Steven B Elliott*

English lawyers have watched over the past 20 years as courts elsewhere in the Commonwealth have shown a renewed willingness to issue compensatory relief for breach of fiduciary duty.[1] This head of equitable jurisdiction has been virtually dormant in England since *Nocton v Lord Ashburton*[2] in 1914, doubtless because of the resistance of English jurists to enlarging the province of fiduciary law. *Swindle v Harrison*[3] is notable for the Court of Appeal's full-blooded affirmation that "Equitable compensation may be awarded for breach of fiduciary duty." Judging from the experiences of other jurisdictions, the open recognition of this remedy may herald a series of English cases in which plaintiff advisees try to capitalize on the wide rules of recovery thought to obtain once a fiduciary breach is made out. In view of this possibility, the critical task faced by the court in *Swindle v Harrison* was to lay a sound foundation by explaining the difference between compensatory damages for breach of fiduciary duty and common law damages. The calculation of relief was not argued in *Nocton v Lord Ashburton*, and so Haldane LC was content to say that it "may not always be the same as in an action of deceit or for negligence".[4]

The judgments in *Swindle v Harrison* are ambitious and raise several difficult questions about the character and availability of damages for breach of fiduciary duty. The purpose of this comment is to consider the proposition expounded by both Evans and Mummery LJJ that the basic difference between damages for breach of fiduciary duty and damages for common law negligence consists in the former being awarded "on what may be called the restitutionary basis" (which I will call the "restitutionary characterisation").[5] The judges offered this restitutionary character in explanation of the relatively liberal rules of remoteness that limit recovery of damages for breach of fiduciary duty, and of certain powerful presumptions favouring wronged principals. The idea that damages for breach of fiduciary duty are restitutionary has been gaining currency elsewhere in the Commonwealth.[6] The position taken in this comment is that the coin is false. There is no worthwhile sense in which equitable compensation can be said to be

---

* Merton College, Oxford.
[1] Most of the Commonwealth cases are cited in M Tilbury, "Equitable Compensation": ch 22 of P Parkinson (ed), *Equitable Principles*, (LBC Information Services, Sydney, 1996).
[2] *Nocton v Lord Ashburton* [1914] AC 932 (HL). The only other English cases in this century in which damages have been awarded for breach of fiduciary duty are *Woods v Martins Bank Ltd* [1959] 1 QB 55 and *Mahoney v Purcell* [1996] 3 All ER 61, discussed PBH Birks [1997] RLR 72.
[3] *Swindle v Harrison* [1997] 4 All ER 705, 733 (CA); noted L Ho (1997) 11 TLI 72; H Tijo & T M Yeo (1998) 114 LQR 181. One of the justices, Hobhouse LJ, refused to accept that breach of fiduciary duty evokes compensatory relief, or at least compensation for consequential losses. The claimant Harrison's submission was "not reasoning which equity recognises. It is not restitutionary." (726).
[4] *Nocton v Lord Ashburton* [1914] AC 932, 958.
[5] *Swindle v Harrison* [1997] 4 All ER 705, 715.
[6] Eg Breach of fiduciary duty: *Canson Enterprises Ltd v Boughton & Co* [1991] 3 SCR 534, 547, 577; *Hodgkinson v Simms* [1994] 3 SCR 377, 440; (1994) 117 DLR (4th) 161, 199; *Hill v Rose* [1990] VR 129, 144; Breach of trust: *Re Dawson* [1966] 2 NSWR 211, 216; *Bartlett v Barclays Bank Trust Co Ltd (No 2)* [1980] Ch 515, 543–544; *Target Holdings Ltd v Redferns* [1994] 2 All ER 337, 348–349, CA; *Guerin v R* [1984] 2 SCR 335, 360–362; Texts: DJ Hayton, *Underhill and Hayton Law Relating to Trusts and Trustees*, 15th ed, (Butterworths, London, 1995), 825-831; JE Martin, *Hanbury & Martin's Modern Equity*, 15th ed (Sweet & Maxwell, London, 1997), 634; IE Davidson, "The Equitable Remedy of Compensation" (1982) 13 MULR 349, 351–353; RP Meagher, WMC Gummow & JRF Lehane, *Equity Doctrines and Remedies*, 3rd ed, (Butterworths, Sydney, 1992), ¶2304; J Glover, *Commercial Equity — Fiduciary Relationships*, (Butterworths, Sydney, 1995), ¶6.117.

restitutionary. The restitutionary characterisation has tended to obscure the true justification of the phenomena it purports to explain, which is a policy of deterring fiduciary misconduct. This stifles discussion of that policy's defensible limits. The restitutionary characterisation is also concerning because it blurs the conceptual distinction between gain and loss-based pecuniary relief.

The alleged restitutionary character of damages for breach of fiduciary duty needs to be considered together with the character of compensation for breach of trust. Because of their shared jurisdictional provenance, these forms of relief are often grouped together under the label "equitable compensation", and are thought to be computed on a like basis. The idea that compensatory damages for breach of fiduciary duty are in some sense restitutionary was born out of the earlier idea that compensation for breach of trust is restitutionary. This was most famously articulated in 1966 in the Australian case *Re Dawson*,[7] which needs to be revisited. There are important differences between damages for breach of fiduciary duty and compensation for breach of trust that the use of a common label can lead us to overlook, but the applicability of the restitutionary characterisation is not one of them. I will argue that the restitutionary characterisation of damages for breach of fiduciary duty is misconceived for the same reasons that the restitutionary characterisation of compensation for breach of trust is misconceived.

The decision

Swindle v Harrison concerned the liability of a solicitor who deals with his client and inadvertently fails to disclose material information. The solicitor Swindle acted for Harrison in the purchase of a restaurant business in Warwick. Part of Harrison's financing fell through shortly before completion. Alternative funds could not be found. Harrison faced losing her deposit and outlays she had already made improving the premises, as well as being exposed to a contract claim in a falling market. In an act of "extreme indiscretion", Swindle's firm offered at the eleventh hour to lend Harrison the money she needed. There was no time for independent advice. The terms of the loan were fair, but Swindle neglected to disclose details of the profit his firm was making and another "marginal" but material fact. The business failed and Harrison was ruined. Crucially, Harrison would have acted in the same way and suffered the same losses if she had been fully informed. If Harrison had been independently advised, she would have been told to take the firm's loan. She was therefore precluded for want of causation, if for no other reason, from recovering her losses against Swindle in negligence. Harrison turned to equity. She contended that, since Swindle was prohibited as a fiduciary from dealing with her without making adequate disclosure, he was liable to make good all of her resultant losses without regard to what would have happened if he had properly discharged his duties and without regard to remoteness.

Harrison's submission was unsuccessful in both the trial court and the Court of Appeal. The three judgments differ markedly. Each of the judges accepted that Swindle had breached fiduciary duties in making inadequate disclosure. Both Evans and Mummery LJJ reasoned that these wrongs did not cause Harrison's losses because she would have taken the same disastrous course if proper disclosure had been made. Evans LJ thought that Harrison would have been entitled to recover if Swindle's breach had been "equivalent to fraud", which seems to require advertent infidelity. He explained that damages for breaches of fiduciary duty that are "equivalent to fraud" are, in his language, restitutionary and therefore unlimited by the ordinary rules of remoteness and causation, although "the chain of causation can be broken by some independent and untoward event".[8] Damages for less turpitudinous breaches are subject to the same rules of remoteness and causation as damages for common law negligence. Mummery LJ accepted that, by virtue of its "restitutionary" character, Swindle's liability was not subject to remoteness limita-

[7] [1996] 2 NSWR 211.
[8] *Swindle v Harrison* [1997] 4 All ER 705, 718.

tions, and also that "it is no defence . . . that compliance with the duty would not have altered the decision of Mrs Harrison to proceed with the bridging loan".[9] He nonetheless concluded that Harrison's loss "did not flow from [Swindle's] breach of fiduciary duty".[10] This, Mummery LJ wrote, was because the risk that the restaurant business would fail was not within the "scope" of Swindle's duty. Hobhouse LJ agreed that Swindle's non-disclosure did not cause Harrison's losses, but preferred to put his decision on the basis that breach of fiduciary duty does not sound in damages.

Gain-based restitution

The term "restitution" is primarily used by private lawyers to describe a remedial response whereby a defendant is directed to give some benefit he has received up to a plaintiff.[11] Restitution is concerned with stripping illegitimate gains. There are two restitutionary patterns of pecuniary liability. The first pattern consists in a defendant's being obliged to give the value of a benefit back to the plaintiff. The second pattern consists in a defendant's being obliged to disgorge the value of a benefit obtained from a third party but at the plaintiff's expense. The conventional remedies for breach of fiduciary duty — constructive trust, rescission and account — have or can have restitutionary patterns. They either direct the errant fiduciary to restore property or value obtained from the principal or to disgorge profits made at the principal's expense. This meaning of the term "restitution" must be contrasted with the normal meaning of "compensation". Whereas restitution is measured by the defendant's gain, an award of compensation directs the defendant to pay a sum of money calculated to make good a loss suffered by the plaintiff.

Where a trustee has appropriated trust property to his own purposes, a claim by the beneficiaries for equitable compensation resembles an action for restitution in the usual sense. Having taken a benefit belonging to the beneficiaries, the trustee must restore it to them. This is a fortuitous resemblance. The trustee's duty to compensate his trust holds equally where he has wrongfully appropriated trust property to his own purposes, as in *Re Dawson*,[12] and where he has lost trust property through careless mismanagement, as in *Bartlett v Barclays Bank Trust*.[13] Lord Browne-Wilkinson was unequivocal in *Target Holdings Ltd v Redferns*:[14]

> "Equitable compensation for breach of trust is designed to achieve exactly what the word compensation suggests: to make good a loss in fact suffered by the beneficiaries and which, using hindsight and commonsense, can be seen to have been caused by the breach."

Compensation for breach of trust is not restitutionary in the usual sense.

A fiduciary's gain similarly mirrors his principal's loss when, as in *McKenzie v McDonald*, the fiduciary purchases property from his principal at an undervalue.[15] A pecuniary award of the difference is ambivalent between restitution and compensation. The loss-based character of equitable compensation is unambivalent, however, in cases such as *Swindle v Harrison*, in which the alleged loss is not reflected by an enrichment of the fiduciary. Harrison did not call Swindle's firm to account for the modest profit generated by its loan to her; rather, she sought compensation for the large consequential trading losses she sustained in the failed restaurant venture. In

---

[9] *Ibid*, 733.
[10] *Ibid*, 735.
[11] PBH Birks, *An Introduction to the Law of Restitution* (Oxford University Press, Oxford, rev ed, 1989) (hereafter "Birks"), 9–16.
[12] *Re Dawson* [1966] 2 NSWR 211.
[13] *Bartlett v Barclays Bank Trust* [1980] Ch 515.
[14] *Target Holdings Ltd v Redferns* [1996] 1 AC 421, 439.
[15] *McKenzie v McDonald* [1927] VLR 134; in England, *Mahoney v Purcell* [1996] 3 All ER 61.

Canson Enterprises Ltd v Boughton & Co,[16] where the plaintiff also sought relief from the consequences of relying on wrongful advice, Stevenson J wrote "This case is not about profit making and restitutionary concepts do not fit." This observation applies equally to *Swindle v Harrison*.

Loss-based restitution?

Exponents of the restitutionary characterisation must be using the term "restitution" in an unusual sense. It is plain that they take it to express a distinctive feature of equitable relief. A claim for equitable compensation is said to be "in a different and higher category than a claim which merely sounds in damages at common law" because it is restitutionary.[17] The restitutionary characterisation identifies an "approach" to quantifying pecuniary liability.[18] The restitutionary approach is sometimes thought to proceed from an analogy with restitution of property: "equity awards compensation in place of restitution *in specie*, by analogy for breach of fiduciary duty with the ideal of restoring to the estate that which was lost through the breach."[19] Liability is calculated according to different criteria from damages for common law negligence. Mummery LJ said in *Swindle v Harrison*[20] that "Foreseeability and remoteness of damages are, in general, irrelevant to restitutionary remedies for breach of trust or breach of fiduciary duty." Evans LJ said that this can be otherwise expressed in terms of the appropriate comparisons that must be made in measuring loss.[21] On his view, whereas ordinary compensation aims to put the plaintiff in the position he would have occupied if he had not sustained the wrong, restitution for breach of fiduciary duty aims to put the plaintiff in the position be occupied before the wrong was committed.

These statements suggest that equitable compensation differs in some fundamental way from common law damages, but Lord Browne-Wilkinson emphasised their kinship in *Target Holdings Ltd v Redferns*:[22]

> "Under both systems liability is fault-based: the defendant is only liable for the consequences of the legal wrong he has done to the plaintiff and to make good the damage caused by such wrong. He is not responsible for damage not caused by his wrong or to pay by way of compensation more than the loss suffered from such wrong. The detailed rules of equity as to causation and quantification of loss differ, at least ostensibly, from those applicable at common law. But the principles underlying both systems are the same."

The compensation principle is captured in several formulations. Compensatory awards aim to make the plaintiff whole; or to achieve *restitutio in integrum*; or to put the plaintiff in the position he occupied before the breach; but the leading articulation is Lord Blackburn's in *Livingstone v Rawyards Coal*:[23]

> "where any injury is to be compensated by damages, in settling the sum of money to be given for reparation of damages, you should as nearly as possible get that sum of money which will put the party who has been injured, or who has suffered, in the same position as he would have been if he had not sustained the wrong . . ."

It is a mistake to think, as Evans LJ did in *Swindle v Harrison*, that anything turns on this phraseology. These formulations express the same rudimentary idea and have generally been used

---

[16] *Canson Enterprises Ltd v Boughton & Co* [1991] 3 SCR 534, 590.
[17] *Re Dawson* [1966] 2 NSWR 211, 214.
[18] *Ibid*, 215; *Hodgkinson v Simms* (1994) 117 DLR (4th) 161 (SCC), 199.
[19] *Canson Enterprises Ltd v Boughton & Co* [1991] 3 SCR 534, 547, *per* McLachlin J.
[20] *Swindle v Harrison* [1997] 4 All ER 705, 733.
[21] *Ibid*, 714.
[22] *Target Holdings Ltd v Redferns* [1996] 1 AC 421, 432.
[23] *Livingstone v Rawyards Coal Co Ltd* (1880) 5 App Cas 25, 39.

interchangeably.[24] Compensation is calculated in different ways for different purposes, but the substance of these differences is not captured in the wording of these verbal formulae. In any event, we know because both the House of Lords and the Supreme Court of Canada have told us that Lord Blackburn's formulation of the compensation principle applies in equitable compensation cases.[25]

As with common law damages, equitable compensation is compensatory and is limited to those losses actually caused by a defendant's wrong. The restitutionary characterisation does not identify a radically distinct pattern of liability. Brightman J said in *Bartlett v Barclays Bank Trust*,[26] a trust case, that "The so-called restitution which the defendant must now make to the plaintiffs . . . is in reality compensation for loss suffered . . . not readily distinguishable from damages except with the aid of a powerful legal microscope." Pecuniary awards for breach of equitable duties can nonetheless be more severe than damages for common law negligence, because more generous rules of remoteness obtain and because of special presumptions that operate against equitable wrongdoers. Whereas recovery in negligence is limited to foreseeable losses, recovery of equitable compensation is not, although the courts have not yet articulated the remoteness limit that does apply.[27] Whereas recovery in negligence is dependent on proof by the plaintiff of factual causation, *Brickenden v London Loan & Savings Co*[28] is sometimes taken to have decided that, once it is shown that an advisor breached a fiduciary duty by failing to disclose some fact his principal was entitled to know in connection with a transaction, it will be irrebutably presumed that this non-disclosure caused the principal to act as he did. If the restitutionary characterisation has explanatory force, it must be in organising and accounting for these and similar "detailed rules".

The idea that the severity of trustee liability is due to its restitutionary character was first expressed in *Re Dawson*.[29] The beneficiaries sought an order directing their trustee to compensate the trust for the value of wrongfully abstracted New Zealand money. The court was at that time obliged to give its award in Australian currency, and so a question arose whether the sum owing should be converted at the time of the breach or the time of the judgment. The New Zealand pound had appreciated relative to the Australian pound during the intervening period, and so the later date was favourable to the beneficiaries. The common law rule was that obligations incurred in foreign currencies are converted at the date of breach on the theory that the effects of currency fluctuations are too remote.[30] Street J decided that the common law rule did not apply and that the sum owing should be converted at the date of judgment.

"The obligation of a defaulting trustee", Street J said, "is essentially one of effecting restitution to the estate".[31] This obligation is "of a more absolute nature than the common law

---

[24] *Swindle v Harrison* [1997] 4 All ER 705, 713–714. There are innumerable examples of the phrases "put the plaintiff in the position he occupied before the breach" and "put the plaintiff in the position he would have occupied if he had not sustained the breach" being used interchangeably, but two are: Rogers, WVH, *Winfield & Jolowicz on Tort*, 14th ed, (Sweet & Maxwell, London, 1994), 645 and *Canson Enterprises Ltd v Boughton & Co* [1991] 3 SCR 534, 577, 579. JD Davies warns that using the phrase "restore the plaintiff to the position he was in before the breach" may engender confusion between measurement and remoteness of damage, which seems to have occurred in Evans LJ's judgment in *Swindle v Harrison*: "Equitable Compensation: 'Causation, Foreseeability and Remoteness'": ch 14 of D Waters (ed), *Equity, Fiduciaries and Trusts* (Carswell, Scarborough, 1993), 302–303.
[25] *Target Holdings Ltd v Redferns* [1996] 1 AC 421, 432; *Canson Enterprises Ltd v Boughton & Co* [1991] 3 SCR 534, 577; *Hodgkinson v Simms* (1994) 117 DLR (4th) 161 (SCC), 199; see also *Re Dawson* [1966] 2 NSWR 211, 215; *Hill v Rose* [1990] VR 129, 143–144. Evans LJ also thought that a different formulation applied in fraudulent misrepresentation cases, but the House of Lords applied Lord Blackburn's dictum in the leading case *Smith New Court Securities Ltd v Scrimgeour Vickers* [1997] AC 254, 262.
[26] *Bartlett v Barclays Bank Trust* [1980] Ch 515, 545.
[27] *Canson Enterprises Ltd v Boughton & Co* [1991] 3 SCR 534.
[28] *Brickenden v London Loan & Savings Co* [1934] 3 DLR 465 (PC).
[29] *Re Dawson* [1966] 2 NSWR 211.
[30] The common law is now more flexible: in England, see especially *The Despina R* [1979] AC 685 (HL).
[31] *Re Dawson* [1966] 2 NSWR 211, 214.

obligation to pay damages for tort or breach of contract".[32] By this he meant that it is unlimited by remoteness. "Considerations of causation, foreseeability and remoteness do not readily enter into the matter".[33] Street J cited several nineteenth century cases in support of this contention. The most prominent of these was *Caffrey v Darby*, in which Sir William Grant MR said obiter that a negligent trustee is liable for losses made possible by his carelessness even if they were unforeseeable and immediately precipitated by some event beyond his control.[34] From this Street J inferred that the common law rule that the effects of currency fluctuations are too remote does not apply in a breach of trust case. He added in support of this conclusion that the obligation to pay compensation is "tantamount to an obligation to effect restitution *in specie*".[35] The trustee must either restore the lost asset or give a pecuniary equivalent:

> "The obligation to restore to the estate the assets of which he deprived it necessarily connotes that, where a monetary compensation is to be paid in lieu of restoring assets, that compensation is to be assessed by reference to the value of the assets at the date of restoration and not at the date of deprivation. In this sense the obligation is a continuing one and ordinarily, if the assets are for some reason not restored in specie, it will fall for quantification at the date when recoupment is to be effected . ."[36]

Street J used the term of "restitution *in specie*" in an unusual sense. In conventional legal usage, to say that a defendant is under an obligation to make restitution *in specie* implies that the claimant has a right to recover the actual property. This could only be because the claimant's legal title or beneficial interest in the property never passed to the current holder. All trustees fall in due course under an obligation to transfer the actual trust property to their beneficiaries. That is not, however, the obligation with which Street J was concerned. Street J's contention was that a trustee must make restitution *in specie* of property that has been lost through a breach of trust, or make a payment in lieu. In these situations, the trustee's primary duty is not to restore the actual lost property to the trust estate. By hypothesis this property is no longer in his hands. What Street J meant was that the trustee's primary obligation is to *replace* the lost property by going out into the market and purchasing a substitute. The cases Street J referred to in which a trustee had been ordered to restore lost trust property in kind rather than cash all involved fungible financial instruments.[37] Compensation is necessary when no substitute is available.

A primary obligation to replace lost trust property in kind seems pointless. The trustee is liable to pay the same sum and the trust is reconstituted to the same extent whether the estate is replenished in cash or kind. On closer analysis, the actual replacement of the lost trust assets was not itself a significant feature of the trustee's liability in the cases to which Street J referred.[37a]

---

[32] *Ibid*, 216

[33] *Ibid*, 215. Street J's mention of causation is misleading. He added further on that trustee liability is not limited by causation, but then qualified this by writing that "the inquiry in each instance would appear to be whether the loss would have happened if there had been no breach": *ibid*, 215. Lord Browne-Wilkinson rightly observed in *Target Holdings Ltd v Redferns* [1996] 1 AC 421, 434, that asking whether a loss generating event would have occurred but for a breach is a causal inquiry. Street J seems to have meant that losses are only recoverable if they would not have occurred but for the trustee's breach, but that the chain of "but for" consequences does not have a remoteness cap.

[34] *Caffrey v Darby* (1801) 6 Ves 488; 31 ER 1159. See also *Salway v Salway* (1831) 2 Russ & M 215; 39 ER 376 and *Clough v Bond* (1838) 3 My & Cr 490; 40 ER 1016.

[35] *Re Dawson* [1966] 2 NSWR 211, 216, *Cf Target Holdings Ltd v Redferns* [1996] 1 AC 421, 434.

[36] *Re Dawson* [1966] 2 NSWR 211, 216.

[37] *Kellaway v Johnson* (1842) 5 Beav 319, 49 ER 601; *Re Massingberd's Settlement* (1890) 59 LJ Ch 107. Street J also referred to *Phillipson v Gatty* (1848) 7 Hare 516, 68 ER 213, but in that case the trustees were not ordered to actually replace the stock, but rather to make up the difference between its present market value and what the improper investments could be sold for.

[37a] See *Ministry of Health v Simpson* [1951] AC 251, 273.

The motivation of these decisions was that the trust should take the benefit of any extraordinary appreciation or returns the trust investments would have generated if they had been retained. According to the analytical approach favoured by the House of Lords in *Target Holdings v Redferns*, the question to ask is whether on the facts known at the time of judgment, the loss of these profits can be said to have been caused by the trustee's breach.[38] A defaulting trustee's liability is quantified at the date of judgment, but that is not because of its alleged restitutionary character. Liability is quantified at the time of judgment because events between then and the date of breach may have increased or decreased the loss attributable to the trustee's wrong.[39] A trustee's obligation to compensate his trust is only "continuing" in the sense that the liability of any wrongdoer to make good a loss continues until it is discharged. The same general analysis applies when a bailee misappropriates or loses bailed goods.[40] The usual measure of damages is the market value of the goods at the time of the wrongful conversion, but the bailor may ordinarily recover as consequential loss any subsequent rise in their value.[41] The true analysis of *Re Dawson* is that, if the trust funds had not been abstracted, they would have been denominated in New Zealand pounds and would consequently have appreciated in value relative to Australian pounds. If the sum owing was converted into Australian currency at the date of the breach, the beneficiaries would have lost the benefit of a strengthened New Zealand pound. The choice of the later date reflects the court's decision to treat this loss as not too remote.

Trustee liability can be relatively severe out of a concern to ensure that people managing the property of others are kept up to their duty. This has been obscured by the restitutionary characterisation articulated in *Re Dawson*, but is apparent in earlier cases such as *Caffrey v Darby*.[42] The trustees failed to duly collect periodic payments owing to the estate. The payor went bankrupt and the trust's security was held to be worthless. While careless in failing to insist on prompt payment, the trustees had acted in good faith. They defended a claim for compensation on the basis that the immediate cause of the trust's loss was the payor's bankruptcy and the "doubtful" judicial decision not to recognise their security. These precipitating events, the trustees said, were neither foreseeable nor their fault. Sir William Grant MR thought the loss was a foreseeable consequence of the trustees' mismanagement, but added that trustees are in any event liable for the unforeseeable loss of trust property where "the property would not have been in a situation to sustain that loss, if it had not been for their negligence".[43] Sir William Grant MR explained that a harsh approach is justified by equity's policy of deterring trustee misconduct. A milder rule "would be an encouragement to bad motives; and it maybe impossible to detect undue motives".[44] The rubric of restitution conceals the underlying policy question in compensation for breach of trust cases, how strict does trustee liability need to be in order to achieve an efficient level of deterrence?

All of this applies *a fortiori* in fiduciary duty cases such as *Swindle v Harrison*. These cases do not involve lost property except incidentally, and so there is no sense in which a fiduciary could even be thought to be under a primary obligation to make restitution *in specie*. Nonetheless, Evans and Mummery LJJ followed courts elsewhere in the Commonwealth in characterising the fiduciary's obligation as restitutionary. As the term is used in *Swindle v Harrison*, it stands for nothing more than the fact that damages for breach of fiduciary duty are subject to more generous rules of recovery than common law damages for negligence. The restitutionary characterisation stands for these rules, but it does not explain them. Their generosity is due to equity's

---

[38] *Target Holdings Ltd v Redferns* [1996] 1 AC 421, 439.
[39] *Ibid*, 437.
[40] H McGregor, *McGregor on Damages*, 16th ed (Sweet & Maxwell, London, 1997), para 1384-1392.
[41] *Sachs v Miklos* [1948] 2 KB 23 (CA).
[42] *Caffrey v Darby* (1801) 6 Ves 488; 31 ER 1159.
[43] *Ibid*, 495–496.
[44] *Caffrey v Darby* (1801) 6 Ves 488, 496; 31 ER 1159.

deterrent policy. This policy justification was openly recognised in the Supreme Court of Canada's most recent pronouncement, *Hodgkinson v Simms*.[45] The plaintiff Hodgkinson invested in certain real estate developments on the advice of the defendant accountant Simms. Simms breached a fiduciary duty in taking secret commissions from the developers. The investments were otherwise unobjectionable when made, but the property market subsequently crashed. Simms argued that Hodgkinson was only entitled to disgorgement of the secret commissions, which is presumptively the amount by which Hodgkinson overpaid. Hodgkinson's investment loss, Simms contended, was too remote, and must be taken to have been the direct result of the general economic recession. This measure of relief, the court held, would not vindicate its policy of deterring fiduciary misconduct:[46]

> "Like-minded fiduciaries in the position of the respondent would not be deterred from abusing their power by a remedy that simply requires them, if discovered, to disgorge their secret profit, with the beneficiary bearing all the market risk. If anything, this would encourage people in this position in effect to gamble with other people's money, knowing that if they are discovered they will be no worse off than when they started."

Simms was ordered to make good the entire loss Hodgkinson sustained in the market collapse. Such has been the influence of *Re Dawson* that the court felt obliged to add that its conclusion accorded with "the principle that a defaulting fiduciary has an obligation to effect restitution in specie or its monetary equivalent".[47]

Terminological confusion

The term "restitution" has sometimes been used to mean nothing more than that the errant fiduciary's liability is compensatory. La Forest J expressed the difference between common law damages and equitable relief in these words in *Canson Enterprises Ltd v Boughton & Co*:[48] "Damages are a monetary payment awarded for the invasion of a right at common law. Equity aimed at restoring a person to whom a duty was owed to the position in which he or she would have been had the duty not been breached." The latter he described as a restitutionary approach. La Forest J shortly admitted that "in the case of simple compensation not involving the restoration of property" the difference in practical result between damages and compensation was difficult to discern.[49] He nonetheless said three years later in *Hodgkinson v Simms*[50] that "It is well established that the proper approach to damages for breach of fiduciary duty is restitutionary. On this approach, the appellant is entitled to be put in as good a position as he would have been had the breach not occurred." This passage echoes the formulation of the compensation principle in *Livingstone v Rawyards Coal*.[51]

In ordinary parlance the word "restitution" carries two different meanings of immediate interest. We sometimes speak of restitution of a person to a proper state, and we sometimes speak of restitution of a thing to a person. When we use "restitution" in the sense of restoring a person to a proper state, we are saying that they should be compensated for some improper deteriora-

---

[45] *Hodgkinson v Simms* (1994) 117 DLR (14th) 161, 208–209.
[46] *Ibid*, 209.
[47] *Ibid*, 208.
[48] *Canson Enterprises Ltd v Boughton & Co* [1991] 3 SCR 534, 577.
[49] *Ibid*, 577.
[50] *Hodgkinson v Simms* (1994) 117 DLR (4th) 161, 199, SCC.
[51] *Livingstone v Rawyards Coal* (1880) 5 App Cas 25, 39 (HL). Compare also "By analogy with restitution, [equitable compensation] attempts to restore to the plaintiff what has been lost as a result of the breach": *Canson Enterprises Ltd v Boughton & Co* [1991] 3 SCR 534, 556, *per* McLachlin J; ". . . the method of computation will be that which makes restitution for the value of the loss suffered from the breach.": Davidson (1982) 13 MULR 349, 351.

tion in their position. Restitution payments to an aggrieved minority for past political persecution, or to the victims of a natural disaster, are intended to make good the injury they suffered. While "restitution" can be used to mean compensation, there are good reasons for insisting on a sharp distinction in legal usage between compensation and restitution. Whereas compensation is the generic description of loss-based relief, restitution should only be used as the generic description of gain-based relief. Strict insistence on this distinction allows us to identify gain-based relief by a simple and unambiguous label. This accords with Spencer Bower's first law of scientific terminology, "that each term should express a distinct concept, and one only, and should always be used in one and the same sense".[52] If "restitution" is used to identify or describe compensatory relief we will have no word for gain-based relief.[53]

The risk of error is exacerbated by the emergent respectability of the term "restitutionary damages", which identifies money awards measured by the defendant's gain rather than the plaintiff's loss. After fermenting in the academic literature for some time, the term "restitutionary damages" was in 1997 commended to our use by the Law Commission in its report on exceptional measures of damages[54] and used by the Court of Appeal in *Attorney-General v Blake*.[55] Whether or not one agrees with the Law Commission, it is easy to see the needless danger in the same terminology being used to identify different forms of relief operating in close quarters. One of the principal remedies the Law Commission says we should call restitutionary damages is account of profits earned by reason of a fiduciary's position. Using the term "restitution" in connection with compensatory damages for breach of fiduciary duty as well may lead us to overlook two points in particular. The first is that exemplary awards are not appendable to gain-based awards responding to breaches of fiduciary duty, but are appendable to loss-based awards elsewhere in the Commonwealth.[56] While in England exemplary awards are not presently appendable to awards of damages for breach of fiduciary duty,[57] they will be if the Law Commission's recommendation is accepted.[58] The second is that a plaintiff may not normally claim both his losses and the defendant's gains arising from the same breach.[59] If loss and gain-based awards are treated under the same rubric we may forget they are elective. Clear thinking requires that these patterns of relief be kept apart.[60]

Conclusion

Swindle v Harrison propagates the idea that equitable compensation is awarded on a restitutionary basis. Evans and Mummery LJJ mistakenly accepted that the restitutionary characterisation of equitable compensation distinguishes it in some rudimentary way from common law damages. As Lord Browne-Wilkinson observed in *Target Holdings Ltd v Redferns*, equitable compensation is awarded according to the same basic principles as common law damages. They both aim to compensate a plaintiff for losses resulting from a defendant's wrong. Compensation for breach

---

[52] G Spencer Bower, *The Law of Actionable Misrepresentation* (Butterworth, London, 1911), para 462.
[53] Birks, 9–16.
[54] Law Commission, "Aggravated, Exemplary and Restitutionary Damages" (Law Com No 247, 1997), 51–52.
[55] *A-G v Blake* [1998] 2 WLR 805 (CA).
[56] *Vyse v Foster* (1872) LR 8 Ch App 309, 333; *Norweb v Wynrib* (1990) 92 DLR (4th) 449 (SCC), 505–507, per McLachlin J; see D Jensen, "Punitive Damages for Breach of Fiduciary Obligation" (1996) 19 U Queensland LJ 125.
[57] *AB v South West Water Services Ltd* [1993] QB 507.
[58] Law Commission, *Aggravated, Exemplary and Restitutionary Damages*: Law Com No 247 (1997), 111–113.
[59] *Tang Man Sit (dec'd) v Capacious Investments Ltd* [1996] 1 AC 514 (PC); *Warman International Ltd v Dwyer* (1995) 182 CLR 544, 559; *United States Surgical Corp v Hospital Products International Pty Ltd* [1982] 2 NSWLR 766, 816; see also Law Commission, "Aggravated, Exemplary and Restitutionary Damages" (Law Com No 247), 47–49.
[60] See also C Rickett & T Gardner, "Compensating for Loss in Equity: The Evolution of a Remedy" (1994) 24 VUWLR 19.

of trust and damages for breach of fiduciary duty are available on a more generous basis than damages for common law negligence, but this is because of a policy of deterring trustee and fiduciary misconduct. Open recognition that a deterrent policy motivates the severity of trustee and fiduciary liability would allow for honest debate about the proper limits of that policy. The restitutionary characterisation is also objectionable because it tends to blur the conceptual distinction between compensation and restitution. This is especially worrisome now that jurists are starting to use the term "restitutionary damages" to identify monetary awards measured by a defendant's gain. It is regrettable that the Court of Appeal allowed the restitutionary characterisation of damages for breach of fiduciary duty to confound English law.

Subrogation, Unjust Enrichment and Remedial Flexibility

(Banque Financière de la Cité v Parc (Battersea))

Charles Mitchell*

Banque Financière de la Cité v Parc (Battersea) Ltd[1] is notable amongst other things for the statement by Lord Steyn that "unjust enrichment ranks next to contract and tort as part of the law of obligations [as] an independent source of rights and obligations",[2] and for his approval of the view that "the place of subrogation on the map of the law of obligations is by and large within the now sizeable corner marked out for restitution".[3] Lord Hoffmann, too, found that one party can confer subrogation rights on another by contract, but that "the term [subrogation] is also used to describe an equitable remedy to reverse or prevent unjust enrichment which is not based on any agreement or common intention of the party enriched and the party deprived."[4] Lord Griffiths[5] and Lord Clyde[6] agreed with Lord Hoffmann. The majority of their Lordships therefore held that outside of contract, subrogation is best understood as a remedy of general application awarded to reverse or prevent unjust enrichment. In this regard, their speeches constitute a significant departure from Lord Diplock's well-known findings in *Orakpo v Manson Investments Ltd*,[7] that "there is no general doctrine of unjust enrichment in English law", that subrogation "takes place in a whole variety of widely different circumstances", and that "this makes particularly perilous any attempt to rely upon analogy to justify applying to one set of circumstances which would otherwise result in unjust enrichment a remedy of subrogation which has been held available for that purpose in another and different set of circumstances."

Lord Hoffmann's statement that subrogation can be awarded to prevent as well as to reverse unjust enrichment also bears out the view that there is no perfect quadration between unjust enrichment and restitution: Professor Birks has recently argued in this connection that restitution can be a response to events other than unjust enrichment;[8] Lord Hoffmann's dictum indi-

---

* Lecturer in Law, King's College London.
[1] [1998] 2 WLR 475; [1998] 1 All ER 737.
[2] [1998] 2 WLR 475, 479A. At 478H, Lord Steyn also uses, and by implication approves, the Birksian terminology of "unjust enrichment by subtraction" and "unjust enrichment by wrongdoing".
[3] *Ibid*, 480D.
[4] *Ibid*, 483E
[5] *Ibid*, 480F
[6] *Ibid*, 489G.
[7] [1978] AC 95, 104.
[8] P Birks, "Misnomer", chap 0 of W R Cornish et al (eds), *Restitution: Past, Present and Future* (Oxford, 1998). See too P Birks, "Property and Unjust Enrichment: Categorical Truths" [1997] NZLR 623, 626-627. Professor Birks previously thought otherwise: P Birks, *An Introduction to the Law of Restitution* (Oxford, 1985), 17–18, 46, 54.

cates that there can be responses to unjust enrichment other than restitution.[9] His words are also consistent with the argument that there are essentially two different types of subrogation awarded by the courts in different situations for different reasons: a claimant is allowed to take over extinguished rights of action via "reviving subrogation" in order to reverse the unjust enrichment of the party who was formerly liable to the right-holder and/or those of his creditors whose position has been improved by the extinction of the right-holder's claim; a claimant is awarded "simple subrogation" to subsisting rights of action in order to prevent the unjust enrichment that would otherwise follow, either of the right-holder or of the party liable to him, according to whether or not the right-holder decides to enforce his rights for himself.[10]

The present case was concerned with reviving subrogation: the appellant sought to be subrogated to rights which had been extinguished by its payment. It is often said in cases of this sort that the extinguished rights will be "kept alive" in favour of a successful claimant, so that he can enforce them for himself by "standing in the shoes" of the right-holder. These are metaphors. They serve a useful purpose to the extent that they explain how the parties in such cases stand in relation to one another, but in a famous phrase, "metaphors in law are to be narrowly watched, for starting out as devices to liberate thought, they end often by enslaving it".[11] Professor Birks has warned that "the language and image of substitution" used by the courts in reviving subrogation cases can obscure the fact that it is an open question in such cases whether the claimant's position following the award of the remedy should be "selectively or exactly like the [right-holder's]".[12] And something very like this happened in the present case. The Court of Appeal refused reviving subrogation to the appellant because it assumed that the remedy could only operate to give the appellant a security enforceable against all the world, as the right-holder's had been, and the court was not prepared to go so far on the appellant's behalf. This all-or-nothing view of the remedy's operation appeared to be consistent with the metaphorical imagery of substitution, but in fact it was a misconception. There is in fact nothing to prevent the courts from holding that a claimant should be treated as though he were entitled to enforce the rights previously enjoyed by a right-holder against a particular person, but that he should not be treated as though he were entitled to enforce those rights against anyone else. And in the event, the House of Lords made precisely such an order.[13]

---

[9] Other examples are: (i) an order that a principal debtor pay his creditor and thereby exonerate his surety from (secondary) liability for the debt: *eg National Commercial Bank v Wimborne* (1978) 5 BPR 11,958; and see discussion in J O'Donovan and J Phillips, *The Modern Contract of Guarantee*, 3rd ed (1996), 560–577; (ii) an order that co-sureties pay their shares of a principal debt directly to the creditor and thereby exonerate the plaintiff surety from (secondary) liability for more than his share: *Wolmershausen v Gullick* [1893] 2 Ch 514, 528–529, *per* Wright J; and see discussion in O'Donovan and Phillips, *supra*, 577–580; (iii) an order that the victim of a wrong committed by jointly and severally liable wrongdoers recover a portion of his loss from each: *Gluckstein v Barnes* [1900] AC 240, 255, *per* Lord Macnaghten; and see discussion in C Mitchell, "The Civil Liability (Contribution) Act 1978" [1997] RLR 27, 31.
[10] C Mitchell, *The Law of Subrogation* (Oxford, 1994) (hereafter "Mitchell"), 4–12.
[11] *Berkey v Third Avenue Railway Co* (1926) 244 NY 84, 94, *per* Cardozo J. Restitution lawyers may prefer Lord Mansfield's version, "Nothing in law is so apt to mislead as a metaphor": *Knox v Gye* (1872) LR 5 HL 656, 676, *per* Lord Westbury (giving no source for the quotation). See too RA Posner, *Law and Literature: A Misunderstood Relation* (London, 1988), 3: "The metaphor elides the reasoning process that might indicate both the aptness and the limits of the analogy that the metaphor (a compressed analogy) conveys." American case studies are: M Boudin, "Antitrust Doctrine and the Sway of Metaphor" (1986) 75 Georgetown LJ 395; B Henly, " 'Penumbra':The Roots of a Legal Metaphor" (1988) 15 Hastings Const LJ 81; S L Winter, "The Metaphor of Standing and the Problem of Self-Governance" (1988) 40 Stanford LR 1371; S J Safranek, "Can Science Guide Legal Argumentation? The Role of Metaphor in Constitutional Cases" (1994) 25 Loyola U Chicago LJ 357.
[12] P Birks, *An Introduction to the Law of Restitution* (Oxford, 1985), 95.
[13] It is only fair to note that the appellant specifically asked to be subrogated to a security enforceable against all the world at first instance and on appeal, and only attenuated its submission when it came before the House of Lords, to argue that it should be subrogated to the former security-holder's rights as against one particular party alone: see n 24 and text *infra*.

A second misleading legal fiction was also in issue. In a number of previous cases, the courts have held that claimants should be entitled to reviving subrogation because, in Lord Jenkins' words, "where a third party pays off a mortgage he is presumed, unless the contrary appears, to intend that the mortgage shall be kept alive for his own benefit."[14] This supposed general rule has always been suspect as a matter of authority, for the reason that it ultimately derives from a more narrowly conceived rule concerned with the rights of part-owners of real property who have paid off prior charges on the property.[15] It is also inconsistent with the view that reviving subrogation is a restitutionary remedy, because it does not require a claimant who has paid off a mortgage to show that it is unjust for the mortgagor and/or his creditors to take the benefit of the claimant's payment before he can be entitled to the remedy.[16] Nonetheless, Lord Hutton attempted to analyse the facts of the present case by reference to Lord Jenkins' formulation whilst simultaneously asserting that "one of the elements which gives rise to the right of subrogation is the unjust enrichment of the defendant at the expense of the plaintiff".[17] Lord Hutton agreed with the others in the result of the case, and some of his reasoning is in fact consistent with the restitutionary analysis which they adopted. However, to the extent that he thought that the appellant should be entitled to reviving subrogation because it could be fictionally presumed that the parties had intended that result, his analysis and the cases from which it was derived must now be viewed as incorrect as a matter of authority. For in his leading speech, Lord Hoffmann precisely identified and condemned as a misapprehension the view that, where there is no express contract between the parties, a plaintiff's entitlement to subrogation necessarily depends upon the intentions of the parties, fictional or otherwise. In Lord Hoffmann's words:[18]

> "[It] is a mistake to regard the availability of subrogation as a remedy to prevent unjust enrichment as turning entirely upon the question of intention, whether common or unilateral. Such an analysis has inevitably to be propped up by presumptions which can verge on outright fictions, more appropriate to a less developed legal system than we now have . . . [It] should be recognised that one is here concerned with a restitutionary remedy and that the appropriate questions are therefore, first, whether the defendant would be enriched at the plaintiff's expense; secondly, whether such enrichment would be unjust; and, thirdly, whether there are nevertheless reasons of policy for denying a remedy."

The significance of these matters in the specific context of the present case will be best understood once the facts of the case have been described.

The facts

Parc (Battersea) Ltd ("Parc") and Omnicorp Overseas Ltd ("OOL") were members of a group of companies called the Omni Group. To finance the purchase of property in London, Parc borrowed money from Royal Trust Bank (Switzerland) ("RTB") and from OOL, which were

---

[14] *Ghana Commercial Bank Ltd v Chandiram* [1960] AC 732, 745. See too the cases cited in Mitchell, 12, n 28.
[15] Mitchell, 13–14.
[16] *Ibid*, 14–15.
[17] [1998] 2 WLR 475, 490C.
[18] *Ibid*, 485F–H. At 492E, Lord Hutton acknowledges that "the concept of mutual intention, whether actual or presumed, can be artificial in a case such as the present one, where the claim to subrogation arises because the security intended by the lender has proved to be defective", but he goes on to say that "in such circumstances the doctrine of subrogation is to be applied unless its application will produce an unjust result". This would place the burden of proof on the defendant, but Lord Hoffmann clearly envisages that it should be for the plaintiff to make out a case before subrogation can be awarded as a restitutionary remedy: *cf* his statement at 486B that "if it is recognised that the use of the plaintiff's money to pay off a secured debt and the intentions of the parties about whether or not the plaintiff should have security are only materials upon which a court may decide that the defendant's enrichment would be unjust, it could be argued that on general principles it is for the plaintiff to make out a case of unjust enrichment."

respectively given first and second charges over the property. Subsequently, the controller and the general manager of the Swiss holding company of the group, Mr Rey and Mr Herzig, approached a Swiss bank, Banque Financière de la Cité ("BFC") to borrow £10 million with which to reduce Parc's debt to RTB, which then stood at £20 million. Because the Bank had already lent money to another company in the group, Swiss banking law required that the Swiss regulatory authorities approve any loan to Parc, a requirement which Mr Rey and Mr Herzig wished to sidestep. It was therefore agreed that BFC would instead lend the money to Mr Herzig, who in turn would lend it to Parc on the security of a deep discount promissory note which Mr Herzig would assign to BFC. Unknown to Parc and OOL at the time, Mr Herzig also gave BFC a letter ("the postponement letter") which was written on the holding company's writing paper and which stated: "This is to confirm that we and all companies of our group will not demand any repayment of loans granted to Parc (Battersea) Ltd, London, until the full repayment of your loan [to Mr Herzig]".

The £10 million was paid by BFC directly to RTB. Later, the balance of Parc's debt to RTB was paid off with further money lent by OOL, and RTB's charge was thereby extinguished. Parc then defaulted on the terms of the promissory note, and BFC issued proceedings as assignee of the note seeking payment of principal and interest, and a declaration that any indebtedness of Parc to OOL was postponed to or ranked after Parc's indebtedness to BFC on the note. BFC obtained judgment under RSC Ord 14 against Parc in these proceedings, but in separate proceedings OOL then also obtained judgment against Parc in respect of the various sums which it had lent the company. The issues which therefore fell to be decided in the current action were (i) whether the postponement letter was understood by BFC to be legally binding on OOL and Parc, (ii) if so, whether OOL and Parc were bound to its terms by dint of the holding company's actual or apparent authority to enter such an agreement on their behalf, and (iii) if not, whether BFC could be subrogated to RTB's rights as first charge-holder in order to acquire priority over OOL's claims against Parc.

At first instance, Robert Walker J held that the postponement letter was understood by BFC to be binding on Parc and OOL along with all the other members of the Omni Group, but that in fact neither the holding company, nor Mr Herzig, nor Mr Rey, was actually or apparently authorized to sign it on their behalf, with the result that it was not binding on them. He also held that BFC was entitled to be subrogated to a proportionate share of RTB's first charge, on the ground that, although the directors of Parc knew nothing of the postponement letter, what they did know was "sufficient to permit a mutual intention to be presumed, and to allow the doctrine of subrogation to apply."[19]

OOL appealed, and the Court of Appeal found in its favour. In Morritt LJ's view, the postponement letter was not understood by BFC to be an agreement by all the members of the Omni Group, but was rather understood by BFC to be a warranty by the holding company that the other members of the group would not enforce their rights against Parc before BFC was repaid. He also held that BFC could not be entitled to subrogation to a share of RTB's charge because: (i) the parties had specifically considered the creation of a charge over Parc's property to secure BFC's loan to Mr Herzig and rejected it in order to avoid disclosure of the loan under Swiss banking regulations; (ii) the holding company's breach of warranty had been due to BFC's failure to take the precaution of checking with OOL that it agreed that its debt should be postponed; (iii) there had been no misrepresentation by Parc or OOL; (iv) BFC could not have had the right to be subrogated to a proportionate share of RTB's security at the time when its £10 million was paid to RTB, because the award of the remedy at this time would have prejudiced RTB's right to recover the outstanding balance of its debt from Parc, and there was "no reason why the

---

[19] Transcript, 66. His view of the basis on which reviving subrogation is awarded was therefore similar to that espoused by Lord Hutton in the House of Lords, and for reasons which have already been discussed, this understanding of the factors entitling a claimant to the remedy was held by the majority of the House of Lords to be mistaken.

[subsequent] payment of the balance by OOL should generate in BFC a right to subrogation in circumstances where the earlier payment financed by BFC did not do so"; and (v) subrogation to RTB's charge would give BFC better rights than the ones it had bargained for — the rights of a mortgagee of Parc's property which would be "considerably more immediate and efficacious than the negative pledge they sought." BFC appealed.

The House of Lords' decision

Their Lordships held unanimously that the postponement letter was thought by BFC to be a binding negative pledge by all the members of the Omni Group, but that in fact the letter was not binding on Parc or OOL.[20] In other words, they agreed with Robert Walker J's findings on this point, and disagreed with Morritt LJ's finding that BFC thought it was getting a warranty by the holding company alone. They also held unanimously that BFC was entitled to be treated as though it had been subrogated to a proportionate share of RTB's rights against Parc, to the extent that subrogation to these rights would enable it to acquire priority over OOL in Parc's insolvency, but to no further extent than that. So far as Parc and its other creditors were concerned, BFC's status was to remain that of an unsecured creditor only.[21] Their Lordships therefore reinstated the order made by Robert Walker J, but amended it to provide that BFC was only entitled to be subrogated to RTB's position *as against OOL*.

The main reason why the House of Lords was prepared to award subrogation to BFC whereas the Court of Appeal was not is that the two courts had different conceptions of the way in which the remedy works. Morritt LJ assumed that the effect of allowing BFC to acquire RTB's rights via subrogation must be to give BFC a security which would be effective not only against OOL, but also against Parc and the other creditors seeking to prove in Parc's insolvency, and this led him to refuse subrogation to BFC because he thought it would be inequitable to put the bank into a better position vis-à-vis Parc than the one it had bargained for.[22] The House of Lords did not disagree with him on the latter point. They had no more desire than Morritt LJ to improve BFC's position vis-à-vis Parc and Parc's other creditors. For, although Parc had undoubtedly been enriched at BFC's expense when half of RTB's charge was extinguished, it could not be said that this enrichment was unjust, since BFC had expressly agreed that it should have no greater right as against Parc than the right to recover on the promissory note, and that was what it had got.[23] Where the House of Lords differed from the Court of Appeal was in recognising that an order subrogating BFC to RTB's rights did not have to put BFC in a position to enforce its subrogated rights against the whole world. This insight was made easier for their Lordships by the fact that on appeal BFC specifically argued for the first time that in principle it should be possible for the courts to award subrogation on the basis that a plaintiff should be allowed to enforce

---

[20] [1998] 2 WLR 475, 478B–F, *per* Lord Steyn, 480F, *per* Lord Griffiths, 486D–E, *per* Lord Hoffmann, 489F, *per* Lord Clyde, and 491E–F, *per* Lord Hutton.

[21] *Ibid*, 480E, *per* Lord Steyn, 480F, *per* Lord Griffiths, 488E-F, *per* Lord Hoffmann, 489G, *per* Lord Clyde, 496G and 497E, *per* Lord Hutton.

[22] In a note on the Court of Appeal's decision, the present writer argued that Morritt LJ might have been wrong to reach this conclusion because the desirability of giving BFC priority over OOL might have outweighed the undesirability of improving BFC's position vis-à-vis Parc and Parc's other creditors: [1998] LMCLQ 14, 18. This argument was predicated on the same mistaken assumption as that made by Morritt LJ, that it was impossible to achieve one of these outcomes without also achieving the other. Lord Hoffmann's analysis of the way in which reviving subrogation works evidently renders the argument otiose.

[23] In this respect, the case must be distinguished from a long line of cases in which subrogation has been rightly awarded as against both a property owner and an intervening chargee, in favour of a claimant who has paid off a first charge over the property in the mistaken belief that the owner has executed a valid new first charge in his favour, and who has then discovered the existence of the intervening chargee against whom his new security is ineffective: see the cases cited in Mitchell, 117, n 43, 120, n 53, 123, n 62.

its subrogated rights against some parties and not others.[24] But even so, it was an insight of great importance, since it means that in future cases the courts need not be inhibited by considerations of the kind which troubled Morritt LJ. As has been said already, Morritt LJ may have been misled by the metaphorical imagery of substitution which is repeatedly encountered in reviving subrogation cases. Lord Hoffmann's speech is an object lesson in the avoidance of this pitfall, in particular the following passage:[25]

> "In my view, the phrase 'keeping the charge alive' needs to be handled with some care. It is not a literal truth but rather a metaphor or analogy . . . When judges say that the charge is 'kept alive' for the benefit of the plaintiff, what they mean is that his legal relations with a defendant who would otherwise be unjustly enriched are regulated *as if* the benefit of the charge had been assigned to him. It does not by any means follow that the plaintiff must for all purposes be treated as an actual assignee of the benefit of the charge and, in particular, that he would be so treated in relation to someone who would not [otherwise] be unjustly enriched."

The question remains, of course, why their Lordships thought it appropriate to award BFC reviving subrogation as against OOL. The majority thought that BFC was entitled to this because OOL had been enriched by the increase in the value of its security over Parc's property which resulted when BFC paid off half of RTB's charge,[26] and this enrichment was unjust because BFC would not have paid RTB but for its mistaken belief that OOL had agreed not to enforce its security against Parc until after BFC had been repaid.[27] It did not follow from the fact that BFC had agreed to lend the money to Mr Herzig who in turn had agreed to lend it to Parc that OOL's enrichment was not at BFC's expense, because BFC could easily trace its payment into the partial extinction of RTB's security: it had paid RTB directly.[28] The fact that BFC's mistake was not induced by any misrepresentation by OOL was irrelevant: in Lord Steyn's words, "restitution is not a fault-based remedy".[29] It was also irrelevant that BFC acted negligently in failing to check whether the holding company, Mr Rey or Mr Herzig were in fact authorised to bind OOL to the terms of the postponement letter.[30] BFC's participation in a scheme which was designed to avoid Swiss banking law did not amount to illegal behaviour of a kind sufficiently grave to disable it from asking for equitable relief.[31] And it did not follow from the fact that BFC had extinguished only part of RTB's charge that it should be denied reviving subrogation lest it hinder RTB's efforts to recover from Parc, in the first place because the balance of Parc's debt to RTB had since been paid off by OOL, and in the second place because BFC was anyway not asking to be subrogated to a security enforceable against Parc — all it wanted was a right enforceable against OOL.[32]

---

[24] [1998] 2 WLR 475, 478H, *per* Lord Steyn: "on appeal to your Lordships' House counsel for BFC attenuated his submission by making clear that BFC only seeks a restitutionary remedy against OOL", and 489D, *per* Lord Clyde: "the more modest claim which [BFC] now make . . . seems to me to have been made out."
[25] *Ibid*, 487G and 488A.
[26] *Ibid*, 479B, *per* Lord Steyn, and 486F, *per* Lord Hoffmann.
[27] *Ibid*, 478F and 479E, *per* Lord Steyn, and 486C-E, *per* Lord Hoffmann.
[28] *Ibid*, 479B-C, *per* Lord Steyn, 486F-H, *per* Lord Hoffmann, 489E, *per* Lord Clyde, and 490G-491A, *per* Lord Hutton.
[29] *Ibid*, 479G. See too 487B, *per* Lord Hoffmann, and 494A-D, *per* Lord Hutton.
[30] *Ibid*, 479H, *per* Lord Steyn, and 487A-B, *per* Lord Hoffmann. This finding was consistent with *Kelly v Solari* (1841) 9 M & W 54 and the other cases cited in G Jones (ed), *Goff & Jones on the Law of Restitution*, 4th ed (1993), 126, n 32. Lord Hutton reaches the same conclusion in different terms at 493H.
[31] *Ibid*, 486H, *per* Lord Hoffmann, and 497B-E, *per* Lord Hutton.
[32] *Ibid*, 479H-480A, *per* Lord Steyn, 487C-488F, *per* Lord Hoffmann, and 494F-496B, *per* Lord Hutton.

Equitable Title and Common Law Conversion: The Limits of the Fusionist Ideal

(MCC Proceeds v Lehman Bros)

Kit Barker*

For anyone who has followed the Maxwell litigation in general and the case of *MacMillan Inc v Bishopsgate Investment Trust Plc (No 3)*[1] in particular, the recent Court of Appeal decision in *MCC Proceeds Inc v Lehman Brothers International (Europe)*[2] will be of significant interest. In the first of these cases, the plaintiff, MacMillan (M), had sought to recover in equity shares which Mr Maxwell had first persuaded it to transfer into the name of a family company, Bishopsgate Investment Trust Plc (B) and then wrongfully pledged to a number of financial institutions, by way of security for the debts of his ailing business empire. One of the defendants in this action was a company by the name of Shearson Lehman Brothers (SLB), which had acquired some of the shares from their original pledgee, Lehman Brothers International (LB), an associated company. The claim against SLB failed on the basis that LB had acquired the shares from B bona fide, for value and without notice of M's equitable interest, so that SLB's derived title to them was clean. M subsequently went into Chapter 11 insolvency and we might have thought that there the matter would rest.

Not so. In *MCC Proceeds Inc v Lehman Bros*, the trustee of the Maxwell Realisation Liquidating Trust, MCC Proceeds (MCC), to whom M's rights had been assigned, recommenced proceedings on a different tack. Dropping the equitable claim to the shares themselves, it instead brought an action at law against LB for conversion of five of the relevant share certificates.[3] By accepting these from B pursuant to the latter's pledge; and by subsequently cancelling them[4] before selling the shares to SLB, LB had, MCC claimed, wrongfully converted them to its own use and was therefore strictly liable for their value. The fact that LB had obtained a good legal title to the shares from B was not, it was alleged, fatal to this conversion claim. M's equitable interest in the certificates, combined with its right to demand their return from B under the terms of the original transfer, sufficed to ground an action at law.

This was a straightforward action for compensatory damages, not for restitution. The difficult issues of legal classification which arose in the first set of proceedings[5] were therefore not resurrected. It did, however, raise two questions, one procedural and the other of crucial substantive importance.

The procedural question

The procedural question related to the application of the doctrine of *res judicata*. Space precludes more than cursory consideration here. Given that it had been determined in the first action that LB had obtained a good legal title to the shares from B; given that a conversion claim in respect

---

* Lecturer in Law, University of Southampton. My thanks to William Swadling for his helpful comments upon an earlier draft of this piece.
[1] [1995] 1 WLR 978 (Millett J), affirmed on different grounds [1996] 1 WLR 387 (CA).
[2] [1998] *The Times*, January 14.
[3] Cert Nos 234, 243, 245, 246, 347.
[4] This occurred when LB transferred the shares into the paperless central depository system of the Depository Trust Co in New York.
[5] On which, see Bird [1995] LMCLQ 308, [1996] LMCLQ 57; Briggs [1996] RLR 88; Swadling [1996] LMCLQ 63; Stevens (1996) 59 MLR 741; Virgo (1996) 10 TLI 20.

of a share certificate[6] had been made against SLB in that case, but dropped; and given that no prior attempt had been made by M to join LB as a party to proceedings, two members of the Court of Appeal[7] were of the view that MCC's claim constituted an abuse of process, to be struck out on that basis. Although the current claim was against a different party (LB, not SLB) in respect of different property (certificates, not shares), the issues which were key to its success had, in substance, already been adjudicated upon and should not be reopened.

On reflection, this seems a little unfair. Although it must be correct to say, as Mummery and Pill LJJ did, that decisions about abuse of process should be taken with an eye on substance, not form, MCC were very careful not to challenge the substantive conclusion reached in the first case, that LB had obtained a good legal title to the shares from B. Rather, their argument was that this did not matter because an action for conversion will in some circumstances lie even against a legal owner.[8] This was a fresh argument (albeit one that in their own circumstances was highly unlikely to succeed[9]). Moreover, the first trial was already so heavily loaded with parties and issues that, even if M had joined LB in those proceedings, so as to enable the point to be argued, the trial judge might well have directed that it be dealt with separately, after completion of the main trial. On this basis, Hobhouse LJ preferred to describe the claim as without foundation, rather than as an abuse of process.

The substantive issue: equitable title and common law conversion

Of the two views, the latter is preferable. But whatever the procedural rights and wrongs of MCC's claim, all three members of the Court of Appeal were clear that it should be struck out on the separate ground that it had no realistic prospect of success. MCC's title to the shares was equitable only and could not ground an action at law. This conclusion appears uncontroversial, but is important precisely because it reaffirms an orthodoxy (that we should draw a sharp line between ideas developed in equity and at law) which in some contexts is under open attack.[10] In this sense, the decision feeds into a long-running, but recently re-invigorated debate about the meaning, desirability and feasibility of the fusionist ideal; and it describes important limitations upon that ideal.

(a) Orthodoxy: legal remedies, legal rights

On the orthodox view, a plaintiff seeking to succeed in an action at law for conversion must prove possession or an immediate legal right to possession.[11] As the Court of Appeal was quick to point out, MCC could point to neither. Since M had originally transferred the shares to B as (bare) trustee, it could not realistically claim an immediate right to possess them, or the certificates which represented them. This right lay with B. The fact that the terms of the transfer

---

[6] Cert No 425. This was hence different to those mentioned at n 3, *supra*. It was issued to SLB when the shares were purchased from LB. It was never in the possession of either M or B.
[7] Mummery, Pill LJJ.
[8] *Roberts v Wyatt* (1810) 2 Taunt 268, 127 ER 1080; *Nyberg v Hendelaar* [1892] 2 QB 202.
[9] *Infra*.
[10] *Infra*.
[11] Brazier, *Street on Torts*, 8th ed (Butterworths, London, 1988), 37; Heuston and Buckley, *Salmond & Heuston on the Law of Torts*, 20th ed (Sweet & Maxwell, London, 1992), 112; Rogers, *Winfield & Jolowicz on Tort*, 14th ed (Sweet & Maxwell, London, 1994), 498; Cane, *Tort Law and Economic Interests*, 2nd ed (Clarendon, Oxford, 1996), 30. There is a contrast between *Street* and *Salmond & Heuston* on the issue whether an equitable owner has title to sue: *Street*, 37 n 14, suggests that equitable ownership is "no disqualification" from suit, provided the plaintiff can make out a right to possess, whereas *Salmond*, 112, states that equitable title suffices, in contrast to a mere contractual right. These accounts are based on different interpretations of the case of *International Factors Ltd v Rodriguez*, *infra* n 18.

reserved to M the right to call for the shares back from B on provision of written notice did not alter this fact. Nor did the fact that B had, in pledging the shares to LB, fundamentally breached the terms of the arrangement. Those cases, cited by MCC,[12] which suggested that a fundamental breach of this kind might automatically re-vest the legal right to possession in M, were cases of bailment, not cases of trust. Moreover, since the primary function of the certificates was as an incident of legal title,[13] it was quite unrealistic to treat them separately from the shares to which they related and to suppose that the intention of the parties had somehow been to create a separate bailment of them. They too were held on trust, with the consequence that the immediate legal right to their possession also lay with B.

The consequence of this is, of course, a certain irony. Although the personal duties of a trustee are more stringent than those of a bailee, the creation of a trust, with the transfer of legal title which it entails, is apt to remove from the equitable owner the immediate right to possession and the protections attendant upon that right. This is entirely a product of the equitable owner's own intentions. The point of the trust arrangement is to enable the trustee to hold and manage property; and this can usually only be done if he obtains the possession right as well as the legal title to the property. Since the equitable owner assented to this, he cannot then legitimately complain about a deprivation of possession; only about a breach of trust by the trustee, or interference with his beneficial ownership rights; both of which give rise to their own, distinct remedies.[14] Conversion being a tort concerned with the protection of possession, not ownership, it is not its function to deal with these matters. There *is* an action at law which could deal with damage to ownership rights, which has probably survived the Torts (Interference with Goods) Act 1977 — an action for damage to a person's reversionary title to property[15] — but this was not available to MCC, because M had no legal title to be harmed by the shares' disposal.[16]

(b) Heresy: legal remedies, equitable rights

The only other way in which MCC might have succeeded was by advancing the heresy that their equitable title to the certificates was itself sufficient to ground a claim for conversion at common law. This would involve a merger of equitable and common law ideas and the Court of Appeal was, on the facts, right to reject it.

As a matter of authority, there were a number of cases which might have suggested that the heresy had a claim to truth. *Healey v Healey*[17] and *International Factors Ltd v Rodriguez*[18] were two of these, sufficient to convince Professor Palmer, writing in 1986, to suggest that a *cestui que trust* might indeed sue in conversion in some circumstances, and that this rule might need to be reconsidered by the House of Lords.[19] In fact, *Healey* was subsequently dealt with by the House

---

[12] *North Central Wagon & Finance Co Ltd v Graham* [1950] 2 KB 7; *Union Transport Finance Ltd v British Car Auctions Ltd* [1978] 2 All ER 385.

[13] Mummery and Hobhouse LJJ.

[14] MCC's practical problem was that the personal action against B and/or Maxwell for breach of trust was of little to no practical use. The equitable property claim in respect of the shares themselves had been defeated by the defence of bona fide purchase; and if a personal, restitutionary action been brought against LB or SLB for knowing receipt of trust property, it would currently have failed owing to the latters' innocence of M's interest. Even if it had not failed on this ground, there are good arguments to suggest that it, too, would have been barred by the bona fide purchase defence. See, *infra* n 44.

[15] *Mears v London & South West Railway Co* (1862) 11 CB (NS) 850, 142 ER 1029.

[16] As Hobhouse LJ observes, MCC's attempt to rely upon this line of authority was therefore misplaced. Its claim for damage to its "reversionary interest" in the shares was indistinguishable from an attempt to rely upon equitable title as the basis of a personal action at common law.

[17] [1915] 1 KB 938.

[18] [1979] 1 QB 351.

[19] Palmer, "The vindication of commercial security over commodities: equitable pledges and conversion" [1986] LMCLQ 213, 228.

in *The Aliakmon*.[20] Lord Brandon's speech in that case,[21] together with arguments put in an influential recent article by Professor Tettenborn,[22] were sufficient to convince the Court of Appeal that the claim must fail. *Healey* was a case in which the equitable owner had been in actual possession of the goods at the time they were converted and should be read in that light. In *Rodriguez*, the terms on which debts were factored to the plaintiff gave it an immediate legal right to the possession of the cheques which the defendant had wrongly diverted.[23] Buckley LJ's view in that case,[24] that the existence of the trust was immaterial to the conversion, was correct; and to the extent that Sir David Cairns' judgment suggested otherwise[25] (which it is fair to say that it did), this was based on a misunderstanding of both *Healey* and the fusionist idea set out in the Judicature Acts.

This line of reasoning led the Court of Appeal to a vigorous restatement of orthodoxy. The "short answer" to MCC's claim, said Mummery LJ, was "rooted deep in English legal history: conversion is a common law action and the common law did not recognise the equitable title of the beneficiary under a trust."

This conscious choice for orthodoxy contrasts importantly with a number of recent judicial statements in the law of restitution. In *Westdeutsche Landesbank Girozentrale v Islington London Borough Council*,[26] both Lords Goff and Woolf (dissenting) were of the clear opinion that equitable principles should be available in common law claims, if justice so requires.[27] This proposition is consistent with the views of Atkin LJ in *Banque Belge v Hambrouck*[28] and (more recently) Millett LJ in *Jones v Jones*[29] about the way tracing rules should work. It also represents the opening sentence in a distinct, more ambitious claim made by many restitution lawyers,[30] that common law and equitable rules should now be fully integrated. In *Lord Napier and Ettrick v Hunter*,[31] Lord Goff let slip his sympathy with this grander goal. The "task nowadays," he said, "is to see the two strands of authority, at law and in equity, moulded into a coherent whole."[32] Integration was also Millett LJ's ultimate ideal in *Jones*;[33] and it lies at the heart of recent calls, not least by Millett LJ himself, for rationalisation of the liabilities of the recipient of misdirected funds. Indeed, in *El Ajou v Dollar Land Holdings Plc*,[34] where the latter issue was raised, the adoption of a common approach at law and in equity was deemed by Millett J (as he then was) to be a precondition of any credible claim by the law to be logical or coherent. This is not, of course, a universal view,[35] but it is one with which Maitland himself would not have been entirely

---

[20] *Leigh & Sillavan Ltd v Aliakmon Shipping Co Ltd (The Aliakmon)* [1986] 1 AC 785, 812, *per* Lord Brandon.
[21] *Ibid.*
[22] Tettenborn, "Trust Property and Conversion" (1996) 55 CLJ 36.
[23] Beyond this, there is a good argument to the effect that the plaintiffs were legal as well as equitable owners of the cheques: Tettenborn, *ibid*, 39-40.
[24] [1979] 1 QB 351, 360.
[25] *Ibid*, 357–358.
[26] [1996] AC 669.
[27] This was the foundation of their mutual belief that equity's jurisdiction to award compound interest should be invocable in an action for money had and received. Justice required this on the facts, since otherwise the defendants would be left unjustly enriched by the receipt and subsequent enjoyment of the money obtained from the plaintiff.
[28] *Banque Belge pour l'Etranger v Hambrouck* [1921] 1 KB 321, 335.
[29] *Trustee of the Property of FC Jones and Sons (a firm) v Jones* [1997] Ch 159, 712. These views are strongly supported in principle by Birks, *An Introduction to the Law of Restitution* (Clarendon, Oxford, 1985, rev'd 1989), 361–362.
[30] See *eg* Beatson, *The Use and Abuse of Unjust Enrichment* (Clarendon, Oxford, 1991), ch 9.
[31] [1993] AC 713.
[32] *Ibid*, 743D.
[33] *Supra*, n 29.
[34] [1993] 3 All ER 717, 739. See also Sir Peter Millett, "Tracing the Proceeds of Fraud," (1991) 107 LQR 71, 76–83.
[35] Contrast *Associated Japanese Bank (International) v Credit du Nord* [1989] 1 WLR 255, 267, where Steyn J describes the perpetuation of distinct (contractual) doctrines of mistake at law and in equity as "entirely sensible and satisfactory."

out of sympathy[36] and it is a vision which is central to the ambitions of modern restitutionary taxonomies.

This point was openly recognised by Hobhouse LJ. But, whilst his Lordship accepted the case for greater integration within the law of restitution, he did not view the current case as an appropriate laboratory for the same experiment. This cannot simply be because this was not a restitution case. For one thing, it could so easily have been, had MCC sought to waive the tort, instead of suing for damages.[37] For another, there is no indication that the integration project is (or should be) unique to unjust enrichment law. The need for rationalisation may be particularly pressing in that area; and the subject's youth may present a useful opportunity for re-jigging the way we think about it. It is always easier to influence analytical development at its early stages, than it is to undo accepted wisdom. But the arguments for integration (which are arguments about coherence), though they may be stronger in some areas of law than in others, are of general, not specific application.

Why, then, was the current case not an appropriate one for integration? There are several possible answers, only one of which is ultimately persuasive. This would clearly have gone beyond the type of *procedural* merger contemplated by the Judicature Acts.[38] It would also have gone beyond the bounds of the project entailed by a merger of tracing rules, since such rules describe neither substantive rights, nor remedies, but evidential presumptions for following value through different forms.[39] Their merger does not impact — or impacts only indirectly[40] — upon substantive issues and ought, therefore, to be less controversial.

Neither of these distinctions is fatal to the argument for integration in the current instance, since there are clear examples of cases within the law, where *substantive* integration has shown itself to be both desirable and attainable. Hobhouse LJ himself cites the example of restitution for mistake. It makes no sense that, at law, restitution is available only for mistakes of fact, when in equity it is available for mistakes of law as well.[41] There is a strong case for rationalisation of the two lines of authority under a single rule.[42]

On the current facts, however, a merger of equitable title with the right to claim damages for conversion would have produced what Hobhouse LJ refers to as "anomalies and absurdities". One of these is that it would have allowed MCC to undercut the bona fide purchase defence which LB would have had against any claim to the shares (or certificates) themselves. A title which had been defeated for the purposes of any proprietary claim would have been resurrected as the basis of a personal action for loss. This would have undermined the policy of transactional security which the bona fide purchase defence endorses, with unfortunate repercussions for commercial confidence in exchange transactions. It is little reassurance to a pledgee to be told that it is safe against claims for the property pledged (or the proceeds of its sale), if it remains strictly liable in conversion for the property's loss. It is significant to note, in this respect, that none of the cases cited by MCC for the view that equitable title suffices in conversion involved a bona fide purchaser.[43]

---

[36] Beatson, *supra*, 257.
[37] As, for example, in *Lamine v Dorrell* (1701) 2 Ld Raym 1216, 92 ER 303.
[38] On which, see *Joseph v Lyons* [1884] 15 QBD 280, *per* Cotton LJ.
[39] *Boscawen v Bajwa* [1996] 1 WLR 328, 334, *per* Millett LJ (tracing is process, not a claim or a remedy); Birks, *supra*, 358–375 (tracing is an identification technique).
[40] This qualification is important, because process always affects a party's capacity to realise substantive rights. In the law of restitution, unless a party can satisfy tracing rules, he may be unable to demonstrate that a given enrichment was received (or is retained) at his expense.
[41] Contrast *Bilbie v Lumley* (1802) 2 East 469,102 ER 448 with *Gibbons v Mitchell* [1990] 1 WLR 1304.
[42] Law Commission, *Restitution: Mistakes of Law and Ultra Vires Public Authority Receipts and Payments: Law Com No 227* (1994).
[43] In neither *Healey* nor *Rodriguez* was there any suggestion that the defendant had given value.

A fairly straightforward solution to the above anomaly, which is consistent with the integration strategy, would be to extend the ambit of the bona fide purchase defence to cover personal actions at law based on equitable title.[44] This would, however, overlook a far more serious logical incoherence inherent in such a claim; which is that it would allow a party to use one type of right (equitable ownership) as a basis for claiming a remedy for the infringement of a different type of right (possession). Conversion is a wrong to possession, *not* to ownership; beneficial ownership having historically nothing to say about possession rights. For the Court of Appeal to have allowed a conversion remedy based on the plaintiff's equitable title alone would have been to countenance an unacceptable exercise in legal cherry-picking. It would have permitted MCC to "pick-and-mix" the most attractive aspects of two entirely different legal species, so as to produce a hybrid action of its own. An ownership right from equity would be tailored to a personal remedy for wrongful possession, derived from law. Both the rationality and desirability of this are highly questionable and it goes well beyond the types of cautious exercise in substantive fusion advocated anywhere to date. Far from adding to the coherence of the law, it allows the plaintiff to create its own Frankenstein's monster.

It is important to stress that this is not simply a concern about crossing the law/equity divide, or about allowing the common law to undercut liability-standards in equity, though both these would clearly also be consequences of admitting the claim.[45] There are, I suggest, acceptable examples of both of these types of development in the law.[46] Rather, it is a point about preserving the logical integrity of causes of action — whether described at law, in equity, or by both. Beneficial ownership rights and possession rights are different and we mix ideas about them at our peril. Having determined that the right to possession of the certificates lay with B, not M (which conclusion happens, historically, to have been made at law), it would have made no sense to have allowed MCC's claim to go to trial on the basis of equitable title. On the facts, this was particularly obvious, given that that title had been defeated in the previous (ownership) claim. But it would equally have been the case, even if that title had survived.

There is one further matter which it is necessary to consider. Professor Palmer[47] has rightly raised a query about the Torts (Interference with Goods) Act, s 8(1). This section purports to allow one who is being sued for conversion to raise by way of defence the interest of a third party. If, as he suggests,[48] this includes third party *equitable* interests, then is it not anomalous that such interests cannot themselves provide the basis for a conversion action? Does the Act then assume a partial[49] fusionist strategy? If so, how can it be rational to reject that strategy? None of their Lordships considered this point, which was simply not argued.

One possible explanation is that s 8, being designed to deal with problems of double recovery, multiplicity of actions and unjustified windfalls,[50] was not intended to extend conversion actions to equitable owners. Rather, it was necessitated by the fact that more than one person could have

---

[44] Tettenborn (1996) 35 CLJ 36, 40-41. There is a good case for saying that, wherever the defence applies to defeat a proprietary claim, it should also apply to defeat personal claims in respect of the same property. See Birks (ed), *Laundering and Tracing* (Clarendon, Oxford, 1995), 213, 332–333.
[45] On which, see Tettenborn (1996) 35 CLJ 36.
[46] For an example of the former, see Atkin LJ's approach to tracing rules in *Banque Belge v Hambrouck* [1921] 1 KB 321. For an example of the latter, see *Lipkin Gorman v Karpnale Ltd* [1991] 2 AC 548 (undercutting current liability standards for knowing receipt with strict personal liability at common law). This undercutting is only acceptable in the short term; and there are strong arguments for now bringing equity into line: Birks, "Misdirected Funds: Restitution from the Recipient" [1989] LMCLQ 296.
[47] [1986] LMCLQ 218.
[48] *Ibid*, 229.
[49] Partial only, because it does not provide a freestanding, *active* claim for the equitable interest-holder.
[50] See Brazier, *supra* n 11, 41.

a *legal* interest in goods sufficient to support a conversion claim.[51] This would mean that a court under s 8 is concerned only with third party legal interests. Another explanation, perhaps more consistent with the language of the section,[52] would be that, whilst the defendant is indeed entitled to bring third party equitable interests before the court, this is to allow all competing claims in respect of the goods to be considered, not just different conversion claims. A third party claim to beneficial ownership of the goods might well affect the extent of the actual loss caused to a legal claimant by their conversion and therefore bear upon the windfall issue.[53] The conclusion consistent with this line of reasoning is that s 8 does allow equitable interests to be taken into account, but that it does not mean that those with mere equitable interests can claim in conversion. Whichever of these interpretations is correct, the inability of an equitable owner to bring a claim for conversion is readily explicable. The anomaly to which Professor Palmer refers may not, in fact, be an anomaly at all.

Conclusions

The true import of the *MCC Proceeds* case lies in what it tells us about the limits of the fusionist ideal. This lesson is important for all audiences, but especially, perhaps, for restitution lawyers, where that ambition enjoys particular popularity.

1. It was not the purpose of Judicature Acts to achieve an immediate substantive fusion of law and equity.[54] Nonetheless, in some parts of the law (and in some more than others), that goal is clearly on the agenda. There is no necessary objection to this. Indeed, despite the difficulties which it raises,[55] it is wholly desirable to the extent that it increases the coherence of legal claims, defences and remedies. Hobhouse LJ goes further in recognising the acceptability in principle of this idea than either Mummery or Pill LJJ, and in this detail he is to be applauded.

2. At the same time, all three members of the Court of Appeal are entirely right to have exercised caution and to have concluded that the current claim must fail in the instant case. The most important limitation upon the goal of integration is, it seems, described by the principle which underpins it. The project should be pursued to the extent — but *only* to the extent — that it increases coherence in the law. It is not an aim which has intrinsic value in and of itself; and it cannot be held out as a justification for the merger of different species of ownership and possession right.

---

[51] This state of affairs flowed from the fact that both those with actual possession and those with an immediate legal right to possession could sue, *eg* both the bailee at will of goods (actual possession) and his bailor (with the immediate right to possession).

[52] s 8(1)(b) states that a plaintiff in an action for wrongful interference with goods may be required to identify "any person who, to his knowledge, has or claims *any* interest in the goods" (emphasis added).

[53] If the legal possessor were able to claim the full value of the property, without regard to the beneficial ownership of another, he might be left with an amount in excess of his loss.

[54] *Joseph v Lyons* (1884) 15 QBD 280; *Hallas v Robinson* (1885) 15 QBD 288.

[55] For a detailed exposition of which, see *Beatson, supra* n 30.

Failure of Consideration and Reliance in Contract

(Stocznia Gdanska v Latvian Shipping)

Peter Jaffey*

The restitution point

A plaintiff suing for breach of contract is entitled to the expectation measure of damages. Sometimes the expectation measure is difficult to determine, and the plaintiff is instead permitted to recover for ascertainable losses incurred in reliance on the contract. But here his claim is in principle limited to the expectation measure so far as it can be determined.[1] There is good reason why a contracting party should never be put in a better position than he would have been in if the contract had been performed — ie, why he should in principle always be limited to the expectation measure. The contract entails an allocation of risk; each party takes the risk that the cost of his own performance and his own reliance on the contract and the value to him of contractual performance or its pecuniary equivalent turn out to be such that he would not have chosen to contract. This is the rationale for the expectation measure cap on recovery. The rationale does not of course apply where a contract is void or voidable and rescinded. Here the parties should not be held to the contract, and it is appropriate for them to have restitutionary claims that have the effect of unwinding or reversing the contract, and, if the contract would have turned out to be a bad one for the plaintiff, he will end up better off than if the contract had been performed.

There is, however, one isolated example known to the common law of a claim arising from the termination of a valid contract that allows the plaintiff to recover more than the expectation measure. This is the claim to recover a prepayment in the event of a total failure of consideration. "Total failure of consideration" is conventionally understood to mean that the contract has terminated in circumstances in which no benefit has been received by the plaintiff under it. Typically the plaintiff has contracted to buy goods and the goods have never been delivered or they have been delivered and the plaintiff has rejected them in accordance with the contract.[2] Here the plaintiff can recover his prepayment even if it exceeds the expectation measure, as where the market value of the goods has fallen. What is the explanation of this claim and what can be the justification for allowing this exception to the principle stated above? One approach is, broadly speaking, that whenever a contract terminates for breach the plaintiff can make either a contractual claim or in the alternative a quite distinct restitutionary claim.[3] The contractual claim is limited to the expectation measure, but the restitutionary claim is not. The restitutionary claim reverses the transfer of value from the plaintiff to the defendant under the contract, more or less as if the contract had been void, or voidable and rescinded. This is sometimes described as "restitution for breach", although it is better described as "restitution for non-performance", because the claim is thought to arise from the fact of non-performance whether

---

* Lecturer in Law, Brunel University.
[1] *C & P Haulage v Middleton* [1983] 1 WLR 1461; *CCC Films (London) Ltd v Impact Quadrant Films* [1985] QB 16.
[2] *Giles v Edwards* (1797) 7 TR 181; *Fibrosa Spolka Akcyjna v Fairbairn Lawson Combe Barbour* [1943] AC 32. For an account of many of the old cases on failure of consideration, see S Stoljar, "The doctrine of failure of consideration" (1959) 75 LQR 53.
[3] Peter Birks, *Introduction to the Law of Restitution* (Clarendon, Oxford, rev ed 1989), 100-108 and ch VII; Andrew Burrows, *The Law of Restitution* (Butterworths, 1993), ch 9; Ewan McKendrick, *Contract Law*, 3rd ed (Macmillan, 1997), 20.5.

this constitutes breach or not — for example, where the contract is frustrated there is non-performance but not breach.

There are two serious objections to this approach. The first is that the availability of the claim in restitution undermines the contract law rules, in particular the rules on remedies (which reflect the contractual allocation of risk). It is argued that there is no inconsistency with the law of contract because the restitutionary claim arises only once the contract has terminated; but this argument must be wrong, because, after all, it is after termination when the rules that cap recovery to the expectation measure come into effect. The second problem is that the approach does not easily account for the rule that the claim arises only in the case of *total* failure of consideration. The analysis implies that there should be a restitutionary claim whenever the contract is not fully performed, not just where the defendant has not performed at all. Of course, if the defendant has also given value to the plaintiff, he should himself have a restitutionary claim (sometimes called counter-restitution) that must be offset against the plaintiff's. The explanation for the limitation to total failure is then sought in the difficulty of measuring the value transferred (for the purposes of the claim for counter-restitution) in a case other than the clear case where the plaintiff has transferred a sum of money to the defendant and the defendant has done nothing in return, *ie*, where there is total failure of consideration. But it is difficult to accept that this could ever have been the reason for rejecting the general availability of a claim for "restitution for breach" if such a claim was thought to be appropriate in principle.

If this analysis in terms of "restitution for breach" is misconceived, how is the claim arising on total failure of consideration to be explained? Should the plaintiff not be limited to his expectation claim in all cases where a valid contract is not fully performed? One answer is that the defendant should not be able to invoke the contract, and the contractual allocation of risk, to limit the plaintiff to the expectation measure where the defendant has himself never genuinely relied on the contract — for example, where he has never delivered goods, and arguably where following rejection he still has the goods. In such a case, the court in effect disregards the contract and allows a restitutionary claim just as if the contract were void or voidable and rescinded. On this approach the claim is not an example of a general claim for "restitution for breach"; it is a restitutionary claim that arises exceptionally where there is total failure of consideration in the sense that the defendant never began to perform the contract.

The nature of the claim arising on total failure of consideration has arisen recently in the House of Lords in *Stocznia Gdanska SA v Latvian Shipping Co*,[4] a case that in this respect was very similar to *Hyunadi Hyundai Heavy Industries v Papadopoulos*.[5] In *Stocznia*, the plaintiff shipbuilders had contracted with the defendant buyers to build a ship. The contract provided for the payment of instalments at intervals during the course of construction and delivery. The first instalment, due on the making of the contract, was paid, but the second instalment, which became due on "keel laying", was not. The shipbuilders then terminated the contract under Clause 5.05, which expressly gave them the right "to rescind" (used to mean terminate, not rescind *ab initio*) in the event of non-payment of an instalment. They then became entitled to damages on the basis set out in the clause. It seems that, in addition to starting proceedings for damages, the shipbuilders wanted to get immediate payment of the second instalment (in effect as an immediate payment of part of the total sum due in damages), and began RSC Ord 14 proceedings for payment of the instalment as an accrued debt. The buyers argued that the debt had not accrued (or was not payable) because if it had been paid it would have been recoverable by them for total failure of consideration.

According to the conventional understanding of total failure of consideration, as meaning that there has been no actual benefit to the party seeking to recover the prepayment, the buyers' argument seems to be correct. This understanding is consistent with the restitution for breach

[4] [1998] 1 WLR 574.
[5] [1980] 1 WLR 1129.

analysis, on the basis that the claim arises only where there is no counter-restitutionary claim by the recipient of the prepayment in respect of value transferred to the payor. On the other hand it is inconsistent with the absence of reliance approach, because the shipbuilders had begun to perform the contract even though no benefit had yet accrued to the buyers. Furthermore, it is inconsistent with *Hyundai*, where on similar facts the House of Lords held that there was not a total failure of consideration. One might have expected Lord Goff, who gave the leading speech in *Stocznia*, to be inclined to reconsider *Hyundai* — the restitution for breach approach is after all more or less assumed in *Goff & Jones*[6] — but he refused to do so. Instead, following *Hyundai*, Lord Goff said that "failure of consideration does not depend upon the question whether the promisee has or has not *received* anything under the contract . . . In truth, the test is not whether the promisee has received a specific benefit, but rather whether the promisor has performed any part of the contractual duties . . ."[7] This is consistent with the absence of reliance approach. The approach based on absence of benefit received would, Lord Goff said, "be apposite if the contract in question was a contract for the sale of goods . . .", but not where it was for the design, construction and sale of goods.[8] In the sale of goods case, there is no difference between the benefit and reliance approaches if the goods are standard goods, so that the seller does not do any significant work referable exclusively to the contract in issue; but, if the contract is for the design, construction and sale of goods, the seller relies on the contract long before there is any benefit to the buyer. Both in *Hyundai* and now in *Stocznia* the House of Lords seemed to say that different tests of total failure should apply in these two types of case, but it is obviously preferable to have a single test that accounts for both types of case, and the appropriate test is surely absence of reliance.

Furthermore, it seems that the buyers might also have argued, in line with the restitution for breach approach, that their claim for restitution should not depend on there having been a total failure of consideration. As mentioned above, the total failure requirement seems to be arbitrary on the restitution for breach approach, and a number of commentators have for this reason argued for abandoning it. This is the view expressed in *Goff & Jones*; and recently in *Westdeutsche Landesbank Girozentrale v Islington Borough Council*[9] Lord Goff suggested that the total failure requirement might be due for reconsideration. Lord Goff did refer to "the continuing debate among scholars and law reformers as to the circumstances in which, and the basis on which, a party in breach of contract can recover a benefit conferred by him on the innocent party under the contract before it was terminated by reason of his breach".[10] But he concluded,[11] "I am content to approach this aspect of the case on the premise, common to both parties, that the issue is one of total failure of consideration since, as I understand it, this is consistent with the approach of the majority in *Hyundai Heavy Industries v Papadopoulos* . . ." The retention of the total failure requirement is also consistent with the absence of reliance approach, but arguably not with the "restitution for breach" approach.

In the light of his approach in *Stocznia*, it is important to reconsider Lord Goff's remarks in *Westdeutsche* about the desirability of abandoning the total failure requirement. *Westdeutsche* concerned not a valid contract that had not been performed, but a void contract that the parties

---

[6] Lord Goff of Chieveley and Gareth Jones, *The Law of Restitution*, 4th ed (Sweet & Maxwell, 1993), Part D.
[7] At p 588, italics in the original. To get around this problem for the "restitution for breach" approach, it has been suggested that the law should recognise for this purpose a constructive or deemed benefit where the recipient of the payment has begun work on the contract: eg Birks, *supra* n 3, at p 232.
[8] At p 588.
[9] [1996] AC 669, 683, referring to Peter Birks, "No consideration: restitution after void contracts" (1993) 23 UWALR 195; WJ Swadling, "Restitution for no Consideration" [1994] RLR 73–85; Andrew Burrows, "Swaps and the Friction between Law and Equity" [1995] RLR 15-29. This is also the view expressed in Goff & Jones, *supra* n 6, 445, 468. For a different view, see J Beatson, *The Use and Abuse of Unjust Enrichment* (Clarendon, 1991), ch 3.
[10] At p 588.
[11] *Ibid*.

had partly performed, or purported to perform.[12] As mentioned above, there is no reason at all why, in the case of a void contract, the restitutionary claim to reverse transfers under the putative contract should be limited to cases where the parties have not performed. On the contrary, the extent of performance should not affect the ground of restitution,[13] because the claim arises not from a failure to perform the void contract but from the voidness of the contract or at least the parties' ignorance of its voidness. It would make no sense for a claim arising from the fact that a contract was void to depend on whether it had been performed. Unfortunately, the expression "failure of consideration" seems always to have been used for both types of case — *ie*, for both void and voidable contracts and also for valid but unperformed contracts. It would be a great advance if the two types of case could be distinguished. The distinction would be clear if the true ground for the claim arising out of a void contract were recognised as mistake of law. Alternatively, it may be right to describe it as "absence of consideration", following Hobhouse J at first instance in *Westdeutsche*.[14] However, Professor Birks has argued that English law has only recognised one type of claim, which he (along with others) understands to be a claim along the lines of "restitution for breach", where the non-performance of the contract gives rise to a non-contractual restitutionary claim either where a valid contract terminates early or where the contract was void, or voidable and rescinded.[15]

The termination and mitigation point

The case raised other awkward points for the House of Lords, in particular the issue of mitigation before contract termination. This does not concern restitution, but it does indirectly relate to the discussion of reliance above. There were actually six contracts in the same terms between the plaintiff shipbuilders and the defendant buyers, providing for the construction of six ships. Two ships had reached the "keel laying" stage, so that the second instalments had became due. When the instalments were not paid, these contracts were rescinded under Clause 5.05, leading, for both contracts, to the issue discussed above. When the buyers failed to pay the instalments due on the first two contracts, it was of course immediately clear that the buyers were unable or unwilling to proceed not only with contracts 1 and 2 but also with contracts 3 to 6, since the contracts were all in the same terms. In any case this was apparently understood by the shipbuilders. It was thus open to the shipbuilders to accept the buyers' anticipatory repudiation and sue for damages on contracts 3 to 6 as well, which they eventually did. But the shipbuilders were in a worse position (at least with respect to immediate recovery) under contracts 3 to 6 because on these the second instalment had not become payable. The shipbuilders attempted to secure a right to the second instalment on the remaining contracts by reassigning the keels already laid under the first two contracts (now terminated) to the other contracts. Thus they claimed the second instalment on all the contracts, although only two keels were ever laid. One would hardly expect Latvian shipping companies or Polish shipbuilders to come to the English courts if such a ploy could succeed. Lord Goff rejected the argument, relying on the construction of the clause of the contract that governed the accrual of liability for the second instalment. He took the view that the intention of the clause was that for the second instalment to become due it was necessary not only that there should be a specified keel of the required specification in existence, but that the specified keel should have been constructed and laid pursuant to the contract in question.

---

[12] Like the old annuity cases discussed in Stoljar (1959) 75 LQR 53.
[13] Although it will be relevant to the change of position defence.
[14] [1994] 4 All ER 890, 924.
[15] (1993) 23 UWALR 195. For a defence of the "absence of reliance" approach and criticism of the "restitution for breach" approach, see Peter Jaffey, "The restitutionary conditional transfer theory and the death of contract" [1998] Edinburgh LR 23.

This may have been the correct construction of the contract. If so, this was fortuitous; a contrary construction is plausible, but the scheme to generate a right to the instalments should fail in any case, and disposing of the issue as a matter of construction of the contract leaves a wider issue unaddressed. The wider issue would have been clearer if the shipbuilders had started to build a third keel, in disregard of the buyers' refusal to continue with the contracts, and then claimed the second instalment in due course; or if they had declined to exercise the right to rescind on the contracts in respect of which the second instalment had become due, and continued to build the ships in order to claim the successive instalments of the contract price instead of suing for damages. One might think that the shipbuilders would be precluded from increasing the total liability of the buyers in this way under the principle of mitigation of damages. But mitigation is said to apply only once the contract has terminated in consequence of the "acceptance" of the breach.[16] Before this, the contracting parties are understood to be allowed to continue to act on the basis that the contract is in force, if this is possible without the other party's co-operation. This is the case where there is anticipatory repudiation, the defendant declaring that he is withdrawing from the contract before any performance is due from him. This was the issue that arose in *White & Carter (Councils) Ltd v McGregor*,[17] and there the House of Lords accepted that there was no rule of mitigation that precluded a plaintiff from continuing on the basis that the contract was in full force, unless, possibly, according to Lord Reid, it had "no legitimate interest, financial or otherwise" in doing so. It is very doubtful that a rule that allows a contracting party to persist in treating a contract as in force when the other party has made clear that he will not or cannot perform reflects good commercial practice or gives effect to what the parties would have agreed to beforehand.[18] On the contrary, it would surely be better if the rule were that a contracting party cannot continue to rely on the assumption that the other party will continue to perform if the other party has made it clear that he will not. This might suggest that more generally contract law should be understood to protect reliance on a contract and not to enforce an agreement as if it consisted of an exchange of promises. Such an understanding is, it is interesting to note, also consistent with the doctrine of total failure of consideration as explained above in terms of absence of reliance, for if contract law protects reliance it is maybe understandable to disregard the contract as against a party who has never relied on it. On the other hand an analysis in terms of enforcing promises suggests both that a contracting party should not have to mitigate unless he has first "accepted" the breach, and also possibly that claims arising out of a valid contract should be limited to the expectation measure (the value of the promise) even where there has been no performance.[19]

---

[16] *Howard v Pickford Tool Co Ltd* [1951] 1 KB 417; *White & Carter (Councils) Ltd v McGregor* [1962] AC 413.
[17] [1962] AC 413.
[18] Some would point out that it is liable to be wasteful, but it is doubtful whether this is a ground of any force in itself if the parties nevertheless agreed or would have agreed to it.
[19] There have been a number of attempts in the past to defend the reliance theory, in particular, of course, by PS Atiyah. For a defence of this approach see Peter Jaffey "A new version of the reliance theory" [1998] NILQ (forthcoming).

Transfers into an Overdrawn Account in Breach of Trust — The Bank's Liability for Receipt

(Citadel General Assurance Co v Lloyds Bank Canada)

Craig Rotherham*

Unless he or she is a bona fide purchaser for value, one who is in receipt of assets that are identifiable as trust property is obliged to respect the beneficiary's proprietary rights.[1] However, English courts have been reluctant to impose personal liability to account upon innocent recipients who no longer have trust property in their possession. As the law stands, personal liability attaches only to those who, at the very least, ought to have been aware that the property they received was impressed with a trust.[2] This might be contrasted with the common law of mistake, where liability follows from receipt, regardless of knowledge, unless a defence is available.[3] Some have decried the lack of symmetry of law and equity in this respect.[4] Yet the reluctance to make liability in equity strict was understandable, given the traditional lack of defences to restitutionary actions.[5] In cases such as *Re Montagu's Settlement Trusts*,[6] where a considerable period of time had passed between receipt of property and the bringing of an action, the unfairness that would have resulted from the imposition of personal liability on the innocent recipient is manifest. However, since the recognition of a change of position defence in *Lipkin Gorman v Karpnale Ltd*,[7] there has been growing support for the removal of any requirement of knowledge for personal liability for receipt of trust property.[8] Against this background, it is interesting that, while Canadian law recognised the change of position defence some time prior to its acceptance in English law,[9] in *Citadel General Assurance Co v Lloyds Bank Canada*,[10] the Canadian Supreme Court rejected an opportunity to take this step. The case raises interesting questions about the nature of "receipt" and the liability of banks where misdirected funds are paid into overdrawn accounts.

The salient facts of the case were as follows. Drive On (D) sold insurance to auto dealers with the policies being underwritten by the appellant insurance company. At the end of each month, after collecting premiums and paying commissions, D was obliged to pay the balance to the appellants. D was a wholly owned subsidiary and both it and its parent banked with the respondents. Subsequently, the bank was instructed to transfer all the funds in D's account to the parent company's account at the end of each day. As the latter account was in overdraft, the effect of these transfers was to reduce the parent company's indebtedness to the bank. Eventually, D failed to account to the appellants for two consecutive months and then ceased trading. The appellant's action to make the bank account for the outstanding insurance premiums succeeded at trial. However, the Court of Appeal for Alberta allowed the bank's appeal.

---
* Fellow, Conville and Caius College, Cambridge.
[1] See *eg Re Montagu's Settlement Trusts* [1987] Ch 264, 276.
[2] See C Harpum, "The Basis of Equitable Liability" in Birks (ed), *The Frontiers of Liability*, vol 1 (1994), 9.
[3] *Kelly v Solari* (1841) 9 M & W 54.
[4] P Birks, "Misdirected Funds: Restitution from the Recipient" [1989] LMCLQ 296.
[5] Until recently, at law, the only way in which a recipient who had received money for his own use could avoid liability was by establishing detrimental reliance on a representation by the plaintiff to the effect that the defendant was entitled to the benefit: *Holt v Markham* [1923] 1 KB 504. There was no general defence of change of position in either law or equity: *Baylis v Bishop of London* [1913] 1 Ch 127; *Re Diplock* [1948] Ch 465.
[6] [1987] Ch 264.
[7] [1991] 2 AC 548.
[8] Harpum, *supra* n 2, at 24-25.
[9] *Mobil Oil Canada v Rural Municpality of Storthoaks* (1975) 55 DLR (3d) 1.
[10] (1997) 152 DLR (4th) 411.

Before the Supreme Court of Canada, the appellants claimed that the bank was liable for both assistance and receipt. Following its decision in *Air Canada v M & L Travel Ltd*,[11] La Forest J, who gave the court's only substantive judgment,[12] held that actual knowledge, wilful blindness or recklessness was required for liability for assistance. On the basis of the trial judge's findings, he concluded that the bank did not have a sufficient level of knowledge to be liable on this cause of action.

Thus the focus of the judgment moved to the question of receipt. Two issues assumed central significance. First, the court had to determine whether the bank could be said to have received trust property. Secondly, if this question were answered in the affirmative, the court had to determine the degree of knowledge required for liability for receipt.

Receipt

When trust money is misdirected into a bank account that is in credit, the received view is that the bank acts merely as the customer's agent and does not receive property for its own benefit. Here, the primary liability for receipt lies against the customer; the bank's liability is as an accessory for assistance of a breach of trust.[13] On the other hand, where money is paid into an overdrawn account, it is generally accepted in English law that the bank does benefit from the payment and may be liable for receipt.[14] In *Citadel*, however, the respondent argued that, because the payor also banked with it, the transaction involved "an off-setting of debt obligations"[15] rather than a physical transfer of property.[16] Thus, the bank argued that it "was not receiving trust property but simply transferring credits from one account to another".[17] La Forest J responded that the debt was a chose in action owned by the appellant and thus represented trust property receipt of which could give rise to liability as a constructive trustee. Presumably, the bank received the chose in action when it set it off against the parent company's indebtedness, at which point the subsidiary company's chose in action was extinguished by being subsumed by the bank's larger chose in action. This description has a rather unfortunate metaphysical flavour, and La Forest J recognised that this issue illustrated "a difficulty with the traditional conception of 'receipt' in 'knowing receipt' cases".[18] Wisely, he preferred to conceptualise the matter in terms of unjust enrichment; this allowed him to characterise the issue in terms of receipt of a benefit, rather than receipt of a thing.

Degree of knowledge

La Forest J noted that judicial opinion tends to be divided in favour of either constructive or actual knowledge as a prerequisite for liability for receipt and that there is also strong academic opinion in support of making liability strict, although subject to defences. Accepting the view of

---

[11] [1993] 3 SCR 787.
[12] Gonthier, Cory, McLachlin, Iacobucci and Major JJ concurred, while Sopinka J agreed subject to his reasoning in *Gold v Rosenberg* (1997) 152 DLR (4th) 385 (Can SC), a decision on knowing assistance issued concurrently with *Citadel*.
[13] See P Millett, "Tracing the Proceeds of Fraud" (1990) 107 LQR 71, 83. This explanation is not entirely convincing, given that the bank receives title to any money deposited with it. Perhaps the law could be better explained on the basis that the bank is a bona fide purchaser.
[14] See *eg Thomson v Clydesdale Bank Ltd* [1893] AC 282; *Westpac v Savin* [1985] 2 NZLR 41. See also Millett (1990) 107 LQR 71.
[15] At pp 423–424.
[16] The complication is perhaps more apparent than real. Where a bank receives payment from an outside source it acquires title to the money and its obligation to its customer is merely as a debtor. Thus, the reality is that the process of setting-off a deposit against an existing indebtedness always involves "an off-setting of debt obligations": the debt which the bank owes the customer against a debt owed to it by the customer.
[17] At p 424.
[18] At p 424.

the Privy Council in *Royal Brunei Airline Sdn Bhd v Tan*,[19] La Forest emphasised that knowing receipt and knowing assistance are fundamentally different: the former being liability for unjust enrichment, and the latter a form of secondary liability. He concluded that, "whereas the accessory's liability is 'fault-based', the recipient's liability is 'receipt-based' ".[20] While one might have thought that this characterisation would lead to the conclusion that fault is not necessary for liability for receipt, ultimately La Forest J took the view that constructive notice was the appropriate standard for liability. He then concluded that the circumstances of the transfers were sufficiently suspicious to have put the respondent bank on notice; as a consequence, it was personally liable to the appellant.

While the conclusion that notice should be a prerequisite for liability for receipt is not indefensible, La Forest J's reasons for reaching it are not entirely convincing. To a large degree, his conclusions logically follow from his elaboration of the concept of unjust enrichment. He recalled[21] his dictum from *Lac Minerals Ltd v International Corona Resources Ltd*[22] that "the determination that the enrichment is 'unjust' . . . flows directly from the finding that there was a breach of a legally recognised duty for which the courts will grant relief." His conceptualisation of the process in this way analytically entailed his conclusion that "[i]n 'knowing receipt' cases, relief flows from the breach of a legally recognised duty of inquiry".[23] All that remained to be determined was the content of this duty of inquiry (*ie* what degree of knowledge was required). With respect, there is a flaw in the premises of this argument. La Forest's location of the unjustness of enrichment in a breach of a duty is consistent with *Lac Minerals*—a breach of confidence case. However, a breach of duty is not a necessary ingredient in all restitution claims. There is no such duty in mistake cases; nor is it obvious why it should be required in cases involving the receipt of trust property.

In dealing with the view that liability for misdirected funds should be strict subject to defences, La Forest J reasoned that a distinction must be made between unjust deprivation and unjust enrichment. Thus, in his view, liability must be understood as involving defendant-sided as well as plaintiff-sided factors. He concluded that:[24]

> "To show that the defendant's enrichment is unjustified, one must necessarily focus on the defendant's state of mind not the plaintiff's knowledge, or lack thereof. Indeed, without constructive or actual knowledge of the breach of trust, the recipient may very well have a lawful claim to the trust property. It would be unfair to require a recipient to disgorge a benefit that has been lawfully received. In those circumstances, the recipient will not be unjustly enriched and the plaintiff will not be entitled to a restitutionary remedy."

Yet, it is not obvious why this should be so. Again, it is not regarded as unfair to require restitution in common law mistake cases. If a defendant unknowingly comes into possession of trust property without having purchased it and does nothing to change his or her position, there is a good argument that the plaintiff should have a claim for compensation. There needs to be a reason for excusing the defendant from making restitution; the fact that the defendant was at the time of the transfer ignorant of the plaintiff's claim is hardly a compelling justification. If such a reason is to be found, presumably it will be along the lines that it would be unreasonable to expose innocent recipients to a liability protected only by a defence (change of position) that may be difficult to make out. According to this view, it would be preferable to put the onus on beneficiaries to take precautions to ensure that their assets are not misapplied.[25]

---

[19] [1995] 2 AC 378, 386.
[20] At p 433.
[21] At p 434.
[22] [1989] 2 SCR 574, 670.
[23] At p 434.
[24] At p 435.
[25] In support of this view, see S Gardner, "Knowing Assistance and Knowing Receipt: Taking Stock" (1996) 112 LQR 56.

Why was the court so reluctant to hold the bank strictly liable in this context? Perhaps we might learn something from US law in this area. The early recognition of the concept of unjust enrichment and the development of a change of position defence encouraged strict liability for beneficial receipt. A defendant could avoid liability only if he or she could rely on a defence of bona fide purchase or change of position.[26] It is accepted as good law in most states that, where it has quite innocently set off trust monies against a customer's existing indebtedness, the bank will have a complete defence if it acted bona fide and without notice.[27] This is somewhat surprisingly, but it is consistent with the controversial but well established view that acceptance of a payment in satisfaction of a debt may constitute giving value.[28] While it is debatable whether such acceptance, in itself, constitutes a material change of position, the policy behind the rule is understandable.[29] Even given the presence of a change of position defence, it could conceivably place an undue strain on banks were they always potentially subject to restitutionary claims for money paid into overdrawn accounts in circumstances in which they had no reason to suspect any impropriety. The US experience confirms that the life of the law is not logic, and that the case for universal strict liability for receipt is not quite as compelling as it might appear at first sight.

A Trace of *Chase Manhattan* in the Netherlands?

(Ontvanger v Hamm qq)

*HLE Verhagen and NED Faber**

In contrast with Roman Dutch law applicable in certain parts of the Netherlands before the period of the great codifications, the Dutch Civil Code of 1838 did not recognise a general action for restitution in cases of unjust enrichment. The 1838 Civil Code did recognise the *condictio indebiti*, for payments made when not due to the payee. In addition, the Code recognised other specific cases that could be characterised as involving unjust enrichment. In its landmark decision *Quint v Te Poel*[1] the *Hoge Raad* (Supreme Court of the Netherlands) held that in unjust enrichment cases for which there is no express statutory basis, an action for recovery may nonetheless be awarded if this fits in the "system of the law" and if it can be linked with cases which have been expressly dealt with by statute. The new Dutch Civil Code (*Burgerlijk Wetboek*, BW) of 1992 does contain a general enrichment action. The wheel has come full circle. This general enrichment action exists alongside the condictio indebiti,[2] which is *not* regarded as an enrichment action.

One of the most challenging questions the courts and legal doctrine are now facing is how to structure the Dutch law of restitution, given the generality of the wording of BW art 6:212. In our opinion the *Quint v Te Poel* decision remains extremely important in this respect. "Unjust factors" which have been recognised by statute or case law should continue to play an important role, as well as the systematic analysis which the *Hoge Raad* considered crucial in the *Quint v Te*

---

[26] AW Scott and WF Fratcher, *The Law of Trusts* (Boston: Little Brown and Co, 1989), §292.2.
[27] *Ibid*, §305.3.
[28] See *eg* the *Restatement of Restitution* (1937), §137.
[29] For a view that the conclusion that value is given in these circumstances "is inevitably circular", see JP Dawson, "Restitution Without Enrichment" (1981) 61 Boston ULR 563, 566. Underscoring the difficulties in dealing with this particular context, Dawson notes that German law initially took the same approach as that favoured by US law, "but then became persuaded that some more serious sacrifice or prejudice was needed".
* HLE Verhagen is Professor of Civil Law at the Catholic University of Nijmegen. NED Faber is Lecturer of Civil Law at the Catholic University of Nijmegen. The authors are members of the staff of the Business and Law Research Centre (*Onderzoekcentrum Onderneming & Recht*).
[1] HR 30 Jan 1959, NJ 1959, 546.
[2] BW art 6:203.

Poel decision. There is a danger, however, that the concept of unjust enrichment will be invoked in all sorts of cases in which it should have no role. It will be interesting to see how the courts will deal with these situations.

In the last few years the *Hoge Raad* has rendered several judgments on unjust enrichment. The judgment we discuss in this paper is the most recent.[3] The other decisions we hope to discuss in a future general study on the Dutch law of restitution.

The facts

The facts of this case were as follows. Wolfson Informatica BV ("Wolfson") was declared bankrupt on 4 September 1992. Hamm was appointed as curator in bankruptcy (*faillissementscurator*). In July 1993 Wolfson received a letter from the tax collector, stating that Wolfson was entitled to restitution of tax and premiums, amounting to fl 12,069. The letter was accompanied by a form for Wolfson to indicate how it wanted to receive this repayment. On 4 August 1993 this form was sent back by the curator, giving the account number to be paid. By the end of August 1993 the money was transferred to this account. Later it turned out that the tax collector had made a mistake. The rebate of tax and premiums should have been made to Wolfson's parent company, Wolfson Groep BV. In a letter dated 12 October 1993 the tax collector requested repayment of the amount of fl 12,069 from the curator, which he refused. The tax collector sued in the district court of Rotterdam, claiming from the curator (in his capacity as such) payment of fl 12,069 and interest from 1 September 1993. The tax collector also requested a "declaration of law" (*verklaring voor recht*) from the district court, stating that the collector's claim against the estate for undue payment (*condictio indebiti*) had to be paid out in full from the available Wolfson funds, in priority to all other creditors of the bankrupt estate.

The judgment of the district court: no preferential status

In its judgment,[4] the district court of Rotterdam held that the claim to recover undue payments made to the curator during the bankruptcy of the payee was a non-preferred claim against the estate (*concurrente boedelvordering*). Claims against an estate (*boedelvorderingen*) are claims with a special status. They are claims which originate during bankruptcy and which arise by operation of law or as a consequence of certain acts carried out by the curator (*eg* the conclusion of contracts). Claims against the estate have to be paid out before "ordinary" claims (pre-bankruptcy claims). If the available funds of the estate are insufficient fully to satisfy all creditors with a claim against the estate, those creditors have to be paid *pro rata* the extent of their respective claims. This is different if there are creditors of the estate with a statutory right of priority, such as secured creditors or privileged creditors (*preferente boedelcrediteuren*). According to the district court the claim against the estate arising from the undue payment (*condictio indebiti*) does *not* have priority over the other claims against the estate. The curator is not at liberty to change the statutory order of priority between claims, no more in the case of unjust enrichment than in any other. The judgment of the district court of Rotterdam leapfrogged to the *Hoge Raad* (*sprongcassatie*). In its judgment,[5] the *Hoge Raad* annulled the judgment of the district court and referred the matter to the Court of Appeal of the Hague.

The judgment by the *Hoge Raad*: (1) pre-bankruptcy payments

The *Hoge Raad* distinguishes between several situations. When a payment has been made "without legal cause" *before* bankruptcy and the recipient of the payment has not satisfied his duty to

[3] HR 5 September 1997, JOR 1997/102 (*Ontvanger v Hamm qq*).
[4] 30 May 1996, JOR 1996/89.
[5] 5 September 1997, JOR 1997/102.

restore the payment,[6] the payor can file his claim with the curator in bankruptcy. The *condictio indebiti* then has to be characterised as an "ordinary" non-preferred pre-bankruptcy claim.[7] The *condictio indebiti* is not a privileged claim, and there is no statutory basis for regarding these claims as having priority. Therefore — if we understand the decision correctly — in case of undue payments made to the payee before the latter's bankruptcy, there is no reason to suppose that the *condictio indebiti* is to be treated any differently from other ordinary non-preferred claims.

The judgment by the *Hoge Raad*: (2) payments after the declaration of bankruptcy

As far as concerns claims which arise from undue payments made to either the bankrupt or to the curator *after* the opening of bankruptcy proceedings, the *Hoge Raad* now makes a distinction between different payments. On the one hand, there are situations identical to the *Floritex* case.[8] There the legal cause of the payment ceased to exist *after* the payee had been declared bankrupt, with retroactive effect *(ex tunc)* from before the declaration of bankruptcy. The *condictio indebiti* was in this situation characterised by the *Hoge Raad* as a non-preferred claim against the estate (*concurrente boedelvordering*). If the available funds are insufficient, the *condictio indebiti* cannot then be fully satisfied. In contrast to this, there are situations where no legal relationship exists or existed between the bankrupt payee and the payor, pursuant to which the payment was made, and where the payment is only the consequence of an *obvious mistake* (*onmiskenbare vergissing*). By way of example the *Hoge Raad* mentions a payment to the wrong person, *ie* a payment which was caused by a mistake as to the identity of the person to whom the payment should be made.

In this second category a special rule applies. The curator must make full restitution of the amount which was paid by mistake. The *Hoge Raad* argues that when he is aware of an obvious mistake the curator acts in accordance with the standards prevailing in social intercourse[9] if he undoes that mistake. The court takes the view that, because of his special position, the curator must be expected not to allow third parties to become victims of accidental, in practice often unavoidable, mistakes. The fact that there is neither a statutory privilege for these claims nor any other statutory basis for according priority to them does not justify the conclusion that the curator may add the mistaken payments to the bankrupt estate. There is therefore no justification for treating the claim for recovery of the mistaken payment as a non-preferred claim against the estate or for allowing the curator to apply the mistaken payment for the benefit of the other creditors with a claim against the estate. That course of conduct by the curator would lead to an enrichment of those creditors at the expense of the person who has made the payment by mistake.

The *Hoge Raad* comes in this way to the conclusion that there is no justification for such a course of conduct and certainly none in the system of the Bankruptcy Act (*Faillissementswet*). The *Hoge Raad* pushes its argument on to the conclusion that reasonableness then requires the party who has made a payment to the curator through an obvious mistake must obtain restitution of the enrichment of the estate. By virtue of BW art 6:212 (unjust enrichment) the curator, having received the mistaken payment and having concluded that a mistake has been made, has the obligation to make a payment to the payor out of the available funds of an amount equal to the amount with which the estate has been enriched. Moreover, the curator must in the circumstances fulfil this obligation as soon as possible, without waiting for the winding-up of the estate

---

[6] BW art 6:203(2): *indebitum solutum*.
[7] BW arts 3.277(1) and 3.278.
[8] HR 14 December 1984, NJ 1985, 288.
[9] Note that under BW art 6:162 a delict is committed, *inter alia*, where a person causes damage to another person, by acting contrary to standards prevailing in social intercourse. The wording used by the *Hoge Raad* almost exactly matches with BW art 6:162.

and without regard to claims of the other creditors. Thus, the *Hoge Raad* does not consider the unjust enrichment claim as a non-preferred claim against the estate, but rather as a "super-preferred" claim against the estate.

Applying this, there had been in this case an *obvious mistake*. The curator was therefore obliged to make restitution of the payment made by the tax collector to the bankrupt. The claim of the tax collector was to be satisfied before any other creditor of the estate or any pre-bankruptcy creditor received anything out of the estate. Furthermore, if the amount received as a consequence of the undue payment had already been paid on to one or more creditors of the estate, the tax collector could, following the *Hoge Raad*'s line of thought, institute an action on the basis of unjust enrichment against those creditors. It is also conceivable that in this situation the payor can hold the curator personally liable for restitution of the mistaken payment.

Some observations

This judgment has not received undivided approval in legal writing. Although the outcome of the proceedings is in accordance with the sense of justice of many persons (including many curators), the reasoning of the *Hoge Raad* can be criticised in many ways. This criticism concerns, *inter alia*, the wholly novel interpretation given by the *Hoge Raad* of the system of the Bankruptcy Act and the significance attributed by the *Hoge Raad* to the principle of "reasonableness". Furthermore, one could doubt whether it is correct to attribute a special status to a claim based on unjust enrichment in situations where the enrichment is caused by an undue payment made during bankruptcy as a consequence of an obvious mistake. Why should there be a different treatment of "obviously mistaken" payments made *before* and those made *after* declaration of bankrupty? What is the difference between an *obvious* mistake and an *ordinary* mistake? Where exactly is the borderline between ordinary mistakes and obvious mistakes? The reasoning was result-led: in order to achieve the result desired, the *Hoge Raad* laboured to find an argument which justify the result.

We are not convinced by the reasoning of the *Hoge Raad*. In our view the *Hoge Raad*'s judgment should be regarded as an *ad hoc* decision. It should not be regarded as the final answer to all questions relating to the preferential status of claims for the recovery of mistaken payments; there are many issues which still need to be solved. Nor should this judgment in our view be regarded as the Dutch reception of the constructive trust, although it cannot be denied that there are similarities between the outcome of the proceedings and the results achieved under a constructive trust.

REGIONAL DIGEST

Asia Pacific
(Brunei, Hong Kong, Malaysia and Singapore)

*T M Yeo**

The past year has seen a healthy number of cases dealing with problems in or related to the law of unjust enrichment, but no significant pronouncement of principle as such. The language of unjust enrichment and restitution is evidently gaining judicial currency, although the underlying principles are not always expressly articulated.

CASES

1. *Chekiang First Bank v Fong Siu Kin* [1997] 2 HKC 302 (HK CA: Litton VP, Godfrey and Ching JJA); affg Unrep (HC: Bokhary J).
Undue influence – setting aside mortgage – unconscionability.
D1 had mortgaged her property to secure a loan by P, a bank, to D2. D2 defaulted on the loan, and P sued both defendants on the loan. D1's arguments that there had been undue influence by P were rejected by the High Court. Upon appeal, D1 raised additional arguments that D2 had exercised undue influence on her.

Held: A bank's security may be set aside where the bank has actual or constructive notice that the security transaction had been procured by the undue influence of another.

Decision: The appeal was dismissed. D2 had not exercised any undue influence, nor was there presumed undue influence, and in any event there was no evidence that P could be fixed with constructive notice of any such undue influence.

Dictum: *Per Godfrey JA*: "The law does not save people from the consequences of their own folly or improvidence. It does, however, save them from being imposed upon by the unconscionable conduct of others."

2. *Cheng Lim Landscaping v Chew Eu Hock Construction* (18 Apr 1997) Unrep (Sing HC: HT Chao J).
Quantum meruit – request – request conveyed to third party – benefit.
Two actions were consolidated. The defendant in both actions, CEHC, was a sub-contractor. In turn, CEHC sub-contracted certain works to the plaintiff in the first action, SH. SH's claim arose from CEHC's deduction in contract price for SH's alleged failure to carry out certain turfing work, which SH argued did not fall within the sub-sub-contract. CEHC had instructed the managing director of SH to carry out the turfing work, and he had in turn requested that CLL, a firm in which he was a partner, to do so. CLL was the plaintiff in the second action, claiming in *quantum meruit*. CEHC had been paid by the main contractor for the turfing work.

Decision: The turfing work did not fall within the sub-sub-contract, and the deductions against SH were thus wrongly made. CLL's claim in *quantum meruit* succeeded as CLL had done the work at the request of the managing director of SH who had been instructed by CEHC to do the works, and CEHC had clearly benefited from the work done by CLL, even though there was no contract between CEHC and CLL.

* Senior Lecturer, Faculty of Law, National University of Singapore. I am grateful to Asst Prof Lusina Ho, Dept of Law, University of Hong Kong, without whose invaluable assistance the Hong Kong section would have been deficient.

Held: A *quantum meruit* claim lies in respect of benefit conferred by the plaintiff on the defendant at the defendant's request.

Comment: This case shows that a request relayed to a third party can found a claim for *quantum meruit* by the third party (at least in the absence of officiousness).

3. *Chien Mateo, Padilla v Chan Choi Hing* [1997] HKLRD 539 (HK HC: Stone J).
Economic duress – bona fide demands – sums due.
As a result of a dispute, P and D entered into a agreement whereby D agreed to guarantee a judgment debt owing by D's firm to P's firm, and to pay the sum to P in eight monthly instalments. D failed to maintain the payments, and P sued for the balance due. D argued *inter alia* that the agreement was procured by economic duress, in that D had undertaken personal liability as she had no practical choice but to do so to save her firm.

Decision: P was entitled to judgment. Economic duress had not been shown, and in any event D had affirmed the agreement after it was entered into.

Held: In a case where there is a demand for money admittedly due and owing, or where there has been a bona fide belief that money is so due, it would be very difficult, though not impossible, to maintain a claim of economic duress in the context of arm's length commercial dealings between the parties (*CTN Cash and Carry Ltd v Gallaher Ltd* [1994] 4 All ER 714; [1994] RLR §134 applied).

4. *Chinese United Establishments Ltd v Cheung Siu Ki* [1997] 2 HKC 212 (HK HC: Rogers J).
Breach of fiduciary duty – appointment of receiver to protect assets.
D, with other investors, formed a company, P, to purchase a 50% share of a taxi company in China. The other 50% was subsequently offered to P, who used a holding company, B, owned entirely by D, to make the purchase. D later sold a 50% share in B to one of the original investors. P applied for the appointment of a receiver of the share of P in B held by D, arguing that P had acted in breach of fiduciary duty in using B to purchase the remaining share of the taxi company, that the taxi company was in financial difficulties, and that it was necessary to suspend the operations of the taxi company to prevent disposition of its assets pending the outcome of the trial.

Decision: P had made out a strong arguable case that D was profiting from a breach of his fiduciary duty to P. A receiver was appointed.

Held: A receiver would be appointed if on the facts an interlocutory injunction would have been granted, or on the basis that the aim of the court is to preserve the assets over which a receiver is sought to be appointed if it is thought to be necessary to put both parties in as good a position as possible when it comes to a court deciding the justice of the case at trial.

Comment: The case did not expressly decide that D's interest was subject to a proprietary claim by P. However, the grant of the receivership order would appear to be consistent only with a proprietary claim, as it would otherwise bypass the need to obtain a *Mareva* injunction.

5. *Chong Kwok Tung v Liu Chong Hing Bank Ltd* (11 Apr 1997) Unrep (HK HC: Le Pichon J).
Money had and received – conversion of money.
P had, with the help of D2, an employee of D1, a bank, opened a number of accounts at D1. P signed several authorisation forms allowing D2 to move the money from one account to another. D2 exceeded his authority, and transferred the money to an account in his own name, from which he conducted his own business of moneylending. P claimed in conversion, money had and received, and deceit. The action only proceeded against D2.

Decision: D2 was liable for money had and received and deceit but not conversion.

Held: No action lies for conversion in respect of money once it has passed into currency. The claim in such cases lies in money had and received.

Comment: The basis for the claim in money had and received was not explained. Probably, it lay in common law tracing from P's legal chose in action against D1 to the value received by D2 in his own account.

6. *Cosmic Insurance Corp Ltd v Ong Kah Hoe t/a Ong Kah Hoe Industrial Supplies* (20 Sept 1997) Unrep (Sing HC: Rubin J).
Recoupment – payment to third party under compulsion of law – whether obligation of defendant discharged.
D2, an employee of D1, was driving D1's lorry while his licence was suspended, and caused the death of a cyclist. The estate successfully obtained a judgment against D2, but D1's insurer, P, avoided liability under the Motor Vehicles (Third Party Risks and Compensation) Act (Cap 189, 1985 Ed), on the basis of D2's disqualification. P was later directed by the Motor Insurers' Bureau of Singapore (MIB) to pay the estate of the cyclist in respect of the judgment obtained, pursuant to an agreement between the MIB and a group of insurers in Singapore, including P. P did so, and then demanded payment from D1, both under the insurance policy as well as on restitutionary grounds.
Decision: P could not recover under contract because as a matter of construction the relevant recovery clause did not extend to a case where the insured was not found to be liable. The claim in restitution also failed as P had not established that D1 was vicariously liable for D2's actions.
Held: A plaintiff should recover in restitution whenever he made, under legal compulsion, a payment which discharges the defendant's liability to a third party so that the defendant obtains the benefit of the payment by the discharge of his liability.
Comment: The claim against D2 was not seriously pursued as he was penniless.

7. *D & C Property Pte Ltd v Four Seas Construction Co Pte Ltd* (20 Aug 1997) Unrep (Sing HC: LM Tan J).
Dishonesty – meaning – accessorial liability – change of position.
The plaintiffs, property developers, were suing the defendants, contractors as well as one director of one of the plaintiffs, for conspiracy, breach of contract, and diversion of corporate opportunity.
Decision: The defendants were found liable for breach of contract, but there was insufficient evidence on the facts to found the claims in conspiracy, breach of fiduciary duty and breach of duty not to disclose confidential information.
Held: (with regard to accessorial liability) "As a general rule, commercial transactions cannot be properly conducted on the basis that a person who is dealing with a company's agent is, without more, obliged to take steps to convince himself that the agent in question is not breaching his fiduciary duty."
Comment: In *obiter dicta,* Tan J considered the level of knowledge required to make strangers to a breach of fiduciary duty liable for encouraging the breach. While accepting *Royal Brunei Airlines Sdn Bhd v Tan Kok Ming* [1997] AC 378; [1996] RLR §15 to be applicable, the learned judge also considered the meaning of dishonesty as adopted in the Singapore Court of Appeal in *Seagate Technology Pte Ltd v Goh Han Kim* [1995] 1 SLR 17; [1995] RLR §16 as the test for barring the change of position defence in restitutionary claims, implicitly suggesting that the same meaning of dishonesty may be applicable in both types of situations.

8. *Fernhill City Investments Pte Ltd v Lee Keng Huat* (31 Aug 1996) Unrep (Sing HC: SC Lai J).
Equitable subrogation by sub-purchaser to purchaser's payment of deposit – prevention of unjust enrichment.
P, a property developer, entered into a contract of sale with a purchaser, who paid the first 10% of the purchase price as booking fee, and who subsequently entered into a contract of sub-sale to D. This was an application by P for a declaration that *inter alia* it had validly terminated the contract for breach by D, in failing *inter alia* to pay the first 10% of the purchase price.

Decision: The declaration was denied, and the contract of sub-sale was ordered to be specifically performed. The allegations of breaches were either unfounded or did not justify the termination of the contract.

Held: There was an equitable subrogation by the sub-purchaser to the purchaser's payment of the booking fee once the latter was reimbursed by the former, otherwise the vendor would be unjustly enriched at the sub-purchaser's expense.

9. *Kwai Hung Realty Co Ltd v Kung Mo Ng* (24 Dec 1997) Unrep (HK HC: W Waung J).
Common law tracing – mixture of funds – defences – ministerial receipt – change of position.
This was an application by some of the plaintiffs, P, to re-amend the statement of claim against one of the defendants, D, a bank. P were a group of companies. A fraudulent employee had forged a large number of P's cheques drawn on various accounts of P at various banks including D. One set of claims was for money had and received in relation to cheques drawn on P at two banks in favour of a third party's account at D (the collecting bank), on the basis of a mistake of the paying bank in making the payment thinking it had the mandate to do so when it did not. D argued against the amendments on the basis that there was no arguable claim as the money had been mixed in the clearing system and could not be traced to D, or alternatively, that there was an unarguable defence of receipt as agent or change of position.

Decision: The amendments were allowed as there were triable issues in respect of the claims and the defences.

Held: The claim based on common law tracing was arguable on the basis of following a chose in action or, alternatively, following money through the clearing system in spite of mixture. The defence of payment over to principal was arguable as there were triable issues as to whether the benefit had indeed been paid over and whether the book entries could be reversed without affecting the substance of the transaction. The change of position defence was not unarguable as there were issues to be tried relating to whether the change of position was bona fide, whether the recipient was a wrongdoer or had acted negligently, and whether change of position was in reliance on the receipt.

Comment: The court did not address the issue of P's reliance on the paying bank's mistake as the basis of its claim. Presumably it was on the basis that the bank paid out the money as P's agent. Nor did the court draw a distinction between following the cheque and the proceeds of the cheque. In *obiter dicta*, the holding in *Agip (Africa) Ltd v Jackson* [1990] Ch 547, that the common law could not trace through electronic transfers or when there had been an intervening payment out in anticipation of a payment in, was said to be arguably inconsistent with the principles of common law tracing stated in *Banque Belge Pour L'Etranger v Hambrouck* [1921] 1 KB 321.

10. *Pacific South (Asia) Holdings Ltd v Million Unity International Ltd*
[1997] HKLRD 1238 (HK CA: Nazareth VP and Godfrey JA, Mayo JA dissenting); affg Unrep (HC).
Relief against forfeiture – unconscionability in assertion of contractual rights – rescission.
The purchaser, P, had tendered payment in respect of a property, before completion, to the vendor, D, in the form of a personal cheque, which D returned without objecting to the nature of the tender D knew that P thought it was because it was premature, but did nothing to disabuse P. The cheque was presented at the time of completion but was rejected by D. P obtained an order for specific performance in the High Court, and D appealed.

Decision: D was estopped from objecting to payment by cheque, after misleading P into thinking that the objection to the tender was on some other ground.

Held: A vendor is not entitled to rescind a contract on the basis of the payment not complying with the contract if he had misled the purchaser that he is objecting on other grounds.

Comment: In *obiter dicta*, Nazareth VP considered the effect of *Union Eagle Ltd v Golden*

Achievement Ltd [1997] AC 514; [1997] RLR §8 (PC HK) and stated that estoppel should be the preferred basis in cases such as the present, but that unconscionable conduct as the basis for granting specific performance will only be granted in "increasingly exceptional and special circumstances". However, he would have been willing to rest his decision on unconscionability. *Cf Wellfit Investments Ltd v Poly Commence Ltd* [1997] HKLRD 857; *infra*, §15.

11. *Segar Oil Palm Estate Sdn Bhd v Tay Tho Bok* [1997] 3 MLJ 211 (Mal CA: Shaik Daud, Norma Yaakob and Mahadev Shankar JJCA); rvsg Unrep (HC).
Recovery of deposit – party in breach of contract – fraudulent misrepresentation.
The vendors of a piece of land, V, had fraudulently represented to the purchasers, P, that certain fixtures in the form of water pipes and electricity cables were outside the land. P found out the truth before completion, and tendered a reduced price in payment. V returned the cheque and forfeited the deposit. P obtained from the High Court an order rectifying the contract to reflect the reduced purchase price and a decree of specific performance. V appealed.
Decision: The appeal was allowed on the basis that P could not rescind the contract partially, and that the purported partial rescission amounted to a total repudiation which had been accepted by V when they returned the cheque. However, V was not entitled to keep the deposit.
Held: The court will not permit a vendor of property to be unjustly enriched by the retention of the deposit when the reason for the purchaser's repudiation of the contract of sale was the fraudulent misrepresentation of the vendor.

12. *Sintalow Engineering Pte Ltd v Nishimatsu Lam Chang JV (Construction & Civil Engineering) Pte Ltd* (30 Nov 1997) Unrep (Sing HC: CR Rajah JC).
Anticipated contract that did not materialise – quantum meruit – free acceptance – total failure of consideration – mistaken conferment of benefits – estoppel.
P were distributors of a prefabricated ceiling system. They were encouraged by D, who were the main contractors of a building project, to construct a mock-up (as requested by the architects of the project), for the owners to assess the suitability of the system for the building project. This encouragement went on even after D had clearly decided that, though they were very interested in the ceiling system proposed, P were not up to the task and that the project should be given to another sub-contractor. In accordance with industry practice, and also according to an express understanding between P and D, the cost of the mock-up was to be borne by P. After P failed to get the contract, P claimed in *quantum meruit* for work done for the mock-up.
Decision: D had benefited from the mock-up as they were under an obligation to have one as requested by the architects. P had a legitimate expectation of a reasonable chance of getting the contract in providing the mock-up, and D was under a duty to inform P if P were to provide the mock-up completely free. P was therefore entitled to *quantum meruit*.
Held: A party who confers a benefit for free on the understanding that it stood a reasonable chance of bidding for a contract is entitled to recovery on a *quantum meruit* basis where the recipient of the benefit had encouraged the first party's belief knowing it to be untrue.
Comment: The basis of the claim was not explained. It could be: (1) mistake in the provision of the services; (2) total failure of consideration in the provision of the services; (3) possibly, unconscionable free acceptance; or (4) that D was estopped by his conduct from relying on the industry practice and express agreement that P would bear the cost.

13. *Siswanto, Frans Bimbang v Coutts & Co AG* (1 Nov 1996) Unrep (Sing HC: HT Chao J).
Total failure of consideration – conflict of laws – proper law of contract.
The Indonesian plaintiffs, who had, in Singapore, opened a Swiss bank account with the defendants (Swiss bankers), sued the defendants in Singapore for breach of contract as well as for money had and received, after losing money in investments. The main question before the court

was whether it was the appropriate forum to hear the case. One of the arguments raised was that the claim for total failure of consideration would not be governed by Swiss law.

Decision: The action would be stayed as Switzerland was the more appropriate forum in all the circumstances.

Held: (In respect of the law governing the restitutionary claim) The governing law of a contract determines whether there has been a total failure of consideration for a restitutionary claim.

Comment: It is not clear whether the court decided that the proper law of the contract governed any restitutionary claim made in consequence of its breach, or that the law of the contract governs the issue whether there has been a total failure of consideration to the exclusion of the law governing the restitutionary claim.

14. ***Teck Seng Beng Pte Ltd (In Liquidation) v Chia Puay Teck*** (16 May 1997) Unrep (Sing HC: CR Rajah JC).
Misappropriation of company funds – money had and received – whether return to shareholders is a defence.
The defendants, D, were shareholders and managing directors of the plaintiff company, P. D had committed breach of trust. The other shareholders, when informed of the fraud, sought to recoup their losses by compelling D to purchase their shares at a significant overvalue, on threat of a police report. D complied. Not having enough money to carry this out, D procured, with the consent of the other shareholders, interest-free loans from P. D could not pay up completely in spite of this, and gave themselves up to the police. D petitioned for a winding up, and the liquidators claimed $520,000 from D as money had and received to the use of P, that D had taken from the company either as loans or otherwise, arguing that any benefits conferred on the shareholders were to be disregarded.

Decision: D was not liable as they had returned more than the sum claimed to the other shareholders, who in this case (where the creditors could all be paid off without taking into account the money claimed in the action) could not be distinguished from the company.

Held: (*Semble*) A defendant is not liable in an action for money had an received if he no longer remains unjustly enriched by returning the sum of enrichment to the plaintiffs, or persons who can be regarded as the real plaintiffs.

Comment: Although the language used has the flavour of change of position, that defence would be unavailable to directors who knew they were not entitled to use the company's money. It is therefore not clear whether the decision is based on: (1) the lifting of the corporate veil; (2) the avoidance of multiplicity of actions (by allowing the claim, and then letting D claim back the repaid money on failure of consideration, though this may be subject to an illegality defence); or (3) an analysis that it was not at the expense of the real plaintiffs. The juristic basis of the claim for money had and received was also not addressed, although it was probably based on the unauthorised taking of money belonging in law to P, or the failure of consideration in the purported loans to D.

15. ***Wellfit Investments Ltd v Poly Commence Ltd*** [1997] HKLRD 857 (PC HK: Lord Browne-Wilkinson, Lord Lloyd of Berwick, Lord Nolan, Lord Cooke of Thornton and Lord Clyde); affg [1996] HKLY 251 (CA); rvsg [1996] HKLY 654 (HC).
Sale and purchase contract – whether unconscionable or inequitable to terminate contract – whether jurisdiction to relieve against forfeiture applicable.
R1 had entered into a contract of sale with R2. In turn, R1 entered into a sub-sale with A, with a time specified for completion before the completion of the main contract, in accordance with the Law Society's guidelines, to enable R1 to finance his main contract. A failed to produce the money on time and R1 rescinded the sub-contract, and arranged alternative financing for the main contract. A asked for specific performance, arguing *inter alia* that R1's conduct in rescind-

ing the contract was unconscionable. The claim was upheld in the High Court, but the decision was reversed in the Court of Appeal.

Decision: Appeal dismissed. Time was of the essence, and there was no suggestion by R1 otherwise that could found a waiver or estoppel. R1 was entitled to rely on his contractual rights and was not acting unconscionably.

Held: A vendor is not acting unconscionably where he exercises his contractual right to rescind a contract where the purchaser fails to meet the time for completion.

Comment: The Board left open the question whether the court has jurisdiction to relief against "forfeiture" consequent upon the rescission of contract on the grounds of unconscionable or inequitable conduct. *Union Eagle Ltd v Golden Achievement Ltd* [1997] AC 514; [1997] RLR §8 (PC HK) was not cited in the opinion.

ARTICLES

16. *Sarwar, MI, "Equity and Commerce: An Alternative Perspective"* [1997] 3 MLJ cxlix.
The author discusses the role of equitable principles in commercial transactions, including principles relating to restitution for unjust enrichment, arguing that the application of the equitable principles does not give rise to unacceptable uncertainty in commerce.

17. *Shariff, NA, "Equitable Doctrine of Undue Influence — Reflections on Recent Cases"* [1997] 3 MLJ lxxxiii.
The author surveys the recent English developments in the law relating to undue influence, arguing that there has been too much emphasis on formalistic requirements at the expense of the fundamental principles of equity.

18. *Soh, KB, "Deposits and Reasonable Penalties"* [1997] SJLS 50.
The writer deals with the rationale and difficulties in drawing the line between deposits and penalties as well as the problems in relief against forfeiture and restitutionary claims. In relation to restitution, he notes that, although the enrichment, being monetary, will not be in question, there may be difficulty in identifying the unjust factor, and measuring the quantum of restitution. He also notes that, although there is a useful role for the law of unjust enrichment identified in *Union Eagle Ltd v Golden Achievement Ltd* [1997] AC 514; [1997] RLR §8, the case may raise as much uncertainty as it seeks to avoid.

OTHER INFORMATION

19. *Lee, EB and Yeo, TM, "Recent Developments in the Law of Restitution"*
Seminar organised by the Singapore Academy of Law and the Faculty of Law, National University of Singapore, at the Singapore Academy of Law, 7 March 1998.

NOTER UP

Kartika Ratna Tahir v PT Pertambangan Minyak and Gas Bumi Negara [1994] 3 SLR 257: [1995] RLR §20; followed in *Choy Chee Keen Collin v Public Utilities Board* [1997] 1 SLR 604 (Sing CA), in the holding that a principal has a proprietary claim against an agent in respect of bribes received, and any profits made from such bribes.
Rajagopal, Mookha Pillai v Chopra, Khushvinder Singh [1996] 3 SLR 457; [1997] RLR §6; noted Lim, KW (1997) 18 Asia Bus LR 85.
Royal Brunei Airlines Sdn Bhd v Tan [1995] 2 AC 378; [1995] RLR §15; noted Panesar (1997) 12 JIBL 175; Clark (1996) 14 CJIL 467.

Union Eagle Ltd v Golden Achievement Ltd [1997] AC 514; [1997] 2 WLR 341; [1997] 2 All ER 215; [1997] HKLRD 366; [1997] 1 HKC 173; [1997] RLR §8; noted Heydon (1997) 113 LQR 385.

Australia

Peter Butler*

The remedy of rescission has been a predominant feature of many of the cases in this period. The most important case is that of *Maguire v Makaronis* §34 from the High Court of Australia. *Akron Securities* §22 provides an interesting illustration of flexible statutory relief that may be ordered under the *Trade Practices Act 1974 (Cth), s 87,* for an actionable misrepresentation as an alternative to equitable rescission as traditionally administered. Associate Professor NY Nahan §57 examines the fundamentals of rescission and the bars to it, and concludes that the present rules should be replaced. In *Commonwealth v SCI Operations* §26 the High Court has rejected the availability of an interest award in relation to provisions of the *Customs Act 1903* (Cth) dealing with refunds of duty. Another High Court decision, *Hill v Van Erp* §40, concerning an ineffective testamentary disposition, invites consideration of the possibility of shaping a restitutionary remedial solution where a negligent solicitor incurs tortious liability in damages at the suit of the disappointed intended beneficiary; see Tapsell §58.

CASES

21. *A & G International Pty Ltd v Collector of Customs* (1995) 129 FLR 23 (Vic SC: Ormiston J).
Mistake of law – restitutionary claim for interest – recovery of customs duty – duty not paid under protest – effect of statute – Customs Act 1901 (Cth), ss 163, 167, 273GA.
The plaintiff paid customs duty under the mistaken belief that the goods were correctly classified. The payments were not made under protest. A court found that the goods fell within a category which was subject to a lower rate of customs duty. The defendant refunded the sums paid by the plaintiffs, but refused to pay interest. The plaintiff brought a claim to recover the interest. The defendant claimed that no interest was payable as there was no right of action to recover the duty because of the *Customs Act 1901 (Cth)* ss 167(4) and 163. Section 167(4) provides that no action shall lie for the recovery of any sum paid as customs duty unless the payment is made under protest and action is commenced within the time-limit stated. Section 163 gives the defendant a discretion to refund payments of duty which have been made under a "patent misconception of the law". Section 273GA allows an appeal to the Administrative Appeals Tribunal against decisions made under s 163.
Decision: The plaintiff had no cause of action for the recovery of the interest.
Held: (1) No proceedings lie to recover any excess duty paid unless that right is explicitly or impliedly conferred by the *Customs Act*. There is no enforceable right to recover any excess duty paid unless the provisions of the *Customs Act* (Cth), s 167, including that the payment be made under protest, have been complied with. Section 167 must be read down to the extent necessary to enable s 273 GA to have effect, but not further. Section 273GA does not have the effect that a failure to exercise the defendant's powers under s 163 gives rise to a cause of action for recov-

---

* Senior Lecturer in Law, University of Queensland. I acknowledge with thanks the able assistance provided by Mr Rafal Zakrzewski, Articled Clerk at the Brisbane office of Mallesons Stephen Jaques, Solicitors, and Mr John Trone, PhD Student, Law School, University of Queensland.

ery of overpaid duty. No money had been wrongly held by the defendant; only a power to give a refund had not been properly exercised according to law. Therefore, the plaintiff did not have a cause of action for repayment of money that carried with it a right to recover interest. (2) Section 163 provides for a discretionary power, not an obligation, of the collector to refund duty, in respect of which an owner has a right to compel the Collector, by way of review, properly to exercise his discretion. Section 163 does not give rise to a remedy in restitution.

22. *Akron Securities v Iliffe* (1997) 41 NSWLR 353; (1997) 143 ALR 457 (NSW CA: Mason P, Priestley and Meagher JJA).
Misrepresentation – statutory remedy – appropriateness of rescission – requirements of restitutio in integrum – taxation benefits – Trade Practices Act 1974 (Cth), ss 52, 87.
The acquisition of a share in an investment scheme involved the entry into a lease agreement with the manager of the scheme and a loan agreement with the appellant for the total of the repayments due under the lease. Only interest was to be payable under the loan until the scheme came to an end. Entry into the scheme gave the investors a significant tax benefit for a small outlay. The investors were also given an option, which the respondents took up, of purchasing "insurance" whereby the manager would guarantee a sufficient return to cover the lease rental payments and the repayment of the loan. The scheme collapsed and the manager became insolvent. The appellant sued the respondents, who were investors, to recover the amounts owing under the loan agreements. At first instance, the respondents successfully argued that the appellant's employee had misrepresented to them that a third party backed the minimum return guarantee. This was a breach of the *Trade Practices Act 1974 (Cth)*, s 52. The trial judge made an order under s 87 of the Act setting aside the agreements ab initio and requiring repayment of the money invested together with interest. The remedy was challenged on appeal.

Decision: Appeal allowed. The majority (Mason P, Priestly JA agreeing) held that the trial judge erred either by assuming that a breach of s 52 automatically led to the conclusion that the respondents should be retrospectively relieved of their contractual obligations, or by not considering whether alternative relief was more appropriate. The rescission orders would be set aside on the condition that the appellant honour the "guarantee" that was misrepresented by its employee.

Held: Per Mason P with whom Priestly JA agreed: (1) Section 87 is not to be given a restrictive interpretation. The court has an unfettered discretion to make such orders as the court thinks appropriate. (2) Unlike s 82, which is concerned only with compensation for actual loss or damage, s 87 extends to the prevention and reduction of loss or damage which is likely to be suffered, where "likely" means "real chance or possibility", and goes beyond permitting orders for pecuniary recovery as understood in the law of tort. (3) The general law principles relating to rescission give guidance as to the exercise of the statutory discretion but they are not determinative. (4) Faced with findings of reliance by the innocent party upon misleading or deceptive conduct, and clear evidence of likely loss or damage that would attract s 87, a trial judge should consider the range of available remedies, recognising that s 87 may allow the defendant's as well as the plaintiff's interests to be taken into account in moulding a just response to a proven contravention. (5) The need to consider all the circumstances relevant to the remedy includes an obligation to have some regard to the extent of loss or damage flowing from the misleading or deceptive conduct. The remedial loss should be proportionate to the wrong, without necessarily having to reflect the extent of the plaintiff's loss or damage. (6) Avoidance of the contracts should not be subject to the repayment of the loan principal in this case because of the circumstances and nature of the loan contract. It was part of a package of interlocking arrangements all of which were induced by the misrepresentation. Furthermore, the money went into the venture, some of it went back to the appellant, and the balance went to the appellant's co-venturer, the manager. If it were required to be repaid, this would add to the respondents' loss flowing from the misrepresentation. (7) The misrepresentation went to a discrete aspect of the whole transaction and not the whole transaction itself. Its precise value could be ascertained. As the loss or damage suffered by the respondents was no more than the lack of the guarantee, it was inappropriate to unravel the whole venture. (8) Rescission was inappropriate as the respondents had gained significant tax benefits that they would not have to account for to the appellant and were unlikely to be forced to disgorge by the Commissioner of Taxation.

Per Meagher JA dissenting: (1) The trial judge did not err in making orders which had the effect of reversing the transaction as the transaction would not have been entered into had the misrepresentation not been made. (2) Adequate provision had been made for *restitutio in integrum*. (3) The benefit of the tax deduction could be disregarded because there was a real question whether the tax would be required to be paid following rescission. (4) The respondents should not be required to repay the principal of the loans as they were not independent of the venture and the respondents retained no part of them.

Dicta: *Per Mason P*: (1) The plaintiff's choice of the statutory remedy may exclude legal and equitable remedies. If plaintiffs can resort to the statutory remedy to avoid inadequacies of equitable rescission, then defendants should be able to resist its possible excesses. (2) Equity, in effecting *restitutio in integrum*, would not have required the respondents to disgorge the collateral taxation benefits as these were not acquired at the appellant's expense.

Comment: There was a stark difference in the measure applied by the majority on the one hand and the dissenting judge and the trial judge on the other. The former attempted to place the parties in the position that they would have been in had the representation not been false, whereas the latter sought to place them in the position they would have occupied had the representation not been made.

23. *Baird v BCE Holdings Pty Ltd* (1996) 40 NSWLR 374 (NSW SC: Young J).
Rescission – share transfers executed and registered under mistaken belief as to tax consequences – when rescission by agreement possible – time from which rescission by agreement operates – rescission and rectification on basis of mistake – accident as a ground of equitable relief – effect of rectification of register – Corporations Law, s 216H.
Share transfers were executed in the belief that no significant tax liability would attach to the transaction. It was a mistaken belief and all the parties claimed that they would not have entered into the transaction had they known the true position. The parties sought a declaration that the share transfers were void and rectification of the company share register.

Decision: The court had no power to make the orders sought.

Held: (1) Discharge by rescission can only occur if the contract is in force, even if it has been partly performed as long as it has not been fully performed. In the present case, as the transfer of shares had been registered and there was nothing left to do under the contract, the contract was at an end and there was nothing that could be rescinded. (2) A rescinded contract is void ab initio but the rescission agreement may itself set up additional terms. (3) A distinction must be drawn between the motive for the transaction, the intention to enter into the transaction and the transaction itself. Mistakes that motivate the transaction are not vitiating factors on which the transaction can be rescinded. In this case, no error was made in putting the parties' agreement into effect. It was an error as to the consequences of the operation of the instrument of a remote kind and, as such, it was not a type of error that amounted to a mistake justifying rectification. The parties were seeking rectification of the transaction and not the documents. (4) The equitable remedy of cancellation was inapplicable on the facts, as was the "accident" ground for relief. (5) The *Corporations Law*, s 216H, which allows an aggrieved person to apply to the court for a rectification of the company register, does not broaden the court's equitable power of rectification. (6) If rectification of the company register were ordered, it would operate retrospectively and hence no capital gains tax would have been payable. (7) Equitable relief would not have been denied, if it were available, merely because the Crown would be deprived of tax.

24. *Bank of South Australia v Ferguson* (1998) 72 ALJR 551 (HC : Brennan CJ, Gaudron, McHugh, Gummow and Kirby JJ); [1998] HCA 12. Rvsg (1996) 66 SASR 77; [1997] RLR §15.
Whether mortgage and loan contract unenforceable and liable to be set aside for operative statutory fraud under Torrens system – whether consequence of statutory fraud that loan irrecoverable – Real Property Act 1886 (SA), s 69.

The *Real Property Act 1886 (SA)*, s 69, relevantly provides: "The title of every registered proprietor of land shall ... be absolute and indefeasible, subject only to the following qualifications: I. Fraud. In the case of fraud in which case any person defrauded shall have all rights and remedies that he would have had if the land were not under the provisions of this Act ..."

In 1990 the defendant F executed a mortgage over his farmland to the plaintiff bank in anticipation of loans being made by the bank. The bank advanced $400,000 in accordance with terms set out in its letter of offer, to which F signed his acceptance. The bank approved the advance for that amount on the basis of documentation prepared by its local branch managers, in which one manager had forged F's signature and the other had altered material details of F's property, all without his knowledge. In 1994, when just over $500,000 was outstanding on the loan, the bank, following default by F and service of notice of intention to exercise its power of sale over the land, claimed an order for delivery of possession of the land. F by way of defence pleaded that the mortgage was void for the plaintiff's fraud in terms of the *Real Property Act*, s 69, and counter-claimed for damages for innocent and negligent misrepresentation and fraud, to which the plaintiff counter-claimed for $509,169.79 with interest as a debt or damages for breach of the loan contract, or restitution as money had and received. The trial judge dismissed the plaintiff's claim and counterclaims to F's counterclaims. He also dismissed F's counterclaims for failure to establish any loss, and declared that the plaintiff could not enforce the mortgage due to fraud. The plaintiff appealed and F cross-appealed unsuccessfully to the Full Court. The plaintiff appealed further.

Decision: Appeal allowed. F had not been under a serious mistake or misled. Even if a case for rescission had been made out, no reason appeared to deny the application of the requirement of *restitutio in integrum*. Cross-appeal, with special leave, allowed.

Held: (1) Section 69 [Iota] of the Act requires identification of the rights and remedies which a person "defrauded"should have had if the land were not under the provisions of the Act. The legislation recognises the principle that an equity arising from the conduct of a registered proprietor before or after registration may be enforced against that registered proprietor notwithstanding the indefeasibility of registered titles. (2) Section 69 [Iota] operates to qualify the general principle of indefeasibility only if the case answers the statutory description of "fraud". Not all species of fraud which attract equitable remedies will amount to fraud in the statutory sense. Statutory fraud embraces less, not more, than the species of fraud which, at general law, founds the rescission of a conveyance; and statutory fraud is not itself directly generative of legal rights and obligations, its role being to qualify the operation of the doctrine of indefeasibility upon what would have been the rights and remedies of the complainant were the land held under unregistered title. (3) To be operative, fraud must operate on the mind of the person to have been defrauded and to have induced detrimental action by that person.

25. *Commissioner of Stamp Duties (NSW) v Carlenka Pty Ltd* (1995) 41 NSWLR 329 (NSW CA: Mahoney AP, Sheller JA and McLelland AJA).
Rectification – mistake – amendment of discretionary trust deed – intended addition of income beneficiary – inadvertent addition of capital beneficiary and taker in default – adverse stamp duty consequences –intention required for rectification – Stamp Duties Act 1920 (NSW).

The respondent, a trustee of a discretionary family trust, sought to add a company to the class of potential income beneficiaries. A deed was prepared and executed which enabled any companies nominated by the trustee to be added to the list of beneficiaries. However, as all beneficiaries were entitled to share in the capital of the trust on the vesting date in default of appointment, the deed operated as a re-settlement of the property and was liable to stamp duty under the *Stamp Duties Act 1920 (NSW)* at *ad valorem* rates. The respondent sought rectification of the deed of amendment by the addition of words that would not permit the company to share in capital of the trust upon its vesting. Rectification was ordered at first instance. The Commissioner of Stamp Duties appealed. In reliance on *Maralinga Pty Ltd v Major Enterprises Pty Ltd* (1973) 128 CLR 336, the Commissioner argued that the mistake was as to the document's effect and not its contents. It was asserted that the document contained words that the party executing it had purposely used under a mistaken belief that the words had a different legal effect and that rectification was not available in such circumstances.

Decision: Appeal dismissed.

Held: (1) Per curiam: Rectification requires disconformity between the form or effect of the document and the intention of the party who executed it. Proof of the intention must be convincing but is not limited to evidence of outward acts (dictum of Denning LJ in *Frederick E Rose (London) Ltd v William H Pim Junior & Co Ltd* [1953] 2 QB 450 disapproved). (2) The plaintiff must show that there is disconformity between the intention and the written instrument and that the intention continued to the time of execution of the agreement. The plaintiff must displace the hypothesis that the written instrument embodies the true intention of the parties. *Per Mahoney AP*: The term "intention", in the context of rectification, refers to what was subjectively seen as to be brought about and the consequences of it. Intention is that which is subjectively foreseen and intended to be effected by the document. It does not include that which was foreseen as likely or certain to occur but not wished for, nor can it include consequences which the parties did not actually have in their mind. *Per McLelland AJA*: Rectification is available where the intention as to the effect that the instrument would have is inconsistent with the effect the instrument as executed has. "Effect" in this context means the legal and factual operation of the instrument according to its true construction, but does not include legal or factual consequences of the operation of the instrument of a more remote, or collateral, kind (for example, its liability to stamp duty).

26. Commonwealth v SCI Operations Pty Ltd (1998) 152 ALR 624 (HC: Brennan CJ, Gaudron, McHugh, Gummow, Kirby JJ), [1998] HCA 20. Rvsg (1996) 139 ALR 595 (NSW FC Full Ct: Beaumont, Einfeld, Sackville JJ), [1997] RLR §29; affg (1995) 63 FCR 21 (NSW FC: Wilcox J). *Interest entitlement – customs duty paid and lawfully retained – refund of duty on grant of retrospective Commercial Tariff Concession Order ("CTCO") – whether interest on monies received under statutory right to refund – whether a right independent of statute to recover interest where defendant has been unjustly enriched by use of plaintiffs' money – whether interest payable from date of application for CTCO – Acts Interpretation Act 1901 (Cth), s 9 – Customs Act 1903 (Cth), s 163, Pcrt XVA, ss 269C, 269N – Customs Tariff Act 1987 (Cth), Pt III Sch 4 – Customs Regs (Cth), rr 126(f), 127(1), 128, 128A – Federal Court of Australia Act 1976 (Cth), s 51A.*

Between 1 Sep 1987 and 29 Feb 1992 the respondents imported and paid customs duty on certain goods. In Sep 1987 the respondents applied to the Comptroller-General of Customs for a Commercial Tariff Concession (CTCO), on the basis that goods serving similar functions to the imported goods were not manufactured in Australia. After prolonged litigation a CTCO was made on 3 Jun 1994, pursuant to the *Customs Act 1901* (Cth), s 269C, which was expressed to have come into effect on 1 Sep 1987. Its practical effect was that from 1 Sep 1987 customs duty was first payable at a reduced rate and was then duty free. The respondents conceded that they were liable to pay customs duty when the goods in question were originally imported, and that the Comptroller-General was both entitled and obliged to retain such duty on behalf of the Commonwealth until the making of the CTCO on 3 Jun 1994. On that date the respondents commenced proceedings to recover the difference between the duty paid and the duty payable, on the basis that the order came into effect on 1 Sep 1987, together with interest. Shortly after, on the same date, the Commonwealth paid the principal amounts refundable and some interest pursuant to conditions imposed in earlier litigation. The respondents pursued their interest claims under the *Federal Court of Australia Act 1976* [the Federal Court Act], s 51A, or the general law of restitution. The trial judge rejected the claims. On appeal the Full Court, by majority, held that the respondents were, unless good cause in the form of a "windfall" defence were shown to the contrary, entitled to an order for interest under s 51A(1)(a); or, if this were inappropriate, an order for interest in a lump sum amount under s 51A(1)(b). The Commonwealth further appealed. The respondents sought leave to cross-appeal seeking deletion from the order of the reference to the "windfall defence".

Decision: Appeal allowed. Cross-appeals granted special leave to proceed and dismissed.

Held: (1) *Per Brennan CJ, Gaudron J, McHugh and Gummow JJ*: There was no foundation for any application of s 51A of the Federal Court Act. *Per Brennan CJ*: Whatever be the nature of the relief to which the importers were respectively entitled, neither was entitled to a refund prior to the making of the CTCO. If a cause of action arose, it arose on the same date as the date on which the money paid as duty was refunded. As there was no period during which either importer was kept out of money which it was entitled to have, there was "good cause shown" why no interest should be awarded on the principal sums sued for. Even if the payment of those principal sums were to be regarded as the equivalent of judgment entered for the purposes of par (a) of s 51A(1), and even if the entitlement to the refund were properly to be seen as the arising of a cause of action, there was no "period between the date when the cause of action arose and the date as of which judgment is entered" so as to satisfy the condition on which the power to order interest under par (a) depends. If no amount could have been calculated in accordance with par (a), there was no room for the application of par (b). *Per Gaudron J*: The refund provisions (*Customs Act*, ss 269N and 167(1), and *Customs Regs*, rr 126, 127, 128, 128A) conferred a right to payment of a refund subject to satisfaction of specified conditions. The provisions were to be taken as conferring a right enforceable by an action for debt rather than by an administrative remedy. As the specified conditions had not been satisfied, no cause of action had arisen when the proceedings were commenced, so that there was no foundation for judgment under s 51A(1). *Per McHugh and Gummow JJ*: The concession order made pursuant to s 269N was not retrospective in the sense that it provided that, as at a past date, being 1 Sep 1987, and thereafter, the law was to be taken to have been that which it was not. Rather, the result was that, on 3 Jun 1994, there were brought into existence fresh rights or liabilities in respect of matters or transactions which had occurred on or after 1 Sep 1987. The legislation imposed a duty or obligation to make a refund of the duty paid in the nature of a debt to pay money enforceable by an action of debt. The statutory scheme represented a balance struck between the competing interests of importers, local producers, and the revenue. It did not include an additional obligation to make a payment in the nature of interest. As the duty was refunded on the day on which the CTCO was made, there was no period in which debts in respect of the refunds were due and owing but unpaid. The payments having been made on 3 Jun 1994 when there arose the causes of action (uncompleted because the stipulated procedural steps had not been taken), there was no sum for which judgment was given or could be given within the meaning of s 51A(1).

(2) *Per Gaudron J, McHugh and Gummow JJ*: As the right or entitlement to the repayment of duty paid was based wholly in statute, restitutionary principles could not convert a statutory right to obtain a refund of money into a right to obtain a refund with interest.

Per Kirby J: The claim for interest must be rejected on a more fundamental ground than that the language of the Federal Court Act did not attach for various textual reasons. An entitlement to a refund was provided for with particularity by a comprehensive statutory scheme which effectively codified the importers' entitlements, once a CTCO was made under the *Customs Act*, s 269N. Such a scheme, in which no express provision had been made to allow interest to be recoverable, excluded a supplementary entitlement to interest. General statutory provisions such as the Federal Court Act or common law principles could not expand the importers' rights.

Dicta: *Per Gaudron J*: There may be included in the "sum for which judgment is given", in the terms of s 51A(1), interest pursuant to par (a), or a lump sum in lieu of interest pursuant to par (b). *Per McHugh and Gummow JJ*: The existing state of authority does not favour acceptance of a "free-standing" right to the recovery of interest where the defendant has had the use of the plaintiff's money in circumstances which indicate an unjust enrichment at the expense of the plaintiff.

27. *Esanda Finance Corp Ltd v Tong* (1997) 41 NSWLR 482 (NSW CA: Handley JA, Santow and Simos A-JJA).
Unjust contract – limited guarantee – principal creditor proffering unlimited guarantee as replacement -relief limited to enforcing limited guarantee – Contracts Review Act 1980 (NSW), s 7.
A guarantee to cover leasing finance was limited as to one guarantor, by way of mortgage, to $105,000. Parties who were not fluent in written or spoken English but, so far as the lender knew, were independently advised by a solicitor, agreed to provide replacement security and signed an unlimited mortgage. The trial judge found that the mortgage was substantively unjust under the Contracts Review Act 1980 (NSW), because it did not contain the term which had limited the liability to $105,000, and ordered that the substitute guarantors be relieved from any obligations. The lender appealed.
Decision: Appeal allowed. Mortgage covering the substituted unlimited guarantee should be limited to $105,000.
Held: (1) The Contracts Review Act 1980, s 7, gives powers to the Court to grant civil remedies that are neither penal nor disciplinary. Once injustice to the weaker party has been remedied, the court should not further interfere with the rights of the parties as interference beyond that point will cause injustice to the other party. (2) A court granting equitable relief for a severable misrepresentation may refuse to allow the innocent party to rescind the entire contract.

28. *FAC v Aerolinas Argentinas* (1997) 147 ALR 649 (NSW FC Full Ct: Beaumont, Whitlam and Lehane JJ)
Ultra vires – fixing of charge by government corporation – recovery of money at common law – whether "review" proceedings necessary before common law claim for recovery of money could proceed – whether legislative or administrative act – Federal Airports Corporation Act 1986 (Cth), s 56 – Administrative Decisions (Judicial Review) Act 1977 (Cth), s 11.
The appellant was a statutory corporation whose function was to manage Federal airports. It was vested with various statutory powers. It purported to fix a charge for landing at particular airports. The respondents, a number of airlines, initially protested against the new charges but went on to pay them. Two years later, the respondents alleged that the charge was invalid and brought an action to recover the sums they had paid. The corporation argued that the proceedings could not proceed until the charge had been challenged in administrative law proceedings under the *Administrative Decisions (Judicial Review) Act 1977 (Cth)* and that the time for bringing such proceedings had expired. At first instance, the court found that the respondents could maintain an action seeking recovery of the monies without either first, or simultaneously, challenging the validity of the determination in administrative law proceedings because the respondents were alleging a jurisdictional error. Additionally, the court held that the respondents were permitted to commence administrative law proceedings. The corporation appealed. The respon-

dents cross-appealed against the finding that the fixing of the charge had been an administrative rather than legislative act.

Decision: Appeal and cross-appeal dismissed.

Held: (1) The corporation was a commercial government undertaking and the charge in question was to be in the nature of a fee for services, therefore the fixing of the charge was administrative in character. (2) The bringing of a common law claim is not conditional on the prior establishment of invalidity in proceedings commenced under the judicial review legislation and is not contrary to the provisions or policy of the *ADJR Act*. (3) Section 10 of the *ADJR Act* preserves the right which existed prior to the enactment of the *ADJR Act*, to bring an action for repayment of monies paid under an invalid determination without first obtaining a declaration as to its invalidity. It is not necessary to impugn an *ultra vires* determination in separate "review" proceedings prior to, or at the same time as, bringing a claim for the recovery of money paid under the *ultra vires* determination. (4) It would have been possible to bring the proceedings prior to the enactment of the *ADJR Act*. Consequently, as the Act expressly preserves other rights of review, proceedings of the present kind can be maintained. (5) The trial judge did not err in refusing to make the finding that the application under the *ADJR Act* had not been made within a reasonable time. There is no error in taking into account, as a relevant consideration, the limitation period applicable to the common law claim.

29. ***Fitzgerald v F J Leonhardt Pty Ltd*** (1997) 143 ALR 569; (1997) 71 ALJR 653 (HC: Dawson, Toohey, McHugh, Gummow and Kirby JJ); affg (1995) 5 NTLR 76 (NT CA : Martin CJ, Angel, Thomas JJ).

Illegality – contract to drill water bores – owner of land not in possession of permit required by statute -whether contract unenforceable by driller – Water Act 1992 (NT), ss 56, 57.

The respondent, a licensed driller, agreed to drill bores for the appellant on the appellant's land. The appellant did not obtain the correct permits for the bores because he misconstrued the requirements of the *Water Act 1992 (NT)*. The respondent drilled the bores with no intention of acting illegally and, after the appellant refused to pay, sued for the contract price. The appellant argued that the respondent was seeking to recover money under an illegal contract because there were no permits for the drilling of the bores. The court held in favour of the appellant at first instance but the respondent was successful in two subsequent appeals. An appeal was brought to the High Court.

Decision: Appeal dismissed. The contract was not unenforceable for illegality. The court stated that this was a plain case.

Held: (1) The section which prohibited an owner or occupier of land from causing or permitting the drilling of bores without a permit was not directed at the driller. The statute did not prohibit drilling and did not contain an express or implied prohibition against the making of the contract in question. (2) The terms of the contract did not require the commission of any illegal act and the contract was not made to effect an unlawful purpose. The performance of the contract did not require an illegal act because the contract would have been performed legally had the owner obtained the relevant permit. (3) The court found that, having regard to the scope and purpose of the legislation, permitting the enforcement of the contract by the respondent driller would not be against public policy. *Per Dawson and Toohey JJ*: A contract which is in itself legal will not be unenforceable merely because something illegal is done in its performance. In this case, the purpose of the statute would not be served by rendering contracts unenforceable if their performance involved a breach of the relevant section. The maxim *ex turpi causa non oritur actio* had no application in the present case because the driller did not have to rely on any illegality to establish its cause of action. *Per McHugh and Gummow JJ*: The case is not to be approached by considering any general *in pari delicto* doctrine. Instead the approach to be taken to determine whether contracts were unenforceable for illegality is that laid down for trusts by McHugh J in

Nelson v Nelson (1995) 184 CLR 538. *Per Kirby J*: The first question to be asked is whether, as a matter of construction, the Act either expressly or by necessary inference prohibits the contract as formed or because of the way it was performed. The second question is whether, as a matter of public policy, the court should refuse to enforce a contract in circumstances where, as performed, illegality has been demonstrated. His Honour answered both questions in the negative. In answering the second question, His Honour considered that, were the court to withhold relief to the respondent, it would result in a windfall gain to the appellant which was unmerited and itself would be an affront to the public conscience.

Dictum (Per McHugh and Gummow JJ): The flexibility attending the administration of equitable relief is not readily available where what is claimed is a legal remedy in aid of a legal right and there is no equity to qualify or displace, wholly or partly, enforcement of that legal right. But what may now be classified as restitutionary remedies may be available to assist in the striking of a balance

30. *Halgido Pty Ltd v DG Capital Co Ltd* (1996) 34 ATR 582; (1996) 97 ATC 4060 (NSW FC: Tamberlin J).
Recovery of payments – withholding tax – recovery under statute – mistake – discharge of another's liability – recoupment – Income Tax Assessment Act 1936 (Cth), ss 221YQ, 261
The applicant borrowed Swiss francs from a non-resident bank, the respondent. The applicant was required to pay and paid the withholding tax that was levied upon the interest. The clause requiring payment by the borrower was rendered void by the *Income Tax Assessment Act 1936 (Cth)* s 261. The applicant sued to recover the sum of the withholding tax claiming that: it had discharged the bank's liability to the Australian Taxation Office and therefore it was entitled to recover that sum plus interest under the *Income Tax Assessment Act*, s 221YQ(2), (which provided that the person who paid the tax could recover it from the lender); it had paid the full interest to the bank under a mistake of law because, as a result of s 261, the bank was only entitled to 90% of the interest and as a result the bank had been unjustly enriched; or, alternatively, the bank was unjustly enriched because the applicant discharged the bank's legal obligation to pay the tax.
Decision: Claim allowed.
Held: (1) The tax payments fell within s 221YQ(2) and were recoverable on that basis. A clause in the agreement which stated that the borrower waived its rights to recover withholding tax payments from the bank was rendered void by s 261. (2) The payments had not been made under a mistake of law. The language of the clause requiring the payments to be made showed that the parties were aware that the clause may be void, and furthermore the parties had received legal advice to a similar effect. The applicant was found to have made the payment even though it knew that the provision requiring them may be invalid and that it was prepared to assume the validity of the obligation and make the payments irrespective of its validity. (3) The fact that the liability of the applicants and of the bank to make the payments was distinct rather than joint did not affect the applicant's right to recover the payments. (4) The recoupment claim succeeded because the applicant had acted under compulsion, not officiously, and it would be unjust for the bank to retain the benefit of the payments that discharged its liability.

31. *Hill v Van Erp* (1997) 188 CLR 159; (1997) 142 ALR 687; (1997) 71 ALJR 487 (HC: Brennan CJ, Dawson, Toohey, Gaudron, McHugh, Gummow JJ).
Misdirected payment – testamentary disposition ineffective – loss of benefit to intended beneficiary by reason of solicitor's negligence – whether duty to intended beneficiary – whether enrichment of next of kin at the expense of intended beneficiary – Succession Act 1981 (Qld), s 15(1).
A solicitor prepared a will for a client upon the client's instructions that it was to include a testamentary disposition to a friend of the client. When the will was being executed, the solicitor asked the husband of the intended beneficiary to attest it. The attestation attracted the *Succession*

Act 1981 (Qld), s 15(1), which had the effect that the disposition was null and void. After the death of the client the intended beneficiary sued the solicitor for damages in negligence. After being adjudged liable at first instance and in the Court of Appeal, the solicitor appealed further.

Decision: Appeal dismissed. *Per Brennan CJ, Dawson, Toohey, Gaudron and Gummow JJ, McHugh J diss*: The solicitor was in breach of a duty of care owed to the intended beneficiary and hence was liable in damages for the value of the intended disposition.

Dictum: *Per Gummow J*: Mrs Van Erp (the intended beneficiary) is correct in not framing her complaint as one against the next of kin, alleging their unjust enrichment at her expense. There has been some support in the academic literature for development of a remedy to force the party taking under the unaltered or unrevoked will to transfer the benefit in question to the intended beneficiary, at least where that party knew of the later and, in the event, unfulfilled intentions of the testator. But in the present case the qualifying or vitiating factor would be negligence of Mrs Hill, something for which the next of kin bore no responsibility. Moreover, the judgment of Peter Gibson LJ in *Halifax Building Soc v Thomas* [1996] Ch 217, 227, and the writings of the commentators suggest that a claim of this nature would fail for additional reasons. The enrichment of the next of kin was not "at the expense of" Mrs Van Erp. At best she was a volunteer. Nor is it clear that the wealth in question would "certainly" have vested in Mrs Van Erp had it not been "intercepted" by Mrs Hill and diverted to the next of kin whilst "en route" from the testatrix. Moreover, it appears that much restitutionary theory is concerned with restoration of benefits subtracted from the wealth of the plaintiff rather than with provision of a means of fulfilling expectations.

32. *KT & T Developments Pty Ltd v Tay* (1995) 13 WAR 363 (WA SC: Parker J).
Caveatable interest – failure of joint venture between members of company – whether constructive trust over company's property – equitable charge or lien.

The plaintiff company was the sole registered proprietor of a lot. It brought proceedings seeking the removal of a caveat that had been lodged over the lot by the two defendants. The first defendant was a member of the company. The second defendant was a company that had lent money to the plaintiff for the purchase. The relationship between the members of the plaintiff company broke down and the first defendant's shareholding was diluted by allotments to other members. The defendants claimed to have an interest in land as beneficiaries under a constructive trust which was said to arise from the joint endeavour between the plaintiff's members to develop the property. Secondly, they claimed to have an interest in the land in the form of an equitable charge or lien to secure the repayment of the loan to the second defendant.

Decision: There was no serious question to be tried as to the existence of either a constructive trust or an equitable charge or lien. Application allowed.

Held: (1) The principle identified by Deane J in *Muschinski v Dodds* (1985) 160 CLR 583, *viz* that a constructive trust can be imposed where a joint endeavour breaks down and one of the parties owns property in circumstances in which it would be unconscionable to deny the interest of the other party in the property, was inapplicable in the present case. This was because the plaintiff company, which was the owner of the property, was not a party to the joint endeavour between its members. Essentially, the plaintiff was the joint endeavour. (2) Ownership of shares in a company gives no proprietary interest in the property of the company. If successful the defendant's argument would cut across the regulation effected by the *Corporations Law*, for example, by placing the interests of shareholders in the company's property above the rights of creditors. (3) Even if a fiduciary relationship existed between its members, the plaintiff company was not a party to it. It could only be liable as a constructive trustee if it fell within the second rule in *Barnes v Addy* (1874) 9 Ch App 244. (4) It fell outside that rule because the defendants could not show a breach of fiduciary duty by the other members; the dilution of the first defendant's shareholding may have been a fraud on a power but it was not a breach of fiduciary duty.

Secondly, even if there had been a breach, the plaintiff company could not be said to have participated in the breach so as to derive a benefit which could be subjected to a constructive trust. The only persons who stood to benefit from the allotment of shares were the other members. (5) There was no serious question to be tried as to the existence of an equitable charge or lien because the facts were found to be that the loan by the second defendant was an unsecured loan to the plaintiff for various purposes rather than a payment specifically in respect of the property.

Dictum: If it were possible to impose a constructive trust over the property of a company in favour of its member, the potential effects on the ordinary incidents of corporate regulation and the rights of creditors of the company would require the existence of exceptional circumstances before such a remedy would be ordered.

33. *Led Builders Pty Ltd v Eagle Homes Pty Ltd* (1996) 70 FCR 436 (NSW FC: Lindgren J).
Account of profits – copyright – election between alternative remedies – entitlement to discovery of documents for purposes of election – Copyright Act 1968 (Cth), s 115 – Federal Court Rules 1979 (Cth), O 15, rr 5, 15.
The respondent was found to have breached the applicant's copyright in plans for project homes. The respondent was ordered to disclose information relating to the contract price and the cost of the houses that had been built in accordance with those plans. The respondent filed an affidavit setting out these matters in broad terms. The applicant sought discovery of all relevant documents such as contracts, invoices and financial records. The respondent refused stating that the applicant was bound to elect whether to seek damages or an account of profits. The applicant argued that it was entitled to defer its election until after a further hearing had taken place or until reasons for judgment had been given.

Decision: The applicant was entitled to discovery of the documents so that it could make an informed decision as to election

Held: (1) A distinction must be drawn between "an inquiry into" damages or an account of profits and the order itself. The court cannot be required to conduct an inquiry into both damages and profits. There is no principle or authority which requires the copyright owner to be "informed" to this extent. (2) In the ordinary case, election has to be made before the hearing because the owner of copyright or other intellectual property will be able to be adequately informed by the interlocutory procedures of discovery and interrogatories. The fact that in earlier cases the defendants may have allowed a hearing to proceed without having insisted on election does not affect this principle. (3) However, a copyright owner cannot make an informed election in relation to an account of profits in the absence of any information about the infringer's overheads.

34. *Maguire v Makaronis* (1997) 188 CLR 449; (1997) 71 ALJR 781; (1997) 144 ALR 729 (HC: Brennan CJ, Gaudron, McHugh, Gummow and Kirby JJ); rvsg (1995) VConvR 54-533 (Vic SC (App Div): Brooking, Nathan and Smith JJ).
Fiduciary duty– solicitors taking mortgage from clients – failure by solicitors to disclose conflicting interest – rescission – scope of equity of rescission – relevance of causal link between breach of fiduciary duty and execution of mortgage – rescission conditioned on payment of principal and interest.
The respondents wished to purchase a poultry farm and required finance to complete the purchase. The appellant solicitors, who acted for the respondents, had an arrangement with a bank for the provision of credit facilities to their clients. Bridging finance was arranged for the respondents for a procurement fee. As part of the arrangement, the appellants advanced the required sum (which was provided by the bank) and guaranteed the repayment of the sum to the bank. The respondents executed a mortgage in favour of the appellants to secure repayment of the debt. The respondents defaulted on the loan and the appellants sought to enforce the mortgage. The respondents claimed that the appellants had failed to disclose that the mortgage was being executed in favour of the

appellants as mortgagees and by doing so they had breached their fiduciary duties to avoid a conflict of interest and duty and not to act for their own benefit. The trial judge found that there had been a breach of fiduciary duty and ordered the mortgage to be set aside. An appeal was dismissed by the Appeal Division of the Supreme Court of Victoria. Nathan J of the majority held that to require the principal to be repaid as a condition of relief would be to condone the breach of fiduciary duty, because the practical effect would be that no relief would be afforded to the respondents. Smith J also refused to impose such a condition, stating the appellants or the bank could sue the respondents to recover the principal debt on the basis of unjust enrichment. The solicitors appealed to the High Court. They submitted that there was no equity in the respondents for a remedy of rescission in the absence of proof by the respondents of loss by reason of entry into the transaction, and that there could be no loss because the respondents would have gone ahead with the transaction even if the appellants had not been in breach of their fiduciary duties.

Decision: Appeal allowed. A new order was substituted making the setting aside of the mortgage conditional on the repayment of the principal sum owing together with interest at commercial rates, and not the higher rate provided under the mortgage.

Held: (1) *Per Brennan CJ, Gaudron, McHugh, Gummow JJ*: (1) Where a solicitor's fiduciary duty prevents him from entering into a transaction without the fully informed consent of his client, and that consent is lacking, the equity for rescission is immediately generated by the preceding breach of fiduciary duty. Such equity entitles the client to have the transaction set aside, subject to restitution. It is irrelevant whether the breach of fiduciary duty causes loss to the client. Consequently, such circumstances do not provide any occasion for testing the rule in *Brickenden v London Loan & Saving Co* [1934] 3 DLR 465. *Per Kirby J*: The rule in *Brickenden* was applicable to the present case. The rule requires that, where "material" facts are not disclosed by a fiduciary, the fiduciary is liable for breach of duty regardless of whether the loss was caused by the breach. Facts will be "material" if but for their existence the relevant loss would not have occurred. The court can take the existence of a causal connection between the breach and the loss into account when it is fashioning an appropriate remedy. (2) The equity for rescission entitles the client to have the whole transaction rescinded and the parties remitted to their original position as far as possible. In the case of mortgagor borrowers seeking such equity, that requires, as a condition of relief, that they do equity by submitting to payment of principal and interest. Otherwise they would be left with the fruits of the transaction of which they complain. (3) Where there is no evidence before the court as to whether the fiduciary would derive a profit at the rate of interest charged, the interest payable as a condition of obtaining relief should be at commercial rates as allowed from time to time by the Supreme Court and not the higher rate provided under the mortgage.

Dicta: *Per Brennan CJ, Gaudron, McHugh, Gummow JJ*: (1) What is required for a fully informed consent is a question of fact in all the circumstances of each case. The circumstances may include (as they would have here) the importance of obtaining independent and skilled advice from a third party. However, there was no duty as such on the fiduciary to obtain an informed consent from the client. Rather, the existence of an informed consent would have gone to negate what otherwise was a breach of duty. (2) Issues of "causation" may arise in limited cases of rescission; for example, rescission for fraudulent misrepresentation in the context of a sale of a business. (3) The other equitable remedies such as an account of profits, compensation or a constructive trust require "causation" between the breach of duty and the profit derived, loss sustained or asset held.

35. ***Natural Extracts Pty Ltd v Stouter; GG Jay Investments Pty Ltd v Doveka Pty Ltd*** (1997) 24 Aust Corpns & Securities R 110 (NSW FC: Hill J)
Fiduciary duty – director – misuse of corporate opportunity – account of profits by director's family trust.

The defendant was a director of the plaintiff company. The plaintiff was attempting to develop and promote an investment scheme based around a tea tree plantation. It obtained an option over a suitable property but was unable to raise sufficient funds to complete the purchase. The defendant, without the knowledge of the other directors, commenced negotiations with the owner of the property for the use of the property for an alternative tea tree oil investment scheme. The defendant then resigned as director and sought a release from his obligations to the company, indicating to the others that he would only continue to do some minor consultation work for the owner of the property. In fact, he negotiated a joint venture with the property owner and together they developed a successful tea tree oil investment scheme around the property. Later, the defendant's interests acquired the property owner's half share in the venture. The defendant had used the plaintiff company's promotional materials to promote the new scheme. The plaintiff company sued the defendant, and his family trust's companies which were involved in the tea tree oil businesses, claiming a constructive trust over the profits that resulted from the defendant's breach of fiduciary duty. The defendant sought to defend the claims by arguing that the plaintiff company had given its consent to his actions, that it had stood by and allowed the defendant to conduct the business at his risk, that the opportunities were not available to the plaintiff, that he made no gain personally but that it fell to his family trust, and that it would be unconscientious to require all the profit of the business to be disgorged because of the time and effort that the defendant had put into the projects.

Decision: An account of the profits made by the defendant's family trust was ordered.

Held: (1) The obligation to account may extend beyond the fiduciary directly to others who actually participated in any fraudulent conduct of the trustee. (2) Although the tea tree oil scheme envisaged by the plaintiff company and that pursued by the defendant were not identical, they were sufficiently similar for there to be a breach of fiduciary obligation. (3) The constructive trust over the profits should not be limited to the defendant's first venture. The fact that a business acquired in breach of fiduciary duty expands even as a result of the work and skill of the fiduciary is no defence to the imposition of a constructive trust. The fiduciary's contribution to the success of the business will be recognised by an appropriate allowance for his time, energy and skill. (4) There had been no informed consent to the defendant's actions on the part of the plaintiff company because the defendant concealed his actions and misrepresented his intentions. (5) It could not be said that the plaintiff stood by and took no action because, shortly after the defendant's actions came to light, legal advice was obtained and the action commenced. (6) A fiduciary duty may continue after a director's resignation, particularly in circumstances where that resignation may fairly be said to have been prompted or influenced by the desire to obtain the corporate opportunity. (7) The plaintiff does not have to prove a positive valuation of assets when seeking a constructive trust. If there is a difficulty in a precise identification of the assets over which the trust extends, then that difficulty ultimately works out against the fiduciary rather than in favour of the fiduciary. (8) The corporate opportunity taken amounted to 50% of the venture with the owner of the property. Therefore, the constructive trust did not extend to shares in the venture later acquired by the defendant from the owner of the property because that acquisition of property was too remote.

36. *Newitt v Leitch* (1997) 6 TAS R 396 (Tas SC: Wright J).
Failure of consideration – mistake – ignorance – partnership agreement – purchaser of interest in unprofitable business seeking restitution – Real Estate Agents Act 1959 (Tas).

The respondent operated a real estate business. He held a sales licence under the *Real Estate Agents Act 1959 (Tas)* but did not hold a real estate agent's licence. As this was required for a real estate business, the business was conducted under an arrangement with a company that held such a licence and that company's principal who was a licensed manager under the Act. The company was also the registered proprietor of the business name. About a year after the business commenced, the appellant entered into a partnership with the respondent. The respondent agreed to pay, and partially paid, a price for an interest in the business. The business became unprofitable and ceased to operate. The respondent claimed the balance of the purchase price. The appellant defended this claim by arguing that a compromise agreement had been entered into. He also made a cross-claim alleging that the respondent purported to sell a share of a business in which he had no interest because the respondent did not hold the real estate agent's licence and was not the proprietor of the business name. The appellant sought recovery of the sum already paid on the basis of total failure of consideration, or alternatively on the basis that it was a payment made under a mistake. At first instance, the claim and counter-claim failed. The appellant sought to have the decision as to the counter-claim reversed.

Decision: Appeal dismissed.

Held: (1) The partnership agreement did not infringe any applicable legislation in a way that would render it illegal or void. (2) The appellant agreed to make the payment in exchange for the right to share in the profits of the business and the right to participate in its management and control. The fact that the business actually made no profit did not lead to a total failure of consideration. The appellant received what he had bargained for, a right to share in the profits and management of the business. (3) There was no severable consideration attributable to an unperformed part of the contract. (4) The rights that the appellant had received had value because, prior to commencement of the proceedings, he had sold his partnership interest to a third party. (5) The appellant was ignorant of the business name and licensing arrangement. However, although ignorance can be a "mistake" for the purposes of the legal principles that govern the recovery of money paid under a mistake of fact, those restitutionary principles were inapplicable in the present case because there was a subsisting contract that governed the parties' rights. *David Securities Pty Ltd v Commonwealth Bank of Australia* (1992) 175 CLR 353 provides no authority for the proposition that a person who has entered into a contract under a misapprehension as to relevant facts may go behind the contract and seek restitution of the consideration provided. (6) No claim was made to rescind the partnership agreement on the basis that the "mistake" was so fundamental as to vitiate the agreement. No evidence was given that the "mistake" induced the appellant to enter into the contract.

Dictum: By selling his partnership interest, the appellant had affirmed the contract and therefore may also have disentitled himself from relief on that basis.

37. *O'Connor v Leaw Pty Ltd* (1997) 42 NSWLR 285 (NSW SC : Rolfe J).
Quantum meruit claim – building contractor – Building Services Corporation Act 1989 (NSW), s 10(1)(a).
An owner disputed the right of a builder to enforce any claim or remedy under a written building contract and in arbitration proceedings, because it did not hold a relevant licence as required by statute. The Building Services Corporation Act 1989, s 10(1) provides : "(1) A person who enters into a contract in contravention of s 4 (unlicensed contracting) or who is unable to enforce a contract because of s 6 (contracts to be in writing): (a) is not entitled to damages or to enforce any other remedy in respect of a breach of the contract committed by any other party to the contract; but (b) is liable to damages and subject to any other remedy in respect of a breach of the contract committed by the person".

Decision: Application to stay the arbitration dismissed.

Held: (1) A claim by an unlicensed contractor based on quantum meruit is not a remedy "in respect of a breach of the contract" and thus is not prohibited under the Building Services Corporation Act 1989, s 10(1)(a). (2) A reference to arbitration is not a remedy or the enforcement of a remedy in respect of a breach of contract, which s 10(1)(a) prohibits. (3) A claim referring to arbitration any dispute or difference "concerning this agreement" is wide enough to encompass a claim on a quantum meruit.

38. *Pedashenko and Others v Blacktown City Council* (1996) 39 NSWLR 189 (NSW SC: Hodgson J)
Fiduciary duty – conflict of interest and duty – duty owed by purchaser council to inform vendor of land of proposed changes to zoning – consent not fully informed – appropriate remedy.
The plaintiffs sold two lots of land to the local council. The council told the plaintiffs that part of one of the lots was required for road widening and the rest for open space, that the lot would be resumed if it were not sold, and that the other lot had no development potential. While negotiations with the plaintiffs were occurring, the council was considering the adoption of a new development plan for the area. That plan was adopted two years later and the lots were zoned special business. This substantially increased the value of the lots. The plaintiffs sued for an order setting aside the transactions or compensation, being the difference in value, claiming that they would not have sold the land to the council had they been aware of the re-zoning proposal.
Decision: The council was ordered to account for the profit made on the purchase.
Held: (1) The council innocently misrepresented to the plaintiffs that there was no reasonable prospect of a more favourable zoning and that it was in the plaintiffs best interests to sell both lots to the council. However, the contract could not be rescinded on this basis as the sale had been completed. (2) The council owed a fiduciary duty to the plaintiffs because the council undertook to act in the interests of the plaintiffs in providing information as to the development potential of the land and advice as to the desirability of the sale to the council. (3) The council's duty and interest were in conflict. There was no fully informed consent to this conflict because the plaintiffs were not told of the proposed new development plan. (4) There was a breach of fiduciary duty both in entering and completing the contract. Consequently, the council was unable to raise a limitations defence. (5) The most appropriate remedy would have been to set aside the contract and order a reconveyance of the property subject to certain adjustments. However, because of the capital gains tax implications that would have for the plaintiffs, an account of profits was ordered based on the current value of the land and the net cost of the land to the council.

39. *Plumor Pty Ltd v Handley* (1996) 41 NSWLR 30 (NSW SC: McLelland CJ in Equity).
Rescission – special condition in contract permitting rescission where certain condition not met – one party resisting rescission – incidence of onus of proving that the non-fulfilment of the condition was self-induced -Foreign Acquisitions and Takeovers Act 1975 (Cth).
The defendant contracted to purchase land from the plaintiff. A substantial deposit was paid under the contract. As the defendant was a foreign person, the consent of the Foreign Investment Review Board had to be obtained under the *Foreign Acquisitions and Takeovers Act 1975 (Cth)*. It was a condition of the contract that either party could rescind the contract if the Foreign Investment Review Board did not give its consent to the purchase within 14 days of the execution of the contract. The consent was not obtained and the defendant purported to rescind the contract. The plaintiff then purported to terminate the contract on the basis that the defendant had wrongly repudiated it. The defendant sued to recover the deposit.
Decision: As materials requested by the Foreign Investment Review Board were not promptly provided, the non-obtaining of the consent resulted from a breach of the defendant's obligations. The plaintiff was entitled to terminate the contract and retain the deposit.
Held: (1) A party cannot seek to rescind a contract for the non-fulfilment of a condition where that condition was not fulfilled because of that party's own wrongful act. (2) The onus of proof of whether the failure of the condition resulted from the rescinding party's breach rests on the party resisting rescission.

40. *Shepherd v ANZ Banking Corp* (1996) 41 NSWLR 431 (NSW CA : Meagher JA, Giles and Abadee A-JJ A).
Failure of consideration – deposits paid to company – whether company incurred debt – personal liability of company officers – Companies (New South Wales) Code, s 556(1).
The appellants each entered into supply contracts with H, whereby H undertook to supply and/or erect kit homes or kit garages, and the appellants paid deposits. Performance was to take place within a reasonable time. H did not perform within a reasonable time or at all. Following the appointment of a provisional liquidator it was ordered to be wound up. The appellants commenced proceedings in which they for the first time terminated their contracts with H. They claimed the amounts of the deposits from the respondents, whom they alleged to be deemed directors of H, a company in liquidation (within the terms of the *Companies (New South Wales) Code*, s 556(1). The basis for liability under s 556(1) was that H incurred debts in the amount of the deposits when, immediately before the time when the debt was incurred, there were reasonable grounds to expect that the company could not pay its debts as and when they fell due. The appellants' case alleged that the time at which H incurred the debts was when it received payment of the deposits, alternatively at the expiry of reasonable times for performance of the contracts, or alternatively again, when H went into liquidation. Bryson J held that H did not incur debts within the meaning of s 556, at any of the alleged times. The appellants appealed.
Decision: Appeal dismissed.
Held: (1) Where an amount is prepaid by way of a deposit under a contract with a company for the supply and erection of a kit home, where the kit home is not supplied or not supplied and erected within a reasonable time or at all, the company does not "incur a debt" for the purposes of the *Companies (New South Wales) Code*, either : (a) at the date of the acceptance of the deposit under the contract; or (b) at the expiration of a reasonable time for performance of the contract; or (c) at the time of appointment of a provisional liquidator. (2) *Per Abadee A-JA, Meagher JA agreeing*: A restitutionary remedy does not arise under the contract, and arises only if and when the payer by election terminates future performance of the contract for total failure of consideration and seeks recovery of the money paid under it. The restitutionary obligation then imposed is "incurred", if at all, only at that time. (2) Whilst the creation of a contingent liability *may* be an incurring of a debt, not every obligation which may ultimately crystallise as a debt or judgment debt upon the occurrence of subsequent events will as a matter of law be an obligation characterised at the time of its being incurred as the incurring of a debt within the meaning of s 556. Each case will turn upon its own facts. (3) It seems to strain the language of s 556 to include within the scope of the incurring of debts a situation where a company does an act which could conceivably result in it owing an obligation of a debt on the basis of a claim in restitution, but which primarily exposes it to an obligation to render performance or in lieu thereof pay unliquidated damages under contract.

41. *Stowe and Anor v Stowe* (1995) 15 WAR 363; (1995) 127 FLR 25 (SC WA: Ipp, Owen and White JJ).
De facto spouse claiming half of all property owned by other spouse – constructive trust based on common intention – relevance of promises to marry where promisor already married – constructive trust based on unconscionable conduct – unjust enrichment – promissory estoppel – relevance of personal relationship to availability of specific performance and promissory estoppel – Marriage Act 1961 (Cth), s 111A.
The appellant and the respondent lived in a de facto relationship for 10 years. After the relationship broke down, the respondent brought an action against the appellant claiming a half interest in all his property on the basis of a constructive trust, unjust enrichment and promissory estoppel. The facts alleged to support these claims were that the parties had a common intention to pool their resources for their mutual benefit and that the appellant had made various promises

and representations, including promises to marry. The appellant sought to have the claims struck out on the basis that they could not be sustained.

Decision: Appeal allowed. The general claims were struck out, but leave was given to amend the pleadings to claim an equitable interest in particular property.

Held: (1) A constructive trust arising out of the common intention of the parties to pool their financial and non-financial resources (such as labour for the benefit of the family) could arise. However, in this case none of the matters pleaded supported an inference of such an intention. (2) A promise to marry is incapable of giving rise to an inference that the parties intended to pool their financial and non-financial resources for their mutual benefit. (3) Allegations of promises to provide for the respondent and promises that certain property would be the family home were also not capable of giving rise to the inference that the parties had an intention to "pool" all their assets. Non-financial contributions to the family welfare and the appellant's business also did not support such an inference. (4) Similarly, the promises and contributions claimed could not give rise to a constructive trust based on unconscionable conduct over *all* the appellant's property. Contributions to particular property could give rise to an interest in that property. (5) Although some of the appellant's acts were done when the appellant was still married to a third party, public policy would not preclude the recognition of equitable claims based on those acts. (6) There was no substance to the claim based on unjust enrichment as the allegations in the statement of claim did not show that *all* the properties of the appellant were benefitted by the actions of the respondent. However, an argument could be maintained that the appellant was unjustly enriched because particular properties were improved by the respondent at the appellant's request. (7) The claim based on promissory estoppel was struck out because the appellant could not be said to have impliedly promised that the respondent would be entitled to such an interest in his property as if they had been married. For public policy reasons, promises made when the appellant was still married could not give rise to an equitable estoppel. (8) The respondent was seeking some orders which only the Family Court had jurisdiction to make in a matrimonial cause. The parties could not by their actions vest the Supreme Court with jurisdiction it did not have. (9) Promissory estoppel could not be used to enforce a contract of marriage contrary to the *Marriage Act 1961 (Cth)*, s 111A. The respondent could not obtain by promissory estoppel something that she could not obtain by contract. A contract to grant an interest in the property to the respondent on the basis of the parties' relationship would not have been specifically enforceable because of its personal nature.

Comment: The question whether it is possible for there to be a constructive trust over an equitable interest was referred to but not decided.

42. *Tutt v Doyle* (1997) 42 NSWLR 10 (NSW CA: Meagher JA, Handley JA, Brownie A-JA); affg with some variation (16 Sep 1993) Unrep (NSW: SC Young J) [1994] RLR §9.
Mistake by vendor as to area of land transferred – purchaser aware – retention of excess by purchaser unconscionable – retransfer ordered.
Between the making of a contract for the sale of land and completion, the vendor, to the knowledge of the purchaser, made a mistake as to the size of the lot to be transferred in a plan of subdivision. As a result the transfer registered by the purchaser gave him a larger lot than was contracted for (2.76 hectares or 6.75 acres instead of 2.2. hectares or a little over 5 acres). The trial judge ordered the purchaser, on terms, to retransfer the additional .56 of a hectare to the vendor. The purchaser appealed.

Decision: Appeal dismissed subject to further correcting orders.

Held: (1) Where one contractual party knows or has reason to know of the other's mistake prior to completion, it is unconscientious for the first party to avail himself of the advantage obtained. Where rescission is impracticable, the count can order retransfer of the area of land equivalent to the excess. (2) A transferor who claims a mere equity based on unilateral mistake and not an equitable estate or interest in land bears the onus of establishing that the transferee knew, or had reason to know, that the transferor was, or might well be, mistaken.

43. *Tweedvale Investments Pty Ltd v Thiran Pty Ltd* (1996) 14 WAR 109 (WA SC: Malcom CJ, Ipp J, Steytler JJ).
Fiduciary relationship – purchase from negotiator of deal who was undisclosed vendor – account of profits – equitable compensation – exemplary damages.
The first appellant (A1) held all the shares in the second appellant company (A2). A2 entered into a contract for the purchase of land for $530,000 and then, prior to settlement, contracted to sell the land for $670,000. Both of these contracts were rescinded on separate grounds. Subsequently, A2 signed another contract for the purchase of the land for $530,000. A1 then met the first respondent (R1), who was a director and shareholder of the second respondent (R2), and informed him about the property in question. A1 made a number of misrepresentations to R1, namely: that the property was being purchased by a client of his for $670,000; that A2, which was said to belong to a person from Singapore, had acquired the property for $610,000; that the purchasers of the property from A2 were backing out of the deal; that he, as one of the directors of the putative purchasers, would be involved in litigation unless another purchaser was found; and that he had dealings with a director of A2. R1 became interested in the property and asked A1 to inquire whether A2 would lower the price. The next day, A1 stated that A2 was willing to drop the price to $650,000 and that this was a good price. R1 arranged for R2 to make an offer of $630,000. A1 returned with a counter-offer from A2 at $650,000 and the suggestion that another buyer was offering $670,000. Following discussions with A1 and upon his advice, R1 directed R2 to make a further counter-offer of $640,000. This counter-offer was accepted. R1 was never aware that A1 was the owner of A2, nor that A2 had contracted to purchase of the property for $530,000. R1 did not think that A1 was acting for the owner of the property. When R1 asked A1 what benefit he would receive from the sale, A1 said that he would charge him a consultancy fee of $24,000 for overseeing the development of the land. The trial judge found that a fiduciary relationship existed and ordered an account of profits and the payment of equitable compensation. A1 and A2 appealed.
Decision: Appeal dismissed.
Held: (1) A fiduciary relationship existed between A1 and R2 and A1 acted in breach of his duties which flowed from their relationship. The evidence showed that A1 had suggested that he would look after R1's interests and could be trusted to deal in good faith with the vendor. There was sufficient evidence for the trial judge to find that A1 undertook to negotiate on behalf of R1 (or more accurately R2) and that there was a relationship of trust and confidence between A1 and R2. A1 had a special opportunity to act to the detriment of R2, which had been persuaded to repose trust in him. A1 exercised his power to the detriment of R2 by purchasing the property for $530,000 and on-selling it to R2 at a large profit without disclosing his interest in the sale. (2) The trial judge did not err in ordering the appellants to account to R2 for $110,000 (*viz* the difference in price at which A2 had purchased the land and the price for which it was sold to R2). The appellants argued, on the basis of *Tracy v Mandalay Pty Ltd* (1953) 88 CLR 215, that, as A2 had entered into the first contract for the purchase of the land prior to the commencement of the fiduciary relationship, R2 could have opted to rescind its contract, but because it elected to affirm, it could not obtain an account of profits. The argument was rejected because the interest that enabled the land to be sold to R2 was acquired by A2 after the fiduciary obligations had arisen (*ie* A2's second purchase contract was entered into while the fiduciary relationship was in existence). Therefore, an account of profits was the appropriate remedy. (3) The trial judge did not err in ordering the appellants to pay equitable compensation of $4695, which was equivalent to the loss that R2 suffered in paying the higher price. It was the difference in stamp duty and land transfer registration fees payable on a transfer of a property for $530,000 as opposed to

$640,000. (5) The trial judge did not err in refusing to award exemplary damages. The question whether there is jurisdiction to order exemplary damages in proceedings where the principal relief sought is equitable was left open.

44. *Unioil International Pty Ltd v Deloitte Touche Tohmatsu* (1997) 17 WAR 98 (SC WA: Ipp J).
Restitution for wrongs – solicitor and client – national partnership – conflict of interest and duty – confidential information.
The plaintiffs retained two defendants (DTT and CCW), respectively a firm of accountants and the Perth office of a national firm of lawyers, to carry out a due diligence investigation into a group of companies (UFI) in which the plaintiffs were considering making an investment. At the same time a partner, D, in the Sydney office of CCW, had been asked by BSC, a state statutory body, to act in a financial transaction between BSC and UFI, and to keep secret any information as to the detail of the transaction. D advised the Perth partner, C, of the retainer and its potential contentious nature with UFI, and that BSC had told him that CCW could only continue to act on the basis that there was no information flow between the Sydney and Perth offices. Following advice from the defendants, the plaintiffs made an investment of $1.88 million in UFI which was worthless by the time of trial. The plaintiffs, among other claims, sued CCW for breaches of fiduciary duty: first, that the Perth partner, C, acted for the plaintiffs in performing the due diligence investigation when his duty to them was in conflict with his interest, as a member of the national firm, in protecting and not disaffecting the solicitor client relationship that existed between BSC and the Sydney office; and, secondly, because D, a partner of CCW had information relevant to the work that CCW were doing for the plaintiffs, therefore, CCW had that information, and should either have disclosed that information to the plaintiffs, or ceased acting for them.
Decision: Claim succeeded on conflict of duty and interest, but was not upheld on CCW's alleged failure to disclose information known to D.
Held: (1) A solicitor who acts in a fiduciary position is not to allow his interest stemming from his membership of a legal partnership to conflict with his duty. (2) The presumption that the knowledge of one partner is to be regarded as the knowledge of his or her other partners is rebuttable. (3) A firm of solicitors does not necessarily owe a duty to its clients to reveal, to each client, and use for each client's benefit, any knowledge possessed by every one of the firm's partners or staff.

45. *Yamabuta v Tay (No 1)* (1995) 16 WAR 254 (WA SC: Comr Pringle QC).
Restitution for wrongs – breach of fiduciary duty – principal and agent – whether purchase by agent in course of agency – remedies – whether jurisdiction to award punitive equitable damages.
A principal brought an action against its agent in respect of alleged breaches of fiduciary duty concerning real estate transactions entered by the agent.
Decision: Claim allowed.
Held: If a principal with knowledge of the facts elects to keep property sold to it by his agent, not being property acquired within the scope of the agency, the principal is without a legal remedy notwithstanding the breach of fiduciary duty. (2) If an agent acquires property during the period of his agency, and then, without disclosing that he is the owner, sells it to his principal, the agent will be treated as having purchased the property on the principal's behalf, and will hold his profits from the on-sale on trust for his principal. (3) It is not open to the court to award punitive damages in equity for breach of fiduciary duty.

ARTICLES

46. Byrne, Hon Justice D, "Restitution for Work Done in Anticipation of Contract" (1997) 13 Building and Construction Law 4.
Considers the difficulties involved in fitting a cause of action based in pre-restitution days on an implied contract into one with an entirely different basis, and suggests an adjustment to the restitution principle that involves a generous interpretation of "benefit" and "receipt" and of the rules as to valuation of such benefit.

47. Cooper, Justice RE, "Between a Rock and a Hard Place: Illegitimate Pressure in Commercial Negotiations" (1997) 71 ALJR 686.
The article examines the principles applied in admiralty cases to set aside salvage agreements obtained by practical compulsion and considers the applicability of those principles to the modern common law doctrine of economic duress. The thesis of the article is that the salvage cases provide reasoned guidance in the uncertain area where what is complained of as amounting to economic duress is the exercise or threatened exercise of a lawful right.

48. Dal Pont, GE, "Equity's Chameleon – Unmasking the Constructive Trust" (1997) 16 Aus Bar Rev 46.
The chameleon-like character of the constructive trust has generated confusion as to the nature, use and ramifications of constructive trusts and trusteeship. The aim of this article is to derive greater consistency in constructive trust jurisprudence by suggesting that, across the spectrum of situations in which constructive trusts may arise, the court does not simply recognise and enforce the constructive trust – it also creates it in order to give effect to a pre-existing obligation which the constructive trustee has breached. This approach serves to distinguish constructive trusts from express trusts and resulting trusts, and brings into question whether some so-called constructive trusts in fact merit that title.

49. Dines, M, "Valuation of Recovery — Partially Performed Discharged Contracts" (1997) 25 Aus Bus Law Rev 89.
This article discusses the recent judicial approach to the valuation of the innocent party's recovery in partially performed discharged contract cases, then examines the question in light of the law of restitution. It is concluded that incontrovertibly beneficial enrichments should be valued without reference to the contract price. Enrichments freely accepted or bargained for should generally be valued with reference to the terms of the discharged contract. However, in cases of part performance it is debatable whether a pro rata valuation rule should apply.

50. Edelman, J, "Restitution for a Total Failure of Consideration : When a Total Failure is not a Total Failure" (1996) 1 Newc LR 57.
The doctrine of total failure of consideration, now part of the distinct law of restitution, has, from its inception, always been regarded as only applicable where the failure of the promised performance is complete or total. Any partial performance has always been seen as a complete bar to recovery under this doctrine. This work examines recent decisions which, over the last five years, have consistently allowed restitution for a total failure of consideration despite part performance in terms of conferral of a monetary benefit. It is now argued that logic, consistency and equity demand that the total failure of consideration doctrine now encompass a partial failure of consideration. It is argued that such a doctrine must extend to benefits received, either monetary or non-monetary, and that the High Court is now in a position where this must necessarily be accepted.

51. Edelman, J, "The New Doctrine of Partial Failure of Consideration" (1996–97) 15 Aus Bar Rev 229.
For a hundred years or more the common law has struggled with the recoverability of money or money's worth where the benefit of a promise given in return (as the "price" or "consideration") for it has not been received. According to received "doctrine" the disappointed promisee cannot recover the price paid for the promised performance unless there has been a "total failure of consideration"; that is, a total failure by the promisor to perform the promise or, put differently, to provide the promised benefit. The "doctrine of total failure of consideration" appears at times to have been honoured in the breach or distinguished (where, for example, the promised performance and the price paid for it can be discretely apportioned) so as to permit part of the price to be recovered for a partial failure to perform the promise. In the development of the modern law of restitution there appears to be emerging a "doctrine of partial failure of consideration" according to which a court can permit a disappointed promisee to recover consideration given for a promise partly performed if the promisee accounts to the promisor for benefits received from the partial performance. Thus, in a substantive sense, a promisee's claim for restitution may be met by a counterclaim for restitution asserted by the promisor, entrusting to the court the task of adjusting the entitlements of the parties to achieve justice in the particular case. This article examines the concept of "a partial failure of consideration". It suggests that the time is ripe for the courts to undertake a general, not merely an incremental, review of the law governing failures of consideration.

52. Levine, J, "Does Equity Treat as Done that Which Ought to be Done? The Consequences Flowing from the Timing of the Imposition of a Constructive Trust" (1997) 5 Aus PLJ 74.
The article explores the problem of at what time a constructive trust should take effect. After an examination of the current law, conflicting academic opinion, arguments of logic and a discussion of competing policy considerations, it seeks to demonstrate that, in the context of domestic relationships, constructive trusts should, except only in extraordinary cases, be held to arise from the date of the "defining circumstances".

53. Lipton, J, "Lender Liability in Unjust Enrichment to Third Party Service Providers" (1997) 20 UNSW LJ 101.
The article examines situations where a lender may potentially be held liable in an unjust enrichment claim in relation to services provided to its borrower for which the borrower is unable or unwilling to pay. The usual case will be where the services provided to the principal borrower have in some way increased the value of the lender's security interest over a particular part of the borrower's property. As a context for its examination, it first considers the basic underlying concepts, cases arising from "ineffective contracts" for services provided, and the relevance of privity of contract doctrine. In its specific examination of the position of third party lenders, reference is made to relevant US jurisprudence.

54. McInnes, M, "Advancement, Illegality and Restitution" (1997) 5 APLJ 1.
In examining the High Court's recent decision in *Nelson v Nelson* (1995) 184 CLR 538, the article addresses three matters: (i) the application of the traditional presumptions of advancement and resulting trust to a mother's transfer of property to her child; (ii) the effect of illegality upon a claimant's ability to establish beneficial title by means of the presumption of resulting trust; and (iii) the restitutionary character of a claim for beneficial title under a resulting trust.

55. McInnes, M, "'Passing On' in the Law of Restitution: A Re-Consideration" (1997) 19 Syd LR 179.
The article aims to determine whether or not the defence of passing on should find a home in the law of restitution. After setting the context for discussion by means of a summary of the High

Court's recent decision in *Royal Insurance* (1994) 182 CLR 51, it is argued that the defence should have been accepted in theory but rejected on policy and practical grounds. The final section examines the availability of restitutionary relief as between a party who passes on an expense and a party to whom an expense is passed.

56. Mulheron, R, "Quantum Meruit upon Discharge for Repudiation" (1997) 16 Aus Bar Rev 150.
Examines a number of vexed issues in relation to the availability of a restitutionary remedy where services are tendered or goods supplied under a contract which is terminated for a serious breach. Part I debates the right of a contractor to elect to pursue a restitutionary remedy at all, Part II analyses critically the crucial threshold element of "benefit", and Part III examines the diverse and conflicting views as to qualification of the quantum meruit claim. Particular attention is given to the recent decisions of *Renard Constructions* (1992) 26 NSWLR 234, *Iezzi Constructions* [1995] 2 Qd R 350, and *Gino D'Alessandro Constructions* [1987] 2 Qd R40.

57. Nahan, NY, "Rescission: A Case for Rejecting the Classical Model?" (1997) 27 UWALR 66.
When is a person "barred" from rescinding his or her contact? Lawyers have given much consideration to this question, but have rarely asked whether it is necessary to have the bars at all. In this essay, the author examines the fundamentals of rescission, and the bars to it, and concludes that the present rules are outmoded and should be replaced. A new scheme of "pecuniary rescission", which would operate between the original parties to the contract, is suggested as an alternative to the existing law.

58. Tapsell, K, "The Negligence Juggernaut and Unjust Enrichment" (1997) 16 Aus Bar Rev 79.
Considers the recent High Court decision of *Hill v Van Erp*, where a solicitor was held tortiously liable in negligence to compensate a disappointed intended beneficiary, who was deprived of a benefit under a will by reason of non-compliance with statutorily prescribed formalities. The writer offers a strained argument for the availability of a restitutionary remedy to the solicitor against a co-beneficiary who gained a corresponding windfall benefit.

BOOKS

59. Cato, C, *Restitution in Australia and New Zealand* (Cavendish Publishing, Sydney : 1997). Reviewed Grantham [1998] RLR 295.
A comprehensive discussion of relevant English, Australian and New Zealand developments at common law and in equity with particular emphasis on Australian and New Zealand precedent and statute law.

60. Cope, M, *Proprietary Claims and Remedies* (Federation Press, Sydney: 1997).
Examines within the context of bankruptcy and insolvency, the nature of equitable proprietary claims and the range of equitable proprietary remedies, including the tracing process.

61. Davenport, P, and Harris, C, *Unjust Enrichment* (Federation Press, Sydney: 1997).
Explains where unjust enrichment currently and potentially fits with particular reference to claims arising out of construction work.

OTHER INFORMATION

62. Eighth Annual *Journal of Contract Law* **Conference, "Contractual and Proprietary Remedies".** 15 Aug 1997, Windsor Hotel, Melbourne; 18 Aug 1997, Hyatt Hotel, Auckland. Includes the following papers: JW Carter & MJ Tilbury, "Remedial Choice and Contract

Drafting"; M Bryan, "Recovering Misdirected Money from Banks: A Problem of Ministerial Receipt at Law and in Equity".

NOTER UP

National Australia Bank v Garcia (1996) 89 NSWLR 577; [1997] RLR §24; noted Duggan (1997) 19 Syd LR 220.
Nelson v Nelson (1995) 184 CLR 538; [1996] RLR §23; noted Cockburn (1997) APLJ 86; Kremer (1997) 19 Syd LR 240; DMM (1997) 71 ALJ 185.
Pyramid Building Soc v Scorpion Hotels Pty Ltd [1998] 1 VR 188 (CA); noted Chambers [1998] RLR 126; rvsg (1996) 136 ALR 166, [1997] RLR §28.
Torrens Aloha Pty Ltd v Citibank NA (1997) 144 ALR 89; [1997] RLR §30.

Canada

Lionel D Smith* and Kenneth W Fitz**

ANNUAL SURVEY

This has been an uncharacteristically inactive year for this jurisdiction. The cases that were decided contain a few points of interest. In *Air Canada v Ontario (Liquor Control Board)* §64 the Supreme Court of Canada was clear that a plaintiff seeking recovery from an agency of the Crown need not prove any fault or bad faith on the part of the defendant. In *Citadel General Assurance Co v Lloyds Bank Canada* §65 and *Gold v Rosenberg* §66, the same court made clear that liability for knowing receipt of trust property requires fault on the part of the defendant, albeit a lesser degree of fault than knowing assistance. In the former case, La Forest J, in trying to fit "knowing receipt" into an unjust enrichment model, said that fault is required on the part of the defendant in order to make the defendant's enrichment unjustified. This seems directly contrary to *Air Canada,* unless we are to reconcile them by saying that fault is required except when suing the Crown. More likely, the attempt to understand knowing receipt as a type of unjust enrichment is misconceived; it is rather a species of equitable wrongdoing.

In *Beloit Canada Ltd v Valmet-Dominion Inc* §67, the Federal Court of Appeal has settled that an accounting of profits is available in Canada for infringement of a patent, even though the governing legislation was unclear on the point. It held that this remedy is however subject to a wide discretion in the trial judge. The difficulties generated by applying unjust enrichment to three-party cases, which have been commented upon in previous Annual Digests, are illustrated again this year by *Toronto-Dominion Bank v Carotenuto* §71 and *Hussey Seating Co (Canada) Ltd v Ottawa (City)* §75; in both cases, the matter is not simplified by reasoning in terms of "juristic reason." The Ontario Court of Appeal had to consider reviving subrogation in three separate cases related to security interests in land. Finally, a number of cases show that the autonomous nature of unjust enrichment is not always taken into account by the drafters of statutes (*Canada Safeway Ltd v Canada* §68; *Ukrainian (Fort William) Credit Union Ltd v Nesbitt, Burns Ltd* §80) and insurance policies (*Moore (Township) v Guarantee Co of North America* §77).

---

* Fellow of St. Hugh's College, Oxford.
** Associate with the Edmonton office of the law firm McLennan Ross.

CASES

Cases from the Supreme Court of Canada are followed by decisions of the Federal Court of Canada; the provincial jurisdictions then appear in alphabetical order.

A. Supreme Court of Canada

64. *Air Canada v Ontario (Liquor Control Board)* [1997] 2 SCR 581; 148 DLR (4th) 193 (La Forest, L'Heureux-Dubé, Sopinka, Gonthier, Cory, McLachlin and Iacobucci JJ); affg (1995) 24 OR (3d) 403; 126 DLR 4th 301; [1996] RLR §85 (CA: Robins, Osborne and Weiler JJA); varying (21 Mar 1995) Unrep (Gen Div: Saunders J).

Mistake – fees incorrectly charged – time from which liability to refund unlawful fees arises – compound interest.

Under the statutory scheme the defendant had a monopoly on sales of alcoholic beverages ("alcohol") in the province. All alcohol imported into the province was the property of the defendant until sold to licence holders or consumers. The plaintiff airlines imported alcohol to serve on flights. The alcohol was held in bonded warehouses. In order to serve alcohol in flight, the defendant required the plaintiffs to hold licences issued by it, under the Liquor Licence Act, RSO 1990, c.L.19. When the plaintiffs removed alcohol from the warehouses to place it on aircraft making domestic flights, they were required to pay the defendant (i) "mark-ups," in the nature of a wholesaler's profit margin, and (ii) "gallonage fees," in the nature of a fee charged to all licence holders. A third airline, Wardair, had questioned the validity of this scheme and, following discussions with the defendant, Wardair was not required to pay mark-ups or gallonage fees after 1 Jan 1984. In 1989, Wardair was taken over by one of the plaintiffs, which then learned about this arrangement. The plaintiffs then sued to recover all mark-ups and gallonage fees they had paid. The defendant counterclaimed for mark-ups and gallonage fees not paid by Wardair from 1984. The trial judge allowed the claim and dismissed the counterclaim; he ordered the repayment of all mark-ups and gallonage fees paid after 1 Jan 1984. The defendant appealed. The airlines cross-appealed, seeking recovery of payments made before 1 Jan 1984. The appeal was allowed in part and the cross-appeal dismissed. The plaintiffs were subject to the defendant's statutory monopoly and the mark-ups had been properly paid. Since licences were not required to sell alcohol in flight, gallonage fees had to be refunded. The date from which they had to be refunded was 1 Jan 1984, as that was the date from which the defendant was aware that the charges might be improper. The plaintiffs appealed, seeking (1) recovery of mark-ups; (2) recovery of gallonage fees paid before 1 January 1984; (3) punitive damages (4) compound interest. Constitutional law points are not digested.

Decision: Appeal allowed in part: mark-ups were properly paid, but all gallonage fees were recoverable without limit of time.

Held: (1) Canadian law has never required a showing of bad faith on the part of a defendant as a precondition to the recovery of money collected by a governmental agency under an inapplicable law. (2) Awards of punitive damages and compound interest are discretionary, and an appellate court should not interfere with a trial judge's exercise of discretion unless it was based on a mistake of law or was so clearly wrong as to amount to an injustice.

65. *Citadel General Assurance Co. v Lloyds Bank Canada* (1997) 152 DLR (4th) 411 (La Forest, Sopinka, Gonthier, Cory, McLachlin, Iacobucci and Major JJ); noted Rotherham [1998] RLR 162; Smith (1998) 114 LQR 394; rvsg (1996) 37 Alta LR (3d) 293; [1996] 5 WWR 9 (CA: Kerans JJA); rvsg (1993) 12 Alta LR (3d) 114; [1993] 8 WWR 118; [1994] RLR §48 (QB: Marshall J).

Trusts – knowing assistance in a breach of trust – degree of knowledge required – receipt of trust property – knowing receipt – what constitutes receipt – knowledge required.

The plaintiff sold insurance through an agent. The agent collected insurance premiums, paid commissions and any settled claims, and remitted the balance monthly to the plaintiff. This was done through the agent's sole bank account, which was with the defendant. The agent ran into financial difficulties, and from April 1987 its account was usually in an unauthorized overdraft. Money was transferred to and from another company's account at the same bank, to pay overdrafts. In June the bank was told to empty the account daily and transfer the money to the other company. A large amount of premiums were not remitted to the plaintiff and the agent became insolvent. The Insurance Act (RSA 1980, c. I-5), s 124(1), provides that premiums collected by an insurance agent are held on trust for the insurer. The plaintiff sued the defendant for the amount of the premiums. At trial, the action was allowed on the basis that the bank had been wilfully blind. The defendant's appeal was allowed on the basis that its knowledge was insufficient for liability. The plaintiff appealed.

Decision: Appeal allowed.

Held: (1) To be liable in "knowing assistance," a defendant must have actual knowledge, recklessness or wilful blindness as to the breach of trust. (2) To be liable in "knowing receipt," a defendant must receive or apply trust property for its own use and benefit. (3) A bank receives trust property where a credit in an account at that bank, which is held in trust, is applied against a debt owing to the bank. (4) The mental element which will suffice for liability in such a case is less than in "knowing assistance." A defendant will be liable if it had actual knowledge of facts which would put a reasonable person on inquiry and failed to make inquiries.

66. *Gold v Rosenberg* (1997) 152 DLR (4th) 385; 35 OR (3d) 736 (La Forest, Sopinka, Gonthier, Cory, McLachlin, Iacobucci and Major JJ); noted Smith (1998) 114 LQR 394; affg (1995) 25 OR (3d) 601; 129 DLR (4th) 152; [1997] RLR §67 (CA: Dubin CJO and Abella and Laskin JJA); rvsg (9 Dec 1993) Unrep (Gen Div: Haley J).

Trusts – knowing assistance in a breach of trust – degree of knowledge required – degree of assistance required – receipt of trust property – knowing receipt – what constitutes receipt – knowledge required.

The plaintiff Gold and the defendant Rosenberg were executors and trustees of an estate, the principal assets of which were shares in two estate corporations, E Ltd and P Ltd. Gold and Rosenberg were equal beneficiaries of the estate, and were the directors of the two corporations. Gold was a university student and was the nephew of Rosenberg. In May 1985, at Rosenberg's request, Gold gave him a power of attorney. Rosenberg also controlled a corporation, T Ltd, for business purposes of his own. This corporation needed to borrow money. The defendant TD Bank, which was also banker to the estate and the two estate corporations, agreed to lend money to T Ltd if it received (in addition to other real and personal security) a guarantee from P Ltd. It required that this guarantee be secured on land held by P Ltd, and also that a mortgage held on other land by E Ltd be postponed to that of the bank. Rosenberg asked Gold to sign a directors' resolution of P Ltd authorising the guarantee; this was also signed by Rosenberg and the transaction was completed. The law firm which drafted the resolution also acted for the estate, the two estate corporations, and the bank. Gold commenced proceedings to have Rosenberg removed as executor and the issues expanded to include the validity of the guarantee of P Ltd, and the liability of Rosenberg and the law firm in case the guarantee should be enforced. The trial judge held that the guarantee, and also the mortgage securing it, and the postponement of E Ltd's mortgage, were enforceable only against Rosenberg's 50% interest in the estate. The bank's appeal was allowed by the Court of Appeal and the plaintiff appealed. The case was argued at trial and on appeal as one of knowing assistance, but in the Supreme Court of Canada it was also argued as one of knowing receipt.

Decision: Appeal dismissed. The claim in knowing assistance was dismissed unanimously. As to knowing receipt, it was held by a majority (4-3) that the bank received trust property in the relevant sense; but it was held by a differently constituted majority (4-3) that the bank did not have a sufficient level of fault for liability.

Held, unanimously: (1) For liability in "knowing assistance," the trustee's breach must be fraudulent and dishonest. (2) Moreover, the defendant must have actual knowledge, recklessness or wilful blindness as to the breach of trust. (3) Liability in knowing receipt requires one of the following states of mind as to the breach of trust: (i) actual knowledge (ii) wilful blindness (iii) wilfully and recklessly failing to make such inquiries as an honest and reasonable person would make (iv) knowledge of circumstances which would indicate the facts to an honest and reasonable person (v) knowledge of circumstances which would put an honest and reasonable person on inquiry.

Held, by La Forest, Gonthier, Cory and Iacobucci JJ: (1) The taking of a mortgage over trust property constitutes a receipt of trust property sufficient to attract liability in knowing receipt.

Held, by Sopinka, McLachlin and Major JJ (dissenting on this point): (1) One who takes a mortgage over trust property does not receive trust property. Knowing receipt requires taking physical control of trust property.

B. Federal Court

67. *Beloit Canada Ltd v Valmet-Dominion Inc* [1997] 3 FC 497 (CA: Isaac CJ and Stone and Desjardins JJA); varying [1993] 2 FC 515; 47 Can Patent Rep (3d) 448; [1994] RLR §41 (TD: Rouleau J).

Infringement of patent – accounting of profits – limitations – whether accounting of profits is a separate cause of action or an alternative remedy – discretionary nature of accounting of profits.

The plaintiff Beloit succeeded in defending its patent against attacks by the defendants, and claimed against them for infringement, seeking injunctions, damages and accountings of profits against each of them. The defendants argued that the claim was prescribed by the passage of time (Civil Code of Lower Canada, art 2261(2)), and that an accounting of profits was not an available remedy under the Patent Act, RSC 1985, c.P-4, which only provides for "damages." The trial judge held that several of the claims were prescribed, while others were established; but the plaintiff was awarded only compensatory damages and not an accounting of profits. He held (1) that an accounting of profits is not a separate cause of action from a claim for compensatory damages; it is merely a different remedy for the underlying wrong. Thus, the limitation period is the same in either case. (2) Although the Patent Act does not provide expressly for the remedy of accounting of profits, it is available for infringement of patent. (3) Nonetheless, this is an equitable remedy and its availability is for the discretion of the court. A plaintiff's choice is not binding on the court. (4) The complexity of an action, and a plaintiff's delay in enforcing its rights, were reasons which might justify the court's refusal to award an accounting. The plaintiff appealed and the defendant cross-appealed.

Decision: Some of the trial judge's holdings were varied but on the points digested his judgment was upheld.

Held: (1) An accounting of profits is a remedy not a cause of action; the applicable limitation period for infringement is the same whether the plaintiff seeks compensation or an accounting. (2) Even though the Patent Act does not refer specifically to an accounting of profits, while both the Trade-marks Act, RSC 1985, c.T-13 and the Copyright Act, RSC 1985, c.C-42 do so, nonetheless the court has jurisdiction to make such an award. (3) The award is a discretionary one. It is not the case that a plaintiff is entitled to elect, subject only to the equitable doctrines of clean hands, laches and acquiescence. Rather, a judge may consider other factors.

68. *Canada Safeway Ltd v Canada* (1997) 154 DLR (4th) 449 (CA: Linden, Letourneau and McDonald JJA); affg (1996) 97 Dominion Tax Cases 187 (Tax Ct: Bell J).
Income tax – whether recovery in restitution is taxable income.
The taxpayer made a successful objection to certain sales taxes which it had paid in 1985–89. It received a refund of $2.8m during taxation year 1994. The Minister of National Revenue argued that this amount was taxable income for the 1994 taxation year, as it was a "reimbursement" within the Income Tax Act, SC 1970-71-71, c.63, s 12(1)(x)(iv).
Decision: Appeal dismissed.
Held: (1) "Reimbursement" does not include a refund. (2) Such a refund should be treated as diminishing the expenses claimed by the taxpayer for the taxation years during which the taxes were improperly paid.

69. *Semiahmoo Indian Band v Canada* (1997) 148 DLR (4th) 523 (CA: Isaac CJ, McDonald JA and Gray DJ); noted B Freedman (1997) 36 Alta L Rev 218; rvsg (1996) 128 DLR (4th) 542 (TD: Reed J).
Restitution for wrongs – breach of fiduciary obligation – remedial constructive trust – precondictions for establishment of.
Certain land was held as a reserve for the plaintiff Indian Band. In 1951 some land was surrendered to the federal Crown in exchange for a payment, found by the trial judge to be at market value, on the basis that it was needed for customs facilities. It was never so used. The Band made inquiries during the 1960s about recovering the land. In 1990 the plaintiff issued a statement of claim alleging breach of fiduciary obligation in the original surrender. The trial judge held that there had been such a breach in that the Crown should have provided for the return of the land in the event that it was not needed. The trial judge held, however, that the claim was statute-barred. The plaintiffs appealed and the defendant cross-appealed.
Decision: Appeal allowed; cross-appeal dismissed; constructive trust declared.
Held: (1) "Given the unique value placed upon land by the First Nations in general, and upon the Surrendered Land by the Band in particular, a monetary award *simpliciter* would be an inadequate remedy for the respondent's actionable breach of fiduciary duty."

C. Alberta

70. *Principal Group Ltd (Trustee of) v Anderson* (1997) 147 DLR (4th) 229; 7 WWR 336 (CA: Hetherington, Cote and O'Leary JJA); (1994) 164 AR 81; [1996] RLR §67 (QB: Cairns J)
Change of position – applicability to voidable preference.
A corporation made some payments to its employees shortly before becoming bankrupt. The trustee in bankruptcy applied for the transactions to be set aside. The judge held that the payments were, under the terms of the relevant statute, "void as against the trustee in bankruptcy" and this was affirmed on appeal. It was argued for the employees that they should be allowed to raise the defence of change of position, but the judge held that the defence could not apply. The employees appealed this holding, arguing that they had changed their position in the six years which had ensued before recovery was sought.
Decision: Appeal dismissed. The change of position defence was incompatible with the legislative provisions of the Bankruptcy and Insolvency Act, RSC 1985, c.B-3.
Held: A statute can only affect the operation of the common law principles of restitution and bar the defences of estoppel or change of position where there exists a clear positive duty which is incompatible with the operation of those principles.

D. British Columbia

71. ***Toronto-Dominion Bank v Carotenuto*** (1997) 154 DLR (4th) 627 (CA: Ryan, Donald and Newbury JJA); varying (1996) 66 All Canada Weekly Summaries (3d) 644 (QB: Kirkpatrick J).
Juristic reason for enrichment and deprivation – burden of proof – what constitutes.
The plaintiff bank agreed to advance $500,000 to C in order that C could repay a loan owing to two people who had invested in a real estate project (the defendants). The plaintiff agreed to provide C with two bank drafts totalling $500,000 in return for cheques payable to the bank in the same amount, drawn by a company controlled by C for next day payment. The drafts were issued to the defendants and immediately deposited by them to accounts at their respective banks. The cheques provided by C to the plaintiff failed to clear the next day or on any subsequent day. The plaintiff did not take any steps to stop payment on the drafts that had been issued to the defendants. The plaintiff obtained a judgment against C. The plaintiff also initiated action against the defendants on the basis that they were unjustly enriched by their receipt of the drafts or their proceeds. Both parties applied for summary judgment but the applications were dismissed; both parties appealed on an agreed set of facts.

Decision: The action for unjust enrichment was dismissed. The defendants had a juristic reason for their enrichment.

Held: (1) It is for the plaintiff to prove the absence of juristic reason for a defendant's enrichment. (2) In order for there to be a juristic reason for a defendant's enrichment, there is no requirement that a contractual obligation have existed between the plaintiff and the defendant. Nor need there be consideration flowing from the payor to the ultimate payee. (3) A "commercially reasonable expectation" of receiving an enrichment can constitute a juristic reason.

Comment: The Court also rejected an argument that questions of unjust enrichment are affected by which party has deeper pockets.

E. Manitoba

72. ***Rillford Investments Ltd v Gravure International Capital Corp*** (1997) 118 Man R (2d) 11; 7 WWR 534 (CA: Scott CJM, Lyon and Monnin JJA); affg (1996) 111 Man R (2d) 252 (QB: Darichuk J).
Contract as juristic reason for enrichment and deprivation.
The plaintiff was in the business of facilitating mergers and acquisitions. A contract was entered into with the defendant in which the latter agreed to pay the plaintiff a commission of $200,000 in the event that a transaction at a net price of $35 million was agreed between the defendant and a party introduced by the plaintiff. The contract contained a "60/365 day clause" which expressly limited the duration of the contract. The plaintiff introduced the defendant to a potential buyer (Hofmann) but a transaction did not materialise. Two and one-half years later, the defendant and Hofmann agreed a transaction for a gross purchase price of $66 million. The plaintiff requested compensation, the defendant declined and litigation commenced. At trial, the plaintiff's claim was dismissed. On appeal, the plaintiff argued that its efforts extended beyond the "four corners" of the contract and hence recovery on the basis of unjust enrichment was not precluded by the 365-day cutoff provision.

Decision: Appeal dismissed.

Held: An express contractual stipulation that remuneration is not payable in the events which occurred excludes a claim in unjust enrichment. A contract can constitute a juristic reason for an enrichment.

F. Ontario

73. *Armatage Motors Ltd v Royal Trust Corp of Canada* (1997) 34 OR (3d) 599; 149 DLR (4th) 398 (CA: Brooke, Osborne and Austin JJA); affg (1995) 45 Real Property Rep (2d) 204 (Gen Div: Desmarais J).
Mistake – subrogation – effect of statute – effect of innocence of defendant and negligence of plaintiff.
The Sawyers, holders of an estate in land, mortgaged it to C Ltd and then gave a second mortgage to the plaintiff. In 1991 the Sawyers then agreed another loan from the defendant, intended as a refinancing of the debt owing to C Ltd. The defendant was aware of the mortgage to C Ltd but not of that to the plaintiff; and the solicitor's search (via an agency) did not reveal it. The defendant registered its mortgage and advanced its loan, which was used to pay the debt owing to C Ltd; C Ltd's mortgage was discharged. In 1992 a principal of the plaintiff took legal advice as the Sawyers were delinquent on their loan; he was told that his position was secure since the plaintiff's mortgage was now first. He advised the Sawyers but not the defendant. The Sawyers defaulted on both loans and the plaintiff sought a declaration that its mortgage had priority over the defendant's. The trial judge granted the declaration and the defendant appealed.
Decision: Appeal dismissed.
Held, by the majority (Austin and Osborne JJA): Subrogation is a remedy, not a right, and a discretionary remedy at that. Where the party who will be adversely affected by this remedy has relied to its detriment on its priority position, the remedy will be denied, at least where the party seeking it has another remedy (*ie* against its solicitor).
Held, by Brooke JA (dissenting): (1) A person cannot take advantage of another's error to better his priority position, where he is aware of that error. (2) Neither the negligence of a plaintiff's solicitor, nor the statute governing priority, provide a reason to deny subrogation.

74. *Bullock v Key Property Management Inc* (1997) 33 OR (3d) 1 (CA: Robins, Doherty and Austin JJA); applic for leave to app to SCC dismissed (27 Nov 97) File No 26074; rvsg (1992) 46 Estates and Trusts Rep 275 (Gen Div: Valin J).
Trusts – involvement in a breach of trust – degree of knowledge required.
A company managed rental units for the plaintiff and was a trustee of funds received. The funds were paid into an account with the defendant bank. The company breached the trust in various ways and the plaintiff sued the company and the defendant bank, alleging that the latter was liable for assisting in the breach of trust. The trial judge held the bank liable on the basis that, given what it knew, it ought reasonably to have made inquiries which would have led it to know of the breaches of trust. The bank appealed.
Decision: Appeal allowed.
Held: (1) Liability for involvement in a breach of trust requires actual knowledge, recklessness or wilful blindness. (2) Wilful blindness requires the existence of a suspicion as to the facts in question.
Comment: The court did not clearly distinguish between knowing receipt and knowing assistance. To the extent that this was a case of knowing receipt, the holding cannot stand with *Citadel General Assurance Co v Lloyds Bank Canada* §65.

75. *Hussey Seating Co (Canada) Ltd v Ottawa (City)* (1997) 145 DLR (4th) 493 (Gen Div: Adams J)
Enrichment by improvements – contract as juristic reason for enrichment and deprivation – availability of unjust enrichment where plaintiff improved defendant's land under a contract between plaintiff and third party.
The defendant leased a football stadium to a football club. The lease obliged to the club to improve the seating. Pursuant to this obligation the club contracted with the plaintiff for the

installation of new seats at an agreed price of $75,528.93. The seats were installed but the club went bankrupt. The plaintiff now sued the defendant in unjust enrichment, and moved for summary judgment.
Decision: Motion and action dismissed.
Held: Contractual arrangements can constitute a juristic reason for an enrichment and corresponding deprivation.

76. *Midland Mortgage Corp v 784401 Ontario Ltd* (1997) 34 OR (3d) 594 (CA: Brooke, Osborne and Austin JJA); rvsg (15 Nov 1993) Unrep (Gen Div: Jarvis J).
Mistake – subrogation – effect of statute – effect of innocence of defendant and negligence of plaintiff.
Following a series of refinancings, a junior mortgagee's interest was registered prior in time to that of the plaintiff, whose mortgage was intended to refinance the prior first mortgage, also held by the plaintiff. The funds advanced under the refinancing were used in part to pay out the loan secured by the prior first mortgage. The junior mortgagee refused to postpone its mortgage in favour of the plaintiff. The plaintiff sought a declaration that its interest had priority over that of the junior mortgagee, despite the fact that it was registered later in time. The trial judge refused the declaration. The plaintiff appealed.
Decision: Appeal allowed. Plaintiff granted priority for the amount of the discharged debt, at the rate of interest agreed on that debt.
Held: (1) Subrogation applies not only in favour of third parties but also in favour of a first mortgagee who refinances its mortgage. (2) The negligence of a party's solicitor does not deny subrogation to that party. (3) Subrogation is not implicitly abolished by the land titles registration legislation in Ontario; an express abolition would be necessary.

77. *Moore (Township) v Guarantee Co of North America* (1995) 26 OR (3d) 733 (CA: Houlden, Osborne and Weiler JJA); rvsg (1991) 4 OR (3d) 556 (Gen Div: Eberle J).
Insurance – whether a claim to recover overpaid taxes is a claim for "damages".
A taxpayer which carried on business in the plaintiff municipality and paid municipal taxes launched a claim against the plaintiff alleging that it had overpaid taxes. The claim was settled for $41,430.38 plus costs. The plaintiff sought to recover this sum from the defendant insurer. The policy required the defendant to indemnify the plaintiff against "loss", defined as any obligation to pay "damages" on account of "wrongful acts". The defendant denied coverage. The trial judge found for the plaintiff and the defendant appealed.
Decision: Appeal allowed.
Held: A claim to recover taxes is not a claim for "damages".

78. *Mutual Trust Co v Creditview Estate Homes Ltd* (1997) 34 OR (3d) 583; 149 DLR (4th) 385 (CA: Brooke, Osborne and Austin JJA); affg (1994) 28 Can Bankruptcy R (3d) 208; 41 Real Property Rep (2d) 217; [1995] RLR §117 (Gen Div: Adams J).
Mistake – subrogation – effect of statute – effect of innocence of defendant and negligence of plaintiff.
A bank held first and second mortgages on a house which was jointly held by Mr and Mrs Shamas. The respondent had pending litigation against Mr Shamas, who transferred his interest in the house to Mrs Shamas for no consideration. The respondent brought proceedings to have this set aside as a fraudulent conveyance, and obtained a certificate of pending litigation against the house. The applicant refinanced the mortgages, advancing $230,000 which was used to pay out the bank's mortgages. It did not take an assignment of the bank's mortgages, but registered new ones, which were therefore prima facie subordinate to the certificate of pending litigation. The applicant applied for a declaration that it enjoyed the priority formerly held by the bank, by subrogation. The trial judge allowed the application, and the respondent appealed.

Decision: Appeal dismissed.

Held: (1) The trial judge was right to say that "the fundamental principle underlying the equitable doctrine of subrogation is one of fairness in light of all of the circumstances. Within this principle is an understanding that no injustice is done by the appropriate subrogation of a party to the rights of original mortgagees;" and, that the doctrine can apply in respect of a certificate of pending litigation. (2) Negligence on the part of the claimant or its solicitor does not disentitle it to subrogation. (3) Subrogation is not implicitly abolished by the land titles registration legislation in Ontario; an express abolition would be necessary.

79. *Stewart v Canadian Broadcasting Corp* (1997) 150 DLR (4th) 24 (Gen Div: Macdonald J).
Restitution for wrongs – breach of fiduciary obligation – disgorgement.

The defendant was a lawyer who defended the plaintiff on charges of criminal negligence in a high-profile case in 1979. In 1991 the lawyer participated in a television programme on the administration of justice in which the client's case was discussed and the client's culpability exaggerated. The client sued alleging that there had been a breach of fiduciary obligations which had caused him to suffer loss and from which the defendant had profited.

Decision: Action allowed; equitable compensation of $2,500 and disgorgement of $3,250 ordered; punitive equitable compensation denied.

Held: Fiduciary obligations may subsist after the relationship which gave rise to them is at an end.

80. *Ukrainian (Fort William) Credit Union Ltd v Nesbitt, Burns Ltd* (1997) 152 DLR (4th) 640 (CA: Brooke, Osborne and Austin JJA); applic for leave to app to SCC granted (7 May 98) File No 26422; rvsg Unrep (Gen Div: Farley J).
Defences – statutory defence – whether third party claim for contribution is a "proceeding for damages".

The plaintiff was suing the defendant financial advisor in negligence. The defendant sought to add as a third party the Deposit Insurance Corporation of Ontario (DICO), seeking contribution and indemnity in the event of the defendant being found liable. The Credit Unions and Caisses Populaires Act 1994, SO 1994, c.11, s 253(1) provided "no action or other proceeding for damages shall be instituted against" DICO for anything done or not done by it in good faith. DICO moved for a determination that the defendant's third party claim was barred by s 253(1), and the motion was allowed at trial. The defendant appealed.

Decision: Appeal allowed.

Held: (1) A third party claim is "an action or other proceeding". (2) However, a claim for contribution is not a claim for damages.

Comment: The Court's decision seems difficult to justify where (as here) the claim being made seeks to establish the regulator's liability in negligence (as opposed to a claim which seeks contribution to adjust the burden of liabilities otherwise established).

G. Québec

81. *Namerow Investments Ltd v Commission Scolaire Des Laurentides* [1997] Recueil de Jurisprudence du Québec 2960 (CA: Proulx, Robert and Zerbisias (ad hoc) JJ); rvsg (26 Sep 1995) Unrep (Sup Ct: Bergeron J).
Modes of restitution – nullity – judicial sale set aside – effect on third parties.

In 1983 the defendant school board obtained a judgment for unpaid taxes against the plaintiff. The judgment was not paid and the defendant attached an immovable belonging to the defendant. In 1984 there was a judicial sale of the immovable. The defendant was the only bidder and acquired the immovable. In 1986 it sold it to C Inc. The immovable was the subject of subdivisions and further sales. Several buildings were erected by buyers. In 1991 the plaintiff commenced an action alleging that the judicial sale in 1984 was void due to various irregularities. It sought a declaration of nullity and rectification of the register, and asked that the judgment be enforceable against C Inc, which was made a third party to the proceedings. In 1995 the defendant and C Inc moved for the dismissal of the claim, arguing that since the immovable had been sold to a good faith third party, art 1707 of the Civil Code of Québec (see [1995] RLR 279) applied and prevented restitution. The judge granted this motion and the plaintiff appealed. It argued that art 1707 might prevent specific restitution but did not bar the claim for a declaration of nullity.

Decision: Appeal allowed.

Held, unanimously: Under arts 1700-1701, if specific restitution is impossible, restitution by equivalent value is appropriate. Art 1707 can operate in favour of a third party to prevent specific restitution, but this will not relieve the party originally bound to make restitution of its duty to do so by equivalent value.

Held, by Proulx J, dissenting on this point: Art 1707 has no bearing on the question of nullity and consideration of it is premature until that issue has been determined.

Held, by the majority (Robert and Zerbisias JJ): A holding of nullity affects the title of third parties and so art 1707 must be considered. When a declaration of nullity is sought the appropriate procedure is to request a fixing of the monetary value of restitution so that if art 1707 operates then restitution by equivalent value can be ordered. All issues should be considered together.

H. Saskatchewan

82. *Robert Lemmons & Associates Ltd v Gannon Bros Energy Ltd* (1997) 148 Sask R 181; [1997] 2 WWR 688 (CA: Vancise, Wakeling and Sherstobitoff JJA); applic for leave to app to SCC rfsd (16 Jun 1997) File No 25731; affg (1995) 130 Sask R 51 (QB: Halvorson J).
Mistake – mistake of law.
The defendant located an oil drilling prospect and decided to drill the property. A contract was executed whereby the plaintiff was the consultant and engineer on the project and the defendant was the operator. The defendant paid certain monies to the plaintiff in respect of engineering services provided. It later transpired that the plaintiff had allowed its engineering licence to lapse. The defendant sought *inter alia* repayment of fees paid to the plaintiff for engineering services while the latter was unlicensed, on the basis that these payments were made under mistake of law.

Decision: Recovery denied.

Held: (1) There is no distinction in Canada between errors of fact and errors of law. Restitution should be accorded in either case unless other factors present indicate that an inequity would result. (2) Restitution will not however be ordered where it would create an unjust enrichment of the payor.

ARTICLES

83. Gesser, A, "Disrespecting Your Elders or Getting What is Rightfully Yours? Unjust Enrichment in Estate Litigation" (1997) 17 Estates and Trusts J 37.
Examines recent decisions involving unjust enrichment claims in estate cases. Attempts to isolate the principles emerging which determine when an unjust enrichment has taken place and what relief is likely to be available.

84. Hadfield, G K, "An Incomplete Contracting Perspective on Fiduciary Duty" (1997) 28 Can Bus LJ 141.
An economic analysis of the incidence of fiduciary obligations.

85. Hoegner, S, "How Many Rights (or Wrongs) Make a Remedy?" (1997) 42 McGill LJ 437.
Argues that by moving toward the idea of the remedial constructive trust for subtractive unjust enrichment, Canadian courts are restricting their ability to rely on the institutional constructive trust in cases where there may be profitable wrongdoing but no subtractive unjust enrichment. Advocates the return to recognising both kinds of constructive trust so as to prevent this.

86. McCamus, J, "Prometheus Unbound: Fiduciary Obligation in the Supreme Court of Canada" (1997) 28 Can Bus LJ 107.
Examines the development of the fiduciary concept in the Supreme Court of Canada, urging caution lest developments in equitable compensation should lead to an unprincipled ability to circumvent the principles governing recovery in tort or breach of contract.

87. Moran, M, "Rethinking *Winnipeg Condominium:* Restitution, Economic Loss, and Anticipatory Repairs" (1997) 47 UTLJ 115.
In *Winnipeg Condominium Corp No 36 v Bird Construction Co* [1995] 1 SCR 85, 121 DLR (4th) 193 the Supreme Court of Canada held that someone who repairs a dangerous defect in a building can recover in negligence the cost of repair from the party whose negligence gave rise to the defect. The author argues that this recovery should be understood as restitution for unjust enrichment. The repairer having been legally bound to repair, by doing so also discharged a liability of the negligent party; the crucial point is how it can be decided that as between these parties, this liability should properly be borne by the latter.

88. Roebuck, L D, "Prometheus Unbound: A Practitioner's Perspective" (1997) 28 Can Business LJ 155.
A practioner's perspective on the Supreme Court of Canada's recent pronouncements on fiduciary law.

89. Youdan, T G, "Liability for Breach of Fiduciary Obligation" [1996] Special Lectures of the Law Society of Upper Canada 1 (Toronto: Carswell, 1996).

NOTER UP

Lubrizol Corp v Imperial Oil Ltd [1997] 2 FC 3; 71 Can Patent Rep (3d) 26; [1997] RLR §51 (CA: Hugessen, Stone and Décary JJA); affg (1996) 69 Can Patent Rep (3d) 173; 117 Fed Trial Rep 197 (TD Muldoon J).
Soulos v Korkontzilas [1997] 2 SCR 217; 146 DLR (4th) 214 (La Forest, Sopinka, Gonthier, Cory, McLachlin, Iacobucci and Major JJ); noted L Smith (1997) 76 Can Bar Rev 539; L Smith (1998) 114 LQR 14; affg (1995) 25 OR (3d) 257; 126 DLR 4th 637; [1996] RLR §98 (CA: Catzman, Carthy and Labrosse JJA); rvsg (1991) 4 OR (3d) 51 (Gen Div: Anderson J).
Télébec Ltée v Québec (Régie des télécommunications) [1996] Revue Légale 607; [1996] RLR §101 (Sup Ct: Bernard J).

England and Wales

*William Swadling**

CASES

90. *A-G v Blake (Jonathan Cape Ltd, third party)* [1998] 2 WLR 805; [1998] 1 All ER 833 (CA: Lord Woolf MR, Millett and Mummery LJJ). Noted Hedley (1998) 148 NLJ 723; Jaffey [1998] LMCLQ (Nov); Virgo [1998] RLR 118. Rvsg [1997] Ch 84; [1996] 3 WLR 741; [1996] 3 All ER 903 (Sir Richard Scott V-C).
Restitution for wrongs – duty of confidence – whether breach of fiduciary duty – breach of contract – recovery of profits.
The defendant, a member of the British Secret Service, was also an agent for the Soviet Union. On joining the service, he signed an agreement not to disclose information which came into his possession by virtue of his position without first obtaining permission to do so. He was later convicted of unlawfully communicating information and sentenced to a term of 42 years imprisonment. He subsequently escaped from prison and made his way to Moscow. There he wrote his biography, which was to be published by the second defendants. The book contained information which by the time of publication was no longer confidential. The Crown did not seek any restraint on the publication of the book. Instead, they sought to recover advances against royalties which the publishers had agreed to pay to the defendant on the ground that the defendant owed a fiduciary duty (i) not to use his position as a former member of the security services so as to make a profit for himself and (ii) not to use the Crown's property, including intangible property such as originally confidential information, for his own benefit. At first instance, the claim for profits failed. The Attorney-General appealed, advancing (after prompting from the court) an additional claim for relief in public law based on his duty, as guardian of the public interest, to oversee the enforcement of the criminal law.
Held: Appeal allowed.
Decision: There was no breach of fiduciary duty as the information disclosed was no longer secret or confidential. However, disclosure was a criminal offence under the Official Secrets Act 1989. The court's power to grant injunctive relief in support of the criminal law, on an application by the Attorney-General, was not limited to restraining the commission of a criminal offence, but extended, where a criminal offence had already been committed, to enforcing public policy with respect to the consequences of the commission of that crime, *eg* restraining receipt by the criminal of a further benefit as a result of that crime. Accordingly, the court would grant an injunction restraining the defendant from receiving any further royalties from the publication of his book.
Comment: For restitution lawyers, the interest in this case lies in the court's comments on any private law claim for profits. Although the court found that Blake was in breach of his contract of employment in revealing the information, the Crown, despite encouragement from the bench, declined to make a claim to the profits on this ground. So the point was not argued. Nevertheless, the Court of Appeal held that such a claim, had it been advanced, would have been successful. While affirming the orthodox position that the normal measure of recovery for breach of contract was compensation, the court held that in exceptional circumstances a restitutionary award might be made. Those circumstances were twofold: (1) the case of "skimped performance", as typified by the Louisiana case *City of New Orleans v Firemen's Charitable Association* (1891) 9 So 486; (2) adopting the views of Birks at [1987] LMCLQ 421, 434, the case where the defendant has

---
* Fellow of Brasenose College, Oxford.

obtained his profit by doing the very thing which he contracted not to do, which was exactly the case here.

91. Banque Financière de la Cité v Parc (Battersea) Ltd [1998] 2 WLR 475; [1998] 1 All ER 737 (HL: Lord Steyn, Lord Griffiths, Lord Hoffmann, Lord Clyde and Lord Hutton). Noted Mitchell [1998] RLR 144. Rvsg (29 Nov 1996) Unrep (CA); noted Bridge [1998] JBL 323; Mitchell [1998] LMCLQ 14.

Subrogation – mistaken payment – third party "enriched" by payment – money used to discharge prior encumbrance – Whether subrogation available so as to give mistaken payor priority over subsequent encumbrancers.

BFC lent DM30m to Parc to enable Parc to repay part of a loan from another bank (RTB) secured by a first charge on land it owned in Battersea. The transaction did not contemplate that Parc would provide any security. It was, however, an express condition of the advance that other companies in the group to which Parc belonged would not demand repayment of their loans until BFC had been repaid. One such company was Omnicorp Overseas Ltd (OOL), which was owed £26.25m, secured by a second charge over the property. The persons who negotiated the transaction had no authority to commit OOL to such an undertaking and it was not binding on it. Parc was insolvent and, if BFC had no priority over OOL's second charge, it was unlikely to be repaid. The question was whether, as against OOL, BFC was entitled to be subrogated to the first charge to the extent that its money was used to repay the debt which it had secured. The Court of Appeal had held that, though OOL was enriched at the expense of BFC, that enrichment was not unjust. BFC had not bargained for security and should not be given it via the remedy of subrogation. Indeed, the remedy of subrogation would give them more than if the letters of postponement were binding. There was no mutual intention that BFC have the priority they claimed.

Held: Appeal allowed.

Decision: Although intention might be relevant to the question whether or not an enrichment had been unjust, it was a mistake to regard the availability of subrogation as a remedy to prevent unjust enrichment as turning entirely on the question of intention, whether common or unilateral. In the absence of subrogation, OOL would be enriched at BFC's expense and prima facie such enrichment would be unjust. Moreover, subrogation as against OOL, which was all that BFC claimed in the action, would not give it greater rights than it had bargained for; all that would happen would be that OOL would be prevented from being able to enrich itself to the extent that BFC's money paid off the RTB charge. That was fully within the scope of the equitable remedy.

Comment: The reasoning in this case is somewhat obscure, as seems usually to be the case where subrogation is involved. However, it appears that the "unjust factor" relied upon by the plaintiffs was mistake. As Lord Steyn said, "But for BFC's mistaken belief that it was protected in respect of intra-group indebtedness, BFC would not have proceeded with the refinancing". The fact that this was arguably a mistake of law seems nowhere to have been noticed. The case is also unfortunate because of the failure of the same judge to see subrogation as merely a route to restitution. Thus, Lord Steyn said: "In my view, on an application of established principles of unjust enrichment, BFC are entitled to succeed against OOL. But, if it were necessary to do so, I would reach the same conclusion in terms of the principles of subrogation." This, despite the fact that Dr Mitchell's thesis, *The Law of Subrogation*, was cited to and mentioned by the House. His Lordship should, however, be congratulated for his introduction of the four-fold Birksian enquiry at the highest level of decision. Lord Hoffmann, with whom Lords Griffiths, Steyn and Clyde all agreed, did not fall into the error of seeing restitution and subrogation as different categories in the law. But, though he located the doctrine of subrogation squarely within the law of restitution (and also made the very helpful observation that there is such an animal as contractual subrogation and that the two were not to be confused), his analysis of the unjust factor is no better than that of Lord Steyn. The case is also unfortunate in that it seems to give normative force to the word "unjust": much of the discussion concerns the question why OOL's enrichment was not unjust, with no reference to the usual unjust factors but instead to questions of abstract justice, a discussion reminiscent of the Canadian approach to restitution. If anything, this case shows that the time has now come to substitute the word "reversible" for "unjust".

92. Barclays Bank Plc v Boulter [1997] 1 WLR 1; [1997] 2 All ER 1002 (CA: Leggatt, Mummery LJJ and Sir Brian Neill); pet all [1998] 1 WLR 472. Noted K Barker, ch 5 of FD Rose (ed), *Restitution and Banking Law* (Mansfield Press, Oxford, 1998) §146; Birks and Swadling [1997] All ER Rev 391; Birks (1998) 12 TLI 2.
Setting aside mortgage – security induced by misrepresentation of husband – whether mortgagee bound by husband's misrepresentation – whether burden of proof on mortgagee to show that it did not have notice of misrepresentation.
The bank held a mortgage over the Boulter matrimonial home. The mortgage had been executed by both Mr and Mrs Boulter. The debtor was Mr Boulter. Upon his default, the bank brought proceedings for possession. Mrs Boulter resisted and counterclaimed for a declaration that she held her half share free of the legal charge. Her pleading alleged, *inter alia*, that Mr Boulter had procured her signature by misrepresentation and that he had been the bank's agent to obtain it. It did not allege that the bank had constructive notice of the misrepresentation. The bank therefore maintained that she had confined herself to the agency point and could not attempt to bring herself within the principle in *Barclay's Bank Plc v O'Brien* [1994] 1 AC 180. The judge upheld that objection. Mrs Boulter could have amended her pleading. She did not want to, since if she won only on the pleadings as amended she would face an order for all prior costs. She appealed instead.
   Held: Appeal allowed. It was not incumbent on the plaintiff to plead and prove that the bank had notice of the misrepresentation.
   Decision: The court held that, on the authority of Lord Browne-Wilkinson's speech in *O'Brien* and on well-established equitable principles, the burden was not on Mrs Boulter to plead and prove that the bank had constructive notice: it is on the bank to plead and prove that it did *not* have constructive notice. It is well established at this level of decision that the doctrine of *bona fide* purchaser for value without actual or constructive notice is a defence which can be raised to defeat a claim of an equitable right or interest and that the burden is on the person raising that defence to plead and prove *all* its elements: it is a "single defence" '.
   Comment: This decision is clearly wrong. The defence of *bona fide* purchase is an exception to the principle *nemo dat quod non habet*, yet that principle was not infringed, the plaintiff having good title to the asset she charged. But given the obscurity of the reasoning in *O'Brien* itself, the court's confusion is perfectly understandable.

93. Barclays Bank Plc v Caplan [1997] *The Times* Dec 12 (Jonathan Sumption QC).
Undue influence – series of guarantees – independant legal advice obtained for first guarantee but not later guarantees – whether later guarantees could be set aside even though first guarantee binding.
A wife granted a charge over the matrimonial home to guarantee her husband's debts. She later sought to have the charge set aside against the lender on the ground that it had been procured by the undue influence of her husband. The judge found that it had indeed been so procured but that, since the bank had taken adequate steps to ensure that she received independant legal advice, the bank were not fixed with notice of the wife's right to have it set aside. However, there had been further agreements in respect of further loans, and in respect of these the bank had failed to ensure that the wife had received independant legal advice. The question was whether the two sets of transactions could be severed.

Held: It was possible for the court to sever from an instrument affected by undue influence the objectionable parts, leaving the part uncontaminated by undue influence enforceable.

Decision: In the two cases in which the court took an all or nothing approach (*Allied Irish Bank v Byrne* (1994) and *TSB Plc v Camfield* [1995] 1 WLR 430), a decision to sever would have amounted to a rewriting of the contract. However, neither of those cases was authority for the proposition that setting aside was invariably an all or nothing process, even in a case where the objectionable features of the document could readily be severed from the rest without rewriting it.

94. *Brennan v Brighton Borough Council (No 2)* [1997] *The Times* May 15 (CA: Pill LJ and Sir Christopher Slade).
Limitation – action to strike out – corporate veil – fraudulent misrepresentation – whether arguable case made out.
B, who wished to develop a tennis centre on land used by a squash club, entered into negotiations with BBC, owners of the land; it was agreed that a lease for 31 years would be forthcoming. BBC insisted that B should personally control the operation through the medium of the club, to be formed into a company; B acceded. Substantial sums were invested by B in development work, and BBC provided a contractual guarantee. After the development work had been substantially completed, BBC, breaching the contract with B, refused to grant the lease, took possession of the centre following a winding up order, and then opened it for business. It was claimed that BBC had acquired the centre for about half its estimated value. B issued a writ claiming damages for fraudulent misrepresentation, which he subsequently sought to amend, after the limitation period had expired, to claim that BBC had been unjustly enriched and that the interests of justice required restitution. B's application for leave to amend was dismissed and his statement of claim was struck out as disclosing no reasonable cause of action. B appealed.
Held: Appeal dismissed.
Decision: The decision not to allow amendment of the writ after the expiry of the limitation period could not be faulted. However, it was not necessarily obvious that B had no arguable case in restitution so that striking out was merited. Although, given that the club was a separate legal entity, B's claim would seem to involve subversion of the doctrine of privity of contract, in view of the relationship between B, the club and BBC it was not certain that, in all the circumstances, a court would have ruled out a restitutionary claim.

95. *Bristol & West BS v Mothew* [1998] Ch 1; [1997] 2 WLR 436; [1996] 4 All ER 698 (CA: Staughton, Millett and Otton LJJ).
Solicitor acting for mortgagor and mortgagee – Breach of duty by solicitor – Extent of liability of solicitor to mortgagee for subseqent loss.
A solicitor acted for both mortgagor and mortgagee in the purchase of a house. The mortgagee provided a loan of £59,000 towards the total purchase price of £73,000. The mortgagee sought an assurance from the solicitor that the remainder of the purchase money was being provided by the mortgagor personally without resort to further borrowing. The solicitor advised that this was the case. In fact, £3,350 was owed by the mortgagor to his bank, and this amount was to be secured by a second charge over the mortgaged property. The mortgagee advanced the money to the solicitor, who advanced it to the mortgagor's vendor on completion of the purchase. When the mortgagor later defaulted on the loan, the property was sold but realised less than £53,000. The mortgagee sought to recover its loss from the solicitor, alleging, *inter alia*, breach of trust. It argued that the advance of the monies having been obtained by a misrepresentation, the mortgagee's consent to the payment away of the money was vitiated. The mortgagee had therefore committed a breach of that trust for which he was strictly liable. The argument was accepted by the trial judge.

Held: Appeal allowed.

Decision: Misrepresentation makes a transaction voidable not void. It gives the representee the right to elect whether to rescind or affirm the transaction. The representor cannot anticipate his decision. Unless and until the representee elects to rescind, the representor remains fully bound. The solicitor's misrepresentations merely gave the mortgagee the right to elect to withdraw from the transaction on discovering the truth. But on rescission, the equitable title does not revest retrospectively so as to cause an application of trust money which was properly authorised when made to be afterwards treated as a breach of trust. There had therefore been no breach of trust in this case.

96. ***BSE Trading Ltd v Hands*** (1998) 75 P & CR 138 (CA: Peter Gibson, Stuart-Smith and Thorpe LJJ). Noted Mitchell [1998] Conv 133.
Landlord and tenant – co-sureties of tenant's obligations – payment of rent by one surety – claim for contribution by other surety – whether paying surety could have recovered against defaulting tenant by being subrogated to landlord's right to forfeit the lease.
BSE Trading Ltd and Hands were sureties who guaranteed the obligations of a tenant, Zastrava Cars (GB) Ltd, under a lease. When Zastava defaulted on the rent, the landlord turned to BSE, which paid several outstanding instalments, then negotiated the surrender of the lease by Zastava to the landlord, and made a further payment to the landlord in consideration of the landlord's agreement to release Zastava from all outstanding liability for breaches of covenant. BSE applied to recover a contribution from Hands and was awarded summary judgment. Hands appealed to the Court of Appeal, arguing *inter alia* that Hands would only be liable if it was first shown that BSE could not have recovered against Zastava, and that they could indeed have recovered against Zastava if they had asserted their entitlement under the Mercantile Law Amendment Act 1856, s 5 to be subrogated to the landlord's right to forfeit the lease and re-enter the property.

Held: There was no right to be subrogated as claimed.

Decision: It was impossible to see how the right of re-entry could be utilised by a surety. That would terminate the lease, and would therefore be inconsistent with the landlord's ongoing right to payment of rent in the future.

97. ***Corporacion Nacional Del Cobre De Chile v Sogemin Metals Ltd*** [1997] 1 WLR 1396 (ChD: Carnworth J).
Bribery of employee – claim for restitution – whether plaintiff had duty to investigate employee's conduct – whether recovery of gains to be reduced because of failure to investigate.
The plaintiff, a copper producer and trader in metals futures, brought an action against the defendants, who were commodity brokers, an associated company and its employees, alleging that they were parties to a conspiracy to bribe the head of its futures department to enter into contracts on terms which were unfavourable to the plaintiff and which included excessive or unnecessary commissions or charges. The plaintiff sought restitution in respect of the value of the bribes and damages for fraud, conspiracy and procuring breach of contract. It also claimed that the defendants had dishonestly assisted in breaches of trust and were liable to account to it as constructive trustees for the amounts of the bribes and the profits it made on the contracts. The defendants sought to reduce their liability by pleading that the plaintiff was partly responsible for its own losses in that it had not competently supervised or overseen its employee's trading activities and that its senior executives knew or should have known of the terms of the contracts but failed to take the opportunity to investigage.

Held: The defence would be struck out.

Decision: The essence of the plaintiff's claim was the dishonest subornation of the plaintiff's employee. In the absence of any allegation in the defendant that the plaintiff knew of or had reason to suspect dishonesty or that it was put on notice of any irregularity, the mere fact that the plaintiff had the opportunity to discover the fraud but failed to take it was insufficient to constitute a defence or a ground for reducing damages.

Comment: That must be right. The essence of a fiduciary relationship is that one person trusted, and was entitled to trust, another to put that other's interest before his own. If one was under a duty to check that that trust was properly placed, the essence of the fiduciary relationship would be destroyed.

98. *Dunbar Bank Plc v Nadeem* [1997] 2 All ER 253 (ChD: Robert Englehart QC, sitting as a Deputy Judge of the High Court). Noted Birks and Swadling [1997] All ER Rev 405. Rvsd [1998] *The Times*, Jul 1 (CA: Millett, Morritt and Potter LJJ).
Undue influence – setting aside of security – whether duty to make counter-restitution.
A loan was taken out by both Mr and Mrs Nadeem. Some of the borrowed money immediately went to settle Mr Nadeem's debts; the remaining £210,000 was used to purchase a new matrimonial home in both their names. Mrs Nadeem having shown that the all-monies charge over the home had been obtained as a result of undue influence of which the bank had notice, the question remained whether she could have it set aside without making counter-restitution.

Held: She must return benefits actually received.

Decision: This was interpreted as meaning that she must pay back that part of the loan with which she had obtained her own share of the house. She had to make counter-restitution of £105,000.

Comment: The protection offered by *Barclays Bank v O'Brien* may be thought not to warrant denial of counter-restitution in those cases in which the wife has obtained an immediate benefit to herself; and that is the conclusion at which *Nadeem* arrives. But consistency will not be achieved until the cases exempting a party from counter-restitution are considered as a group. The law of restitution still has difficulty in thinking in terms of principles and in identifying from its different fragments the cases which reflect and underpin those principles. In *Dunbar v Nadeem* not one other instance of exemption was brought to the attention of the court.

99. *Dunbar (administrator of Dunbar (decd)) v Plant* [1997] 3 WLR 1261; [1997] 4 All ER 289. Noted Birks and Swadling [1997] All ER Rev 401; Bridge [1998] CLJ 31.
Suicide pact – whether rights of survivor forfeited under Forfeiture Act 1982 – test for exercise of discretion.
A young couple, deeply in love, set up home together. A house was bought with the aid of a mortgage and conveyed to them as joint tenants at law and equity. An insurance policy was taken out on the man's life and written in favour of the woman. She later had trouble at work. She was accused by her employer of false accounting and theft, and threatened with imprisonment. She decided to commit suicide. He could not face life without her. So they agreed to commit suicide together. But they only partly succeeded in their plans. Although he managed to hang himself, her simultaneous attempt failed. On the facts, and though never prosecuted for the offence, she was found to have aided and abetted his suicide. Did she in consequence forfeit a half-share in the home and the proceeds of the insurance policy? Until recently, the rule at common law was simple, if strict: no criminal could retain a benefit which accrues to him from crime: *Re Crippen* [1911] P 108. It was relaxed by statute as a result of a case in which a blameless widow who killed her husband was denied social security benefits. The Forfeiture Act 1982 now gives the court a power to modify the application of the forfeiture rule in a particular case, but only if "it is satisfied that, having regard to the conduct of the offender and of the deceased and to such other circumstances as appear to the court to be material, the justice of the case requires the effect of the rule to be so modified in that case." The trial judge prevented the forfeiture rule operating as regards the house, but not the insurance policy. In exercising his discretion, he said that he was attempting to do justice between the parties, they being the woman and the family of the deceased.

Held: The forfeiture rule should have been prevented from operating both as regards the house and the proceeds of the insurance policy.

Decision: The Court of Appeal said that the trial judge had adopted the wrong approach. The real question was whether the justice of the case required the benefits to be forfeit. The public interest would only rarely call for forfeiture in the case of a survivor of a suicide pact. The survivor will normally deserve sympathy, not punishment.

100. *Foskett v McKeown* [1998] 2 WLR 298; [1997] 3 All ER 392 (CA: Sir Richard Scott V-C, Hobhouse and Morritt LJJ); pet all. Noted Birks and Swadling [1997] All ER Rev 402; Chambers (1997) 11 TLI 86; Mitchell [1997] LMCLQ 465; Nolan [1997] CLJ 491; Smith (1997) 113 LQR 552.

Tracing – trusts monies used to purchase life assurance policy – whether beneficiaries of trust had ownership or only lien over proceeds of policy.

In 1986 Murphy took out a life assurance policy on his own life. The annual premium was £10,220. He paid the premiums for 1986, 1987, 1988, 1989 and 1990. In 1989 he transferred the policy to three trustees, one of whom was himself. The beneficiaries were his wife and children. In 1991 he died. The insurers paid the death benefit of £1 million to the trustees. It then transpired that in 1989 and 1990 he had found the premiums from a fund which he held on another trust of which he was a trustee. It was a disputed question whether the same was true of the 1988 premium. The plaintiff was a beneficiary under that trust. He sought a summary judgment against the surviving trustees of the policy, claiming that his trust was entitled to the £1 million as the traceable product of the money misapplied by Murphy. At first instance Laddie J found that the trust which had been pilfered was entitled to 53.46% of the death benefit.

Held (Morritt LJ diss): The trial judge ought to have gone no further than to allow the plaintiff a lien on the £1 million for the amount of the premiums actually taken from the trust, together with interest.

Decision: Sir Richard Scott V-C answered the tracing question in favour of the plaintiff: "Since the purchasers can trace their money into the proceeds of the policy, the next question is as to the nature of the interest in the proceeds that they can claim". He nevertheless concluded, on the claiming question, that the trust was only entitled to a lien for the amount of the premiums. Hobhouse LJ held that, construing the terms of the policy, it was incorrect to say that the money of the plaintiff's trust was traceable to the £1 million, because, under those terms, the death benefit had already been earned by the payment of the earlier premiums. The payments were factually and legally irrelevant to the right under the policy to recover the £1m. The proceeds of the policy were not increased by the use of the trust monies. Nevertheless, the trust was entitled to a lien for the premiums, either "directly" or "by way of subrogation" to the rights of indemnity and lien of Mr Murphy.

Per Morritt LJ, dissenting: The death benefit was traceably the product of all five premiums, so that the plaintiff could trace into it to the extent and in the proportion that he could show that those premiums had been taken from the trust (pp 327G–H, 332H). On that basis the claiming question was determined by the analogy of the purchase of any ordinary asset with trust money or partly with trust money and partly with the trustee's own money (pp 331B–333B). The plaintiff's trust was therefore entitled to a proportionate share in the £1 million.

Comment: As will be apparent, the judgments in this case are confused, and it as well that the case is going to the House of Lords. Scott V-C's conclusion that the plaintiff's had only a lien is based on reasoning which contradicts his answer to the tracing question. As to Hobhouse LJ, in the light of his position on the tracing question, it is difficult to see how the lien could be explained as arising "directly". The only defensible position is that taken by the dissentient, Morritt LJ.

101. *Ghana Commercial Bank v C and Others* [1997] *The Times* Mar 3 (ChD: Peter Leaver QC).
Application for service out of jurisidiction – action to recover stolen monies or proceeds of stolen monies – personal and proprietary claims – whether fiduciary relationship necessary for tracing claim.

This was an application for leave to serve out of jurisdiction. RSC Ord 11, r 1(1)(t) allows such applications where *inter alia* "the claim is brought for money had and received or for an account or other relief against the defendant as constructive trustee, and the defendant's alleged liability arises out of acts committed, whether by him or otherwise, within the jurisdiction". The plaintiff bank had sent 12 books of bankers' drafts from their office in London to their head office in Accra. Only 11 of the books had arrived. The bank contended that, through a series of transactions, part of the proceeds of the missing drafts had been transferred into the account of the first and second defendants, and another part had been paid into the account of the third defendant. The bank now sought to recover monies in the defendants' accounts or to trace those monies into other accounts into which transfers had been made or into other property purchased with those monies. The plaintiff did not assert that any of the defendants knew of the theft of the drafts at the time of transfers. While conceding that there could be no personal liability at the time of transfer, the bank argued that the fiduciary relationship necessary for a tracing claim in equity would arise from the theft of the bankers draft. Thus the bank had a proprietary claim from the moment of receipt and a personal claim from the moment of knowledge thereafter.

Held: Leave to serve out of jurisdiction granted.

Decision: The bank had demonstrated a good arguable case that the defendants were constructive trustees within Ord 11, r 1(1)(t) and that their alleged liability arose out of acts committed within the jurisdiction. The words "constructive trustee" should be construed as referring to a constructieve trustee against whom a personal claim could be made as well as one against whom a proprietary claim could be made.

102. *Guinness Mahon v Kensington and Chelsea RBC* [1998] 2 All ER 272 (CA: Morritt, Waller and Robert Walker LJJ).
Void contract – contract completely exectuted – whether unjust enrichment claim lies.

This was an interest rate swap agreement which, unlike that in *Westdeutsche Landesbank Girozentrale v Islington LBC* [1996] AC 669, had completely run its course by the time the House of Lords in 1991 had declared such agreements ultra vires and void. It was therefore a "closed" rather than an "open" swap. The Court of Appeal in *Westdeutsche* had held that there was a common law claim to restitution in the case of an open swap; that finding was not challenged on appeal. The question now for the Court of Appeal was whether payments made under a closed swap were likewise recoverable. The local authority argued they were not, on the ground that the open swap cases were examples of recovery on the ground of a failure of consideration, albeit a partial failure of consideration, whereas in the case of a closed swap the condition for the payment could in no way be said to have failed.

Held: No distinction was to be drawn between payments made under an open swap and those under a closed swap. Recovery was to be allowed in both cases.

Decision: In the case of a contract void from the start there must for that reason be a total failure of consideration. The very fact that the contract is ultra vires constitutes the total failure of consideration which justifies the remedy of money had and received or restitution for unjust enrichment. If partial performance of that assumed obligation in the case of an open swap does not preclude a total failure of that consideration, then there is no basis on which complete performance of a closed swap could do so.

Comment: The Court of Appeal has once again fallen into the trap of using the contractual rather than the restitutionary meaning of the word "consideration", despite the correction of this mistake more than fifty years ago by the House of Lords in *Fibrosa Spolka Akcyjna v Fairburn Lawson Combe Barbour Ltd* [1943] AC 32. The sooner a substitute is found for this misleading word the better. See further §103 *Comment*.

103. *Kleinwort Benson Ltd v Birmingham City Council (No 2)* Hearing 9–16 Mar 1998 (HL: Lords Goff of Chieveley, Browne-Wilkinson, Lloyd of Berwick, Hoffmann and Hope of Craighead); leapfrog appeal from QB (Langley J in Chambers).
Bank entering into interest rate swap agreements with local authorities – agreements ultra vires local authorities – bank bringing restitutionary claims to recover monies paid under a mistake of law – availability of restitutionary remedy – limitation – Limitation Act 1980, s 32(1)(c).
  Comment: Not to be confused with *Kleinwort Benson v Birmingham City Council* [1997] QB 380, this case comprises consolidated leapfrog appeals from an unreported judgment in Chambers by Langley J, providing the House of Lords with the opportunity to reconsider the rule in *Bilbie v Lumley* (1802) 2 East 469 against the recoverability of payments made under mistake of law and its ramifications, which will also affect the decision in *Guinness Mahon v Kensington & Chelsea RBC* §102. At the time of writing, the House of Lords has not handed down its judgment, which will be reviewed in P Birks (ed), *Lessons of the Swaps Litigation* (Mansfield Press, Oxford, forthcoming) §148.

104. *Kleinwort Benson v Glasgow City Council* [1997] 3 WLR 923; [1997] 4 All ER 641 (HL: Lord Goff, Lord Mustill, Lord Nicholls, Lord Clyde and Lord Hutton). Noted: Dickinson [1998] RLR 104; Peel [1998] LMCLQ 22; Pitel [1998] CLJ 19.
Void contract – conflict of laws – whether English court has jurisdiction where defendant Scottish – whether claim a "matter relating to contract".
In 1982 a Scottish local authority entered into a number of interest rate swap agreements with an English bank. In 1991 the House of Lords declared that such agreements were ultra vires the powers of the local authorities and void. The bank thereupon brought an action in restitution in England to recover sums it had paid over pursuant to the void contract. The local authority challenged the jurisdiction of the English courts to resolve the dispute, arguing that, since it was domiciled in Scotland, it should be sued in that country. The bank argued, it was excepted from the normal rule that a defendant be sued in his place of domicile because the claim was in respect of matters relating to a contract the place of performance of which was England within the terms of the Convention on Jurisdiction and the Enforcement of Judgments in Civil and Commercial Matters 1968, art 5(1).
  Held: The English courts did not have jurisdiction to entertain the bank's claim.
  Decision (Lords Mustill and Nicholls dissenting): A claim could only fall within art 5(1) if it was based on a particular contractual obligation, the place of performance of which was within the jurisdiction of the court. In the instant case, however, the plaintiff's claim was for the recovery of money paid under a supposed contract which in law never existed and so was not based on a contractual obligation but was a claim for restitution based on the principle of unjust enrichment. Accordingly, since no express provision was made in respect of such claims in art 5, and it was legitimate to infer that that omission was due to the absence of any connecting factors consistently linking such claims to any jurisdiction other than the defendant's domicile, it followed that the plaintiff's claim did not fall within art 5(1).
  Comment: The reason why the bank wanted to sue in England rather than Scotland was because of more beneficial limitation provisions. First, the limitation period in England is six rather than five years. But second, and more importantly, for a claim based on mistake, the limitation period in England does not begin to run until the mistake was or should have been discovered. On the facts of the case, therefore, no limitation period whatever would have applied had the case been brought in England, assuming of course that mistake of law is a good ground

of restitutionary claim in England. That question is at present being litigated in the case of *Kleinwort Benson v Birmingham (No 2)* §103.

105. *Mohamed v Alaga & Co (a firm)* [1998] 2 All ER 720 (Ch D: Lightman J).
Illegality – void contract – claim for work done under contract – whether restitutionary claim would defeat the policy lying behind the invalidity of the contract.
The plaintiff, a leading member of the Somali community in the United Kingdom, agreed with the defendants, a firm of solicitors that he would introduce refugee Somali nationals to them, that they would apply for Legal Aid on the refugees' behalf, and that they would pay over to the plaintiff one half of all fees so received. Although 243 such refugees were introduced by the plaintiff, the defendants did not honour their side of the agreement. To the plaintiff's contractual and restitutionary claim the defendants relied on the fact that the sharing of solicitors' fees was prohibited by statute.

Held: The plaintiff had no claim in either contract or restitution.

Decision: No claim in restitution was available where statute forbade the making of the contract and the grant of the remedy was a method of nullifying the statutory provision. A claim in restitution had to be limited, by virtue of the provisions of the contract, to a payment out of the fees received from the referred clients, and any such payment had therefore to involve a sharing of those fees, which was itself prohibited. Even if the payments were not necessarily to be paid out of the fees received, none the less it would in substance be a payment in consideration of the introduction of clients. Such payment accordingly would be in breach of statute.

Comment: It is hard to see why the content of the restitutionary claim should be thought of as governed by the illegal contract. The claim was simply for reasonable remuneration for the work done in introducing clients to the firm. It seems correct, however, that the claim was denied as one which, if allowed, would circumvent the policy of the statute which rendered the contract void.

106. *Rochester upon Medway City Council v Kent County Council* [1998] *The Times* Mar 5 (QBD: Sullivan J).
Ultra vires payments – whether recoverable as paid for "no consideration".
Kent County Council (County) had proposed the Third Medway Crossing, by way of a tunnel, in the mid-1980s so as to relieve traffic congestion in the Medway towns and to encourage the economic regeneration of that part of Kent following the closure of the Chatham Royal Navy base in 1984. On the assumption that central government funding would not be available for such a project, Rochester upon Medway City Council (City) agreed to make annual contributions towards the costs incurred by County under a lease finance initiative (the main agreement), and, under the Highways Act 1974, s 274, to make two advance lump sum payments of £2 million towards existing highway schemes in the area on the basis that, in return for such payments, City's annual contributions under the main agreement would be reduced (the side agreement). The purpose of the latter was to avoid government-imposed forward funding restrictions. When central government subsequently agreed to support the Medway crossing, the need for contributions from City ceased and they sought restitution of the payments already made.

Held: The payments were recoverable.

Decision: It was unnecessary to decide whether the change in funding arrangements had resulted in the obligations under the main and side agreements being frustrated because, in any event, the power to make contributions under the Highways Act 1974, s 274 only extended to existing highway schemes. The contribution here was therefore an unlawful exercise of the council's powers. Accordingly, City were entitled to claim that there had been no consideration. County were not justified in retaining the money, which was to be repaid in full.

Comment: Although the judge relied on Lord Goff's speech in *Westdeutsche Landesbank Girozentrale v Islington LBC* [1996] AC 669 for the proposition that "absence of consideration" is a ground of restitutionary claim, even the briefest of readings of that case shows that that proposition is far from secure.

107. *Royal Bank of Scotland Plc v Etridge* [1997] 3 All ER 628 (CA: Hobhouse and Mummery LJJ). Noted Birks and Swadling [1997] All ER Rev 397; Price (1998) 114 LQR 186.
Undue influence – solicitor acting for wife and mortgagee – Whether wife had obtained independant legal advice.
This is yet another case from the *Barclay's Bank v O'Brien* stable. Mrs Etridge sought to set aside a security she had granted on the ground that the solicitor from whom she obtained advice was not independent of her husband and had never advised her other than in her husband's presence. In interlocutory proceedings, the trial judge ruled that this was not an arguable defence and granted a possession order to the bank.
Held: The possession order was discharged.
Decision: Where the solicitor was also appointed by the bank to act for itself in completing the mortgage, the bank had to be taken to know of any defects in the process. Since the bank delegated their task to their own solicitor, they were responsible for his discharge of that duty. If he did not discharge it, then they must accept that situation since they are in the same position as their agent. The only evidence was, at present, from the wife, who says that he did not.
Comment: This case was decided *per incuriam* the court's earlier but at the time unreported decision in *Barclay's Bank Plc v Thomson* [1997] 4 All ER 816, in which the Court of Appeal seems to accept that solicitors in advising a wife are acting for her and not as the agent of the bank.

108. *Silverwood v Silverwood* (1997) 74 P & CR 453 (CA: Nourse, Peter Gibson LJJ, Sir Patrick Russell).
Resulting trust – illegality – evidence of fraudulent design led to counter allegation of gift – whether evidence properly admitted.
A woman aged 88 transferred money into the names of her grandchildren with the intention of defrauding the Department of Social Security of Income Support payments. The fraud was successful and the benefits were paid. On her death, the plaintiff, the will beneficiary, claimed to be entitled to the monies so paid on the basis that, since voluntary, the payments were held by the grandchildren on resulting trust. The grandchildren argued that the payments had been made as a gift. The plaintiff led evidence of the fraud to counter this contention. The grandchildren argued that the trial judge was wrong to admit the evidence of fraud.
Held: The monies were held on resulting trust for the deceased's estate.
Decision: The test established by the House of Lords in *Tinsley v Milligan* [1994] 1 AC 340 was whether of necessity reliance was placed by a claimant on illegality in proving his claim. It would be absurd as well as unjust if a claimant, claiming a resulting trust, could not lead evidence of fraud in order to disprove a spurious defence. The relevance of the plaintiff's evidence was that it rebutted the defence of gift. Therefore, as the plaintiff was not forced to plead or rely on illegality in order to establish the estate's claim, he was entitled under a resulting trust.
Comment: This is a logical and uncontroversial extension of *Tinsley v Milligan*. However, it also shows the absurd results to which the reasoning in that decision can lead, for, as Nourse LJ pointed out, this being an executed fraudulent design, had the payments been made by the deceased to her son rather than her grandchild, the presumption of advancement would have applied (query whether this is correct – the orthodox view of English law is that there is no presumption of advancement between *mother* and child) and the payments could have been retained.

109. *Stocznia Gdanksa SA v Latvian Shipping Co* [1998] 1 WLR 574; [1998] 1 All ER 883 (HL: Lord Goff, Lord Lloyd, Lord Hoffmann, Lord Hope and Lord Hutton); noted Jaffey [1998] RLR 157; McMeel [1998] LMCLQ 308; Beatson & Tolhurst [1998] CLJ 253.
Shipbuilding contract – rescission – whether instalments due before rescission still payable – whether total failure of consideration.
The plaintiff shipbuilders entered into several agreements to design, build, complete and deliver ships for the defendant. Under each agreement property in the vessel did not pass to the defendants until delivery. The price was to be paid in four instalments, with 20% being paid after the plaintiffs gave notice that "the first and second sections of the Vessel's hull had been joined on the berth where the vessel is being constructed". After the keel of vessel 1 had been laid, a keel laying notice was served on the defendants and, when they failed to pay the instalment, the plaintiffs served a notice exercising their contractual right to rescind the contract "if the Purchaser defaults in the payment of any amount due to the Seller". The same happened with vessel 2. The plaintiffs commenced an action against the defendants, claiming the second instalment in respect of vessels 1 and 2. The judge granted the plaintiffs summary judgment in respect of the second instalments of the price for vessels 1 and 2, holding that the instalments remained due and owing despite the rescission of the two contracts. The defendants had argued that these payments, if made, would be immediately recoverable on the ground that they were paid for a consideration which had totally failed. However, the judge held that there had not been a total failure of consideration, because the contacts were not just for the sale, but also for the construction of the vessels. After a successful appeal to the Court of Appeal on another point, a further appeal was taken to the House of Lords.
Held: The appeal on this point would be dismissed.
Decision: Where a shipyard's contractual duties under a shipbuilding contract included the design and construction of the vessel, as well as the duty to transfer the finished object to the buyers, the design and construction of the vessel formed part of the consideration for which the price was to be paid. Accordingly, the fact that the contract had been brought to an end before the property in the vessel or any part of it had passed to the buyers did not prevent the shipyard from asserting that there had not been a total failure of consideration in respect of an instalment of the price which had been paid before the contract was terminated, or that an instalment which had then accrued due could not, if paid, be recoverable on that ground. Since in the instant case the design and construction of the vessels formed part of the plaintiff's duties under the contracts, it followed that they were entitled to assert that there had not been a total failure of consideration, notwithstanding that property in the vessels had not passed to the defendants.
Comment: The only remarkable thing about this case is that, in the light of *Goss v Chilcott* [1996] AC 788, it seems to have been assumed by all concerned that nothing less than a total failure of consideration was enough to trigger restitution, for there can be no doubt that there was a partial failure on the facts of the case.

110. *Taylor v Dickens* [1997] *The Times* Nov 24 (ChD: Judge Weeks QC).
Estoppel – promise to leave property by will – whether requirement of belief that will would not be revoked before death.
In 1988 the deceased told the plaintiff, her part-time gardener, that she intended to leave him her house in her will, whereupon he declared that he would not receive any payment for his gardening or the other help he provided thereafter. The deceased subsequently executed at least three wills, in which she left her residuary estate to the plaintiff. However, in her fourth and latest will she left him nothing, although she did not inform the plaintiff of this change of mind. During the seven years prior to her death, the plaintiff provided care for the deceased in many ways and received no remuneration for his services. He now claimed to be entitled to the residuary estate on the basis of proprietary estoppel.

Held: The claim failed.

Decision: Where one person believed that he would be granted a right over another's property in the future in a situation where the promisor still had a right to change his mind, in order to establish the requisite unconscionability for proprietary estoppel, the promisee had to prove that the promisor had created or encouraged a belief that he would not exercise that right and that the promisee had relied on that belief. In the present case, the plaintiff knew that the wills were revocable and that the deceased might change her mind.

Comment: This decision is clearly wrong, for the judge seems to have forgotten that the whole point of estoppel claims is that they concern promises which, since they are unsupported by consideration, are initially revocable. What later makes them binding, and therefore irrevocable, is the promisee's detrimental reliance on them. Once that occurs, there is simply no question of the promisor changing his or her mind. The case as pleaded had nothing to do with the Law of Unjust Enrichment, though it is possible to speculate as to the availability of a restitutionary claim on the facts in the light of the failure of the expectation claim.

LAW REFORM

112. Law Commission: *Damages for Personal Injury: Collateral Benefits* (LCCP 147) (1997).
This Consultation Paper seeks views on the issue whether a personal injury tort victim should be forced to give credit to the tortfeasor for benefits received from another source. Its main proposal is that, subject to cases where the provider of the collateral benefit has a right to recover the value of the benefit from the tortfeasor by being subrogated to the victim's undischarged tort claim, collateral benefits, unless essentially coincidental, should be deducted from damages which meet the same aim. The Commission also seek views on the question whether the provider of the benefit should have an automatic right of recovery against the tortfeasor. They say that the arguments both for and against are finely balanced. The full text of this consultation paper is available free on the Internet at: http://www.gtnet.gov.uk/lawcomm/homepage.htm

113. Law Commission: *Aggravated, Exemplary and Restitutionary Damages* (LC 247) (1997).
The Law Commission makes various recommendations concerning reform of the law of aggravated and exemplary damages. As to restitutionary damages, the Commission recommends no legislative intervention but favours judicial development. The report does contain, however, a very useful account of the incidence of restitutionary damages in the present law. The full text of this report is available free on the Internet at: http://www.gtnet.gov.uk/lawcomm/homepage.htm

114. Law Commission: *Limitation of Actions: A Consultation Paper* (LCCP 151) (1998).
In this consultation paper the Law Commission recommends a "core regime" for the topic of limitation of actions, included in which are "restitutionary actions". The central features of such a regime would be fourfold: (1) there would be an initial limitation period of three years that would run from when the plaintiff knows, or ought reasonably to know, that he or she has a cause of action; (2) there would be a long-stop limitation period of 10 years, or in personal injury claims of 30 years, that would run from the date of the act or omission which gives rise to the claim; (3) the plaintiff's disability (including supervening disability) would extend the initial limitation period; adult disability would not extend the long-stop limitation period, though deliberate concealment (initial and subsequent) would; acknowledgements and part payments should start time running again but not once the initial or long-stop limitation period has expired; (4) the courts would *not* have a discretion to disapply the limitation period. The full text of this consultation paper is available free on the Internet at: http://www.gtnet.gov.uk/lawcomm/home page.htm

ARTICLES AND NOTES

115. Bant, E, " 'Ignorance' as a Ground of Restitution – Can it Survive?" [1998] LMCLQ 18.
The author takes issue in particular with Grantham and Rickett in [1996] LMCLQ 465 and more generally with Birks over whether there is a ground of restitution called "ignorance".

116. Barnsley, D G, "Conveyancing Liens" [1997] Conv 336.
Of interest to restitution lawyers is the extensive treatment of the lien of the purchaser of land for the return of his deposit.

117. Birks, P, "Notice and Onus in *O'Brien*" (1998) 12 TLI 2.
A detailed search for the exact juridical basis of the doctrine in *Barclay's Bank Plc v O'Brien* via the recent decision of the Court of Appeal in *Barclay's Bank Plc v Boulter* §92.

118. Birks, P, and Swadling, W, "Restitution" [1997] All ER Rev 385.
A discussion of all restitution cases reported in [1997] All ERs.

119. Burrows, AS, "Restitution: Where Do We Go From Here?" (1997) 50 CLP 25.
This lecture, given as part of a series entitled "Law and Opinion at the End of the Twentieth Century", asks three questions: (1) where have we got to with the law of restitution? (2) how have we got to here? (3) where do we go from here?

120. Coote, B, "Contract Damages, *Ruxley*, and the Performance Interest" [1997] CLJ 537.
A general discussion of the question of damages measured by the cost of cure, including a short examination of whether a claim to the defendant's saving of expense would be an explanation of the phenomonem.

121. Degeling, S, "Carers and Victims: The Law's Dilemna" (1997) 11 TLI 30.
This article sets out to defend the highly anomalous finding of a trust in favour of a carer over the damages award made to an accident victim in *Hunt v Severs* [1994] 2 AC 350. The author suggests that the result is explicable in terms of the rules of subrogation by drawing an analogy with the position of an indemnity insurer.

122. Evans, Sir William, edited by Smith, LD, "Essay on the Action for Money Had and Received" (1802) [1998] RLR 1.
An edited republication of an Essay from *Essays: On the Action for Money Had and Received, on the Law of Insurances, and on the Law of Bills of Exchange and Promissory Notes* (Liverpool, 1802) by Sir William Evans, apparently the first writer in the common law tradition to accept that unjust enrichment can be a source of obligations. The structure of the Essay appears to have been derived from a passage in *Moses v Macferlan* (1760) 2 Burr 1005, the decision in which, in the light of the principle of *res judicata*, is criticised. There is also discussion of recoverability of payments under void contracts, including analysis of the annuities cases, the importance of which has recently been rediscovered: *eg Guinness Mahon v Kensington & Chelsea RBC* §102. Most topically, the author gives an invaluable account of the law on restitution for mistake of law, which the author supported, immediately prior to *Bilbie v Lumley* (1802) 2 East 469. The rule has been reconsidered this year in *Kleinwort Benson v Birmingham City Council (No 2)* §103, in the hearing of which this Essay was considered.

123. Forsyth, C, "Characterisation Revisited: An Essay in the Theory and Practice of the English Conflict of Laws" (1998) 114 LQR 141.
Although directed mainly at conflicts lawyers, this article will be of interest to restitution lawyers

because of its use of *Macmillan Inc v Bishopsgate Investment Trust plc (No 3)* [1996] 1 WLR 387 as its central example.

124. Martin, J, "Recipient Liability After *Westdeutsche*" [1998] Conv 13.
The author's thesis is that, despite Lord Browne-Wilkinson's *obiter* comments on the fault-based nature of the constructive trust in *Westdeutsche Landesbank Girozentrale v Islington LBC* [1996] AC 669, there is still room to argue for a regime of strict liability for the recipients of misdirected funds.

125. Millett, Sir Peter, "Equity's Place in the Law of Commerce" (1998) 114 LQR 214.
In the first part of this two-part article, the author expands on his judgment in *Bristol & West BS v Mothew* §95 and discusses the question of liability for breach of fiduciary duty, in particular the questions of causation and remoteness. The second part of the article will discuss Restitution and Constructive Trusts.

126. Panagopoulos, G, "Cross-Border Tracing" [1998] RLR 73.
There is no clear guidance on the question of how to treat international tracing, *ie* tracing in the context of claims involving international elements. Tracing has been described as a process; yet for the purposes of private international law tracing should be characterised as a substantial and not a procedural issue. There is no logic in applying the different tracing rules of the *lex fori* in circumstances where the *lex causae* would or would not have allowed a claim contingent on tracing. Furthermore, although a substantial issue, tracing should not be characterised as a separate issue, thereby attracting its own choice of law rule. Tracing is not a source of rights. It is an extension of rights with an independent source. The logical approach is to apply the choice of law rule applicable to the claim contingent on tracing. Thus, where the relevant issue arising under a claim is characterised as restitutionary, this will be the law of the restitutionary obligation; where the issue is characterised as proprietary, this will be the choice of law rule in relation to the particular property to which the claim relates. The above approach should apply irrespective of whether the tracing rules at law or equity apply. The existence of distinct tracing rules should be inconsequential as a matter of private international law.

127. Rose, FD, "General Average as Restitution" (1997) 113 LQR 569.
A short note in which the author considers whether the law of general average can be considered as part of the law of restitution.

128. Rose, FD, "Illegality Limited" (1998) 8 KCLJ 69.
An account of those situations in which the defence of illegality will not be available to restitutionary claims.

129. Smith, SA, "Contracting Under Pressure: A Theory of Duress" [1997] CLJ 343.
The author presents a framework for understanding pressure cases. Three related arguments run through it. First, the fact that a party contracts under pressure raises two factually related but conceptually distinct concerns, one for wrongdoing and one for autonomy. Second, the concept of free choice or consent is meaningful in its own right and thus is distinct not only from the notion of wrongdoing but also from other normative concepts such as wealth maximisation, distributive justice and substantive unfairness. Third, it is crucial to maintain a clear distinction between a concern for wrongdoing and a concern for autonomy because while they often support the same result in particular cases, their scope and force are not identical.

130. Stagg, P, "The Social Security (Overpayments) Act 1996" (1997) 4 *Journal of Social Security Law* 155.
The author considers the implications of the Social Security (Overpayments) Act 1996. He explains the application of the recovery provisions and highlights the new procedural pitfalls facing those seeking to challenge overpayment recovery decisions.

131. Tettenborn, A, "Absolving the Undeserving: Shopping Centres, Specific Performance and the Law of Contract" [1998] Conv 23.
The article focuses on the recent decision of the House of Lords in *Co-operative Insurance Society Ltd v Argyll Plc* [1998] AC 1 to refuse specific performance of a "keep-open" clause in a lease of a shopping centre. One of the reasons for doing so was the fear that the plaintiff would be "unjustly enriched" in that they could extract for the release of the order a sum greater than their actual loss from non-performance. The author questions whether on the actual facts of the case such a mismatch was likely to occur.

132. Tettenborn, A, "Third Party Cheques — Security or Snare" [1998] RLR 63.
The author examines payments made by means of building society cheques, under which the received wisdom has it that payment is guaranteed. He examines whether such confidence might be misplaced, and considers the argument that in two situations at least, where the payer obtained the instrument from the building society by fraud, or where, even in the absence of fraud, the consideration provided by the payer for the issue of the instrument fails, the building society would be entitled not to pay out on the cheque. He concludes, however, that as long as the payee gives consideration (other than by accepting it in discharge of a pre-existing obligation) for the instrument he can enforce it and can have neither fraud nor failure of consideration pleaded against him.

133. Ulph, J, "The Proprietary Consequences of an Excess Delivery" [1998] LMCLQ 4.
This short note considers the proprietary consequences of an excess delivery, and, where the vendor is acting under mistake, considers whether any restitutionary questions need to be resolved.

134. Virgo, GJ, "The Law of Restitution and the Proceeds of Crime — A Survey of English Law" [1998] RLR 34.
This article seeks to show that there is a coherent body of law founded on the principle that no criminal should be allowed to benefit from the commission of the crime and that this properly forms part of the law of restitution. The author surveys the law on restitution of the proceeds of crime in three particular circumstances. First, where the victim of the crime wishes to bring proceedings to recover the proceeds of crime from the criminal, the author suggests that the victim's restitutionary claim can be founded on the commission of the crime itself and contemplates that the development of the constructive trust will be of particular importance in this area. Secondly, the statutory mechanisms for depriving the criminal of the proceeds of crime are examined. Finally, the author examines the circumstances when the criminal can be prevented from obtaining the proceeds of crime at all, with particular reference to the forfeiture rule.

BOOKS

135. Birks, P, (ed) *Privacy and Loyalty*. OUP, Oxford, 1997. Reviewed DM MacLean (1998) 72 ALJ 317.
This book contains the papers from two conferences. Those from the second, concerned with Fiduciary Relationships, will be of most interest to Restitution lawyers. The papers are: Fiduciary Obligations and Fiduciary Powers – Where Are We Going? (*Charles Harpum*); The Flight to Fiduciary Haven (*Laura Hoyano*); Constructive Fiduciaries? (*Lionel Smith*); The Identification of Fiduciaries (*John Glover*); Fiduciaries in Context: An Overview (*David Hayton*).

136. Birks, P, (ed) *The Classification of Obligations.* OUP, Oxford, 1997.
Of particular interest to restitution lawyers will be the editor's essay entitled "Definition and Division: A Mediation on *Institutes* 3.13".

137. Burrows, A, and McKendrick, E, *Cases and Materials on the Law of Restitution.* OUP, Oxford, 1997. Reviewed by Hedley [1998] CLJ 220; O'Dell [1998] RLR 287.
A case-book of over 900 pages on the Law of Restitution.

138. Cranston, R, (ed) *Making Commercial Law: Essays in Honour of Roy Goode.* OUP, Oxford, 1997. Reviewed by Munday [1998] CLJ 222.
A collection of essays on commercial law offered as a *Festschrift* to Roy Goode. Of particular interest to readers of this *Review* will be the essays by Peter Birks, "The Necessity of a Unitary Law of Tracing", and Ewan McKendrick, "Local Authorities and Swaps: Undermining the Market?".

139. Dagan, H, *Unjust Enrichment: A Study of Private Law and Public Values.* CUP, Cambridge, 1997.
The author's blurb for this book reads as follows: "This book presents a comparative analysis of the doctrine of unjust enrichment in the North American and Jewish legal systems and in international law. . . . Applying both theoretical analysis and comparative legal techniques, the study claims that the choice of compensation [sic] arising from a claim of unjust enrichment is not a matter of legal technicality. Instead, it describes how the legal choice of a pecuniary remedy can be seen to embody a choice between competing values. This decision . . . is implicated in the prevailing background ethos of the society at issue, and is deeply influenced by its own complex conceptions of self and of community."

140. Fehlberg, B, *Sexually Transmitted Debt.* OUP, Oxford, 1997.
An empirical study of the problem of wives standing surety for their husband's debts.

141. Harris, J, (ed) *Property Problems: From Genes to Pension Funds.* Kluwer, London, 1998.
A collection of essays on the law of property, including W Swadling, "Property and Unjust Enrichment", in which the argument is made that restitution should almost never be effected by the award of rights *in rem*.

142. Palmer, NE, and McKendrick, E, (eds) *Interests in Goods.* 2nd ed, Lloyd's of London Press, London, 1998.
A revised and updated collection of essays on Personal Property. Of particular interest to restitution lawyers will be the following: Bona Vacantia (*Andrew Bell*); Mixtures (*Peter Birks*); The Title Obligations of the Seller of Goods (*Michael Bridge*); Conditional Gifts (*Robert Chambers*); Pledge (*Norman Palmer and Anthony Hudson*); Solicitors' Liens (*Anthony Hudson*); Conversion, Tort and Restitution (*Andrew Tettenborn*); Money Claims for Misuse of Chattels (*Anthony Hudson*); Restitution and the Misuse of Chattels (*Ewan McKendrick*); Improving Stolen Chattels (*Norman Palmer and Anthony Hudson*); Equitable Liens (*John Phillips*).

143. Rose, FD (ed), *Blackstone's Statutes on Contract, Tort and Restitution* **(9th ed).** Blackstone Press, London, 1998.
This edition includes the text of the Late Payment of Commercial Debts (Interest) Act 1998 and the Draft Damages Bill appended to the Law Commission Report on *Aggravated, Exemplary and Restitutionary Damages* §113.

144. Rose, F (ed), *Failure of Contracts: Contractual, Restitutionary and Proprietary Consequences.* Hart Publishing, Oxford, 1997. Reviewed Tettenborn [1998] RLR 290.

Contains the proceedings from a conference held in Cambridge in September 1996. The papers were: Loss and Gain at Greater Depth: The Implications of the *Ruxley* Decision (*Janet O'Sullivan*); Remedies for Breach of Contract: Specific Performance and Restitution (*Richard Nolan*); The Proprietary Consequences of Contract Failure (*Sarah Worthington*); Restitution Under Article 85(2) of the EC Treaty: Can it be Done? (*Felicity Toube*); Restitution for Termination of Contract in German Law (*Gerhard Dannemann*); Failure of Long-Term Contracts and the Duty to Re-negotiate (*Erich Schanze*); Le Mythe de la Responsabilité Contractuelle en Droit Francais (*Christian Lapoyade Deschamps*); Contract, Unjustified Enrichment and Concurrent Liability: A Scots Perspective (*Hector MacQueen*); Contracts and Restitution: A Few Comparative Remarks (*Eltjo Schrage*); Restitution: Contract's Twin? (*Steve Hedley*). The book also contains commentaries on most of these papers and a bibliography of the publications of Professor Sir Guenter Treitel.

145. Rose, FD, *General Average: Law and Practice.* LLP, London, 1997.

An integrated account of the common law and practical rules governing a subject at the intersection of Carriage of Goods by Sea, Marine Insurance and Restitution.

146. Rose, FD (ed), *Restitution and Banking Law.* Mansfield Press, Oxford, 1998.

The revised and expanded proceedings of the SPTL Restitution Section Seminar on *Restitution and Banking Law* held at Warwick in Sep 1998. Papers include "Unauthorised Payment and Unjust Enrichment in Banking Law" (Justice Deon van Zyd), "Distributing the Burden of Alternative Coextensive Liabilities" (Charles Mitchell), "Undue Influence and Misrepresentation after *O'Brien*: Making Security Secure" (Janet O'Sullivan and Graham Virgo), "*O'Brien*, Notice and the Burden of Proof" (Kit Barker), "Cross-Border Security Enforcement and the Conflict of Laws" (Gabriel Moss QC and Felicity Toube), "Cross-Border Security Enforcement, Restitution and Priorities" (Nick Segal), "Tracing and Electronic Fund Transfers" (Lionel Smith), "Assisting a Breach of Duty by a Fiduciary, the Common Law and Moneylaundering" (Michael Tugenhat QC), "Recovering Misdirected Money from Banks: Ministerial Receipt at Law and in Equity" (Michael Bryan) and "Overview" (Professor Peter Birks QC).

147. Swadling, W, (ed) *The Limits of Restitutionary Claims: A Comparative Analysis.* British Institute of International and Comparative Law, London, 1997, available direct from BICCL, 17 Russell Square, London WC1B 5DR for £25.00. Reviewed Evans-Jones [1998] RLR 291.

This book contains the papers (suitably updated) given at a meeting in 1993 of common and civil lawyers. They are: Unjust Enrichment Claims: A Comparative Analysis (*Brice Dickson*); Change of Position and Surviving Enrichment (*Peter Birks*); Change of Position and *Wegfall der Bereicherung* (*Heinrich Dörner*); Restitution and Bona Fide Purchase (*William Swadling*); Bona Fide Purchase, Property and Restitution: *Lipkin Gorman* in German law (*Carsten Zülch*); The Effect of Illegality on Claims for Restitution in English Law (*Graham Virgo*); Illegality: The Case for Discretion (*Nili Cohen*); Mistake of Law – Time for a Change? (*Ewan McKendrick*); Mistake of Law: English and Roman Comparisons (*Laurens Winkel*).

OTHER INFORMATION

148. Lessons of the Swaps Litigation. The first Mansfield Symposium, held at All Souls College, Oxford on 29 Nov 1997.

Papers included "The Ground for Restitution" (Professor Ewan McKendrick), "Implications for the Law of Property" (WJ Swadling), "Implications for Contrast and Tort" (Hubert Picarda

QC), "Implications for the Conflict of Laws" (RH Stevens), "Implications for Tracing" (Dr LD Smith) and "Defences to Restitutionary Claims" (Professor PBH Birks QC). The papers will be published by the Mansfield Press in a book (ed P Birks) together with a paper on "Interest" (Professor FD Rose) and a review of the House of Lords decision in *Kleinwort Benson v Birmingham City Council (No 2)* §103.

149. Resulting Trusts: Practical Issues. The second Mansfield Symposium, held at St John's College, Cambridge on 20 Apr 1998.

Papers included "Equitable Ownership and Equitable Interests: Equities and Resulting Trusts" (R Davern), "On the Classification of Trusts" (N McBride), "Dispositions Involving Fiduciaries: The Equity to Rescind and the Resulting Trust" (RJ Nolan), "Resulting Trusts in the Conflict of Laws" (RH Stevens), "A Hard Look at *Hodgson v Marks*" (WJ Swadling) and "Resulting Trusts and Illegality" (GJ Virgo and J O'Sullivan). The papers (ed P Birks), together with a reprint of "Restitution and Resulting Trusts" (P Birks), will be published by the Mansfield Press.

NOTER UP

Banco Exterior Internacional SA v Thomas [1997] 1 WLR 221; [1997] 1 All ER 46; (1996) 75 P&CR S. Noted Birks and Swadling [1997] All ER Rev 393.
Barclay's Bank Plc v Thomson [1997] 4 All ER 816; [1997] 1 FLR 156. Noted Thompson [1997] Conv 217; Price (1998) 114 LQR 186; Birks and Swadling [1997] All ER Rev 396.
Box v Barclays Bank Plc (24 Mar 1998) [1998] *The Times* Apr 30; noted Virgo [1998] (2) *Company, Financial and Insolvency Law Review.*
Cargill International SA v Bangladesh Sugar and Food Industries Corp [1998] 2 All ER 406 (CA). Affg [1996] 4 All ER 563; [1996] 2 Lloyd's Rep 524; [1997] RLR §80.
Co-operative Insurance Society Ltd v Argyll Stores Plc [1998] AC 1; [1997] 2 WLR 988; [1997] 3 All ER 297. Noted McMeel (1998) 114 LQR 43.
Credit Lyonnais Bank Nederland NV v Burch [1997] 1 All ER 144; (1996) 74 P&CR 384. Noted Birks and Swadling [1997] All ER Rev 394.
Hillsdown Holdings Plc v Pensions Ombudsman [1997] 1 All ER 862. Noted Birks and Swadling [1997] All ER Rev 388.
MCC Proceeds Inc v Lehman Bros International (Europe) [1998] *The Times* Jan 14; noted Barker [1998] RLR 150.
Nelson v Rye [1996] 2 All ER 187. Noted J Stevens [1997] Conv 225.
Swindle v Harrison [1997] 4 ALL ER 705; Noted Elliott [1998] RLR 135; Ho (1997) 11 TLI 72.
Ashe, M, and Rider, B, (eds), *International Tracing of Assets* (FT Law & Tax, London, 1997). Reviewed Panagopoulos [1998] RLR 293.
Birks, P (ed), *Laundering and Tracing* (Oxford: OUP, 1995). Reviewed Ogilvie (1997) 76 CBR 275.
Chambers, R, *Resulting Trusts* (OUP, Oxford, 1997). Reviewed Lord Millett [1998] RLR 283.
Howard, C (Gen ed), *Butterworths Moneylaundering Law* (Butterworths, London, 1997). Reviewed Panagopoulos [1998] RLR 294.
McMeel, G, *Casebook on Restitution* (Cavendish, London, 1996). Reviewed O'Dell [1998] RLR 287.
Smith, LD, *The Law of Tracing* (Oxford: OUP, 1997). Reviewed Gillese (1997) 36 Alta LR 285; Sir Robert Walker [1998] RLR 286; Mitchell (1997) 11 TLI 116; Nolan (1998) 114 LQR 331; Tettenborn [1998] CLJ 218.
Tettenborn, AM, *The Law of Restitution in England and Ireland*, **2nd ed** (Cavendish, London, 1997). Reviewed White (1998) 148 NLJ 794.

European Union

Alison Jones*

I. WHERE COMMUNITY LAW REQUIRES A RESTITUTIONARY REMEDY IN PRINCIPLE – RESTITUTION OF CHARGES LEVIED BY A PUBLIC AUTHORITY UNDER NATIONAL RULES IN BREACH OF EUROPEAN COMMUNITY LAW

A. The right to restitution

The case-law of the European Court of Justice (ECJ) has established that, in some situations where Community law and Community rights have been infringed, Community law demands that a plaintiff must, *prima facie*, have a right to restitution. It is settled law that entitlement to the recovery of charges levied by a Member State in breach of Community law is a consequence of, and an adjunct to, the rights conferred on individuals by the Community provisions. The Member State is required, in principle, to repay charges levied in breach of Community law (see *EU Digest* [1996] RLR 190, 192–200, esp §176 *Amministrazione delle Finanze dello Stato v San Giorgio (Case C-199/82)* [1983] ECR 3595).

In the absence of a Community provision (such as a Regulation) governing the matter, however, the principle of national procedural autonomy applies. The relevant national legal system determines the procedural and substantive rules governing the right of recovery subject to the proviso that any rule barring or limiting the right to restitution (a) must not be less favourable than those relating to similar claims of a domestic nature (the principle of non-discrimination) and (b) must not make it virtually impossible or excessively difficult to exercise the right that the national courts are obliged to protect (the principle of effectiveness). This means that, where charges have been levied contrary to Community law, national courts must ensure that those charges are *prima facie* recoverable under the national rules. "Since *Factortame (Case 213/89)*, there can no longer . . . be any doubt that in certain cases Community law may itself directly confer on national judicial authorities the necessary powers in order to ensure effective judicial protection of those rights, even where similar powers do not exist in national law" (Mischo AG in *Francovich v Italy (Cases C-6/90 and C-9/90)* [1991] I ECR 5357, para 53; *R v Secretary of State for Transport, ex p Factortame (Case C-213/89)* [1990] I ECR 2433; see also [1997] RLR 147, 148–149, [1996] RLR 190, 199-200).

Even if no ground of recovery were available in English law, an English court would therefore have to adapt or extend the law to ensure that a restitutionary remedy was available. This obligation may be of particular significance to the English courts since English law does not recognise a general cause of action for restitution for unjust enrichment (the recognition in *Lipkin Gorman (a firm) v Karpnale Ltd* [1991] 2 AC 548 that the principle of unjust enrichment unites all restitutionary claims does not absolve a court from determining the basis of a particular restitutionary claim: Goff and Jones, *The Law of Restitution* 4th ed (1993), 15). Further, the court would be obliged to set aside any rule of national law limiting or barring the right of recovery which could be said to impair the effectiveness of Community law.

---

* Solicitor, Lecturer in Law, King's College, London.

B. National rules and procedures not to be discriminatory and to ensure the effectiveness of Community law

1. Unjust enrichment of the applicant – passing on

In *Just v Danish Ministry for Fiscal Affairs (Case 68/79)* [1980] ECR 501; [1996] RLR §175), the ECJ held that Community law would not prevent a national legal system from disallowing restitution of charges improperly levied where recovery would lead to the "unjust enrichment of the applicant". Furthermore the Court accepted that unjust enrichment of the applicant might occur where the burden of the unlawful charge had been passed on to the plaintiff's customers. The Court has been asked to elaborate on its ruling in several cases subsequent to *Just*: see *eg San Giorgio*. In *Comateb* §150 the ECJ has again been asked to answer questions concerning the compatibility of national rules with Community law.

150. Société Comateb v Directeur Général des douanes et droits indirects (C 192-218/95) [1997] I ECR 165 (Request for a preliminary ruling from the Tribunal d'Instance, Paris).
Dock dues levied contrary to Community law – recovery of charges – legislation requiring the charges to be passed on – damages.
27 companies brought actions against the Director-General of Customs and Indirect Taxes for repayment of dock dues ("*octroi de mer*") levied contrary to Community law. The national court referred questions to the ECJ asking, in essence, whether a Member State could legitimately object to the repayment of the charge on the ground that it has been passed on to the purchaser. In that case the State's legislation actually required the charge to be passed on.

Held: (1) Council Regulation (EEC) No 1430/79 on the repayment or remission of import or export duties applied only in relation to charges etc created by various Community provisions and collected by Member States on behalf of the Community. It did not apply to national taxes, even when levied in breach of Community law (*San Giorgio* [1983] ECR 3595, para 20). (2) Nonetheless the Member State was in principle required to repay charges levied in breach of Community law. Entitlement to the repayment of charges levied by a Member State in breach of Community law was a consequence of, and an adjunct to, the rights conferred on individuals by the Community provisions prohibiting such charges: *San Giorgio*. (3) However, as an exception to that principle, the protection of the Community rights did not require repayment of duties levied in breach of Community law where it was established that the person required to pay such charges has actually passed them on to other persons (see esp *San Giorgio*). In such a case the burden of the charge had been borne not by the trader but by the purchaser to whom the cost had been passed on.

(4) Even if the taxes were designed to be passed on, were normally passed on, or if legislation obliged the tax to be passed on, it could not be assumed in any case that the charge had actually been passed on (even where failure to comply with an obligation to pass on the tax carried a penalty). In the case of indirect taxes it could not be assumed, nor could there be a presumption, that they had been passed on (see *Bianco and Girard v Directeur Général des Douanes et Droits Indirects (Case 378/95)* [1988] ECR 1099). It was for the national courts to determine, in the light of the facts of each case, whether or not the tax had been passed on and, if so, whether reimbursement of the trader would amount to unjust enrichment. If the burden of the charge had only been passed on in part, the national authorities would have to repay the trader the amount not passed on.

(5) If the final consumer could obtain reimbursement through the trader of the amount of the charge passed on to him, that trader must in turn be able to obtain reimbursement from the national authorities.

(6) Even where it had been established that the burden of the charge had been passed on in whole or in part to a purchaser, repayment of the charge would not necessarily lead to the unjust

enrichment of the applicant. It would be compatible with the principles of Community law for national courts to take into consideration the damage which an importer had suffered as a result of the reduced sales and increased prices caused by the unlawful provisions (see *Just* [1980] ECR 501, para 26); (7) The levying of the dock dues could have made the price of products from other parts of the Community significantly higher than the price of local products (which were exempt from the dues) with the result that importers suffered damage. In such circumstances the trader could justly claim that, although the charge has been passed on to the purchaser, the inclusion of that charge in the cost price had, by increasing the price of the goods and reducing sales, caused him damage which excluded, in whole or in part, any unjust enrichment which would otherwise be caused by reimbursement. Where domestic law permitted the trader to plead such damage in the main proceedings, it was for the national court to give such effect to the claim.

(8) Further, irrespective of whether or not the importers had passed on the charges, the traders had, subject to the conditions laid down in *Brasserie du Pêcheur and Factortame (Cases C-46/93 and C-48/93)* [1996] I ECR 1029, to be able to apply to a national court for reparation of loss caused by the levying of charges not due.

Comment: The ECJ has been criticised for accepting that passing on may operate as a defence to a restitutionary claim, since the application of the defence is fraught with difficulties (see [1997] RLR 147, 149). In *Comateb* the Court seems to recognise the difficulties which will arise in the application of the defence and attempts to confront some of those problems. In particular the Court stressed that it had actually to be *established* that the wrongly levied charges have been passed on. It would not be sufficient for a Member State simply to point to legislation which required the charge to be passed on. This reinforces its finding in *San Giorgio* that the onus of establishing that the unlawful levy paid has not been passed on must not be placed on the plaintiff.

Further, the Court recognises that the successful application of a defence of passing on might be precluded where it can be established that, although the sums had been passed on, the application of the higher prices had effected the volume of sales made by the plaintiff and consequently had an out of pocket impact on the plaintiff's profits. However, it seemed to leave the question of whether this factor should be taken into account in the context of the restitutionary claim to the relevant domestic law.

Finally, the Court emphasised that a trader also had to be able to bring an action against the Member State for *damages* in respect of any loss suffered in consequence of that state's breach of its Treaty obligation. The case is thus a further ruling in the line of cases beginning with *Francovich v Italy (Cases C-6/90 and C-9/90)* [1991] I ECR 5357. In these cases the ECJ has recognised the right of individuals to seek compensation from a Member State for loss or damage caused by a failure to implement a directive (*Francovich* itself) or by some other breach of Community law (see esp *Brasserie du Pêcheur* and *Factortame*). To establish liability the plaintiff must show that: the rule of law infringed was intended to confer rights on individuals; the breach of Community law was sufficiently serious; and that there was a direct causal link between the breach and the loss.

The *Comateb* judgment "recognises that repayment or entitlement claims against state authorities and damages claims against the state may co-exist as independent remedies in matters of taxation... Repayment or entitlement claims and damages claims are claims of a different nature, and what is recoverable under each may differ": *Fantask* §152, para 81, Opinion of Jacobs AG.

The restitutionary claim has the advantage that there is no need to establish loss. The action is merely for the recovery of taxes overpaid and the amount recoverable is relatively easy to calculate. However, various defences may bar the claim. For example, the ECJ accepts that Member States may, in the interest of legal certainty and to avoid severe disruption to public finance, impose short limitation periods for the commencement of such claims: *Rewe-Zentralfinanz eG v Landwirtschaftskammer für das Saarland (Case 33/76)* [1976] ECR 1989 and *Bv v Produktschap voor Siergewassen (Case 45/76)* [1976] ECR 2043; [1996] RLR §172. Several Member States apply extremely short time limits in this context (in *Comet*, for example, the Dutch authorities alleged that the claim in respect of charges levied contrary to Community law was barred since no action had been brought within the 30 days prescribed). Alternatively, the claim may be barred where it has been established that the charges have been passed on.

It is now clear that where this occurs the plaintiff may seek instead, bring a damages claim as an *alternative* to the restitutionary claim. "The existence of a wholly independent claim for damages, subject to longer time limits than the comparatively short ones prescribed for restitutionary and enforcement claims in many Member States, is consistent with the different nature of the claim. Its basis is not merely unjust enrichment of the state resulting from simple error ... but a serious violation of individual rights calling for a re-appraisal of the balance between such rights and the collective interest in a measure of legal certainty for the state": *Fantask* §152, para 83, opinion of Jacobs AG. The claim will however, be dependent on complying with the appropriate procedures of national law and satisfying the three criteria set out by the ECJ in *Brasserie du Pêcheur and Factortame*. In a case where charges have been levied contrary to Community law a plaintiff should have no difficulty in establishing that the rule of law infringed was intended to confer rights on that plaintiff. However, there may be some difficulty in establishing that the breach of Community law was sufficiently serious, and severe difficulties in establishing loss and that it was the breach of Community law that caused the loss.

The Court also clearly envisaged that the damages action might be brought *in addition* to a successful restitutionary claim. Thus, a national court will be obliged to ensure that plaintiff is able to recover in respect of loss suffered over and above the amount recovered in the restitutionary claim (see Treitel, *Remedies for Breach of Contract* (1988), 98–100; Birks "Inconsistency between Compensation and Restitution" (1996) 112 LQR 375).

151. ***GT-Link A/S v De Dankse Statsbaner (DSB) (C 242/95)*** [1997] 5 CMLR 601 (Reference from Denmark by the Østre Landsret (Eastern Regional Court) under Article 177).
Compatibility with Community law of surcharge on goods imported from abroad into certain maritime ports and of system of port duties – EC Treaty, arts 95 and 86 – recovery of charges – damages.
The case concerned charges levied by De Dankse Statsbaner (DSB), the Danish state railway (a state-owned undertaking) and the owner of some Danish ports. GT-Link operated ferry routes from ports owned by DSB. Under the terms of the contract conferring on GT-Link the right to use the port, GT-Link was required to pay shipping and goods duties to the port in accordance with regulations in force.

Held: (1) Certain of the charges were contrary to EC Treaty, art 95 (see also *Haahr Petroleum (Case C-90/94)* [1998] 1 CMLR 771). (2) Further, a public undertaking which owned and operated a port and occupied a dominant position in a substantial part of the common market, would be in breach of EC Treaty, art 90, read in conjunction with art 86, where it levied unreasonable port duties. (3) Rules relating to the burden of proving that the conditions for application of art 86 had been satisfied had, in principle, to be governed by national rules. The same principles applied whenever it was necessary to prove breach of a provision of Community law which, like art 86, was capable of having direct effect. The domestic legal system had to determine the rules governing any action brought to safeguard rights which individuals derived from the direct effect of art 86. However, they could not be less favourable than those governing similar domestic actions nor render virtually impossible or excessively difficult the exercise of rights conferred by Community law. Any requirement of proof which has the effect of making it virtually impossible or excessively difficult to secure that repayment of charges levied by a Member State in breach of Community law, was incompatible with Community law: *San Giorgio*. (4) Even within the framework of art 90, art 86 had direct effect and conferred on individuals rights which the national courts had to protect. Persons on whom duties, incompatible with art 90(1) in conjunction with art 86, had been imposed by a public undertaking were in principle entitled to repayment of the duty unduly paid. Entitlement to repayment of those charges was a consequence of and an adjunct to the rights conferred on individuals by the Community provisions prohibiting such charges (*Comateb* §150). The public undertaking (which was responsible to the Danish Minister of Transport and whose budget was governed by the Budget Act) was therefore in principle required to repay charges levied in breach of Community law, except where it was established that the person required to pay such charges has actually passed them on to other persons. (5) Traders could not be prevented from applying to the courts having jurisdiction, in accordance with the appropriate procedures of national law, and, subject to the conditions laid down *Brasserie du Pecheur* and *Factortame*, for reparation of loss caused by the levying of charges not due.

Comment: At first sight this case merely follows the same pattern as in *Comateb* §150. The Court reiterated that Member States must in principle repay duties levied in breach of Community law. What is striking about this judgment, however, is the fact that it concerned one of the Treaty's competition provisions and not one of the Treaty provisions dealing with free movement of goods (such as arts 12, 30 or 95). This is the first judgment in which the ECJ has clearly stated that, where money is paid under a contract which infringes one of the competition rules, that money must, in principle, be repaid.

A key difference between the competition and free movement of goods provisions is that the former impose obligations on both public *and* private entities (they are capable of having horizontal direct effect), whereas the latter imposes obligations only on state entities (they only have vertical direct effect: see *eg Apple and Pear Development Council v KJ Lewis Ltd (Case 222/82)* [1983] ECR 4083). The question thus arises whether this judgment will have any significance in proceedings concerning a contravention of the competition rules which involves only private parties (see also discussion in *infra*, Part II below).

It is possible that the Court intended its statements to be confined to cases where charges are levied by a Member State or state entity. Indeed the Court stressed that the right to repayment arose when the charges had been levied by a Member State or public undertaking responsible to a national ministry and whose budget is governed by the Budget Act. It is well established that the Member State must, in principle, repay sums levied in breach of Community law. Further, the charges had not merely been agreed as a result of contractual negotiations between GT-Link and DSB but were dictated by state regulations.

However, it is possible that its statements can be interpreted more broadly. The Court stated that, where it was necessary to prove breach of a provision of Community law capable of having direct effect (as both arts 85 and 86 were) the same principles applied as those it had set out in *San Giorgio* [1983] ECR 3595, para 26. National substantive and procedural rules apply subject to the proviso that the rules are not discriminatory and do not render the exercise of the Community rights ineffective. The Court then went on to stress the rights that individuals derived from the direct effect of art 86 (see paras 24–27) and indicated that the right to repayment of charges levied contrary to art 86 was "a consequence of and an adjunct to the rights conferred on individuals" by that provision which prohibited the charges. Any rule which had the effect of making it virtually impossible or excessively difficult to secure repayment of the charges levied would, therefore, render the exercise of the Community rights ineffective and be incompatible with Community law.

The importance that the Court attached to the rights derived from art 86 suggest that it was not so much the fact that the charges were levied by a Member State, but the infringement of the individual's rights which led it to conclude that the unlawful charges had to be repaid. If this is the case, a party to a contract with a private dominant undertaking who had been obliged to pay unfair prices for services or goods conferred under that contract may be able to rely on *GT-Link* in proceedings to recover those excessive payments. The levying of those sums would be in breach of the claimant's directly effective Community rights and repayment would be necessary as "a consequence of and an adjunct to the rights conferred on individuals" by art 86, which prohibits the charging of unfair selling prices.

A wide interpretation of the Court's decision is supported by the opinion of Jacobs AG. It is "settled law that art 86 creates direct rights in respect of the individuals concerned which the national court must safeguard . . . it is for the domestic legal system of the Member State concerned to determine the conditions governing actions to defend those rights, subject to the requirements of equivalence with actions to defend rights deriving from domestic law and of effectiveness, namely *that it must be possible in fact to recover*" (para 176, emphasis added). The implications of this case will be considered in the discussion *infra*, in Part II. In particular it seems likely that the case will lend strong support for an argument that payments conferred under a contract which is void for infringing EC Treaty, art 85 should also be recoverable (see *infra*, Part II, esp II (D)(2)(a)(i)–(ii)).

The Court also stated, as it had in *Comateb* §150, that a trader had also to be able to bring an action for *damages* in respect of any loss suffered in consequence of the State or public undertaking's breach of its Treaty obligation. Again this is the first time that the ECJ has stated that an action for damages must be available in case of a breach of the EC Treaty competition rules. The reference to the conditions of liability set out in *Brasserie du Pecheur and Factortame* (see comment *supra*, at §150) perhaps indicates that the Court intended only to extend the existing cases of state liability for breaches of Community law. However, the reference to rights conferred on individuals by art 86 also suggests that this judgment might have wider repercussions. It may be a step towards recognising that a system of damages for breach of the competition rules is inherent in the Treaty (see discussion *infra*, Part II (D)(2)(b)).

ii. Excusable error and limitation periods

152. *Fantask A/S v Industriministeriet (Case C-188/95)* [1998] 1 All ER (EC) 1 (Reference to the ECJ from the Østre Landsret, Denmark).
Charges levied contrary to the terms of a Community directive – recovery of charges – rule precluding recovery where charges paid over a long period of time in circumstances where payer and payee were unaware of illegality of charge – limitation periods.
Fantask had paid charges on the registration of new and private limited companies and on the capital of such companies being increased. It claimed that the charges were contrary to a Community directive on indirect taxes on the raising of capital.

Held: (1) The directive only authorised the levy of charges where those charges were calculated on the cost of the formalities in question. They could also cover the costs of minor services performed without charge. (2) Entitlement to the recovery of sums levied by a Member State in breach of Community law is a consequence of, and an adjunct to, the rights conferred on individuals by the Community provisions as interpreted by the Court: *San Giorgio*. The Member State is therefore in principle required to repay charges levied in breach of Community law: *Comateb*, §150. (3) Accordingly, whilst recovery of such charges may, in the absence of Community rules governing the matter, be sought only under the substantive and procedural conditions laid down by the national law of the Member States, those conditions must nevertheless be no less favourable than those governing similar domestic claims nor render virtually impossible or excessively difficult the exercise of rights conferred by Community law (see *Peterbroeck v Belgium (Case C-312/93)* [1995] I ECR 4599, at para 12) (4) A general principle of national law under which the courts of a Member State should dismiss claims for the recovery of charges levied over a long period in breach of Community law in circumstances where neither the authorities of that State nor the persons liable to pay the charges had been aware that they were unlawful, does not satisfy the above conditions. Application of such a principle in the circumstances described would make it excessively difficult to obtain recovery of charges which are contrary to Community law. It would, moreover, have the effect of encouraging infringements of Community law which have been committed over a long period.

(5) A Member State could, however, rely on a limitation period under national law which ran from the date at which the unlawful duties became payable in so far as the period satisfied the principles of non-discrimination and effectiveness set out in para (3) above. The five year limitation period could not be regarded as rendering virtually impossible the exercise of rights conferred by Community law, even if the expiry of those periods necessarily led to the dismissal, in whole or in part, of the action brought. The Danish five year time limit was reasonable (see *Haahr Petroleum (Case C-90/94)* [1998] 1 CMLR 771) and was applied without distinction to actions based on Community law and those based on national law. The periods were necessary in the interests of legal certainty, which protected both the taxpayer and the authority concerned, *Rewe (Case 33/76)* [1976] ECR 1989; *Comet (Case 45/76)* [1976] ECR 2043, paras 17-18; and *Palmisani v Istituto Nazionale della Previdenza Sociale (Case C-261/95)* (10 Jul 1997) ECJ Transcript, para 28). It therefore satisfied those requirements. (6) The fact that the Danish Government had failed to transpose the directive, in breach of which the charges had been levied, properly did not preclude it from relying on such a reasonable and non-discriminatory limitation period: *Johnson v Chief Adjudication Officer (Case C-410/92)* [1994] I ECR 5483; *Steenhorst-Neerings v Bestuur van de Bedrijfsvereniging voor Detailhandel (Case C-338/91)* [1993] I ECR 5475; followed *Emmott v Minister for Social Welfare (Case C-208/90)* [1991] I ECR 4269 distinguished.

Comment: (1) This case does not add much novel. However, it gives another example of a national rule which would render the exercise of a Community right of recovery impossible and which, consequently, may not be applied by a national court (point (4)). (2) Further, it is another case in a line with retreats from the Court's judgment in *Emmott* (see *Johnson, Steenhorst-Neerings* and *Haahr Petroleum (Case C-90/94)*). This line of cases clearly establish that a Member State may rely on a reasonable, non-discriminatory limitation period to resist actions based on rights derived from a Community directive even if that Member State has not properly implemented the directive (and even if the individual concerned did not, consequently, have a clear knowledge of his rights set out in the Directive). The Court distinguished *Emmott*, holding that it did not support the view that a Member State could not rely on a limitation period under national law as long as the directive, in breach of which charges had been wrongly levied, had not been properly transposed into national law. The ruling in *Emmott* was justified by the particular circumstances of the case. It would only apply where a time-bar had the result of depriving an applicant of any opportunity to rely on rights derived from the Community directive. This line of cases appears, therefore, to have effectively overruled the decision in *Emmott*.

II. BREACH OF EC TREATY, ARTICLE 85

A. Introduction

A dispute arising between private parties to a contract may raise issues of both restitution and Community law. For example, a claimant might bring a restitutionary action before an English court seeking to recover benefits conferred under a contract alleged to be void for infringing the EC Treaty, art 85 (part of the EC competition rules). Broadly, art 85(1) prohibits agreements between independent undertakings which prevent, restrict or distort competition. Any clause in a contract affected by the prohibition, which has not been exempted under art 85(3), is void. Further, the agreement as a whole will be void where the invalid clauses are not severable from the remaining terms of the agreement (the sanction of nullity is set out in art 85(2), as interpreted by the ECJ: *Société Technique Miniere v Maschinenbau Ulm GmbH (Case 56/65)* [1966] ECR 235, 250).

National courts are obliged to consider arguments raised before them concerning art 85. It creates rights in individuals which the national courts have a duty to safeguard: *Belgische Radio en Televisie v SV SABAM (Case 127/7)* [1974] I ECR 51, 62. However, the application of the provision raises a number of significant practical difficulties. In particular, the question whether a contracting party is entitled to recover benefits conferred under a contract, or a contractual term, which contravenes art 85 is a question of extreme importance.

In the last few years a number of cases involving payments made under contracts purported to be in infringement of art 85 have arisen for decision in the English courts all at first instance and unreported: see esp **Inntrepreneur Estates (CPC) Plc v Milne** (30.7.93, QB), **Inntrepreneur Estates (GL) Ltd v Smyth** (14.10.93, QB), **Scottish and Newcastle Plc v Bond** (25.3.97, QBD), **Gibbs Mew Plc v Graham Gemmel** (29.10.97, QB), **Matthew Brown Plc v Campbell** (11.11.97), **Star Rider Ltd v Inntrepreneur Pub Co** (8.12.97, Ch), **Parkes v Esso Petroleum Co Ltd** (11.2.98) and **Trent Taverns Ltd v Sykes** (17.2.98, QB) (the "unreported cases"). Most of these cases (with the exception of *Parkes*, which concerned a licence agreement under which the plaintiff was to sell Esso motor fuel from Esso's service station) have involved disputes arising out of tenancy agreements concluded between brewers and their publican-tenants. The disputes have raised the validity of the exclusive purchasing commitment imposed in the agreement, obliging the tenants to buy beer and other drinks from named suppliers. Broadly, the tenants have *inter alia* sought to recover excessive payments made for beer supplied under the agreements. However, instead of, or, in some cases, in addition to, bringing a restitutionary action, most of the cases referred to above have been pleaded in tort.

B. The tortious claim

1. The cases

In these cases the tenants have sought damages from the brewer on the grounds of breach of statutory duty. They have sought to recover, for example, the difference in value between the price paid for the beer and the fair market price that would have been paid in the absence of the tie and the loss of profits/income that would have been made had the tenant been able to charge lower prices and/or or improve the state of the premises and thereby increase turnover. The cases establish, however, that, at least where an action is brought by a *party* to an anti-competitive agreement, the tortious claim for damages will not lie. In *Trent Taverns* Steel J concluded that this point had now to "be regarded as settled at first instance. Thus, those seeking to rely on the point must expect to find it dealt with summarily pending any expression of dissent from the Court of Appeal." Unfortunately the cases were decided in the course of interlocutory proceedings and the reasoning adopted, especially in the earlier cases, is unclear. There would seem to be three possible reasons for rejecting such a tenants' claim: (a) In the context of a breach of art 85 no private action for damages for breach of statutory duty lies; (b) Although a breach of art 85 could give rise to a damages action for breach of statutory duty, the statutory duty is not owed to a claimant/ co-contractor; or (c) Although a breach of art 85 could give rise to a damages action for breach of statutory duty, any such action would be defeated by the defence of illegality.

(a) Breach of statutory duty

In English law not every breach of a statutory duty gives rise to a private action for damages suffered in consequence of it. However, it seems to be fairly well accepted that a tortious action for damages will lie against an entity that infringes EC Treaty, art 86 and that the appropriate cause of action is breach of statutory duty (see *Garden Cottage Food v Milk Marketing Board* [1984]

AC 130, 141 *per* Lord Diplock, *obiter*; the statutory provision breached is in fact the European Communities Act 1972, s 2). In order for such an action to be successfully brought it will, consequently, have to be established that (1) the duty under the statute was owed to the plaintiff; (2) the damage suffered was of the kind which the statute intended to prevent; (3) the damage was sustained in circumstances contemplated by the statute; (4) the defendant was in breach of his statutory obligation; and (5) the breach of duty caused the damage.

One might expect the position to be the same in cases of breach of art 85 (arguably both arts 85 and 86 are aimed not only at promoting the general economic prosperity of the common market as a whole but also the protection of private individuals to whom loss or damage may be caused by breach of the prohibition). Indeed, it was the view of Morritt J that "a breach of art 85 is, in English law, the equivalent to the breach of a statutory duty imposed for the benefit of private individuals to whom loss of damages is caused by a breach of that duty" (*Plessey v Siemens* [1988] ECC 384, paras 37–38). The unreported cases are not conclusive on whether or not the damages action is available in the context of proceedings involving art 85. In *Milne* Mitchell J considered the case of a breach of statutory duty on the hypothesis that the duty existed. Further, in *Brown* Michael Tugendhat QC, sitting as a Deputy High Court Judge, felt that the existence of the statutory duty had not been established. However, the cases appear to have proceeded on the basis that it was arguable that such a breach could, in principle, give rise to an action for breach of statutory duty but that there were other "insuperable hurdles" to the mounting of such a claim.

(b) Duty owed to a co-contractor

Some of the cases suggest any action for breach statutory duty could not be brought by a party to a contract who was also in breach. A party to a contract would not be someone to whom the duty contemplated by the statute was owed – one of the requirements for establishing a breach of statutory duty (criterion (1) above). In *Milne* Mitchell J held "that a *third party* might have a cause of action against either party to the agreement because of the contravention of art 85" (emphasis added). However, where the agreement was one entered into freely by each party, the statutory duty, if it existed, not to enter into agreements contravening art 85, applied to both parties to the agreement. Similarly, in *Brown* Michael Tugendhat QC, sitting as a Deputy High Court Judge, stated that there was no authority to support the argument "that art 85 gives rise to a cause of action by one party to a void agreement against the other . . . where a person . . . has agreed to enter into a contract under which he or she accepts a competitive disadvantage . . . he or she is, of course, entitled to disregard those provisions if and in so far as they are void, but if that person complies which such void provisions he or she cannot claim damages against the other party for the consequence suffered as a result."

(c) Illegality

On balance, however, the cases suggest that the real reason for refusing the claim for breach of statutory duty is its "illegality". Any claim founded on an illegal act should fail: *ex turpi causa non oritur actio*. "[O]n the basis that the tie provisions are void, they must also be illegal . . . In principle where both parties, contracting on equal footing, are aware of the illegal nature of the contract . . neither party can recover anything paid or transferred thereunder" (*Milne, per* Mitchell J). In *Smyth* Sir Peter Pain, sitting as a judge of the High Court, considered that it passed "all understanding how contracts freely entered into could give rise to a cause of action in one of the parties entering into it, on the ground that the other party was in breach of duty . . . the contract is an illegal contract. The parties entering into it are *in pari delicto*". In *Parkes* Sir Richard Scott V-C relied on *Milne*, *Smyth* and *Brown* in support of his conclusion that "the proposition that a party to an illegal agreement can claim damages from the other party for loss caused to him by being a party to the illegal agreement, cannot, in my view, be right."

2. The position in principle

It will be argued *infra* Part C that the defence of illegality has been applied too rigidly in these cases (see(C)(2)(b)(iv)). It will also be argued (in Part D) that the national courts may be obliged, as a matter of Community law, to ensure that an action for damages is available. This may be necessary in order to ensure the effective protection of a tenant's rights and to redress a serious violation of those rights.

C. The restitutionary claim

1. The Cases

(a) The beer tie cases

Some of the difficulties that arise in relation to a tortious claim may be bypassed where a restitutionary claim is brought. Obviously a restitutionary action would not be defeated by any of the objections to the tortious claim set out in points (B)(1)(a) and (b) above. The tenant will not have to establish either that a private action for damages lies or that the duty under the statute was owed to that tenant. Perhaps partly because of the difficulties confronting the tortious claim the tenant has, in some of the cases, also claimed to be entitled to restitution of the sums overpaid for purchases under the void tie agreement. These claims have, however, presented difficulties of their own and have fared no better than the tortious ones. In *Trent Taverns* Steel J found the claim that the tenant was entitled to restitution to be a "well worn argument" and, although not so frequently canvassed, to be "just as hopeless as the damages claim".

In *Brown* the tenant had overpaid for beers and other products bought under the void tie and sought to recover all sums so paid save to the extent that the brewer could prove value given. Counsel appears to have relied upon *Westdeutsche Landesbank Girozentrale v Islington LBC* [1996] AC 669 and *Lipkin Gorman v Karpnale* [1991] AC 548 as authority for the assertion that money paid under a void contract is recoverable. Michael Tugendhat QC, sitting as Deputy High Court Judge, accepted that the tie provisions in the lease might infringe art 85 and that the tenant had paid higher prices for beer and other supplies as a result of this tie. However, he rejected the restitutionary claim, finding that the money had been paid under a separate contract for the sale of the beer and not under the void tie provision. It was unarguable that a separate contract (entered into pursuant to a void restriction) should also be void.

In *Gibbs Mew* the reasons given by Anthony Thompson QC, sitting as a Judge of the High Court, for rejecting the claim were somewhat different. That case concerned a dispute between a small and regional UK brewery and one of its tenants. As a consequence of the size of the brewer involved, the judge held that the agreement did not infringe art 85(1) at all. He took account of the Commission's view that the ties of the small and regional UK brewers, taken individually, did not significantly contribute to the foreclosure of the UK on-trade market and that the agreements did not fall within the scope of art 85(1). However, even if wrong about this, the judge considered that the restitutionary claim was "totally unsustainable". The defendant had had the beer delivered to him. It was, therefore, wholly untenable to try and advance an argument based on total failure of consideration. It was impossible for the tenant to restore to the brewers the beer which had been supplied.

In *Trent Taverns* Steel J, fortified in his view by the failure of the claims in *Gibbs Mew* and *Brown*, dismissed the claims. He gave several reasons for his conclusion. First, the individual sale contracts were unaffected by the sanction of nullity set out in art 85(2). Secondly, there had been no failure of consideration (there had been full performance) and, thirdly, the illegality of the agreement created a bar to restitution.

(b) The petrol tie

Parkes concerned not a beer tie but a petrol tie. Under the terms of a licence agreement the plaintiff, Parkes, had to sell motor fuel as agent of Esso at a site owned by Esso (there was no sale of fuel by Esso to the plaintiff). The plaintiff received a commission dependent on the volume of petrol sold through the site. In return, he was obliged to pay a Site Facilities fee. In addition, the plaintiff was to sell goods from the Service station shop and to operate the car wash and vacuum cleaning facilities. In return for this right, Shop, Car Wash and Car Vacuum fees were to be paid. The plaintiff was obliged to stock in reasonable quantities and display various Esso products, such as lubricants, antifreeze and car care products, in the shop. He had to purchase these products from Esso for resale. In addition to bringing claim for damages, the plaintiff sought restitution, broadly in respect of the various fees paid to Esso and the excessive amounts paid for the lubricants etc under the alleged tie. Sir Richard Scott V-C comprehensively rejected the restitutionary claims.

The claim in respect of the Site Facilities fee failed on a number of grounds (the same objections applied in respect of the claim for the shop, car wash and car vacuum fees). In the first place the payments had been paid as a consequence of a clause which was not void under the Treaty rules (it did not restrict competition within the meaning of art 85(1)). Secondly, the fee had been paid as consideration for allowing the plaintiff to sell its motor fuel from the site, which the plaintiff had done. The agreement was fully executed on both sides. *Westdeutsche* was thus distinguishable as a case in which the contract had not been fully executed. Thirdly, Esso had a defence of change of position. Esso changed its position in reliance of the fees by allowing the plaintiff to remain in occupation of the site for the full period for which the fees were paid. Finally, Scott V-C noted that there might be illegality objections to the award of a restitutionary remedy.

Similarly he considered that no action could be brought to recover payments made for lubricants under a term of a contract (a tie) which made it impossible for the plaintiff to acquire products from competitors of Esso. Although accepting that the clause might infringe art 85, he considered that since each independent sales contract had been executed no question of restitution could arise. Presumably, he also believed that the illegality objection would apply.

2. *The position in principle*

(a) Recovery of money paid under a void contract or contractual provision

Authority does not support the view that money paid to another is recoverable simply on the ground that it was paid under a void contract (see the argument of counsel in *Brown* set out above). A ground for recovery must still lie. However, where monetary payments have been made under a contract or contractual provision which is void for infringing EC Treaty, art 85, an action for unjust enrichment by subtraction may lie.

(i) Nullity. It will be necessary as a preliminary issue to establish that any payments were made under a void contract or contractual provision. Where the payments are made under a clause of the contract which restricts competition within the meaning of art 85(1), in circumstances where the agreement has not been exempted under art 85(3) (and there is no application for exemption pending), that clause is clearly null and void. Where the payment is made under a clause which does not so restrict competition, that clause is not void unless the clauses which offend art 85(1) cannot be severed from the remaining terms of the agreement. In such a case the whole agreement will fail (see *Société Technique Minière* [1996] ECR 235 and *Chemidis Wavin v TERI* [1978] 3 CMLR 514).

In *Parkes* Scott V-C was of the view that the various Site fees etc had not been paid under "offending provisions". He did not, however, rest his conclusion on this point alone. He conceded that "it may arguable that if Article 85 strikes at all then the whole agreement goes."

In the cases dealing with the tenancy agreements concluded between the brewers and publicans, it seems to have been assumed for the purposes of argument that, save where concluded by small and regional brewers, the beer ties in issue might be in contravention of art 85 and consequently void (see *Gibbs Mew* discussed above). Despite this, it was held, in both *Brown* and *Trent Taverns*, that the individual contracts for the sale of beer were unaffected by the nullity. They were severable from the tie. "[I]n argument [it was] recognised that the tie provisions of the lease were not a contract for sale of the beer and other goods supplied, but that there were separate sale contracts with the suppliers." Thus Michael Tugendhat QC in *Brown* considered that the argument for recovery "could only succeed if art 85(2) makes void separate contracts (with the same and with other parties) which were entered into pursuant to a restriction which is void, even if they are fully executed by the supply of drinks which have presumably been consumed long ago. No authority for this was cited, and in my view it is not arguable".

With respect, this conclusion must be wrong. Even though the impact of a void clause on another agreement made on the basis of that clause is, *prima facie*, to be determined by national, not Community, law *Société de Vente de Ciments et Bétons de l'Est SA v Kerpen & Kerpen GmbH & Co KG (Case C-234/89)* [1991] I ECR 935), it must be correct in principle that the English courts should find that the individual sales contracts are void. It was the void tie provision which obliged the tenant to conclude the sales contract. If it had not been for the tie, the tenant would not have concluded the contract. The tenant would have been free to purchase the beer from the brewer, or other brewers, at a lower price and on more favourable terms. The sales contracts should, therefore, be regarded as a part of the larger tenancy and tie arrangement. If the tie falls, the agreements concluded in consequence of the tie should also fall. The sanction of nullity prescribed for contraventions of art 85(1) would be meaningless if a valid agreement could be concluded exploiting a void provision in another contract.

In addition, it will be argued below that, although the ECJ has *prima facie* left this matter to be resolved by national courts, the non-discriminatory national rules may only be applied in so far as they do not render the exercise of the rights conferred on individuals under art 85 ineffective. The whole purpose of art 85 would be undermined if agreements concluded in furtherance of the objective of a void term were not also affected by the sanction of nullity set out in art 85(2). Thus it may be necessary, as matter of Community law, for a national court to find that the parasitic sales agreement is void in order to ensure that it can comply with its obligation to provide effective legal protection for the tenant's rights derived from Community law (see discussion in *infra*, Part D).

(ii) Grounds of recovery — an action for money had and received. Where money has been paid under a provision which is void under EC Treaty, art 85(2), that money should be recoverable in an action for money had and received on the grounds of either failure of consideration, mistake or illegality.

Failure of consideration: It was at one time thought that a total failure of consideration could not be established if benefits had been conferred under a void contract by both the plaintiff and defendant. However, it now seems clear that this ground may be invoked even where a counter-payment has been received under the contract: see *Westdeutsche Landesbank Girozentrale v Islington LBC* [1996] AC 669, 714, (Lord Browne-Wilkinson), 683 (Lord Goff), *Goss v Chilcott* [1996] AC 788 and *Guinness Mahon & Co Ltd v Kensington and Chelsea RLBC* [1998] 2 All ER 212. In the latter case the Court of Appeal held that a party to an apparent swap contract which was *ultra vires* and void was entitled to recover the amount by which what he had paid exceeded what he received on the grounds that there had been a total failure of consideration. It therefore recognises that the ground may be invoked even though payments have been made "both ways" under the contract. It would, therefore, be tenable to advance an argument based on total failure of consideration (contrast the view set out in *Gibbs Mew*). Although a tenant would not be able to restore to a brewer the beer which had been supplied, this should not defeat the claim. A credit could be given in respect of that beer (a *quantum valebat*). By giving such a credit, the purchaser could offer substantial *restitutio in integrum,* which is normally sufficient: see in *Smith v Scrimgeour Vickers* [1997] AC 254, 262, *per* Lord Browne-Wilkinson, *obiter,* and discussion of counter-restitution below.

Mistake: It is probable that the rule precluding recovery of payments made under a mistake of law will soon be judicially abrogated (the House of Lords have been invited to review the rule in *Kleinwort Benson v Birmingham (No 2)* §103). However, until such a time recovery will only be possible on the grounds of mistake where the mistake is one of fact or where a qualification or exception to the mistake of law rule applies. In particular, a payer will be able to recover money paid under a mistake of law if he mistakenly concluded an illegal contract and was not *in pari delicto* with the payee. "If there is something more in addition to a mistake of law — if there is something in the [payee's] conduct which shows that, of the two of them, he is primarily responsible for the mistake — then [money paid] may be recovered back": see *Kiriri Cotton Co v Dewani* [1960] AC 192, 204 (PC, *per* Lord Denning).

Illegality: Irrespective of the existence of a mistake, a claimant may nonetheless be able to recover benefits conferred under an illegal contract where the plaintiff is a member of the vulnerable class for whose protection the illegality was created. "Where contracts . . . are prohibited by positive statutes, for the sake of protecting one set of men from another set of men: the one, from their situation and condition, being liable to be oppressed or imposed upon by the other: then the parties are not *in pari delicto*; and in furtherance of those statutes the person injured after the transaction is finished and completed may bring his action and defeat the contract" (*Browning v Morris* (1778) 2 Cowp. 790, 792, *per* Lord Mansfield). Further, property transferred under an illegal contract will be recoverable where the transferor withdraws from the contract within the *locus poenitentiae*: *Hastelow v Jackson* (1828) B&C 221, 226. This rule encourages the abandonment of contracts contrary to public policy but does not apply once the contract has been partly performed: *Kearley v Thomson* (1890) 24 QBD 742; see also *Tribe v Tribe* [1996] Ch 107.

It seems to have been accepted in the unreported cases that contracts concluded in contravention of art 85 are illegal for the purposes of the *in pari delicto* rule (although the conclusion of such a contract is not a criminal offence: see A Jones, "Recovery of Benefits Conferred under Contractual Obligations Prohibited by Article 85 or 86 of the Treaty of Rome" (1996) 112 LQR 606, 612–614). Further a strong case could be constructed to show that an objective of art 85, when applied in the field of beer supply agreements, is the protection of a vulnerable class of individuals (publican-tenants) from exploitation by powerful corporate groups (brewers) (see discussion *infra*, Part C(2)(b)(iv)). However, it will only be in rare circumstances that withdrawal will have occurred within the *locus poenitentiae*.

(iii) Counter-restitution. Any action for money had and received would, of course, be subject to the general requirement of counter-restitution. Even though the tenant would be unable to restore the beer, substantial *restitutio in integrum* could be offered by giving credit in respect of money or other benefits received from the other party (see discussion of total failure of consideration above). The *quantum valebat* would be assessed by taking the market value of the beer and/or other drinks which willing parties would have agreed upon on delivery

(iv) Fully executed contracts. In *Brown, Trent Taverns* and *Parkes* the judges, in their decision to reject the restitutionary claims, attached importance to the fact that the benefits claimed had been conferred under contracts which had been fully executed on both sides. In *Parkes* Scott V-C distinguished *Westdeutsche* on the grounds that it was a case in which the contract had not been fully executed. This conclusion is, however, insupportable in the light of *Guinness Mahon v Kensington and Chelsea RLBC* [1998] 2 All ER 212. In this case the Court of Appeal held that there was no principle which could be used to justify drawing a distinction between a closed swap and an open swap. "The fact that the swap contract, though ultra vires and void, has been fully

performed does not constitute a defence or bar to the recovery of the net payment as money had and received for the recipient had no more right to receive or retain the payment at the conclusion of the contract than he did before": *ibid*, 225, *per* Morritt LJ. Thus, rather than distinguishing *Westdeutsche* on the grounds that the contract had not been fully executed, the Court of Appeal relied on it in support of its conclusion.

It is possible that this aspect of the Court of Appeal's decision will be reconsidered by the House of Lords in *Kleinwort Benson v Birmingham (No 2)* §103. There is considerable support for the view that there is "no compelling reason to allow a plaintiff to recover the value of his performance if he has received in exchange for it all that he expected" (Birks, "No consideration: Restitution after Void Contracts" (1993) 23 UWAR 195, 206; see also *Davis v Bryan* (1827) 6 B&C 651).

Even if the House of Lords were to conclude that payments made under a fully executed contract were irrecoverable, however, it is still not evident that this rule would bar recovery where payments have been made in consequence of a void beer tie. The sales contracts cannot be severed from the terms of the main agreement obliging the publican to purchase beer from the brewer, but must be regarded as part of the larger whole. Whether or not the agreement is fully executed will, therefore, depend on whether the main agreement containing the tie has been fully executed or whether it is a continuing agreement which has been concluded for a period of time, some of which has still to run.

(v) A proprietary claim? Following the House of Lords' decision in *Westdeutsche*, a recipient of a benefit conferred under a void contract will not normally hold that property on trust for the transferor. Only if the property was identifiable in the hands of the recipient at the time when his conscience was impressed with the knowledge of the fact that the contract was void might the court be persuaded to impose a trust on that recipient: [1996] AC 669, 714-715, *per* Lord Browne-Wilkinson.

(b) Defences

(i) Limitation. An action for money had and received will be barred six years from the date of payment: Limitation Act 1980, s 5. However, where the ground of recovery is mistake, "the period of limitation shall not begin to run until the plaintiff has discovered . . . the mistake . . . or could with reasonable diligence have discovered it": s 32(1)(c).

(ii) Change of position. The defence of change of position operates as a complete or *pro-tanto* bar to any restitutionary claim. The defence is not available to those who are not in good faith or who are wrongdoers (*Lipkin Gorman v Karpnale Ltd* [1991] 2 AC 548, 580, *per* Lord Goff). It is therefore unclear whether or not the defence would be available to a brewer that has received sums under a void tie agreement. It was suggested in *Parkes* that the defence of change of position might validly be raised by a party to a void contract that was in a superior bargaining position. However, it is possible that Scott V-C's concerns in that case could have been more appropriately met in other ways. The acknowledgement that Esso had allowed the licensee to remain in occupation of the site simply recognised that that licensee should make counter-restitution in respect of the benefits received under the void agreement: see *supra*, Part C(2)(a)(iii).

(iii) Passing on. There would be no possibility of a brewer raising an argument that the excessive payment has been passed on to the publican-tenant's customers. The Court of Appeal has held that the defence of passing on is not available in cases involving the private law of restitution: *Kleinwort Benson Ltd v Birmingham City Council* [1997] QB 380.

(iv) The in pari delicto defence. Even if an action for money and received is available to a tenant, the restitutionary claim may, like the tortious one, be subject to a claim that the action was barred by the principle of *in pari delicto*. In *Parkes*, Scott V-C noted that there were "illegality objections to permitting a restitutionary remedy in a case such as this." In *Trent Taverns* Steel J also felt that the illegality of the agreement would create a bar to restitution. This defence will

not, however, bar the recovery of benefits if the ground of recovery itself is "illegality" (*supra*, Part C(2)(a)(ii)).

It is submitted that the principle of *in pari delicto* is applied too stringently both as a general rule in English law and specifically in the unreported cases. In general, the rigid application of the rule has in the English courts has been justified on a number of grounds: the moral obliquity of the plaintiff, the desire that the court should not soil its hands "by adjusting among dishonest men the results of their unholy speculations" (*Gravier v Carraby* (1841) 17 La 118; 38 Am Dec 608) and the desire to punish a claimant for its wrongdoing. However, since the operation of the defence leaves the undesirable consequence of leaving a wrongdoer with an undeserved windfall, the bar should be applied, if at all, only where denial is clearly dictated by the illegality or there is gross turpitude on the plaintiff's behalf. This would rarely (if ever) be so in the case of a breach of the competition rules. An approach attempting to distinguish the differing degrees of iniquity of those in infringement of the competition rules would be fraught with difficulties. Breach of the rules is not a crime and the rules are enforced to achieve a broad range of objectives. In most cases it will therefore be hard to establish that an undertaking in breach is morally culpable. In particular, it would seem impossible to characterise a tenant-publican that has mistakenly, ignorantly or unwillingly infringed the rules as being guilty of such moral turpitude as to require a denial of the restitutionary remedy.

More specifically, the defence of illegality will not bar recovery where it is established that the parties are not *in pari delicto*, that the transferee withdrew from the transaction within the *locus poenitentiae* or where the illegality is not pleaded.

Non in pari delicto. In *Trent Taverns* Steel J merely cited one case, *Stergios Delimitis v Henninger Bräu AG (Case C-234/89)* [1991] I ECR 935, in support of his conclusion that art 85(1) was "for the protection of potential competitors, not of a party to the anti-competitive agreement." In the other unreported cases in which the illegality defence was discussed, it appears simply to have been assumed that the parties were *in pari delicto* and that the claim was barred. In cases involving a dispute between an individual publican–tenant and a large brewer, however, it is possible that a tenant could successfully establish that the primary obligation of observing art 85 was placed on the brewer and not the tenant. Article 85 was intended to be applied for the protection of the tenant. The parties are not *in pari delicto* so that the action lies (*Kiriri Cotton Co Ltd v Dewani* [1960] AC 192).

It is undoubtedly the case that art 85 has been applied to protect a party to a contract which is in a weaker bargaining position. Although art 85 is intended to ensure "that competition in the internal market is not distorted" (EC Treaty, art 3(g)), the competition rules have been construed teleologically against the wider backdrop of the Treaty and applied to give effect to the tasks and aims of the Treaty as a whole. They have thus been used with the aim of protecting small and medium sized undertakings (they have also, for example, been used as an instrument of single market policy).

Numerous decisions, judgments or other acts of the Community institutions are explicable in their application of art 85, at least partly, by a desire to protect "smaller" competitors from the exploitation of an aggressive and larger one. The Commission recognises that distributors are frequently smaller undertakings which may be oppressed in bargains concluded with larger and more powerful manufacturers. Thus, in some decisions finding an infringement of art 85 the Commission has reserved fines for the principal beneficiaries of the unlawful activity and has declined to impose fines on distributors that have acted unwillingly or against their own economic interest (see *eg* the Commission's decision in *Adalat* [1996] OJ L201/1). Commission Regulation No 1475/95 governing motor vehicle distribution and servicing agreements was partly enacted to give dealers greater commercial independence *vis-à-vis* manufacturers. In addition, and crucially to the cases being discussed, the Special provisions for Beer Supply Arrangements set out in Regulation 1984/83 clearly stipulate that the limit on the scope and duration of the exclusive purchasing obligation is made, at least partly, in order to protect the resellers (tenants) commercial freedom (see recital 18). The Commission's policy in regulating these agreements thus reveals "the intention of affording better protection of the competitive freedom of contracting parties in a weaker economic position": *Delimitis (Case C-234/89)* [1991] I ECR 935, Opinion of van Gerven AG.

Withdrawal within the locus poenitentiae. It has already been seen that property transferred under an illegal contract will be recoverable where the transferor withdraws from the contract within the *locus poenitentiae* (*supra*, Part C(2)(a)(ii)).

Where the illegality is not pleaded. Where a party to an illegal contract relies on a proprietary right in money, the court is not entitled to reject the claim unless the illegality of necessity forms part of the case. Thus, a party to an illegality will be able to recover if he can establish an equitable proprietary interest in the money without relying on his own illegality. This may be possible where the Court imposes a trust on the recipient of money conferred under a void contract: see *supra*, Part C(2)(a)(iv) and *Tinsley v Milligan* [1994] 1 AC 340.

It seems clear, therefore, that in assuming that because the contract was illegal, no party could recover anything paid or transferred thereunder, the cases discussed above failed adequately to consider the position under English law. Further, the question of whether the parties are or are not *in pari delicto* depends on the purpose of art 85, the interpretation of which is a matter of Community law. The national court should, therefore, *either* have made a thorough examination of both the case law of the ECJ and the practice of the European Commission before ruling on the issue *or* made a reference to the ECJ under art 177. Since the latter court would be in a better position to give a purposive interpretation of art 85 (and to determine whether its objective in the context of beer supply agreements was to protect the weaker party to the bargain or some wider Community interest). it is submitted that the latter course of action would have been preferable (see *infra*, Part D).

D. The position in EC law

1. Introduction

It can be seen from the series of unreported cases that the English courts have denied tenants a right to recover in respect of overpayments made in consequence of a void beer tie. The courts have given short shrift to claims that a tenant should be able to recover these sums in either restitutionary or tortious proceedings. Rather the judges appear to have been influenced by their belief that the tenants were utilising the EC competition rules to avoid the consequences of a bargain which turned out to be economically adverse to his or her interests. "Art 85 is not concerned with furnishing a remedy for an improvident agreement" (*Trent Taverns,* per Steel J). Any such view may have been formed partly as the issue has arisen in proceedings brought against tenants which had fallen behind in their rent payments. The requests for restitution or damages have only arisen as counterclaims. The judges may, therefore, have considered that the tenants were raising spurious Euro-defences to avoid the full consequences of the landlords' claims.

Arguably, this position is indefensible as a matter of English law (see the discussion in *supra,* Part C, esp C(2)(b)(iv)). In addition the cases ignored the fact that the disputes arose within the sphere of European Community law. Community law dictates that the provisions of art 85 are directly effective *Belgische Radio en Televisie v SABAM (Case 127/73)* [1974] ECR 51, 62), when a contract or contractual provision infringes art 85(1) and at least some of the consequences that arise from such an infringement (for example, that that contract or contractual provision is void and that those in breach may be liable to a fine). The impact of Community law should not have been ignored.

2. An effective remedy

The ECJ has not yet ruled on the controversial question of whether, as a matter of Community law, sums conferred on a private individual under a contract which is void for infringing art 85 must be repaid. It has also not ruled on the question of whether an action for damages should be available in cases of breach of the competition rules by a private individual. (Contrast the position where a Member State or a state entity is in breach of its Treaty obligations: see *eg GT-Link* §000 and *Brasserie du Pêcheur and Factortame* [1996] I ECR 1029).

The European Commission is undoubtedly of the view that private actions should be available to encourage the private enforcement of the EC competition rules at the national level ("Commission Notice on co-operation between national courts and the Commission in applying arts 85 and 86 of the EEC Treaty" [1993] OJ C39/6, esp at para 16). Similarly, in *Banks v BCC (Case C-128/92)* [1994] I ECR 1209, van Gerven AG expressed the view that the competition prohibitions were "aimed at safeguarding undistorted competition and freedom of competition for undertakings operating in the common market, with the result that breach of that system must be made good in full." Further, the ECJ has made it clear that, when dealing with a breach of a provision of Community law which is capable of having direct effect (as both arts 85 and 86 are), the national court may only apply its national procedural and substantive rules in so far as those rules do not infringe the principles of non-discrimination and effectiveness (see esp *GT-Link*, §151). Thus, although the ECJ has been obliged to leave it to the national courts to protect rights arising from the directly effective Community provisions, it has stressed, relying on EC Treaty, art 5 (the obligation on Member States to facilitate the achievement of the Community's tasks), the duty of the national courts to ensure the effective protection of Community rights and Community law.

(a) A restitutionary remedy

In particular, it seems likely that, in order to comply with the Community principle of effectiveness, a claimant should, *prima facie*, have a right to restitution (an action for money had and received must be available). Such a right would be necessary to ensure the effective protection of the tenant's directly effective Community rights and/or to ensure that the fundamental objectives of the Community are not thwarted. Any rule of national law barring the right to recover, such as the principle of *in pari delicto*, could only then be applied in so far as it did not render the exercise of the Community rights excessively difficult or virtually impossible.

(i) Effective protection of the tenant's directly effective Community rights. The ECJ has held that, where taxes have been levied by a Member State contrary to Community law, entitlement to the repayment of those charges is a consequence of, and an adjunct to, the rights conferred on individuals by the Community provisions prohibiting such charges (see *Amminstrazione delle Finanze dello Stato v San Giorgio (Case 199/82)* [1983] ECR 3595; *EU Digest* [1996] RLR §176).

Similarly, the ECJ may consider that repayment of benefits conferred under a void beer supply contract is necessary to ensure the effective protection of the tenant's rights. The ECJ has held that an entitlement to the repayment of charges levied by a state entity contrary to rules set out in art 86 (read in conjunction with art 90(1)) which is a consequence of and an adjunct to the rights conferred on individuals by that article: see *GT-Link* §151. Although dealing with duties demanded by a public undertaking, it has already been noted that the Court, in reaching its conclusion that the charges should be repaid, clearly looked to and stressed the rights conferred on individuals by art 86. Further, the duties imposed in that case had been levied under the terms of an agreement concluded between the ferry operators (GT-Link) and the port owner (De Dankse Statsbaner). Consequently, it is to be expected that the conclusion would have been the same had the unfair selling prices been imposed in a contract concluded between two private individuals. The rights conferred on the payer under art 86 would have been the same in each case (the right not to be exploited by an undertaking in a dominant position).

Article 85 also confers rights on individuals. "As the prohibitions of arts 85(1) and 86 tend by their very nature to produce direct effects in relations between individuals, these articles create direct rights in respect of the individuals concerned which the national courts must safeguard": *Belgische Radio en Televisie v SABAM (Case 127/73)* [1974] ECR 51, 62. In *GT-Link* the Court accepted that these rights might be infringed, even where that individual is a party to an agreement concluded in contravention of those rules, *eg* where the competition rules are intended to protect a weaker party to the contract. This may frequently be the case when dealing with art 86 since a dominant undertaking is, by definition, in a position to exploit its market power and charge its customers excessive prices for its products/ services. Further, it has also been seen that art 85 has been applied to protect the commercial freedom of a party to a contract, such as a publican-tenant, that is in a weaker bargaining position (see *supra*, Part C(2)(d)(iv)).

Were the ECJ of the view, therefore, that the objective of protecting the weaker tenant-publican, was a sufficiently important objective of art 85, in the context of beer supply agreements, the national court would be obliged to provide an effective remedy to protect the tenant's directly effective Community rights. A restitutionary action would have to be available and the *in pari delicto* bar to recovery could not be applied.

(ii) The broader objectives of Community competition law. It is possible that the ECJ would conclude that the Community policy in this sphere is to protect a larger public interest which goes beyond the mere protection of individuals harmed by the action. The limitation on the scope and duration of the exclusive purchasing arrangement is not only about maintaining the reseller's commercial freedom but, perhaps more importantly, ensures access to the retail level of distribution on the part of other suppliers (see Regulation 1984/83, Recital 18; *cf Trent Taverns*, where Steel J considered that art 85(1) was for the protection of potential competitors, not parties to an anti-competitive agreement).

However, even were it considered that art 85 was intended to serve a wider Community interest, the tenant should still be entitled to recover any benefit conferred under the void contract. Article 85 is intended to prevent anti-competitive behaviour and private enforcement of the rules should be encouraged. The *San Giorgio* line of cases achieves a dual objective (see *EU Digest* [1996] RLR 190, 192-200). If a Member State levies charges contrary to the Community rules on free movement of goods (as the Italian authorities did in *San Giorgio*), the levy not only infringes the individual's right derived from the Community provision but it thwarts one of the essential Treaty objectives. From a Community perspective, the obligation to ensure that a restitutionary remedy exists not only protects individuals from the unlawful demands of a national authority but serves the important purpose of ensuring that the free movement rules are enforced by individuals at a national level and that a national authority in breach of Community law is not entitled to benefit from its breach. In *Fantask* §152, the Court specifically noted that a rule which made it excessively difficult to recover charges levied contrary to Community law would have the effect of encouraging infringements of that law.

Similarly, in the context of art 85, a right to repayment would ensure that competition in the Community was not distorted. The availability of the restitutionary remedy would encourage a tenant to abandon an anti-competitive beer supply agreement. The private proceedings would have the effect of enforcing the competition rules and ensuring that a brewer in breach of art 85, would not be enabled to retain a windfall received as consequence of its breach. A national court would, therefore, be obliged to ensure that the benefits were, in principle, recoverable. Further, it seems likely that the application of the *in pari delicto* rule would be viewed by the Court as a rule which renders the exercise of the Community right to recover excessively difficult or virtually impossible.

(b) A tortious remedy

The objectives of Community law set out in (i) and (ii) above support the view that, in order to comply with the Community principle of effectiveness, a tortious action should, in principle, be available. In particular, a tortious claim for damages should also be available to a tenant who has suffered loss over and above the amount recovered in a restitutionary claim (the excessive price of beer has effected the volume of sales and profitability of the publican's business). However, the nature of the tortious claim is different from that of the restitutionary one. "Its basis is not merely unjust enrichment . . . but a serious violation of individual rights": *Fantask* §152, Opinion of Jacobs AG, para 83. It may be the case, therefore, that the ECJ would hold that a national court is only obliged to award damages in proceedings against an undertaking that has committed a *sufficiently serious* breach of the competition rules. If so, the ECJ will need to set out guidelines indicating what factors a competent court should take into consideration in assessing the seriousness of the breach. Factors such as the clarity and precision of the rule breached, whether the breach was intentional or involuntary and whether any error or law was excusable or inexcusable may be relevant: see *Brasserie du Pecheur and Factortame (Cases C-46/93 and C-48/93)* [1996] I ECR 1029, esp paras 51–66. Further, it must be anticipated that a tenant will have serious difficulties in establishing loss and a causal link between the brewer's breach of Article 85 and the damage sustained. These difficulties may mean that, in most cases, it will be more attractive for a tenant simply to pursue a restitutionary claim.

D. Conclusions

A publican-tenant who has purchased beer from a brewer in consequence of a void beer tie should be able to recover excessive payments made for that beer. The unreported cases have failed to give adequate consideration to the points raised by the publican-tenants in argument. As a matter of English law, it should have been recognised that, since these payments had been made under a void contract or contractual provision, they were recoverable in an action for money had and received. Further, that the defence of illegality does not apply where the parties are shown not *in pari delicto*. In addition, the courts failed to recognise that the case had a Community perspective. A national court when acting to protect rights conferred by a directly effective Community provision, such as art 85, is obliged to comply with the Community principles of non-discrimination and effectiveness. National courts may therefore be obliged, as a matter of Community law, to ensure that a tenant is able to recover excessive payments made in consequence of an invalid provision in a contract. Where a tenant has suffered loss over and above the amount recovered in the restitutionary claim, it may be that a tortious claim for damages must also lie.

ARTICLE

153. Verse, DA, "Improvements and Enrichment: A Comparative Analysis" [1998] RLR 85.
To establish an enrichment, and hence the first requirement of a restitutionary claim, can constitute an arduous task. The root of the difficulty lies in the commitment which, it is argued, English law adopts towards the issue of "subjective devaluation". The aim of this essay is to explore the exact scope of this concept for one important group of cases where subjective devaluation is frequently invoked, namely cases of unrequested improvements of another's property. For the purpose of this analysis, a comparative method will be used. Civil law countries have long been granting restitutionary claims for unrequested improvements, and they have thus been facing exactly the same problems as those now arising in the emerging English law of restitution. The issue of "imposed enrichment", as most civilians would refer to it, has been broadly discussed, especially by German lawyers. It will be shown that their solutions of the enrichment issue are often quite similar to those advocated in the common law jurisdictions. Nevertheless, there are differences in detail which give reason to rethink the exact boundaries of subjective devaluation.

NOTER UP

154. *Ontvanger v Hamm qq* HR 5 Sept 1997, JOR 1997/102 (Hoge Raad); noted HLE Verhagen and NED Faber [1998] RLR 165.

Israel

*Daniel Friedmann**

155. ***Atlantic Fishing and Shipping Co Ltd v Day Frost Industries Ltd*** (1996) 50(4) PD 471 (SC: Tal J).
The principle of unjust enrichment – competition – increasing market share by breach of statutory duty – whether unjust enrichment.
The plaintiff (Atlantic) claimed that it was engaged in distant fishing and imported a haul of fish into Israel. This import was exempt from custom duty. The defendant was also a fish importer who obtained an exemption from custom duty. This exemption was based on another provision in the custom regulations and its extent was subject to the approval of the Director General of the Ministry of Agriculture. Such an approval was granted and it related to 3,000 tons of fish. It was, however, claimed that it was used in order to import much greater quantities which were sold at dumping prices. As a result, the plaintiff suffered substantial losses that led to its financial collapse. The action was based on breach of statutory duty and on unjust enrichment. The present decision was rendered on a preliminary motion to strike out the statement of claim. The facts have not yet been determined and the decision was based on the facts as described in the statement of claim.
  Held: (1) The claim in tort should be struck out. Fiscal provisions may be enacted not only in order to provide a source of revenue but also to further a social and economic policy, or even the support of certain segments of the economy. Nevertheless, breach of such a provision is a matter that should be dealt with by the public authority. It does not provide a competitor or any other private party with a cause of action against the party in breach. (2) However, a different approach was adopted with regard to the claim in restitution. It is unreasonable that a merchant or a businessman who evades taxes will be exposed to a competitor's claim on the ground that the tax evasion offers him a competitive advantage that is detrimental to the competitor. But in the present instance there was a specifically defined market in which the plaintiff was the sole supplier. Afterwards, the defendant was granted a limited access to this market. The claim that the defendant enriched himself, at the plaintiff's expense, by disregarding the legal limitations upon his share in such a specifically defined market, stated a cause of action in restitution.

156. ***Levy v Mabat Bniya Ltd*** (1993) 47(4) PD 49 (HC).
Termination for breach – restitution to the party in breach – the injured party's claim for damages – its effect on restitution to the party in breach – the rule against double recovery.
The plaintiffs purchased an apartment from the defendant corporation. During the winter, rain water leaked into the apartment. The defendant was unable to repair the building and the plaintiffs terminated the contract and claimed damages. The district court awarded them performance damages in the amount of $138,750, which reflected the value of such an apartment had it been properly constructed. From this amount the district court deducted the sum of $16,000, as quantum meruit for the use of the apartment during the period which it was in the plaintiffs' possession. On appeal:

* Professor of Law, Tel-Aviv University and The College of Management.

Held: (1) Under the Contract Law (Remedies for Breach of Contract) 1970, s 9, upon termination of the contract or the ground of its breach both parties are entitled to restitution of the benefits conferred under the contract. These include not only money or property transferred but also the value of its use (quantum meruit). In the present case the party in breach was, therefore, entitled to recover the apartment which was sold to the injured party as well as the value of its use. (2) The injured party is, however, entitled to performance damages. In the present case, had the apartment conformed to the requirements, the plaintiffs would have had the apartment and as owners they would have enjoy its use free of charge. The loss of such free use also constitutes part of the plaintiffs' damages. Hence, the plaintiffs are entitled to the full value of the apartment and there is no room to deduct from their claim an amount representing the value of the use of the apartment. The plaintiffs are entitled to recover the value of the apartment, while the right of the party in breach to restitution of the value of its use can be set off against the plaintiffs' loss of use of a properly built apartment.

Comments: (1) The Contract (Remedies for Breach Law) 1970, s 9 is set out in [1994] RLR 172. (2) Under Israeli law, upon the termination of a contract on the ground of its breach, the injured party can obtain restitution as well as damages for breach. It is however clear that he is not entitled to double recovery. He may not recover both restitution and damages for the same item. Thus, *eg* in the present case the plaintiffs could not recover in restitution the amount they paid for the apartment and also damages representing its full value. (3) The plaintiffs were also entitled to damages for the loss of the use of a properly built apartment. But they should be denied recovery of a corresponding item (either as damages or in restitution). In the present case it seems that the corresponding item is interest on the sum awarded as damages. The plaintiffs are not entitled to interest on the damages representing the value of the apartment for the period that the apartment was in their possession. Had they bought a properly built apartment, the could have freely used it, but they would not have received interest on its price or on its value. The question of interest was not, however, discussed in this case.

157. *Maya v Panford (Israel) Ltd* (1994) 48(5) PD 705 (SC).
Economic duress – illegality – threat of breach of contract – good faith in negotiation.
The appellant (M) was the director and shareholder of Maya Corp, which acquired from the respondents diamonds for $1.5 million. Payment was made by post-dated cheques which were not honoured. M went abroad and the respondents were unable to get in touch with him and did not know his whereabouts. Before leaving the country M authorised B to negotiate a compromise with the respondents. B offered the respondents a certain quantity of diamonds in final settlement of the debt. The value of these diamonds was substantially less than the amount due to the respondents. But B stated that, if they do not agree to the offer, they would receive nothing. After taking legal advice the respondents agreed to the compromise and signed a waiver document. After receiving the diamonds in accordance with the compromise the respondents initiated bankruptcy proceedings against M and applied for the appointment of a receiver. The district court allowed the application. M appealed.

Held (by a majority): Appeal dismissed.

Per M Chechin J: (1) The respondents were entitled to rescind the compromise agreement on the ground of economic duress. It is not always easy to distinguish between legitimate pressure in contractual and economic relations and pressure that goes beyond the permissible lines. To find the proper balance regard must be had to the question to what extent does the conduct deviate from proper business morals as well as to the degree of pressure that it exerted on the other party and whether it left him a reasonable alternative other than yielding to the pressure. In the present instance the threat of breach of contract by M, who was abroad and his whereabouts were not known, amounted to duress. The respondents had no reasonable alternative other than to accept his offer and they are entitled to rescind the compromise and the waiver on the ground of duress. (2) M is personally liable for the loss which the respondents suffered. Although the contract was made with Maya Corp, M was active in the negotiations. He committed a breach of the duty of good faith in negotiations (see the Israel Contract Law, s 12) since he knew that Maya Corp would not be able to perform the contract. He is, therefore, personally liable in damages. Furthermore, this is a case in which it is proper to "lift the corporate veil" and impose personal liability on M.

Per Shamgar J: There was no duress, as the respondents failed to show that the breach by M would lead to their financial collapse. In addition, they could initiate proceedings against M's property in Israel and also try and enforce a judgment against him abroad. However, the conduct of M and Maya Corp was clearly anti-social and *prima facie* amounted to an offence. The compromise and the waiver agreement are against public policy and are void under the Contracts (General Part) Law, s 30. M is personally liable in fraud and also for breach of the duty of good faith in negotiations.

Per Goldberg J (dissenting): There had been no duress.

Comment: (1) On the duty of good faith in negotiation in Israeli law see N Cohen, "Good Faith in Bargaining and Principles of Contract Law" (1990) 9 *Tel Aviv University Studies in Law* 249. (2) The decision has no *ratio decidendi*. The majority reached the conclusion that the respondents are entitled to disregard the agreement. But each of the majority judges offered a different reason for such a result and none of the reasonings commands a majority. (3) It is submitted that the better reasoning is that of M Chechin J. The case is concerned with the situation in which the consent of one party has been vitiated by the misconduct of the other party. There are, however, few Israeli decisions which dealt with this type of situation in accordance with the rules on illegal contracts. The reasoning of Shamgar J is in line with this approach. *Cf* also Sir G Treitel, *The Law of Contract*, 9th ed (1995), 344-345.

158. *Mimsav Corp v Sodagal Ltd* (1996) 50(3) PD 35 (SC).
The principle of unjust enrichment – profits gained by inducing breach of contract – competition.
The case is concerned with issues similar to those which arose in *Sodagal Ltd v Spielman* (1994) 47(3) PD 459; [1996] RLR §234. Indeed some of the parties to the previous litigation were also involved in the present one. Both cases are concerned with competition between parties in the business of supplying and refilling gas containers for home made soda water. However, the result reached in the present action is the very opposite from that reached in the previous case.

The plaintiff in both cases supplied gas containers on which there was a label stating that the container remained in the full ownership of the plaintiff and that the customer's payment was a mere deposit. The customer, after using the gas, returned the container, received another one full with gas and paid for this service (this payment actually reflected the price of the gas and the service of refilling the container). The defendants acquired empty containers from the consumers and from distributors, filled them with gas and sold them back. Many of the containers were originally put on the market by the plaintiff and the plaintiff claimed that by doing so the defendants infringe its property right and are liable in conversion and also in unjust enrichment.

Held: (1) The claim was dismissed. The Supreme Court reiterated the conclusion, reached in *Sodagal v Spielman* [1996] RLR §234 that the transaction between the plaintiff and its customers is that of a sale and not bailment. There is, therefore, no ground for an injunction to prevent the acquisition by the defendants of containers which originated from the plaintiffs. (2) In the absence of proof of inducing breach of contract or other unfair business practices, the plaintiffs have no cause of action in unjust enrichment. The mere fact that containers, which were originally sold by the plaintiff, are acquired by the defendants and used in the course of their business, does not suffice in order to ground an action either in torts or in restitution. A cause of action may, however, be available where the plaintiffs have a contract with distributors which requires these distributors to return the empty containers to the plaintiffs. Acquisition by a competitor of such containers from these distributors may constitute a tort of including breach of contract and provide ground for a claim in restitution.

Comment: (1) The court did not expressly overrule the decision in *Sodagal v Spielman*. It seems, however, that the part of that decision which allowed the claim in restitution, where there has been no interference with the plaintiffs' contractual relations, is confined to the facts of that case. (2) The other parts of reasoning of *Sodagal v Spielman*, including the possibility of recovering in restitution in cases of inducing breach of contract, of course, remain in force.

159. *Nehushtan Investment Co v Shindler Lifts Ltd* (1996) 50(5) PD 72 (SC).
Distribution agreement – competition by manufacturer after termination – whether unjust enrichment.
In 1936 the parties signed a contract under which P became the sole distributor and supplier of maintenance service in Israel to lifts manufactured by D. Under the terms of the contract each party could terminate it by three months notice. The contract remained in force for 57 years. In September 1993 D gave notice that the contract was to be terminated, the termination to be effective after one year. P sought an injunction to enjoin D from providing maintenance service to D's customers. P contended that its "customers portfolio" constituted "property" and that, by competing with P, D will be unjustly enriched, notably in view of the advantage which D enjoys as a manufacturer of the lifts supplied by P. The district court dismissed the claim. P appealed.

Held: (1) P has a legitimate interest in its customers portfolio. This, however, does not bar competition with regard to customers whose contract of service with P had expired. (2) P has an expectancy to continue its relations with its customers. However, the mere fact that this expectation will be frustrated by competition is insufficient to substantiate a cause of action in restitution. In order to found a claim an additional element is required, notably impropriety or fault in the way the competition is carried out. (3) In the present case D gave fair notice of termination and P has no ground to prevent competition.

160. *Zagoori v The National Labour Tribunal* (1995) 49(4) PD 749 (SC, sitting as a High Ct of Justice: Bwak J).
Illegality – retirement agreement – severance payment by a public authority exceeding the amount authorised by statute – agreement performed in part.
The applicant (Z) was employed by a municipal corporation. The parties reached an agreement under which Z would take an early retirement and receive 200% severance compensation, *ie* an amount equal to two monthly salaries for every year of employment. This agreement was contrary to the Budget Law 1985, which prohibited changes in salaries and other terms of employment in legal entities whose budget is supported by public funds, unless certain conditions are met. In the present case the agreement had to be confirmed by the Minister of Finance. But such confirmation was not obtained.

Z retired from his work but received only half the amount of compensation agreed upon. Z sued the corporation. The Labour Tribunal recommended that the corporation would consider either to take him back to work or apply to the Minister of Finance to confirm the agreement. The Minister declined to confirm the agreement while the corporation was unwilling to re-employ him.

The National Labour Tribunal held that under the Budget Law the retirement agreement was void. Each party was entitled to restitution. Z was entitled to restore the compensation which he received. Upon doing so he might resume his employment and receive his salary from that date. However, by the time the decision was rendered, Z reached the age of 65 so that the possibility that he would resume employment was excluded. Z applied to the High Court of Justice.

Held: (1) The agreement was illegal. When it was formed the parties had no intention to obtain the confirmation of the Minister of Finance. The contract was contrary to the provisions of the

Budget Law and was therefore void for illegality. (2) The Contracts (General Part) Law, ss 30–31, relating to illegal contracts are applicable to contracts illegal under the Budget Law, even though the Budget Law makes no reference to these provisions of the Contract Law. The provisions of the Contract Law are intended to be of general application, but the mode in which they will be applied in the context of a specific statute depends on the wordings, the purpose and the policies of that statute. (3) The Contract Law, s 31 requires the parties to a contract void for illegality to make restitution, though the court in its discretion may relieve a party from liability to restore the benefits received under such contract. In addition s 31 provides that, if one party has fulfilled his obligation under the illegal contract, the court may order the other party to perform "the whole or part of the corresponding obligation". (a) In the present situation the employee has fulfilled his part of the contract and the question arises whether provisions of the Budget Law, which declare the contract to be void, preclude the application of the discretion, granted to the court under the Contract Law, s 31, to order the performance of the corresponding obligation. This question should be answered in the negative. But the court, when using its discretion, must pay due regard to the policies of the Budget Law. (b) The need to deter from making such contracts has to be taken into account and it is also clear that an order requiring the corporation to pay the full amount stipulated in the contract would undermine the policy of the Budget Law. On the other hand, justice between the parties involved should also be considered and such consideration is not to be wholly excluded by the Budget Law. In the past the Ministry of Finance confirmed or was willing to confirm agreements under which employees of this municipal corporation received 170% severance compensation. (c) Under the circumstances the court used its discretion to order the performance in part of the obligation of the municipal corporation, namely to pay 170% severance compensation (rather than 200% as was originally stipulated in the void contract).

Comment: On illegal contracts in Israeli law see D Friedmann, "Consequences of Illegality under the Israeli Contracts Law (General Part) 1973" (1984) 33 ICLQ 81; N Cohen, "Illegality: The Case for Discretion", ch 7 of WJ Swadling (ed), *The Limits of Restitutionary Claims: A Comparative Analysis* (1997) 186 (*infra*, §291).

ARTICLES

161. Cohen, N, "Illegality: The Case for Discretion", ch 7 of WJ Swadling (ed), ***The Limits of Restitutionary Claims: A Comparative Analysis*** (1997) 186.
(1) A comparative analysis of the different attitudes of English and Israeli law with regard to the issue of illegality. The Israeli Contracts (General Part) Law 1973, s 30 states that "a contract the making, contents or object of which is or are illegal, immoral or contrary to public policy is void". This provision reflects the pre-existing law, which drew heavily on English Law. (2) The major innovation, however, has been in respect of the consequences of an illegal contract. The Contracts Law, s 31 provides the parties to an illegal contract with two remedies: first, restitution which is the primary remedy though the court has discretion to "relieve a party of the whole or part of the duty" to make restitution and, secondly, insofar as the party has fulfilled his obligation under the illegal contract, the court may "require the other party to fulfill the whole or part of the corresponding obligation". (3) The article refers to the similarity between Israeli law and the New Zealand Illegal Contracts Act 1970, though the latter offers a wider range of remedies (including compensation and variation of the contract). (4) The main emphasis of the article is a comparison with regard to the way Israeli and English courts have applied their discretion in granting remedies where a contract is tainted with illegality. The English case of *Tinsley v Milligan* [1994] AC 340 is closely scrutinised showing that there is a gap between the rhetoric of the courts and the way it actually rules. This case applied a pragmatic approach to the issue of illegality although the court rejected the "public conscience test" adopted by the Court of Appeal

as a guide for the exercise of discretion with regard to illegal contracts. (5) The article concludes by commenting that the Israeli legislative reform has proven to be satisfactory and by recommending that a similar discretionary regime be explicitly applied in English law.

162. Dagan, H, "The Entitlement to the Profits of Breach of Contract: An Anatomy of Judicial Legislation" (1997) 20 Tel-Aviv Univ LR 601 (Hebrew).
The article focuses on the desirability of allowing a promisee to claim the profits derived by the promisor through a breach of contract as an alternative pecuniary remedy of wide applicability. Three conventional arguments often raised in the debate over restitutionary damages are addressed: prevention of unjust enrichment, protection of proprietary rights and promise keeping. Doubts are raised as to the ability of these arguments to substantiate the doctrinal conclusions they purport to support. The article discusses two additional considerations that are helpful to the discussion: enhancement of efficiency and performance of contractual obligations in good faith. It is submitted that, in order to settle the debate over restitutionary damages for breach of contract, a choice must be made between the instrumental conception of contract and its more cooperative alternative.

163. Dagan, H, "Protecting Another Person's Interest" (1995) 25 Mishpatim 463 (Hebrew).
Claims made by good Samaritans for reimbursement of expenses, remuneration for time, efforts, and expertise, and compensation for losses they incur as a consequence of their intervention are traditionally treated by the common law with suspicion. In contrast, in certain defined conditions, Israeli law supports these claims. The article vindicates the position taken by Israeli law. The author also challenges the restrictive approach regarding remuneration for the time, efforts, and expertise of intervenors. He maintains that recovery should not be limited to professional rescuers who protect life or limb and that the appropriate measure of recovery in such claims should be the benefactor's opportunity costs rather than the fair market value of his services. Finally, the author explains the normative appeal of the Israeli statutory scheme, which requires beneficiaries, subject to judicial discretion, to compensate their benefactors for proprietary damages they incur as a consequence of their intervention.

164. Grosskopf, O, "Buyer-Seller Relationships and Their Effect on the Rights of the Original Owner" (1998) 4 HaMishpat (Hebrew).
(1) The author examines a way by which the law of unjust enrichment can take some of the burden from the controversial issues relating to market overt in situations similar to those presented before the Israeli Supreme Court in *Cnaan v USA* (1997) Unrep (a further hearing of that case is now pending). In that case Ms Cnaan paid 250 New Israeli Shekels (NIS) for two paintings which she bought in the flea market. They turned out to be original paintings by Rubin, which were lost while on exhibition in the USA. The paintings were worth over US $100,000 and the USA government (as the insurer who compensated the original owner) claimed them. The Supreme Court, by a majority, decided that the conditions of market overt (Sale of Goods Law, 1968 s 34) had not been fulfilled because the vendor in the flea market was not engaged in the business of selling original paintings and because the payment of NIS 250 does not constitute sufficient consideration. The claim of the US government was, therefore, upheld. (2) The article submits the proposition that, if a seller performs the sale contract by delivering property belonging to a third party, then that third party should be entitled to every benefit the seller had received through the contract, including the right to rescind the contract and sue for restitution. The main argument in support of this broad proposition is that the seller, by using property belonging to another in order to perform the sale contract, has enriched himself at the expense of the original owner. He should, therefore, be accountable before him for any right or power he had acquired in connection with the contract. (3) In *Cnaan v USA* the sale contract had been formed under a mutual

mistake, since neither the vendor nor the purchaser knew that the paintings were original. Under the Contracts (General Part) Law 1973, s 14(b) the court has a discretionary power to rescind such a contract. If the seller was entitled to apply to the court to request rescission of the contract, then according to the above proposition this possibility should have been open to the original owner, who ought to be subrogated to the rights of the original owner. It is clear that, if the sale contract could have been rescinded, then the difficult questions concerning market overt would have been avoided.

NOTER UP

Tempo Beer Industries Co v The Director of Purchase Tax (1997) Unrep (SC); rvsg [1993] RLR §180.
On appeal to the Supreme Court it was decided to allow new evidence which might prove the evidence submitted by the taxpayer were not truthful. The decision of the district court was, therefore, squashed. The case was remanded to the district court to hear the additional evidence an give a new decision.

New Zealand

*Peter Watts**

The last year has been a quiet one for the law of restitution in New Zealand. The Equiticorp litigation, which raised innumerable issues of restitution law (see [1997] RLR §§171–172 for first instance decisions), was scheduled for hearing in the Court of Appeal in February 1998, but it settled.

CASES

165. *Carey v Norton* [1998] 1 NZLR 661 (CA: Thomas, Keith and Williams JJ).
Will – undue influence – benign intentions of influencer no bar to avoidance.
M executed a new will within a month of her death. She had been advised as to an appropriate division of the assets by a brother and half-brother, whom she was to appoint as executors. The result was an alteration to the beneficiaries from just a sister and one neice to all nephews and neices. M had for a year been agitating with her wider family the prospect of changing the will, but the trial judge found that in the events which occurred M was unusually dependent upon, and deferential to, the brothers' advice. One of the brothers also accompanied M to the solicitor to have the will executed. Although the brothers were found to have acted with the utmost rectitude and the outcome of their advice was not unfair, the judge concluded that M did not exercise her own free and informed judgment in making the will.
Decision: Appeal dismissed. Will set aside for undue influence.
Held: It does not matter that advice is innocent and well-meaning if it results in the testator's not exercising an independent and informed judgment in making the will.
Comment: The trial judge had followed the authorities which hold that in order to have a will set aside it is necessary to prove on the balance of probabilities actual undue influence, unlike the position with inter vivos dispositions. This finding was not appealed, though the principal case relied upon (*Craig v Lamoureux* [1920] AC 349) was considered by the court.

* Associate Professor of Law, University of Auckland.

166. *CN & NA Davies Ltd v Laughton* [1997] 3 NZLR 705 (CA: Richardson P, Gault, Henry, Thomas and Keith JJ); noted Scott (1997) 7 BCB 4; Maxton [1998] NZ Law Rev 37, 46.
Misrepresentation leading to mortgage – unilateral alteration of deed by mortgagee – effect of registration of mortgage under Land Transfer Act 1952.
This was an appeal from a refusal to discharge an interim injunction issued to prevent a mortgagee sale. For the purpose of the proceedings, the mortgagors were conceded to be guarantors only and to have entered into the deed as a result of a misrepresentation. It was also assumed that a unilateral alteration to the deed would ordinarily have discharged the mortgage. However, the applicant argued that registration of the deed under the Land Transfer Act 1952 gave it an indefeasible title even inter partes. The mortgagors argued that indefeasibility did not require that the underlying personal covenants, including those to honour the guarantee, be enforceable in the events which had occurred, and that in any event any liability they had was countered by an *in personam* liability on the part of the mortgagee.
Decision: Interim injunction maintained.
Held: (1) The efficacy of statutory registration would not necessarily protect the mortgagee against an attempt to cancel the agreement for misrepresentation under the Contractual Remedies Act 1979. (2) It was arguable that the mortgagors never came under a liability or were discharged from it by the alleged material alteration of the deed by the mortgagee. In such circumstances it would be unconscionable for the mortgagee to rely on its registered title.
Comment: This case, and another decided a month later, *Duncan v McDonald* [1997] 3 NZLR 669, deal with complicated issues as to the effect of the 1952 Act, and this case is noted here simply to give an indication of the complexities that are likely to arise where rescission and direct restitutionary remedies are pursued in cases when registered property interests arise from the contract.

167. *Fisher v Mansfield* [1997] 2 NZLR 230 (HC: Heron J).
Mutual wills – tracing trust assets into exchange product.
Despite imperfect drafting, the court in this case was to conclude that there had been agreement between a husband and wife as to the making of mutual wills respecting *inter alia* a jointly owned home. The wife survived the husband and later remarried. Having sold the relevant house, it was assumed for the purposes of the case that she had used the proceeds in contributing to the purchase of another home with her new husband. The intended beneficiaries of the mutual will obligations lodged a caveat on the title of the new home, which the wife sought to have removed in the present proceedings. She acknowledged in her affidavit in support that she was fully aware of her obligations "both morally and legally", but argued that the caveat could not be sustained. She had failed before a Master and sought to have his decision reviewed.
Decision: Caveat sustained.
Held: (1) The elements of an enforceable agreement to make mutual wills had been established. (2) The interest of the beneficiaries under the agreement was traceable into the new house, which became subject to a constructive trust in their favour. (3) It was not important that the class of beneficiaries was not yet closed. (3) If any breach of fiduciary duty were necessary to establish a constructive trust, it had been established by the wife's having failed to keep the trust property separate.

168. *Fortex Group Ltd v Macintosh* (30 Mar 1998) Unrep (CA: Gault, Henry, Keith, Blanchard, and Tipping JJ); rvsg *Macintosh v Fortex Group Ltd* [1997] 1 NZLR 711; [1997] RLR §173.
Restitutionary remedial constructive trust – employer deducts employee contributions from salaries and wages but fails to pay deductions and own contributions into superannuation trust – no trust awarded over assets subject to a security interest.
The appellant employer constituted itself trustee of two superannuation funds, into which both employer and employee contributions were to be paid. Employee contributions were to be made

by way of deduction from salary and wages with corresponding transfers by the employer to the fund. In the case of the principal fund at issue the payments into the fund were to be made monthly, but the defendant developed the practice, without the consent of the employees, of paying the total contributions into the fund only annually. It intended to do so at the end of a relevant year, but went into receivership before doing so. The trial judge held that although the facts could not support either an express trust or an institutional constructive trust, a remedial constructive trust, to the extent that the appellant was at all times within its overdraft limits, should be declared over the assets securing the overdraft.

Decision: Appeal allowed. A remedial trust was not appropriate on the facts.

Held: (1) Dismissing a cross-appeal, there was no evidence to support an express trust. (2) Similarly, an institutional trust failed for lack of subject-matter. (3) Assuming that the remedial constructive trust exists in law, then all that is required as to subject-matter is that the defendant have some assets over which the trust might be declared. (4) No remedial trust can be declared over assets beneficially owned by a secured creditor unless it can be shown that it would be unconscionable for the creditor to rely on its security. (5) The secured creditors were simply relying on their security in order to get their money back, and hence were not enriched, let alone unjustly enriched. No other basis for an unconscionability finding could be established (*Space Investments Ltd v Canadian Imperial Bank of Commerce Trust Co (Bahamas) Ltd* [1986] 1 WLR 1072, PC, distinguished).

Dicta: (1) The constructive trust arising in de facto relationship cases is an institutional one. (2) Any use of a remedial constructive trust must take account of the need not to vary settled insolvency rules on too loose a basis. (3) (*Per Blanchard J*) The fact that the employer was itself a trustee of the superannuation scheme did not entail that its contractual obligation to pay into the scheme was a fiduciary one. The appellant's claim was no more compelling against unsecured creditors than it was against the secured creditor.

169. *New Zealand Forest Products Ltd v The Accident Rehabilitation and Compensation Insurance Corp* (17 Nov 1997) Unrep (HC: Ellis J).
Overpaid accident compensation levies – refunded without interest – claim to interest at common law.
As a result of a successful appeal to the Privy Council, the plaintiff was found to have been overcharged for levies due under New Zealand's statutory accident insurance scheme. Those levies were then refunded but without interest. The plaintiff sought to recover interest. It did so on a number of bases, including claims at common law and equity based on unjust enrichment. In the present proceedings the defendant applied to strike out the claims.

Decision: The claims should not be struck out.

Held: Although there was no scope for interest to be awarded under the Judicature Act 1908, s 87, the common law and equitable claims, including those based on unjust enrichment should not be struck out.

Comment: This decision should be compared with *Commonwealth of Australia v SCI Operations Pty Ltd* [1998] RLR §26.

170. *Parkin v Alabaster* (8 Apr 1998) Unrep (CA: Gault, Henry and Tipping JJ); rvsg *Alabaster v Parkin* (1997) 6 NZBLC 102,009; [1997] RLR §167.
Partnership – hotel business – opportunity to purchase and shift hotel building not part of partnership business – no constructive trust or account of profits.
This appeal was decided on its facts. No partnership in respect of the relevant opportunity was found to exist (*Aas v Benham* [1891] 2 Ch 244 discussed). The result was that the profit-stripping remedies given at first instance were no longer appropriate.

171. *R v Ellerm* [1997] 1 NZLR 200 (CA: Eichelbaum CJ, Gault and Heron JJ); criticised Simester and Brookbanks, *Principles of Criminal Law* (Wellington, Brooker's, 1998), 594-595.
Theft – logs on bottom of lake bed.
This case can be briefly noted for its consideration of the property rights of an owner of a lake, here the Crown, in respect of logs found on the bottom of the lake. The court held, on the assumption that the logs had been abandoned by their original owner, that the Crown had a sufficient special property in the goods to support a charge of theft under the Crimes Act 1961 (*Hibbert v McKiernan* [1948] 2 KB 142; *Parker v British Airways Board* [1982] QB 1004 followed).

172. Re *Tamaki Manufacturing Ltd* (1998) 18 NZTC 13,550 (HC: Giles J).
Sale of assets subject to fixed charge – resulting chose in action held on constructive trust – elements of express trust also established.
Tamaki sold most of its assets in exchange *inter alia* for a promise to pay, secured by debenture. Many of the relevant assets were subject to a first fixed charge in favour of X & Y. X & Y appeared to have consented to the sale on the basis that their position not be prejudiced by the sale. Tamaki went into liquidation 6 weeks later. The Inland Revenue claimed priority for unpaid tax over the monies still owing by the purchaser by virtue of revenue statutes that confer priority over floating charges and unsecured creditors.
Decision: X & Y had priority to the monies owing by the purchaser to the extent that they represented the proceeds of the assets subject to the fixed charge.
Held: (1) If X & Y had not consented to the sale, the proceeds would be held on constructive trust for them, ahead of the revenue (*Bank of New Zealand v Elders Pastoral Ltd* [1992] 1 NZLR 536 followed). (2) Whether or not holding an equitable proprietary interest is sufficient to justify tracing that interest into proceeds, there was a fiduciary relationship between Tamaki and X and Y. (3) The evidence did support the submission that Tamaki had agreed to assign the purchase rights to X & Y or otherwise to hold them on trust for X & Y in return for a consent to the sale of the assets.

173. *Wilkinson v ASB Bank Ltd* [1998] 1 NZLR 674 (CA: Richardson P, Henry, Keith, Blanchard and Tipping JJ); noted Maxton [1998] NZ Law Rev 37, 41; Rickett (1968) 8 BCB 56.
Undue influence – husband, wife and son – secured guarantee given to bank.
This was an appeal from a successful summary judgment application where it had been conceded for the purposes of the application that a husband, aged 73, had exercised undue influence over his wife, aged 70, in the giving of a secured guarantee to the respondent bank of the borrowings both of an accountancy practice in which her husband was a principal and of a company in which the husband held 15% of the shares and their son the remainder. The bank also conceded that it was put on inquiry as to the possibility of the undue influence. The company was in financial difficulties at the time, although the bank appeared to have been unaware of that fact. The bank stipulated for independent advice to be given to the appellant. Certified advice was given to her by a senior partner of a firm of solicitors. The husband was present when the advice was given, but the bank was also unaware of this. The firm had, to the bank's knowledge, acted on occasion for the borrowers. In the present case, however, another firm acted for the borrowers and for the bank.
Decision: Appeal dismissed. Guarantee therefore enforceable.
Held: (1) It is not to be assumed that, because a solicitor has had some involvement with the principal debtor, he or she is unable to function independently in advising a guarantor. Depending on the circumstances, the solicitor may be in a better position than a stranger to give balanced advice. (2) This was not one of the rare cases where no reasonable solicitor could have advised a client to enter the transaction. The court should not overlook the indirect personal advantages which family members may be deriving from the business of the borrowing relative.

There were such indirect advantages on the facts. (3) In the circumstances, the independent advice overcame any constructive knowledge of the undue influence which the bank otherwise had. (4) (*Per Tipping J*) The steps which a lender must take to overcome constructive knowledge of the possibility of undue influence do not so much remove the notice as satisfy the lender's equitable duty to clear its conscience by taking sufficient steps to see that the guarantor was protected from the possible effects of the influence.

Comment: The case contains a full survey of recent English, Australian and New Zealand authorities, and contains general observations about the existing law, together with some guidelines for lenders.

173A. *Solicitor-General v Reid* [1997] 3 NZLR 617 (HC: Paterson J).
Proceeds of crime – receipt by third party – liability under Proceeds of Crimes Act 1991.
This case may be briefly noted for the Court's refusal to give the beneficiaries of a discretionary trust relief against a forfeiture order respecting property derived directly or indirectly from the commission of an offence by their relative, Reid (the same Reid involved in *A-G for Hong Kong v Reid* [1994] AC 324; [1994] RLR §202 but fresh act of bribe-taking). The beneficiaries were volunteers and family members and hence were not seen as appropriate recipients of the court's discretion.

ARTICLES

174. Birks, P, "Property and Unjust Enrichment: Categorical Truths" [1997] NZ Law Rev 623.
A major article on many aspects of the interrelationship of the law of unjust enrichment and the law of property, legal and equitable. Amongst other conclusions is one that property and unjust enrichment intersect, insofar as an unjust enrichment can give rise to property rights. Property rights arising from unjust enrichment are more fragile than others, being subject to "change of position" and other defences. The event of unjust enrichment can occur even when no title passes from the plaintiff to the defendant in the relevant asset. Property rights resulting from the tracing process are based on unjust enrichment. Considerable space is devoted to aspects of *Macmillan Inc v Bishopsgate Investment Trust Plc (No 3)* [1996] 1 WLR 387; [1996] RLR §131; and *Westdeutsche Landesbank Girozentrale v Islington LBC* [1996] AC 669; [1996] RLR §139.

175. Carter, JW and Tilbury, MJ, "Remedial Choice and Contract Drafting" (1998) 4 NZ Bus LQ 14.
A wide-ranging essay on remedies following breach of contract, including restitutionary damages for breach of contract, and recovery of prepayments.

176. Grantham, RB and Rickett, CEF, "Property and Unjust Enrichment: Categorical Truths or Unnecessary Complexity" [1997] NZ Law Rev 668.
A response to Birks §174. It is primarily directed to countering Birks' argument that unjust enrichment has a role to play in the recovery of the value of property when no title in the property has passed from plaintiff to defendant. The authors argue that owning property is an event in itself, and that Birks' analysis downgrades ownership from an event to a response. Where no title has passed, they argue that the owner's property rights are logically prior to any possible ones based on unjust enrichment. Further, there is no need for unjust enrichment where those property rights exist.

177. McLauchlan, DW, "Analysing Mistake" (1997) 3 NZ Bus LQ 194.
Provides an analysis of when there is a "mistake" for the purposes of the operation of the Contractual Mistakes Act 1977.

178. Smith, H, "The Principle of Unjust Enrichment in English and German Law" (1997) 9 Otago LR 144.
A comparative overview of the concept of unjust enrichment in English and German law.

179. Spillane, C, "Unjust Enrichment and De Facto Relationships: The End of a Marriage of Convenience" (1997) 8 Auck ULR 301.
Argues that unjust enrichment concepts, such as free acceptance and incontrovertible benefit, are not appropriate vehicles for determining at common law the economic position of parties to a failed de facto relationship.

180. Watts, P, "Property and 'Unjust Enrichment': Cognate Conservators" [1998] NZ Law Rev 151.
A response to Birks §174 and to Grantham and Rickett §176. It argues that both sets of analyses in those articles are flawed in their assumptions that non-tortious restitutionary actions are based on unjust enrichment, and are therefore separate from actions to vindicate ownership. It argues that both tortious and non-tortious restitutionary actions are underpinned by a common principle designed to ensure the integrity of transfers of ownership and possession. However, in the event that unjust enrichment is the basis of non-tortious restitution, it is argued, with Birks, that the concept can operate even where no title has passed from the plaintiff.

BOOKS

181. Cato, C, *Restitution in Australia & New Zealand* [Sydney: Cavendish Publishing. 1997. Paperback]. Reviewed Grantham [1998] RLR 295.

NOTER UP

Alabaster v Parkin (1997) 6 NZBLC 102,009; [1997] RLR §167; rvsd [1998] RLR §170.
Goss v Chilcott [1996] AC 788; [1996] RLR §248; [1997] RLR 183; further noted Beehag (1997) 8 J Bank & Fin L 289; Carter and Tolhurst (1997) 11 JCL 162.
Gray v Chilton St James (1996) 8 NZCLC 261,306; noted Watts [1997] NZ Law Rev 319, 321.
Macintosh v Fortex Group Ltd [1997] 1 NZLR 711; [1997] RLR §173; rvsd [1998] RLR §168.
National Bank of New Zealand Ltd v Waitaki International Processing (NI) Ltd [1997] 1 NZLR 724; [1997] RLR §174; noted Grantham and Rickett [1997] RLR 83.

Scotland

*William J Stewart**

None of this year's cases are of enormous general importance but all contribute to the continuing development of the subject. They mostly speak for themselves, though see *Shilliday v Smith* §186.

CASES

182. *ELCAP v Milne's Exr* 1998 GWD 263 (Ct Sn (OH): Lord Penrose).
Services rendered – recompense.
The pursuers, a charity, took over a hospital unit (from the National Health Service) in which Milne was staying and ran it as a nursing home. A year before the hand-over the pursuers inti-

* Solicitor, Macmillans, Glasgow.

mated to the defender that there would be charges. Milne stayed at the home and was cared for until his death without paying. The pursuers sued in implied contract and restitution for the cost of care until Milne's death.

Decision: Contract case dismissed. Proof before answer (trial of facts reserving legal arguments on relevancy) allowed on the recompense case.

Held (on the restitution point): The curator bonis allowed the estate in his care (that of Milne) to enjoy the services knowing that the pursuers did not intend to provide them gratuitously (although a charity) and so it could be found that the estate was lucratus to the extent of the pursuers' ordinary charges.

Comment: It is not normally the case that the defender's knowledge of the benefit is considered in Scots cases of this kind; rather it is the pursuers intentions that are examined. Those (few) Scots lawyers who think that a more essential analysis involves a consideration of the idea of free acceptance (in this case appearing like an unjust factor) will look forward to publication of the full report. The note says the decision to allow proof before answer was taken "with some regret" and it might just be the case that it the unconscientious receipt which overcame the dislike of allowing a charity to claim for services.

183. *Fife Scottish Omnibuses Ltd v Tay Bridge Joint Board* 1997 GWD 1180 (Ct Sn (IH): Lord Prosser, Lord Cameron of Lochbroom, Lord Murray).
Overcharges – judicial review – repetition – illegality as a defence.
The pursuers, a bus company, sought judicial review of decisions taken by the defenders which precluded the pursuers from obtaining a lower toll rate on the toll bridge operated by the defenders. They failed at first instance (1996 GWD 1645) on the main point of interpretation of the key legislation under which the defenders exercised their powers, *viz* the Tay Road Bridge (Revision of Tolls) Order 1991. It was observed by Lord Marnoch that, in any event, the mode of registration adopted by the pursuers, being a device to avoid the application of the Drivers' Hours (Harmonistation with Community Rules) Regulations 1978, was such that it would be inequitable to allow repetition. The pursuers reclaimed (appealed).

Decision: Reclaiming motion allowed (appeal granted). Proof before answer (trial of facts reserving legal arguments on relevancy) allowed. Illegality averments excluded from the proof.

Held (on the restitution point): Repetition would normally be available on the facts of a case such as this one and the illegality suggested was irrelevant because the citizen is allowed to arrange his affairs in such a way as to mitigate the effects of statute.

Comment: Opinions were reserved on the matter of equitable considerations (in the non-technical use of that term which applies in Scotland). Lord Prosser's obiter dictum, that it was doubtful whether there were cases which could be categorised as unjustified enrichment which a priori excluded the possibility of specialities which made repayment inequitable, is tantalising. This case is close to a "no taxation without Parliament" case and one wonders what "equities" ought to be allowed in such cases. If one is to retain nominate heads, as Scotland does, they could be at least useful if the relevant equities, if any, were incorporated within their respective doctrines.

184. *Mortgage Corporation (The) v Mitchells Roberton* 1997 SLT 1305 (Ct Sn (OH): Lord Johnston).
Solicitors acting for borrowers – receipt of monies – constructive trust.
The pursuers advanced money to solicitors acting on their behalf as lenders on condition that they only parted with it for a good security. These solicitors passed the money to the borrowers' solicitors on condition that it be treated as undelivered pending receipt of the security documentation. They passed the money to the borrower without a security. He dissipated it.

Decision: Proof before answer (trial of facts reserving legal arguments on relevancy) allowed.

Held (on the restitution point): The borrower's solicitors could be taken as having known both the source of the money and the circumstances in which it had been handed over. The action was not bound to fail.

Comment: His Lordship's own opinion is comment enough: "I confess an almost instinctive abhorrence of the notion of constructive trusts in the law of Scotland, being concerned substantially with rights, be they real or personal, not subject to, with certain exceptions, overriding equitable considerations . . . but I have to recognise that the animal is identifiable within the law of Scotland in circumstances where a third party, either gratuitously or with knowledge of breach of trust, acquires property belonging to a trust. However, I am further concerned that to apply this notion in the context of what was otherwise a normal solicitor transaction is introducing a foreign body."

185. *Michael v Carruthers* 1997 SCLR 1005 (Ct Sn (OH): Lord Hamilton).
Improvements to property – recompense.
The essence of the case is rooted in the Scots law of the tenement and the feudal system of landholding still applicable. The defender took a title to a basement flat which had been created from his parents' flat utilising the whole basement area below. The other owners sued for reduction of his title and for removal. The restitutionary point is in the counter-claim by the defender that, if the pursuers were successful in removing him he (the defender) was entitled to be paid for the refurbishments and improvements he carried out to the basement flat.

Decision: Under the law of property the defender had no good title to the basement but proof before answer allowed on the plea of delay and acquiescence by the owners and the counterclaim for recompense.

Held (on the restitution point): The law was developing and the relevant criteria and parameters are not fixed. There was an implication of loss. There were averments that the defender believed himself the proprietor. Even though he had not averred a gain, on the face of it converting a dilapidated basement into a habitable dwellinghouse suggested an enhancement to the proprietors. The works were not *in suo*. There was no alternative remedy. The equity of the situation was uncertain. The question of onus in the general field of unjust enrichment was not clearly settled. The facts had to be examined.

Comment: The academic community, the Scottish Law Commission and the Inner House having blown up the complete certainty of the nominate heads of quasi-contract, many practitioners on and off the bench are at a loss as to what to do. It is hard to see what precisely it is that the pursuers have gained in a practical sense. While objectively a flat is more valuable than a basement void, normally an ordinary flat dweller would rather be able to sell his flat (with a share in a basement) rather than become a member of a consortium of mini-property developers. His Lordship expressly said that the work did not appear to be carried out in suo "in the sense of the authorities." Some more detailed explanation of that would have been welcome. Incidentally, the passive receipt by the proprietors of the renovations was argued as a personal bar matter rather than as free acceptance under enrichment.

186. *Shilliday v Smith* (2 Apr 1998) Unrep (Ct Sn (IH): Lord President Rodger, Lord Caplan, Lord Kirkwood).
Payments made to repair work on another's property in contemplation of marriage – recompense – condictio causa data causa non secuta – unjust factors – qualification – non-materialisation.
The parties moved in together into the pursuer's cottage. Two month's after that the defender bought a house and the parties discussed getting married. Later they became engaged but continued to live together as man and wife in the pursuer's cottage. When the defender bought the house it was in state of disrepair. They moved into the defender's house and repaired it. Various works were carried out including the installation of central heating, renovation of the bathroom

and the addition of a conservatory and a garden wall. Just when the work was almost complete the parties were no longer getting along and one night the pursuer came home and was locked out of the house and was homeless for six months. The pursuer made a substantial contribution to the repair works. She also paid sums to the defender, who then used it to pay for materials and work. She also brought a number of the items to the house and garden which she had to leave behind. She obtained Decree for her expenditure before the Sheriff. The Sheriff Principal refused an Appeal. The defender appealed.

Decision: Appeal refused.

Held: Enrichment not being seriously disputed, because the condition upon which the payments were made was the reciprocation by marriage, which did not take place, retention by the defender would be unjust.

Comment: This is a modernising decision and intellectually revolutionary for Scots law. It will be a blow for those who would prefer to see the law structured along revived civilian lines. The Lord President expressly commended Professor Birks work: "Anyone who tries to glimpse the underlying realities must start from the work of Professor Peter Birks ... — in particular his book *An Introduction to the Law of Restitution* (paperback ed 1989) and his two groundbreaking articles on Scots Law, "Restitution: a View of the Scots Law" (1985) 38 CLP 57 and "Six Questions in Search of a Subject — Unjust Enrichment in a Crisis of Identity" 1985 JR 227." He then, without dissent from the rest of the division, decided the case on the basis of Birksian principle – particularly by identification of an unjust factor: "She does not argue that the defender should pay her the sum in the crave ["plea"] simply because she paid money to him and spent money on his house from which he has derived benefit. The pursuer points, rather, to a particular factor which makes the defender's enrichment unjust. Where such a relevant factor exists, the factor, rather than the mere fact of expenditure by the pursuer and benefit to the defender, constitutes the ground of action. So in *Newton v Newton* 1925 SC 715 the pursuer was allowed to recover from his former wife money which he had spent on a house which actually belonged to her, but which he had mistakenly thought belonged to him. The critical factor in the pursuer's ground of action was his mistake about the title: he recovered because his wife was benefiting from sums which he would not have spent if he have been aware of the true position. In the present case also the pursuer does not simply rely on the fact that she spent money on the defender's property from which he has benefited. On the contrary, the critical factor in her ground of action is that she acted as she did in contemplation of the parties' marriage, which did not take place. That is why she asks to be recompensed." At a practical level it was not necessary to use the old latin tags.

It will take a lot of effort to restructure the Scots law with this "new" analysis and "taxonomy", identifying two unjust factors. An attempt to do so (Stewart, *The Law of Restitution in Scotland* (Green 1992); Supp (1995)) was seen by some leading commentators as unpatriotic — smuggling in foreign English doctrine. Practitioners will not be sorry to see the back of the old analysis and old taxonomy.

187. *Transocean Maritime Agencies SA Monegasque v Pettit* 1997 SCLR 534 (Greenock Sh Ct: Sir Stephen Young).

Employment contract – condition – condictio causa data causa non secuta – recompense.

The defender granted an undertaking to his employers in consideration of sponsorship expenses incurred by his employers during his cadetship to guarantee to remain with the company for at least two years on completion of his training. When qualified he took up work elsewhere in breach of his undertaking. The pursuers sued in contract and restitution under the nominate heads of recompense and the *condictio causa data causa non secuta*.

Decision: Action dismissed.

Held: (1) The averments concerning contractual breach were irrelevant and lacking in specification. (2) It is only in exceptional circumstances that a claim for recompense can succeed where there is an available remedy under statute or common law. (3) The condictio could not apply following *Connelly v Simpson* 1994 SLT 1096, which, while difficult to apply because of the different approaches in the Inner House, on any reading was against a claim like this one where it was either precluded by the possibility of a contractual claim for damages or because the payments when made for the trainee were due and payable and were not of the nature of advances.

Comment: This is even more unfortunate than *Connelly*. The pursuers in *Transocean* at least tried their best to sue in contract but were simply unable to provide enough specification (particulars) — they were not, on the face of it, trying to subvert a contractual result with a restitutionary claim. That position is internally justifiable to the extent that the pursuer can appeal, amend to improve the contract case on the way to the appeal and thereafter have the appeal granted, the technical specification defects being cured. At the level of the Sheriff Court at first instance it is asking too much to expect a fundamental review of the effect of *Connelly* (and the cases which suggest or show traces of a subsidiarity doctrine in regard to recompense). An appeal to the Sheriff Principal was abandoned. It is submitted that this is the very kind of case in which a restitutionary analysis would have been the best way to make the defaulter pay for having taken the training and run off in breach of a clear undertaking given in consideration and guaranteed. The two nominate heads would not necessarily produce the same sum – the condictio might have faced similar difficulties as the contract claim, there being a need to specify the sums or value he received. The recompense claim is usually to be assessed equitably *in quantum lucratus* and that would allow the court to fix a sum on a broad brush basis. Finally, the pursuer did, correctly it is submitted, take advantage of *Morgan Guaranty Trust Company of New York v Lothian Regional Council* 1995 SLT 299; [1995] RLR §258 to argue the same case both by reference to recompense and a condictio.

188. West Dunbartonshire Council v McGoughan 1998 GWD 94 (Dumbarton Sh Ct. Sheriff Fitzsimons).
Use of heritable property – recompense.
The council sued for six years rent and repairs after removing the defenders. It seems that the defenders were in occupation as a result of being the daughter and son-in-law of the deceased tenant, who had, before she died, applied to exercise her right to buy. The negotiations with the descendant defender continued but never concluded.

Decision: Order made for payment of the "rent" only.

Held: The defenders were unjustly enriched by the non-payment of rent.

ARTICLES

189. Blackie, J, "Enrichment, Wrongs and Invasion of Rights in Scots Law" in Visser,D, (ed), *The limits of the Law of Obligations* (Juta 1997) 284.
A search for marks or notes in the Scots case law for anything like an *Eingriffskondiktion*. An appraisal of the benefits of such if it can be found and of the obstacles to its recognition and development. A conclusion is that law reform might be needed.

190. Evans-Jones, R, "The claim to recover what was transferred for a lawful purpose outwith contract (condictio causa data causa non secuta)" in Visser, D (ed), *The Limits of the Law of Obligations* (Juta 1997) 139.
A rigorous demarcation of the proper scope of the eponymous *condictio* including a valuable contrast with the other *condictiones*, especially the *condictio indebiti*. Many relevant Scots cases are reviewed. There is a review of what is meant by "cause" in contract. There are concluding remarks on the merits of a mixed system in this context. And a lot more besides.

191. Gretton, G, "Constructive Trusts II" (1997) 1 Edin LR 408.
The published version of the second part of the provocative and essential text noted at [1997] RLR §204.

192. MacQueen, HL, "Contract, unjustified enrichment and concurrent liability: A Scots perspective" in Visser, D (ed), *The Limits of the Law of Obligations* (Juta 1997) 176.
A broad survey of the "interface" between these two branches of obligations concluding *inter alia* that unjustified enrichment has a legitimate part to play in contract failures and that attempts to find contractual solutions are self-defeating and indeed dangerous for the law of contract.

193. Wolffe, WJ, "Contract and Recompense: *ERDC Construction Ltd v HM Love & Co*" (1997) 1 Edin LR 469.
An article of vital importance to practitioners and considerable value to academics. It discusses *inter alia* the eponymous *ERDC* [1994] RLR §257 and *Fox v Hendrie* [1997] RLR §191.

NOTER UP

Dollar Land (Cumbernauld) Ltd v CIN Properties Ltd [1996] RLR §263; 1996 SC 331; 1997 SLT 260; affd (16 Jul 1998) unrep (HL).
Elf Enterprise (Caledonia) Ltd v London Bridge Engineering Ltd [1997] *The Times* Nov 28; [1998] 1 CL 604.
Smith v Bank of Scotland [1997] SC 111 (HL); [1997] SCLR 765; noted CEF Rickett (1998) 114 LQR 17; rvsg.
Mumford v Bank of Scotland 1996 SLT 392; [1995] SCLR 839; noted E McKendrick [1996] RLR 100; affg [1994] SC 613; 1994 SLT 1288.

South Africa

*Daniel Visser**

CASES

194. *Hubby's Investments (Pty) Ltd v Lifetime Properties (Pty) Ltd* 1998 (1) SA 295 (W).
Builder's improvements of landowner's immovables – contract between builder and employer – no contract between builder and landowner or between employer and landowner – employer's default – builder's enrichment claim or lieu against landowner.
The applicant had entered into a contract with a certain company (Sentinel Building Supplies (Pty) Ltd) in terms of which it undertook, against payment by Sentinel, to erect sectional title factories on land owned by the respondent. In the contract the applicant is referred to as the "contractor", while Sentinel is described as the "employer". The applicant built the factories, but received no payment from Sentinel. The applicant avers that Sentinel is an empty shell and that it has an enrichment claim against the respondent as owner of immovable property on which improvements had been made. On the return day of a rule *nisi*, placing the respondent under provisional winding up at the instance of the applicant, the respondent argued *in limine* "that the applicant has, *ex facie* the founding affidavit, no *locus standi* to bring the application as it is not, as it alleges, a creditor of the respondent".
Decision: The respondent's point *in limine* was dismissed.

---

* Professor of Law, University of Cape Town.

Held: (1) *Buzzard Electrical (Pty) Ltd v 158 Jan Smuts Investments (Pty) Ltd* [1997] RLR §213 distinguished between cases where the plaintiff had made improvements to property as a subcontractor and cases where the plaintiff had made improvements to property pursuant to a contract with a third party, but without there having been a contractual relationship between the third party and the owner. In the first instance, *Buzzard* held, there could be no claim by the plaintiff against the owner; in the second instance, however, it was possible that an enrichment lien or claim (as the circumstances demand) would lie. (2) Where there is no indication whether the particular instance fell within the first or the second situation described in *Buzzard* it must be held that an enrichment claim exists in principle.

195. ***Kunneke v Eerste Nasionale Bank van Suidelike Afrika Bpk*** 1997 (3) SA 300 (T) (Stafford J); noted De Waal (1997) De Rebus 538.
Bank appropriating investment made with it by a surety to cover cheques supposedly drawn by the principal debtor but not properly signed – right of the surety to recover the amounts of the cheques from the bank.
A close corporation, the West-Transvaal Computer College CC, held an account with the defendant bank. The plaintiff had bound himself as surety for and co-principal debtor with the close corporation up to an amount of R50,000 and had invested R60,000 with the defendant as security. The close corporation's mandate to the bank was to pay only cheques signed or co-signed by the plaintiff. During December 1992 the defendant used R52,865.88 of the plaintiff's investment to erase the close corporation's overdrawn account. Included in this amount was a sum of R32,322.80 which the defendant had debited against the current account of the close corporation on the strength of cheques on which the signature of the plaintiff did not appear. The plaintiff thereupon instituted an action to recover the R32,322.80 from the defendant.
Decision: By ignoring the terms of the mandate the defendant had paid out the cheques irregularly and the plaintiff was accordingly entitled to judgment.
Held: (1) *London Intercontinental Trust Ltd v Barclays Bank Ltd* [1980] 1 Lloyd's Rep 241 presented some authority for the contention that a bank which did not honour its client's mandate regarding payment could nevertheless debit the client's account if, contrary to the payment instructions contained in the mandate governing the account, "actual authority" had been given to one of the authorised signatories to sign on his or her own. In the present case, however, no such "actual authority" had been given. (2) The principle enunciated in *Standard Bank Financial Services Ltd v Taylam (Pty) Ltd* 1979 (2) SA 383 (C), namely that a bank would have an enrichment claim against its client if it were to make a payment contrary to the instructions of the client while acting as a *negotiorum gestor*, was not applicable in the present case. The *Taylam* principle required that the bank's action should not amount to "indiscriminate meddling" and that such meddling should be necessary "in order to do justice between man and man", but in the present case the bank's action amounted to the exact opposite of what was required to do justice between man and man. (3) Therefore when, as in the present case, the principal debtor does not owe a bank any debt at all but the bank has used the funds of the surety to cover a supposed debt, the surety is entitled to reclaim those funds from the bank on the basis of unjustified enrichment.

196. ***Wilkens NO v Bester*** 1997 (3) SA 347 (SCA) (Van Heerden, [E M] Grosskopf, Marais, Schutz JJA, Streicher AJA).
Conditional debt – payment thereof in the mistaken belief that it arose unconditionally – whether reclaimable with the condictio indebiti.
Bester was an employee (as well as the managing director) of a company and a member of its pension fund. The administrators of the pension fund paid him two amounts totalling just more than R1,3m, being the actuarial value of his share of that fund. This was done in terms of an amendment to the pension fund's rules (agreed to by all the relevant parties, but not approved by the

Registrar of Pension Funds, nor registered as required by the Pension Funds Act 24 of 1956, s 12(1)). In making the payment the administrators of the fund laboured under the mistaken belief that Bester had an unconditional right to payment of the amount, whereas in fact, because the amendment had not properly been made, his right to payment was still governed by the pre-amendment rules and therefore subject to two conditions, namely (a) the future solvency of the fund and (b) his own survival beyond the termination of his services. Bester invested R800,000 of the amount that he had received with a financial institution. Shortly thereafter the company was liquidated and, as a result thereof, Bester's estate was sequestrated. The curators of Bester's insolvent estate attached the R800,000, whereupon Bester brought an application against the curators on the ground that that amount was "pension moneys" and therefore, according to the provisions of the Insolvency Act 24 of 1936, s 23(7), did not fall within his insolvent estate. He later abandoned this line of reasoning — and the application based thereon — in favour of bringing an application against the liquidator of the pension fund (which its managers had decided to dissolve) for the payment of R1,99m (to which his share in the pension fund had grown), now arguing that the R1,3m that he had previously received had been irregularly made and therefore did not amount to pension moneys, making him entitled to receive the full amount of R1,99m from the fund. The liquidator of the pension fund and the Registrar of Pension Funds opposed this application, arguing, in turn, that the R1,3m indeed amounted to pension moneys and that it could, therefore, be set off against the full amount of Bester's claim against the pension fund. The court of first instance found that the R1,3m was pension moneys, but that set-off could not operate because Bester's claim against the fund had not been liquidated and granted Bester's application. An appeal was lodged.

Decision: The appeal was upheld.

Held: (1) Van Heerden JA, delivering the majority judgment, agreed with the court *a quo* that set-off could not operate in these circumstances. His reason for this view, differing from that of the court below, was that upon sequestration the debt (which was the converse of the right to reclaim payments) had vested in the respondent's estate, but the respondent's right to his share in the fund had not thus vested as a result of the provisions of the Insolvency Act 24 of 1936, s 23(7). (2) Nevertheless, the application had not been correctly granted. The essence of the court's reasoning was as follows. The payment by the administrators was *ultra vires* and they had initially had the right to reclaim this sum. However, this right fell away the moment that the respondent obtained an unconditional right to payment of his share of the pension fund, that is to say when the conditions were fulfilled on dissolution of the fund. (3) The law is clear that, if a conditional debt were to be paid in the mistaken belief that the condition in question had been fulfilled, (a) the *condictio indebiti* would be available to reclaim that payment but (b) would fall away as soon as the condition was fulfilled. The legal position should be no different if, as in the present case, the payment was not made in the mistaken belief that a condition had been fulfilled, but in the mistaken belief *that the debt was unconditional*: here, too, the *condictio indebiti* is available only until the condition has been fulfilled. (4) An important corollary of this was, however, that retrospectively the payment amounted to a (partial) payment of an unconditional debt, which reduced by operation of law the respondents claim to the rest of the pension moneys by R1,3m.

ARTICLES

197. Blackie, J, "Enrichment, Wrongs and Invasion of Rights in Scots Law" 1997 Acta Juridica 284.
A consideration of the emerging category of unjustified enrichment arising from "invasion of rights" in Scots law.

198. Evans-Jones, R, "The Claim to Recover What was Transferred for a Lawful Purpose Outwith Contract (*condictio causa data causa non secuta*)" 1997 Acta Juridica 139.
An analysis of the application of an enrichment action, the *condictio causa data causa non secuta*, in the field of contract and the difficulties that arise from this application.

199. Fombad, C M, "The Principle of Unjust Enrichment in International Law" (1997) CILSA 120.

200. Hutton, S, "Restitution after Breach of Contract: Rethinking the Conventional Jurisprudence" 1997 Acta Juridica 201.
A consideration of the juristic basis of the claim for restitution after termination for breach in South African law.

201. MacQueen, H L, "Contract, Unjust Enrichment and Concurrent Liability: A Scots Perspective" 1997 Acta Juridica 176.
An analysis of the intricate relationship between contract and unjustified enrichment in Scots law.

202. Smits, J M, "Van wil, causa en verrijking: over een alternatieve route naar de contractuele gebondenheid" ["Of will, causa and enrichment: about an alternative route to contractual liability"] 1997 Stellenbosch L R 280.
Explores the "theory of good cause" as a means of identifying the true foundation of the binding force of contract and well as the role of unjustified enrichment in this theory.

203. Van Zyl, D H, "Enrichment and Wrongs in South African Law" 1997 Acta Juridica 273.
Explores the borderline between delict and enrichment and comes to the conclusion that (a) there is no category in South African law that can be equated with the English "enrichment based on a wrong", nor with the German *Eingriffskondiktion*, but that (b) the *actio negotiorum gestorum contraria* might provide a remedy in certain instances.

204. Zimmermann, R, "Restitution after Termination for Breach of Contract in German Law" 1997 *Acta Juridica* 121.
An inquiry into the nature of restitution after breach of contract in German law, leading to the suggestion that it might be appropriate that the law of unjustified enrichment should govern this matter.

BOOKS

205. Visser, D, (ed), *The Limits of the Law of Obligations* [Cape Town: Juta & Co. 1997. Paperback R210. First published as 1997 Acta Juridica.]
This book contains chapters by contributors from England, Scotland, South Africa and Germany and it investigates the boundaries between the law of enrichment, contract and delict.

NOTER UP

ABSA Bank Ltd t/a Bankfin v C B Stander t/a CAW Paneelkloppers [1997] RLR §210; now reported 1998 (1) SA 939 (C); noted Sonnekus (1997) TSAR 383.
ABSA Bank Ltd v Standard Bank of SA Ltd 1995 (2) SA 740 (T); [1996] RLR §286; affd on appeal 1998 (1) SA 242 (SCA); approved: *Hubby's Investments (Pty) Ltd v Lifetime Properties (Pty) Ltd 1998* (1) SA 295 (W); [1998] RLR §194.

Bowman, De Wet and Du Plessis NNO v Fidelity Bank Ltd 1997 (2) SA 35 (A); [1997] RLR §212; noted Schulze (1997) De Rebus 316.

Buzzard Electrical (Pty) Ltd v 158 Jan Smuts Investments (Pty) Ltd 1996 (4) SA 19 (A); [1997] RLR §213; noted Smith (1997) Juta's Business Law 5; followed: *Hubby's Investments Ltd v Lifetime Properties Ltd 1998* (1) SA 295 (W); [1998] RLR §194.

USA

Andrew Kull*

CASES

206. ***Amoco Production Co v Smith*** (1997) 946 SW 2d 162 (Tex Civ App).
Mistaken payment – theory of the action – statute of limitations.
From 1985 to 1992 Amoco remitted to HW Smith (and his estate) royalty payments intended for another payee, also named HW Smith. The trial court dismissed Amoco's suit to recover the mistaken payments, holding that an action for money had and received is governed by a two-year statute of limitations.

Decision: Reversed. Amoco is entitled to judgment on a theory of unjust enrichment. The case is remanded for determination of the amount of principal and interest due under a four-year limitations period.

Held: (1) "Unjust enrichment is not an independent cause of action but rather characterises the result of a failure to make restitution of benefits under circumstances which give rise to an implied or quasi-contractual obligation to return the benefits." (2) An action for money had and received is, in effect, a cause of action for debt not evidenced by a writing. (3) Former Texas statute applied a two-year limitations period to debt "not evidenced by a contract in writing", resulting in holdings that an "action for unjust enrichment" was subject to the two-year statute. A 1979 amendment brought all actions for debt, whether or not evidenced in writing, under a uniform four-year limitations period. The overpayment to HW Smith created a debt in favour of Amoco that is governed by this four-year statute of limitations.

207. ***Brookside Memorials Inc v Barre City*** (1997) 702 A 2d 47 (Vt).
Tax – mistaken payment on excessive assessment – unjust enrichment of municipality – voluntary payment – payment over.
Brookside paid municipal sewer rates exceeding $3500 annually, although as a stonecutter it was entitled to a flat rate of $100 per year. When the facts came to light, the City agreed to apply the lower rate in the future and offered a refund of one year's excess payment. Brookside sued to recover the excess paid within the six-year statute of limitations. The superior court gave summary judgment for the City on the grounds that Brookside "paid voluntarily without protest and could have discovered the problem through reasonable diligence". Brookside appealed.

Decision: Reversed.

Held: (1) "If money is paid to a municipality which in justice and good conscience it ought to return, it is generally liable for repayment on an implied contract." (2) Rule denying recovery of voluntary payments protects reliance of public authorities on anticipated revenues. (3) Voluntary payment rule does not apply where plaintiff paid without full knowledge of the facts, and where City was in the better position to discover and correct the error. (4) City may not limit its liability to the extent of funds still held at the commencement of suit, where payments went

* School of Law, Emory University.

"directly to City's Water and Sewer Department, and not to any other nonparty governmental entities from which they could not be recovered".

208. *Commerce Partnership 8098 LP v Equity Contracting Co* (1997) 695 So 2d 383 (Fla CA).
Benefits conferred under agreement with third person – unpaid subcontractor v owner – requirements of action.
Equity as subcontractor made improvements to property of Commerce; Equity was never paid by the general contractor, which settled its litigation with Commerce and has since become insolvent. Equity sued Commerce to recover the contract price for the work. At trial, Commerce attempted to present evidence as to amounts it had previously paid directly to other unpaid subcontractors; the court excluded this evidence and gave judgment for Equity. Commerce appealed.

Decision: Reversed and remanded. Commerce must be allowed to prove that it has already expended (whether in payments to the general contractor or directly to subcontractors) an amount greater than the original contract price for the work.

Held: (1) Under Florida statute, failure to perfect a mechanic's lien does not preclude an unpaid subcontractor from suing the owner on a theory of unjust enrichment. (2) In such an action the subcontractor must prove that (a) it has exhausted its remedies against the general contractor and (b) the owner has received the benefit without payment of consideration. These requirements "limit the cause of action to those situations where the enrichment of the owner is truly unjust when compared to the uncompensated subcontractor". (3) Equity failed to prove at trial that Commerce made no payment to anyone for the benefits conferred by Equity. (4) If payments by the owner exceed the contract price, an unpaid subcontractor's claim that the owner has been unjustly enriched must fail.

Comment: The court makes it clear that an owner will be liable in restitution when it has paid no part of the price attributable to an improvement: this is "a windfall benefit, something for nothing". It is likewise clear that the owner cannot be liable in restitution if it has paid the full contract price, even if the subcontractor has received nothing. The opinion gives no explicit direction for the most likely case – partial payment for the work of the unpaid subcontractor, in some unknowable proportion – but seemingly leaves the trial court to determine the extent, if any, to which the owner has been unjustly enriched by the claimant's work.

209. *Cooley v Fredinburg* (1997) 146 Or App 436; 934 P 2d 505.
Judgment subsequently reversed – improvements to property during temporary possession – set off against liability for rents.
By court order, amid complex foreclosure proceedings, a junior lienor was allowed to redeem real property over the objection of the owner; lienor went into possession and owner appealed. During the pendency of the appeal, lienor received rents and made improvements. Held, on this first appeal, that the order permitting redemption had been erroneous. Owner recovered possession and commenced an action to recover rents received in the interim; lienor claimed the right to set off the cost of its improvements or the increase in value attributable thereto. The trial court dismissed owner's claim for rents, finding that the cost of lienor's improvements was greater than the rent received. The Court of Appeals reversed, and both parties petitioned for reconsideration.

Decision: Adhered to as modified. The lienor may set off against rents expenses necessarily incurred in the protection of the property, but neither the cost nor the value of any improvements.

Held: (1) *Restatement* §42(1) states that a mistaken improver may set off the lesser of the cost or value of improvements against his liability to the owner for mesne profits. (2) Recent Oregon decisions allow restitution for the value of improvements made in good faith, on the principle of avoiding unjust enrichment: *Coos County v State* (1987) 303 Or 173; 734 P 2d 1348, and

Sugarman v Olsen (1969) 254 Or 385; 459 P 2d 545. (3) By contrast, *Restatement* §74(e) provides that, where property has been taken from a judgment debtor, pursuant to a judgment subsequently reversed, the debtor is entitled to specific restitution plus the value of the use, diminished by taxes and necessary expenses but with no allowance for improvements. (4) The choice between competing rules depends on the circumstances. Lienor was on notice that the initial order allowing redemption was subject to appeal: pending a final resolution, it assumed the risk that it might lose ownership. "In cases where neither party has sought a legal determination of its rights, and there are mere unlitigated claims to the property, the equities are in equipoise if the claims and improvements are made in good faith. Here, because of the pending appeal, the equipoise no longer existed when [lienor] made its improvements."

210. ***Curtis v Becker*** (1997) 941 P 2d 350 (Idaho CA).
Benefits conferred in pursuit of claimant's interest – improvements to property not desired by owner.
The original developer of a subdivision sold an unimproved lot to Becker for $20,000, then sold the rest of the property to Curtis, another developer. Curtis obtained the approval of municipal authorities for a change in the subdivision plan on condition that he complete specified improvements, including the street and sewers abutting Becker's lot. Becker refused to authorise the improvement to his lot and tried to obstruct the work, which Curtis performed anyway. Becker later sold his lot for $38,000. Curtis sued Becker to recover the value of the improvements; the trial court awarded Curtis $18,000 and costs. Becker appealed.
Decision: Reversed.
Held: (1) By his agreement with the municipality, Curtis was obliged to obtain Becker's consent to the improvements. Because he proceeded without Becker's consent, Curtis's restitution claim is barred by the doctrine of unclean hands. (2) No rule of law "allows one party to alter the property of another and impose upon that property owner an uninvited financial burden merely so that the first party can use his own property as he deems most desirable and profitable" (Lansing J, concurring specially).

211. ***Demoulas v Demoulas Super Markets Inc*** (1997) 424 Mass 501; 677 NE 2d 159.
Breach of fiduciary duty – corporate opportunity – remedy.
Shareholders' derivative suit alleged diversion of corporate opportunity by corporate officers and others. The superior court found defendants liable and ordered relief including (i) imposition of constructive trust on assets and liabilities of companies controlled by defendants, and (ii) repayment to plaintiff corporations of certain cash disbursements made to defendants. Defendants appealed.
Decision: Reversed in part and remanded.
Held: (1) Where a corporate fiduciary obtains a gain or advantage through a violation of his duty of loyalty, a court may properly order restitution of the gain, so as to deny any profit to the wrongdoer and prevent his unjust enrichment. (2) In making restitution of assets and liabilities of companies to which benefits were improperly directed, defendants are entitled to credit for amounts that they personally invested in these enterprises (assuming, of course, that such funds are not themselves traceable to violations of fiduciary duty toward the plaintiff corporation). Burden of proof is on defendants to show what part of any entity's assets is not the direct or indirect result of violations of duty. (3) Repayment to plaintiff corporation of certain cash distributions to defendants may be made net of income taxes paid by defendants in respect of such distributions, since the object of restitution is to recover only the [net] gain from the wrongdoing. If repayment to the plaintiff results in any tax benefits to defendants, these benefits must be traced and transferred to plaintiff to avoid unjust enrichment. (4) The superior court correctly ordered that repayment of such cash distributions bear interest at six per cent from the date of each distribution to the date restitution is made.

212. *Dixon v Smith* 1997 Ohio App Lexis 2005.
Benefits conferred in anticipation of contract – commingling of assets in contemplation of marriage – necessity of tracing – prejudgment interest.
During the nearly five years they were engaged to be married, Dixon and Smith decided successively: to cohabit; to commingle assets in a joint bank account; to go into the horse-breeding business together; and to make improvements to Smith's real property, using money obtained from a first-mortgage loan on Dixon's property. Following the termination of their engagement, Dixon sought to recover $18,750 expended on these property improvements, as well as $50,000 she had paid to service Smith's debts during the period of their cohabitation. Smith moved to dismiss, arguing *inter alia*: that he had never intended to marry Dixon; that her financial contributions had been gifts; that his debts had been greater at the conclusion of their relationship than at the outset; and that Dixon's action was an impermissible attempt to recover damages for breach of promise to marry. The trial court gave judgment for Dixon in the amount of $18,750, and both parties appealed.

Decision: Affirmed.

Held: (1) The statute prohibiting the recovery of damages for breach of promise does not preclude the recovery of property transferred in reliance on a promise of marriage. In order to avoid the unjust enrichment of the recipient, such a transfer is treated as a conditional gift. (2) One who transfers property on the strength of the recipient's promise to marry does not do so as a "volunteer". (3) Transfer of property by Dixon in the belief that she and Smith were to be married was the result of a relievable mistake of fact. (4) Dixon's claims to recover additional amounts via constructive trust were properly denied, because the proceeds of these expenditures were not specifically traceable. "A constructive trust is not a right to recover on a debt owing, it creates a right to recover property wrongfully held." (5) Trial court did not abuse its discretion in denying prejudgment interest. Although interest ordinarily accrues on a liquidated claim from its due date, the amount of recovery in unjust enrichment is by its nature uncertain until the court determines the amount of the benefit to the defendant. Here the amount of enrichment to Smith resulting from Dixon's expenditures was not "capable of ascertainment by mere computation".

213. *Estate of Campbell* (1997) 704 A 2d 329 (Maine).
Confidential relation – constructive trust reaches property in which person reposing confidence had no interest or expectation.
John procured transfer of Blackacre to him by his mother, then 85 years old and in failing health. On mother's death siblings sought to obtain property for her estate. The probate court found an abuse of confidential relation and imposed constructive trust. Appealing this finding, John also asserted a separately derived title to Blackacre on the grounds that (i) because deed to Mary in 1951 omitted reference to "heirs", it conveyed only a life estate, and (ii) after Mary's death John had obtained valid deed from sole heir of original grantor.

Decision: Affirmed.

Held: (1) "The salient elements of a confidential relation are the actual placing of trust and confidence in fact by one party in another and a great disparity of position and influence between the parties to the relation." Probate court did not err in finding abuse of confidential relation and unjust enrichment. (2) Assuming without deciding that Mary had only a life estate in Blackacre, subsequent deed to John does not defeat imposition of constructive trust. "John's fiduciary obligation arose out of his confidential relationship with Mary during her life, and we are presented with no compelling argument that the obligation should not continue for the benefit of her estate at her death. John's procurement of the curative deed occurred while he was subject to this obligation and has no effect on the equity power of this court to impose a constructive trust in these circumstances."

214. *Fireman's Fund Insurance Co v Wilshire Film Ventures Inc* (1997) 52 Cal App 4th 553; 60 Cal Rptr 2d 591.
Insurance – subrogation – claim of casualty insurer against person otherwise obliged to indemnify against a given loss.
Wilshire leased camera equipment, undertaking to return it by a specified date or to pay full replacement value. The equipment was stolen from Wilshire's possession. When Wilshire refused to pay for the stolen equipment, Fireman's (the lessor's insurer) paid replacement value to the lessor, then sued Wilshire to recoup this payment via subrogation. Fireman's had judgment at trial. Wilshire appealed, arguing (on the basis of *Patent Scaffolding Co v William Simpson Constr Co* (1967) 256 Cal App 2d 506, 514) that "when two parties are contractually bound by independent contracts to indemnify the same person for the same loss, the payment by one of them to his indemnitee does not create in him equities superior to [those of] the non-paying indemnitor, justifying subrogation, if the latter did not cause or participate in causing the loss".
Decision: Affirmed.
Held: (1) An insurer that pays a loss for which the defendant is liable to the insured has a claim by subrogation against the defendant only where, *inter alia*, the insurer's equitable position is superior to that of the defendant: *Meyers v Bank of America* (1938) 11 Cal 2d 92, 101. (2) Fireman's and Wilshire do not occupy the same position vis-à-vis the lessor, nor were they bound "to indemnify the same loss". Wilshire had an obligation, which it has breached, to return the equipment or pay its value. The obligation of Fireman's, which it has honoured, was to insure the lessor against loss of the equipment. As between the parties, the equities are with Fireman's.
Comment: A simpler analysis might begin by observing that it was evidently not the intent of the parties to give Wilshire the benefit of the lessor's insurance.

215. *Glick v Barclays de Zoete Wedd Inc* (1997) 300 NJ Super 299; 692 A 2d 1004 (App Div).
Unenforceable agreement – quantum meruit recovery in favour of discharged attorney.
Attorney was engaged to represent plaintiffs in a suit alleging employment discrimination. Although the parties evidently intended that this representation would be on a contingent-fee basis, the formal agreement as to contingent fees required by New Jersey rules was never concluded. Attorney was later discharged; plaintiffs retained new counsel; the underlying litigation was eventually settled. Original attorney moved for an award of fees. The trial court held that there was no valid fee agreement, and that absent such agreement the attorney could not recover in quantum meruit for services rendered. Attorney appealed.
Decision: Reversed in part and remanded. Failure to obtain a contingent fee agreement as required by the rules of professional conduct does not bar an attorney from recovery in quantum meruit.
Held: (1) Where an attorney renders services without any agreement as to remuneration, the law implies a promise to pay a just and reasonable compensation. (2) The dismissed attorney must demonstrate that the former client would be unjustly enriched by the retention of a benefit without compensation. (3) The amount of recovery as restitution is properly determined by the lawyer's contribution to advancing the client's cause, not by his usual hourly rate. Where an attorney is dismissed for good cause, he may be entitled to no recovery other than reimbursement of reasonable expenditures. (4) Absent wrongful or unethical conduct by the discharged attorney, to deny any compensation for failure to obtain a written fee agreement would be excessively harsh.
Comment: The question is whether furtherance of the policy underlying the contingent-fee rules makes it appropriate to deny restitution in such a case. A different panel of the NJ Appellate Division recently held that it did, refusing to "sanction circumvention of the rule by permitting recovery on a quantum meruit basis": *Estate of Pinter v McGee* (1996) 293 NJ Super 119; 679 A 2d 728.

216. *Hanigan v Trumble* (1997) 252 Neb 376; 562 NW 2d 526.
Fraud – following property into its product – joint tenancy as fraudulent conveyance.
Brockman, who had acted for many years as Hanigan's attorney, accountant, and financial adviser, eventually advised Hanigan to lend him $200,000, without security, as interim financing for the construction of Brockman's new house. The house was constructed on a lot previously purchased by Brockman, taking title with his wife as joint tenants. At the time of all these transactions, Brockman was hopelessly insolvent. Some but not all of the money borrowed from Hanigan was in fact used for construction expenses. After repeated and unmet promises of repayment, Hanigan commenced suit on Brockman's promissory notes; Brockman committed suicide, and title to the house passed to his widow by survivorship. The district court gave summary judgment for Hanigan in the amount of the notes plus interest. In subsequent proceedings, the court held that the Brockman house was subject to a constructive trust [strictly speaking, an equitable lien] in favour of Hanigan, so that Hanigan might collect the whole of the judgment by levying on the house. Mrs Brockman appealed.
Decision: Affirmed in part, reversed in part, and remanded.
Held: (1) Mrs Brockman's claim that she had no knowledge of her husband's wrongdoing does not make her a bona fide purchaser. She would be unjustly enriched if permitted to retain the property of another. (2) Of the total amount advanced to Brockman, Hanigan can trace only $96,000 to the construction of the house. The house can be subject to constructive trust [equitable lien] only to this extent. (3) On the other hand, by taking title to the real estate in joint tenancy, while insolvent, Brockman made a conveyance in fraud of creditors. Hanigan is entitled to have this conveyance set aside; in effect, to satisfy his judgment from the real property as if it had been held by Brockman individually. (4) Hanigan may levy on the property only to the extent it is not exempt. Mrs Brockman and her children may be entitled to homestead and other exemptions pursuant to statute.

217. *Hunnicutt Construction Inc v Stewart Title and Trust of Tucson* (1996) 928 P 2d 725 (Ariz CA).
Priority of liens – mortgagee as bona fide purchaser takes free of constructive trust, while judgment lienor does not.
Owner fraudulently induced plaintiff builder to furnish labour and materials for improvements to real property. By the time builder obtained a judgment for the amount owing, owner had mortgaged the property to defendant; and defendant had purchased the property at its own foreclosure sale. A magistrate granted summary judgment to the builder, declaring that the property was subject to a "first lien" constructive trust securing the amount due; this constructive trust he declared to be "prior in right and time to all other liens on the real property", specifically including defendant's recorded mortgage. Thereafter, a trial court determined that the mortgage to defendant made it a bona fide purchaser without notice of the builder's claim; that the defendant's lien was accordingly senior to the plaintiff's constructive trust interest; and that the plaintiff's equitable interest was extinguished when the defendant's first mortgage was foreclosed. Plaintiff appealed.
Decision: Affirmed.
Held: (1) Unrecorded equitable interests (including constructive trust and equitable lien) are enforceable against judgment lienors but not against bona fide purchasers. "Unlike a BFP or lender for value, a judgment creditor has not relied on the recorded title in purchasing or extending credit on the property": *Restatement* §173 cmt j. (2) By contrast, bona fide purchase may have the effect of cutting off a constructive trust already existing; and a mortgagee maybe a purchaser for this purpose: *Restatement* §172 cmt a & c.

USA

218. *Jordan v Mitchell* (1997) 705 So 2d 453 (Ala Civ App).
Improvements to property of one unmarried cohabitant with funds of another – no presumption of confidential relation.
Jordan and Mitchell lived together for five years after their divorce, building a house on property owned by Mitchell. Following their eventual separation, Jordan sued to recover $20,000 she had contributed from her own funds to the construction of the house. The circuit court gave judgment for Mitchell. Jordan appealed.
Decision: Affirmed.
Held: (1) In the absence of mistake or misreliance by the donor, or wrongful conduct by the recipient, the recipient may have been enriched, but he is not deemed to have been unjustly enriched. Plaintiff's theories of mistaken improvement, equitable lien, constructive trust, money had and received, and quasi-contract all fall on the same ground. (2) If a confidential relationship is shown, "the burden of showing that the transaction was fair and righteous is on the one receiving the benefit". But the existence of a confidential relationship is not established merely by proof that the parties had a "close and affectionate" connection. There is no presumption that a confidential relation exists between unmarried cohabitants.

219. *Keller v O'Brien* (1997) 425 Mass 774; 683 NE 2d 1026.
Judgment subsequent reversed – new rule of law with prospective application – retention of payment not inequitable.
Keller paid alimony to O'Brien pursuant to a divorce decree entered in 1990. When O'Brien remarried in May 1992, Keller filed a complaint seeking to terminate alimony. In February 1994 the trial court dismissed the complaint, finding no change in O'Brien's economic circumstances sufficient to warrant a modification. On Keller's first appeal the Supreme Judicial Court reversed and remanded, announcing as a new rule that remarriage terminates alimony except in extraordinary circumstances: (1995) 420 Mass 820; 652 NE 2d 589. On remand, Keller for the first time sought restitution of alimony paid since the date of his original complaint in 1992. The trial court terminated Keller's alimony obligation in August 1995 but denied restitution. Keller appealed again.
Decision: Affirmed.
Held: (1) Restitution of a benefit is available only where its retention would be unjust. (2) Keller's failure to seek restitution prior to remand in July 1995 deprived O'Brien of "any meaningful opportunity to adjust her standard of living in anticipation of any income reduction". (3) The rule announced in this case as to the effect of remarriage should be given prospective application only. (4) Restitution of payments pursuant to a judgment subsequently reversed will be denied where it would be inequitable or involve substantial hardship. See *Restatement* §74 and cmt c.

220. *Kerin v United States Postal Service* (1997) 116 F 3d 988 (2d Cir).
Breach of contract – profitable breach not causing direct damage.
Landlord sued Tenant for breach of various lease covenants, including violation of a provision fixing the maximum occupancy of the premises. The district court gave judgment for Landlord, awarding (i) damages for injury to the premises and (ii) $65,000 in respect of Tenant's unjust enrichment. In calculating this latter sum as the value to Tenant of its overuse of the premises, the court stated that it had "taken care not to duplicate plaintiff's recovery or compensate him for items for which he had been compensated elsewhere." Tenant appealed.
Decision: Affirmed as to damages, reversed as to the recovery in restitution.
Held: "Because [Landlord] has not proved that the benefit enjoyed by [Tenant] harmed him beyond the contract damages he obtained, he is not entitled to an additional sum."
Comment: The case is noteworthy for its facts and for the outcome in the district court,

notwithstanding the complete failure of the Second Circuit to appreciate what was before it. It is exceedingly rare that a real-life case presents so lucidly the issue of restitution to recover the profits of an "efficient breach". The facts here are particularly suggestive in that breach of a lease clause concerning maximum occupancy so closely resembles the intentional surcharge of an easement, for which restitution is available without regard to harm. See *Raven Red Ash Coal Co v Ball* (1946) 185 Va 534; 39 SE 2d 231.

221. *Klein v Fidelity & Deposit Co of Am* (1997) 117 Md App 317; 700 A 2d 262.
Insurance – expenditure by insured averts claim for which insurer would have been liable.
Klein was president and sole shareholder of Merritt Savings & Loan, insured by Fidelity under a standard directors' and officers' liability policy. In 1985 Merritt was rescued from near failure, amid charges of mismanagement by Klein and threats of litigation, by a sale of all its outstanding shares to Chase. Klein claimed reimbursement of expenses incurred in negotiating the sale. Fidelity denied coverage and Klein brought suit, asserting a claim under the policy and a claim in restitution. The circuit court ruled in favour of Fidelity. Klein appealed.
Decision: Affirmed.
Held: (1) Warnings and threats of Klein's potential liability in connection with the near-failure of Merritt did not constitute a covered "claim" within the coverage of the D&O policy. (2) Although the sale to Chase conferred great benefit on Fidelity, Klein is not entitled to restitution because Fidelity's retention of the benefit is not inequitable. (3) Restitution to an insured for preventive measures that benefit the insurer is not available where the insured would have undertaken the same measures purely from self-interest: *McNeilab Inc v North River Ins Co* (1986) 645 FS 525 (DNJ), affd (1987) 831 F 2d 287 (3d Cir). (4) Proof that expenditures were made "in an emergency situation" is a *sine qua non* for recovery in such cases. Here there was no consultation with Fidelity and no claim for reimbursement until more than a year after the sale to Chase was completed.

222. *Lackey v Lackey* (1997) 691 So 2d 990 (Miss).
Breach of fiduciary duty – insurance policy purchased with stolen trust funds – tracing through commingled fund into insurance proceeds – burden of proof.
Buster Lackey as trustee diverted large sums from a trust account into his own personal and business accounts, where they were commingled with funds from other sources. Premiums on a life insurance policy in the amount of $1.1 million were paid from these commingled funds. Following Buster's death, beneficiary Ellen Lackey brought suit to recover misappropriated trust assets, seeking *inter alia* a lien on the insurance proceeds. The chancery court gave judgment for Ellen against Buster's estate in the amount of $1.6 million but denied her claim to execute against insurance proceeds: while the premiums were likely paid in large part with stolen trust funds, it was impossible to determine in what proportion. Ellen appealed.
Decision: Reversed. Ellen may satisfy her judgment out of insurance proceeds except to the extent that the policy beneficiaries (Buster's children) can establish that premiums were not paid with stolen funds.
Held: (1) Statutes providing that life insurance proceeds are exempt from the claims of creditors do not apply to insurance purchased with stolen funds. (2) "Where commingling of trust property with other property is through the fault of the trustee, the entire mass will be treated as trust property or funds, except insofar as the trustee may be able to distinguish the two". *State v Harvey* (1968) 214 So 2d 817, 820. Application of the rule to the present case makes it appropriate that Buster's children (the insurance beneficiaries) bear the burden of establishing what proportion of the premiums, if any, was paid with Buster's own funds. (3) There is no windfall to Ellen, since her recovery is limited to the amount that will make her whole.

223. ***Lumbermens Mut Cas Co v Department of Rev & Fin*** (1997) 564 NW 2d 431 (Iowa).
Subrogation – embezzlement by employee of tax authority – funds recovered by imposing tax on employee's illegal income.
Surety issuing fidelity bond to state tax department paid $600,000 to restore funds embezzled by Department employee. Department assessed income tax in respect of embezzled funds, attached all available property of the employee, and collected $145,000 in tax. Surety sued Department to recover this money on a theory of subrogation. The trial court gave summary judgment to Department. Surety appealed.
Decision: Affirmed.
Held: (1) Surety is entitled by subrogation to funds recovered by Department through restoration of money wrongfully taken, but not to funds collected as delinquent taxes. (2) Tax collected on employee's illegal income does not reduce the loss to the Department as the result of embezzlement by employee. (3) Department's action in exhausting employee's assets by tax liens did not violate its contractual obligation to do nothing to impair Surety's right of recovery by subrogation.
Comment: This puzzle has a solution. To the extent that the assets subjected to lien were the traceable proceeds of the embezzled funds, Department (in its capacity as employer, not tax collector) had an equitable interest that should have been exempt from a lien for employee's taxes. See *Atlas Inc v United States* (1978) 459 FS 1000 (DND). If Surety had acted promptly, it might have claimed this equity for itself via subrogation.

224. ***Mobile Telecommunications Technologies Corp v Aetna Cas & Surety Co*** (1997) 962 FS 952 (SD Miss).
Mistaken payment – threat of litigation – payment with knowledge of the facts or in conscious ignorance.
Mtel paid $2 million in legal fees for its defence against claims of securities fraud, then sought reimbursement from Aetna under "directors and officers" liability coverage. Aetna made a provisional payment of $1 million. Six months later, Mtel sued Aetna to recover the balance of its expenditure. Aetna counterclaimed to recover an unspecified portion of the sum previously paid, alleging that payment had been made under duress and by a mistake of fact as to the amount due. Mtel moved to dismiss the counterclaim.
Held: Motion granted.
Decision: (1) Mississippi treats as "voluntary" a payment that is made "without compulsion or fraud, and without any mistake of fact, of a demand which the payor does not owe, and which is not enforceable against him, instead of invoking the remedy or defence which the law affords against such demand, and when there has been no agreement between the parties at the time of payment, that any excess will be repaid": *McLean v Love* (1934) 172 Miss 168; 157 So 361. (2) Mtel's implicit threat to sue Aetna for damages resulting from a delay in payment cannot constitute compulsion in this context, since the threat of litigation to enforce a good-faith claim is not improper coercion. (3) Conscious ignorance of facts that would reveal what portion of Mtel's legal fees were covered by insurance does not constitute relievable mistake as to the amount of liability. (4) Aetna could have sought declaratory judgment of the amount due.

225. ***Nappi v Nappi Distributors*** (1997) 691 A 2d1198 (Maine).
Subrogation – corporation discharges gratuitous obligation of its deceased president.
The president and principal shareholder of a company undertook, in his personal capacity and gratuitously, to construct an addition to a house occupied by an invalid friend. He died when the work was under way but before it was completed and paid for. The company thereupon caused the project to be finished and paid the associated expenses, despite notice from the decedent's widow and executrix that she authorised no such expenditure. When the widow later demanded

payment to the estate of certain promissory notes of the company, the company asserted a right of set-off in the amount expended to complete the construction project. The widow sued for the balance of the notes. The trial court held that the company was entitled to the claimed set-off via subrogation. The widow appealed.

Decision: Affirmed.

Held: (1) Former president's promise to pay the costs of the improvements in question, although gratuitous, was an enforceable obligation under the doctrine of promissory estoppel, inasmuch as the owners of the realty had permitted the project to proceed in reliance on such promise. (2) Company did not act voluntarily or officiously when it paid the costs of the project to protect its own reputation and interest. (3) Evidence that "it would have reflected badly on the business if the project were not completed", and that company faced a threat of litigation because its name appeared on some of the contractors' bills, was sufficient to establish that in paying these debts the company did not act as a stranger to the transaction.

226. *Parker Motor Freight v Fifth Third Bank* (1997) 116 F 3d 1137 (6th Cir).
Good-faith receipt – change of position – bank set-off of deposit claimed by third party – interline obligations between motor carriers as trust property.
Pursuant to an "interline agreement" between motor carriers Parker and OK, OK received payments from shippers that were owed in part to Parker. Payments were deposited by OK in its account at Bank; Bank set off these funds against OK's debt to Bank under a defaulted loan. Parker sued Bank to recover its share of OK's deposits. The district court gave summary judgment for Bank. Parker appealed.

Decision: Reversed and remanded. The trial court must determine whether Bank changed position as a result of the setoff.

Held: (1) By federal common law, a payment of freight to one railroad for "interline" transportation is held in trust by the payee for the other carriers to the extent of their entitlement. The same rule is here held to apply to payments for interline services by motor carriers. (2) By the majority rule, a bank exercising a right of set-off takes its depositor's funds free of the equities of third parties of which it has no notice. (3) Ohio follows a minority rule according to which a bank, even without notice of a third party's claim to a deposit, "cannot apply such funds to the individual indebtedness of the depositor, where such lack of knowledge has not resulted in any change in the Bank's position and no superior equities have been raised in its favour".

Comment: The case turns on a fundamental question about the affirmative defences to restitution. On the division of US authority in the particular context of a bank's set-off of funds in which a third party asserts an interest, see the Annotation at 8 ALR 3d 235.

227. *Perlman v Prudential Life Ins Co of America* (1997) 686 So 2d 1378 (Fla CA).
Rescission – measure of recovery to policyholder on rescission of life insurance for fraudulent inducement.
Perlman purchased insurance on the lives of his elderly parents. Following a dispute about the amount of premiums due, Perlman refused to make further payments; Prudential terminated the policy and refunded its cash value. Perlman sued to rescind the policy, alleging that he had been induced to buy it by fraudulent misrepresentations about the scheduled premiums. Prudential moved to dismiss, arguing that Prudential would be entitled in any event to retain its earned premium for the period the policy was in effect; while the balance, or cash value, had already been refunded. The trial court accepted this reasoning and dismissed the claim. Perlman appealed.

Held: Reversed and remanded. Prudential is entitled to retain only the actuarial value of the insured risk, without compensation for its expenses, commissions, and profits.

Decision: (1) It appears to be the majority rule that, if a policy is rescinded for misrepresentation or wrongful cancellation by the issuer, the insurer is liable to refund all premiums plus interest: Annotation (1970) 34 ALR 3d 245, 312-323. But we reject this outcome as inconsistent with the requirement that, on rescission, the parties be restored to the status quo ante. (2) Better authorities credit the insurer with the value of the insurance for the period the policy was in force. (3) Value for this purpose is measured, not by premiums, but by the actuarial value of the covered risk, specifically excluding the insurer's expenses, costs, profits, and commissions paid to others. (4) Insurer has the burden of establishing the relevant allocation.

228. *Reidling v Holcomb* (1997) 225 Ga App 229; 483 SE 2d 624.
Mistaken improvements – restitution denied.
Reidling, a builder, was shown an unimproved lot in a new subdivision; he walked the boundaries of the property with a representative of the developer, who gave him a copy of a survey on which the parcel in question was identified as Lot 4. Reidling agreed to purchase Lot 4. The seller delivered a deed to Lot 4 in which the property was identified by reference to the recorded plan of subdivision: the recorded plan was a later version of the survey shown to Reidling, on which the former Lot 4 was renumbered as Lot 1. This Lot 1 was sold to Hulsey. When Reidling had completed 75% of the construction of a house on the property, Hulsey required him to vacate; Hulsey completed construction of the house himself. Reidling brought an action against the developer for negligence and against Hulsey on a theory of restitution. The trial court gave summary judgment for the defendants. Reidling appealed.
Decision: Affirmed.
Held: (1) The "sole proximate cause" of Reidling's loss was his negligence in failing to examine the deed and search title before purchase. (2) Unjust enrichment requires knowing receipt and conscious failure to reject the benefit. But there is no evidence that Hulsey stood by while aware of Reidling's error.
Comment: (1) If Hulsey, like Reidling, was a professional builder who completed the house in order to sell it, the denial of restitution against Hulsey is indefensible. (2) If, instead of vacating, Reidling had defended a suit in ejectment, he would have had the statutory right to "set off the value of all permanent improvements placed on the land in good faith". Hulsey would then have had the option either (a) to pay Reidling for the value of the improvements or (b) to surrender title to Reidling in exchange for the value of the unimproved land: Ga Code Ann (1982) §44-11-9.

229. *Rush v Alaska Mortgage Group* (1997) 937 P 2d 647 (Alaska).
Mortgages – prior lien discharged without intent to subordinate – subrogation.
Rush held a note secured by a first mortgage on Blackacre, which she exchanged for a new note and a new mortgage that was seventh in priority. When the first mortgage was extinguished, Rush's attorney (if not Rush herself) had actual knowledge of the intervening liens. Upon subsequent foreclosure by one of the other mortgagees, Rush sought to be restored to her prior position as senior creditor. The trial court gave summary judgment against Rush, holding that (1) actual notice of intervening liens defeated her claim to equitable subrogation, and (2) her intent to subordinate the original lien might be inferred from this actual notice, combined with the fact that she received higher monthly payments under the substitute note. The court found a "business decision" to favour higher monthly payments over lower monthly payments with higher security.
Decision: Reversed and remanded. It was error to grant summary judgment against Rush where the critical issue turns on her intent to subordinate her first-mortgage security.
Held: (1) Equitable subrogation prevents unjust enrichment as a result of the inadvertent release of a security interest in land. Under this doctrine, a senior creditor who releases a mortgage in exchange for a new one, though without an agreement for subordination of intervening liens, is not subordinated to those intervening encumbrances absent either an intent to

subordinate or "paramount equities" in favour of junior creditors. (2) Constructive notice and negligent ignorance of the intervening lien are immaterial to whether the equitable reinstatement of a prior lien should be allowed. (3) Even actual notice is not dispositive of equitable subrogation, being at most evidence of the creditor's intent to subordinate: "priority is simply not lost by substitution unless that is the intent of the parties".

Comment: By a large majority, US jurisdictions adhere to the rule that actual notice of intervening liens bars subrogation, notwithstanding the unjust enrichment of junior encumbrancers at the expense of the claimant. For a recent example, see *First Fidelity Bank v Travelers Mortgage Services* (1997) 300 NJ Super 559; 693 A 2d 525.The more liberal position here adopted by the Alaska court accords with the recommendation of the new mortgage *Restatement*, to the effect that "knowledge is not necessarily fatal to the grantee's claim of subrogation, if equity would nonetheless dictate the recognition of subrogation": *Restatement Third, Property (Mortgages)* (1997) §7.6, comment d.

230. *Sharon Steel Corp v Aetna Casualty & Surety Co* (1997) 931 P 2d 127 (Utah).
Insurance – contribution between insurers with common liability to defend – statute of limitations – effect of settlement – method of allocation.
Sharon sued several liability insurers to compel them to assume the defence of certain environmental protection claims. Aetna ultimately expended substantial amounts in defence of Sharon; Aetna sought contribution from Hartford, another insurer, arguing that the two companies had an equal obligation to defend their policyholder. Consistent with its view of its policy liability, Hartford tendered only 5% of defence costs; Aetna paid the remainder. Hartford then settled with Sharon, obtaining a complete release from further liability under its policy. Aetna sued Hartford for contribution (here denoted "equitable subrogation"). The trial court gave summary judgment for Hartford on the ground that, "since an insurer's subrogation right is derivative of the rights of its insured", Sharon's settlement with Hartford extinguished any claim that Aetna might have had for contribution. Aetna appealed.
Decision: Reversed.
Held: (1) An insurer that settles a claim for which another insurer is liable may recover via equitable subrogation: *State Farm Mut Auto Ins Co v Northwestern Nat'l Ins Co* (1996) 912 P 2d 983 (Utah); [1997] RLR §256. (2) Although the authorities are not all in agreement, the tendency of the decisions is to allow an insurer, "under the doctrines of contribution or equitable subrogation", to recover costs incurred in the defence of its policyholder from other insurers that were equally obliged to defend yet failed to do so. Aetna has a claim for equitable subrogation to compel Hartford to contribute its fair share of defence expenditures. (3) Aetna's cross-claim against Hartford is not time-barred, even though it was not asserted within the applicable (four-year) period of limitations from the date Aetna first made a payment entitling it to contribution. Because a cross-claim for contribution is "not an independent action for affirmative relief", it "relates back" to the date of filing of the original complain (by Sharon against its insurers) and was therefore timely filed. (4) Hartford's settlement with Sharon is no defence to Aetna's claim via subrogation, where Hartford had notice that Aetna had paid more than its share of defence costs for which both insurers were liable. (5) On remand, the trial court shall allocate defence costs between the companies in proportion to their respective periods of coverage multiplied by their applicable policy limits from time to time.
Comment: Calling this liability "equitable subrogation" instead of simply "contribution" leads to unnecessary difficulties, particularly as the court suggest no reason why the action should not simply be viewed as one in contribution. The generous ruling on the limitations issue – reflecting the current enthusiasm for equitable loss allocation between insurers – will not help an insurer that undertakes a single-handed defence of its policyholder without first being sued.

231. *Shield Benefit Administrators v University of Michigan* (1997) 225 Mich App 467; 571 NW 2d 556.

Mistaken payment – insurer pays claim exceeding policy limits – good-faith receipt.

Insurer paid hospital for services provided to policyholder, discovering later that the claim exceeded policy limits. Hospital refused to return the payment, and Insurer sued in restitution. The trial court gave summary judgment for Insurer. Hospital appealed.

Decision: Reversed.

Held: (1) Payment made under a mistake of fact is ordinarily recoverable without regard to the payor's negligence, absent detrimental reliance on the part of the recipient. (2) Court hereby recognises an additional affirmative defence in favour of a "third-party creditor" who receives payment without notice of the mistake, notwithstanding the absence of detrimental reliance. See *Restatement* §14(1).

Comment: Mistaken payments by insurers to hospitals have brought expanded recognition of the affirmative defence of good-faith receipt, sometimes called a "good-faith creditor exception" to restitution for mistaken payments. (The defence is what *Restatement* §14 calls "Discharge for Value".) *Federated Mut In Co v Good Samaritan Hosp* (1974) 191 Neb 212; 214 NW 2d 493 is often treated as the leading case.

232. *Sholer v State ex rel Dep't of Public Safety* (1997) 1995 OK 152; 1997 Okla Lexis 85; 945 P 2d 469.

Void taxes and assessments – statutory notice requirement – statute of limitations – sovereign immunity.

Following suspension of their driver's licences, plaintiffs were charged a separate "reinstatement fee" for each offence; they brought suit to recover amounts paid in excess of the single reinstatement fee authorised by statute. At an earlier stage of the case the Oklahoma Supreme Court held that (1) multiple fees were unauthorised; (2) plaintiffs might recover the overcharge by an action for money had and received; (3) such an action was governed by the three-year statute of limitations applicable to an action on a contract express or implied: 1995 Okla Lexis 64. The State moved for a rehearing, arguing for the first time that the courts had no jurisdiction to hear the claim where plaintiffs had failed to comply with a statute regulating the recovery of fees or taxes alleged to be "in whole or in part unconstitutional or otherwise invalid"; the statute requires written notice at the time of payment stating the grounds of complaint and that suit will be brought for recovery. The Supreme Court granted a rehearing and issued a supplemental opinion.

Decision: Affirmed.

Held: The plaintiffs do not challenge the constitutionality or validity of the statute under which the fees were collected; their theory is that the State misinterpreted a valid enactment. Under the circumstances the statutory requirement of protest has no applicability.

Per Lavender J (dissenting): (1) An action to recover unauthorised fees is an action in restitution, available to prevent unjust enrichment. (2) Because the claim does not depend on implied contract, it is properly governed by Oklahoma's five-year statute of limitations applicable to "an action for relief, not hereinbefore provided for". (3) Because the action is not founded on a tort (for which a statute provides the mode of recovery), nor a contractual obligation (for which the State is now presumed to have waived its immunity from suit), the issue of sovereign immunity to a claim in restitution must be directly addressed. "Reason no longer supports the use of sovereign immunity by the state to obtain unjust enrichment at the expense of a citizen." The doctrine should accordingly be abolished in restitution cases.

Comment: The holding on rehearing is interesting in itself, as a distinctly liberal interpretation of a common form of protest requirement that often bars restitution in such cases. But the most useful part of this obscure case is the dissenting opinion of Lavender J.

233. State v Mitchell (1997) 930 P 2d 1284 (Alaska).
Judgment subsequently reversed —payment of child support by one not the father – intermediary agency not liable for amounts properly paid over to mother.
State of Alaska sued Mitchell, alleging his paternity of an infant, to enforce duty of child support; Mitchell did not answer, and State obtained default judgment. From 1990 to 1994, State collected some $14,000 through garnishment, of which it remitted $9,000 to the child's mother. In 1993 the superior court set aside the default judgment, when blood tests conclusively determined that Mitchell could not be the child's father. Noting that the State was partially to blame for the erroneous judgment – in that it had not presented all relevant evidence to the court that issues the default judgment – the superior court ordered that all funds obtained from Mitchell be reimbursed, including those funds paid over to the mother. State appealed.

Decision: Reversed in part and remanded. The State is not liable to reimburse that portion of the funds properly paid to the child's mother.

Held: (1) State would be unjustly enriched if it were permitted to retain monies paid by Mitchell under a vacated judgment. (2) As to funds paid over by State to mother, State is in the position of an agent whose duty is to remit funds to a disclosed principal. (3) "An agent is not liable to a person who is entitled to the return of money paid to the agent in his representative capacity, if the latter has in good faith and without notice or knowledge or the other's right to reclaim, paid the money over to his principal." (4) Mitchell has a potential claim for reimbursement against those persons whose obligation of child support he has discharged.

234. State Farm Fire & Cas Co v East Bay Mun Utility Dist (1997) 53 Cal App 4th 769; 62 Cal Rptr 2d 72.
Insurance – subrogation – insurer paying loss not covered by policy does not do so as a volunteer.
State Farm paid a claim under its standard homeowner's policy for damage caused by a ruptured water main, although coverage of such losses was apparently precluded by applicable policy exclusions. State Farm then sued East Bay, the utility company responsible for the damage, on a theory of subrogation. The trial court gave summary judgment for East Bay: because its policy did not cover the loss, State Farm acted as a volunteer in paying the claim; as such it was not entitled to subrogation. State Farm appealed.

Decision: Reversed.

Held: (1) Modern, expansive view of subrogation extends the claim to one who pays in order to protect his own rights or interests, and whose payment is favoured by public policy, even where payment is not in performance of a legal duty: *Employers Ins Co v Pacific Indem Co* (1959) 167 Cal App 2d 369; 334 P 2d 658. (2) Insurer need not present ironclad proof of its policy liability to defeat a finding that it has made a "voluntary" payment to its insured. (3) Where the nature of the loss is within the basic scope of policy coverage, an insurer that pays a claim is not necessarily a volunteer even if it acts in the face of judicial authority suggesting that applicable exclusions would enable it to deny liability. (4) When East Bay was disputing the amount of its liability, and the insured required prompt settlement of its claim to make necessary house repairs, State Farm acted in a reasonable and morally responsible manner by timely paying the claim and then seeking subrogation. (5) Denial of subrogation on the grounds that State Farm acted as a "volunteer" would frustrate public policy favouring the prompt settlement, in good faith, of legitimate insurance claims.

235. State Farm General Ins Co v Stewart (1997) 288 Ill App 3d 678; 681 NE 2d 625.
Insurance – vendor and purchaser – subrogation of insurer to collateral contract rights of insured.
DeFrancesco contracted to sell Stewart improved real property for a price of $75,000 plus assumption of a $20,000 indebtedness. Stewart paid $5,000 down and agreed to pay the balance when she obtained financing. DeFrancesco delivered a deed and possession of the property. By

the terms of the contract (and Illinois statute), the risk of loss passed to Stewart upon execution of the contract. On the day that Stewart obtained a loan for the balance of the price, the building was destroyed by fire; Stewart refrained from payment "until we figured out what the insurance companies were going to do." Both parties were insured against loss by casualty to the property. State Farm paid DeFrancesco $79,000 (its policy limits); Hartford paid Stewart $130,000. State Farm thereafter brought this action against Stewart, asserting that it was subrogated to DeFrancesco's contract rights, seeking payment of the balance of the contract price. The circuit court gave summary judgment for State Farm. Stewart appealed.

Decision: Reversed.

Held: (1) Although the authorities are sharply divided, we favour the view that a casualty insurer may not be subrogated to collateral contract rights of the insured against a third-party vendee of the property. (2) Equitable subrogation requires that the insurer's payment extinguish the debt of a third party primarily liable to the insured for the insured loss. Here, DeFrancesco was the beneficiary of two distinct obligations, one on the policy, the other on the contract. (3) There is no unjust enrichment or windfall to Stewart, where nothing would prevent DeFrancesco from enforcing the contract against her in a separate action.

Comment: An unsatisfactory addition to the rich store of cases on this complex topic: see Palmer §23.2. The chief lesson of the opinion is that it is wrong to generalise about a rule (insurer's subrogation to "collateral contract rights" *vel non*) without distinguishing the different circumstances in which the question arises. A decision denying subrogation on more typical facts (*eg* vendor has insurance, purchaser has none, property is destroyed before passage of title) bears little analogy to the unusual situation here, in which two insurers have evidently paid for the same loss. It is true that the insurer's assertion of "collateral contract rights" will not fit the usual model of subrogation arising on discharge of another's obligation, and in the more typical case it may be an error to regard these problems as part of restitution at all: the answer (one way or the other) might be better explained as a function of the parties' implicit contractual allocation of risks. Here, by contrast, the problem seems genuinely restitutionary because State Farm has paid a claim by mistake: at the time of the fire, DeFrancesco appears to have had no insurable interest in the property and no casualty loss. Allowing State Farm to assert DeFrancesco's contract claim against Stewart would ensure that neither DeFrancesco nor Stewart was unjustly enriched in consequence of State Farm's mistake. Whether a restitution claim should be barred on the grounds that payment was made with knowledge of the facts is a separate, pertinent issue that the court does not address.

236. ***Wilhm v Ekan Properties*** (1997) 262 Kan 495; 939 P 2d 918.

Tax refund – refund paid to prior owner, where taxes paid in part from proceeds of foreclosure sale.
Partnership owned Blackacre, subject to mortgage; property taxes for three years had been paid in part only, the balance being delinquent; Partnership had challenged the tax valuation as excessive. Partnership defaulted, Mortgagee foreclosed and purchased Blackacre at auction; sheriff paid the delinquent taxes from the sale proceeds before paying the balance to Mortgagee. Mortgagee thereafter sold Blackacre to Buyer. After the foreclosure sale, the tax authorities had reduced their assessment of Blackacre; and, following the sale to Buyer, the county treasurer refunded to Partnership a portion of the tax collected for the three years in question. Buyer sued Partnership to recover a portion of the tax refund. The trial court gave summary judgment for Buyer. Partnership appealed.

Decision: Affirmed.

Held: (1) Where a mortgagee is entitled to all the proceeds of a foreclosure sale (because they do not exceed the secured indebtedness), if proceeds are used in part to discharge taxes the mortgagee acquires a claim to share in an eventual refund. (2) Mortgagee's inchoate right to refund was assigned to Buyer. (3) Trial court properly allocated refund between the parties in the proportion that each had contributed to tax payments under the original assessment. (4) Partnership was not entitled to set off, against its liability to Buyer, a portion of its legal expenses in pursuing the refund claim.

Comment: A simpler allocation would give the refund to the mortgagor to the extent he had overpaid taxes under the revised assessment, with the balance to the mortgagee.

237. ***Wolff v Ampacet Corp*** (1996) 284 Ill App 3d 824; 673 NE 2d 745.
Performance of contract with third party – common fund – attorney seeks fee from strangers benefited by judgment obtained.
Wolff, an attorney, commenced an action on behalf of himself and three clients, all creditors of a bankrupt corporation, to obtain reinstatement in the bankruptcy proceeding of claims that had been dismissed for procedural reasons. The action was ultimately successful; Wolff received the agreed-upon contingent fee from his three clients. The judicial ruling obtained by Wolff had the effect of reinstating the claims of numerous other creditors in the same proceeding, none of whom had taken any action to challenge the dismissal of their claims. Wolff now demanded a legal fee from an unspecified number of these other creditors, including Ampacet, which ultimately recovered some $65,000 as an indirect consequence of Wolff's efforts. Ampacet refused to pay, and Wolff brought suit on a theory of restitution. The trial court gave summary judgment for Ampacet. Wolff appealed.

Decision: Affirmed.

Held: (1) The doctrine of "common fund" recovery permits a party or an attorney to recover the expenses of litigation from the fund created thereby, so that the expense is borne equitably by those benefiting from the successful suit. It has no application to the present case, in which no fund was created by Wolff's efforts. (2) Recovery in quasi-contract depends on the existence of a duty owed by the party to be charged. Where there was no relationship between Ampacet and Wolff there could be no obligation in restitution.

NOTER UP

Humphrey v O'Connor [1997] RLR §242; cert denied (1997) 940 P 2d 1015 (Colo CA).
Mohamed v Kerr (1996) 91 F 3d 1124 (8th Cir); [1997] RLR §248, enforced on subsequent appeal *sub nom* ***Mohamed v Unum Life Ins Co*** (1997) 129 F 3d 478 (8th Cir).

REVIEW ARTICLE

RESULTING TRUSTS[1]

Equity lawyers do not lack for textbooks which deal with equitable doctrines, many of which, such as election or donatio mortis causa, are seldom encountered today. But they have long lacked an up to date textbook which satisfactorily explains equity's core concepts and special techniques. As a result commercial lawyers, who have discovered the apparent advantages of alleging breach of trust or fiduciary duty, can obtain little guidance from the textbooks on the nature or scope of these concepts. The result can be seen in the recent mortgage fraud litigation. Equity lawyers have been challenged to define their own concepts, and have found great difficulty in doing so. They have been compelled to acknowledge that many of the terms which they use are ambiguous and that, as always, ambiguity of expression has concealed confusion of thought.

The relentless advance of the law of restitution, however, has brought help from an unexpected quarter. Thirty years after the publication of Goff and Jones' great work, and ten years after Professor Birks gave the subject a formal structure, his former pupils are producing a torrent of monographs on the concepts which lie at the intersection of restitution and equity. They have thrown light on the constructive trust, fiduciary obligations, subrogation, and tracing. Now Dr Chambers, another of Professor Birks' former pupils, has given us a monograph on resulting trusts. It is the first book to explore this subject in depth. Yet it lies at the very heart of equity and, as its author convincingly demonstrates, plays a major role in the law of restitution. For far too long the resulting trust has lain neglected in the shadow of its invasive neighbour the constructive trust. Dr Chambers has attempted to cut back the tangled undergrowth of the constructive trust and let in light to allow the resulting trust to grow. As a long-time member of the resulting trust supporters' club I am naturally biased, but I believe that he has substantially succeeded. If I have any criticism, it is that he may have gone too far.

Dr Chambers begins his book with an analysis of the nature of the resulting trust. He recognises that, like the constructive trust, it arises by operation of law, but that, unlike the constructive trust, it gives effect to intention. His central thesis, which he develops at length, is that a resulting trust arises whenever there is a transfer of property in circumstances in which the transferor (or more accurately the person at whose expense the property was provided) did not intend to benefit the recipient. This was Professor Scott's view, but it has not previously been the received wisdom in England. What Dr Chambers articulates with great clarity is that the resulting trust responds to the absence of an intention on the part of the transferor to pass the beneficial interest, not to a positive intention to retain it.

This provides much needed rationalisation and simplification. It explains how the resulting trust can arise where the person at whose expense the property was provided lacks capacity to create a trust or is unaware of the transfer; and even where he positively does not wish to retain a beneficial interest (as in *Vandervell v IRC* [1967] 2 AC 291, where the retention of a beneficial interest by the transferor destroyed the effectiveness of the tax avoidance scheme which he was aiming to implement).

In *Vandervell (No. 2)* [1974] ch 269, Megarry J sought to explain this apparent anomaly by divining that there are two categories of resulting trusts, one which is presumed and one which

---

[1] RESULTING TRUSTS. *Robert Chambers.* Oxford: Clarendon Press. 1997. xxx and 244 pp, plus 12 pp Bibliography and 4 pp Index. Hardback £45.

is automatic. This curious classification has been accepted by several academic writers, but it has now been rejected by the House of Lords in *Westdeutsche Landesbank v Islington LBC* [1996] AC 669,708. Dr Chambers demonstrates that it is wrong. There is no distinction between the cases. The resulting trust arises by operation of law (*ie* automatically) whether or not the provider of the property intended to retain a beneficial interest, since it responds to the absence of any intention on his part to pass the beneficial interest to the recipient. The absence of any such intention may be affirmatively proved or presumed from the circumstances. Dr Chambers rightly insists on the distinction between the resulting trust itself and the presumption which is one means by which it may be established, an essential distinction which Megarry J's nomenclature blurs.

Some commentators have considered Dr Chambers' analysis to be inconsistent with that of William Swadling, who has shown that it is not necessary to prove that the transfer was by way of gift in order to rebut the presumption of resulting trust; it may be rebutted by proof of any circumstance which shows that the property transferred was not intended to be held on trust. Swadling himself appears to be of this number. I do not agree. Proof, for example, that a payment was made by mistake (*eg* to repay a non-existent debt) will defeat the resulting trust on Dr Chambers' analysis also, since it shows that the transferor did intend (albeit mistakenly) to pass the beneficial interest to the recipient. A man who pays a debt does intend the creditor to take the money beneficially in discharge of the debt. His intention to dispose of the beneficial interest in the money is not affected by the fact that he is mistaken in believing that he owes the money. It is perfectly possible to accept Dr Chambers' analysis of the resulting trust and yet hold that a mistaken payment is not held in trust by the recipient.

Dr Chambers then analyses the nature of the *Quistclose* trust. I have naturally found this part of the book the most disappointing and the least persuasive, for he goes out of his way to reject my own (now unfashionable) explanation that it is merely a resulting trust for the transferor with a superadded mandate to the transferee to apply the money for a stated purpose. It is difficult to understand why Dr Chambers finds it necessary to reject this analysis, which would sit comfortably with his own exposition of the resulting trust. There is no doubt that the transferor retains a proprietary interest which is extinguished only when the money is applied for the designated purpose or returned; and that if the transferee has a beneficial interest at all in the meantime (which I do not accept) it is minimal. He must keep the money separate; he cannot apply it for his own benefit; he cannot refuse to return it to the transferor if demanded, and in the meantime must apply it for the stated purpose or any other purpose which the transferor may substitute; and if he becomes bankrupt the money does not vest in his trustee in bankruptcy. The money must be applied for a purpose specified by the transferor; and if the transferor becomes bankrupt his trustee in bankruptcy can revoke the transferee's mandate and demand repayment. If there is any content to beneficial ownership at all, the transferor is the beneficial owner and the transferee is not.

It is, of course, not necessary that the payment should be by way of loan; Lord Wilberfoce clearly envisaged the possibility of a *Quistclose* trust superimposed on an outright payment. A common example of this occurs when a prospective mortgagee pays the mortgage advance to its own solicitor. The money is obviously trust money and must be paid into the solicitor's client account. It is paid for a particular purpose and, unless his instructions are revoked, must be applied by the solicitor in or towards completion of a specified purchase and mortgage of land. On any analysis the trust is a resulting trust which arises at the moment the money is received by the solicitor. Why should the analysis of the position in equity be any different where the trust for repayment is reinforced by a legal obligation to repay?

Equity lawyers will be pleased that Dr Chambers rejects Lord Browne-Wilkinson's unorthodox use of the doctrine that "equity acts on the conscience" and the unduly narrow view which he took of the resulting trust in consequence. His reinstatement of the previous case law and his criticisms of the reasoning in the *Westdeutsche Landsbank* case are convincing. The fear that the resulting trust would entail the injustice of imposing fiduciary duties on the recipient of misdirected property was always unjustified.

Restitution lawyers will be similarly grateful to Dr Chambers for his thesis that the resulting trust is a response to unjust enrichment and not merely an instrument for vindicating rights of property. This is a controversial question of categorisation upon which it would be unprofitable (and unwise) for the judges to enter. But he presents compelling arguments for categorising the trust which arises in the three party cases (where the ground for restitution is variously described as "ignorance" or "powerlessness" but is really want of title) as a resulting and not a constructive trust. This is a view which I have always championed. Dr Chambers even suggests that the equity to rescind a disposition, which is another equitable response to unjust enrichment, is in reality "a resulting trust in disguise."

Here I think he goes too far, largely because he rejects the distinction between property transferred in breach of trust or fiduciary duty (the three party case) and property transferred by means of a transaction which is voidable for mistake, misrepresentation and so on (the two party case). Yet there is a real distinction between property obtained, albeit improperly, with the knowledge and consent of the beneficial owner, and property obtained without his knowledge or authority by a fiduciary exploiting his position for his own benefit. The doctrine of equity is that equitable ownership is not affected by a breach of trust or fiduciary duty. A transfer of property in breach of such a duty does not pass the beneficial interest to the transferee; equity's response is to raise a resulting trust in favour of the transferor. In the final chapters of his book Dr Chambers argues that the position is the same where the transfer is made without breach of trust or fiduciary duty but is voidable in equity.

These are some of the most difficult and to my mind least successful chapters in the book. In the absence of a breach of trust or fiduciary duty, a voidable transfer passes a defeasible title to the transferee. Whether the transfer is voidable at law or only in equity, it is effective to pass the equitable ownership pending divestment. Equity's response is rescission and (sometimes) retransfer in specie, not a resulting trust. The problem is to know when retransfer in specie will be ordered, and (in the absence of a resulting trust) why. I have suggested a possible answer elsewhere. It may not provide the solution, but it is better than requiring the resulting trust to do work for which it is not fitted.

My criticisms, however, are my own. Others will not share them. All will agree, however, that this is an excellent book in every way. It points the way to a better understanding of one of equity's core concepts. If it succeeds in restoring it to its proper place at the heart of equity it will also bring order to an important area of the law of restitution.

Peter Millett,
A Lord of Appeal in Ordinary.

BOOK REVIEWS

THE LAW OF TRACING. *LD Smith. Oxford: Clarendon Press. 1997. xliv and 396 pp, plus 8 pp Index. Hardback £50.*

This is an important work but it is not easy going for the general reader. It has well-defined and ambitious aims: to restate the principles of the law of tracing (and claims which tracing supports) in such a way as to demonstrate their rationality, unity and justice. The work is divided into four parts: foundations; following; tracing; and claiming. Dr Smith rightly insists on the distinction between the process of tracing and the claim to which it gives effect. The fourth part (on claiming) is an addition to what was originally a doctoral thesis. Its appended character is evident in a certain amount of repetition (for instance the supposed need for a fiduciary relationship is dealt with at pp 123-128 and again, in little more detail, at pp 340-347).

There is a full citation of overseas authorities, especially from the United States, Canada and Australia. Indeed they appear to be in the majority, and a large majority in the interesting section on following (no doubt reflecting North America's traditional concerns with oil and grain;the English court has not yet had to consider commingled North Sea gas in offshore or onshore transit systems). Dr Smith suggests (p 284) that in the field of claiming North American jurisprudence has pulled ahead of the "misconceived doctrinal conservatism" of other jurisdictions, and (p 128) that the courts of England and New Zealand are remiss in continuing the charade of seeking a fiduciary relationship as the necessary foundation to a claim involving equitable tracing. However, it seems possible that the House of Lords may go beyond the inconclusive case of *Westdeutsche Landesbank Girozentrale v Islington LBC* [1996] AC 669 and recognise the tracing process as part of equity's auxiliary (as opposed to exclusive) jurisdiction.

The book's virtues include a coherent plan, consistent terminology (although the usage of "disgorgement" may not be universally accepted) and thorough citation and clear discussion of the authorities. These are, however, made less accessible by repetition, frequent cross-references (to sub-divisions of chapters rather than to pages) and by much important material being in footnotes rather than the text. That may reflect the flood of recent cases which must have made completion of the manuscript exceptionally difficult.

There is also some unevenness in the treatment of incidental topics. For instance, the text has (p 58) a very simplified account of bankruptcy accompanied by a footnote suggesting that possession (without ownership) of a chattel is an asset which vests in a trustee in bankruptcy. That seems doubtful and is in any case a confusing distraction. There is a interesting section on "tracing in transit" and a discussion on banking and payment systems which shows that the author is in touch with the practicalities of modern life. But he seriously underestimates the problems facing the expert forensic accountants when he appears to suggest (p 268) that the problems in *Barlow Clowes International Ltd v Vaughan* [1992] 4 All ER 22 (where over 10,000 would-be investors subscribed over £100m for a fraudulent scheme run through ten bank accounts in three jurisdictions) could easily have been solved by a "short algorithm of a few lines run on a modest microcomputer".

The decisions of the Court of Appeal in *Foskett v McKeown* [1998] 2 WLR 298 and *A-G v Blake* [1998] 2 WLR 805 are too recent for any notice, and Dr Smith cannot have had long to consider the significance of the *Westdeutsche* case. Perhaps this book has come at the best of times and the worst of times in that the English courts are now, after a long period of inactivity, making rapid progress in clarifying the rules of tracing and claiming (and in doing so is paying due attention to the wealth of academic material now available). Dr Smith's work is a valuable but inevitably inconclusive attempt to digest what is, for the moment, an indigestible subject-matter.

Robert Walker,
A Lord Justice of Appeal.

CASES AND MATERIALS ON THE LAW OF RESTITUTION. *AS Burrows and EG McKendrick. Oxford University Press, Oxford. 1997. lxiii and 901 pp, plus 10 pp Index. Hardback £55; paperback £27.50.*
CASEBOOK ON RESTITUTION. *G McMeel, Blackstone Press, London. 1996. xxix and 547 pp, plus 11 pp Index. Paper £22.95.*

An advertisement for varnish is currently being shown on television, in which it is claimed that the product "does exactly what it says on the tin". This virtue is also shared both by *McMeel* and by *Burrows and McKendrick*. The former is, as it describes itself, a book on the law of Restitution which brings together an extremely useful collection of well-edited extracts from the leading English cases on the subject. The latter is, as it describes itself, a book on the same subject which brings together not only a similar collection of extracts from leading cases but also adds significant extracts from academic material, all interwoven into and connected by means of an extensive superstructure of notes and questions. Furthermore, whilst the primary focus of *McMeel* is upon English cases, and thus frequently has one or a few more English cases on a topic than do *Burrows and McKendrick*, the latter authors not only provide often more lengthy extracts from the cases which they have in common with *McMeel*, but they also supplement their English cases and academic materials with a host Commonwealth resources.

In their chapters and extracts, the authors of both books have very capably rounded up the usual suspects. As to *McMeel*, there is (in chap 1) a lucid introductory chapter, describing not only the genesis of the principle against unjust enrichment (which principle is the basis of the organisation of the book), but also explaining the origin of — and any modern relevance of — the common counts and equitable and proprietary restitutionary techniques, and concluding with extracts from various articles and cases on the issue of enrichment. The book then goes on to map out (in chaps 2, 3 and 4) the causes of action in mistake, compulsion and failure of consideration, managing to take in along the way rescission of contracts for mistake, and the contested notions of ignorance, and free acceptance, without losing coherence of structure. The last three chapters (6, 7 and 8) continue the theme of the usual suspects by covering, respectively, wrongs, tracing and proprietary remedies, and defences. All of this is very well done: mindful of the approach which he sketched in the Preface simply "to identify the established grounds of recovery, and the limitations upon such recovery" (p viii), the author begins his treatment of each topic from the cases. As he himself went on to observe "[c]riticism and categorisation come later" (*ibid*) and in the well thought out notes and questions to the cases, he has provided references to, and occasionally extracts from, relevant academic analyses: in particular, at the end of each main section, there are page references to *Birks*, *Burrows* and *Goff & Jones*. Occasionally — and much too infrequently — the author allows himself some greater latitude in the text of his notes to explain, commentate upon, and criticise the cases extracted: for example, the explanation (at p 269) of the decision of Goff J at first instance in *BP* v *Hunt (No 2)* [1979] 1 WLR 783 is very clear, as is the consideration of the vexed question of the extent to which rescission is restitutionary (at pp 110–111) and the discussion, primarily by means of notes and text (at pp 491-494) of the defence of *bona fide* purchase.

Readers will have spotted that there is no reference in the above description of the book to chapter 5 of *McMeel*: it bears what the author describes in the Preface (p viii) a "heading of convenience: 'Restitution and Public Law' " in which he has a section on *Woolwich* v *IRC (No 2)* [1993] 1 AC 70 and a section on the *Westdeutsche* and related litigation (up to and including the decision of the Court of Appeal in *Westdeutsche Landesbank* v *Islington LBC* [1994] 4 All ER 890; though perhaps this would have been improved by the addition of some of the excellent judgment of Hobhouse J at first instance in that case). This chapter exemplifies the strengths of this book. It contains apt extracts and good references to the academic debates on these two fraught areas, without succumbing to what the author would no doubt see as the temptation of building yet another theoretical edifice.

Burrows & McKendrick shares a similar structure, but is constructed upon a different philosophy. Chapter 1, on unjust enrichment and competing theories, is an excellent introduction to the evolution of the principle against unjust enrichment; and chapter 2 explains how that principle organises the modern law of restitution (and also the subsequent structure of the book). In particular, the section on benefit in that chapter is extremely useful. The extracts in these two chapters are extremely well chosen, allowing the reader to understand the theoretical basis of the subject, from which can come acceptance, criticism or rejection. But, whilst that may be a useful consequence of *McMeel*, it is the intended result of *Burrows & McKendrick*. Therein lies the difference in philosophy between the two books: the former is for the most part content to be descriptive, the latter aims also to be and is theoretical and provocative. With that aim in mind, in its subsequent chapters *Burrows & McKendrick* also continues the theme of the usual suspects, containing chapters on the causes of action (mistake, ignorance, failure of consideration, illegitimate pressure, undue influence, discharge, necessity, *ultra vires* demands by public authorities: respectively chaps 3 to 9, and 12), on restitution for wrongs, tracing and proprietary restitution, and defences (respectively chaps 13 to 15). The full — and excellent — chapter in this list on ignorance (as against a short section in *McMeel* (chap 2, section 5; see also chap 6, section 5)) reflects the fact that many topics are done in more detail in *Burrows & McKendrick*. The examples could be multiplied: the analysis of the meaning of (failure of) consideration (chap 5, section 6), the detailed discussion of free acceptance (chap 5, section 7) and of exploitation (chap 7, sections 4 to 5), and the extensive notes on and discussion of *Westdeutsche* (the House of Lords decision in which ([1996] AC 669), with the advantage of the later publication of *Burrows & McKendrick*, the authors were able to include). On the other hand, there are some occasions upon which the honours on this front are with *McMeel*, as for example in his more detailed treatment of rescission of contracts for mistake and misrepresentation.

Readers will have spotted that there is no reference in the above description of the book to chapters 10 and 11 of *Burrows & McKendrick*. The material presented in these chapters allows a consideration of the question whether, respectively, illegality and incapacity constitute unjust factors (as well as defences, an issue considered later (chap 15, sections 7 and 8)). These chapters are two further examples of the greater depth of detailed coverage which *Burrows & McKendrick* often enjoys over *McMeel*. However, although the chapters present relevant material, there would seem to be little attempt in either chapter to relate illegality and incapacity as unjust factors to any of the emerging organisations of unjust factors which had earlier been sketched in chapter 2. For example, if there are three good reasons for restitution (impaired consent, unconscientious receipt, and policy; see *Burrows & McKendrick*, 91–94), chapters 10 and 11 could, and perhaps should, have presented an argument as to why either of illegality and incapacity satisfies — or not — one of those three reasons.

In the context of restitution of benefits transferred under a contract void for illegality, I have argued previously in this *Review* that analysis ought to proceed along the following threefold pattern of enquiry: (i) is the contract void (for illegality), (ii) is there is an unjust factor calling for restitution, and (iii) does the illegality continue on to deny the action in restitution ([1995] *RLR* §207)? Assume a contract void for illegality. As to the second point — unjust factors — the case law on illegality provides examples of the traditional unjust factors such as mistake or duress grounding restitution (*eg* respectively *Oom* v *Bruce* (1810) 12 East 225 and *Smith* v *Cuff* (1817) 6 M & S 160). It is more than arguable that the *locus poenitentiae*, which forms the basis of chapter 10 of *Burrows & McKendrick*, provides an example of failure of consideration as an unjust factor (this, as the authors note at 521, n 7, is Graham Virgo's suggestion at [1996] CLJ 23, 25); though it is also possible that, especially in the light of *dicta* in *Tinsley* v *Milligan* [1994] 1 AC 340 and *Tribe* v *Tribe* [1996] Ch 107, it may more properly be regarded as an example of policy-motivated restitution (*eg* Birks, 299). As to third point — the policy underlying the illegality continuing on to deny restitution — the case law on illegality provides examples of how the traditional unjust factors such as mistake or failure of consideration may *prima facie* have grounded restitution but the policy which rendered the contract void continued on to deny restitution (*eg* respectively, *Morgan* v *Ashcroft* [1938] 1 KB 49 and *Boissevain* v *Weil* [1950] AC 327). Consequently, though there is clearly room for a re-analysis of the illegality cases along lines similar to the above, there would seem to be little room for illegality as an independent unjust factor.

On the other hand, there is probably room for incapacity as an unjust factor. Let us return to first principles: one of the three principles organising unjust factors holds that an enrichment is unjust because the plaintiff did not consent to the defendant's having the enrichment: the plaintiff was compelled or mistaken or simply did not know (ignorant). Similarly, where the law says that the plaintiff *could not* know or consent, he or she likewise did not intend the defendant to have the enrichment; consequently, the defendant has been as unjustly enriched where the plaintiff could not consent as where the plaintiff did not consent. This explanation probably encompasses and unifies the cases discussed in chapter 11 on infancy, mental incapacity, the legal incapacity of a company (and in some cases a public authority) acting *ultra vires*. (However, in some public authority cases, the type of policy which motivates restitution from the executive to an overpaying taxpayer also motivates restitution from an overpaid citizen to the executive probably better explains restitution of money paid *ultra vires* the authority). But to argue against illegality or in favour of incapacity as unjust factors is to point up one of the strengths of *Burrows & McKendrick*: it allows, indeed provokes, such theoretical debate and comment.

Reviewers of cars road-test them under various conditions and then report on how the car performed. Over the course of one academic year, I took the opportunity similarly to road-test *McMeel*, and over the course of the following year similarly road-tested *Burrows & McKendrick*. I consulted *McMeel* for the purposes of revising a course of lectures for undergraduates, and never failed to mine a nugget which could be produced for discussion in class; my students found it an excellent compendium of the cases and really liked the cross references to the leading textbooks, which made it all the easier to use the book in conjunction with them for preparation for classes or examination. Similar cross-references in *Burrows & McKendrick* performed a similar function. Indeed, the idea of the authors (as they state in their Preface, at p vii) is that *Burrows & McKendrick* should be used alongside one of the leading texts, and that, for readers who have no access to a sufficiently well stocked law libraries or who choose to study or research elsewhere, the often quite lengthy extracts from the leading cases and materials should form a sufficient basis for comprehension of the subject. From my road-test of their book, I can state that in this twin aim, the authors succeed admirably. I consulted *Burrows & McKendrick* both for the purposes of revising a course of lectures for postgraduates, and as the basis of my postgraduate seminar tutorials; it never failed to disclose an issue for class or to provoke debate in the seminar, much as it did in the previous two paragraphs. In such situations, the superb selection of Commonwealth cases and academic materials, coupled with the well-written, apt and often provocative notes and comments, really proved their worth. Furthermore, I used both books as starting points for research, especially when I needed something to give to colleagues and practitioners who had run up against a restitution issue in another area of the law and needed a good quick resource; again, invariably, they too went away happy. I found particularly useful for

Chancery lawyers the analysis from a restitution perspective of the liability to account as a constructive trustee for receipt of trust funds presented in *Burrows & McKendrick* (at chap 4). Furthermore, Professor Birks has recently commented on "the new emphasis on defences . . . Of the four crucial questions . . . it is suddenly the unobtrusive fourth to which we have to bend our energies" (Birks (ed), *Laundering and Tracing* (Oxford, 1995) 322–323). Reflecting this, both books contain an extensive chapter on defences, which on more than one occasion proved invaluable in explaining the difference between the absence of a claim in principle and a claim in principle met successfully with a defence.

From the perspective of English law, it might be said that *McMeel* completes the set, taking its place alongside the work of authority (*Goff & Jones*), the theoretical analysis (*Birks*) and the clear introductory texts (*Burrows*, and *Tettenborn*). Nevertheless, at a time when the subject is growing in the entirety of the common law world, it might have been thought that some more non-English material would have made *McMeel* even more useful to non-English users, and would in any event have been more representative of the nature of the subject's evolution. This point is admirably met by *Burrows & McKendrick*, which can not only take its place alongside the same English works of authority, theory and introduction, but can also perform the same function alongside the leading texts on the law of restitution elsewhere in the common law world.

Eoin O'Dell,
Trinity College Dublin.

FAILURE OF CONTRACTS: Contractual, Restitutionary and Proprietary Consequences. *FD Rose (ed)*. Hart Publishing Ltd, Oxford. 1997. xxvi and 283 pp, plus 6 pp Appendix and 4 pp Index. Paperback £30.

This, like most collections of conference papers, is a mixed bag with not all that much in common save a vague connection with the law of contract. A clear, if laborious, exposition of the German rules of unjust enrichment applicable after termination of a contract rubs shoulders with a perceptive though impressionistic account of how the French have got to grips with — and increasingly come to ignore — their supposed fundamental distinction between contractual and delictual liability and the principle of *non-cumul* that goes with it. Richard Nolan's wide-ranging and sceptical analysis of what, if any, theories might justify restitutionary damages for breach of contract clashes nicely with Felicity Toube's eminently practical discussion of restitution as it affects agreements nullified by the EEC Treaty, art 85(2). Following a modern trend, most of the papers are followed by shorter Comments, though in this instance the organiser's hope that the comments will stimulate the reader with diametrical disagreement seems to have been largely unfulfilled. But for all this variety the result is a readable, entertaining and thoroughly scholarly collation, and was undoubtedly worth the effort of organising and producing.

In a short review it is difficult to do justice to all the pieces concerned, and hence I hope the participants will forgive me for omitting specific reference to some of them. I found particularly stimulating Janet O'Sullivan's account of what was going on in that newish contractual *enfant terrible*, *Ruxley v Forsyth* [1996] AC 344, and in particular her suggestion that there is a lot to be said for regarding the "consumer surplus" as something valuable in itself rather than trying to shoehorn it into categories such as disappointment and vexation. Equally thought-provoking was Sarah Worthington's attempt to make sense of proprietary restitution in cases of contract failure since the *Westdeutsche* saga. Her view, which will be familiar to readers of her PhD thesis, is that the key to the problem is whether equity would enforce a retransfer of the very asset by which the defendant has been unjustly enriched: if, and only if, the answer is Yes, then a proprietary remedy will be granted. I personally am not sure whether this ought to be a sufficient criterion for preserving the claimant's rights in the face of a bankrupt defendant. But that, of course, is beside the point. Steve Hedley's view that recent scholarship has allowed the supposed law of unjust enrichment to wax too fat at the expense of old-fashioned contract is well-known and long-standing, but none the worse for that: his chapter here on "Restitution: Contract's Twin" is decently (and closely) argued, and ought to be taken on board by any over-enthusiastic restitutionist. And the Scots are not forgotten: see in particular a highly instructive analysis of the sometimes unhappy relation between the concepts of contract and unjustified enrichment north of the Tweed.

In short, a well-written, informative and well-edited book for both academic and practitioner. Both will find it difficult not to enjoy: and the former will find it a welcome opportunity to combine pleasure with scholarship.

Andrew Tettenborn,
Bracton Professor of English Law, University of Exeter.

THE LIMITS OF RESTITUTIONARY CLAIMS: A Comparative Analysis. *William Swadling (ed)*. London: British Institute of International and Comparative Law/UKNCCL. 1997. xxii and 256 pp, plus 3 pp Index. Paperback £25.

The aim of this book is to identify and explore how the Common law and the Civil law restrict claims for the reversal of unjustified enrichment both through the operation of defences and through the denial of recovery where the cause of action is based on mistake or error of law which, within both traditions, has, or still does, operate to inhibit claims. Apart from an introductory overview provided by Dickson of the law of restitution in English law and the law of unjustified enrichment in Civilian systems the book comprises studies which deal roughly with the same subject matter taken from the point of view of each of the two different legal traditions.

The first pair of essays deal with the defence of change of position in English law, where it has only recently been introduced, and in German law where it has a long history. Dörner provides a detailed study of the operation of the defence in German law. Birks argues that, because of the possibility of tracing in English law, the conclusion that the introduction of the defence allows the plaintiff to recover only "surviving enrichment" must be understood differently in English and German law.

Two essays examine the operation of the defence of *bona fide* purchase in the context of claims of unjustified enrichment with particular reference to *Lipkin Gorman v Karpnale Ltd* [1991] 2 AC 548, where the defence was raised. The defence of *bona fide* purchase concerns whether a transferee has acquired title to property. Yet the fact that a person has acquired property is not a defence to a claim of restitution so, argues Swadling, *bona fide* purchase cannot be relevant as a defence in such a context. He justifies the consideration of this defence in *Lipkin Gorman* on the grounds that the claim on that occasion was in fact one for vindication of property rights. The complementary essay by Zülch, by reference to two parallel German cases, examines the facts of *Lipkin Gorman* from the point of view of German law. The issue of *bona fide* purchase arises less centrally in this contribution. Zülch shows that in German law a claim of unjustified enrichment would lie on (one view of) the facts and that, although it is not called a defence of bona fide purchase, the purchaser for value in German law would have a defence which "constitutes a corollary in the law of restitution to the rules of *bona fide* purchase in the law of property". The solution is a policy one. In the law of property the position of the purchaser for value is sometimes preferred over that of the original owner. The circumstances in which this is the case is determined by the operation of the defence of *bona fide* purchase. But the same policy would be undermined if the purchaser for value was not also given a defence against an enrichment claim brought by the original owner. If the policy is to be sustained the purchaser for value must be protected both in the law of property and obligations.

The next pair of essays examine the different positions taken by English and Israeli law concerning the recovery of benefits transferred under illegal transactions. The comparison is a useful one. English law treats such benefits as irrecoverable in principle subject to a number of rigidly operated exceptions. Israeli law, on the other hand, both allows recovery of benefits in principle and it gives a large degree of discretion to the courts in determining the circumstances in which recovery should sometimes be denied. Cohen's illuminating study examines the operation of the Israeli law which was introduced relatively recently by statute. Her conclusion is that the law works well in practice. Virgo, by contrast, is highly critical of English law. He shows how English law adopted the rule, which originated in Roman law, that recovery is barred when the parties are equally at fault (*pari delicto*). Consistent with the terms of its formulation, the rule was operated flexibly by English judges in the eighteenth century and recovery was permitted under some illegal transactions. Later, however, the rule came to be operated inflexibly. The critical factor appears to be that the courts have come to attribute equal fault to each party from their mere involvement in an illegal transaction. Recovery, as a rule, is therefore normally denied unless the plaintiff's claim falls within one of a number of recognised exceptions. The Roman jurists probably operated the *pari delicto* rule in an equally inflexible manner with the critical difference that they did not apply it to transactions which were merely illegal if there was no turpitude involved. It is interesting, therefore, that Virgo argues that there should be recovery as a matter of principle under illegal transactions in English law provided that there has been no gross moral turpitude on the part of the plaintiff.

The last two essays in the collection examine the position taken by English law and the Civilian tradition towards error of law as a bar to restitution. McKendrick makes out a convincing case for the abolition of the bar in English law while warning of consequent problems. Winkel's erudite contribution concludes that epistemological premises provide the irrefutable grounds on which to dispense with a distinction between error of fact and error of law as a bar to restitution.

Dickson, in his introductory overview, was not optimistic about the benefits of comparing the Common and the Civil law in this field. Nevertheless this book certainly does enhance an understanding of the approaches taken by these different traditions to common issues. The essays are, without exception, extremely impressive. However, perhaps inevitably, sometimes some of the essential points are missed. Justinian treated error of law as a bar to recovery with the *condictio indebiti*. Since his view was recorded in the *Digest* it necessarily has had an important influence on the Civilian tradition. However, as modern Civilian systems came to cohere to the view that claims like the *condictio indebiti* concern the recovery of what is undue, the role of error was diminished. If error is not part of the cause of action, there is little reason to distinguish between different types of error as a bar to restitution. Also, critically, a legal system which adopts the "system" of the *condictiones* must necessarily be more liberal than the Common law in allowing a cause of action in cases where there has been an error of law. Since each *condictio* is specific to one particular fact situation, if error of law bars the *condictio indebiti* there is no other alternative claim to which the plaintiff can turn. In English law, on the other hand, the plaintiff who is barred by a mistake of law has another ten unjust factors on which he may be able to base his claim and thereby avoid the harsh consequences of the rule. It is only through the bitter experience of a "mixed" legal system like that of Scotland that the lesson is really learnt that the rule is far more severe in one legal tradition than another.

Robin Evans-Jones,
Professor of Jurisprudence, University of Aberdeen.

BOOK REVIEWS

INTERNATIONAL TRACING OF ASSETS. *Edited by Michael Ashe QC and Barry Rider.* FT Law & Tax, London (1997). 2 vols looseleaf.

International Tracing of Assets is a monumental work about a topic of monumental proportions. Until recent times, the topics of laundering, tracing and claiming had not been properly examined as a unitary theme. They were to be found sporadically in various texts dealing with a variety of topics. (See however P Birks (ed), *Laundering and Tracing*: Clarendon Press, Oxford, 1995); LD Smith, *The Law of Tracing*: Clarendon Press, Oxford, 1997). *International Tracing of Assets* seeks to encompass these various topics that is the law and practice of identifying, tracing and then controlling assets with particular focus on their international dimension. The work is principally directed at the practitioner who requires a concise, practical and topical account of the law and practice relating to the identification and tracing of assets across a broad spectrum of situations.

International Tracing of Assets consists of two volumes in a loose-leaf form which examine the legal issues from both a national and international perspective. There are 49 contributors to the first volume, of which Mr Michael Ashe QC and Professor Barry Rider are the general editors. It is primarily concerned with the issues as they arise at domestic level and the various topics are dealt with under separate sections. There is a survey of the law of tracing and then those areas of law which may give rise to a claim contingent or related to tracing *ie* under criminal law, financial services law, banking law, matrimonial law, civil law (that is in tort, restitution, contract and for breach of trust), insolvency law, tax law, corporate law and administrative law, as well as a separate survey of defences. There are also separate examinations of the criminal and civil liabilities for the controlling, handling or being associated with money laundering operations, as well as modes of identifying and tracing assets under both criminal and civil law. The law relating to the seizure, confiscature and forfeiture, of the proceeds of criminal activity and the freezing of assets under civil law, are also dealt with. There are separate examinations of various procedural matters such as the enforcement of interim orders and judgments, the commencement of international proceedings and evidentiary matters pertaining to tracing. Finally, there are a series of summaries of the relevant law and practice in a number of key jurisdictions.

The second volume, which is under the general editorship of Mr Andrew Keltie and Mr Nick Pearson, has a total of 47 contributors, covering 47 jurisdictions, in addition to England and Wales. It aims to provide advice and guidance on the measures available in various jurisdictions, which may be relevant to the tracing and recovery of assets. The contributors are all practitioners in the relevant jurisdictions and a standard methodology has been adopted in relation to each jurisdiction of a list of key questions. In this way, the examination of each jurisdiction does not necessarily provide a detailed summary of the relevant laws, but rather concise statements and descriptions which answer the key questions, whilst still making reference to relevant laws. There are also questions on whether certain relevant conventions and treaties are in force in the relevant jurisdictions. It is therefore of great value to any practitioner who may wish to refer to what the position may be under a particular jurisdiction on one of the key questions relating to tracing and recovering assets. As such, despite the fact that the relevant law and practise of certain key jurisdictions is examined in the first volume, there is little overlap as the respective examinations are significantly different. Finally, the texts of a number of useful treaties and acts (or at least the relevant provisions) appear at the back of this volume, together with various court precedents.

International Tracing of Assets is an impressive work in the field relating to identifying, tracing and claiming of assets both internationally and domestically. One is also impressed by the degree of continuity throughout the various sections, something difficult to achieve in a work covering such a broad range of issues by such a large number of contributors. It would be difficult for a work seeking to encompass an area of this magnitude to have exhausted all the potential issues which may arise. Nevertheless, the absence of any discussion of the role of the conflict of laws in relation to this area does seem to be a significant deficiency. This is particularly so for a work which describes itself through the phrase "International Tracing". Although the relevant areas which may give rise to a tracing exercise and possible claim are given a thorough examination as a matter of English domestic law, the question of how they might be treated under the conflict of laws is avoided. There is, of course a discussion of service ex juris (Vol 1, K), the enforcement of orders and judgments (Vol 1, J), as well as certain international interlocutory procedures, such as mareva injunctions (Vol 1, E2). However, some of the central issues of private international law are not dealt with. Presumably, an international claim of the sort envisaged by the editors will contain sufficient international elements so as to raise potential issues of private international law, *ie* questions of jurisdiction, characterisation and choice of law. It may be that being in the form of a loose-leaf such additions may be incorporated in time, together with other developments in the law relating to the theme of the work.

George Panagopoulos,
Hertford College, Oxford.

BUTTERWORTHS MONEY LAUNDERING LAW. *General Editor Chris Howard, Wilde Sapte. London: Butterworths. 1997. Looseleaf £150.*

The topic of money laundering is one that has received increasing attention in recent times. Prompted by the sheer scale of the problem and the obvious need to legislate against those seeking to launder proceeds of criminal and other illegal activities, the UK government has, over the last five or so years, enacted an abundance of legislation dealing with this matter. *Butterworths' Money Laundering Law* examines the topic of money laundering both from a practical and legal point of view. It seeks to provide a reference work, containing a detailed analysis of the relevant UK law. Under the general editorship of Chris Howard, the work is aimed at practitioners but also people in sectors of industry, such as banking, where issues of money laundering may be relevant.

From a practical point of view the work introduces the reader to the international problem of money laundering. Following the introductory division, the second division of the book examines the processes and methods of money laundering, describing the factual scenarios, the various stages, as well as explaining the relevant terminology. The methods and processes of money laundering can at times be very complex and intricate. An examination of money laundering methodology is therefore essential in properly understanding this subject.

The work then goes through the relevant UK statutory provisions and regulations, in particular the provisions of three key acts: namely the Criminal Justice Act 1988, the Drug Trafficking Act 1994, and the Prevention of Terrorism (Temporary Provisions) Act 1989, as well the Money Laundering Regulations 1993, which were enacted in compliance with the European Council Directive on money laundering. The relevant statutory provisions appear towards the end of the work. However, although the text of the Council Directive on money laundering is included, it seems odd that the text of the Money Laundering Regulations is not.

The topic of money laundering has an important international aspect. As such, it is only fitting that there be included an examination of the various international initiatives as well as a comparative analysis. In relation to the comparative analysis, there is a summary of the position under the law of 11 other jurisdictions. These comparative sections have been written by practitioners from the relevant jurisdictions and provide a useful summary of the relevant laws relating to money laundering under the law of these jurisdictions.

There are several proposed sections of the work, the material of which is intended to be published in future issues. These include matters of confiscation, specimen compliance and forms and precedents. Being in the form of a loose-leaf, the work will have the advantage of being regularly up-dated and having new sections added as well as old ones altered. In particular, it will also be possible to add further jurisdictions in the comparative analysis. These considerations are of great importance in an area of law that is highly mobile and likely to see many new developments, both domestically and internationally.

George Panagopoulos,
Hertford College, Oxford.

RESTITUTION IN AUSTRALIA AND NEW ZEALAND. *Charles Cato. Cavendish, Sydney and London. lxiii and 362 pp, plus 6 pp Index. Paperback £34.95.*

If nothing else, the law of restitution can at least claim to be one of the fastest growing areas in the civil law. The rapid pace of its growth, however, would not have been possible without the intellectual and doctrinal foundations provided in the works of Lord Goff and Professor Jones, and Professors Birks and Burrows. It is in these footsteps that *Restitution in Australia and New Zealand* seeks to follow.

Perhaps the most striking feature of the book is its organisation. In sharp contrast to other works on this subject, it is principally concerned with the contextual relevance of the law of restitution. The book thus proceeds to examine the scope of restitutionary recovery under such diverse headings as unsolicited benefits, the discharge of another's debt, ineffective transactions, mistake in contract, illegal contracts and breach of fiduciary duty. In doing so the author draws on English and Canadian authorities but, true to its title, the book is primarily focused on the application of restitutionary causes of action in the often unique legal landscape of Australia and New Zealand.

In seeking to describe the law simultaneously in both jurisdictions the author has undertaken an unenviable task. Despite the historical associations between Australia and New Zealand, the jurisdictions have diverged significantly in recent years. While the Australian courts have been less enthusiastic proponents of an approach based on a unifying principle of unjust enrichment, New Zealand jurisprudence has more readily adopted unjust enrichment terminology taking its lead, somewhat schizophrenically, from both England and Canada. The difficulties in describing the law in both jurisdictions are, furthermore, exacerbated by the substantial statutory modifications made to the common law in New Zealand. The Contractual Remedies Act 1979, the Contractual Mistakes Act 1977 and the Illegal Contracts Act 1970 purport to regulate many aspects of the law of restitution. While it can be argued with some justification that these statutes, with their wide judicial discretions, are a positive hindrance to the development of coherent principles, they are nevertheless a fact of life. The book thus has some value as the only current work attempting to integrate these statutes into a wider restitutionary framework.

Although England has benefited from a number of excellent works, the antipodes have been less well served. In New Zealand, in particular, judges, practitioners, academic and students have been forced to muddle along without a single coherent account of the law. From this perspective *Restitution in Australia and New Zealand* is to be welcomed for its attempt to redress this oversight. Its collection of Australian and, especially, New Zealand case law will no doubt be greeted by practitioners with some sense of relief. In many respects, however, the book is disappointing. Historically, the development of the law of restitution has been hindered by the difficulty in identifying the proper theoretical and doctrinal constructs upon which the specific causes of action and remedies sit. *Restitution in Australia and New Zealand* unfortunately offers very little in the way of theory. Apart from a short introductory chapter, which sets out the broad outlines of the dominant model of restitution, the book seems solely concerned to describe the law. In itself this failing could be forgiven. There is clearly room for an uncluttered description of the law, if only for student use. However, its entirely contextual organisation may positively impede the coherent development of the law. For example, its separate chapters on unsolicited goods, mistake within contract and ineffective transactions suggests divisions and distinctions which are misleading and counter-productive.

Likewise, there is little overt recognition of the crucial doctrinal distinctions between what has come to be called autonomous unjust enrichment and restitution (disgorgement) as a purely remedial response to other causes of action. While the author may be aware of the distinction, there is little guidance for the uninitiated, who, having been told in the opening chapter that restitutionary remedies are a response to unjust enrichment, will quite justifiably, but incorrectly, assume that restitution in respect of a breach of fiduciary duty (ch 11) and a tort (ch 12) are also necessarily responses to unjust enrichment.

In final analysis, *Restitution in Australia and New Zealand* is a book which those interested in the law of restitution in Australia, New Zealand and elsewhere will probably acquire. It is a useful summary of the principal features of the law in both jurisdictions and as Goff and Jones' work paved the way for more theoretical accounts, so *Restitution in Australia and New Zealand* will hopefully pave the way for a more sustained account of the law in New Zealand.

Ross Grantham,
Senior Lecturer in Commercial Law, University of Auckland.

THE HISTORY OF QUASI-CONTRACT IN ENGLISH LAW. *RM Jackson. Wm W Gaunt & Sons Inc, Florida. xxxv and 130 pp, plus 4pp Index. Hardback.*

Restitution is the fastest growing subject in the common law, attracting and stimulated by a burgeoning literature. It nonetheless remains a controversial area and it is important that the foundations of the modern law are known and properly understood. In 1936, Professor Jackson remarked both that there was no adequate account of quasi-contract in English law and that there was no detailed historical account of it. The latter he attempted to remedy with the current book, which was, until recently at least, essential reading for those coming to the law of restitution for the first time. The difficulty with older books, however is their accessibility, or lack of it. It was recently brought to the attention of members of the Restitution Discussion Group (majordomo@maillist.ox.ac.uk) that Gaunt have remedied the problem by republishing Professor Jackson's book. All serious students of the subject will be grateful that they can now easily obtain a copy of this important work.

FDR.

NEW 5th Edition

Goff & Jones
The Law of Restitution

Professor Gareth Jones, Q.C. FBA

♦ Unbeatable coverage   ♦ Fully revised
♦ Now included in **Sweet & Maxwell's** prestigious Common Law Library

In the five years since the last edition of **Goff & Jones**, there has been increasing judicial acceptance of the law of restitution - in the Court of Appeal, the House of Lords and the Judicial Committee of the Privy Council.

This new fifth edition has been substantially rewritten and expanded to reflect the many developments and cases in this field of law, meaning **Goff & Jones** remains the title to be relied upon.

Four reasons why you need the new 5th edition of Goff & Jones: The Law of Restitution

- **Fully revised chapters** - substantially rewritten since the fourth edition in 1993, you can depend upon this work to be up-to-date.

- **Important new cases** - the repercussions of the most important decision of the last five years, that of the House of Lords in *Westdeutsche*, are being felt in many areas of the law of restitution, and are given due consideration here, along with *Banque Franciere*, *The Trident Beauty* and *Blake*, plus 6 decisions of the House of Lords.

- **No competition** - we don't think you will find another title on this topic that can compare to the depth and completeness of coverage offered in this important work.

- **An author of importance** - Professor Gareth Jones, Q.C. FBA has taken sole responsibility for this latest edition, bringing you guidance from one of the leading lights in restitution law. A Professor at the University of Cambridge and a Fellow of Trinity College, he has written widely on related topics.

Contents: Introduction, The Right to Restitution - Where the defendant has acquired a benefit from or by the act of the plaintiff, Mistake, Compulsion, Necessity, Ineffective Transactions, Where the defendant has acquired from a third party a beneficiary for which he must account to the plaintiff, Where the defendant has acquired a beneficiary through his own wrongful act, Defences

October 1998   0 421 60800 5   £175

Arlidge, Eady & Smith on Contempt

Also publishing this year

2nd Edition

Edited by **The Honourable Mr Justice Eady and Professor A T H Smith**

Since the last edition of **Arlidge & Eady on Contempt** there has been a vast amount of case law in the area of contempt. This new edition has hence been substantially updated, ensuring that the book remains at the forefront of contempt law literature, and now forms part of Sweet & Maxwell's highly respected Common Law Library.

December 1998   0 421 45910 7   c. £175

ORDER YOUR COPY TODAY, CALL 0171 449 1111

Order Source Number: 3250 J

Sweet & Maxwell

Restitution From Blackstone

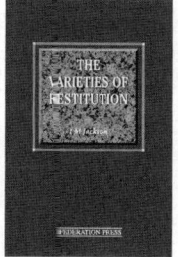

The Varieties of Restitution I.M. Jackman
Published April 1998 : 212 Pages : £22.50

The law of restitution is commonly described as 'unjust enrichment at the plaintiff's expense'. Jackman challenges this view, revealing that much of the law of restitution does not concern cases where the defendant has been 'enriched' or where the plaintiff has suffered 'expense'. He identifies three distinct categories of legal thought in this area:

- the reversal of non-voluntary transactions
- the fulfilment of non-contractual promises
- the protection of the private legal facilities of proprietary rights and fiduciary relationships.

Unjust Enrichment P. Davenport & C. Harris
Published November 1997 : 152 Pages : £19.95 (HB)

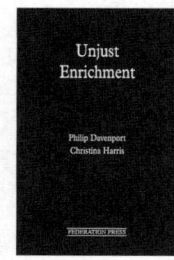

Unjust enrichment offers splendid rewards for those who understand it and grave dangers to those who do not. This books explains clearly and concisely the use and dangers of the doctrine. The authors draw primarily upon examples in construction law, where unjust enrichment has had its greatest impact, while pointing out that the principles in the book are of general application.

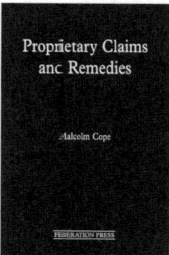

Proprietary Claims & Remedies M. Cope
Published November 1997 : 232 Pages : £29.95 (HB)

This book deals with a major problem for practitioners working in bankruptcy and insolvency: the nature of equitable proprietary claims, the range of such remedies and the rules and presumptions developed for tracing. The book is split into two parts. The first highlights the effect of claims and the prerequisites for their successful establishment. The second is devoted to problems of both common law and equity, particularly the equitable rules and presumptions developed to identify the subject matter of a remedy.

Casebook on Restitution G. McMeel
Published June 1996 : 588 Pages : £22.95

This book guides the reader through the often impenetrable language to an appreciation of the leading cases and a clearer understanding of the practical difficulties of restitution claims. Cases extracted cover issues ranging from the deceptively simple example of mistaken payments to the complicated fall-out of corporate collapse, as in the *Barlow Clowes*, *Polly Peck* and *Maxwell* cases.

These titles will be of interest to all those studying and working in the area of restitution.

To order your copy contact Blackstone Press on
Tel: 0181 740 2277 Fax: 0181 743 2292

BLACKSTONE PRESS LIMITED
Aldine Place London W12 8AA E-mail: sales@blackstone.demon.co.uk

RESTITUTION AND CONTRACT

Andrew Skelton
Solicitor, Kensington Swan

Essential to their understanding, development and practical application is the relationship between the Law of Restitution and the Law of Contract. The most important and most difficult point of contact is where a contract is prematurely discharged for breach and a plaintiff who has conferred a money or non-money benefit on the defendant has a choice of remedies for breach of contract and unjust enrichment.

The central question is whether and to what extent the plaintiff's recovery in restitution is subject to a ceiling based on the terms of the discharge contract. The issue has troubled courts throughout the common law world and the case law is in a mess.

The author examines the authorities in England, Australia, Canada, New Zealand and the USA, demonstrating how the contract influences the claim for unjust enrichment without imposing a general notion of subsidiarity on the restitutionary claim.

Contents

Introduction and Fundamental Concepts

Claims for Money

Claims for Non-Money Benefits:
I: The Position in Case Law
II: Analysis of the Position in Case Law and Proposed Solution

The Position of the Defaulting Party

"The spotlight which the author turns on this difficult subject improves our understanding of it and will help to avoid muddles and wasteful litigation in the future."

From the Foreword by Professor Peter Birks QC

ISBN 0–952649–93–4   Paperback   £23 (overseas £26)
Packing and postage £3
UK customers please add £3 p&p for the first book and £1 for each additional book. Overseas customers please add £3.50 for the first book and £1.50 for each additional book
Payment in sterling net of bank charges

MANSFIELD PRESS, P.O. Box 639, Oxford OX3 7HD, UK

RESTITUTION AND BANKING LAW

Edited by
FRANCIS ROSE
Professor of Commercial and Common Law, University of Buckingham

Many of the difficult problems and the leading cases are the same in Banking Law and the Law of Restitution. Both areas deal with important practical and legal issues. In this book leading practitioners and academic commentators combine their experience to discuss major topical issues.

UNAUTHORISED PAYMENT AND UNJUST ENRICHMENT IN BANKING LAW
Deon van Zyl, Judge of the Cape High Court

DISTRIBUTING THE BURDEN OF ALTERNATIVE CO-EXTENSIVE LIABILITIES
Dr Charles Mitchell, Lecturer in Law, King's College London

UNDUE INFLUENCE AND MISREPRESENTATION AFTER *O'BRIEN*: MAKING SECURITY SECURE
Janet O'Sullivan, Fellow of Selwyn College, Cambridge
Graham Virgo, Fellow of Downing College, Cambridge

O'BRIEN, NOTICE AND THE BURDEN OF PROOF
Kit Barker, Lecturer in Law, University of Southampton

CROSS-BORDER SECURITY ENFORCEMENT AND THE CONFLICT OF LAWS
Gabriel Moss QC and Felicity Toube, Barrister

CROSS-BORDER SECURITY ENFORCEMENT, RESTITUTION AND PRIORITIES
Nick Segal, Solicitor, Partner, Allen & Overy

TRACING AND ELECTRONIC FUNDS TRANSFERS
Dr Lionel D Smith, Fellow of St Hugh's College, Oxford

ASSISTING A BREACH OF DUTY BY A FIDUCIARY, THE COMMON LAW AND MONEY-LAUNDERING
Michael Tugendhat QC

RECOVERING MISDIRECTED MONEY FROM BANKS: MINISTERIAL RECEIPT AT LAW AND IN EQUITY
Michael Bryan, Senior Lecturer in Law, University of Melbourne

OVERVIEW
Peter Birks QC FBA, Regius Professor of Civil Law, University of Oxford

ISBN 9526499–1–8   1998   Hardback £37
Packing and postage £3
UK customers please add £3 p&p for the first book and £1 for each additional book.
Overseas customers please add £3.50 for the first book and £1.50 for each additional book
Payment in sterling net of bank charges

MANSFIELD PRESS, P.O. Box 639, Oxford OX3 7HD, UK